DISCOVERY

Richard E. Byrd, Rear Admiral, U. S. N. (Ret.)

DISCOVERY

The Story of the Second Byrd Antarctic Expedition

RICHARD EVELYN BYRD

ROWMAN & LITTLEFIELD
Lanham • Boulder • New York • London

Published by Rowman & Littlefield
A wholly owned subsidiary of The Rowman & Littlefield Publishing Group, Inc.
4501 Forbes Boulevard, Suite 200, Lanham, Maryland 20706
www.rowman.com

Unit A, Whitacre Mews, 26-34 Stannary Street, London SE11 4AB

Distributed by NATIONAL BOOK NETWORK

Cloth edition originally published by G. P. Putnam's Sons in 1935
First Rowman & Littlefield paperback edition © 2015

British Library Cataloguing in Publication Information Available

Library of Congress Cataloging-in-Publication Data Available

Paperback: 978-1-4422-4166-4
E-book: 978-1-4422-4167-1

∞™ The paper used in this publication meets the minimum requirements of American National Standard for Information Sciences—Permanence of Paper for Printed Library Materials, ANSI/NISO Z39.48-1992.

Printed in the United States of America

TO

EDSEL FORD

INTRODUCTION

AS a life-long friend of Dick Byrd and of his distinguished father before him, I have been asked to set down here some reminiscences of his early youth, and a brief outline of his official record in the Navy before he entered on his career as an explorer. As a member of the Senate Naval Committee for more than twenty years, and more recently as Secretary of the Navy, I have had exceptional opportunities to follow his brilliant career from the day when he entered the Naval Academy as a slender midshipman, until he electrified the world by his magnificent flights across the Atlantic and over the Arctic and Antarctic poles. It is not my intention to praise Byrd, but simply to record some unadorned and unknown facts.

As a boy, Dick got into rather more than his fair share of mischief, and what his exasperated father used to call "reckless deviltry," though when not leading his gang of Winchester youngsters in some new and hitherto unheard-of form of escapade, he was a notably quiet and thoughtful lad. Always the leader of the gang, he maintained his leadership because, no matter what was the physical risk or the still more dreaded danger of parental wrath, he was always ready to "go first" when the challenge came.

At times I think his father's indignant denunciations of foolhardiness were more than justified.

Certainly that was so when as a youngster, with little or no experience in handling boats, he insisted, over the violent protests of his seafaring hosts, on taking a small sailing craft across Hampton Roads in the face of a rising storm, and there and then came within an ace of ending forever his career of adventure.

To this day his old friend, Judge Carson, whom Dick visited in the Philippines on his trip alone around the world before he was quite twelve years old, attributes some of his gray hair to the anxiety accompanying his efforts to locate the young daredevil who had managed to slip away on his Filipino pony and join a sheriff's posse and a detachment of mounted constabulary who were engaged for three days and two nights, in the wilds of the distant province of Sorsogon, rounding up a group of desperate bandits who had broken out of the provincial jail.

But perhaps it was from some of these heedless and ofttimes reckless adventures and experiences of his youth that he learned the need of "preparedness" when anything worth-while is to be accomplished. Without the careful planning which has marked all his activities in later life he could not have achieved his marvelous record of never losing a man on any of his four separate expeditions to the Polar regions; or on the Naval Aviation Station he commanded during the war with a personnel of more than three hundred men; or when, in the early days of the war, he developed and instructed his assistants in the then extremely dangerous art of night flying over water.

And yet I must confess that my reading of the official reports of his personal activities on the Polar expeditions does not encourage me to believe that the leopard has changed his spots, or that Dick Byrd, the man, is any less willing to take a chance than was Dick Byrd, the youth. It has always been his own life, however, that he has placed in jeopardy. His impulsive response to the call of some new adventure has never involved unnecessary danger to the lives, the limbs, or the health of his subordinates, or needless risk to the successful accomplishment of his undertaking.

Before entering the Naval Academy, Byrd spent two years at the Virginia Military Institute and one at the University of Virginia. Although he had missed a year's schooling when he adventured around the world, he was the youngest student at the Institute when he entered at the age of fifteen. The usual age requirement of sixteen years had been waived in his case because of the notable progress he had made in the studies prescribed at the Institute, especially mathematics and elementary physics, and also because of his manifest ability to hold his own with any group of boys of advanced school age.

His exceptional ability as a leader, that innate talent for "leadership" so highly prized in the Army and Navy, began to disclose itself on the very day he entered the Naval Academy. He was elected chairman of his class in his plebe year, and he held more offices during his four years at the Academy than any other member of his class. Greatly devoted to football, Byrd was one of the most reckless players on the team, in the bad old days before the game was "opened up" to make football safe for the undergraduate; and in leading the gymnasium team, of which he was captain, he smashed his ankle in an attempt to perform an exceedingly hazardous feat on the flying rings.

After graduating, this passionate liking for athletics brought about a rigorous régime of exercise and sports, which kept him so physically fit that when leaving on his first expedition his condition was as good as during his Academy days.

But he never got rid, and perhaps he never tried to get rid of the far-away, dreamy look in his eyes for which he was so often reprimanded as a small boy. He sometimes passed an acquaintance without any sign of recognition, an apparent slight which was not always well received until his friends learned to know him better. And we may be sure that he did not get off so easily on a certain memorable occasion when his day-dreaming resulted in his failure to salute the Commandant of Midshipmen; or on another memorable occasion when he appeared in military formation in yellow civilian shoes. Apparently all his years of service in the Navy did not completely cure him of this weakness, if it be a weakness, for I heard not long ago that he appeared on the platform at one of his recent lectures in full evening dress, minus a white vest, which most people hold to be *de rigueur* on such formal occasions.

But what manner of midshipman he was is best told in his class annual, which records the estimate of his classmates after four years of close and intimate contact. Here it is:—

"RICHARD EVELYN BYRD: Athlete, Leader in all right things, Friend, Gentleman. From the time we entered as plebes until the present Dick has been putting his whole heart into everything he does, including the little meeting behind the old Hospital. Most of the time Dick moves around with a far-away look in his eyes. But go where he may he cannot hope to find the truth and the beauty of which he dreams. He has already lived a life rich in experience and he will live a life richer still. But he will always give to life more than he takes."

I know it is telling tales out of school, but it is no secret now that the "affair behind the Hospital" was a memorable fight Dick had with a civilian in Annapolis. This young man had manhandled more than one of the midshipmen, and at a class indignation meeting Dick was selected to challenge the pugnacious youngster. The challenge was accepted. After a tough battle Byrd emerged the victor by a slight margin,—so slight a margin that when they shook hands after the fight they had learned to respect each other profoundly, and from that moment they became friends.

I could fill many pages with the story of Byrd's service in the Navy. But I believe that story is best told by the following extracts from the official record of Lieut. Richard Evelyn Byrd, Jr., United States Navy:

1. Twenty-two detailed reports of fitness on Lieutenant Byrd by different officers in the Navy made since 1917 show him to be above the great majority (the highest mark that can be given) in the following: Coöperative qualities, devotion to duty, education, force, industry, initiative, judgment, justice, leadership, physical energy and endurance, reliability, self-control, discipline of subordinates, loyalty of subordinates, efficiency of personnel (based upon the efforts and results of such efforts of the officer concerned), efficiency of material (based upon the results which the officer concerned has accomplished in keeping up or improving the material under his charge).

2. There follow some quotations from the special remark column of these reports of fitness.

Chief of Bureau of Aeronautics, April 1 to September 30, 1921:

"Lieutenant Byrd is an exceptionally loyal, capable and efficient officer. For his age and length of service he has remarkably good judgment, tact, and an ability to coöperate with others. He is zealous and indefatigable in the performance of his duty, persistent in accomplishing the end in view, and does so without creating friction or opposition. I have no hesitation in saying that he, more than any one else, by his own qualifications had much to do with getting passed the legislation creating the Bureau of Aeronautics in the Navy Department. It was by his knowledge of aviation, its relationship to the Navy, and by his tact and persistence in persuading those opposed to it, and also in making new converts, that the law was passed. His work in this connection was invaluable to the director of aviation and later to the chief of bureau, and to the service. He has a pleasing and strong personality and brings credit to the service in his contact with civilians.

"On account of his original and valuable work in devising instruments and methods for air navigation in connection with the trans-Atlantic flight, he was detailed to go to England to return on the ZR-2 to assist in navigation. He was there during the loss of ZR-2, and rendered prompt and valuable assistance at this critical time, and received letters of thanks and commendation from the British authorities which, it is assumed, have been made a part of this record. . . ."

(The above remarks concerning navigation refer to the first successful trans-Atlantic flight that took place in 1919. Byrd had charge of the navigational preparation for that flight.)

"I consider Lieutenant Byrd one of the most valuable officers I have met in the service, and that his being placed on inactive duty will be not only a loss to this bureau but to the service itself."

Chief of Bureau of Navigation, March 31 to July 12, 1922:

"Lieutenant Byrd (retired) was actively employed under this bureau during the period covered and the performance of his duties were most successfully carried out. He shows tact, knowledge, and ability of a very high order, and his services were of great value not only to the bureau but to the whole Navy. He is always courteous, willing, and earnest, and whatever work assigned him was not only cheerfully but thoroughly well carried out. The bureau regrets to lose his services."

Commandant first naval district, June 14 to September 30, 1923:

"Lieutenant Byrd has performed his duties in a most satisfactory manner. He is one of the most efficient officers that I have been associated with. He is an officer of great judgment, rare ability, rare initiative, and very conscientious. It is a great pleasure to have him associated with me."

From these extracts from Byrd's record it can easily be seen that he made his mark in the Navy long before he became famous.

Perhaps a word of explanation may be in order as to a comment made by the Chief of the Bureau of Navigation in such reports on Lieutenant Byrd's demonstrated "adaptability in handling matters dealing with Congress." Byrd has always said that he owes much of the success which may have come to him in life to the training he received at the Naval Academy and during his period of active service with the Navy. No other officer on the active or retired list is more loyal to the Navy than he. And so it came about that when it was discovered that his "tact, adaptability, and skill in handling matters pending in Congress of special interest to the Navy and its personnel" could be counted upon, the Bureau never failed to call upon him, he never failed to respond, and always gave the best that was in him to the furthering of the interests of the Navy, and of its officers and men, in legislation affecting their well-being, their pay and the supplies and material without which the Navy might prove to be a broken reed in time of need.

All of this I was well able to observe as Chairman of the Senate Naval Affairs Committee, at which time I was in close contact with him. The great majority of his fellow officers knew little of this work, as only the combined knowledge of the ranking officers could really fully tell of his actual accomplishments.

The late Rear Admiral William A. Moffett, U. S. Navy, Chief of the Bureau of Aeronautics, in the course of a most gracefully worded tribute upon Byrd's return from his North Polar flight said:

> "Byrd's polar and trans-Atlantic flights were but incidents in many years of high adventure. He went around the world alone at the age of twelve. After graduation at Annapolis he helped put down two revolutions in the West Indies. He distinguished himself by years of splendid service with our battleship fleet.
>
> "Not the least of all this unwritten record is the fact that he has been officially cited twenty times for bravery or conspicuous conduct. He has received the thanks of Congress as well as the five highest medals the country can give: Congressional Medal of Honor, Congressional Life Saving Medal, Distinguished Service Medal, the Flying Cross and the Navy Cross. Probably no other man has all of these decorations."

And he now has a total of twenty-two citations and special commendations, nine of which are for bravery and two for extraordinary heroism in saving lives.

At the risk of extending this foreword unduly, I cannot resist the temptation to make one personal comment on Byrd's Atlantic and Polar flights.

None of them was sponsored by the Navy Department, although the Navy was always keenly interested and went the limit in furnishing him such moral and material support as was permissible under Navy Regulations.

As a result, in maintaining discipline, Byrd was compelled to rely wholly upon his personal authority as leader of each of those expeditions. His authority began and ended with himself. He lacked the power to court-martial his men. Many, if not most of them, were volunteers without pay. He could not discharge them after they once reached the polar regions. Threats of docking their pay were, of course, meaningless. And yet he has never had a case of direct disobedience to his orders on any of his expeditions.

Of course, there were instances of infractions of regulations. But these never seriously threatened the discipline of any of his expeditions, even to a slight degree. Byrd's rule seems to have been based on a nicely balanced admixture of mutual tolerance and respect, accompanied by that firmness and justice in the leader without which discipline can never be maintained.

After each of these expeditions many of his men found themselves suddenly lifted from obscurity to a place in the public eye, which gave their every word and deed its own peculiar news value. Not all of them were able to keep their heads. Ambition, fame, and an opportunity to capitalize on their membership in these world-renowned adventures beckoned, and not all of them could resist the temptation to "gae their own way." Yet I am in position to know that Byrd has the devoted and loyal friendship of the great majority of the men he took with him on his various expeditions. Rarely indeed have such steadfast loyalty and devotion to the leader been reported in any of the historic records of exploration, and still more rarely in the long history of exploratory adventure in the polar regions.

Another unique phase in the handling of his expedition is the full responsibility that Byrd must bear single-handed. Other expeditions than his have been backed either by their governments or a group of men, whereas, in these enterprises of his, the largest ever sent to the polar regions, the full responsibility rests with him and him alone, to such an extent that the mistakes of any of his men could easily result in the loss of his reputation or plunge him into bankruptcy. He always realized the tremendous chances he was taking in this direction.

One characteristic of Byrd is that he does not take himself too seriously. He feels that his work is relatively unimportant compared with contributions to civilization that are being made by tens of thousands of hard-working citizens. He has worked exceptionally hard all his life and attributes his success to work rather than to any unusual ability. He takes no stock whatever in "this hero business," for he is convinced that the majority of people have great courage which will always show when the test comes; for this reason he dislikes extremely being set up as an example.

It has been said that Byrd's last expedition was the most useful and, from a scientific standpoint, the most productive Polar expedition of all time, and it has occurred to me that his services should have some special recognition by the Navy. True, a joint resolution had been passed by the Congress extending the gratitude of the Nation to Admiral Byrd and to the members of his expedition, and upon his return from that expedition the President of the United States accorded him and his men, for the first time in history, an extraordinary and unprecedented mark of appreciation of the high value of their services to the Nation, by leaving the White House to welcome the party home at the Washington Navy Yard dock, and waiving altogether, in that instance, the prescribed formal first call of the Commander of the expedition. But when I made inquiries as to some appropriate and special form of recognition of Byrd's services to be accorded him by the Navy itself, I found that he had already received every medal and decoration provided by his country for such services, and also had received a special medal voted by Congress and designed by the Navy to commemorate his earlier Polar expeditions.

In this connection I was informed that when the Congress had it in mind to vote him a special medal of honor after his flight to the South Pole on his first Antarctic Expedition, Byrd asked that medals be given to his men instead. It is only necessary to add that Congress broke all precedents by voting medals for every man as he requested.

And now I shall tell one more tale out of school. I myself radioed Byrd at Spitzbergen after his flight over the North Pole that the Navy Department would approve his promotion to the rank of Commodore and that Congress would promote him to the rank of Admiral in recognition of that magnificent achievement. But his reply, absolutely refusing to accept such an exceptional honor on the ground that his exploit did not, and could not justify such an exceptional exercise of the power of Congress, effectively squelched the movement.

After his subsequent flight over the South Pole, the demand from the public for his promotion to the rank of Admiral was so insistent that he was promoted in spite of himself. His promotion was on the retired list, as Byrd wired that under no circumstances could or would he accept an appointment which would have prevented the promotion of a number of his fellow officers, had he been passed over the heads of thousands of officers on the active list.

I may add that, contrary to the widespread belief, his appointment as Admiral on the retired list carries merely a few dollars increase over the pay to which he was already entitled.

I have tried to depict this man as he is known to his friends and his associates, but I feel that no account of him would be complete that omits the story of his long vigil in his advance weather base on his last expedition. I was deeply moved by the account written on the spot when it was still fresh in his mind by Dr. Thomas C. Poulter, his chief scientist and second in command, which was first published in the New York *Times* and reprinted in the Congressional Record of May 7, 1935. I am strongly tempted to include it in toto, but Byrd has so vigorously objected on the ground that his book is about 110 men and not one alone that I confine myself to a few of Dr. Poulter's paragraphs.

> "LITTLE AMERICA, ANTARCTICA.—Our arrival at Commander Byrd's advance-base weather station at the southernmost and coldest spot ever inhabited by man marked the end of a horrible ordeal endured by a man alone, cut off from human aid by a code that he refused to break. . . .
>
> "Though for two months three of us lived there with our Commander, jammed together in his 9-by-13 room, we learned next to nothing from him of his experience, for he told us no more than bare courtesy required. I had expected this, for I knew that the many thousands who heard him lecture on his last expedition were struck by the fact that not once did he mention himself. Therefore, when he writes of this expedition, he will, I am sure, as is his custom, omit the part he played. That his experience may not be entirely lost, I have consented to write this article for the New York *Times*.
>
> "When we first saw him, on August 10, we were shocked at his appearance. Emaciated, hollow-cheeked, weak, and haggard though he was, he met us casually, calmer by far than any of us. 'Hello, fellows,' he said, as if he had seen us only yesterday, but his ghastly condition and husky voice told us that, in spite of this matter-of-factness, he had been through some terrific things. When I learned that his condition had been even worse and that his most desperate time had been many weeks before our arrival, in the very middle of the winter night, I realized dimly what his battle for survival must have been.
>
> "Since that time I have been collecting here and there the pieces that go to make a consecutive story of his trials. Some I have gathered from casual remarks he has dropped from time to time in conversation or in the discussion of his cold-weather problems. Some I have from his old friend Murphy, who received and handled his radioed instructions, and still more from his record, a part of which I had a chance to read. Putting the pieces together I discovered that I have come upon something rare. It is a picture of a mighty trial of manhood and spirit and reveals something of Byrd the man. . . .
>
> "He went much further than his refusal to call for help, and in so doing lessened his chances for survival. Time and again he exhausted the slender reserve of strength he had struggled so desperately to gain in order to keep radio contact. After his engine broke down, he had to hand crank the generator. He knew that, in spite of his instructions to the contrary, his men at Little America would have fought through to him had radio communication with him suddenly ceased. He does not talk of this but the facts show his reasoning. . . .
>
> "But these facts came afterward, we did not know them at Little America. I did not know them when I requested his permission to make a tractor journey to the advance base with the

benefit of improving twilight of late July for meteor observations. His disarming reply to this request said: 'I approve the trip only on condition that you can make it without undue risk to the men on the first attempt.'

"We turned back half-way short of the advance base in obedience to his strictly worded safety precautions. When we did reach the advance base in August we were scarcely two weeks ahead of the sun. His need for aid had passed. He had fought it out alone and wholly within himself in June and, in spite of recurring periods of weakness, he was once more struggling uphill.

"I don't know of anything finer than that in life or literature. The odds were so overwhelmingly against him that he should rightfully have lost his fight. Had he done so, his chivalrous regard for us would have been only too evident. It is natural that he should have our deep gratitude, for what he endured and for his willingness to face the supreme sacrifice in his thoughtfulness for our safety."

CLAUDE A. SWANSON,
Secretary of the Navy.

Washington, D.C.,
October, 1935.

CONTENTS

ILLUSTRATIONS

MAPS

DISCOVERY

THE STORY OF THE SECOND BYRD ANTARCTIC EXPEDITION

Chapter I

PLAN AND PREPARATION

I

MY decision to return to Antarctica with a second exploring expedition was not so much a spontaneous thought as a maturing compulsion bred by the work of my first expedition. Problems of large geographical and scientific importance remained to be investigated, and it seemed desirable—more than that, imperative—to attempt to close them while we still had the momentum of one successful effort, the advantage of a more enlightened public interest in Antarctic research, and while there was still available an Antarctic-trained personnel from whom could be drawn the nucleus for a second and stronger expedition. There is really only one effective training ground for Antarcticists, to borrow Cherry-Gerrard's identification; and that is Antarctica itself. And, finally, there was, at least for me, the intangible attraction of the white continent itself, the pull of discovery, of seeing new lands and fitting into the jig-saw of geography the missing pieces beyond the horizon. No one who has ever seen new lands rising above the prow of a ship, or above a running dog team, or through the shine of a propeller, can easily deny the pull. Of all the continents, Antarctica is the fairest, white and unspoiled, spacious and austere, fashioned in the clean, antiseptic quarries of an Ice Age.

Anyhow, that was the way I looked at it. When I walked out of Little America, in February 1930, to go down to the ship, it was with the firm resolve to go back.

"We'll be back, Bill," I said to Haines, the meteorologist.

"Not me," said Bill, watching the frosty cliffs of the Barrier recede, "once is quite enough."

Well, four years later both of us were to stand again over Little America, in the rare sunshine of its sheltering valley, and Bill was digging furiously down to our old quarters. When at last his chunky frame slid and disappeared into the depths of the Balloon Station, I drew a sigh of relief such as I have rarely had opportunity to indulge.

For a long time the odds were three to one we'd never get back.

The Second Byrd Antarctic Expedition was assembled and departed in the travail of the depression. Indifference, its own poverty, even actual hostility were among the obstacles it had to overcome. In my own files are letters—not the most agreeable correspondence—berating me for stupidity and selfishness in setting forth on such an enterprise when the country was in a bad way. What they were driving at wasn't very clear. I'm quite sure they couldn't have measured Little America as a haven for spirits too sensitive to endure the economic agonies of civilization. The south polar regions are too slashingly severe for a sensitivity of any sort. It was hard to see how the departure of a handful of men, almost entirely supported by what they had been able to beg or borrow, could impair the resources of a country of 120 millions of population, with a national income of 40 billions. On the other hand, there was a certain merit in again advancing the flag, on an errand of discovery and research, to a continent where it was absent for nearly a century.

However, in the full measure, all this is trifling. The difficulties in the beginning made the final success all the more satisfying. Had not the country—the Government in the person of President Roosevelt, the Navy in the person of Secretary Swanson—had not business men and many old friends who supported my previous expeditions, come to our assistance, the ships would never have passed Boston Light. Behind the expedition, as I write this, lie thousands of miles of hazardous voyaging, more than 450,000 square miles of new lands explored or surveyed, and it is proper that these debts should be acknowledged.

The actual cash donations were about $150,000—a meager war chest for an expedition with a million dollar task. It was soon spent. Its other resources were made up of material and stores either given outright or loaned, and (as in the instance of the General Foods broadcast over the Columbia Broadcasting System) payments for services rendered. Nearly one hundred thousand dollars' worth of scientific equipment was loaned to the expedition by various universities, the U. S. Government and scientific institutions.

II

Antarctica has occupied a curious place in geographical history. Though its existence had been forecast in the speculations of Greek philosophers before the time of Christ, to balance their conception of a symmetrical geography, and though Pomponius Mela, forty-three years after Christ, had conferred the name Antichthones (or Antipodeans) upon the inhabitants of this imaginary continent beyond the Torrid Zone of frightful heat, the actual discovery of the continent was more than two thousand years in coming. It was the last of the great land masses to be lifted into the realm of geography. Thirty years after Columbus the whole Atlantic coast of the New World had been felt out by the navigators, from Labrador to Tierra del Fuego. Yet today, nearly 100 years after its discovery, and in spite of all the vaunted methods and implements of modern civilization, there still remains in Antarctica a great stretch of coastline which has yet to be seen, yet to be charted. The Boston Tea Party (1773) was brewing when Captain Cook ushered in "an epoch in the world's history" [1] by crossing the Antarctic Circle. John Bidwell was making ready to set out from Missouri with the first of the covered wagon trains to the Promised Land of California just about the time (1841) the British bombing ships, *Erebus* and *Terror,* dropped their hooks in the mud of Derwent River, Hobart, Australia, and Captain Ross was posting to England the brilliant news of the discovery of the Antarctic Continent. Yet the Spanish-American War was only three years distant when man for the first time (1895) set foot on it.[2]

These convenient, if arbitrary, date-marks are set up merely to show how sluggish, in contrast with the headlong rush of discovery and exploration over the rest of the world, was the evolution of Antarctic geography. Hungry as they were for land, and greedy for discovery, the great circumnavigators of the sixteenth and seventeenth centuries recoiled from the violence of the far southern seas. Though Drake rounded Tierra del Fuego in 1578 and "there was no maine nor iland to be seen to the southwards, the Atlantic Ocean and the South Sea meeting in a most large and free scope," nevertheless two centuries elapsed before a ship's keel pierced the Antarctic Circle. In 1895 the Sixth International Geographical Congress, meeting in London, declared that "the exploration of the Antarctic regions is the greatest piece of geographical exploration still to be undertaken." Which statement is as true today as the day it was propounded. Within the still undiscovered, still unknown, and uncharted interior regions could be secreted the whole of Europe.

I shall not attempt here, as I did in the account of the first expedition, to outline the history of previous Antarctic explorations. That has been done more thoroughly and better than I could do it.[3] As for the original motives, they are familiar enough—weary and disillusioned reflections of the land hunger, the feverish lusts and excitements that animated the tidal wave of discovery after Columbus launched the furious nautical enterprises of European maritime powers toward the New World. The feeling out of the South American coast line in the quest for the strait between the Atlantic and Pacific oceans inevitably forced navigators into high southern latitudes. But after Magellan, for a long period, it was contrary winds and gales blowing ships to the south, rather than the incentive of exploration, which led to further discoveries in Antarctic regions.[4] The far southern seas were too fierce and the climate too inhospitable for adventurers whose minds were

[1] H. R. Mill, *The Siege of the South Pole,* 71.

[2] Ibid., 382.

[3] Readers interested in general histories are recommended: Mill, *The Siege of the South Pole;* Hayes, *Antarctica* and *The Conquest of the South Pole;* Markham, *The Lands of Silence.* In addition there are the accounts of Scott, Amundsen, Mawson, Shackleton and their associates. As fine a book as any is Cherry-Gerrard's *The Worst Journey in the World.*

[4] Sir Clements Markham, *Lands of Silence,* 389.

tuned to the softer enchantments of El Dorado, the Fountain of Youth and the Golden Temple of Doboyba. Ultimately search for the southern continent was an issue in the far-flung struggle of the great European powers for commercial and political supremacy; it was a factor in empire-building, with Australia as one of its products.[5]

But the frenzy passed, chilled by the prophecy of Cook retreating from the ice "countries condemned to everlasting rigidity." Commercially, Antarctica is small change; its only accessible resource is whaling, and even these fishing fields are being depleted. Immense coal deposits exist in the mountains, and traces of commercial ores have been found. But such are the practical difficulties of reaching them, they might as well be on the moon. In this respect, Antarctica is a frozen asset.

Cook was wrong, however, when he exclaimed, "I make bold to declare that the world will derive no benefit from" the finding of the southern continent. During the sixty years since the *Challenger's* dredges, scraping ocean bottom in 1300 to 1975 fathoms of water at the edge of the Antarctic pack ice, hauled up glaciated fragments of gneisses, granites, micaschists, grained quartzites, sandstones and shales,[6] proving that what Ross had found was not an oceanic island but a continent, Antarctica has fulfilled a certain brilliant purpose.

Commercially barren and, for all calculable practical purposes, of no account in the land scrambles of imperial powers, it has quietly entered geography as the common domain, the particular sphere of influence, of world science. In this respect, certainly, it has continental traditions and prospects unique among the great regions of the earth.

The world is small and rapidly getting smaller. These are days of bathyspheres, moon rockets, stratospheric flights and 200-inch telescope lenses. But if the world is shrinking, it is because science is audacious and unsatisfied. And if the Antarctic has shrunk least of all, if it still stands aloof and hidden in glacial fogs, it is because the pack ice and the gales which defend its coasts, and the cold, the blizzards and the unutterable lifelessness of the interior regions are not easily to be subdued.

Looking at it in the broad way, there are few divisions of science, or sections of human knowledge, that cannot be profitably explored in Antarctica.

Geology, glaciology, meteorology, botany, biology and zoölogy, astronomy physics, geography, terrestrial magnetism, oceanography, geophysics and paleontology—these and many others hold open broad avenues of research. In all, the second expedition was equipped to investigate and did investigate some 22 divisions and subdivisions of scientific research.

None of them is esoteric and of narrow and peculiar importance

[5] Mill, op. cit., 1.
[6] Ibid., 360.

to remote places. With varying degrees of intimacy they all have, somewhere, a bearing upon problems world-wide in scope. Just how important are the expedition's findings in these various branches of research it is, of course, impossible to estimate, at least so soon after our return. I believe that we all pride ourselves on having achieved, by a fair margin, the most complete program of scientific research in the history of polar exploration. But polar exploration, by its very definition, is pioneering. It is first of all an instrument geared to penetration, whose primary object is fact-finding and observation. Theory and interpretation, which are the beginnings of enlightenment, come later. There must first intervene a period of painstaking correlation and appraisal.

Take, for example, the single problem of terrestrial magnetism. The revival in the middle nineteenth century of the search for the Antarctic continent had its origins in the clamorous needs of practical navigation for the completion of magnetic charts in the southern hemisphere. Steam was coming in, trade was booming along the routes to China, Australia, and India; and merchants, spurred by the need of making faster voyages, were sending their masters on great circle courses round the Cape of Good Hope and Cape Horn, which necessarily carried ships into high southern latitudes. The treachery of the compasses, owing to the uncertainty of magnetic conditions nearer the South Pole, made navigation hazardous.[7] The discovery of the Antarctic continent by Ross was the culmination of an expedition dispatched primarily on magnetic research.[8]

Nowadays the problem is of much wider scope. The paucity of data from the south polar regions has made our knowledge of the permanent magnetic field of the earth decidedly incomplete. According to recent data, more lines of magnetic force seem to be leaving the earth than entering it, a condition inconsistent with classical magnetic theory. A fascinating possibility was at once opened up. More adequate knowledge of the magnetic field in the vicinity of the South Pole may either indicate that the state of things is in harmony with classical theory, or else stimulate a more intensive search for such theoretical entities as the dirac isolated magnetic pole, with a consequent impact not only upon the science of terrestrial magnetism, but also upon the whole field of physics, notably in nuclear studies and cosmic ray theories. The expedition was equipped to collect data in the three main problems of terrestrial magnetism associated with—(1) the permanent field of the earth, its distribution, secular change and local anomalies; (2) the regular diurnal variation and (3) the irregular variations of storms. Toward this end it was outfitted by the Carnegie Institution of Washington, D. C.

Or take, for example, the problem of glaciology. In the earth's history there is no chapter more enthralling than glaciation. It is also the

[7] Mill, op. cit., 183.
[8] Markham, op. cit., 410.

blankest chapter, a glittering edifice of theories and a painful want of substantive data. Antarctica is the one region on the earth today where ice sheets of continental extent survive almost in their fullest development—where modern ice theories can be put to thorough test [9]—and where we can observe the mechanism of an Ice Age such as in the Pleistocene overwhelmed Europe and the United States, with a profound influence upon the evolution of mankind.

As for meteorology, biology, geology and the other traditional departments of Antarctic expeditions, we were rather strongly equipped both in the matter of men and instruments; the work will be discussed in the proper place later on. It should be pointed out here, however, that the expedition made a number of innovations in Antarctic research, with notable results. It had the distinction of (1) extending cosmic ray research into the highest southern latitudes yet attained in the adventuresome pursuit of this perhaps most exciting of modern phenomena; (2) of initiating meteor observations in association with a world-wide chain of synchronized observatories; (3) of modernizing meteorological observations, including the use of airplanes on high-altitude aërological soundings; (4) of extending the mapping technique introduced by the first expedition, and (5) of introducing the use of seismic instruments, such as are employed in petroleum geophysics, for determining the nature and thickness of the Antarctic Ice Cap, which till then were entirely conjectural. For the suggestion to use the latter I am indebted to Dr. R. A. Daly of Harvard and the Harvard Committee on Geophysical Research; [10] for the construction and loan of a special set of seismic instruments and a complete set of standard equipment I am indebted to the Seismograph Service Corporation of Tulsa, Oklahoma, and the Geophysical Research Corporation.

III

The geographical program was as complete as our ingenuity, skill and perseverance could make it. Perhaps in this connection a statement of policy is in order. Geographical discovery is still, as it always was, the brightest weapon in the explorer's armory; but in the new philosophy of exploration it is principally a tool for getting at something deeper. It attains the dignity of a science only when, rising above the superficial glory of a first penetration, it brings the apparatus of science to bear upon the *unknown* for a truer understanding of a multiplicity of problems.

In the program of the second expedition there was no spectacular objective, no *tour de force* such as a polar flight, that would create great

[9] R. E. Priestley and C. S. Wright, *Some Ice Problems of Antarctica, Problems of Polar Research,* American Geographical Society, 335.

[10] Seismic methods in glacier studies were used, several years before, in the Oetztaler Alps and also in Greenland.

public interest. The nearest we came to that sort of thing was a proposed flight from the vicinity of Peter I Island and across the unknown coast to Little America. This project, however, had to be canceled. The burden of nearly every main flight, surface journey or ship's penetration was exploration of the Pacific Quadrant. Therein is the key to the network of tracks traversing the reconnaissance maps elsewhere in this book. The attacks were intensive and, in many places, interlocking, with one great region as a target.

One of the practical difficulties in writing about unknown lands, and especially about the polar regions, is to set up points of orientation from which the average reader can find his way among unfamiliar places and circumstances. Bold landmarks are comparatively scanty, ice is anonymous and monotonous, and, except to navigators and students, fixes of position, which is to say latitude and longitude, are almost meaningless.

Hence the difficulty in establishing in terms of understandable boundaries the whereabouts of the Pacific Quadrant.[11] For our immediate purposes, it may be sufficient to identify it as the great region of unknown land and sea lying east of Little America, including the unknown seas of the South Pacific Ocean that beat against the unknown coast, thence up through the unknown interior to the Pole. Clear to Hearst Land, south of Cape Horn, discovered by Sir Hubert Wilkins, on the opposite side of the continent, the region was a geographical vacuum. If the interior was completely blank, the coast and its ocean approaches were hardly less so. In the South Pacific between the 150th and 130th meridians West, for example, the horizon of knowledge had barely been pushed beyond the Antarctic Circle—and, astonishingly, the record was Cook's penetration of 1773. The region drew my interest throughout the first expedition. We succeeded in making two successful aërial casts to the east, the first of which located the Rockefeller Mountains, and the second, northeast along the uncharted coast, yielded up the Edsel Ford coastal range of Marie Byrd Land. I considered the results of this flight far more important than the results of our flight to the Pole. Up to that time discovery in this sector was limited to Scott's coasting of the Barrier to King Edward VII Land, approximately 165 miles east of the Bay of Whales, and the overland journey by Lieut. Prestrud of Amundsen's expedition to the Alexandra Mountains in the same vicinity.

Against the Marie Byrd Land region, holding as it did the most substantial American gains on the continent, we proposed to throw

[11] It was Sir Clements Markham who first conceived the idea of dividing Antarctica into four equal quadrants, based upon the Greenwich meridian and identified according to the great land masses or oceans facing them—thus, the American, African, Australian and Pacific Quadrants. A second arbitrary division—East and West Antarctica, likewise based upon the Greenwich meridian—was suggested by Dr. Nordenskjöld and E. S. Balch (Hayes, *Antarctica,* 10).

virtually the full weight of our field resources—to run over it a geographical network of an intensity and range impossible to previous expeditions. With ships, airplanes, dog teams and snow tractors, a broad plan seemed feasible. The idea was to launch a double attack by ship and plane on the way in, having for its principal object the exploration of the unknown coastal regions of the Pacific Quadrant. In the second season (that is to say, the second Antarctic spring and summer) we would press the attack into the interior from Little America, using dog teams, tractors and aviation on a broad front between the coast and the Queen Maud Range buttressing the polar plateau. How extensive these operations were may be judged from the fact that on a north-and-south line a corridor of discovery was driven through the Pacific Quadrant from the Antarctic Circle to the rim of the polar plateau, a distance of 1437 miles. And this was a by-product of various voyages, flights and journeys having special and wider missions.

Apart from the fact the region was unknown, speculation had invested it with several of the most crucial problems of Antarctic geography. First of all, there was the delineation of the coast-line, a primary problem in geography. Associated with it was the challenging possibility of an archipelago or peninsula jutting from the coast in the vicinity of Marie Byrd Land. There was the problem of investigating the trend and structure of the Edsel Fords. Of first-rate importance was the delineation of the eastern shore of the Ross Ice Barrier, the mighty shelf of supposedly largely water-borne ice hinged to the Queen Maud Range on the south and South Victoria Land on the west and fronting upon the Ross Sea. Associated with this was the surmise of a great Ice Strait passing (in theory) between the Ross and Weddell Seas and dividing the continent. No more impressive commentary on the weakness of Antarctic geography could be made than this, that there was question whether Antarctica were one continent or two.

However, these and related objectives will be taken up in detail later on. All this is in the nature of a foreshadowing—or perhaps I should say, in all frankness, an *apologia* for returning with a second expedition. In the course of my travels through this enlightened commonwealth I still meet an astonishingly large number of otherwise well-informed people who wonder what we were doing down there. They seem to have the idea everything could have been cleaned up by a single trip, like a suburbanite's shopping trip to town.

Happily the region we planned to study was so accessible from Little America that the original base in the Bay of Whales could again be used. We thus escaped the enormous risk of having to locate and found a new base on an unknown coast.

IV

We had, therefore, a sound plan, excellent objectives and a personnel trained in Antarctic field methods; all we lacked was money. And in the years of Our Lord 1932-1933, it will be recalled by men not necessarily with long gray beards way down to here, money was rather hard to get. A sense of doom and discouragement was withering the spirit of the country; and even rich men felt themselves so overpoweringly beset that I could not bring myself to ask former benefactors, with one or two exceptions, to come to our help. Still, it's remarkable how far you can go without money.

As I remarked earlier, our capital amounted to about $150,000, donated mostly in small amounts by thousands of people, some of whom got no request from me for funds. The largest contributors were Edsel Ford, an unfailing friend in the past, William Horlick, Colonel Ruppert, Thomas J. Watson, and the National Geographic Society.

The strange tales and untruths that get abroad often make a hard task harder. Contrary to a rather widespread belief, I've never had unlimited backing or support from any individual or organization. Even if such sponsorship had been available, I'm not sure that I would have accepted it unless I were given a free hand; otherwise it might involve too much red tape, too many restrictions, and directions from the "home office." With radio a man in a Fifth Avenue office can nowadays transmit—as easily and swiftly as telephoning—a message to an exploring unit near the South Pole. Successful exploration is pretty much a matter of spot decisions. As a matter of fact, I have found organizations extremely reluctant to take the responsibility for so uncertain an undertaking. As for the government, it would take an act of Congress to allow governmental sponsorship for such a large expedition, and I doubt if such an act could be passed. I have not been unaware of the dangers I have been risking on these expeditions other than those of a physical nature. Personal bankruptcy could easily follow an untoward accident such as the sinking of one of the ships in the ice or in a bad storm, and my reputation as a leader would also be involved. Other expeditions that have approached the size of mine generally had the government back of them to shoulder the responsibility. I have often felt that it is really too much for one man to assume.

I've borne the responsibility and debts of the expeditions I have led. It hasn't always been the gentlest of occupations. It follows a certain remorseless pattern—an exhausting period of preparation and begging, a heavy field campaign, and on top of that a dreary struggle to pay off accumulated debts, piling up like the layers of a cake.

Luckily an expedition has something to sell besides its capacity to collect scientific data. It has, on account of public interest in its career and discoveries, a definite advertising and publicity value. This is one of its principal stocks in trade. In return for the right to advertise their products as being used under rigorous polar conditions, manufacturers will often contribute certain necessary supplies, in the lush days would sometimes make cash contributions, as well. Were it not for this it would be impossible for such an expedition to serve science, for sufficient funds could not be raised to buy the necessary equipment.

Even Columbus worked on a percentage basis. Every navigator that set forth for the New World in the Golden Age of Discovery had an iron-bound contract either with the Crown or his backers. But in polar exploration there is no loot to be divided—no pearls and gold ornaments, spices and silk—as a rule just a handsome debt, as easy to share as an incipient case of leprosy, and a great mass of scientific data that is very costly to work up and publish.

There's a broader way to look at all this. What products we gathered under such arrangements were essential. They passed certain rigid standards. And I know that in many cases the advertising value involved was not the only reason those great corporations contributed to our undertaking. The forward-looking, loyal business of this country is unselfishly interested in the advancement of science.

In this group especially must be listed Mackay Radio and Telegraph and the Tidewater Oil Company. The latter donated fuel for the flagship, for aviation, tractors, and electrical generators. Clarence Mackay and his staff through Mackay Radio and its associated company, Postal Telegraph, handled free of charge all communications between the expedition and the States. Incalculable were the contributions they made. Also in this group falls the help given us by Mr. Seward M. Patterson, shoe manufacturer. The most difficult and important part of the body to protect from cold are the feet. Mr. Patterson worked for over two years to produce for us the proper kind of wearing shoes and ski boots. He was eminently successful. Through my old friend, Charles J. Faulkner, Armour and Company donated a considerable amount of food supplies and the man pemmican. The latter is indispensable for long trail operations. Thomas E. Wilson, president of Wilson and Company, and Gustavus Swift, president of Swift and Company, were very generous in the donation of meat products. Among the thousands of other contributors, many of whom I shall have occasion to mention elsewhere in this book, I must express especially deep obligation to Berwind White Coal Company; Brown and Williamson Tobacco Company; Eastman Kodak Company; General Electric Company; and Plymouth Cordage Company.

We also had another asset—a story to sell. This time radio, after weighing the problem carefully and examining the technical hazards, decided to risk it. A costly gamble for every one if it failed—a 10,000 mile radio telephone circuit, expensive amplification relay hookups at

Buenos Aires, Honolulu, Long Island and San Francisco, and Little America incapable of powering a transmitter of much better than peanut-stand strength compared to the power of average broadcasting stations. However fascinating it might be as a novelty, just an uproar of static from the south polar regions (and it was static, by the way, not the sound of the blizzards and the cracking of ice) couldn't compete with the crooners and the tattlers.

Messrs. Paley and Klauber of the Columbia Broadcasting System, and Chester and Butler of General Foods Corporation took a sporting chance. Happily it came off all right, thanks to the excellence of the engineers all along the line. We are forever indebted for such generous support. The money from the broadcasts kept life breathing in the expedition when the pulse had all but stopped.

Yet all these things which ultimately made it possible to go back hung fire for a long time—for months, even several years. The deepest crevasses and the heaviest gales an explorer has to contend with are financial.

The task of hammering together a second expedition was begun hard upon the demobilization of the first. It moved slowly enough at the beginning. My secretary, Hazel McKercher, and I worked alone at first. Miss McKercher, by her great efficiency and loyalty, has made great contributions to all my undertakings. Warrant Officer Victor F. Czegka, veteran of the first expedition, was made general manager. He took a small office in Boston. His staff consisted of a secretary and Stevenson Corey, who volunteered his services and worked faithfully from the start. The Navy loaned us the use of a storehouse at the Boston Navy Yard.

To fulfill the broad program of geographical exploration and scientific research which alone would justify a return to Antarctica, we required a vast quantity of things—planes, dogs, tractors, ships, food, clothing—all the innumerable things indispensable to the setting up of an expedition on a continent which offers nothing toward existence except seal and penguin meat.

Primus stoves from Sweden; special skis and bindings from Norway; fur clothing (mukluks, parkas, mittens, sleeping bags, pants and inner liners) from Alaska; dogs from Quebec Province, Labrador, Manitoba and the pick of American kennels; bamboo poles (for trail flags) from the tropics, the latest charts from the British Admiralty and from the U. S. Navy Hydrographic Office. The single item of bolts, nuts and screws occupied an inch-sheaf of invoice pages—everything from tiny watch screws to bolts 8-feet long. Czegka's list of categories of supplies covered 52 pages, and each category was necessarily subdivided many times. For instance, we required 27 types of knives, from ice knives to cleavers. The tailor needed some twenty different kinds of needles. So much for little things. To equip an airplane for polar flying and maintain it in the field calls for hundreds of accessories, tools and spares.

It's remarkable how many things you need. Apart from food (sugar—15 tons, flour—30 tons, dehydrated vegetables—2,000 pounds, especially manufactured dog and man pemmican, etc., etc.) there are myriads of other things. 7,000 yards of windproof cloth for clothing, tents and flags; hickory for 50 sledges; 100,000 feet of piano wire for ocean soundings and samplings; 27,000 feet of rawhide for sledge lashings; 750 gross of screws; 2 outboard motors and 3 collapsible boats; 2 sinks and 6 stepladders; 15 stoves and 100 tons of coal; 20 gasoline and kerosene pressure lanterns and over a hundred mattresses; 15,000 yards of canvas and 1,500 pounds of pipe tobacco; chinaware and toilet paper; ski poles and a wind-driven generator; flashlights and batteries; blankets and shirts; 18 tons of rope for this and that, gang lines, sledge lashings, ships' tackle, etc.; 720 pairs of wool mittens and 300 pairs of overalls; 3,000 books and 6 cases of chewing gum; 5 typewriters and four phonographs; 12 telephone poles for radio antennae and a complete machine shop; 1100 pairs of wool socks; 72 brooms; 165 snow shovels (inglorious instrument!); hundreds of charts; 125 cases of soap; and some 60 cases of strong sauces to subdue, when the flesh is weak and the palate flagging, the taste of sealmeat and the eternal salt horse. . . .

I could go on forever, only to prove something which needs no proof: that outfitting a polar expedition is a mean and intricate business.

I seem to remember that Czegka, even after he had drawn up a list of needed things from the memory and experience of the first expedition, painstakingly traveled through the encyclopædic Manufacturers' Catalogue, item by item, just to make sure nothing was left out—a monumental effort by itself.

Thus as early as 1931 we had a clear-cut idea of what we needed. Ships, sealing-wax and anti-scorbutics. But the storehouse was as empty as Mother Hubbard's cupboard.

It would be unforgivably tedious to attempt to chronicle the accumulation of the multitudinous things. We proved ourselves, if nothing else, the world's hardest working beggars. We wrote innumerable times and called upon manufacturers and firms specializing in the things the expedition required. Approximately 30,000 letters were dispatched hither and yon, having for their theme, "Please, sir, would you be so kind . . ." And there were almost as many replies saying, in a word, "Sorry, gentlemen, but business conditions are such . . ." Czegka wrote 127 letters, by honest count, trying to persuade firms to donate overalls; in the end we had to buy them. He canvassed lumber yards for a year before he found a firm willing to donate hickory for the sledges.

Czegka refused to believe they meant no *positively* until he was turned down forty-three times. I never understood why the fatal limit should be an odd figure.

But to Czegka first of all, and next to Corey, later expedition Supply Officer, goes full credit for achieving the impossible. In a large measure the things we sailed with, the gear and stores which made possible the existence of the expedition, were gathered through their industry.

There were others, too. Paul Siple, who had served with me in the Antarctic, Kennett Rawson, who was with me in Greenland in 1925, Pete Demas, veteran of three of my expeditions, joined us later on. To assist in raising supplies and to handle our business interests while we were away, I had the invaluable services of Leo McDonald, an old friend who has been connected with my activities since 1926, and John McNeil. Without these two men we would have been hard pressed indeed.

By the summer of 1933 nearly 100 people, mostly volunteers, were working for us—were struggling to get us ready with a dogged purposefulness and unselfishness that made everything else—the defeats and humiliations, the disappointments and weariness—seem unimportant. Take, for example, the great work of T. S. McCaleb, building radio communication sets when I didn't have a five-cent piece to give him. He was loaned to us by the famous scientist and explorer, Dr. Hamilton Rice.

And as the word traveled round that, with a break or two, the expedition would sail in October, the clans began to gather—June, who had been co-pilot on the flight to the South Pole; Petersen, Blackburn; Johansen from Norway; Noville, executive officer on the North Pole expedition and co-pilot and radio operator on the trans-Atlantic flight; Finn Ronne, whose father had served in the Antarctic both under Amundsen and myself; Innes-Taylor; Bill Haines, meteorologist on both polar expeditions—eighteen men in all who had previously served with me again went south. One of them celebrated by getting married two weeks before he left. After two years I'm still trying to think up a convincing tale for the day I meet his wife.

V

My last two expeditions have been so costly because of our earnest desire and very ambitious plans for scientific work. It was because of this that we needed so much equipment and so many men. We needed ships also, two of them: a big steel ship not alone to transport the bulk of the stores and scientific apparatus, but also to carry on her deck a twin-engined plane with an 82-foot wing spread. An icebreaker, a stout wooden ship, to serve as supply ship and shoulder the brunt of the work in pack ice. Taking a metal ship deep into the Antarctic ice and laying her against ice to unload is always a long risk, which is another reason I wanted a second ship in reserve.

Well, there was no shortage of ships. Harbors, roadsteads and wharfs were lined with vessels driven by the depression from the seas. One day I was offered 50 of them, including a yacht originally owned by a prince. The prices were fair enough, but the treasury gave forth only a hollow sound.

The United States Shipping Board had laid up at Staten Island a number of freighters, mostly of war-time construction, which hadn't been able to earn their keep. The Shipping Board was generous. For a dollar-a-year we got the loan of a three-island, oil-burning outcast from the Pacific lumber trade, named *Pacific Fir.* She looked her age, and the engines hadn't turned for some time. Rechristened the *Jacob Ruppert,* after my friend Colonel Jacob Ruppert, she left the graveyard, with a creaking and groaning in her stiffened members, for a fleeting resurrection in the ice of the far south. But she was a good ship, and the personnel of the Shipping Board could not have been more coöperative.

Locating a trustworthy ice ship was more difficult. Not many are available. The barkentine *City of New York* of the first expedition was past her usefulness; she was reduced to the state of a floating museum, towed ignominiously from one exhibition mart to another. Out in Oakland, California, I came upon another old ice-breaker, a celebrated ship, the barkentine *Bear,* which in April, 1884, had relieved the six survivors of the Greely expedition at Cape Sabine and subsequently served brilliantly in the Arctic. She was recommended to me by my old friend Bob Bartlett. She was the "White Angel" of the whaling fleet and she policed the gold rush to the Yukon. Retired from the Coast Guard in 1928, she had become the property of the City of Oakland. She had been constructed at Greenock, Scotland, in 1874; built of oak, with the frames close together and stoutly braced forward against the shocks of working in ice. First a whaler, she was purchased ten years later by the U. S. Government for the special purpose of breaking through to the Greely party after the relief expeditions of 1882 and 1883 had failed. Later on she was further strengthened against ice pressure with additional beams and truss frames; iron straps were fixed over the stem and secured with through bolts, and filling pieces were inserted to close up the angle between keel and bottom and thus absorb the lateral thrust of the ice and keep the bottom planking from opening up. Water-tight bulkheads were built in forward and aft; and a sheathing of Australian iron bark was laid along the water line to guard her planking. She had auxiliary steam power. She was 200 feet long, with a draught of 18 feet, 2 inches, beam of 32 feet, and 703 tons net register. In her prime she could make 9 knots under steam, according to a report written by Captain Cochran, who commanded her on eight cruises. Well, she never quite did that for us.

Old as she was, the *Bear* was the ship we were looking for. She was still staunch and sound. I asked the City of Oakland if she was available. Very generously the authorities offered to put her up for public auction, as was required by law. It was to be one of those gentlemanly understandings. However, there was a slight miscarriage. The agreeable formality of the auction was suddenly interrupted by a local junkman's startling bid of $1,000. He wanted to break her up for junk. The auction almost broke up. Somebody spoke firmly but discreetly to the junkman. At any rate, it was his first and last bid. We got the ship for $1050, and she was christened *Bear of Oakland,* the least I could do to show my gratitude.

Not long afterwards she was sailed to Boston by a volunteer crew, where she was presently joined by the *Ruppert.* Both ships required extensive overhaul, and here again we came up hard against the question of funds. The labor was volunteer; it is refreshing how many good men will give a willing hand to a rightful purpose. But gear and parts were expensive, and we had to wriggle and squirm to put the ships in condition for sea.

There was the matter of ballast for the *Ruppert,* four thousand tons of headaches. No getting around that: the ship had to be deep in the water to hold her propeller down while working in pack ice. Most of all she would need ballast for the stormy transit back to New Zealand after unloading at Little America. Quite innocently I inquired into the price of the cheapest pig iron. The price was around $50,000. We nearly foundered in high seas then and there.

Even rocks and sand, counting hauling charges, were too expensive. The Navy offered a pile of old guns and armor plate at Portsmouth (N. H.) Navy Yard, but the cost and time required for breaking them up were prohibitive. Finally, through the Chief of Naval Operations, Admiral Standley, who had already assisted in countless ways, the Navy loaned us 500 tons of ancient anchor chain. A beginning. The *Ruppert* would also have to carry upwards of a thousand tons of coal for coaling the *Bear* in the Antarctic ice and at New Zealand. We could count on that. But still 2,500 tons of ballast to go.

An odd sort of a gamble touched with generosity finally saw us through. I remembered seeing great mounds of coal in the yards of the Pocahontas Fuel Company. Taking a shot in the dark, I telephoned the president, Mr. O. L. Alexander, and made a proposition: I asked him if he would lend us several thousand tons of lowest grade coal for ballast, which we would promise to pay for if, through any mishap, we were unable to return it two years hence. Meanwhile he'd have free storage for it, we suggested, hopefully, and perhaps, if prices rose by 1935, a chance for a better price. Mr. Alexander was a sporting gentleman. With his coal, the steaming coal for the *Bear,* the anchor chain and a fair measure of unpaid bills in the office safe, the *Ruppert* was finally ballasted.

For putting the ships in commission, refitting them for long and dangerous voyages, I shall forever be grateful to Lieut. Commanders E. P. A. Simpson and W. K. Queen, Lieut. H. H. Jackson, all of the Naval Reserve, and Mr. E. J. Ropes. We still wonder how they did it with so little money and supplies. Sometimes I hardly dared ask. One of the crew was arrested for "borrowing" another ship's clock he had neglected to ask for. Czegka, thinking of the overalls correspondence, blew up over that. He didn't think it was cricket.

Planes? The field operations called for four—a twin-engined engine for long-range exploration which would be capable of operating from floats and skis; an auto-gyro for short-range reconnaissance and high-altitude aërological flights; and two single-engined planes for intermediate purposes and reserve. Not an extravagant number, as it turned out. I was mindful of the Fokker we lost in the Rockefellers the first season at Little America. This time we were to crash two.

Here, again, the abject maneuverings of the poor and not very meek who were to inherit the ice. Repelled in the attempts to get a big plane by outright donation, and lighting happily upon the ancient truth that the whole is equal to the sum of its parts, we even resorted to the strategy of trying to induce the individual manufacturers of the innumerable parts that make up a modern plane each to contribute his particular unit. We did not get the total plane donated, but we got enough parts to reduce substantially the cost of the plane we finally purchased.

At the critical moment my old friend William Horlick came forward with a substantial cash donation. With what he gave and what we were able to borrow, we got the plane the job called for—a Curtiss-Wright Condor, powered by two supercharged Wright Cyclones (725 H.P.), fitted with skis and floats, and wonderfully handy for exploring. It was, in fact, an exploring instrument, with special fuel tanks for long-range flying, unobstructed vision from all windows, ports for the mapping camera, free passage from the radio installation aft to the pilots' seats forward, dump valves which could empty the cabin tanks of 800 gallons of gas in 75 seconds if a "hot" landing were in order. Capable of lifting a gross load of 19,000 pounds on either floats or skis, it provided the essential elements of load (mapping cameras, repair kits, emergency rations and camping gear, etc., for the flight crew in the event of a forced landing away from base) and range (approximately 1300 miles with a full load). The plane was named the *William Horlick.*

From the Pep Boys of Philadelphia we borrowed a Kellett autogyro, the first time such a machine was taken to the polar regions. It was called *Pep Boy's Snowman!* Mr. Alfred Sloan of General Motors loaned us a single-engined Fokker monoplane, which was named *Blue Blade,* and American Airways generously contributed a single-engined Pilgrim monoplane, which was named *Miss American Airways.* Both of these latter planes had already had hard service. The

Fokker came directly from the air mail, for which it had been especially designed; the Pilgrim came out of passenger service, complete with cushioned seats, lavatory, and ash trays. These gadgets, of course, in spite of the happy speculation they excited among the aviation unit, were eliminated. The planes were reduced to bare essentials, to save weight.

Searching for tractors brought more grief. Edsel Ford contributed two light snowmobiles useful for short hauls. Mr. W. King White of the Cleveland Tractor Company presented a marvelous vehicle, a Cletrac, which was virtually a snow dreadnaught, with a load capacity of 20,000 pounds. But in between these two types, an intermediate design was needed—a comparatively light and fast car for long range exploration. It seemed to me that mechanized transport would be the next great step in south polar transport. The fact that Shackleton, Scott and Mawson had all failed at it early in the century—that our own mild experiment in 1929 had come to grief about 82 miles south of Little America [12]—meant little. The early experiments in the Antarctic were made at a time when motors elsewhere were just commencing to oust the horse and buggy in more congenial climates; and our first car was too light and low-powered to contend with the combination of soft, loose snow and hard sastrugi that made barrier travel so punishing. Given the right amount of power, wide treads and length enough to span the average crevasse, motors ought to be able to go places.

So far as getting a design for our intermediate requirements in 1933, we were practically licked. American manufacturers weren't interested. But in France, after my trans-Atlantic flight in 1927, I had met André Citroën, well-known automobile manufacturer. He built, I knew, an excellent tractor. He was even then sponsoring a tractor expedition exploring the Gobi desert. Investigation revealed that his cars were successfully used on the snow and glacier ice of the Alps. My friend Vincent Bendix heard of my predicament and sent a cable to M. Citroën, whom he knew intimately, and it brought a cordial response. In the end M. Citroën gave us three stock cars, the last arriving in New Zealand just in time to be picked up by the *Bear*. Without them the disembarkation in the Bay of Whales would be a more awful memory of toil and trouble than it is.

Planes and tractors are superb instruments, but there is no getting away from dogs. The Eskimo husky still is, as he always has been, the one absolutely reliable means of polar advance. He can overcome terrain, which a tractor can't penetrate and a plane can't land on. For this reason the scientific field program, involving three long journeys, was to be almost entirely sledging. Additional dogs were required for support, emergency purposes, local reconnaissance, and the multiplicity of

[12] Byrd, *Little America,* 303.

hauls connected with the loading and unloading of the ships. The more dogs, therefore, the better.

Most of the dogs we had to pay for. Norman Vaughan, an experienced sledger with the first expedition, cheerfully gave up his advertising business to organize this branch of transport. He was a wizard with the little money I could turn over to him. When he was obliged to return to business, Captain Innes-Taylor, likewise of the first expedition, stepped in. He had served with the Royal Canadian Northwest Mounted Police and had sledged in the Yukon. He knew dogs, and was an excellent "vet" to boot.

We drew in all directions for dogs—the north shore of the St. Lawrence, Labrador, Manitoba and (indirectly) from Alaska. At Wonalancet, N. H., Milton Seeley had crossed the Alaskan breed of the first expedition with Siberian and wolf, producing a stout sledging dog—short, stocky, well-formed, with good shoulders and paws, the extra speed of the Siberian, and averaging about 65 pounds. We selected some 50 of them. From the north shore of the St. Lawrence and the Labrador region we collected 76 huskies, typical Labrador dogs, motley in coat and blood history with a distant wolf strain, stocky dogs with wide foot pads and strong legs, averaging between 70 and 75 pounds. From John Is-feld at Gimli, Manitoba, came 30 Manitoba huskies, descendants of the dogs used by Sir Ernest Shackleton's second expedition—magnificent animals, large-boned, deep-chested, heavy-shouldered and strong-legged. They weighed between 80 and 100 pounds.

The *Ruppert* left Newport News with 153 dogs and in spite of the killing heat of the tropics, the strain of three months' confinement on shipboard, less than 10 failed to reach the ice—really a wonderful showing for Captain Innes-Taylor's dog drivers.

The dog food, about one hundred thousand pounds, was Ralston's Purina dog-chow,[18] generously donated by the manufacturers, through Mr. William H. Ralston, chairman of the board of that company; and the essential dried milk was contributed by Mr. C. R. Walgreen, president of the Walgreen Drug Company.

VI

One by one, as the summer of 1933 advanced, we cleared the hurdles. But it was all uproar, all uncertainty, a shouting confusion of telephones and telegrams, hammers banging, hand trucks rumbling, orders and counter-orders, wild goose chases. Not until the ships actually slipped their moorings did I dare admit we were really going. Too many matters hung by a thread almost to the last hour.

[18] The ingredients consisted of suet, meat meal, whole wheat, wheat germ, dried milk, cod liver oil, cooked barley groats, corn, molasses and hydrogenated soya bean oil, all compressed into cakes.

Yet, one way or another, the thing was done, the crystallization of uncountable large and small efforts, contributions and assistances. At Newport News, for example, I spotted in the *Ruppert's* hold a pair of shoulders familiar even in the anonymous covering of an ill-fitting suit of dungarees—Dr. Dana Coman, medico for the first expedition, now head of the psychiatry clinic at Johns Hopkins. Unknown to me, he had unostentatiously joined the crew as a stevedore to help get the ships off. He knew what a heartbreaking ordeal are the last few days in the home port.

The *Bear,* being slower than the *Ruppert,* had to get away first, leaving Boston September 25th, 1933, under command of Lieut. (J. G.) Robert A. J. English, U.S.N. Her officers were: sailing master and ice pilot, Captain Bendik Johansen; First Officer Stephen D. Rose; Second Officer Nathaniel B. Davis; Chief Engineer, Leland Barter; Second Engineer, S. A. Pinkham; and Third Engineer, T. E. Litchfield.

The *Ruppert* put out on October 11th. Commander Hj. Fr. Gjertsen of the Norwegian Navy was in command with the title of Commodore. Considered one of the ablest ice pilots in the Norwegian Navy, having served aboard Amundsen's *Fram* during her Antarctic voyages and having also been ice pilot for a whaling factory ship in Antarctic waters, I invited him to join the expedition, feeling the need of a trained ice craftsman to work the unprotected *Ruppert* in the pack. The other officers were: Lieut. (J.G.) W. F. Verleger, U.S.N.R., Captain; First Officer O'Brien;[14] Second Officer Andersen;[14] and Third Officer J. J. Muir. The engineering officers were: Chief Engineer W. K. Queen; First Assistant B. W. Paul; Second Assistant J. A. Ellis; and Third Assistant P. MacCurrach.

En route to Panama, the *Bear* promptly stuck her nose into a hurricane and narrowly escaped foundering off Southport, N. C. Meeting a full gale off Diamond Shoals lightship and warned by radio the main storm was on his course, Lieut. English tried to run for Southport Harbor. On October 4th green seas were breaking over the decks and the ship was taking water through the hatches and companionways. The pumps couldn't handle it fast enough; it rose in the machinery spaces and, finally, with every roll it was swishing in the bunkers, clogging the rose-box suctions of the pumps with fine coal dust.

One after the other the engineers crawled into the bilges, and tried to scrape away the coagulated coal from the strainers with their hands, but the stuff was too thick. The steam pumps stalled for want of suction; and the hand pumps, though stubbornly manned, made no headway. The level rose in the engine room, and to save the shaft bearings and the engine, the engine was stopped. For several hours more, though there was no dry coal, the engineers managed to keep the fires bright.

[14] Resigned at Wellington.

It must have been a terrible night, especially for a green crew. The officers promptly organized four bucket lines—one into the lower reaches of the forehold, a second into the shaft alley aft, a third into the engine room, and a fourth into the stokehold. All night long, with the ship rolling heavily, the crew, scientists, landlubbers, and veterans, steadied themselves on slippery, oily ladders and gratings, passing three-gallon buckets of bilge water to the main deck and lowering empty buckets to the men below. In spite of all they could do the water gained. In the shaft alley, Davis, Callahan and Miller, all six-footers, were in water up to their shoulders. The level rose to the ash pits of the boilers: and the firemen, up to their armpits, hauled the fires, raking the red-hot coal into the water. The situation was serious.

With the boiler secured, the steam generator stopped, and with it all power and lights. Close-hauled, the ship pounded toward Frying Pan Shoals lightship.

After hours of battling, under the able leadership of her commanding officer, the crew finally gained the shore and, with the sea moderating, was anchored safely in eight fathoms of water off the harbor entrance. Out of the fire and into Frying Pan Shoals—a felicitous reversal.

"I can't say too much for the crew," Lieut. English reported. "Landlubbers and all served the buckets as methodically as gunners serving a gun. It was a miserable night, and quite a few of them must have been pretty sure it was all over."

On account of the punishment she took, it was necessary to return the *Bear* to Newport News for dry-docking, where she was joined by the flagship.

After taking aboard the planes and various other gear, the *Ruppert,* on October 22nd, stood down the channel toward the Chesapeake Capes, bound for the Panama Canal and the South Pacific Ocean. The *Bear* set out on November 1st. The two ships were next to meet in the Bay of Whales, more than three months later.

Counting all hands (the volunteers taken aboard in New Zealand and ignoring a handful of defections, either on account of illness, change of heart, or other causes), the expedition numbered 115 souls.

VII

One broad change in plan was forced upon us shortly after passing through the Panama Canal. Mention was previously made of the plan to divert the expedition for an exploratory venture into the Pacific Quadrant before proceeding to Little America. Our immediate objective, as we steamed down the Pacific coast of South America, was Peter I Island, a tiny landfall lying within the Antarctic Circle, southwest of Cape Horn. In that locality Charcot, Wilkins and de Gerlache had made substantial penetrations without raising the continent. The strategy was to attain the deepest southing within the ship's capacity to deal with such ice as she met, and from that point endeavor to gain the coast by aircraft, if possible making a non-stop flight westward to Little America. A successful flight over this utterly unknown region would rub out an enormous stretch of *terra incognita.* The big plane was equipped with floats with this mission in view.

The stumbling block grew out of the fact that, in order to boost the plane's ability to lift from the water a load sufficient to fuel her for such a sustained flight and still fly economically, we had fitted her with variable pitch propellers. According to the best counsel, they were, in spite of being a comparatively new development, altogether reliable. If I have any steady taboo in the calculation of field operations, it is the prejudice against placing a major enterprise, where I can avoid it, at the mercy of an experimental factor.

There are already quite enough incalculable human and natural risks inherent in such operations without taking on the further jeopardy of something which hasn't yet made the grade in civilization. At sea we received a report from the War Department, which had been conducting extensive tests, that while the propellers were generally reliable, nevertheless structural weaknesses had developed in several instances at certain nodes of vibration.

That finished the matter, so far as we were concerned. The risk to the lives of the flight crew was serious enough; but a failure of the initial flight operation might completely wreck the whole program.

Therefore on November 8th, 1933, 1150 miles out of Balboa, C. Z., and 500 miles west of Callao, Peru, we altered course for Wellington, New Zealand.

The decision now was to refuel the ships at Wellington, take aboard various stores, and then attack the Quadrant on a southeasterly slant, ultimately steaming eastward along the front of the pack and making a series of direct thrusts toward the coast by ship and plane. With fixed pitch propellers, which we fortunately had in reserve, this project was feasible.

The washing out of the original project was disappointing, but not a calamity. The alternative, at least in prospect, was of equal geographical importance.

Making between nine and ten knots, the *Ruppert* held on a west-southwest course for Wellington. We saw neither ship nor sail throughout the voyage. It was surprising how barren the Pacific is in these middle latitudes. For days we never saw a bird; not until we drew near land again did the albatross, Mother Carey's chickens and the fulmars collect around the ship in numbers. Dr. Perkins, who was collecting plankton samples from these little-traveled waters by passing a steady stream of sea water from the main circulating pump through a plankton net, remarked on the poverty of life in it.[15] In spite of the great volume of water filtered, there was one 2,000-mile stretch of ocean along the 33rd parallel, between the 122nd and 161st meridian West, from which he derived only two samples, on account of the nearly complete absence of plankton.[16] Compared to the abundance of planktonic "soup" in Antarctic waters, and the masses of pack ice and bergs stained yellow-green at the waterline by diatoms, the amount and variety of life in the middle latitudes, in the zone of transition between the Equator and the Antarctic, is relatively small.

Still the days passed agreeably enough. The passage was somewhat rough, with frequent squalls, rain and mist and a long, rolling swell. But there was compensation in the beauty of the fine Pacific days—quiet and calm, with a blue spaciousness to the sky.

There was one unexpected interlude—a pause at Easter Island the most isolated outpost of the Polynesians. When we changed course, the new direction put it almost on our track, and remembering a bit I had read about its history and the queer, ugly, monolithic gods and monuments, the ideographic script on wooden tablets and the vanished people who created them, I yielded to the temptation to put in there for a day. Easter Island lies about 2,000 miles off the Coast of Chile and 1,100 miles from Pitcairn, nearest inhabited island to the west. Accordingly we altered course a trifle more to fetch up with Cook's Bay, and late in the evening of the 15th we raised the low volcanic headlands. It was too dark and dangerous to approach; so we stood off till morning, while signal fires burned all night on the shore.

This being an account of a polar expedition and its exertions on behalf of science, our casual digression into the culture and customs of the Polynesians may be of some value, if only as an instance of the remarkable adventures that befall explorers on a busman's holiday. Landing innocently enough, we engaged ill-gaited horses that left us aching for days; we visited the stone images and the *ahu* at Rano-Raraku, snapping photographs on every side, and stuffing pockets with ancient adze-like stone chisels and tanged spearheads of obsidian. Amiable as setters, the Kanakas tagged after us, delightfully decked out in unmatched uniform clothing derived, as near as we could tell

15 The vast majority of organisms obtained in the South Pacific between Panama and Wellington, consisted of many species of copepods, strikingly varied as to size, shape and color, diatoms, dinoflagellates, radiolarians, heliozans, colonial hydroids, Sagittae, a few annelids, pterepods and other small gastropods. At Lat. 38° 30′ S., Long. 169° 45′ W., swarms of dinoflagellates distributed in dark brown patches from a foot square to 25 x 200 feet, containing vast quantities of Peridinium, not hitherto seen.

16 This occurred in a transition zone of rapid change in water temperature; on November 20th the temperature was 19.2° C.; on November 29th, when the plankton again became numerous, the sea temperature had dropped to 16° C.

from the insignia, from visiting yachts, British and Chilean warships. One fellow who particularly took our fancy was got up in a British Admiral's cap, a Chilean naval officer's jacket, and a pair of pink pajama pants that must have been of Parisian extraction. In spite of the cosmopolitan variety of his attire and the monocle he carried expertly in his eye, there was a lamentable flaw in his deportment as a gentleman—his trousers, of course, were unbuttoned.

As for the economic philosophy of the natives, naturally, after so brief a stay, I am hardly qualified to discuss it; but it appears to be summed up in a sort of a "share-the-wealth" slogan, "Gimme shirt," which occurs in their language as rhythmically as the surf beating through the gut outside the stone pier. For a shirt you can possess anything—"gimme shirt, me give horse, heemage (we later decided this meant image), wife." I was impressed to find that Captain Cook, about the time of the Revolution, visited Easter Island, and was annoyed by the taking ways of the natives. Well, if in the happy hunting grounds of explorers I should ever happen to meet the good Captain Cook, I shall hasten to tell him that in 150 years their technique has improved. Field glasses, cigarettes, handkerchiefs, hats—they vanished with the slickness of legerdemain. When we finally escaped the place, Dr. Perkins remarked: "That's one place that took the Byrd expedition." They even made off with most of the oarlocks of the lifeboat, leaving the shore party to make their way back to the ship with their coats spread to catch the wind. And this, mind you, while our own crew was sitting on the thwarts. It was all done, of course, with disarming innocence and uncanny skill. Since only one ship calls in a year, the natural assumption is that they must meanwhile practice among themselves.

Altogether the call at Easter Island almost ruined us. One tatterdemalion gentleman appeared alongside the *Ruppert* in a long boat, announcing "me guv'nor." Commodore Gjertsen, having a naval officer's respect for international courtesies, promptly had him piped aboard where he was sipping the Commodore's brandy and inhaling his cigarettes when the real governor, Murdo Smith, a Scotchman, came alongside and attempted to get aboard to pay his respects. It took some time to get that straightened out. Meanwhile the scientists had disappeared into the interior. They failed to return before dark, with the result that some of us who remained ashore to make sure they were all right, were marooned for the night, a gale having blown up and forced the *Ruppert* rather hastily out of the unprotected Bay. The Governor had only two extra beds in the only house on the island. So 11 men had to sleep on the beach, chilled and miserable in a thudding rain. The total nourishment for 24 hours was two chickens for which one of the scientists bartered his shirt. None of us ashore that night will forget the sight of "Ike" Schlossbach, Lieut.-Commander, U.S.N. (Ret.), curled up beside the sputtering fire of driftwood, with his head shoved into a box so the heat wouldn't burn his hair off.

"How long," I asked Governor Smith, "is this gale likely to last?"

"Difficult to say," he said. "It may blow out by morning, or it may last for days."

Lovely thought—the Admiral in command of a polar expedition marooned ashore on a semi-tropical island and his flagship unable to get him off.

Next afternoon, though it was still blowing, I managed to get out to the ship in a boat manned by natives. The *Ruppert* steamed around to the other side of the Island, to gain the lee, opposite Binapu Bay. The half-starved men ashore meanwhile footed it across the island. Even then, when we sent the natives back with the lifeboat, in charge of Second Officer Andersen, the wind was so severe that the five Americans—Andersen, Russell, Healey, Creagh and Dane—had to assist natives at the oars, taking nearly two hours to make the trip. But with the wind at their backs and their coats spread, the castaways breezed out to the *Ruppert* with the run of a cup defender, almost without wetting an oar. It was then that the natives embezzled the oarlocks.

As Commander Noville, the executive officer, came up the ladder, he said:

"Me go bed now. Me give shirt for bed."

VIII

Otherwise the run to New Zealand was uneventful. It took a long time to shake down, largely on account of the fact the ship's company was drawn from all walks of life and all manner of occupations, professions and trades, biologists and seamen, engineers and physicists, aviators and cameramen, and so on through a broad cross-section of society. The ship itself and the life in her were perhaps unlike that of any ship on the seven seas, being in many ways remindful of a small city afloat.

On the after well-deck the big plane, minus wings, was secured abaft the mainmast. Every few days the engines were run to circulate the oil through the parts and prevent rusting. The dogs were scattered over the ship, chained to board walks spread over the decks. Once a day they were fed and watered and, at intervals, exercised on the forward well deck. The drivers took turns watching them throughout the night. Up forward, in a ramshackle stall, were the three cows donated by the Guernsey Cattle Club. Beneath this bucolic scene, in the 'tween-decks, the aviation unit was making the Fokker, Pilgrim and autogyro ready for flight—eliminating extra fixtures where they could, ripping out the passenger seats in the Pilgrim, lagging oil lines, oil tanks and

S.S. "Jacob Ruppert"

S.S. "Bear of Oakland"

(© Paramount Pictures, Inc.)

EASTER ISLAND

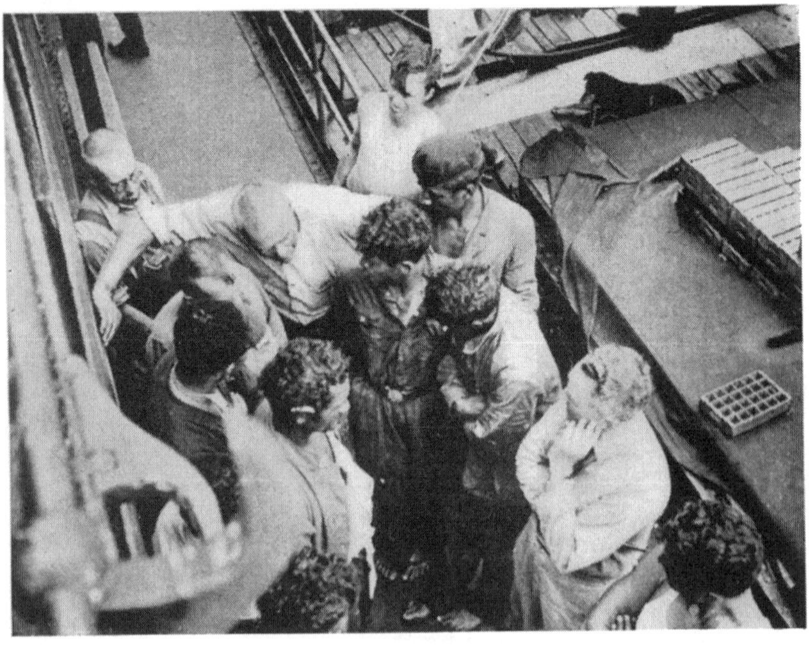

MID-PACIFIC

crankcases with insulation against cold, installing special navigational equipment, replacing wheels with skis, installing larger gas tanks.

Orders called for 50 sledges, 8 light airplane sledges and 42 dog sledges (lead and trailers) for unloading operations on arrival in the Bay of Whales. Czegka, Tinglof and Ronne were assembling these. The sledge parts, bridges, runners, gee poles, etc., had all been made in Boston, but they had to be put together, lashed with rawhide, varnished and rigged. On the flying bridge, behind a flimsy canvas shelter, Dr. Poulter, Dr. Bramhall and Zuhn, the physicists, had set up the cosmic ray apparatus, commencing a series of continuous observations (over 30-40 hour periods) shortly after we crossed the Equator. Anyhow, they called them observations. They hardly ever came below except to eat. But one night the ship heeled heavily to a big swell; a frightful din over the wheel house arose, and the watch dashed out, thinking the cosmic ray apparatus had carried away. The apparatus was intact, but what seemed to be at least a gross of empty coca-cola bottles had pitched to the deck. "So that," murmured Captain Verleger, "is what those guys are doing up there."

So the voyage, in one sense, was not just a stop-gap between civilization and Antarctica: the expedition was gathering strength each day at sea, becoming more unified in purpose, plan and organization. The radio engineers were constructing radio sets for the planes, and field sets for the fall sledging and tractor units. The dog drivers had harnesses to fit, each to its individual dog, with the name written in red paint on the whiffletrees—Pitou, Friday, Navy, Taku, Coal, Cain, Power, etc. They had gear to sort out, more than a thousand trail flags to sew and fit with bamboo sticks, tents to make, and rations to weigh, literally ounce by ounce, and sack in neat bags, each identified and of the right amounts for sledging requirements.

Corey and Siple, among their other jobs, were assembling in a special cache the myriads of stores needed for the Advance Weather Base we proposed to plant far south in Antarctica and occupy throughout the winter night.

In the midst of these activities, on the morning of December 5th (having meanwhile crossed the 180th meridian and lost a day) the lookout shouted, "Land!" and the serrated peaks of North Island, New Zealand, green and lovely, welled over the horizon. Bucking a wind of full gale force funneling through Cook Strait, we made for Wellington, where I was happy again to place our affairs in the capable and generous hands of my old friends, Joe Gardner, of Binnie, Halliburton and Gardner, and Jim Duncan, of Tapley & Co., Ltd. They rendered the first expedition every possible friendship and courtesy, and did no less for the second.

Except for the loss of five dogs (one jumped overboard, and the others died of various physical infirmities) and the gradual disappearance of a dozen chickens picked up at Easter Island (which may have accounted for the well-fed appearance of Boilermaker Mitchell), the flagship made port without casualties.

IX

Meanwhile the *Bear* passed through the Panama Canal, entering the Pacific November 17th. Lieut. English laid a course for Papeete, Tahiti, where he coaled ship, December 12th, for the second leg across the Pacific. All the way across, Roos, the oceanographer, ran a bathymetric profile with her sonic sounding unit along her track, making the striking discovery, while crossing the so-called Aldrich Deep between Tahiti and New Zealand, that the ocean bottom had apparently been upheaved in recent years, probably by an earthquake. The bathymetric charts put it beyond the 500 meter curve, but Roos's soundings (taken at five-minute intervals) showed that the ocean bottom rose from 5,500 meters at lat. 29° 06′ S., Long. 167° 01′ W., to 3,480 meters at Lat. 29° 42′ S., Long. 167° 55′ W., then declined to 5,700 meters at Lat. 30° 09′ S., Long. 168° 34′ W. Previous soundings in this region were few and far between. In crossing the Deep the *Bear* undoubtedly passed over a submarine ridge which commenced in a gentle slope and culminated in a peak about 30 miles distant.

This bathymetric survey, which was conducted by the *Bear* throughout her voyages, was one of her most valuable contributions. On a single stretch of South Pacific Ocean where, in a region as large as the combined territory of the United States and Mexico, the entire submarine topography was based upon only 14 soundings, the ship added 600 soundings.

Chapter II

THE FIRST THRUST

I

HURRY . . . hurry . . . hurry! Like a lash that word is unremittingly laid across the back of a polar expedition; it makes a nightmare of the sleeping and waking hours of its leader. From the hour of birth an expedition is constantly striving against frustrating adversaries—against its own poverty and limitations, against unfavorable storms and tides, against sun and darkness. And always—always it is straining against time. The days a polar expedition can spend in the field are numbered; and a day wasted in port may, through ill luck, cost heavily in the field. So you come to fret over days, then hours, and finally minutes.

In Wellington it was the same old story. Charming and hospitable as the city is (Nature must have had compensations in mind when she endowed New Zealand, last jumping-off place for Antarctic expeditions, with such wonderfully generous people), I desperately measured the time we spent refitting there. It seemed as though we should never get to sea again. Every vanishing hour meant an hour lost on our projected explorations in the Pacific quadrant; an inexorable deadline, fixed by the magnitude of the task of reëstablishing Little America and inaugurating certain field operations before the winter night shut down, governed this enterprise.

But there were sundry things to be done, and all of them were important. We were in truth fortunate that they could be done in eight days, instead of ten, or even more. After all, a polar expedition is a unique enterprise. Once it leaves the last port of call it is drastically on its own. South of Fifty is no place for second-guessing. Either you're ready or sorry.

The long haul across the Pacific had revealed the hidden frailties of the *Ruppert's* old engines. An alarming knock had developed in the intermediate pressure cylinder, leaky tubes needed replacement, and various other faults, notably a heavier fuel consumption than we had counted on, necessitated a general overhaul. So there was no liberty for Commander Queen's engine room gang in Wellington.

Neither was there liberty for June's aviation unit. Soon after the ship was tied up alongside the wharf, the big plane was swung ashore, to be made ready for flight. The huge wing sections were mounted, the variable pitch propellers were removed and replaced by fixed pitch propellers, heater hoods were installed for warming the engines in cold temperatures, and a staunch tiered platform, seven feet high and fabricated of pine baulks a foot square, for cradling the plane, was constructed over No. 5 hatch, on the after well deck.

On this tiered pedestal, directly abaft the mainmast, the plane was cocked fore and aft. The whale-like tail ran high across the poop. The pedestal, which covered the whole square of the hatch, was made fast to the hatch coaming by steel rods; and as a safeguard against the wrenching force of the ship's roll it was further strengthened by long 1½-inch steel rods—three to a side—bolted to the bulwark stanchions. Cocked on this eyrie the plane's lower wing was some twenty-seven feet above the water line, well out of reach of any seas we were likely to encounter. Altogether the structure seemed solid enough. Still, I must confess that I never breathed easily until the plane was safely berthed at Little America. The ship was a trifle down by the stern, having been heavily ballasted aft to keep the propeller from coming in contact with the ice; so the plane was exposed to spray and wash from following and beam seas.

Of course these and other preparations took time; but at last, on the night of December 11th, I saw daylight ahead. Orders were hastily posted instructing all hands to report aboard ship for a 6 A.M. sailing, and couriers were dispatched to notify the men scattered about the city. Let us pass lightly over the few remaining hours. Last night in port is always a unique and memorable experience; and what young men do under these circumstances is a social activity not eligible for inclusion in a narrative of this order. I can only say that, judging by the errant sounds which throughout the early watches eddied from the gangplank, the farewell to civilization must have ranked, as an event, somewhere between a bachelor's dinner and a departure for the front.

Surprisingly, the last man aboard was our senior scientist, Dr. Poulter, whose rectitude is one of the brightest memories of the expedition. He had gone ashore to make final preparations for the care of his three small sons, who had preceded him to New Zealand. One of the boys, as I recall, came down with a toothache during the night; and at dawn or thereabouts the good man curled up in a chair for forty winks. The next thing he knew the telephone was ringing furiously and an angry voice was shrieking: don't you know what time it is, and what the hell do you scientists think a sailing order is! To make amends for the affair at Easter Island, Dr. Poulter had solemnly promised that thereafter his staff would be models of promptness.

Shortly after seven o'clock a taxicab impetuously delivered Dr. Poulter at the gangplank. At 7:38 we cast off.

So it was Southward Ho! at last; I couldn't restrain a feeling of satisfaction as I felt the deck strain to the pulse of the engines. All that had gone before was in the nature of a prelude. Now we were squared away on our mission. As the ship stood out from Cape Palliser we were like a man-o'-war clearing decks for action. The last stray cargo was whisked below, hatches were battened down, and in the holds and on

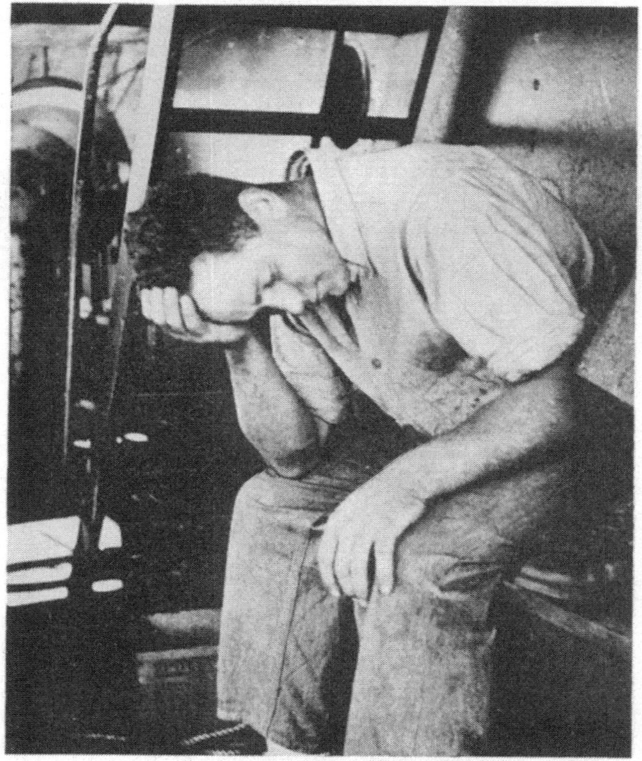

"Mal de Mer"

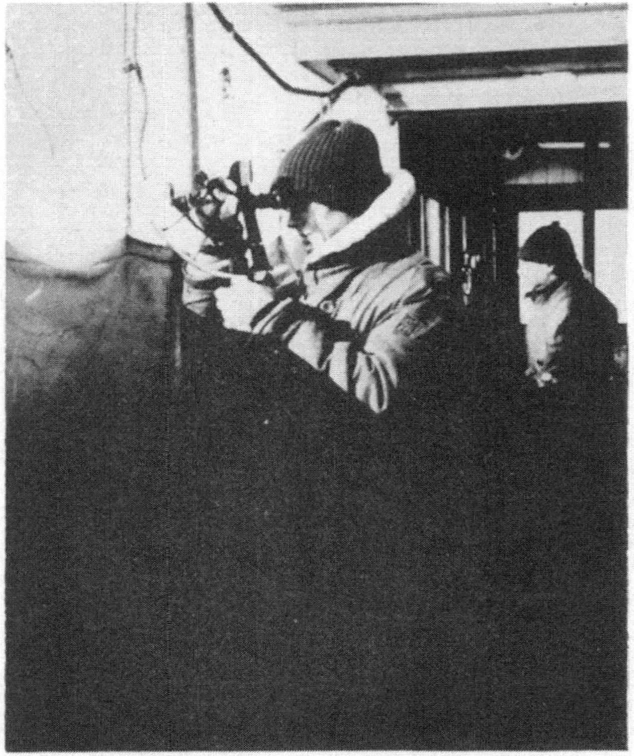

(Photograph by Earle B. Perkins)

Commodore Gjertsen Taking a Sight

THE "WILLIAM HORLICK" ON HER CRADLE JUST BEFORE THE FIRST FLIGHT

SENTINELS OF THE SOUTHERN SEAS

the shelter deck the lashings securing the small mountains of cargo were inspected and reënforced. The decks were nakedly bare. Up forward the engineering force was hurriedly lagging with asbestos the steam lines to all winches, to keep the lines from freezing up in the south.

"All secure for sea," Commodore Gjertsen reported that afternoon. Well, from now on the game would run according to the way we played it and the breaks we got. With the engines wide open and turning up a brave nine knots we steamed toward one of the most formidable areas on the face of the earth. In this same area other expeditions had tried and failed. Yet somehow, as I contemplated the heaving metallic sea, I was quietly confident of the outcome. Where the others had staked all on a single thrust, we had two strings fitted to our bow. The first was the ship. We would speed her to the limit of her penetrating powers. Sooner or later it was inevitable that ice would stop her, as it had stopped every other vessel in the past. When that happened we should fit the second string—the plane. The "mountains of ice" which had flung back Captain Cook and his successors would be trifling barriers to a plane. Soaring in its natural element it could venture with impunity where no ship could live. In the expiring twilight I studied the structure of the plane: the enormous upper wing, 82 feet long, shrunk the 54-foot beam of the ship: and the bulking outline in the shadows conveyed an impression of power that was reassuring.

II

It's a funny thing about a polar expedition, but no matter how much care is given to its organization, it will evoke more surprises than a grab-bag. At Wellington I had instructed the personnel officer to take on nine volunteers. They were to assist in the unloading of supplies in the Bay of Whales and to help work the ship back to Dunedin. Dunedin would again be the winter base for the ships. The first afternoon out all hands were summoned forward for a counting of heads. I discovered then that instead of nine, eighteen men had been signed on. The personnel officer wasn't quite sure how it happened. "Maybe I signed on twins," he said brightly. Nevertheless it was a serious matter. We had little food and clothing to spare beyond our fixed requirements. While I was canvassing this situation, Captain Verleger burst into the cabin.

"There's three more of 'em, Admiral!" he exclaimed.

"Three more what?"

"Stowaways," he said. "In No. 4 lifeboat. When we unshipped the tarpaulin, there they were, tucked in snug as bugs in a rug. What'll we do with 'em—keelhaul 'em on general principles, or throw 'em in the brig till we can think of somethin' better?"

We had no brig, and keelhauling is outlawed by civilized society;

so a different procedure was in order. After thinking the matter over, I resolved to do what seemed to be the fair thing. I called all the new men together and explained to them the circumstances that made the meeting necessary. We were over-manned, I said, and this meant a shortage of food and clothing. Not a dangerous shortage; with careful husbanding and thrift we could get by; but it would mean discomfort. Quarters, too, would be crowded.

"You are in no wise to blame for this," I concluded. "The fault is largely ours. If you find this prospect displeasing and more than you bargained for—if you wish to be returned to Wellington, that action will be taken. Will those men who wish to return please step forward?"

Nobody stirred. If a man had moved one of our most successful operations would have been extinguished at the start. The time lost in returning to port would have ruined all hope of an extended operation in the Pacific quadrant.

"All right," I said. "That finishes it."

The incident had an amusing sequel. A couple of days later Captain English, who had just put out of Tahiti, radioed: "Have just found two stowaways aboard. Please send instructions." I replied: "Suggest you return and try to recruit another. We're one up on you."

The ship's company now numbered ninety-five men, and with quarters originally intended for scarcely a third that number congestion was inevitable. Men alternated watches in order to share bunks. Later on, when the weather turned colder, I saw men coming off watch turn over heavy coats to their reliefs. A dozen new bunks, makeshift affairs, were hastily built on the shelter deck, across from the cows. There was little comfort and more than a little hardship, but the newcomers took it in a commendable spirit. It was a matter of share and share alike; and once the reasonableness of that philosophy permeated the crew all dissatisfaction disappeared. As for the stowaways, fairness compels me to say that the three of them—Pilcher, Christian and Wray—worked like dogs; instead of cursing them we were later to rejoice over the deception that brought them into the expedition.

Except for the discomfort involved, the increased man-power was really a blessing. With extra hands to work the ship it was possible, now, to relieve most of the prospective members of the Ice Party from routine ship's duties and turn them to the job of preparing for the problem of disembarkation in the Bay of Whales. The veterans of the first expedition, whose backs still ached with the memory of an earlier struggle, knew what the tenderfeet could never know without experience: that unloading would be a long, bitter nightmare, and that strategy and planning would save much grief later on.

The problem of organizing the disembarkation I turned over to "Vic" Czegka. This Marine warrant-officer, impatient, but with a gift for precision, knew what it was all about. He had been through the mill before. Czegka's job was to work out a practicable plan of unloading for any of several situations we were likely to meet in the Bay of Whales: and to supervise the reëstablishment of Little America as expeditiously as possible. Assigned to assist and coöperate with him were June, Haines and Innes-Taylor, all veterans of the first expedition, Executive Officer Noville and his assistant, Ken Rawson.

You see, we were devising means to overcome our problems thousands of miles before we came to them. Often we were wrong. Often, too, in this as in similar problems, we spent uncounted hours discussing contingencies that never arose and, in the casual run of things, were hardly likely to arise. But at least we always knew what we were up against and were prepared for the worst. If I have any philosophy at all about polar exploration it flows from this sense of empirical experimentation. A Micawber is soon brought up hard in the polar regions.

The readiness with which the ship shook down after putting out from Wellington was gratifying. Usually, after a long stay in port and especially after the infusion of new blood, a crew is backward about falling into a smooth routine. Instead, the life of the ship moved smartly from the first; and except for the clipped English accents and Cockney twang echoing unfamiliarly in the passageways and the "good-o's" and "right-o's" that responded to an order, the New Zealanders melted easily into the organization. We liked them, and I think they liked us. Two New Zealanders—First Officer Bayne and Second Officer Dempster—were on the bridge.

In the various reaches of the ship a great deal of work, apart from the routine activities of the ship's crew, was gathering speed. Czegka and Ronne were hurrying to finish the assembly of sledges required for unloading operations. On the shelter deck Tinglof was constructing from stock lumber a dozen heavy tractor sledges—heavy, rigid affairs intended to carry loads of several tons. Captain Innes-Taylor and his dog department were putting their gear in order for the punishing grind of hauling cargo into Little America. Cox was building a portable cow barn in No. 3 hold. Up forward in the fo'c's'le, "Sails" Kennedy and Dr. Shirey were busy over the sewing machines, turning out large quantities of windproof clothing, trail tents of various designs, and thousands of orange trail flags fitted to slender bamboo strips. Supply Officer Corey, who was responsible for all general expedition stores, and his assistants were segregating, checking and marking the supplies earmarked for Little America, to facilitate the movement from the ship. These and other related jobs left no time for idleness.

My diary reports:

Wed., Dec. 13, 9:50 P.M.

Noon position: Lat. 45° 05′ S., Long. 177° 43′ E. A heavy fog closed in during the middle watch this morning, and visibility was reduced to half a ship's length. Nevertheless, being well out of the steamer lanes, we are running at full speed. The air is calm and considerably colder. At noon mess Commodore Gjertsen remarked that it has the look of "iceberg weather." It's hardly likely that we should encounter bergs this far north, but to be on the safe side lookouts were stationed in the eyes of the ship. Supply officer Corey is issuing heavy clothing to all men on watch.

We lost our seventh dog today—Watch. He died of strangulation—fell, unobserved, over the side and strangled in his collar. Innes-Taylor, Dane and Moody worked over his body for an hour, but couldn't save him. It is always a tragedy to lose a good dog, but no blame attaches in a case like this. I can't praise the dog department too highly. The mortality rate among the dogs has been surprisingly low—only 7 out of 153. We had expected to lose upwards of twenty per cent in the tropics.

III

Course was laid to fetch us up in the vicinity of the intersection of the Antarctic Circle and the 150th meridian west, where we planned to launch our first attack. Except for the fog the Roaring Forties were good to us. The sea was calm as a millpond. The more sensitive landlubbers began to take heart; at the mess tables there were sly speculations that the infamous reputation of these seas was just a conspiracy contrived by explorers.

"Didn't I promise you fellows a calm voyage!" Captain Verleger roared. "Eighteen years I've sailed the seas, and never a storm. If you stick with me, you'll never have to feed the goldfish."

Bill Haines had been eyeing the barometer. He chuckled softly. "Maybe so, Captain. But I figure that before long you're going to miss a lot of familiar faces at this table."

On our second Thursday December 14th (having again crossed the 180th meridian, we recovered the day lost on December 3rd), the crew got a taste of the strength within these seas. A heaving sea, with an irregular beam swell, set the ship to rolling heavily. We took spray over the decks. Though the sun came through dimly for a few hours during the late afternoon, the fog still held, and during the night watches we were obliged to reduce speed to slow and half. In addition to the routine lookouts stationed on the bridge, two iceberg lookouts, one to port and one to starboard, were assigned to the fo'c's'le, with a bell at hand and certain signals for the bridge. One bell meant iceberg to starboard, two to port, and three dead ahead. As another precaution, the engine room now made hourly reports to the bridge on sea water temperature, an excellent indicator of the presence of the cold current bearing bergs northward.

Fri., Dec. 15, 11:40 P.M.

Noon position: Lat. 55° 01′ S., Long. 172° 27′ W. Day's run (noon to noon 243 miles, the best since leaving port. Moderate south-southwesterly swell: sky still overcast, with furred gray clouds. Light northwesterly winds, which are easing us along.

Again and again, it is impressed upon me that an especially indulgent Providence must watch over the destinies of a polar expedition. For a voyage toward the South Pole is paved with the good intentions of landlubbers. Without a sense of humor I'd be a nervous wreck.

Last night Noville went forward to relieve Paige on iceberg lookout. "Where's the bell?" Noville asked, being unable to find it in the dark. "Right here, sir," said the artist, and promptly struck one bell. Up on the bridge the officer on watch slammed the telegraph to stop, and then bellowed for more information while Noville desperately tried to signal him with a flashlight that it was just a case of artistic license. It took a long time to get that straightened out.

Yesterday a new lookout on the bridge made the same sort of mistake. Toying with the cord, he accidentally struck one bell. Thinking quickly, he glanced at his watch, saw that it was nearly six thirty, and brightly added four bells. But instead of striking them with nautical crispness and a right respect for spacing, he hammered them out in a way that sounded like a general alarm.

. . . Just now one of my most difficult jobs is to impress upon all hands the absolute need for economy. Men can't seem to get it into their heads that everything we have is limited; and that where we're going there'll be no chance for replacement. The stores allocated for the Ice Party have been segregated and plainly identified; the stern unwritten law of the expedition is that these stores shall not be touched, notwithstanding which I discovered today that several boxes had been broken into. It has been necessary to discipline one man for broaching cargo.

The other day a scientist tossed a piece of scrap lumber overboard. Czegka happened to see him do it. "Maybe you wouldn't have been so hasty," the veteran observed, "if you stopped to realize that it would take you a hundred thousand years to grow a piece of wood that size at Little America."

As we pressed southeast I was impressed anew by the profusion of pelagic life in higher southern latitudes, in contrast with the barrenness of the Pacific crossing. From the invisible reaches of these vast wastes of water the ship attracted a whole world of flying life, which it carried along with it. Black-browed albatross, Cape pigeons, white-faced storm petrels, Mother Carey's chickens and fulmars, darting and soaring like clouds of aircraft, hung about the ship, cheerfully joining their errand with its own. Occasionally we overtook small schools of blue penguins, which porpoised out of our path like frightened rabbits. And from time to time we sighted whales.

The fog was somewhat disquieting. We were still in it on the 16th, twelve hundred miles southeast of Wellington. Sometimes it would lift a bit for a few hours, then shut in again, thick as wool. The telegraph moved fretfully from full speed, to half, then slow, then back again to half and full. Commodore Gjertsen and Captain Verleger were constantly on the bridge. Decks, spars and rigging dripped with oozing moisture, and the dogs, hating wet, laid back their ears and whined, night and day.

Sat., Dec. 16, 9:10 P.M.

A bit of excitement last night—a flare-back in the fire box of the midships boiler. The ship trembled with the shock. Colombo, who was standing near the fire box, just escaped being caught by the mass of flame that gushed out. The worst thing was that a shower of sparks from the funnel fell about the *William Horlick,* and several small holes were burned in the fabric. I'm really afraid of the plane catching fire. At rather frequent intervals the engine room is obliged to blow tubes, and the plane consequently is doused with small sparks raining down from the stack. The officers on watch have been instructed to alter course while this is going on, if necessary, so as to bring the wind on the beam, and carry the sparks clear of the plane.

... The wind, still holding in the northwest, is rising, flicking spray from the waves. Barometer dropping fast—from a bulge of 29.84 inches at noon, yesterday, it had dropped to 28.82 inches this afternoon. It's still dropping. Though a drop of this magnitude would mean hurricane warnings in lower latitudes, it very often means nothing here.

However, the rising agitation of the sea points to dirty weather. Exclaiming that it was indecent to keep such a thing in plain view, the less tranquil diners tonight draped the barograph on the sideboard with a black cloth.

We're only several days' steaming from the Midnight Sun; so there are just a few hours of twilight now. This evening the air cleared with great suddenness, and we had a rare taste of sunlight.

Sun, Dec. 17, Midnight.

We're in for it now. Having blithely passed through the Forties and Fifties, we've poked our bow against a wind of close to hurricane force on the threshold of the Sixties. The log dismisses it as a gale, but the aviators tell me that gusts of wind registered a velocity of seventy knots on the Condor's air speed indicator. In all events, we've had our baptism in the elements for which these latitudes are celebrated, and tonight we're lucky to have the plane and dogs intact.

In the wake of the spectacular barometric dip, the storm built up rapidly. The first squalls hit us shortly after midnight. The wind rose violently in the northwest, almost dead astern. The ship made heavy going of it, with the propeller lifting clear and thrashing wildly as the seas tossed the stern. Were it not for the plane, we might have run before it: but being wholly unprotected from following winds, the plane took a bad beating.

Shortly after seven o'clock, after all hands were called, things started to happen fast. The plane, rising and falling on its timbered pedestal, was trembling under the lash of the wind and the strain of the pitch and roll. The ailerons and flippers, which had been set at neutral, were vibrating wildly. There was only one thing to do: to round the ship into the wind and give the plane what little lee the midships boat deck offered. This meant bringing her over into the trough of the seas, a risky and difficult maneuver.

As the ship started around the aviation gang fell to the task of securing the plane. By that time the aileron battens and lashings had been carried away and the control surfaces were all oscillating dangerously. Bowlin, Swan, Smith, McCormick, Schlossbach and Demas now swarmed aboard the plane and struggled to pass wide strips of canvas tape around the wings, to hold the ailerons fast. It was a mean job. Footing was insecure, hail and snow drove into their faces, wind tore at their clothing, and below them green water creamed over the deck. With one hand they clung on, and with the other worked the canvas and lashings around. Once Swan was spun off his feet by a stiff gust and for seconds hung by one hand from a wire before somebody hauled him onto the wing. Three times the deck force assisting them was caught by boarding seas, and sent flying across the deck, before they grabbed something handy.

One wave lifted a dozen dog crates on the starboard side and swept them, dogs and all, clear to the port rail. Innes-Taylor, Buckley, Wade, Paine and Russell, who were on watch, dived in and made them fast before a second wave carried them overboard. Herb, a big Manitoba, who was chained to the deck, was washed over the side. Somebody saw him just in time and hauled him back. The dogs really had a fearful day. I pitied them.

After a long struggle, we finally got the ship headed into the wind, and the danger abated. For two hours we had our bow pointed toward New Zealand. When, in the forenoon, the storm worked into the west, then into the southwest, we followed it round, holding the ship in the wind. This afternoon a short lull came, which was broken by savage squalls. Now the wind is rising again. The sea has a wild aspect. The wind is like a solid force, ripping spray from the waves before they break; and black wind shadows, like cats' paws, rake the sea where they strike. Above the crash of the seas the vibrating flying wires of the plane make a deep, sonorous, thrumming note, like the sound of a plane in flight.

The barometer, having touched a low of 28.26 inches this morning, is rising fast....

Mon., Dec. 18, 10:30 P.M.

The gale blew itself out during the night, and at noon today we resumed our course, with the engines at full speed. The wind has dropped to a fresh breeze, and the seas have moderated. Our noon position was Lat. 61° 29′ S., Long. 162° 06′ W., which put us only 439 miles from the intersection of the Antarctic Circle and the 150th meridian West.

It's getting colder. The air temperature has dropped to 31°, and the sea temperature to 33°. This morning all winches were started, and from now on they will turn slowly all day and all night. It's the best way to prevent them from freezing. Most of the asbestos lagging so patiently wound around the steam lines was washed away yesterday. Ice is already forming on the spars and rigging.

Blue sky this afternoon, and in the evening the sun leapt through the cloud wrack. A good omen. Tomorrow, unless we are stopped by pack, we shall surpass Cook's southing. We're lucky not to have met ice before this.

IV

Tuesday, December 19th, was a notable day. On this day we raised our first icebergs in the early watch; we broke past Cook's track for a new record southing; and we celebrated the arrival of Iceberg, Klondike's bull calf. The first event was an incident, the second a creditable achievement, and the third (though Messrs. Clark and Cox, who had Klondike's destiny in hand, were disinclined to see it that way) was an event over which we had no control.

Say what you will, but of all the natural beauties of the world there can be few lovelier and more stirring to the contemplative traveler than his first glimpse of true Antarctic tabular icebergs. They are something apart, something incredibly unreal, yet so perfectly and instinctively appropriate within their setting that you are moved to exclaim: here is an ultimate definition! It is so meaningless to call them sentinels. They are much more than that. They are mobile extensions of the Antarctic itself, stately white caravels afloat on a painted sea; a sky-filling architecture schemed and wrought by Nature from the marble quarries of the Ice Age. On some we saw the whole of Manhattan could have been disposed, even to its subways. Beyond the rose-flaming horizon lay the undiscovered coast from which the glacial pressures piling up from behind, and the tidal movements working from below, had wrenched these bergs. Now, in the persuasive sway of submarine currents, they drifted softly toward extinction. In these waste waters sailed a doomed fleet, the fairest that ever put to sea.

Dick Russell, on lookout, sighted the first iceberg. At 1:25 A.M., he raised the cry: "Berg on the port bow!" A moment later half a dozen more lifted frosted domes above the horizon. Soon the sea was crowded with them. Two hundred were counted in view at one time: and, at the speed we were making, we were raising a new horizon every hour. The largest was perhaps four miles long and three miles wide. Later on, in the Devil's graveyard, we were to steam past mountains of ice that would make these bergs seem mere cream puffs. But these claimed our awe now.

The day broke beautifully—a lovely golden panel of light pushing

THE "WILLIAM HORLICK" READY TO TAKE THE AIR

(Photograph by Joseph A. Pelter)

THE FLIGHT CREW PREPARING TO BOARD THE PLANE

(Photograph by Joseph A. Pelter)

The Pack Rolls to the Horizon

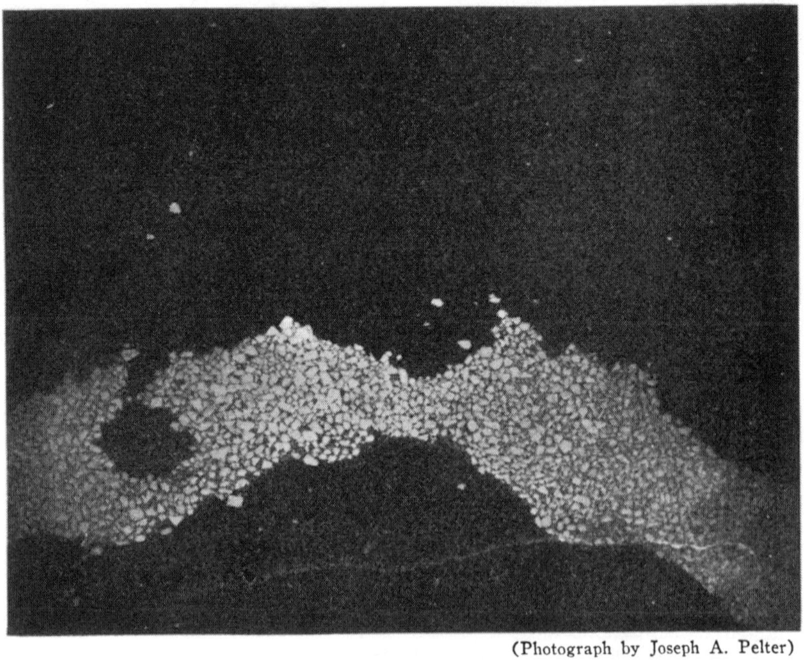

(Photograph by Joseph A. Pelter)

A Mosaic of Pack (from the Air)

through softly furred, gray cumulous clouds. The air stirred under a light, variable westerly wind; the sea was choppy. In the fractured sides of the bergs, in the grottoes and caves worn at their water line, were strange, rich blues, pale delicate greens, and weathered yellows and grays. The sea surged over their submerged spurs, and exploded in shining puffs of surf. The scene was a study in magic. Wherever you looked it faithfully and uncannily reflected whatever phantasy with which you invested it. You could see white sailing ships, with towering canvas set, standing out to sea: you could see turreted castles of fabulous architecture, enormous battlements, steepled and gabled structures cunningly wrought by the weathering hands of wind and sea. One was like a battleship down by the stern, its bow tilted crazily toward the sky, its crumpled upper works strewn across the deck. Another was a breathless reproduction of the Colosseum, weathered and decaying, with three perfectly formed arches, two hundred feet high, through the portals of which the sea surged boisterously. There was beauty there of a rare and infinitely varied pattern.

But we had a job to do, and no time for thumbing Baedeker. We pressed past these shining structures at top speed, steering various courses to pass among them. At 8:30 P.M., at Lat. 65° S., Long. 153° 32′ W., our observations indicated that we had surpassed Cook's southing:[1] that we were at last on the rim of the unknown sea. One hundred and fifty years had passed since a keel had furrowed these blue waters. Instinctively my eyes sought the southern horizon for the yellow-white effulgence of ice blink. No, still a water sky. For a while at least the road south lay open.

But the significance of geographical discovery, I must confess, was largely lost upon the expedition. Almost to a man the crew waited with breathless expectancy for an event which has been common in Nature since the world began. Klondike, one of the Guernsey cows, was about to—well, let's go back to the beginning. When Klondike came aboard at Newport News, she was already in that state which columnists no longer describe as "an interesting condition." In fact, I suspect that this was her outstanding claim to preference, and I suspect, also, there had been some sly counting on the fingers, too.

Anyhow, Cox and Clark were unaccountably eager to have the calf born within the Antarctic Circle. It appears that they had a sublimely confident understanding to that effect with The Guernsey Cattle Club. A calf born in these frosty latitudes, they reasoned, would have a unique claim to immortality. December 19th had been fixed as the date, at which time Cox, Clark and the whole palpitating constituency of The Guernsey Cattle Club calculated the expedition would be well within the Circle. They made the fatal mistake of not reckoning on Klondike.

Nor on the fog, either. As the days wore on the countenances of Cox and Clark grew haggard; they studied the log, scanned the noon posi-

[1] In this longitude as shown on the Admiralty Chart.

tions, checked the day's run, watched the sky for ice blink, consulted the skipper. On the 19th they were up all night. Captain Verleger came upon them on the shelter deck.

"How far from the Circle now?" Cox asked, huskily.

"Three hundred miles," said the skipper, "and if you want that calf born within the Circle, my advice is to borrow the plane and fly the cow across, because it looks to me as if Klondike ain't goin' to wait for mere latitude."

The hours passed, and Cox and Clark breathed easier. They tiptoed topside for a look at the bergs. Suddenly a shout flew over the ship.

Klondike had declined to wait for destiny.

With eleven thousand miles of voyaging behind her, the frost in the air assured her that her journey was about run; and not caring to quibble about a few degrees of latitude, she quietly and definitely achieved the everlasting duty of her sex.

An immediate dead reckoning placed the event just 247 nautical miles north of the Circle. A suggestion from the news correspondent that in view of the peculiar circumstances surrounding the event, the calf be named "Caught Short," was violently resisted. Iceberg it was named.

V

Shortly before midnight, just after the sun set for the last time, we marked the creamy glow of ice blink on the southern horizon. That meant pack ahead. The bergs were thinning out. The ship was running south-southeast. At 6:30 A.M., December 20th, at Latitude 65° 55′ S., Long. 151° 10′ W., 35 miles north of the Circle, we fetched up against the northern rim of the pack. Great fields of loose, pancake ice curved irregularly to the east and west. Southward they extended to the limit of vision. It looked none too promising; neither did it look too bad.

With Commodore Gjertsen on the bridge, giving quick commands to the helmsman, we worked eastward through scattered floes, looking for a feasible passage. Remember, we had an old iron ship which for years had lain unused in a government graveyard. Her plates were only seven-eighths of an inch thick; they were rusty, and there was no telling how much of a strain her rivets could withstand. We went cautiously, side-stepping the heavier floes.

At 8:20 we paused for a manual sounding.[2] A successful sounding would give us a hint of the nearness or remoteness of the undiscovered coast to the south. No bottom at 300 fathoms. We broke through patches of light, new ice. At 9:30 another sounding. No bottom at 300 fathoms. A ribbon of black water unrolled before our bow, and we took a southerly heading through the pack.

[2] During this voyage Morgan made several efforts to get soundings with his seismic apparatus, but the results were generally inconclusive.

It was really exciting. Past the rim of geographical discovery, we felt our way forward, scanning the radiant horizon for the secrets it might at any moment yield. Above the gray flooring of the pack a white cliff, seeming without end, slowly emerged. "Barrier coast," sang out the man in the crow's nest. But he was wrong. Twenty minutes later we marked sky on either side: just a berg. About ten o'clock another monstrous ice structure tempted us. We altered course to approach it, crunching through fairly heavy ice at slow speed. This time I was taken in. For a long time that gleaming dome, with its sheer cliffs, held a tantalizing promise. But what was that odd peak sticking up behind it? Of course. Just two bergs, seven miles, maybe eight miles long.

Disappointed, we stood away. The ship zig-zagged down narrow leads, holding to the south. On a small floe the first Antarctic seal, a Crab-Eater, raised his head resentfully as the swell from the ship disturbed his sanctuary, stared hard with bloodshot eyes, then promptly rolled back on his belly. Flights of snowy petrels, white as the snow against which they flew, were precipitated out of the sky and flickered tirelessly about the ship. Still, it was wonderfully quiet. The pack heaved on a gentle swell, grating ever so slightly, with a sound like that of branches rubbing together in a forest. The ice yielded and parted before the ship's forefoot, and slipped, hissing, with soft protests, along the plates. Otherwise it was utterly peaceful.

By mid-afternoon it was evident that the ice massing in front of us was too heavy to be taken by assault. The ship inched through heavier, older ice. The shocks of impact came more frequently; several times, when we struck masses of hard, blue-green ice, the *Ruppert* trembled the length of her keel. Down in the engine room you could hear the hollow sound of the ice banging against the plates.

Commodore Gjertsen shook his head. "She's an old ship," he reminded us. "It's not as if you had a wooden ship, built for ice. Her plates won't stand much punishment. All we have to do is sheer off a couple of rivets . . ."

The ship was virtually blocked, though we continued to struggle on for a few hours more. There is no sense battering your heads against a stone wall, not if you can vault it. Bill Haines, wise in the lore of Antarctic weather, was appraising the wind, studying the barometer. At six o'clock that evening he came into my cabin.

"The barometer has leveled off, and the wind is in the south," he said. "Looks as if it's going to be pretty good flying weather."

So we made ready to fit the second string to our bow.

Shortly after six, at Lat. 67° 09′ S., Long. 148 ° 00′ W., we turned. On her own hook the *Ruppert* had exceeded Cook's penetration by 148 statute miles. It was up to aviation to renew the assault.

Twenty-eight miles astern I had noticed a wide lake of open water in the pack. It was sheltered, and wide enough to give us a long take-off run in any direction. So we turned back for it, leaving a ribbon of black, roiled water in our wake. Behind us the ice was already closing in, erasing all trace of our passage.

The decision to fly I kept to myself. In the evening the usual Wednesday night movie show was held on the shelter deck. I had already decided on the crew—June, chief pilot; Bowlin, co-pilot; Petersen, radio operator; Pelter, serial mapping cameraman. During the show I took these men aside, one by one, and asked them to be ready to fly in the morning. When the show was over, Noville stood up and quietly asked for volunteers to help lower the motor sailer, which was to act as crash and tow boat.

By that time we had gained the lake. I examined it from the bridge. It was a perfect place for a take-off, clear of ice except for a big berg, which lay about a thousand yards off, tilted on its side. We would have to be careful, however, about drifting fragments of hard ice. Many of these, barely awash, lay scattered about. If struck squarely on a take-off run, any one of them could easily knock a hole through a pontoon.

The crew now sprang to its tasks. The aviation unit made a final check of the plane. Dyer, chief radio engineer, and Bailey, chief radio operator, finished the installation of a homing loop, as an extra navigational safeguard. Up forward a gang was hoisting the big gasoline drums from No. 2 hold, rolling them aft through the shelter deck and hoisting them to the poop. Corey struggled in the lockers, a diminutive figure lost in small mountains of emergency rations, camping equipment, and fur clothing. Flight requirements were: one month's rations, full camping equipment, for five men. Every item had to be checked and re-checked, weighed and carefully stowed.

Barely rolling along the horizon, the Midnight Sun was an amber whorl in golden mist. With infinite, almost imperceptible, slowness the pack worked round the ship: you noticed, when you glanced out from time to time, that the pattern of the ice was constantly altering. But there was little time for small observations. Men worked the clock around. It was a foretaste of what was in store for them. Later on, two or three hours' sleep in forty-eight would be a luxury.

Captain Verleger and June had charge of lowering the plane over the side. McNamara and Dustin, two of the ablest seamen, were posted at the winches. I didn't want anything to miscarry; hoisting that six-ton plane from its berth, swinging it outboard and lowering her gently to the water was a ticklish job. I was none too confident of the tackle. You could make only one mistake. But the thing went off very nicely. The boom was topped to plumb the plane, and then, with the deck force heaving on the guide lines, it was neatly conveyed to its proper medium. The motor sailer towed it astern, where Noville took charge of gassing it, a laborious job, since the gasoline had to be pumped by hand and strained through chamois.

(Photograph by Earle B. Perkins)

SEALS SUNNING ON AN ICE FLOE

(Photograph by Earle B. Perkins)

THE "WILLIAM HORLICK" OVERBOARD

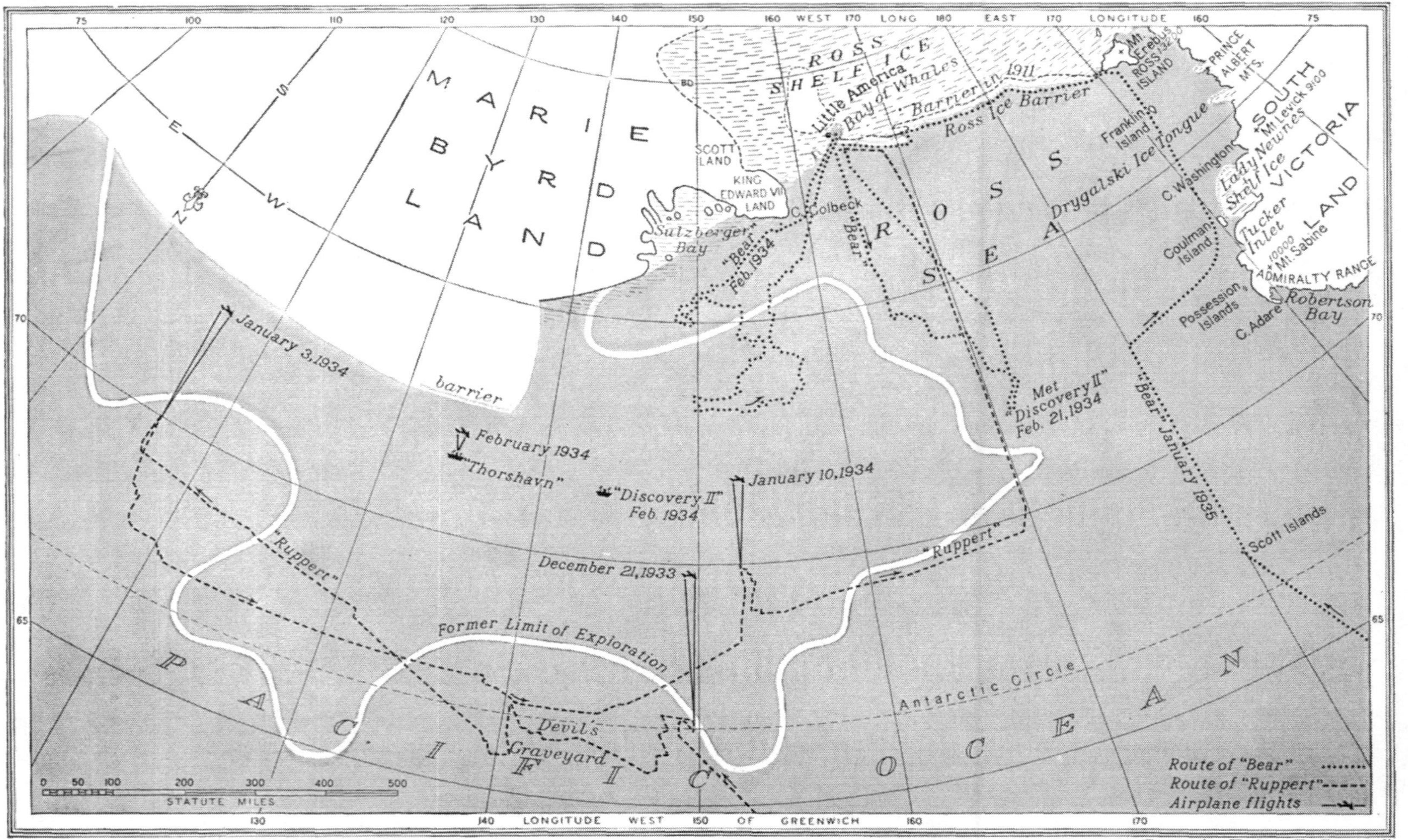

(Constructed by Lieut. (J. G.) R. A. J. English, U. S. N.) (Drawn by Herbert E. Eastwood)

THE ROSS SEA AND PART OF THE SOUTH PACIFIC OCEAN, SHOWING ROUTES OF SHIPS AND FLIGHTS FROM THE "JACOB RUPPERT"

By then it was nearly four o'clock on the morning of December 21st.

One thing or another held us up. On a flight of this sort unexpected details are forever cropping up; but shortly after ten o'clock the flight crew rowed out to the plane.

The morning was incomparably fair, crystal clear, and the big berg on our starboard hand shone like a burnished shield.

VI

At 10:40 o'clock the port engine was started: three minutes later the starboard engine joined in explosively. For twenty minutes we taxied up and down the lake, looking for a take-off stretch clear of ice. We selected one which lay in the lee of the berg. At 10:53, after a run of only twenty-nine seconds, we rose in the eye of a light south-westerly wind, circled and returned over the ship.

Before squaring away on our course we spent an hour making certain preliminary tests. There was the matter of checking the compasses. In high southern latitudes, on account of the proximity of the Magnetic Pole, the magnetic compass is inclined to be sluggish and not wholly reliable. Although I would rely almost entirely upon the sun compass, still there is always a chance you will lose the sun, in which case the magnetic compass is a navigator's mainstay.

We determined the deviation in an interesting way. Before leaving the ship I asked Commodore Gjertsen to head the ship due south by the gyro compass, which had been checked by azimuths. As we circled above the ship I now asked him, by radio telephone, to confirm his heading. "Due south," the answer came back almost immediately. Making broad circles, we passed straight over the ship half a dozen times, each time checking by radio the compass readings.

Up forward June nodded his readiness: the plane was fit. Petersen reported that the homing loop had carried away, but that was a small matter.

At 11:40 A.M. we advised the ship we were starting south. Wheeling, we struck down the 150th meridian.

Chapter III

THE DEVIL'S GRAVEYARD

I

THE flight due south along the 150th meridian was the first of three south-seeking aërial corridors of exploration which we drove into the uncharted ocean of the Pacific Quadrant of Antarctica. The first flight started out to be mainly a test flight, but we were finally tempted to extend it to the limit of the gasoline supply of the plane. The day was perfect—ideal for a flight, with one of the steadiest barometers I have ever seen in the polar regions. The thermometer stood at 40° above.

Making one hundred knots, we roved over the pack. June climbed to 2,000 feet. At that altitude we had vision of about 59 miles. In all directions the pack lay upon the sea, like a curiously tesselated ivory plain, with coal-black lanes of open water twisting through it, filling the interstices. It was mostly light, loose pack, one-year ice. I looked in vain for the heavy, rafted pressure ice which I had expected to find in this region. And this puzzled me, for a while, until the explanation leapt to mind.

Ahead of us a snow squall projected shallow curtains of dirty, whirling mist into the golden sunlight. Still holding steadily to his course, June carried the plane through it. The air turned unsteady and the wings rocked a bit. For a few minutes streams of snowflakes pelted wildly across the wing, and the sun was obscured. But the interruption was short-lived: as abruptly as we left it, we burst into the sunshine.

When we took off it was my plan to fly only a hundred miles or so; then, if conditions were favorable, return and gas up for a longer flight. But a suspicion was working in the back of my mind, and I motioned to June to keep going.

Dead ahead I saw loom above the horizon an extensive ice front, miles off but directly on our course. In the haze of the horizon it had the fine sweeping line, the flat roofing and the seeming permanence of Barrier Coast.

But I declined to be taken in. After you've been tricked often enough by the glittering false imageries of Antarctica, you learn to hold your tongue and your conviction.

Nevertheless, flying steadily at 2,000 feet, we bore toward it.

June leaned back and said that we had exceeded our estimated limits: that we were now using our gasoline reserve. My dead reckoning placed us about 184 miles [1] south of the *Ruppert*. Since our gasoline reserve was 25 percent or more, I felt we could safely run another twenty-five or thirty miles south without undue risk. The sky was now partly overcast: thin patches of stratus clouds from time to time shut out the sun, but visibility was excellent, and we had perfect radio communication with the ship.

In fact, from time to time I reported directly to the *Ruppert* over the radio telephone, receiving weather information and transmitting, in turn, reports on our progress. It was the first time I had ever used radio telephony on a flight of discovery; it was the first time, I believe, the apparatus was ever used in polar exploration, and I was impressed by the possibilities that it offered.[2]

Slowly the enormous ice mass in the south divulged its true identity. As we drew closer, and the perspective changed, we discovered that instead of being a continuous structure it was, in reality, a great column of icebergs, at least three score in number, strung out like warships in a battle line. Over and beyond them stretched the pack-littered sea.

At 1:40 P.M., having reached the outward limit of our gas, we turned at Lat. 69° 51′ S., Long. 149° 45′ W., and headed back for the ship. At our altitude we had visibility of at least 50 miles, and therefore well beyond the 70th parallel.

A theory, growing out of my observations and study of the best scientific opinion, had already matured.

The absence of pack—on the contrary, the comparative openness of the sea—strongly argued against the existence of the archipelago or a peninsula of the continent supposed by some to project into this area. If land existed, there must have been larger quantities of heavy bay ice than we have seen. After all, a steady current with a westerly set [3] was continuously wafting pack down from the ice coast to the eastward: and any extensive land mass lying athwart that current was bound to accumulate and dam back the immense pack for which this region was fabled.

It was possible, of course, that this was an unusually light ice year in this sector; but opposed to this reasoning was the fact that Ells-

[1] Except where otherwise indicated all distances are given in statute miles.

[2] The main transmitter in this plane was a standard commercial aircraft transmitter slightly modified by Dyer. It delivered 50 watts of crystal-controlled power to the antennae over a frequency range of 2,000 to 9,000 kilocycles on either telephone or telegraph. A dynamotor run from the plane's 12-volt circuit furnished power for the transmitter. An auxiliary transmitter—consisting of a self-excited oscillator delivering 25 watts to the antennae over the same frequency range—was carried as a precaution against failure of the main unit. Two antennae were available, one fixed and the other a trailing wire.

[3] On December 19th the westerly set of the current was measured and estimated to be about .9 knots.

worth's ship, the *Wyatt Earp,* in the Ross Sea to the westward, was bucking heavy pack en route to the Bay of Whales.

No, it seemed to me, as I turned the facts over in my mind on the way back to the *Ruppert,* that the first explanation was apt to be the right one. The huge lobe of uncharted white space bulging between the 140th and 160th meridians West must be nearly all Pacific Ocean. With a little effort later on, perhaps with a fair measure of luck, it could be erased from the map and the land be defined as falling within the then known coasts of Marie Byrd Land and King Edward VII Land. This had already been forecast by the best geographical opinion.

A more profitable point of attack was in the vicinity of the 120th meridian West, where a deep embayment in the pack seeming to persist year after year and shoal soundings indicated the proximity of the unknown coast.

While Bowlin took his trick at the wheel, June and I discussed. Time was the controlling element. We couldn't afford to delay arrival in the Bay of Whales later than the middle of January; and, taking all things into account, I didn't see how we could spare more than a fortnight to take up the attack farther east. Besides, the ship's oil reserves allowed no greater margin. The region was notoriously inhospitable. The seas were rough, and earlier navigators had reported that the sun was rarely seen through the fog. Maybe we were off on a wild goose chase.

However, exploration is less a matter of waiting for breaks than of creating them. It was decided that immediately after landing, the plane would be hoisted aboard and the ship sent eastward.

The flight was completed without incident. The sun being obscured by clouds, we asked for a radio direction bearing from the ship. It checked nicely. Then, dead on our course, a smudge of smoke on the horizon—the *Ruppert.* At 2:55 P.M. we raked over it, fore and aft. At 3:03 P.M. June eased the floats into the quiet water.

Three hours later, with the plane cradled on its tier, the *Ruppert* was steaming northward at full speed through a widening breach in the pack.

Of that evening my diary reported:

> It is nearly midnight, and sea and sky and ice pack are perfect harmonies of color. It is beauty of a sort that will stop you in your tracks. No use to cast about for words to describe it. The artist, Paige, standing lookout watch, had been watching it for a long time. "Why don't you paint it?" I suggested.
>
> "I could paint it, all right," he said with a smile. "But what's the use? Nobody would believe it. Who ever saw a sky like that?"
>
> How can you describe a sea that's like no sea that ever was, or ever will be again? A disembodied sea, having no relation to winds, or tides, or currents: but just living colors, like the colors that dwell in rich wines, brimming in pack ice and icebergs of the whitest white? How can you describe a sky that's so china-like that a single sharp sound might shatter it; and a ship running

through it, with deserted decks, exhausted men asleep in whatever attitudes they hit, and no sound except the soft rhythm of distant machinery, the hiss of water along the sides?

Paige said another wise thing, too. "Nature puts her price on beauty," he said. "I've knocked around the world, looking for things to paint, and I've just found that you've got to go far—you've got to leave the beaten track to find beauty like this." ... I've just finished calculating the geographic gains of our first operation. By ship and airplane we made a new record southing of 350 statute miles, and explored approximately 30,000 square miles of previously unknown area. A promising start. Luck was with us. Dyer told me this evening that when he examined the electrical system on the plane he found that the dynamotor had torn itself apart. It must have happened just as we landed. Otherwise we should have lost all communication with the ship. I noticed a queer, new sound just as June banked for the turn—a sound like millions of tons of water rushing.

... Poulter took another sounding in the pack just before we got underway. No bottom at 570 fathoms.

II

Through the night of December 21st and the morning and afternoon of the next day we retreated through the pack, always angling, when we could, to the eastward. The pack was largely formed of fields of pancake ice, which were too closely crowded to persuade Commodore Gjertsen to force the ship. At times we profited by great open lanes, brimming with slick black water. Other times we had to jockey the ship through streams of heavy, crumpled ice. First the gyro compass failed, then one of the ship's generators broke down. We struck the worst ice just a few miles south of the open sea. At seven o'clock on the evening of the 22nd the *Ruppert* stubbed her toe against a floe with shock enough to bring every man to his feet. Luckily everything held. For the next hour or so, we backed and filled, maneuvering for an exit. The engine room telegraph belled constantly, and the crack of ice giving before the bow and rumbling along the sides came with disturbing frequency. Jockeying this way and that, you stand a good chance of breaking the propeller blades against a block of ice.

At last we extricated the ship and, breathing easier, bore north of east through lighter ice. Shortly after eight o'clock, at Lat. 65° 51′ S., Long. 147° 20′ W., the ship broke clear of the pack and gained open sea. Coasting the face of the pack, which now curved irregularly on our starboard hand, we steered eastward, altering course occasionally to evade the tentacle-like streams and belts of ice extending from the main mass.

The respite was short-lived. The glass dropped sharply. The wind, which had been holding in the east, whistled into east-northeast and stiffened. Then a white fog arose, and wet snow came slanting through it. The night turned sodden. Out of the mist, heaving on the long swell, lurched the out-riders of a ghostly fleet of icebergs. Speed dropped to half, then to slow. All night long the chilled men in the crow's nest, and up in the eyes of the ship, were calling: "Berg off the starboard bow," or "Berg close aboard to port."

Though the name was to come later, we had entered the frontiers of that region which, for the members of the Second Byrd Antarctic Expedition, shall forever be remembered as the Devil's Graveyard. You'll probably never see that name on any chart. Like Scylla and Charybdis, or the Symplegades—The Clashing Rocks—of the Euxine Sea, it is one of those fabulous, terrifying aspects of Nature which lie in ambush for sailors at the ends of the earth. What we called the Devil's Graveyard lay, roughly, between the 147th and 135th meridians, along the Antarctic Circle. It was a mood of Nature. For days a sleet-oozing, dripping oppressive fog, so thick that the bow at times was lost from the view of the bridge, lay over the sea. And through that smoking pall, like phantom fleets, prowled icebergs past numbering, with the sea sobbing in their basement grottoes. Like a cornered thing, the ship stood among them, stopped and drifting, or maneuvering, with swift alarums and excursions, to evade towering cliffs, emerging with formidable clarity out of the gloom which bore down upon her. Fog alone is oppressive enough at sea, but when it is a veil concealing hordes of preying enemies it becomes malevolent. The telegraph was cocked at standby; lookout watches were doubled: on the bridge, in the eyes of the ship, in the crow's nest, and deep down in the engine room, men waited and watched uneasily. Those days in the fog left a spell on us that will not be lightly shaken off. Months later, George Noville told me, he'd break, with a start, from a sound sleep, with sweat on his palms and forehead, his body braced against an invisible blow, listening for the cry of the lookout and waiting for a reeling impact. That's the way it was in the Devil's Graveyard—a deep, brooding fog which, in Conrad's phrase, was one great circular ambush.

Sat., Dec. 23, Midnight.

Since five o'clock this afternoon the ship has been standing by and drifting in thick fog. We are lying about a mile north of the pack, surrounded by numerous bergs. It has been snowing intermittently, and the decks are slippery as a waxed floor. Wind E.N.E., barometer at midnight 28.40.

In the early afternoon a large glacial growler was wafted by the ship. Its sides were plainly marked with silt and gravel bands. Lowering the small boat, Morgan and Siple went alongside and broke off a number of specimens of igneous rocks, which were blue, green and brown in color. Quite likely this growler is a remnant of a glacier from the coast we are seeking.

Noon position (dead reckoning) Lat. 66° 20′ S., Long. 144° 02′ W.

Sun., Dec. 24, 11:38 P.M.

Christmas Eve. A more god-forsaken place could not be imagined. Ship stopped and drifting all day. The fog still holds, robbing us of irreplaceable hours. It lifted a bit this afternoon, when the wind shifted into south-southwest, but soon closed in again. Snow squalls swirling around the ship every few hours. The bergs about us seem to be increasing in numbers. Our position is really critical. Visibility at times drops to zero, and the bergs rise out of the fog with alarming suddenness. You stare into the shifting vapor, seeing nothing, only dim, uncertain shadows. The tortured shadows part, and a towering white mountain, with cliffs upwards of 150 feet high, cleaves through, scarcely four ship-lengths away. Then the cry floats down from the crow's nest, echoed almost simultaneously from the lookout in the eyes of the ship: "Berg on the port bow." Down in the engine room the engineers on watch spring to their posts, the screw turns, the decks tremble to the motion, and the ship sheers away from the menace. This darting to and fro has been going on all day.

We nearly lost one of the dogs—a wolf dog, Olaf. Buckley and Paine were exercising a team up forward. Lewisohn swore that the dog, having lost all interest in polar expeditions, simply jumped overboard. Anyhow, there he was in the water, paddling violently. Dustin went over the side on a line and tried to grab him by the collar, but the dog, being badly frightened, escaped him and rounded the bow. He couldn't have lived long in that water. Fortunately, he swam into the current of warm water discharging from the circulating pumps, and had the good sense to paddle around there until the men were able to reach him in a small boat. Innes-Taylor gave the dog artificial respiration, and tonight Olaf appeared to be suffering less from exposure than from a hang-over produced by a liberal shot of excellent whiskey. When Innes-Taylor revealed the cure, it was all we could do to restrain the entire ship's company from jumping overboard.

Poulter attempted another sounding today: ran out 10,500 feet of line, and, allowing a foot of drift for every five feet of line, reported no bottom at 9,000 feet: Temp., 31° at noon: barometer 29.14 and dropping.

Mon., Dec. 25, Midnight.

Christmas. In spite of the fog we had a very satisfying day: the tables in the forward and after saloons groaned under an amazing variety of food; there were movies on the shelter deck, and Christmas boxes, bought months ago, were opened with eagerness and their contents shared all around. Except for those on watch, the rules were relaxed, and I doubt if there was anywhere on this earth a gayer Christmas than was celebrated in the Devil's Graveyard. The fog, the damp air, the wet, slimy decks, the menace of the bergs—they were all, for a few brief hours, forgotten, except by the lonely devils shivering on watch. But I dare say there will be a few big heads in the morning.

For a while it looked as if the elements had released their own gift. The fog lifted at 6:15 this morning, and we got under way again, steering east and southeast along the front of the pack. Shortly after 4 o'clock the fog closed in again, thicker than ever. An hour later the air cleared enough to tempt us into a slow advance. With the edge of the pack about two miles off on our right hand, the ship crept ahead for two hours, feeling rather than seeing the way.

Suddenly the fog drained into the sea. It was an eerie experience. One moment we were sliding down a narrow gray corridor, thankful for the lack of bergs. The next moment the fog was sucked away, and hundreds of bergs, many of immense size, cropped up as if by magic. Closely ranked, they extended as far as I could see, so numerous that the sea was broken into rivers coursing among mountains of ice. It was Scylla and Charybdis multiplied a thousand times.

Commodore Gjertsen signaled for a slow speed astern. We backed out a way, then turned. The fog closed in, and we stopped at 9 o'clock. We've been drifting ever since. The barometer is dropping. Wind and sea are making. We're in for bad weather.

Noon position (dead reckoning), Lat. 66° 30′ S., Long. 141° 20′ W.

III

Next day a gale screeched down from the northwest, and for a few hours I thought that the Devil's Graveyard would be the graveyard of the Second Byrd Antarctic Expedition. All day long the ship clawed into the eye of a gale, fighting to protect her own skin as well as the big plane cradled aft. Once she lay helpless, drifting with terrible sureness upon a berg which, had her sides but brushed it, would have sent her instantly to the bottom. The *Ruppert* had no intricate system of inner skins. She was a tramp lumber ship, with a shell of ⅞ inch steel. The berg that sent the *Titanic* to the bottom on a clear night was a pebble compared to those among which the *Ruppert* twisted in fog and gale.

The curious thing is that the storm was kindled in deep fog. Even at the height of the blow, when the Condor's air speed indicator registered a wind velocity of more than 50 knots, the fog thinned but very little. That's what made the situation so critical. For this eggshell of an iron ship lay among a host of bergs, like herself harried and driven by the gale. Disaster might have been the penalty of a single blunder. The ship couldn't retreat. She was caught between the anvil of the pack and the hammer of the bergs. There was no lee anywhere. The ship had to take it and like it. Every third sea rolling under her sent the stern kiting. The propeller rose thrashing; on the poop you could feel the shaft vibrating as the blades strove for substance. To save the shaft we had to cut down engine revolutions. I shudder to think what would have happened if the propeller had shaken off or the rudder jammed; no power on earth could have saved us. She was loggy and the seas were knocking her head around, first one way, then the other, however stubbornly the helmsman labored to hold the ship into the wind. Yet our skins depended upon the ship's speed and maneuverability. There was no telling when an aimless mountain of ice would come out of the mark, across the bow, with the rush of the Apocalypse. Snow squalls cut through the fog, digging their own darker furrows; and the air was lacerating with snow blown off the tops of bergs.

IV

The gale struck during the night. The Cape pigeons, more reliable than a barometer in that area, had given warning. Higher and higher they flew, till they were cutting across the trucks of the foremast—a sign of bad weather. The seas piled up, breaking across the forward and after well-decks.

Shortly after seven o'clock the lookout up forward sang out: "Big berg dead ahead!" Almost the same instant Captain Verleger and Chief Officer Bayne, who were on the bridge, raised a big berg on the starboard bow. The sides were lost in the fog, but two hundred feet in the air, white spires stood clear.

Not caring to steer between them, and unwilling to lay the ship in the trough of the sea to pass them to leeward, Captain Verleger decided to pass them to windward. Heaving on the gale, the ship lunged forward. Just as she drew abeam of the larger berg, her speed fell off. Came a whistle in the speaking tube behind the helmsman. Commander Queen, in the engine room, reported the fires were out. In some way water had gotten into the starboard oil tank; with the pitching and rolling of the ship it had worked up through the oil, been pumped under pressure to the burner nozzles, and put the fires out. Queen had instantly switched to the port tanks and started the fires again, but steam pressure was dropping fast.

Pressure dropped in short order to less than ninety pounds—barely half normal pressure. It wasn't enough to hold her in the wind. She lost steerage way. Slowly the seas cuffed her bow around: then she fell off, beam-on to the storm, and swiftly drifted down wind, rolling like a drunkard.

Just two hundred yards—maybe a little more, maybe less—to the good, we fell past the big berg. Then the mists enveloped it; we saw it no more. "Gor blime," muttered Chief Officer Bayne, under his breath, "I'd just made up me mind where to jump." We weren't clear yet—not by a long shot. The ship fell in among a mess of growlers, scarcely less formidable than the giant bergs of which they were shattered remnants. Masses of hard, blue-green ice, they lay strewn everywhere, heaving with loud crashings on the sea. It was impossible to tell which way they were bearing. The waves would throw them up, revealing twenty feet of green basement, then suck them into the hollows until they were barely awash. You found yourself watching them with a curious fascination. It was like being among countless agitated reefs. If the ship in her helplessness had ever grazed her plates against one of those things, it would have been too bad. We passed some with nothing to spare.

Providence must have been with us that day. Slowly steam pressure rose, and the ship groped her way back into the wind. All the afternoon and evening, and until the storm abated at six o'clock on the morning of the 27th, we held her in the eye of the wind, following it as it hauled into the westward. And all the while these malevolent fleets of ice—with bergs two, three, four miles long and more, of every conceivable shape and form—came wallowing out of the gray mists, stood briefly in view, then vanished, as new ones emerged to take their places. The waves welled and crashed and gushed against their smooth flanks, sending spray clear over their tops. Sometimes the mists would wrap around them, so that you saw only the dripping domes, strangely truncated and floating with baffling buoyancy in mid-air. The sea was littered with brash ice, bergy bits, growlers and half-shattered bergs, as though two giant fleets were fighting an action in the dark.

Whence came these phantom fleets? And whither were they bound? To destruction, of course. For this was a march of death, and in all Nature there is nothing like it. Billions upon billions of tons of ice, like mountains broken from the lands, made drunk by the discovery of their buoyancy, and dancing a wild, but stately parade as they drifted in the compulsion of submarine currents to inevitable extinction in warmer latitudes. You couldn't but stand awed in that shouting confusion of sea and wind, watching that grand procession passing in and out of the obliterating fog. Once we saw a great berg, like a battleship struck in a vulnerable spot, hesitate; then, with a titanic, convulsive movement, roll over on its side, strewing the sea about it with broken ice. Over the crack of the wind there came a remote, rushing sound, like that of an avalanche. Then the fog shut down.

But for all these passing perils life in the ship went on pretty much as usual. Persisting long enough, any danger soon loses the desperate quality of imminence. Solicited by his own minor concerns, the average man will glide with untouched serenity through a crisis which does not directly impinge upon his affairs. Under such conditions you come to appreciate the lasting strength of men. Perhaps with some a lack of imagination is the basis of the outward confidence which reflects this sense of security; others may reason—well, there's nothing we can do about it; let the bridge do the worrying. Anyhow, though only a few of the men had seen the ice of a polar sea before, not even the Devil's Graveyard in its wildest aspect could shake them from their day-by-day routine. You'd think it was the commonest thing in the world for an iron ship to be playing blind man's buff with icebergs in gale and fog. The dog drivers watered and fed their dogs, Cox looked after his cows. In the makeshift laboratory midships Dr. Perkins and Siple leaned over swaying microscopes, studying plankton specimens. In the radio shack, Dyer, Hutcheson and Pierce worked over the radio sets they were building for the trail parties; on the spray-swept flying bridge Dr. Bramhall and Zuhn stood by their cosmic ray apparatus, vigilant lest the heavy pitching and rolling of the ship carry away their instruments. And in No. 2 hold, where the last of the beer was supposedly under lock and key, an unnoticed interloper cheerfully celebrated alone, until the heaving of the ship became too much for him, and he fell into a sound sleep.

But that night, when he took his place at the head of the ward-room table, Commodore Gjertsen spoke soberly: "Gentlemen, you can thank God that you still have a deck under you tonight."

Wednesday morning, the 27th, the sun shattered the fog like a golden lance. The seas moderated, and at 5:00 A.M. the ship was able to resume her easting. Several sights—the first shot at the sun since the 22nd—fixed our position as Lat. 65° 50′ S., Long. 139° 30′ W. Though we had been driving at close to full speed against a northwest wind all the day before, the ship had actually been driven about 60 miles east.

Under a cold breeze pouring in from the west-southwest, the fog vanished, and in the golden sunlight we had our first full view of the white monuments of the Devil's Graveyard. The sea was almost lost for the bergs. There was no end of them. They rose, one upon the other, like skyscrapers in a metropolis. Commodore Gjertsen and Petersen, who had both served with whaling expeditions in the Antarctic, exclaimed they had never seen so many.

Except for narrow belts of scattered ice lying across our course and the brash ice from decaying bergs, the sea was free of pack. We brushed through these minor fields, altering course first to east-southeast, then southeast. About ten o'clock, the wind switched around into the northwest, the skies became overcast, and the seas became boisterous again. Shortly after noon the ship was turned to meet them, to ease the stress on the plane. The squall, however, soon blew itself out. By four o'clock we were steaming southeast.

As the day wore on the bergs, instead of diminishing in number, actually increased: and the wonder we had felt in the morning increased to amazement. Every mile forward brought new columns into sight. They seemed inexhaustible. A grander display of ice-power had perhaps never been seen. In a twenty-four hour period ending December

28th Dr. Poulter estimated we sighted 8,000 bergs.[4] In that single day we passed among 19 times as many bergs as the International Ice Patrol reports in a normal year.[5]

And these were full fledged bergs—not growlers. Making ten knots, it took us close to two hours to steam past one flat-topped structure which lay, like an ivory island, on our port hand. That meant a berg twenty miles long. It was easily ten miles wide (we took bearings on it as we passed by) and from the water's edge to the overhang of its cliff it must have stood 250 feet high. In that single structure Dr. Poulter estimated there were 4½ billion tons of ice and snow—"more or less." There were others quite as large: one or two that might have been larger.

Still, now that the fog had lifted and we were once more driving toward our objective, we could look at these things with greater equanimity. In the evening the sun strove clear again, bathing the sea with amber warmth, and all the delicate, latent lights—the fine blues, the lavenders, the greens—were awakened in these floating creations. You saw whole cliffs glow with that rare, lovely beauty you associate with the light falling through old stained glass in ancient cathedrals. Softened and transformed by the warmth of sunlight and the shy emergence of colors, the Devil's Graveyard was very different from the death prowl it became in the fog. Even the bridge players in the saloon put down their cards and went on deck to watch. It was the ultimate compliment to creation.

V

Thursday December 28th found us making full speed on course 120° true. The day broke fine, and with such excellent visibility the great numbers of bergs were no hazard. In fact, shortly after 6 A.M. they abruptly thinned out. Thereafter, except for a few scattered bergs, the horizon was quite bare.

For a while it seemed that, having passed through the humbling ordeal of the Devil's Graveyard, Fortune would smile on us. Long before us the keels of Cook, Bellinghausen, de Garlache, Charcot and Larsen had cut these same waters, with varying degrees of fortune. Still with the open sea spreading before us, we recrossed the Circle

[4] It is difficult to estimate the largest number of bergs ever seen. Scott reported having sighted them in "numberless" quantities (Scott, *The Voyage of the* Discovery, ii., 382). And Shackleton saw "thousands" (Shackleton, *The Heart of the Antarctic,* i., 65). Not far from what we called The Devil's Graveyard Charcot raised 5,000 in two days (Charcot, *The Voyage of the* Why Not?, 94).

[5] According to the U. S. Coast Guard, the normal number of icebergs annually sighted by the International Ice Patrol is 420. The largest number ever reported for a year was 1,351 (in 1929): the smallest—11 bergs (in 1924).

and broke past the *Norvegia's* track.[6] Noon position was Lat. 67° 30′ S., Long. 133° 10′ W.

In the afternoon the sky became overcast—a light mist rose. The barometer, after rising steadily for forty-eight hours, began to sink. And now, on our starboard hand, we again picked up the white outer reaches of the pack. By six o'clock, having veered in to scan it for an opening, we had it close aboard.

It was our intention, if a promising lead could be found, to drive the ship into it, force her south until she was blocked, and then resume the penetration by air.

But no opening existed. The pack was solidly compacted, a solid wall, with ridges of broken, twisted pressure ice scattered through it. The *Ruppert* couldn't live a minute in that stuff.

"It is impossible," the Commodore said.

Reluctantly we shifted course to the east, to run along the curving edge of the pack. Heart-breaking days were ahead.

All that night—all the next day—the ship felt along the edge of the pack, looking for a south-seeking lead. The sea washing against the pack was white with flotsam, distributed in long curving tongues or broad streams. Through these the ship punched her way. Nevertheless, profiting by the trend of the pack, she was gradually easing southward.

Fri., Dec. 29, 9:30 P.M.

Noon position: Lat. 68° 42′ S., Long. 124° 40′ W. Since noon yesterday we have extended our southing some 72 miles, but we're again well above the *Norvegia's* track. The situation is unimproved. The pack persists impenetrable. we have decided to continue eastward, hoping for a better break. Having come this far we are reluctant to give up until we have had another shot at the coast, even at the sacrifice of time allotted for unloading operations at Little America.

I finally persuaded Commodore Gjertsen to rest tonight. He was on the bridge for thirty hours without sleep. So long as the ship is in ice, he feels that it is his responsibility to con her. Dr. Poulter and Rawson, however, have proved themselves excellent assistant ice pilots.

Tonight we saw our first mirages. A huge, tabular berg loomed astern, where we knew no berg existed. For fully twenty minutes it stood on the horizon, true as life, with the sun shining on its cliffs. Then the sea seemed to rise up and swallow it. When we looked again it was gone. An hour later a mirage lifted a pinnacled berg on our quarter, and the same mysterious lie was solemnly repeated.

[6] *Norvegia* on her circumnavigation in 1929 sailed south of 70° S. for some distance to the eastward of 120° W., then she was forced northward, and the *Ruppert* for over a hundred miles was south of her track.

Shortly before supper, the pack front having angled sharply to the southeast, we gained a stretch of open sea. Three hours later we came up hard against the pack again, and had to resume our easting. We have sighted many large bergs imprisoned in the pack.

The sea is quiet, the wind unsteady in the southwest.

Sat., Dec. 30, 10:45 P. M.

Noon position (dead reckoning), Lat. 69° 12′ S., Long. 116° 42′ W., Bar. 29.34, Temp. 28°. We have reached the limit of our easting—exceeded it slightly, as a matter of fact, since I had set the 120th meridian as the boundary of this eastern operation.

The ship is hove to in a fairly wide bay in the face of the pack. A long curving tongue of ice to the northward forms a natural break-water—an ideal place for a take-off, if we ever get a chance to fly. We reached this point at 9:30 o'clock this morning, and since them have done little but twiddle our thumbs.

Though the sky was clouded there was just enough promise of a break to tempt us to make ready for a flight. The canvas strips lashing the ailerons and flippers were unshipped: the engines were heated: and the aviation crew had just made ready to swing the plane over the side when a snow squall bore in, filling the air with mist.

Siple and several others, who had put out in the small boat on a seal-hunting excursion, were swiftly blotted from sight. A recall signal on the ship's whistle finally brought them back.

The barometer's still dropping: it's snowing steadily and—worse luck—the wind has circled around into the northwest.

These days of waiting—this gloomy, unending fog—are wearing on the spirit. Some of the men were rather depressed tonight.

Sun., Dec. 31, Midnight.

We're pushing south again. At noon, having lain for twenty-six hours at the edge of the pack, we decided to make a last effort. Nothing, certainly, was to be gained by waiting. We had no time for that. Our deadline has come and gone.

So we struck southeast, following a tortuous lead which brought us into a goodish stretch of open water, where we came about smartly to avoid a drifting berg. Since then we've been pushing through loose pack at slow speed, averaging about two knots.

A bleaker prospect could not be imagined—the gray pack, with the gray mist curling over it, wet snow sifting down, and a flat sky with low-lying clouds. The ship is covered with snow.

The barometer is on another wild career: from a high of 29.10 inches yesterday it dropped to 28.51 at noon, but it is rising again. Bill Haines suggests we turn the barograph upside down. "That's one way," he said, "to make it go up."

New Year's Day, 1934, found us still cleaving southward into the pack, though at greatly reduced speed. Sometimes we profited by stretches of open water, but more often we crept through loose, mushy ice, interspersed with heavy floes. Often the ship hardly had way on her, though you could feel the screw thrashing and the fan-tail trembling as the blades fought for a foothold. At noon dead reckoning put the ship at Lat. 69° 57′ S., Long. 116° 35′ W. In twenty-four hours she had run 48 miles through the pack.

As always, when we approached the limits of discovery, the excitement over the possibility of sighting land got the better of the new hands. The flying bridge was clustered with hopeful Columbuses. And there were beguiling hints to whet their hopes—a solitary Emperor penquin moodily measuring his fate on a drifting floe, and a giant petrel wheeling like a startled thing in the fog. These are not often found far from land. Bergs, too, often carry the illusion of coast; in mist they are especially deceptive, and so there were frequent cries of "Land Ho!" which were repudiated almost in the same breath. "Don't get me titillated," complained Second Mate Dempster, "till ye see the smoke curlin' from the chimneys."

By mid-afternoon it was manifest that the *Ruppert* had reached the limit of her southing. The ice got heavier; even with the shaft turning up 40 revolutions, the ship's speed dropped to nothing. The lookouts, conning the pack from the crow's nest, reported heavy ice fields in all directions. Well down on the horizon was a solid wall of bergs, dark as land.

At 3:30 o'clock, at Lat. 70° 02′ S., the ship stopped, backed cautiously and commenced to retreat.

I still hoped to fly. The barometer was rising, and the wind was steady in the southwest. The sky was overcast, but I was prepared to fly without the sun if I had a decent horizon.

Six miles back the *Ruppert* glided to a stop in a stretch of slick black water. Aviation made ready to lower the plane. At the height of the preparations, the motor sailer, carrying the flight crew's emergency rations and sleeping bags, sprang a leak. Third Mate Muir brought it alongside the ship and managed to hook on to the hoist just before the deck sank under him. Luckily we saved the boat, but of course everything in it was soaked.

At 10:15 o'clock the plane touched water, was immediately towed aft and gassed. A light snow was falling, but Haines thought the air might clear. Instead it blew hard, and the plane itself was in danger. The ship was swung broadside to the wind, to make a lee, and all that night the plane lay abaft the stern, held there by a long cable. Smith, Schlossbach and Swan in turn stood watch on the pontoons, fending off the ice that came drifting down. An aching night. The temperature dropped to +24°.

Morning brought no improvement. The wind, if anything, was on the increase, and apprehensive of the safety of the plane I gave orders to have it hoisted aboard. Because the great weight of the plane made it difficult to handle in the wind, 150 gallons of gas in its tanks were dumped into the sea. Shortly after ten o'clock the plane was safely on its cradle. Our disappointment over another broken hope was more than balanced by the satisfaction of getting the plane aboard without damage. Every time we launched the big plane we took a gamble we could not afford to lose.

Still we lingered. We had no sound reason for waiting. In fact, that afternoon Haines and I decided a flight would be impracticable. Visibility was scarcely three miles, ceiling one thousand feet. In that critical temperature ice, it was certain, would quickly collect on the wings.

Yet at eight o'clock that night we were still waiting, seduced by the promise of the thin wafer of sun gliding past the overcast. All that night, while the ship lay sleeping, Haines, shivering in sheepskin coat, kept his finger on the weather's pulse.

Next morning, January 3rd, we flew. No sun, limited visibility, low ceiling, a barometric height of 28.54 inches, and a steady snowfall. Poor conditions for any sort of a flight—abominable for a flight of exploration. Maybe we were just being obstinate. Anyhow, the plane went over the side shortly after 10 o'clock, and at 11:22 A.M. we took off. The start was made from Lat. 69° 57′ S., Long. 116° 35′ W. The flight crew was the same—Chief Pilot June, Bowlin, Pelter, Petersen and myself.

VI

I dare say that much harder flights have been made, but none with the peculiar perils of this one.

Before we squared away we made three quick navigation runs over the ship, to determine the compass error. The error, we found, was about 55°. The sun was obscured, so the sun compass was useless. We'd have to rely on the magnetic compasses. And the ship, surrounded by mist, was a pretty small target to hit.

At 11:33 we struck south along the meridian of 116° 35′ W.

Conditions were anything but encouraging. At 400 feet scud was flying under the floats and six hundred feet above the great orange wing the air was solidly roofed with stratus clouds. It was snowing, too.

Five minutes later, when I looked back, the ship was lost to view. The gray mist had closed in around it.

My last instructions to Haines were to flash us a weather bulletin by radio every fifteen minutes, even if it meant just saying: "Unchanged." Polar meteorology is a curious thing: local conditions change very rapidly, sometimes without apparent rhyme or reason. And when you're on a flight away from base, no matter how reassuring your own horizon may be, one thought is always uppermost in your mind: what's happening back there?

(Photograph by Earle B. Perkins)

FIRST VIEW OF THE BARRIER

A FIRST FAMILY OF ANTARCTICA

The "Jacob Ruppert" Approaches the Bay Ice

(Photograph by Joseph A. Pelter)

A Stately Promenade

I also asked Commodore Gjertsen to keep forcing a heavy column of smoke through the *Ruppert's* stack. If we wandered off our course on the return, a smoke column might be a providential beacon.

On the run south visibility was rarely better than ten miles and often less. The ceiling was never higher than a thousand feet. Most of the way we flew at 400 feet. Even at that altitude we burst through heavy fields of cloud. At this height our drift indicator was quite unreliable. The loss of this check gave me one disturbing moment.

When we took off the wind was faint and a trifle north of west. Yet forty miles south the plane appeared to be drifting to the westward. Only an easterly wind would account for that. But it seemed hardly possible that in so brief a time the wind could have hauled around the compass. Maybe my navigation was off.

To ascertain the true direction of the wind, I opened the door and dropped a smoke bomb. It struck the top of an iceberg, but failed to explode. The second one I held until it burned my hand. It, too, failed to ignite. I checked the compasses. They seemed to be all right. A momentary glimpse of the sun, a dull burning in the fog, reassured me that the sun was where it ought to be.

Now June dropped the ship to an altitude of 50 feet, over a wide lead, and I checked the trend of the ripples. The wind was definitely east. A surprising reversal. The *Ruppert* continued to report a steady westerly wind.

The pack underneath us, and to the right and left, was the heaviest we had yet seen. Occasional lakes and channels appeared, but there were no favorable connecting passages. The *Ruppert* was no ship for that sea.

About 110 miles south we cut across an enormous stretch of ice. At first it had all the appearance of shelf ice, anchored, perhaps, to continental Barrier. In the mist we couldn't tell what lay beyond. We crossed it at an altitude of 300 feet, and presently discovered what it was: a perfectly flat floe of extraordinary size. We estimated it was 20 miles wide. How long it was we couldn't tell; to right and left it extended as far as we could see.

In the middle of that immense slab, on which an army could have maneuvered without being cramped, were two huge Emperor penguins, the only living things we saw. They must have heard our engines, because, after glancing wildly around, they dropped to their bellies and scuttled off. Probably it never occurred to them to look up. For no reason at all I was suddenly bemused by the thought that here was the loneliest couple on the face of the earth. I never realized how well off most of us are until I saw an Emperor penguin.

We were still pressing south when June beckoned me forward. The southern horizon ran black with snow squalls. No sense sticking our necks into that. We turned sharply.

At the turn our latitude was 72° 30′ S., with a vision ten miles south of that, say to Lat 72° 40′. The pack, hard and compacted, continued unbrokenly. The coast still eluded us, but we had at least made a new record southing, and in doing so had nailed a fact. Narrowed were the possible limits of the yet undiscovered coast. Discovery very often is only the last stage of exploration. The way to the positive contributions of discovery is often paved by negatives.

On the homeward leg work was cut out for us.

The sodden clouds pressed down. A brace of snow squalls swelled darkly across our course. Blobs of mist streamed past the windows. The wing tips wallowed in it. Bowlin, whose trick it was at the wheel, rose into the cloud level in search of quieter air. For a little while we flew blind, holding a course by instruments. It was colder at that level. The air speed indicator stopped—ice, of course. Then I noticed the beginning of the thing I was waiting for: ice crystals forming on the fabric of the wing, like dew on summer grass. Bowlin saw it immediately. He bore down through the clouds and leveled off at 100 feet, where the air was warmer.

No great comfort at that level, either. Directly on our course we remembered seeing at least three bergs, two of them over a hundred feet high. Others lay scattered through the pack. Another squall swirled around the plane. Snow fogged the windows. Visibility fell to nearly nothing.

Out of the mist a black shadow loomed and sprang forward. Bowlin yanked up the bow. The plane rose, like a ship's bow flung up by a long wave, and the full force of 1500 horsepower poured into the climb. Some of the rations and gear stowed on the long side seats came loose.

Between the pontoons and the shattered summit of a berg there was just enough room for daylight and a prayer.

After that we held an altitude of 300 feet. Toward the end of the flight the air cleared a bit. Haines having advised that conditions were unchanged in the vicinity of the ship, we were encouraged to make a slight easting to examine more closely a berg which we had distantly sighted from the ship the day before.

A monstrous berg it was, twenty-five miles long if it were an inch. Another great berg, tilted and splintered, lay jammed against it. They had evidently collided.

At 2:18 o'clock we were over the ship, landing three minutes later. The plane was immediately taken aboard. Two hours after we landed a thick snow storm blotted out the whole horizon, and simultaneously the stretch of open water in which we landed filled with pack and bobbing growlers.

"You fellows stole one that time," Haines said to the flight crew as it came aboard.

VII

Nevertheless, still hoping for another chance, we lingered another 24 hours. What deceived us were the winds. During the weeks we cruised off the Pacific Quadrant the wind was shifting to all points of the compass, due to the eastward movement of the cyclonic and anti-cyclonic disturbances over the South Pacific Ocean. What impressed Haines was the fact that when a cyclonic area passed to the northward, causing the wind to shift into the south and southwest, no change in the weather occurred. On the contrary, the snow squalls, the fog and the low clouds persisted. And this was surprising, since a wind off the unknown coast, especially if it was at all elevated, should have been a clearing wind. At Little America south and southwest winds from the high plateaux of the interior were drying winds on account of their downward component, corresponding to the fair north and northwest winds of the northern hemisphere. On the continent they were the only reliable flying winds. And Haines now made the acute observation that these southerly winds, in order to have picked up enough moisture to produce such abominable weather as we encountered, must have blown over several hundred miles of broken pack or more or less open water. Which was the meteorologist's way of framing the converse statement that the unknown continental shore lay at least several hundred miles south of our track.

Our subsequent explorations as far as they went confirmed this theory.

On the afternoon of January 4th we commenced the retreat from the pack. Around nine o'clock that night the weather showed signs of clearing. We stopped again, with everything in readiness for a flight. But after this faint promise the weather again turned foul. At midnight, I regretfully asked Commodore Gjertsen to proceed. In a driving snowstorm the ship steamed for the open sea.

Chapter IV

LITTLE AMERICA REGAINED

I

ALL day Friday, January 5th, we pressed northward through the pack, but angling westward whenever a favorable lead presented itself. The ship made slow progress, and frequently had to back and fill to work a passage through heavy ice. A gentle snow fell throughout the day. Toward evening the pack thinned out. Shortly after midnight, at Lat. 67° 36′ S., Long. 120° 34′ W., we emerged from the pack and set a course for Little America, 3,000 miles away. We faced again the transit of the Devil's Graveyard.

In the few days since we entered this region from the westward many changes had already taken place. Under the influence of wind and current the pack, at least along its northern approaches, had flattened out and dispersed and we were enabled to launch our westing at a higher latitude. We raised numerous bergs—hundreds of them, as a matter of fact, many of which the men were sure they recognized from the eastward transit—but the vaster fleets of the Devil's Graveyard had vanished. They, too, had been scattered northward by winds and currents.

One thing remained unchanged—the fog! Damp, loathsome, clinging and treacherous, the fog persisted. We had to double the lookouts, and at times heave to; but in spite of the most scrupulous precautions we twice narrowly escaped ramming bergs head-on. Rarely did we see the sun, and when we did never more than as a pale coin fleeting through banks of clouds. The ship oozed moisture; and the dogs, hating wet, were forever complaining. If man could howl, I dare say the crew would have added their own melancholy refrain. Sometimes it snowed, and sometimes it blew, but the fog always lay over the sea.

January 7th, having made a noon-to-noon run of 142 miles, the ship's noon dead reckoning position was Lat. 67° 21′ S., Long. 130° 31′ W. The night before, Ellsworth had reported by radio that his ship, the *Wyatt Earp,* was moored in the Bay of Whales, and that two of his men, Balchen and Braathen, both of whom were members of my first expedition, would shortly ski into Little America. We awaited their report with an inexpressible eagerness. So much depended upon it. Had Little America survived the buffetings of the storms? Were the radio towers still standing? Were the shacks hopelessly buried under the rising tide of drift? Or would we have to carve out, in the short season remaining, a new base for the winter party?

Aside from the effect on our plans, we had a sentimental stake in the news as well. When you have wintered in a place like Little America something takes root. As deeply as the land, it will claim your memory.

Next day our questions were answered. Ellsworth advised:

> LITTLE AMERICA IS AS YOU LEFT IT WITH PLANES IN GOOD CONDITION EXCEPT FOR DIGGING OUT. RADIO MASTS OK BUT TREMENDOUS PRESSURE SHOWS IN FRONT OF VER-SUR-MER (INLET) MAKING IT IMPASSABLE FOR DOG TEAMS. (SHIP) DOCKED TWELVE MILES FROM LITTLE AMERICA. NO SIGN OF THAWING THIS SUMMER.

Little America intact! The two planes—the single-engined Fairchild and the tri-motored Ford in which we had flown to the Pole—both safe! Offsetting it were two discouraging circumstances. Impassable pressure in Ver-Sur-Mer Inlet would bar the original approach to Little America from the Bay of Whales. The eastern margin of the Bay was a fearful maze of crevasses and pressure ridges. Unless a passage could be found or created, the task of unloading ship and hauling the stores into Little America would be very complicated. The fact that the ice in the Bay hadn't started to move out and that Ellsworth had to moor his ship twelve miles from the base meant an extension of this difficulty—a long, punishing haul for dog teams and tractors. Still, this last didn't worry me so much. I was quite sure that before long the ice would go out.

Anyhow, there was nothing we could do about it in the Devil's Graveyard.

Mon., Jan. 8, 1934, 11:22 P.M.

Noon position (dead reckoning) Lat. 67° 15′ S., Long. 138° 36′ W. Sky constantly overcast, light northerly winds. The barometer rising steadily—29.36 at midnight.

All day we've been running about three miles north of the pack, frequently brushing through loose fields of ice. Whenever the fog lightens a bit we increase speed to full.

This evening we had one close shave. The fog closed in very swiftly, and we were on a berg before we knew it. The helmsman brought her around hard. We take such things very lightly now. The mess objected to such clumsy steering, complaining that it threw the soup into their laps.

Poulter is engaged in an interesting experiment. For the past week, or more, he has been dropping large numbers of empty corked bottles over the side, containing a mimeographed form asking the finder to notify the expedition and report on the circumstances of its discovery. The form also contains the position at which the bottle was released, and the date. If by luck any of these bottles should be found we will have a valuable hint of the currents flowing through this little known area.

Not having a more appropriate receptacle, Poulter is using empty beer bottles, which we started collecting early in the voyage. My only hope is that a capricious current doesn't carry the whole lot of them down upon some unsuspecting shore. It would be embarrassing to have to explain the number.

Tues., Jan. 9, Midnight.

Noon position (dead reckoning) Lat. 67° 06′ S., Long. 146° 04′ W. Day's run 172 miles. Heavily overcast and foggy most of the day. Numerous bergs and growlers. Wind freshened this evening and approached gale force. This is indeed a sunless world. It has been necessary to heave to three or four times, waiting for the fog to lift. We start and stop, and the bells are constantly ringing for different speeds. Navigation is nerve-wracking. One moment the mist ahead of you is empty; the next it fills with the looming, sleek hull of a mile-long iceberg. Not having been able to get a decent sight in days, and with the innumerable changes in course and speed adding uncertainty to the dead reckoning, we are doubtful of our true position.

However, we're due to cross the 150th meridian shortly after midnight, and I am considering the feasibility of reëntering the pack. I have an idea that we'll find ice conditions greatly improved. If we're successful it may mean a short-cut to Little America. Besides, I'd like to attempt another flight.

At 2:30 o'clock on the morning of January 10th, in half a gale, the *Ruppert* made the turn. It was a foul night, snow and spray flying across the deck in level sheets, and freezing as they struck. During the first and middle watches the course varied between 180° and 220° true. Then the ship was headed due south. The air cleared rapidly, blue rifts appeared in the overcast and suddenly the sun was blazing in a cloudless sky.

But where was the pack? According to the dead reckoning the ship was already well south of the deepest penetration she had been able to make in this same sector only three weeks before. But the horizon-filling fields of ice which had blocked her then were gone. Except for a handful of bergs and growlers the sea was clear.

The noon fix confirmed the miracle—Lat. 69° 02′ S., Long. 152° 21′ W. With open sea ahead of her, with the throttle advanced to full speed, the ship was 137 miles beyond her record southing on the 150th meridian. She was even 19 miles south of the position the dead reckoning had conceded her and within five hours' steaming distance of the *Condor's* record southing on the 150th meridian! Therein lay the miracle: the old *Ruppert,* resurrected from a government graveyard where she had lain rusting, having proved herself unable to earn her keep in the lumber trade, was making history. She was exploring in spite of herself!

It is only in the chart room, where men pore over charts and lay off distances with dividers, that record southings and the like draw much water. Said the cook of the first southing: "Well, couple of miles either way—what the hell!" But that afternoon a new spirit quickened the life of the ship. Maybe it was just the joy of the sun, of escaping at last from the gloom of the Devil's Graveyard. Whatever the reason we were all conscious of a lift.

Even the shifty yellow stain of ice blink recurring along the horizon line failed to dash that sudden exhilaration. By supper time the white front of the pack was visible. At 7:30 o'clock, at Lat. 69° 50′ S., Long. 152° 21′ S., just one mile short of the plane's previous record southing on the 150th meridian—the *Ruppert* fetched up with the edge of the pack.

It was now my intention to attempt a non-stop flight to Little America. In a straight line the base lay about 600 statute miles from the ship. However, I planned to fly due south along the 152nd meridian until we raised the coast, then follow the continental edge westward to Little America. Once we raised the coast we would be over familiar ground. The flight recommended itself for several reasons: (1) it was a logical extension of the investigations we had prosecuted off the Pacific Quadrant; (2) it would definitely settle, once and for all, the speculation revolving around the supposed archipelago.

The ship had hardly lost way before the various departments involved in the flight project had their duties in hand. Corey had the emergency gear and rations stowed in the plane. Captain Verleger's deck force was standing by the winches and guide lines, ready to swing the plane out. Noville's men were rolling gas drums aft. And Bailey had made contact with the Ellsworth Expedition in the Bay of Whales. Lincoln Ellsworth having generously offered to provide us with frequent weather bulletins.

Two and a half hours after the ship stopped June was in the air, calibrating compasses and testing the radio direction finder.

Where the *Ruppert* lay conditions were ideal: a rising glass, a strong, but even wind from the southwest; the right amount of broken water to give the floats of the heavily loaded plane a chance to rise on the steps; and perfect visibility. The Midnight Sun glided to the horizon, and the few high cirrus clouds were like rose petals.

But in the Bay of Whales conditions were anything but ideal. Ellsworth's meteorologist reported snow, a falling barometer, shrinking visibility.

With the plane gassed and secure for flight, we stood by, hoping for an improvement. Instead the reports from the Bay of Whales grew steadily worse: ceiling dropped from 300 feet to 200, then to 50 feet, finally to nothing. Ellsworth's operator added, after transmitting the formal meteorological equation, "Personally, I'd hate to go walking in this stuff."

The original flight plan, therefore, was out of the question. Local conditions meanwhile took a change for the worse. The glass started down again, and the wind sidled into the north. Nevertheless, because visibility still remained good, I resolved to make a try for the coast.

At 3:30 A.M., with a load of 18,400 pounds, we took off. Forty-two minutes later, having completed various tests over the ship, the plane bore south, straight down the 152nd meridian. The flight crew consisted of June, Bowlin, Petersen and myself.

II

In the air we were still chuckling over an amusing incident that preceded the take-off. In all flight operations in the Antarctic you must count on the possibility of a forced landing. If we came to grief I was pretty sure the ship couldn't force its way to us. Moreover, the time lost in a rescue operation might ruin the whole program of the expedition. If we were not disabled by injury, it would be up to the flight crew to start footing it for Little America, while the *Ruppert* steamed at full speed toward the Bay of Whales. There the rest of the expedition could get under way with the establishment of the winter camp and, with probably more hope of success, take such action as was necessary for the flight crew's relief. So I had hit upon the idea of taking two dogs along to help us haul food and stores if the necessity arose.

The dogs that Innes-Taylor selected were two giant Shambouls, the biggest dogs on the ship. They weighed close to ninety pounds, and looked like small ponies. Vaughan came across them somewhere in Quebec Province and was instantly taken by them. A French-Canadian farmer owned the pair, and used them as draught horses, hitching them to the plow in the planting season. They were named Toby and Pierrette. The dog drivers insisted they answered only to French. Maybe that accounts for what happened. Somebody forgot to take the dogs aside and explain, in French-Canadian patois, what was up.

Anyhow, on the morning of the flight Toby and Pierrette were rowed out to the plane and installed in aluminum kennels which Boyd, the machinist, had made for them. Specially designed airplane sledges, very light and very strong, were stowed nearby. All was quiet until the flight crew arrived in furs. There was the devil to pay then. Bursting from their crates, the dogs, beside themselves with excitement, charged up and down the long cabin. Gear flew in all directions. We began to fear for the safety of the plane. Petersen covered his eyes and moaned as Pierrette, in full flight, shot past his delicate radio equipment.

Finally, thoroughly winded, we got the pair under control, and, recalling the work boat, sent them back in disgrace. It was the first—and last—time I ever tried to mix aviation and four-footed surface transportation. Said Bowlin: "I'd sooner rely on my own dogs; they lie quieter."

The flight along the 152nd meridian was accomplished without incident. All the way south I toyed with the idea of striking for Little America if weather improved. While we were in the air, Dyer, back on the *Ruppert,* simultaneously maintained communication with us and with Ellsworth's ship, transmitting weather bulletins to us from Ellsworth's meteorologist. The weather there persisted unfavorable. It would have been folly to try to get through.

Just south of the ship the pack was fairly open; but beyond the floes were larger and densely packed, and the lanes of open water running among them dwindled to delicate traceries.

One hundred miles south a cluster of immense bergs loomed on the western horizon. We altered course to investigate them, then resumed the southing.

The sky slowly became overcast. From the *Ruppert* Haines reported conditions were unchanged, but that a turn for the worse was impending.

At 5.35 A.M.—at Lat. 71° 45′, Long. 152°, we turned.

Just before the turn June rose to 4,000 feet. Because of clouds we could see only some thirty miles to the south—say to Lat. 72° 15′.

Nothing, except for a few scattered bergs, relieved the gray monotony of the pack. North, east, south and west it flowed drearily to the horizon. No sign of the coast. No sign of life, not even the dark lumpish outline of a seal.

We were over the ship at 6:55 o'clock. We rose, then, to 7,000 feet for a careful survey of the pack, to locate the most feasible exit for the ship. North and west of the ship the pack streamed to the horizon, but about thirty miles to the northwest we marked an irregular lead, twisting between lakes of open water. I was anxious to avoid, if I could, a roundabout voyage to Little America merely to gain the favored transit through the Ross Sea along the 178th meridian east. That late in the season, with any sort of a break at all, we stood a good chance of being able to carve out a new route through the back way.

Landing at 7:05, we made the plane fast to the stern and let it float there till noon while we stood by for later weather bulletins from the Bay of Whales. Where we were the air had a pleasing softness to it. The temperature rose to 40° above. On the ship men stripped to the waist. The dogs lay panting, with their red tongues flickering.

Eight hours later a snow squall blustered round the ship, and snow swirled through the passageways. The fog clamped down again. At 1:15 P.M. the deck force, cursing the vagaries of the air, hoisted the big plane aboard.

Thirty minutes later we shoved off for Little America, retreating to gain the westerly leads we had sighted from the air.

My diary reports:

> ... The flight along the 152nd meridian having completed, for the time being, this expedition's operations in the Pacific Quadrant, a brief summary is in order.
>
> The consequence of three record penetrations between the 152nd and 117th meridians west was virtually to extinguish the possibility of an archipelago extending far into the Ross Sea from Marie Byrd Land, at least in the vicinity of the areas we saw. It is likely that the coastal limits of Marie Byrd Land do not extend far beyond Lat. 75°.
>
> Between these meridians we have advanced the Pacific Ocean a substantial distance south, thereby shrinking the possible continental extent of Antarctica.
>
> Another consequence was the demonstration of the effectiveness of the technique of a double assault by ship and plane, the plane carrying on where the ship is stopped. The combination worked perfectly.
>
> It is a pity that the weather did not give us a break during the long easting. Just one fair day was all we needed. But it never came. Whoever gains that remote coast must be thrice blessed by Fortune.

III

Friday, January 12th, we were out of the pack, but steering various courses to evade belts of heavy ice. In the early morning, running through mist, the ship stumbled into a bight the walls of which suddenly pinched around her. Smart maneuvering saved her from a difficult situation. Ken Rawson proved on this occasion that he had a cool head and that his four trips into the Arctic had given him a real knowledge of ice navigation. The ship bore northward to regain open sea, then resumed the westing. In the evening the pall clamped down again; speed dropped to slow. The sea was choppy all day.

That afternoon, too, Ellsworth informed us that an outrush of ice in the Bay of Whales had ruined his plane. The bay ice on which it was moored broke out suddenly; and though the plane itself was salvaged before it went to the bottom, it was badly wrecked. Ellsworth is a gallant gentleman, and we had wished him well. The facilities of our expedition, including one of our planes, we informed him, were at his command. Ellsworth, however, said he had no alternative but to return to New Zealand for repairs. Next day he advised he was steaming northward, and the two ships later passed unseen in the Ross Sea. Ellsworth and I are the only living members of the Polar Legion. To be a member one must have been leader or co-leader of an expedition that has reached either the north or south pole.

Saturday the 12th was carved from the same gray mold as the many days that had gone before it: annoying snow flurries, visibility ranging tantalizingly from fair to impenetrable fog. Full speed in the clear stretches, slow and sometimes stopped in the worst. The noon dead reckoning postion was Lat. 69° 26′ S., Long. 162° 14′ W. In the early afternoon the ice got worse. We threaded immense fields of old ice, jagged and pressure-ridden, bearing the stratification lines of two or three seasons. About one o'clock that afternoon, easing through a swollen fog bank, the ship rammed her forefoot into a cul de sac of heavy pressure ice, folding back to the north and east. The ship was in it before the bridge knew it. Commodore Gjertsen slammed the telegraph to full speed astern, and we avoided collision by inches. The next four hours we groped north by east, fumbling for an exit.

Toward evening the fog drained, and in the southwestern sky, rising from horizon to zenith, swelled the most threatening cloud I've ever seen: black as a thunderhead, shot through with smoky yellow lights, brimming and baleful as a typhoon warning. But it was a hollow threat. The sun strove through, and in a little while the sky was fair. Now we cruised through an interesting variety of ice forms: broken pack, mesa-topped tabular bergs standing 150 feet high; hilled and tented bergs, like drifting islands; and, for the first time, numerous structures of shelf ice, flat and squat and streamlined as aircraft carriers, and a mile long.

Past these the pack thinned out, whereupon we sharply altered course to 265° true, hoping to find a back passage into Little America.

By tradition and experience, as I have said before, the 178th meridian East is regarded as the fastest and safest passage through the pack into the Ross Sea. It was considered foolhardy to attempt a break-through on any other line.

But Ellsworth only recently had been caught for days in heavy pack along that meridian: heavier pack, at any rate, than was good for the *Ruppert*. Rather than expose the ship to that, I resolved to attempt to carve out a new route. Having nothing to lose but a bit of time, it was a worth-while gamble.

The outcome of the move was that we had the amazing good fortune to find an absolutely clear passage along the 169th meridian West. We met no ice at all. The way to Little America was open. It was, in a sense, a new chapter in the navigation of the Ross Sea.

Evading the last scattering of pack, we gradually altered course to due south. Speed was increased to full. The day was overcast, with occasional snow tempests, and the wind ebbed and flowed hesitatingly in the northwest.

Ever since leaving New Zealand the crew had been spasmodically making ready for disembarkation; but now, with Little America only three days distant, these preparations went into high gear. Under Czegka's direction a comprehensive unloading plan was evolved. In fact, three distinct procedures had been worked up, suitable to deal with any of three sets of conditions that were likely to prevail in the Bay of Whales. The unfavorable elements encountered by Ellsworth's expedition were warning to be prepared with a flexible plan. Depending upon conditions, we were prepared to unload (a) directly on the bay ice, or (b) on the Barrier's edge, or (c) in Floyd Bennett Harbor on the western shore of the Bay.

The bay ice was the logical unloading platform. Treacherous as it is, especially in late summer, it is least dangerous to a ship. But Balchen had advised, after investigating the pressure ice between Little America and the Bay, he had seen no passage, which apparently destroyed the possibility of reaching the base from the bay ice. Balchen said that possibly a way through could be found farther south, though it might impose a haul of 20 miles. Such a haul would grind our transport to the ground.

If there were no feasible way of reaching Little America from the bay ice, the alternative was to moor the ship alongside low barrier, on the eastern rim of the Bay, and start unloading there. This method would have the advantage of a short haul, perhaps only three or four miles, but the disadvantage of an infinitely enlarged risk. Low barrier means barrier 20 feet high or more. Like bay ice, it too has an annoying habit of breaking out when you least expect it, but when barrier goes, especially with a ship in the vicinity, watch out! Thousands of tons of ice burst loose in a split second, surging outward with the rush of an avalanche. On our first visit to the Bay of Whales, because we had no alternative, we took the *City of New York* and the *Eleanor Bolling* alongside the barrier. A mass of ice broke off, fell partly across the ships, which were lashed together, and we narrowly escaped losing the *Bolling*. No, we should adopt this second procedure only if the first were absolutely closed.

The third procedure—that is, unloading in Floyd Bennett Harbor—would be a last resort. We should resort to it only if the ship were hopelessly blocked off from Little America. In this event, it would mean founding a new base on the western shore of the Bay of Whales. Fortunately we were equipped to get away with it.

There were seventeen different departments within the expedition, and each was responsible for the packing and identification of its gear and equipment. All stores had to be distinctly marked and identified, with symbols designating their relative importance, to facilitate handling on the ice. All items were divided into three categories: *absolutely necessary, necessary,* and *least necessary.* They were to be unloaded in that order of precedence. The wisdom of this segregation is obvious.

These various tasks occupied the crew during the final run to the Bay of Whales. The aviation crew removed the floats from the big plane and replaced them with skiis. Demas said that his tractors were ready for service. Tinglof had finished building twelve tractor sledges. They were stacked on No. 2 hatch forward. Czegka and Ronne had ready the lighter dog sledges, both single and double-enders. On the

14th Dr. Bramhall and Zuhn terminated the cosmic ray observations, took down their apparatus and crated it for transfer to Little America. In fair weather and foul, so quietly their presence was scarcely ever noticed, these two fine young men stood their punishingly lone watches beside their apparatus on the flying bridge. They commenced their observations on the equator and carried them into record high south latitudes.

Monday January 15th the wind hauled into the east, and stiffened, bringing more snow and rising seas. Speed dropped to half during the evening. The flurry became a blizzard, the blizzard a gale. For five hours the ship lay hove to, with a beam wind piling stinging drift across the decks in flat sheets. We got underway again at 3:34 A.M., January 16th, and at noon were only 150 miles north of Little America.

Now, miraculously, the skies cleared. Under a fine Capri sky we completed our southing. After days of sunless voyaging, the air suddenly filled with flying life—clouds of snowy petrels like white arrows flying, latticed groups of brown Antarctic petrels, checkered mantled Cape pigeons darting across the bow, and overhead, like flights of bombers wallowing among swift pursuit ships, the heavily flying skua gulls. The Ross Sea was blue as a tropical sea. The wind moved into the southwest, and brought a hint of ice. The temperature dropped to + 23°.

At 6:15 o'clock, on the morning of January 17th, we raised the white palisades, the Ross Ice Barrier, on the starboard bow. And men who had been working all night in the holds, getting the last things ready, swarmed up the ladders to have their first glimpse of the Continent. Marbled cliffs under a cloudless blue, it was as beautiful a thing as you could wish to see, like a white cloud resting on the sea.

Three hours later we passed West Cape and stood in at the mouth of the Bay of Whales. A voyage of 13,323 nautical miles was ended. Third Mate Muir closed the log with a triumphant entry.

IV

Looking back on the events of that day, I find it hard to tell exactly what did happen; and in what order. Events were crowded, and we moved from one fresh excitement to the other. Of one thing, I am sure, the day belonged, properly enough, to the veterans. For they had the memories; remembered things came flooding back, to be confirmed or contradicted by what they saw. Any one looking over that wide bay, with its fine sheer cliffs, its gentle rolling swales and smooth eminences, and gleaming, glistening snow, the soft roundness of everything, the infinite reaches of sky, would understand why one is pulled back.

The terrific outrush of ice that had dashed Ellsworth's hopes was told in the masses of ice lying across the mouth of the Bay. Two miles broad, a belt of shattered floes and broken chunks of barrier stretched almost solidly between East and West Capes. We cautiously followed it eastward. Under the brow of East Cape Commodore Gjertsen found a lane of open water. He followed it south, and presently the ship gained the spacious waters of the Bay.

Carl Petersen, scanning the western side of the Bay, suddenly exclaimed: "There's a flag—a flag, by golly, that Blackburn left there!" You could make it out with the help of glasses, a bamboo pole, with a wind-torn shred of orange pennant still clinging to it, showing above a haycock on the heights of Chamberlin Harbor. A moment later Bill Haines marked the beacon atop the north cape of Ver-Sur-Mer Inlet. Four years ago it was a square turret of snow blocks, standing twenty-five feet high. But the winds had worn it down until it was now just a smooth dome barely awash.

If the discovery of familiar things excited the others, it was the changes that bewildered me. Outwardly the Barrier seems as enduring as mountain rock, but is scarcely more permanent than desert sand. Every season, every month, every day, indeed every hour works its change. A cliff shears off under infinite pressure, altering the configuration of a bay. The accretion of snow gradually transforms an inlet into a valley, a valley into high barrier. Capes and harbors born by the calving of bergs are obliterated by the same violent circumstances. In the South Polar regions Nature is forever shaping and reshaping, creating and destroying, striving in an infinite variety of ways toward ends we cannot foresee.

All the ice in Floyd Bennett Bay had gone out. Four years before we would have sworn it would hold fast. "Damn it," swore Vic Czegka under his breath. Fifty tons of valuable stores, for which no room could be found on the *City of New York* in 1930, had been cached there. Much of it was Czegka's machine equipment. On the bottom now, of course. Through the glasses we could see the pressure ice that Ellsworth and Balchen had reported: ridge upon ridge of it, twisted and jumbled, upheaved thirty feet or more above the flooring of bay ice.

Not only was the entrance to Ver-Sur-Mer Inlet blocked off; the Inlet itself appeared to have filled in until it had become merely a shallow depression. Before the north cape was an almost sheer wall fifty feet high. Now the Inlet had filled in with drift, the cliff had disappeared, and only a gentle slope remained.

One circumstance we saw, was greatly in our favor. The recent dispersion of the bay ice made it possible for the ship to approach within three miles of Little America. In 1929 the ships had to lie eight miles from the base. If, by a stroke of luck, we could force a passage through the pressure ice near Ver-Sur-Mer Inlet, the problem of unloading would not be nearly so formidable as it had promised. However, that problem could wait a few hours. The immediate job was to find out if Little America was fit to be reoccupied. Balchen and Braathen, I should add, had not entered the buildings.

Five hundred yards off the east Barrier wall Commodore Gjertsen stopped the ship. The motor sailer was lowered, and fifteen of us went aboard. About three miles north of Little America we made the landing, bringing the boat alongside a gentle incline of ice foot. We waited while the boat returned to the ship to pick up the dog teams. The moment the dogs set foot on the Barrier the Antarctic peace was gone. Bedlam shouted in. Once more on firm land, after three and one half months on a heaving steel deck, the huskies went utterly mad. They yipped, and they barked; they ate snow, and they rolled in it: they wriggled out of harnesses, and tore in wild circles around the landing place. In no time the place was a shambles of broken harnesses, overturned sledges, slithering huskies and exceedingly wrathful drivers.

Leaving the dog drivers to collect their teams, Haines, Petersen, Noville, and I started on foot for Little America. Sinking to the knee at every step we toiled up the slope. Now three black specks slowly lifted above the glistening ridge—the three radio towers! On the crest Little America was revealed—the shallow valley at the head of Ver-Sur-Mer Inlet, the tall steel towers one of which was leaning out of plumb, a cluster of low bamboo antennae poles, and strange, unremembered things that the snows of four winters hadn't covered. A crystal quiet lay over the place, over the smooth and rounded swales running to the horizon; not a snow crystal was out of place, and the surface was smooth as the slickest satinwood.

In a little while we stood over the Administration building. The snow had deepened three or four feet. The ventilators and the stove pipe were barely awash, but the cleated anemometer pole stood a good five feet above the surface; and curiously, a broom, stuck in by the handle, was there, an irrelevant suggestion of domestic felicity.

Bill Haines' face, as he took in these familiar things, was good to see. "Bet I could dig down and find my old theodolite stand," he said. "You're on," I said, "here's the shovel." Bill's face fell. He looked at the shovel with strong distaste. "Listen," he said. "Four years ago, when I put down one of those awful things, I took a pledge—a solemn pledge—that I'd cut off my right arm before I'd touch a snow shovel again. And damned if you don't put one in my hand the moment we land!" It may be a classic phrase that the smell of powder exhilarates old war-horses, but I've never seen a veteran explorer show anything but the deepest melancholia at the sight of a snow shovel.

By that time the dog teams had pulled up, bringing more recruits. Neither Haines nor I was exactly certain where to start digging. We paced off the distance from the stove pipe, trying to remember how many steps we used to take from the stove to the vestibule opening into the tunnels. However, after an argument, a large hole was started.

Three or four feet down, Haines broke through a shell of hard blue ice, and uncovered the tarpaulin roofing the old balloon station. In short order he drove a hole through that, and disappeared. In a little while we heard him chuckling. We plunged in after him.

Fourteen feet down, at the bottom of the square balloon station, with its ledge for the theodolite tripod still intact, we turned left into the vestibule. Bill had left the door open. We could hear him stumbling around in the dark. A faint ghostly fluorescence illuminated the ice packed around the windows. Petersen struck a match. By the light of it I found a fruit jar, half full of kerosene which, surprisingly, was still there. The wick burned, and as the glow strengthened the shadows fell back.

It wouldn't be right to say that the place looked as if we had left it only yesterday. The roof had sagged under the crushing weight of ice. Several of the main beams had cracked. They lay splintered across the top bunks. A film of ice lay over the walls, and from the ceiling hung thick clusters of ice crystals, which were brighter than jewels when the light caught them. The haste with which the building had been evacuated was everywhere in evidence. Torn parkas and windproofs, unmatched mukluks, dirty underwear and odds and ends of all sorts were scattered about. By the looks of it you would have thought a tornado had struck the place. I was a trifle ashamed that we had left that mess behind us, and glad we could do our own housecleaning.

On a table stood a coffee pot, a piece of roast beef with a fork stuck in it, and half a loaf of bread. Four years before, Dr. Coman had lunched off them while he waited for the last sledge to come back for Mason, who lay ill with appendicitis. It evoked queer memories to come upon that. There was a time, back in February 1930, when it looked as if Mason were too ill to be moved, and some of us might have to spend a second year. On the bunk walls were 1929 calendars, with the days scratched off. Haines found a tinfoil medal, big as a pie plate, which the camp had presented to Vanderveer, the cameraman. It was a medal for hardship—hardships that he had cannily managed to escape.

Out of the corner of my eye, I happened to notice Finn Ronne. The young Norwegian was standing beside his father's bunk. Martin Ronne was one of the finest men who ever set foot on the Antarctic continent. He was sailmaker on the first expedition. Nearly twenty years before he had been at Framheim with Amundsen. He died the year before we started south a second time, aged sixty-eight. Finn beckoned to me. When he held the light, I saw that his own name had been printed in large letters on the wall. I couldn't recall having seen it before. Martin must have put it there just before he moved out. Finn's eyes blazed. "The old man must have known I'd come down," he said.

(© Paramount Pictures, Inc.)

Admiral Byrd Steps Ashore

Four Years of Ice Crystals in the Old Tunnel

(Photograph by Joseph A. Pelter)

BLAZING A TRAIL THROUGH THE PRESSURE

ON THE MAIN HIGHWAY TO LITTLE AMERICA

Meanwhile a second group dug down into the Mess Hall, breaking through the roof of McKinley's photographic laboratory. This building lay about two hundred yards west of the Administration Building. We hurried over to have a look. They told me that the door from the photo lab to the main house was open when they got to the bottom. Well, that was another reality out of the past. McKinley was never known to close a door behind him. In the old days you could always tell that good old Mac was in the shack by the cold draught on the back of your neck.

The Mess Hall, perhaps because of its stauncher construction, was in good shape. The roof was undamaged, in spite of the six feet of snow and ice that had accumulated on it. The shack needed a bit of tidying up, that was all. Cans of baked beans, meats, coffee, cocoa, and powdered milk were neatly racked behind the galley stove.

While we were standing there the telephone rang. I'm not joking; it actually rang. If Haile Selassie had crawled out from under one of the bunks, we couldn't have been more taken aback. Nobody moved for a second. "Did somebody miss the boat?" asked George Noville with raised eyebrows. Petersen had found the telephone and pressed the buzzer. We heard him laugh. Poulter answered in the Ad Building. "By yimminy," said Pete, "she works!"

A set of boxing gloves hung from a nail overhead. There was a girl's picture on the wall. Strom's accordion, on which he used to play delightful Norwegian folk songs, was in his bunk. The phonograph was on the long mess table, and the needle was poised over a record. Somebody cranked it. As the first strains issued from the wheezing box, Haines, Petersen and I fell into each other's arms. It was "The Bells of St. Mary's." For fourteen months, Quin Blackburn had played that piece. For him no amount of repetition ever diminished its charms; he played it over and over again, until the glacial echoes of Little America were saturated with its lugubrious essences, till even the most patient man prayed to be delivered from the bells. Quin was standing near by. A slow smile illuminated his face. "Wait a moment—don't tell me—I'll remember it in a second," he said.

Then the most amazing thing of all happened. Petersen idly flipped a switch. The lights went on. Not brightly—just a dim, faint glow in the bulbs, but undeniably they burned.

On the stove were cooking pans full of frozen food. There was coal in the scuttle. A fire was made in the kitchen stove, the food was warmed, and found to be as good as the day we left, four years ago. The seal and whale meat and beef in the tunnel were perfectly preserved.

V

So much for the rediscovery of Little America. It was an agreeable—more than that, an affecting—experience for the men who had wintered there in 1929-1930. It left a spell that lingered for many days, and I dare say that many will remember it long after the larger discoveries in the field have slipped their minds.

Before turning back for the ship I put Dr. Poulter in charge of the job of reclaiming the base and handling the stores which, I hoped, would soon be pouring in. His fine talents had already impressed me, and I had him in mind for second-in-command. Then I dispatched Ronne, the best man we had on skis, and Blackburn, because of his intimate knowledge of the Bay of Whales, to make a quick exploration of the pressure ridges along the east shore of the Bay.

"Look for a feasible passage near Ver-Sur-Mer Inlet," I instructed them. "Remember that it will have to accommodate tractors as well as dog teams." They shoved off immediately.

On the way back to the ship I passed half a dozen dog teams already hauling food, camping equipment and other gear into the base party. Though the temperature was well below freezing, the men were stripped to the waist. In the loose, soft snow the dogs made heavy going of it. Obviously they were badly out of condition. Well, their holiday was ended. From now on it would be all heart and sinew, for them as well as the men. A polar expedition moves forward and survives mostly by brute force and by its capacity for punishment. And the impending struggle to unload would tax these things to the limit.

At ten o'clock that evening I rejoined the ship. An hour and a half later the *Ruppert* was brought alongside the bay ice and moored. The ice anchors that were put out at once demonstrated their worthlessness. The weight of the ship as she worked on the swell tore them loose from the snow. Deadmen, made of hatch covers nailed together and buried at a goodish depth in the snow, were our next experiment. Eight mooring lines—bow, stern and spring lines—were run out to them, and made fast by means of toggles, so that they could be readily slipped if we had to cast off fast. The deadmen held.

The ship lay about two miles east and somewhat south of the mouth of Floyd Bennett Harbor. East and west of her the front of the bay ice ran elliptically between the high barrier walls. This white flooring was from eight to ten feet above the water's edge: soft white snow on top, more densely packed as you went down, and hard blue-green ice at the water level. The total thickness was probably close to thirty feet. This was our unloading platform, our natural dock.

Little America, hidden by the barrier shoulder north of Ver-Sur-Mer Inlet, was about three miles, as the skua gull flies, from the ship's berth. But there was no assurance that we could gain it from this position, not unless Ronne and Blackburn could unravel a trail through the glittering chaos of pressure. From the flying bridge I scanned it with field glasses. A belt of pressure, from a quarter to half a mile wide, ran irregularly along the eastern shore of the Bay. It had neither unity nor symmetry: just great misshapen blocks and ridges and bowlders of ice, upheaved and twisted into tortured attitudes by the incalculable pressures of glacial action. Some of these ridges stood thirty feet high; deep crevasses gaped in the troughs. Where the bay ice ran up to the edge of the disturbance the surface was grossly disturbed, rising and shelving to form a series of mighty bulges, like arrested waves. From where I stood I could see no way through.

Nevertheless we immediately made ready to lower the planes over the side. Planes, at least, could fly over the pressure ridges. The big plane was scheduled to go first.

No one slept that night. From that night on sleep was a dimly-remembered pleasure. The winches were squealing, and hand trucks were rumbling on the iron decks. At 3:30 o'clock on the morning of January 18th the six-ton *William Horlick* touched the bay ice. For the next half hour, while the aviation crew made it ready for flight, I scarcely dared to call my soul my own. The major exploratory mission of the expedition rested on that plane. As it lay there, fairish pieces of ice were breaking off all along the ice front. A strong swell was hastening the disintegration of the bay flooring. One bad break would ruin us. It had happened to Ellsworth. It could happen to us.

At last the engines were started, and the plane taxied away from the crumbling edge. South of the ship the bay ice presented a good runway. June swept off into the wind, rose and wheeled for Little America. A moment later the men watching from the shore were shocked to see first one, then the other of fourteen-foot skis snap down. The pressure of the 90-knot wind surging around them snapped them back against the ski pedestals. They were forced down from horizontal to an angle of 45°. With the skis in that position the plane could no more land than if it were on stilts. And three men were in it—June, Bowlin and radio engineer Guy Hutcheson.

Chapter V

THE WHITE NIGHTMARE

I

DISASTER hovered in the sky that morning. Those on the ground could only stand and watch with that choking sense of futility that freezes a person watching somebody run along the edge of a high cliff. It was barely possible that June was unaware of what had happened, and might attempt to land at Little America. Hutcheson had gone aloft to test the radio installations. I hurried aft to the radio shack and found Bailey already working the plane. "They know about it," he said, "and are trying to figure a soft way to land." Bailey had just completed a schedule with San Francisco. He was standing in the doorway, watching the plane, when he saw the skis flop. Hutcheson was trying to raise him when he made contact.

Both June and Bowlin were experienced pilots, steeped in the craft of flying, cool and resourceful in the wisdom bought of thousands of hours of hard flying. Better than the men on the ground they knew their situation in the air. Dr. Shirey laid out his surgical kit. Innes-Taylor had a dog team hitched up, with fire extinguishers and stretchers aboard. Twenty men were ordered out on the ice, to stand by for a possible crash.

At 500 feet June made a ten-mile swing over Little America. Noville saw the plane coming and fired a smoke bomb, to give the pilot the wind direction for landing. But the instant he saw the skis he doused the bomb with a bucket, to warn them away. June and Bowlin didn't see him. They were too absorbed in their problem. The plane had sagged violently when the skis dropped; it felt as if a great hand suddenly pressed them down, Bowlin said. A glance revealed what had happened.

Taking his life in his hands, Bowlin crawled out on the wing to see what could be done. The wind tore off his cap, he lost a glove. He found that the flexible bongee cords attached to the toes of the skis, which are intended to hold the skis slightly above the horizontal in flight, had stretched. In the haste of getting the plane in the air the preventer wires, which give reënforcement, had been overlooked.

Soon after Bowlin had climbed back into his seat, June brought the plane down on a long, flat glide. He leveled off, and, just before she hit, pulled the nose up, close to stalling angle. The speed fell off perceptibly, and she squashed in. The tail struck first, and the skis flopped up under the pull of the bongee cords. Just at that moment June put her down. In a flurry of drift she safely ran out her momentum. A fine landing.

Two hours later the plane was safely flown to Little America. Our jangled nerves had scarcely recovered from that incident when another event unstrung them.

Ronne and Blackburn, fagged out by hard skiing, had come aboard and reported that the pressure, at least as far south as Cape Manhue, was impassable. The higher ridges, they said, measured thirty feet from crest to trough, and they had come across numerous cracks in the bay ice, three feet wide, with open water showing. The movement of the ice was apparently proceeding at comparatively high velocity, because they could hear loud creakings and groanings deep in the pressure, and several times they had heard masses of ice crash down in the distance. June, who had surveyed the region from the air, confirmed this report. If we persisted in the attempt to reach Little America from the bay ice, it appeared that the only alternative was to lay a trail southward down the Bay, sweep eastward through the lighter pressure traversing Amundsen Arm, and then, having gained high barrier in the vicinity of the Framheim, Amundsen's old base, bear north again to Little America.

No matter how you measured it, that course meant a haul of twenty miles—forty miles for the round trip—to gain an objective scarcely two and a half miles from the ship. And we had our 400 tons of equipment, every pound of which had to be transported to Little America, either by dog team, or tractor, or, if necessary, by plane and man-power. But time was running against us, running with the swiftness of rip tide. If we embarked on such an enterprise it would mean cancelling every other scheduled operation. The expedition would still be hauling stores long after the onset of the winter night. Even under the most favorable conditions the unloading of the ships and the movement of supplies into the main base would be a prostrating effort; but a twenty mile haul meant slavery. Still another factor entered into the equation. The *Ruppert* had to be unloaded and started back to New Zealand by February 5th. The diminishing fuel in her tanks dictated that deadline. Altogether, the situation seemed hopeless.

Against my better judgment, against the solemn warning of previous experience, I decided that morning to cast in our lot with a Barrier mooring. I did so with full appreciation of the peculiar hazards involved; the narrow squeak we had in 1929 was still fresh in mind, and the observations of previous visitors to the Bay of Whales confirmed the fact it was no rare phenomenon.[1] Nevertheless, the Barrier opened the only road straight to Little America.

[1] In 1908 Shackleton had steered for an indentation in the Barrier called Balloon Bight, only to find that a monstrous calving had taken place, creating what is now the Bay of Whales. "It was bad enough to try and make for a port that had been wiped off the face of the earth . . . but it would have been infinitely worse if we had landed there whilst the place was still in existence. . . . The thought of what might have been made me decide then and there that under no circum-

Shortly after breakfast we cast off from the bay ice and headed for the east wall of the Bay. If I required new proof of the inconstancy of this mighty sea-borne ice sheet, it was there for me to read. Eleanor Bolling Bight was greatly changed. A shallow V-shaped bay had appeared, and sharp angles and cape-like projections which I remembered had vanished. All this meant destructive transitions on a grand scale, a broad breaking off here, a creeping forward there. The Barrier ice, in the vicinity of the Bay of Whales is from 300 to 600 feet thick, deep enough to drown all but the tallest buildings in Manhattan. Commodore Gjersten, who had visited the Bay with Amundsen, in 1911, looked at it blankly. He shook his head. "It has changed so much," he said, "as to be almost unrecognizable."

About five miles north of Ver-Sur-Mer Inlet we stood in close to the Barrier. The motor sailer was following astern. Noville was in it, making a survey of the undercutting at the waterline. Very often the swell will gouge deep into the ice, leaving a lightly supported overhang. Usually, too, submarine spurs of hard green ice extend well out, a menace to the sides of the ship. So you have to pick your moorings carefully.

A likely place caught our interest. The wall was smooth, about thirty feet high. Just beyond it the Barrier rose sharply to fifty feet. It seemed solid enough, solid as masonry. Staunchness was deceptively written in every gothic line. But delicacy was there, too, though you couldn't see it; the delicacy of an avalanche poised for the final overbalancing ounce, and when that happens it's a sight to take your breath away.

Bill Haines was on the bridge, standing beside me. "What do you think of that place, Bill?" I asked. "Does it look good to you?"

Before he could answer something happened. No eye was fast enough to catch it all. A slither of snow, a dark line running, and for a quarter of a mile that fine barrier cliff, seemingly so staunch, melted into a tempestuous white waterfall. A sharp, rending crack, prolonged as the break gathered length came to the ship, then the clatter of small bergs hitting the water. The ship creaked to the sudden surge of water. Then silence. The fanning streams of ice, the bergs gently rocking as they settled at equilibrium, the dazzling white slash in the Barrier—these were the only things to attest to the veracity of our eyes. In half an hour the current had scattered these.

Bill Haines got out his answer. "Admiral," he said, "I don't think I should care to tie up there." It was quite enough ice to sink the battle fleet.

Anyhow, that settled it. More than the needs of the expedition, more than the folly of risking everything on a single cast, there were the lives of the men to consider. The ship was turned; we headed back

stances would I winter on the Barrier, and that wherever we did land we would secure a solid rock foundation for our winter home." Shackleton, *The Heart of the Antarctic,* i., 75-76.

to the old mooring place alongside the bay ice. In the last resort, if Little America couldn't be reached, we could still carve out a new base in a sheltered place on the western heights of the Bay. The main problem was to get the stores ashore, and to get them ashore fast.

However, the first thing we did was to dispatch Ronne on another survey of the pressure ridges. We still believed that a patient search would yield a passage.

II

Thursday afternoon, January 18th, was the beginning of the nightmare. The end didn't come till the cold and darkness of May. Long cruel days, unnumbered days, days of aching effort, dragging from one task to the next. The sun made its unhurrying round of the sky, and the pygmies strove underneath. Time was everything, time was nothing, time was something that ran on and on, lacing the dissolving hours with the blinding pain of fatigue; there was no end to it, only a terrible penalty if you allowed it to get the upper hand. Yet time was always the master and you were its creature. That's one thing the Bay of Whales burned into us.

Perhaps at times I cracked the whip too hard. But I had been through the mill before, and I knew something about the job of getting a polar expedition started off on the right foot. The men were drawn from all walks of life, from a wide variety of occupations. We had scientists, aviators, mechanics and artisans of all sorts, engineers, jacks-of-all-trades, an ex-insurance salesman, millionaires' sons, even a deep-sea diver, an archaeologist, an artist, a parachute jumper, a tree surgeon, a song-writer who wanted a taste of adventure, and one man who was, I discovered later, a fugitive from justice. And in the face of a great emergency all these men, these diverse talents, these conflicting temperaments had to be mobilized, organized and launched on a killing job in which sheer man-power, guts, the capacity to take it to the bitter end, and a certain practical aptitude for doing things the right way were the controlling factors. What made it especially difficult was the novelty of the situation. Nearly all these men stood confronted by realities utterly foreign to their experience, not merely in the nature of the task, but in the whole perspective. The aspect of the ice and the peculiar hazards residing in it, the pressing need for haste and the penalty that would crack down on desultoriness, the swift things that could happen and the simple things to remember—these things had no equivalents in their backgrounds. The familiar human frailty of being baffled by the unfamiliar, of being irked and troubled by divergence from routine had to be met. There's only one training ground for polar work, and that's in the polar regions. If I cracked down hard in the beginning it was because I knew that in the end we should have to pay double for piddling.

Fortunately I had a capable nucleus of officers. Czegka, though he had lately been hampered by a chronic illness, had the job of supervising the unloading and seeing to it that the stores were properly allocated. His right hand man was energetic Steve Corey. June, a man with a rare instinct for the right way of doing practical things, was given the responsibility of keeping things moving on the ice. Assisting him were Captain Innes-Taylor, who had charge of all dog-teams and transportation, and Demas, who commanded the tractor unit. Commodore Gjertsen was responsible for the safety of the ship. For him and his watch officers this meant unrelaxing vigilance. Heavy floes and bergs lay scattered on the water. A sudden shift of wind or a rising swell might bring them creeping down, pinning the ship. There was an ever-present danger that the ice alongside which we lay might break out, compelling a trigger-quick getaway. Captain Verleger and his Boatswain's Mates, McNamara and Voight, together with the deck force under them, had the job of breaking out cargo, manning the winches, and keeping the stuff pouring on the beach. Noville, executive officer, had general charge of unloading ship and assigning personnel, which meant drafting work lists, posting watches, keeping everything moving without interruption, and drawing upon man-power already taxed to the limit. It was a difficult, trying job, and Noville was the man for it. His assistant was Ken Rawson, whose competence had been demonstrated in every situation. And, of course, there was Bill Haines. Bill, being first and last a weather man and a trifle suspicious (perhaps in consequence of his calling) of any arbitrary authority, sidled away from the hint of a title. But his husky figure followed the action; one hour you'd see him straining over the heavy gasoline drums in the hold, the next loading sledges on the ice; and from time to time you'd hear his voice, with its colorful and identifying preface of "dammit to hell," reproaching the cock-eyed authority that ordered things done this way or that. Very often Bill was right.

Aboard ship on the afternoon of the 18th we had a conference, principally to agree on procedure in the face of the new circumstances. The decisions were elementary. Unload ship. Keep cargo moving inland from the edge of the ice. Establish a main cache, or dump, about three miles south of the ship, at the edge of the pressure ice. Leave no stores near the edge of the ice, but transfer them instantly from cargo nets to waiting dog sledges. Bend every effort to keep the stuff flowing to the terminal cache, but if it came too fast shunt portions of it to intermediate caches. Once the tractors were safely landed, never risk them nearer than a hundred yards to the edge of the bay ice—too much danger of their being carried out to sea on a breaking floe. Let the lighter dog teams relay on short runs to the tractors: let the tractors, heavier and more powerful, ferry to Pressure Camp, the name we gave to the first main cache.

A simple plan and, therefore, by polar standards, a good one. The grave danger in unloading too rapidly was in accumulating stores on the edge of the ice faster than our transport could move it away. Any such clotting would expose a large portion of our supplies to the risk of being carried off by a sudden outrush of ice. More ice would go out—we knew that; it was as inevitable as the disappearance of the sun on April 19. We reckoned on the likelihood that, in the due course of events, the sea would break past Pressure Camp. But by that time we hoped to have the *Ruppert* safely started for New Zealand, and all our man-power concentrated on the task of pushing the stuff inland. Besides, it was inevitable that the breaking up of the ice and spells of bad weather would force the ship from her berth for long intervals. During the let-ups the men ashore could clear out the intermediate caches and advance the stores toward high barrier.

The remaining rules were equally simple and arbitrary. Unloading ship was an all hands' job. Every man was taxed, and until the crisis passed all other activity was subordinated to it. Such an order meant disappointing the scientists, who were anxious to commence their work. Siple, Dr. Perkins and Lindsey had already entered the pressure in search of seals. We had to recall them. The men were divided into two 12-hour shifts, but the shifts actually overlapped, with men working sixteen-eighteen hours a day. Weather is the only time clock in the Antarctic. In good weather you stick with it as long as you can. You count on resting during the bad spells, when you can best afford it.

Even Commodore Gjertsen, when he came off watch, joined the men at the unloading berths ashore; and Chief Officer Bayne was long enough at the winches to become part of them, an outlandish figure attired in orange windproofs and glossy bowler hat, moving in clouds of steam.

Thurs., Jan. 18, Midnight.

The unloading is in full swing tonight. All five tractors—the two Citroëns, the two snowmobiles and the Cletrac—were safely landed this afternoon and are now hauling stores. The sight of these five vehicles on the ice delighted me. These machines will, I believe, make Polar history.

I must congratulate Demas for the good sense he used in getting his cars ashore. Before the booms plucked a car from the hold, he started the engine. Thus, when the treads hit the ice, the shore crew had only to cast off the bridle and the driver had only to jump in, give it the gun and race off—a work of a few moments.

It was a wise precaution. A crack opened in the ledge behind the unloading berth: just after the last car spun clear the whole ledge sloughed off and crumbled alongside the ship.

Abele narrowly escaped a ducking. Unwisely he lingered near the edge. The piece on which he was standing sheared off, carrying him with it. He found himself flat on his stomach, clutching at a wilding balancing piece of ice which was drifting out to sea.

Fortunately the motor sailer was cruising nearby. Cox and Dustin came alongside and picked him up.

In No. 2 hold the aviation unit is making ready to swing the Pilgrim, the Fairchild and the auto-gyro to the beach. The deck force has been unloading steadily from the shelter deck.

Organization is still imperfect; there are very many unnecessary delays and no end of blunders. We are anything but the last word in efficiency, but time will, I hope, shake these things out. These inefficiencies are really my fault, in the last analysis.

III

Friday, January 19th, was a wild day, a helter-skelter mélange of minor triumphs, narrow escapes and disappointments. South of the ship a pillar of smoke suddenly climbed the sky—a tractor on fire! The cab and cargo compartment crawled with flames. The fire was finally doused with chemical bombs, but not before the whole wooden structure had been consumed. A moment later the second Citroën burst into flames. Same cause: defective gas lines. Thankfully the driver was alert; a well-placed bomb extinguished the blaze before much damage was done. The two lighter snowmobiles broke down. The cast-iron gears turned brittle and cracked, the drivers thought, from cold temperatures. Anyhow, whatever the cause, the fleet of tractors, upon which I had gazed so hopefully only the day before, was eighty percent *hors de combat* at the most critical time. For by that time the deck force and the winchmen had gotten into the swing of the thing, and the food, dog food, clothing and the bales of hay (there were thirty tons of hay alone) were pouring out of No. 1 hold. Even with the equivalent of sixteen nine-dog teams on the ice, Innes-Taylor wasn't able to keep his transport abreast of the outpouring.

The Pilgrim was safely landed and towed inland by the surviving Cletrac. But a Fokker wing section was caught by a gust of wind as the boom whisked it off No. 4 hatch, was spun with such violence as to carry the men hanging to the guide lines off their feet, and was flipped against a boom stay. It was damaged, but could be (and was) repaired.

That day, too, the wind moved into the north, kicking up a moderate sea which jostled the ship against the ice. Where she lay an undershot ledge of green ice rubbed against the hull. Down in the holds you could hear the plates rub and scrape as the ship met and gave to the swell. Not a very pretty sound. The possibility of puncturing the side of the ship while she lay alongside the ice I had always reckoned as one of the most formidable hazards confronting the expedition. We had brought along a number of enormous rubber tires to serve as fenders, and these were lowered and disposed along the length of the ship. They weren't very effective. The ledge jutted out well below the waterline, and its spurs were irregular. While we were considering what further steps to take, Lindley, the electrician, came forward with a suggestion.

Aboard ship were a dozen 45-foot telephone poles. These were to be used for directional antennae for radio broadcasting at Little America. Lindley suggested employing them as shores. It was an excellent idea. Four poles were immediately slung into position along the hull, with the outer ends resting against hatch covers planted in the snow to give a solid backing. The butts rested against wooden buffers dropped over the side, and were made fast. No doubt it was an odd looking arrangement, remindful of clumsy galley sweeps, but it did work like a charm.

In spite of the fact that all but half a dozen crippled or ailing dogs were in harness, our four-footed transport was anything but smooth. The dogs were badly out of condition and wild as March Hares to boot. During the southern voyage the regular dog-drivers had tried to keep the crew from petting the dogs to death, but with no more success than you would expect. All you had to do was to snap your fingers and call a name: and instantly the whole ingratiating pack would break from the trail, utterly oblivious to the shrieks of the driver, and swarm up for petting. Very flattering and all that, but it hardly made for efficiency. Morgan's team dragged him a hundred feet, with his foot caught in a loop of lashing, while his leader galloped up in pursuit of a shipboard acquaintance. "Damn you, Pitou," yelled Duke Dane at his leader, "if you've got any wolf in you, now's your chance to show it!"

For the first few days dog transport was a three-ringed circus. The teams were forever fighting, tangling, breaking away. Two days after we landed there were few drivers with voice enough left to speak above a whisper. The original team combinations that had been settled aboard ship proved impossible in practice. Day by day—indeed, hour by hour—the drivers experimented with new combinations, shifting dogs from file to wheel and wheel to file, and frantically searching their material for that rarest of sledging virtues—a good leader. I dare say that during that first week every dog that showed a spark of intelligence was promoted to, and almost as swiftly demoted from, leadership of one team or another.

It wouldn't be fair to impose the burden of blame on the dogs. The drivers, too, were learning. Not more than half a dozen had ever handled dogs before. Innes-Taylor's organization of dog drivers, permanent and temporary, was a rare mixture of talents—biologist Perkins, Third Engineer McCurrach, mechanical engineer Ronne, lawyer Buckley, banker Russell, advertising man Paine, insurance broker Dane, agriculturist Moody, aerial photographer Pelter, geologist Wade, and Fourth Mate Healy. Is it any wonder the dogs were bewildered, and the drivers at their wits' end? But this weird diffusion of career men ran through the organization.

The third day something happened to the refrigerator. The cook sent a mess boy to the harassed Czegka, with a demand something be done about it:

"All right," said Czegka. "Get Boyd, the machinist. Tell him I said to fix the refrigerator."

"He ain't on board," said the mess boy blandly.

"Where is he?"

"Out at Pressure Camp—cooking."

"The machinist cooking!" yelled Czegka. "Then let the cook fix the refrigerator!"

The confusion notwithstanding, every hour saw matters on the mend. The organization began to function efficiently, and though for a long time it was anything but perfect, still it began to run more smoothly and to better purpose. As the dogs worked into shape the transport quickened. The first day or two even the nine-dog teams rarely carried loads heavier than 500 pounds. These loads were stepped up to 1,000 and 1,200 pounds. Siple's powerful team, backed up by the giant Shambouls, hauled a ton at a clip. And one by one the tractors returned to service, though for a while they were anything but dependable. Demas and his crew of Dustin, Hill, Morgan, Stancliff and Fleming were wonderfully patient. Poor devils, they had to endure a deal of biting quips, especially from the dog drivers. It got so that you could tell a tractor driver by his furtive, half-apologetic air, his frost-bitten fingers, the oil on his pantaloons, and the permanent stoop brought to his shoulders by hours spent under a raised hood.

Sun., Jan. 21, 10:50 P.M.

Tonight the wind is rising in the southwest, and I doubt if we shall be able to hold this mooring much longer. Even with ten mooring lines out, the ship is straining rather hard. One of the shores has already worked loose. We shall probably have to cast off before very long. Sky overcast—and a thick pall of sea smoke fills the Bay.

No. 1 hold empty at last, and the booms are working over No. 2. Unloaded the Fokker from between-decks. It is now ashore, anchored alongside the Pilgrim about a mile south of the ship. No. 2 hold is largely filled with lumber and gasoline and kerosene drums—some 500 drums in all. Frightful things to handle. The drums weigh between 400 and 450 pounds each, and there's nothing handy to take hold of. The ice shelf on which we are unloading is forever crumbling. The men, leaning forward to seize the net, spring back, complimenting themselves on their agility. Next time the boom licks out a little bit farther.

Transport is steadily falling behind. We're unloading ship just about twice as fast as dogs and tractors can move it away. Consequently, to keep the stuff from piling up near the edge, the drivers have been obliged to create four temporary relay caches between the ship and Pressure Camp. A great mound of stuff has accumulated during the past twenty-four hours in a cache a hundred yards from the ship. Rather close for comfort, but the risk must be taken. The tractors are crippled. Only two of them—

a Citroën and the Cletrac—are running, but almost never at once: usually one or the other is out of commission. The dog teams are exhausted. We have put them on eight hour shifts. The dogs must have rest, even more than the men. Fagged-out dogs have been brought aboard ship, where it is warmer.

Just east and south of Pressure Camp Ronne has at last found a likely looking passage. It means tacking through a half mile of upheaved ice, with dangerous crevasses and impassable ridges close aboard on either hand, but by bending and winding through the good spots Ronne thinks the dog teams can get through. He's doubtful about the tractors. There's one water level crevasse, 35 feet wide, with a three-foot crack of open water in its center, across the trail which we'll have to bridge.

From the ship to Pressure Camp it's 3.4 miles; by the new trail it's 3.8 miles from Pressure Camp to Little America, making a total haul of 7.2 miles from the ship's present berth to Little America. Which is better than I had expected. Past the pressure, Ronne said, the trail gains rolling bay ice, then rises steeply over a shoulder of high barrier. From there on it's a straight run across the roof of the Barrier to Little America. We're very, very fortunate.

IV

At 12:30 A.M., January 22nd, the wind, settling down in the east-southeast, drove us from our berth. The wind really kicked up quite viciously; two telephone pole shores were carried away and, not having time to slip the toggles, the shore crew cut the last two moorings with an ax. Until noon the ship lay hove to under the brow of East Barrier, waiting in the lee for the storm to pass. The retreat was actually a tactical gain. It gave the expedition a chance to draw second wind. The men were spent, unshaven, with blood-shot eyes and fatigue showing in hollow cheeks, a number were on the verge of collapse. You could tell it by the way they stumbled, the mechanical way they did things, and the slow way the words formed when they spoke. And nerves were raw, too. While the ship lay drifting only the watch officers were on deck. The others slept heavily, deep in the first real sleep in five days.

But June and Innes-Taylor allowed no halt on the ice. Twenty-five men, mostly dog-drivers and tractor men, were ashore. All night the teams and the tractors nibbled at the caches, inching the stuff south. When the men could work no longer, they turned in, boots and saddles. The two trail tents at Pressure Camp were not large enough to accommodate all. The others piled up bales of hay which they roofed with tarpaulin; they lay down and slept on the snow. When the ship regained her mooring all the stores, with the exception of the hay, had been transported at least as far as the intermediate relay cache 1.5 miles south of the ship, and a substantial quantity was gathering at Pressure Camp.

At 4 P.M. on the 22nd we were again alongside the ice, with ten mooring lines out; the winches were squealing, the cargo nets were swinging out, and men, rubbing the sleep out of their eyes, were stumbling to the beach for another long nightmare. We decided, now to supplement the transport with aviation. The Pilgrim, which had been made ready for flight, was impressed as a cargo-carrier. During the next twenty-four hours she made a flight an hour between the Bay of Whales and Little America, carrying a ton every flight. Such speed and ease were tantalizing. By contrast the crawling dog teams and tractors seemed very slow and laborious. This same afternoon Captain Innes-Taylor and Al Wade drove two empty teams through the pressure to Little America, on a test run through Ronne's passage. It took them more than an hour to make 3.3 miles. The going, they said, was hard and, in spots, dangerous.

However, this was no work for the Pilgrim. Bowlin warned that the rough take-offs and the down-wind landings on rough sastrugi at Little America were severely punishing the landing gear. I had no choice but to withdraw the plane; it was too precious to be risked as a freighter. The burden must be shouldered by tractors and dogs. There's no getting around it; the dogs are to the polar regions what camels are to the desert. There are certain jobs they'll do better than the cleverest piece of machinery yet built.

On the 23rd, mindful of Ronne's warning, I flew with June to look for a passage through for the tractors. We flew 30 miles south, within the irregular, phrigian-capped outline of the Bay of Whales. The prospect was none too encouraging. The pressure rolled against the foot of the East Barrier wall, wave upon wave. Wherever a cape or a cliff projected the pressure at the foot swirled around it in a monstrous whirlpool. The pressure trended southwest with the coast of the Bay, to merge indistinguishably with the rolling uplands and valleys of the inland shelf ice. Fifty miles southwest we could see great blocks of upheaved ice reflecting splinters of sunlight. Unless the tractors made a looping turn into the mouth of Amundsen Arm they seemed to be blocked, as Ronne had said. A détour of twenty miles, as I remarked before, would nullify their usefulness. Twenty miles of hauling to make good three brings you up hard against the law of diminishing returns. But there must be a way; there had to be.

Coming back, we flew low over the pressure just east of Pressure Camp. Ronne's passage was marked with orange trail flags, so we had no difficulty tracing it from the air. No doubt about it: the passage was rough. It scrambled around monstrous ice bowlders and over high shoulders of ice, slanted into deep troughs, zig-zagged past sagging, thinly roofed crevasses, the hollow depths of which were betrayed by the dark skeletal shadows outlined between the lips. But the more we studied the passage the more we became convinced the tractors could get through. The narrower crevasses could be filled in, the broader ones avoided; the hairpin turns could be rounded by hard digging, the razor-backed ridges leveled. The open crevasse in the center of the pressure could be bridged. We had telephone poles. With hatch covers laid across them they would make an adequate bridge for the tractors. We discovered, too, that a second bridge would be necessary. Just beyond Pressure Camp lay another long open crevasse, about fifteen feet wide, running east and west. That also would have to be bridged before the stores could be moved out of the cache. Yet all these things, I reflected, were within our capacity. We had the tools and the men. But did we have the time? Ramming heavy cargo through that bottleneck was bound to be a protracted, killing job.

We made another important observation. During the previous week large quantities of loose ice had collected in the mouth of the Bay of Whales. These drifting masses were constantly replenished by pack drifting down from the northeast, and the ice breaking out of the Bay. So long as this great weight of ice lay across the mouth of the Bay, it tended to dampen the long swell rolling in from the Ross Sea. Now all this ice was gone. The steady drumming of southerly winds had scattered it, and the Ross Sea now had a clean sweep down the Bay. This fact accounted for the recent increasing roughness of the water, the banging of the ship at her mooring, and the accelerating velocity with which the ice was moving out. Just the night before a single floe, upwards of twenty blocks long, had broken out astern of the ship. Conditions forecast another outrush of ice on a scale equal to that which Ellsworth had observed. June had previously reported (and I saw them from the air) many new cracks between the ship and Pressure Camp. Myriads of thread-like fractures fanned in all directions from the pressure. Only three inches wide now, they would broaden from hour to hour. We were instantly impressed with the necessity of advancing to safer ground at once the stores already on the ice. Half a mile south of Pressure Camp an arm of the West Barrier shore of the Bay curved in. The approach to it was gentle. Solid and as nearly permanent as high barrier can be, yet not so high as to tax the dogs and tractors, it was a logical place for an emergency cache. June called my attention to it. That spot next day became the site of West Barrier Cache—the second big cargo dump. Simultaneously we selected a third cache—East Barrier Cache—on the opposite heights of the Bay, a little north of Cape Manhue (named by Amundsen) and about a mile and a half south-southwest of Little America. Pressure Camp—West Barrier Cache—East Barrier Cache, these names were later to be burned into the minds of my men, to become as bitterly unforgettable as the localities of hard-fought engagements to the memories of soldiers. They were strategic points to be fought for, and finally won, after infinite toil and punishment, in the long struggle to reoccupy Little America.

From the air I had a new and instructive perspective of the scope of the struggle. For miles the trampled snow, the enlarging caches, the trail running through the pressure all told of enormous activity. Pressure Camp was a great untidy swirl of crates, boxes, gasoline drums, with two orange-topped tents in the center. Between the camp and the ship ran the road, worn into firmness by the ceaseless pounding of the dogs and tractors. All along the way were nondescript temporary depots, where drivers had dumped their loads to rest fagged-out teams. At all these places the dog teams and tractors, like prodigiously active centipedes, were nibbling, loading and hurrying south to the main dump at Pressure Camp, then flying back empty for another load. There, in a nutshell, was how we finally reoccupied Little America. Literally, we inched our way along Misery Trail, hauling and relaying, making uncountable thousands of small journeys, like so many ants engaged in a stupendous transfer, with a direful threat flogging weary backs. I don't know what it is that gives that aspect of frantic industry to ants: hunger, probably, and a dim sense of doom. What drove us was the thought of the ice crumbling behind our backs, and the sea creeping hour by hour nearer toward our priceless stores.

V

As a result of this brief flight, we made a sudden change in tactics. That afternoon the unloading of ship was summarily suspended. All available man-power on the ship was marched out on the ice and concentrated on the job of advancing stores to the comparative safety of Pressure Camp and high barrier beyond. Simultaneously Innes-Taylor and a tractor party left the ship with three telephone poles in tow, with which to bridge the first crevasse just beyond Pressure Camp. The second bridge could wait. The immediate need was to gain the stable heights of West Barrier Cache with all possible dispatch.

Wed., Jan. 24, Midnight.

We have again been driven from our mooring by heavy seas, this time very suddenly. A succession of blinding snow squalls struck shortly after midnight. While we were debating whether we could hold our berth, the wind settled it for us. Two spring lines parted, all the shores carried away, and the ship surged heavily against the ice. Captain Verleger, who was descending the gangway, very narrowly escaped being knocked overboard by a telephone pole which at that moment was being swung ashore on the after boom. The surge of the ship set the pole spinning, and Verleger ducked out of the way by the breadth of a gnat's eyelash. The heavy gangway wrenched with the ship. As it did the ledge of ice on which it was resting let go suddenly. The gangway hung there for five minutes, just long enough to allow the dog drivers sleeping aboard—Captain Innes-Taylor, Russell, Paine and Healey—to be routed out and sent ashore, with their clothing

An Intermediate Cache

(Photograph by John Dyer)

The Big Haul Goes On

A Dog Team and the "Bear of Oakland"

(Photograph by John Dyer)

Tons of Supplies

under their arms. A line had just been passed around the gangway, and a strain taken on the line when the last supporting ledge crumpled, and the gangplank slipped into the water. It was taken aboard with difficulty. At 5:30 o'clock this morning we cast off and backed away from the ice.

Since then we have been drifting and cruising about the Bay, looking for sanctuary for the ship till the storm blows out. With bottom 350 fathoms deep, there is no anchorage and very little lee. A northeaster is sweeping down the Bay, fanning level sheets of drift from the dome of the Barrier. The air is choked with snow, and visibility drops to nothing. In sunlight no place in the world can be lovelier nor more transquil than the Bay of Whales. In a gale it is hell let loose.

Here the phrase "seeing the world go to pieces before your eyes" has a realistic meaning. In all directions Nature is in the throes of disintegration. Half a mile of Barrier crumpled as if it were a false front. The Bay is crawling with pack ice. From East to West Barrier, in all the small bays, harbors and inlets, along a 20-mile front, the ice is breaking up under the pounding of the gale. You can sometimes hear the sound of the cracking carrying above the drumming of the wind. At noon a squall hit furiously. The air darkened with flying snow. Half an hour later it cleared. We were appalled to see that the whole ice front between East and West Barrier—a stretch nearly five miles long—had broken out. Gone was the ship's berth. Gone, too, the site of the cache we had established 100 yards south of the ship. Just before the squall hit several teams were clearing up the last of the boxes left there. Thinking these men might have been caught, I immediately radioed Innes-Taylor to check all the men ashore. He reported an hour later that all hands were accounted for.

Forty-seven men, including Captain Verleger, are marooned ashore. Instructions have been issued to supply them with food, clothing and sleeping bags from the Winter Party's stores. We'd be helpless without radio. Petersen at Pressure Camp has been in hourly radio communication with the ship.

This afternoon, we steamed into Floyd Bennett Harbor in search of a lee, but were driven out by heavy ice. The ice there was breaking up fast. When we beat back to the east wall we found that a quarter of a mile of the Barrier, to a depth of forty yards, had sloughed off. The Bay is now full of loose ice. Two large bergs are drifting off East Cape. In these black squalls navigation is rather treacherous. Tonight the ship is hove to and drifting in the mouth of the Bay.

Thurs., Jan. 25, 10 P.M.

Wind ESE, force 5, occasionally snow squalls. Still drifting near the mouth of the Bay and no immediate prospects of regaining our berth. At 1 o'clock this afternoon we drew alongside the ice, south of the former mooring, but a heavy swell made it impossible to tie up. Large floes are still breaking out. The ice front is now about 200 yards back of its former position, and Innes-Taylor reports many new cracks north of Pressure Camp. However, he advised that Captain Verleger has thrown a bridge across the first crevasse south of the Camp, and dog teams and tractors are already ferrying stores to West Barrier Cache. The balance of transport was emptying the intermediate caches north of the camp. We could see those teams from the ship, steadily nibbling at the caches, vanishing and reappearing in flurries of drift.

The outlook tonight is discouraging. This condition may last for days. Every hour spent in fruitless cruising cuts into the *Ruppert's* oil reserve. It occurred to me tonight that, if all other avenues are closed, we could unload the last of the stores on the decks of the *Bear*, and use her as a ferry to the shore. Her stout wooden sides could rest against the ice without half the risk. Captain English advised tonight that he expects to reach the Bay of Whales on the night of the 31st.

This afternoon we explored a V-shaped Bay in the East Barrier, about five miles north of Little America. The *Bolling* moored there in 1929. Surprisingly, Haines saw a box half-imbedded in the snow, thirty feet up the face of the cliff which must have been left 200 feet from the water's edge. It had been buried deeply, then the Barrier had broken off, with the line of cleavage through the center of the box.

Friday, January 26th, the wind switched into the southwest and abated. We ventured in again to resume unloading. Steaming down the Bay we passed an outward-bound floe in the center of which reposed 25 bales of hay. If that was all we lost we had reason to be thankful. A tough break for the cows, but a boon to the dog drivers. They never could understand how they were advancing the cause of science by hauling hay. As we approached the edge of the ice, the dog teams and tractors, summoned by radio from Pressure Camp, were snaking toward the ship. Fifty-six hours after she had been driven off, the ship was again moored, this time about a mile west of the former berth, no great distance from Chamberlin Harbor. Eastward the breakup had grossly altered the face of the ice. Before it had made a clean curving line from east to west. Now it was rudely broken and jagged, as if a great ax had hacked at it.

June came aboard to make a report. No casualties, he said, and no losses except for the hay. Colombo had a painful case of snow blindness, and a few men were lightly frost-bitten.

"It's an ill wind," June said, "that blows no good. That storm gave transport a chance to catch up. We've already got eight tons of stuff in West Barrier Cache, and a couple of tons in East Barrier Cache. The dog drivers took it through the pressure. It's pretty hard going. They've built a flimsy bridge over the worst crevasse."

"How long does it take to get through the pressure?" I asked.

"Well, Siple made a test trip. Left Pressure Camp for Little America with a ton on his sledges. Took him five hours. The steep ascent up the Barrier, more than anything, took it out of the dogs. However, with lighter loads and after the trail has been worn down, we ought to be able to cut the time in half."

"How are the men?" I asked.

June smiled. "Fagged out, absolutely. They've lost all track of time and everything else. But those guys certainly can take it."

VI

This new berth we held exactly ten hours.

The ship lay in a bight of ice which bulged sharply just forward of the bow. About 150 yards beyond the edge the dog-drivers had noticed a tiny crack in the snow, paralleling the edge. It was only half an inch wide. Nevertheless the tractors were ordered to heave to on the far side. On a 200-yard line, the Cletrac was bringing the sledges to them from the loading berths. All hands, then, were unloading No. 2 and No. 4 holds.

Cumbersome gasoline drums were rising out of No. 2. The cargo net was dropping them, six at a time, on a ledge of ice. Noville, Dyer, Pierce, Abele, Paige, Lewisohn and several others were lifting them onto the sledges. Lindley was nearby, strengthening the camel's back for one of the shores. I happened to be watching him from the bridge.

"Put a line on, Lindley," I yelled. "You're too close to the edge."

Lindley threw a loop around his waist, and Pierce held the other end.

A moment later Pierce glanced down at his feet. Between his feet a crack was widening—one, two, three inches. Lindley uttered a sharp cry. The ledge on which he was standing collapsed. Pierce coolly dragged him back, and together they scrambled beyond a second fracture. Heedless of their own safety, the men struggled to save the gasoline. Three drums were rolled to a sledge, which the tractor snaked across the crack. Six more were rolled back into the cargo net, and hoisted back on the ship. None too soon the men broke for the gangway.

Then it happened. With an infinite quiet, with a deadly soundlessness unlike any silence in human experience, the front of the bay ice, to a depth of 150 yards, detached itself. Swift as a shadow the crack ran eastward, as if a blade were passing underneath. An obscure, uncertain line, then a dark ribbon, then open water. Eastward it ran, clear to the hills of pressure, nearly four miles away; and all along the ice surged out, dividing easily into massive floes. Not a sound. The swell had diminished. If you can imagine an earthquake without sound, you will sense what it was like. The only sounds were the officers calling to the men casting off the mooring lines, the winches squealing as the gangway came aboard, and the whir of the tractor treads as the drivers beat a retreat with their loads.

At 1:50 A.M. on January 27th, we cast off. Neither that day, nor the next, was the *Ruppert* able to find a stable berth. A dozen times, tempted by passing hesitations in the dispersion of ice, we drew alongside likely spots, only to retire hastily before a fresh outburst. On the morning of the 28th the ice cemented to the barrier shore south of Chamberlin Harbor appeared to be holding. The ship drew alongside, and a party was sent ashore in the motor sailer to sink dead men for the mooring lines. Captain Verleger and Bos'un McNamara were in the party. Having finished their job, they walked inland a way. One hundred yards in they passed a tiny crack. Ten minutes later, recalled by a blast on the whistle, they were barely able to clear that crack with a running jump. The Captain's game leg went back on him, and McNamara's honest face was creased with worry. They skipped with the agility of a couple of elderly Elizas crossing the ice. "You fellows can have the ice," said the skipper. "Give me a solid deck every time."

This is the sort of thing we were up against. By radio June warned that a new crack had appeared between the old intermediate relay cache and Pressure Camp, and he thought the camp might go out within a few days. Ten men were landed in the motor sailer, on the 28th, to reënforce the thirty-four already at Pressure Camp. All stores between Pressure Camp and the edge of the ice, June said, had been collected, and the dog teams and tractors were running between the Camp and West Barrier Cache. More than half of the food, gasoline, clothing and general stores had already been advanced to the latter. A magnificent job. But it was like working against a tide. Already open water had crept within a mile of Pressure Camp. For the first time we could plainly see the camp from the ship. The intermediate relay cache was at the water's edge. Luckily for us, the tractors were now functioning perfectly.

VII

Sunday the 28th, while we lay drifting, was a lovely day. Light snow squalls drifted brightly across the sun. In the evening soft, puffy cumulus clouds turned gold in the declining light of the sun; rose tints crept over the Barrier, long purple shadows gathered in the pressure, and the freezing water, dead calm, was green as absinthe. The 29th brought light northerly winds, a temperature of +12°, and a heavy fog. The white dome of the West Barrier glistened above the low fat rolls of sea smoke.

At 1:45 o'clock the third afternoon, the dispersion of the ice having been arrested, we crept in for another mooring. We held it five hours, just long enough to unload the radio equipment and the autogyro. Then the ice alongside which the *Ruppert* lay surged out, and the ship backed away hard, to port. An hour later, we tied up again in a small bight about a mile to the west. And again the dog teams and tractors, summoned by radio, came wearily down from Pressure Camp.

The conditions were far from auspicious. Uncountable cracks traversed the ice, which restively contracted and expanded over the swell. As the ice heaved the fractured edges ground together and parted with deep sighing noises. Across these the dog teams slammed on the dead run. Flags were jabbed in the snow to mark the cracks, and lookouts were posted over the worst. The tractors, too precious to be risked near the edge, stood off at 200 yards, where the Cletrac was drawing in sledges from the unloading berths on an endless line. Now ship's crew and shore transport fell to it. Temporarily we halted the unloading of gasoline from No. 2 hold. All hands were concentrated on the task of getting the coal out of No. 4, and the meat out of the refrigerator. There were 125 tons of coal alone to be moved. All that night men shouldered heavy sacks of meat down the gangplank, while over their heads the cargo slings flicked out with sacks of coal. Shortly before midnight McCormick took off in the autogyro and checked in at Little America. All four planes were then safely at the base.

We held this berth until 4 A.M. on January 30th, when a new danger threatened from another quarter. The masses of pressure ice that had recently broken out were being wafted down by easterly and northerly winds. They lay distributed in a huge scimitar-curved stream north of the ship. Small hills of gnarled blue-green pressure ice drifted among the plinth-like floes. While we unloaded we kept a weather eye cocked on this stuff. Slowly it pushed closer. Stubbornly we held our position, unloading furiously, until the ice closed in ahead and abeam, leaving only a narrow hole astern. Then we cast off and backed out, full speed astern with the wheel hard over. And with no room to spare. The stern hit the ice a glancing blow, but hard enough to make the plates jingle. We gained open water. Half an hour later, perhaps less, all that ice, thousands of tons of it, was jammed against our berth.

At noon we closed in and moored again, with ice breaking off both ahead and astern of the ship. By supper time the last gasoline drum was out of No. 2 hold, and 35 tons of coal had passed out of No. 4. The sky was overcast, and a light, impalpable haze—that curiously indefinite haze of the polar regions, which makes horizon and snow and sky an indeterminate gray ocean—lay over the Bay.

But at 9:40 P.M. that night a column of smoke climbed over the dull pinnacle of West Cape. The *Bear of Oakland!*

Chapter VI

AGAIN TO THE EASTWARD

I

WITH bare sticks and yards aslant, the *Bear of Oakland* rounded the white tower of West Cape and steamed down the Bay. She had a heavy list to port, due to the fact (Lieut. English told me later) that the bunkers had not been trimmed. The night was fair, cold and crystal clear, contriving a perfect setting for the reunion of these two ships, the famous old veteran of the Arctic heaving down to meet, in the yellow haze of the Midnight Sun at the bottom of the world, the resurrected outcast of the Pacific lumber trade. On the *Ruppert* a hush fell as the winches paused and men scrambled topside to watch the *Bear* come in.

As the *Bear* drew within hailing distance Commodore Gjertsen gave her three welcoming blasts on the whistle. That instant Lieut. English smartly broke out three signal flags which had already been hoisted in stops; the signals spoke the ready response of an officer accustomed to doing things in the Navy way. There was an embarrassing pause while Rawson frantically searched the code book for the meaning of the signals. Lieut. English, he remarked, must have equipped himself with the new international code which went into effect after our departure.

"Welcome to the Bay of Whales," I megaphoned across for want of a more ceremonial reception.

Lieut. English shoved his lanky body, topped by a stocking cap, through the window of the pilot house.

"Thanks," he said. "Glad to be here."

A moment later he announced, through cupped hands: "Knew it was the Bay of Whales, all right. About ten miles north we passed a big floe with a lot of hay on it. We guessed it was yours—unless there's another dairy farm on this coast."

But there was no time for amenities. As the *Bear* rode across our bow and punched her nose into the ice, bow and stern lines came snaking across the gap, and were made fast. Then the wooden ship, a mere chip in the *Ruppert's* lee, was warped alongside. Lieut. English, with his characteristic efficiency, had everything in readiness: fenders disposed along the sides of his ship, mooring lines neatly coiled, deadmen ready, winches turning over, crew standing at their posts.

By 10:30 P.M. the two ships were lashed together, with the *Bear* outboard. In short order the long booms of the *Ruppert* were whipping cargo from the deck of the *Bear* to the waiting dog teams on the ice. The *Bear's* decks were piled high. Tiers of lumber were racked on the fo'c's'le, so tightly crowded there was scarcely access to the running rigging. A Citroën tractor, which had been taken aboard in New Zealand, stood on the after well deck, abaft the galley; the steel straps lashing it down had already been cast off. Presently the *Ruppert's* forward boom flicked the machine across the deck and lowered it, with engine purring, on the ice.

Demas, anxiously awaiting this new reënforcement to his tractor division, made a quick inspection. "How does she sound?" he asked Von der Wall. Von der Wall had worked over the tractor during the southerly voyage.

"Sounds fine to me," said Von der Wall.

"Then you're elected," Demas said. "Drive her into Pressure Camp. You'll see about a million boxes down there. Just take 'em aboard."

"Any other instructions?" asked Von der Wall as he climbed into the cab. Von der Wall—a petty officer in the navy—was an expert deep sea diver. Tractor driving in the Antarctic was probably the last experience he had counted on.

Demas waved him on with a grin. "Stay away from the edge of the ice, and *keep her rolling*—that's all you have to remember."

The little red tractor, its treads musically whirring, rolled down the trail to join the traffic plying furiously between the ship and Pressure Camp, between Pressure Camp and West Barrier Cache.

The arrival of the *Bear,* with her fresh reënforcements, was just the tonic we needed. Fatigue was forgotten; the expedition seemed to lift forward as it drew upon hidden reservoirs of strength. The *Bear's* crew not occupied in unloading their own ship, jumped across to give the *Ruppert's* crew a hand. Some joined the sledge-loading crews on the ice, others went down into the after holds. There was no halting that night. By 3 A.M., January 31st, No. 5 hold was empty; by noon more than half the coal was out of No. 4. A flow and a rhythm came into the effort that were inspiring. For the time being the convulsive movement of the ice was arrested. In the lull the expedition drove home the full power of its resources. Even the distribution of mail was held up, so as not to lose time.

In my cabin, during the small hours of the morning, Lieut. English and I had a quiet talk. He said that they had had a smooth Pacific crossing until the *Bear* drew near the northeast coast of New Zealand. A hurricane hit them then; and with only thirty tons of coal in her bunkers, and riding light, the *Bear* had a second close call. She took green water across the decks, Lieut. English said, and the time-worn timbers worked so much that the pumps never stopped. Fighting for a lee, they turned into Hicks Bay, a narrow unlighted cove on the coast. In the tight channel, with two anchors out and steaming on the engines to hold the anchorage, they finally rode out the storm. When the hurricane subsided they put out for Wellington; but just south of Napier another storm hit them, and they were obliged to put in there for coal. The *Bear* reached Wellington January 6th, taking on lumber, the tractor and other stores; she left on the 11th, and put into Dunedin two days later, where she took aboard the last of the supplies consigned to that port, including the tractor and lumber for several shacks. On January 19th she started south.

Instead of steering directly for the open passage we had found to the eastward, Lieut. English held a course slightly to the west, thinking he would run before the "brave west winds" common to the Forties and let them blow him east of Scott Island. With her heavy deck load the *Bear* rolled nastily in beam seas. However, the westerly gales failed to materialize, so Lieut. English brought his ship down longitude 178° 45′ E. It was a wise decision. He raised no pack, saw a few bergs in the vicinity of the Antarctic Circle, and had the satisfaction of making a record run for auxiliary ships between Dunedin and the Bay of Whales, a twelve days' run which equaled the *Eleanor Bolling's* 1929 passage.

Of course I congratulated Lieut. English on the excellent handling of his ship. He and his officers, Captain Johansen, Ice Pilot and Sailing Master, First Officer Rose and Second Officer Davis, had demonstrated seamanship of the highest order. It took shrewd and careful handling, a sympathetic knowledge of the peculiar strength and weakness of the ancient *Bear,* to bring her safely through. She was respectably old when the *Oregon* raced round the Horn. But there was a fine and indestructible courage of her oak timbering with its sheathing of iron bark, which age and rot could not corrupt. Her crew knew it. With quiet smiles they passed around copies of a scurrilous article in a New Zealand publication which prophesied the *Bear* would never reach the ice: she was too old, too rotten—the seas would break her open and sink her. Well, there she was in the sanctuary of the Bay of Whales; and as I glanced over her and sensed the staunchness in her chunky frame, I took her measure for a trip on which I should soon dispatch her—a trip which would give her a chance to round out her career in gallant style: not as a supply ship, an exalted grocery wagon, but in her true capacity as a vessel of exploration. I had no doubt as to her ability to live in ice.

Wed., Jan. 31, 11:50 P.M.

A nippy southwesterly breeze blowing all day; temperature between + 9 and + 13° during the day. Just enough wind and cold to make it uncomfortable, notwithstanding which we've made excellent progress. There are no longer such arbitrary arrangements as shifts and watches. All men work as long as they are physically able; and whenever their own particular duties slacken, they move unbidden to help another group that may be falling behind. The men have been very good about that. I know they are exhausted. Many of them, I'm sure, are working on nerve alone. There's very little talking nowadays, not even the usual grouching. A sure sign of fatigue.

Except for miscellaneous stores on the shelter deck, a small amount of meat, and the transfer of 250 tons of coal to the *Bear,* the *Ruppert* is practically empty. She ought to be able to pull out by Monday. Tonight we finished unloading the deck cargo of the *Bear,* really a splendid day's work.

However, we've absolutely got to start moving supplies through the bottleneck to East Barrier Cache. I don't like the looks of things. Practically all of our supplies are now jammed up in West Barrier Cache, hundreds of tons of it in jumbled piles on the snow. Tractors and dog teams are now running through Pressure Camp without stopping.

At 10 o'clock tonight June, with twenty men, left the ship in a tractor to throw the second bridge across the crevasse in the heart of the pressure. The tractors are blocked off from Little America until that bridge is built. At Pressure Camp they took in tow the telephone poles and the baulks we had used for the plane's tier on the after well-deck. A hard assignment. Some of these men have not slept in forty hours. But it's got to be done.

II

At 2 A.M., February 1st, with the temperature 15° below zero and a mean southwesterly breeze whipping stinging drift into their faces, June and his crew drove the last nail into the Bridge of Sighs. Made of telephone poles resting on piers of stout timbers, with hatch covers for a flooring, it spanned a crevasse channel of open water. Broken pressure towered round about it; the approaches from either direction were hammered and smoothed with crowbars, ice axes and shovels. At 3:15 A.M. this same morning, June and Stancliff drove the first tractor across, with a heavy Kohler power plant in tow. Thirty minutes later they rolled into Little America. The Kohler plant was required for the radio broadcast. Ten hours later Dyer held a successful test with New York and Buenos Aires, the first time a voice from Antarctica was ever heard in civilization.

Fri., Feb. 2, 10:51 P.M.

Ruppert entirely unloaded now except for personal gear and the transfer of coal to the *Bear.* Boatswain's Mate McNamara, one of the best, a man I can always count on, is in charge of the latter detail—a filthy and always unpopular job. While we coal the *Bear* with the forward booms, we are simultaneously unloading her deck cargo with the after boom.

All spare hands have been dispatched to Pressure Camp and West Barrier Cache to speed up the movement of supplies. About

50 tons of stores still remain in the former. I don't wish to leave anything there a second more than is absolutely necessary. Our transport is now divided into three divisions: one ferrying between the ship and West Barrier Cache, another between Pressure Camp and West Barrier Cache, and a third operating between the latter and East Barrier Cache. Food, clothing, coal, and scientific gear everywhere have right of way.

Dr. Perkins and Lindsey, who for the past week have been exploring the pressure ice in search of seals for dog food, returned to the ship tonight. Both seals and penguins, they said, are extremely scarce. About twenty seals a day was their limit; for they had to penetrate deep into the pressure, dragging their sledges after them, to make a kill. They were tired and concerned about the scarcity of seal.

Sat., Feb. 3, 11:20 P.M.

Today, with Lieut. English and Captain Verleger, I made a tractor trip into Little America for the first formal broadcast from the Antarctic Continent. It took us two hours to reach Little America. Dyer, Hutcheson and Pierce had everything in readiness. The apparatus was housed in a tent on the surface. A strong westerly was blowing, causing the tent to flap violently and sifting drift inside. I silently saluted Dyer. If he could put on a broadcast under such conditions, he was a genius. You can't but admire the cool competence of these modern technicians; springing full-fledged from great scientific universities; soundly trained in their particular specialties, they arrive while still in their early twenties, with a confidence and security no other profession seems able to impart.

"Think it will go through?" I asked Dyer. Dyer chuckled. "No reason why not," he said, "if nothing blows up." "And if something blows up . . . ?" I suggested. Dyer chuckled again. "It will be just too bad." Outside Pierce, dancing up and down to keep warm, stood by the power plant which chugged bravely in the blizzard.

Well, we gathered in the old Mess Hall, by the dim light of kerosene lanterns. Hutcheson fiddled with controls on a monitor board, snapped his fingers across the microphones to test them. And I thought, as I watched these mysterious preparations, how broadly things had changed: how, twenty-two years before, Scott and his whole party had silently died of hunger while his base party, just 160 miles away, awaited his homecoming at Cape Evans; and here we were casually making ready to tell of our prosaic doings to a vast audience in the United States. A momentary misgiving swept over me. When too much talk seems to be the cause of much of the grief in the world, no man could break the isolation of the Last Continent of Silence without a twinge of remorse.

Anyhow, a thing called a cue finally came; each of us went to the microphone to say his piece: and ten thousand miles away (so Dyer reported) the voices came through clear as a bell. Somehow, in the shadows of the Mess Hall, fifteen feet or so beneath the surface, it didn't seem possible.

That afternoon, before returning to the ships, I took stock of the rehabilitation of old Little America. The improvements that Dr. Poulter had accomplished in a fortnight, with only a handful of men, were remarkable. The old buildings were restored, the old caches excavated, and the stores which had lately been flown and hauled in were neatly segregated, each in its proper cache near the center of the camp. Thus the radio department's stores were in one pile, with distinctive pennants to mark the boundaries and identity of the cache; the scientific department's stores were in another, with other identifying markings. In this way, by separating into their proper categories the heterogeneous masses of stores pouring in from the outer emergency caches, much confusion was avoided; and the danger of losing large quantities of stores under rapidly gathering drift was greatly minimized.

The Administration Building was partly rebuilt. Fifty tons of snow were shoveled from the roof alone. The roof was lifted into position and strengthened with new beams; the débris was cleaned out, and four new bunks, making twenty in all, were installed. Very little had to be done, as I said earlier, to the old Mess Hall. But Dr. Poulter invented ingenious escape hatches for both buildings. For exits we had previously depended on slanting tunnels rising to the surface. These had the fault of drifting over and filling during heavy blizzards; also, they tended to shrink under the weight of snow accumulating on top, making it awkward to pass through them. What Dr. Poulter did was to sink vertical shafts to the entrances of both buildings, with ladders rising to the surface, and light wooden hatches to cap them. The hatches were about fourteen feet deep. Of course the veterans scoffed at such novelties. The new arrangement, however, worked very nicely.

The 1,000-foot tunnel which had formerly connected the old buildings (I say *old,* because we fell into the habit of thus differentiating everything identified with the first Little America) was impassable, having either sagged or narrowed; but by digging down from the surface Dr. Poulter and his men reached the old caches. Many items of considerable value were salvaged and later put to good use. In the food caches alone were found two and a half tons of flour, several hundred pounds of butter, quantities of condensed and evaporated milk, canned meats, fruits, fish, preserves and other foods, all in prime condition. The various other caches yielded odd amounts of coal, gasoline, kerosene, lubricating oils, medical supplies, radio equipment, aviation tools, photographic equipment and the like.

Bowlin, Smith and Schlossbach had meanwhile dug down to the old planes—the Ford and the Fairchild—which in 1930 we had anchored on the ridge to the eastward. Both planes were completely buried:

there was just a pale shadow to mark the submerged wing of the Fairchild; of the big Ford only the rudder post and the starboard wing tip were awash. A casual examination confirmed Balchen's report of their being in good condition. I decided, however, to let them lie there until next spring. We had no need for them, and no time to spare for digging them out.

I returned to the ship by dog team, stopping off to examine the caches. The evening had turned bitter, the wind was rising, and drift was pouring in a white waterfall from the lip of the Barrier. But in spite of the numbing wind and drift, the abominable visibility, tractors and dog teams were pluckily shuttling between the dumps. Already a solid bulwark of stores had risen on the heights where East Barrier Cache stood; and teams and tractors were slamming, pounding and dragging through the bottleneck of pressure.

Contemplating this activity I ceased to despair over our seemingly desultory progress. All this had been done in little more than a fortnight. It was something to be proud of. The teeming trail, the regular movement of teams and tractors, the fattening caches, the rebirth of Little America—all these things were proof of a stupendous effort. Sweat, blood, risk and doggedness had gone into the making of the road to Little America. Before the business was done some men would feel that something of themselves, too, had gone into them.

Even the *Ruppert,* when I boarded her, seemed to wear the dowdy dress of fatigue. Her decks were full of débris, her lavatories frozen, odds and ends of rejected things thrown everywhere. The winch packings were all blown out: and either too weary or too hard-pressed to make repairs, the winchmen preferred to stand in clouds of steam, which froze as it struck their faces and hands. Well, it wouldn't be long now. A few more hours and they could go. In the year's waiting at Dunedin both men and ship could rest and refit.

Sunday the 4th was overcast and chilly. The wind gathered gale force in the southwest. A sea of drift poured across the Barrier. The dog teams and tractors tried to shovel through it, but could no longer follow the beacon flags. After several teams had gotten lost, traffic was suspended, whereupon the trail crews sought sanctuary either at Pressure Camp or Little America, whichever was nearer. But not until the *Bear* was unloaded.

That night, both ships, still lashed together, lay empty of cargo and practically deserted, except for the men on watch and the lame and the crippled. The ships were cold and damp and heaved nastily on a choppy sea. Whitecaps were racing across the Bay, and heavy flotillas of ice hovered in eccentric play at the mouth.

III

During the night the *Ruppert's* crew were summarily recalled by radio from Pressure Camp and Little America, where they had been functioning as dog drivers, tractor mechanics, stevedores and Heaven only knows what else. In all thirty-five men were assigned to return. The others I decided to keep to assist the Ice Party in moving the stores toward Little America. They could return with the *Bear*. The *Ruppert* would have a skeleton crew, no more.

During the night the crew straggled aboard one by one, not a few of them, I know, deeply disappointed at leaving us. Sailing, too, were "Vic" Czegka, general manager of the expedition, and Dr. Shirey, the expedition's only medical officer.

This alone was disturbing enough. Dr. Shirey had earlier come to me and said, with disarming candor, that he could not remain with the Ice Party. His health (Dr. Shirey was subject to high blood pressure) forced the decision on him, he explained; he had hoped for an improvement which had failed to come; therefore he thought it wiser that he should leave with the ship, rather than remain and become in all probability a burden upon the Ice Party.

Nothing could be more clear-cut than that.

Still it was a felling blow. By a cruel turn of affairs and through no fault of theirs, a company of men engaged in hazardous operations and to all intents and purposes marooned at the bottom of the world, were abruptly deprived of all medical protection. It was unthinkable that they should be left without that protection for a year.

Yet where—and how—would we get a doctor? The Ross Sea must certainly freeze before long and cut us off. It was barely possible that we could race a ship to New Zealand and back with a doctor, and clear her again before she were beset. But suppose she failed? Suppose she were caught by the ice? A potential disaster, then, for ship and crew.

We had one ace in the hole—James Sterrett, hospital corpsman on the *Bear*, a medical student of several years' training. Sterrett was a conscientious, capable man. That I did not instantly promote him to medical officer was in no wise a reflection on his ability. Rather for the sake of his future career, as well as the morale of the men (a stout-hearted lot, they themselves cheerfully accepted the situation without complaint) I was reluctant to force this great responsibility on him when he was not quite ready for it. It would not have been fair to him.

Never have I felt my responsibility as leader more keenly. I watched the *Ruppert* make ready to sail with a despair in my heart that weighed heavy as dishonor. I felt that in some way I had betrayed these men.

And the recurring thought of the terror this news might strike in distant homes didn't help to mitigate the bitterness of my reflections. I determined then to get a doctor—regardless of cost or consequence—or else cancel the expedition.

For Czegka's going I was forearmed. In fact, it was I who insisted on it. A chronic back disorder had made the last month a long misery, but he had carried on in spite of blinding pain. I knew the fortitude of the man. This same complaint made the first winter night a hell for him. And though it meant mutual disappointment, I refused to let him hurt himself further on my behalf. The wealth of stores on the ice and the expedition's successful reoccupation of Little America were largely the fruits of his planning and enterprise. A good task and a generous heart: who could ask for more? With genuine sorrow I waved him on.

A discouraging night. Captain Verleger suddenly fell ill with pneumonia: one lung was congested: he became slightly delirious with a high temperature. Another worry.

It was blowing hard when the *Bear* cast off and stood across the *Ruppert's* bow, holding her nose against the ice with the force of her engine. Rapidly the shore crew cast off the *Ruppert's* stern and spring mooring cables; but the toggle for the bow line was frozen and couldn't be slipped. While the men struggled with it, the wind caught the side of the ship and smartly wafted her stern around. She was about to smash broadside against the *Bear.*

"Cut the line—cut the line!" Commodore Gjertsen shrieked from the bridge.

Ike Schlossbach, who had his wits about him, seized an ax and hacked the line loose with a couple of hard strokes. Her screws churning, the *Ruppert* backed out, just grazing the *Bear,* came about and stood out for the northern transit to New Zealand. The weary, grimy men lining her rails shouted friendly farewells. Lieut. English gave them a "highball" on the whistle—three long blasts, followed by a short one: then, as the plumes of vapor welled above the *Ruppert's* stacks, Commodore Gjertsen's response floated back.

Half an hour later the *Ruppert* vanished in the fog. The men who had come down to see her off and gather the last of their belongings headed in for Little America by tractor. Counting the *Bear's* crew, ninety-five men were still on the ice. That afternoon I transferred my quarters to the *Bear,* which had slipped into the *Ruppert's* berth.

Mon., Feb. 5, 9:30 P.M.

... I've been wracking my brains trying to figure a way to get a doctor here; the situation seems hopeless. The elements of time and expense are irrevocably set against us. Here's the way I see the situation:

Possibilities	*Objections*
Let the *Ruppert* pick up a doctor in Dunedin, return and be met by *Bear* at edge of pack: let the latter, on account of her stouter hull, risk the double passage of the Ross Sea.	Time element unfavorable. *Ruppert's* bunkers almost empty of fuel. Engines in need of overhaul. Barely possible and can be attempted if all other means fail.
Ask Ellsworth to dispatch *Wyatt Earp,* now at Dunedin, with doctor recruited in New Zealand.	Promising unless Ellsworth has started for the States. Confident I can count upon his coöperation.
Locate the nearest whaling expedition, and ask them for the loan of a doctor.	Very doubtful. No whaling ships operating in the Ross Sea this season. Absurd, too, to ask a whaling expedition, with upwards of 300 men in its care, to relinquish its only doctor.
Petition the New Zealand Government to rush a doctor here on a fast cruiser.	Tempting—but unthinkable except as a last resort.

Now that the knotty problem is behind us it's amusing how easily the situation finally was resolved. Hope of a helping hand from Ellsworth's expedition was instantly extinguished on radio tidings that the *Wyatt Earp* was laid up for repairs, with her engines torn down. A thorough search of the air by radio finally yielded up the S.S. *Thorshavn,* a great Norwegian whaling factory ship. She was then far to the northeast, steaming in the opposite direction; and though her master offered to come to our aid if no alternative remained, the inconvenience and the heavy expense that he would incur through the interruption of his fishing, made me reluctant to press home the seriousness of our plight.

In this posture the natural, the obvious thing occurred to me. I suddenly remembered (kicking myself for obtuseness) that while the *Ruppert* was exploring near the 120th meridian, Bailey had accidentally made radio contact with the British exploring ship *Discovery II.* To our astonishment she was then engaged in scientific investigations, not far to the eastward. Though our courses failed to bring the ships together, nevertheless we exchanged greetings. I remembered that she was on her way back to New Zealand for a brief refitting, and was scheduled presently to resume her operations off the Antarctic continent.

A series of radiograms swiftly located *Discovery II* at Auckland, New Zealand; she was making ready to resume her operations off the continent, and her master, Lieut. Nelson, of the British Navy, was eager to extend a helping hand, if the proper authorizations could be obtained. Through regular channels we made petition to the British and New Zealand governments: the necessary authorizations were immediately forthcoming, as a consequence of which *Discovery II* was instructed to take aboard a doctor and transfer him to the *Bear* somewhere in the Ross Sea. Through our New Zealand agents we advertised in the local press for a doctor. From a plenitude of candidates, Dr. Louis H. Potaka, graduate of Otago University and highly recommended, was swiftly chosen. Curiously, he was just then on the point of accepting a government appointment to Samoa. He chose the polar regions as against the tropics (so he told me later) because the experience promised to be more novel.

No action could have been more generous nor a swifter cutting of red tape than the gesture of the British and Dominion governments in releasing *Discovery II* for her errand, nor shall I ever forget her commanding officer, Lieut. Nelson, for his splendid sportsmanship. These arrangements were not the work of the moment; the last clinching details were riveted in the radio room of the *Bear of Oakland,* when she was hundreds of miles northeast of Little America, and heavily engaged in the last exploratory campaign of the fall season.

We were none too soon. The relay race run by *Discovery II* and the *Bear* through the gales, and fog and ice of the south polar seas to deliver a doctor to Little America must always be for me one of the dramatic high spots of the second expedition. Death, for perhaps two men, might have been the penalty of failure.

IV

The same day that the *Ruppert* pulled out, the dog teams under Innes-Taylor and the tractors under Demas emptied Pressure Camp. Eighty percent of the stores were then assembled on the summit of West Barrier Cache, and the full resources of the shore party were free to be shaped to the task of transferring from West Barrier Cache to East Barrier Cache, and thence to Little America. Anyhow, our stores were beyond the danger of the decaying bay ice.

By the greatest stroke of luck during the seven days the two ships had lain together they were not once obliged to relinquish their berths. But the movement of ice continued at varying velocities. Floes gently detached themselves and were wafted off. Deep in the pressure you could hear restless submarine grindings and grumblings, heavier crashes as ice structures taxed past endurance let go. Where the Bridge of Sighs lay, the edge of the bay ice folding against the pressure was in a steady, almost perceptible drift toward the sea. The wrenching movement carried the western abutment fifteen feet in a single day. Nearly every twenty-four hours June had to haul the bridge into a

(Photograph by John Dyer)

THE CORNICHE ROAD

Uncharted Seas

The "Bear" Returns

new position.[1] Having to contend with such imponderable forces, the men never truly knew the meaning of restfulness, of security, until Little America was battened down in May.

Thursday, February 6th, they struck their tents at Pressure Camp, and June and his crew moved their headquarters to West Barrier Cache, which became the new nerve center of the shore campaign. Ike Schlossbach, Buckley, Stancliff, McCormick and several other men had already anticipated them. They were comfortably ensconced in a den (appropriately termed Hooligan Heim; in deference to our Norwegian collaborators everything remotely resembling a residence was dignified as *Heim*) which was ingeniously fabricated of food boxes, with celotex strips for a roof. The shack even had a swinging door, and a stove, which was kept alive with loose coal frugally scraped up from the droppings of burst coal bags. The fire gave warmth, and the coffee simmering and beer bottles thawing on the stove made it a grateful oasis for the half-frozen drivers swinging past. The new tents were pitched nearby, with accommodations for twenty-four men, and Petersen set up his radio apparatus for communication with the ship and Little America.

That afternoon Demas successfully navigated the six-ton Cletrac across the Bridge of Sighs and ran it safely through to Little America. The telephone poles fairly doubled under the tractor's weight, but Demas made it—another potential headache averted. Thereafter the Cletrac trafficked between East Barrier Cache and the main base. It was too heavy and too essential to later field operations to be risked among the pressure and crevasses of the Bay. Hauling between three and five tons every journey, that squat, creeping vehicle looked handsomer to me than Pegasus.

With all matters at last in hand, I now resolved to execute a project which I had long since determined upon; notably to take the *Bear* on a dash of exploration along the coast of King Edward VII Land into the northeast. If we shoved off promptly, there was time to do it before the freezing of the Ross Sea and the massing of pack would make the voyage dangerous: plenty of time, too, to allow the *Bear* to return and join in any coöperating action necessary to the relaying of a doctor. So on the morning of the 6th I asked Lieut. English to make preparations for departure that afternoon.

The voyage was a logical rounding out of our previous investigations off the Pacific Quadrant by ship and plane; moreover, I was eager to take the old *Bear* on a last thrust into the unknown. The outward limit of the known coast was only 350 miles northeast of Little America, not quite three days' run for the *Bear* if she were lucky

[1] Morgan, the geologist, measured the movement and found that along the western face of the pressure the ice was moving seaward at the rate of between two and four inches per hour, and at times with much greater velocity.

enough to find open seas. No ship in the past had pushed very far beyond the 151st meridian W.[2] Nasty weather and extraordinarily heavy pack had repulsed every attempted penetration. Three times, in 1929, the *City of New York* of my first expedition had tried to make the break-through, only to be knocked back on her heels. The impenetrable pack for which these seas were fabled, as I have said, was supposed by some to derive from the massing of ice around a theoretical archipelago.

But the *Ruppert's* explorations north of the continent, together with the flights and the soundings of previous expeditions, had indicated the archipelago's unlikelihood; and it seemed to me that a successful excursion in the *Bear* ought to foot up the evidence. Anyhow, the conditions seemed unusually auspicious. The pack we had sighted from the plane during the last flight along the 152nd meridian seemed not too dense for the *Bear*. Nor was it pressure ice—another indication of the absence of land. Either the coast was not so heavily icebound as it had seemed, or else this was an unusually lean ice year. On the face of it, the opportunities seemed just right.

The *Bear,* fortunately, was equipped for a thorough hydrographic survey of the region. Hydrographically, the region northeast of the Bay of Whales was one of the least known, if not *the* least known, of the seas contiguous to the Antarctic continent. That purpose alone would have justified the trip. Eddie Roos, oceanographer and veteran of the first expedition, was in charge of this particular branch of research. On the voyage from New Zealand, he had already run one line of soundings across the Ross Sea—the beginning of a bathymetric profile which would ultimately throw a network of soundings across a large part of it.[3]

Geologist Wade was summoned from Little America with a full-strength dog team, complete trail and camping equipment, two months' rations. It was my intention to put him ashore for geological reconnaissance if we were lucky enough to gain land. George Grimminger of the U. S. Weather Bureau, Haines' assistant, who had come down on the *Bear,* was aboard for meteorological observations.

I also had the idea of taking the auto-gyro aboard for the purpose of brief flights of exploration in the vicinity of the ship, and a radio message was sent to McCormick at Little America, asking him to get

[2] The *Discovery* (1902) and the *Terra Nova* (1910) of Scott's expeditions, the *Nimrod* (1908) of Shackleton's first expedition and the *Kainan Maru* of the Japanese expedition (1912) had all attempted to break through the seas off King Edward VII Land, only to be blocked by consolidated pack.

[3] During her various voyages across the Ross Sea in 1934-1935, the *Bear* ran eight different lines of soundings across the Ross Sea, the most complete bathymetric survey ever made of this little known sea. Four lines of soundings were also run from New Zealand to the Ross Sea.

it ready with all possible dispatch. The great merit of this type of plane, especially for high altitude flights over the ship, must be obvious. It could take off from and land on small ice floes. If the ship were beset the pilot could be sent aloft to scan the pack for the most favorable exit. At the plane's ceiling of 11,000 feet he would have complete and instant vision over pack which the *Bear* might require days to penetrate, and perhaps not be able to breach at all.

However, shortly after luncheon, while we were waiting for McCormick, a sudden heavy jar along the side of the ship brought us all to our feet. Along the whole length of the ship and beyond a slab of ice, a dozen yards wide, had broken out and crushed against the ship. Captain Johansen, who was on watch, sped half a dozen men down the teetering gangplank to cast off the mooring lines. The ship backed out through masses of débris.

The swell was on the rise, and I noticed that everywhere the ice front was disintegrating. In a twinkling all mooring places were destroyed. There was no place where we could safely take aboard the auto-gyro: rather than risk it, or waste time in waiting for better conditions, I cancelled the project. As it was, we had to take Wade's dogs, sledges and rations aboard with handlines, while the ship stood in with her bow nosed against the ice.

At 7:44 P.M. the *Bear* was under weigh. As we passed down the Bay I could make out, with glasses, the heavily loaded teams inching along the rim of the Barrier; and Bowlin and Felter, who were aloft in the Pilgrim on a photographic mission, came down to waggle their wings in a gesture of god-speed.

V

The northeasterly cruise in the *Bear* was one of the most interesting cruises of exploration I have ever made, not only because it was very fruitful, but also because of the circumstances in which it was made. There was a joy and spirit to the *Bear's* attack which were lacking in the *Ruppert's*. The *Bear* was a wooden ship: she was built for ice: ice was her meat. She could hit with both hands where the flimsy *Ruppert* had to wheedle and cajole: she could lower her head and bore in where the *Ruppert* had to turn tail and seek a better 'ole. Therein lay the merit of the honorable and ancient *Bear of Oakland*. And she was worked by a smart crew, too, disciplined, keen and loyal to her officers.

Quitting the Bay of Whales, Lieut. English set course for Cape Colbeck. A good part of the way we had the tall white coast of the Barrier on our right hand. Trim as an English hedge, it rose in places to a height of 150 feet. The first morning out (February 7th) the sea was making: the wind rose to a velocity of 35 miles per hour, and the *Bear* pitched and rolled heavily.

Approaching Cape Colbeck, where the Barrier bulges out before it trends at right angles toward Marie Byrd Land, the ship was held off by an extensive unbroken field of ice. Lieut. English skirted it. Past the heavier ice the ship bore in toward Biscoe Bay. About 25 miles northeast of Colbeck we were astonished to raise a line of icebergs directly across our path. It was the regularity of the line that caught our interest: the bergs were strung out on a north and south line as far as we could see, and so close together that there seemed no passage between them.

Roos's soundings, repeated at five minute intervals, along the ship's track, explained the phenomenon. The tell-tale echoes bouncing from the bottom had found and explored a ridge 45 fathoms deep. The bergs were aground! The shoaling had been hinted by the progression of soundings, a gentle rise, then a steepening. Very likely this ridge is a submarine extension of the Alexandra Mountains of King Edward VII Land. On this ridge the deeper-draft bergs had been caught on either side, to be held captive till disintegration and melting lightened them.

Working through these grounded mountains, the *Bear* steered east, on a course intended to fetch up with the area of open water sighted in the vicinity of Lat. 76° S., Long. 148° W., during the flight of December 5, 1929. By noon of the 8th we attained this point: and with the attainment the *Bear* broke past the record northeastings of the *Discovery* and the *Kainan Maru.*

On this course the ship drew abreast of the wide mouth of Sulzberger Bay, which we had discovered by flight in 1929. To our surprise the Bay, which had then been quite open, was now, though summer was nearly over, completely closed by ice. A solid sheet of bay and shelf ice, miles broad, ran to the coast of Marie Byrd Land.

To be so near the coastal margin of Marie Byrd Land and yet find it walled off by impassable ice, was disappointing. Clearly we were in for a difficult time if we persisted in the easting. It occurred to me that here was a possible explanation why the *Ruppert* and the *Bear* had gained the Ross Sea without meeting pack. This region must be the breeding grounds of much of the Ross Sea Pack. Summer had come and gone, and much of the immense reservoirs which fed and replenished the pack was still rigid. Many of the bays were still frozen in, and the ice still largely riveted to the continental rim.

Nevertheless the *Bear* launched a bold thrust to the east. In thickening ice she bore through several degrees of longitude, until, at 1:30 A.M. on the morning of the 9th, she was stopped in her tracks by consolidated pack. Captain Johansen, scanning the sea from the crow's nest, recommended a northeasterly heading.

On this course the ship, easing, ramming and fishtailing through narrow leads, finally strove to Lat. 75° 06′ S., Long. 148° 08′ W.,

100 miles from the Edsel Ford mountains. Solid pack walled her off again.

The ship drew off to the northwest and at a trifle lower latitude she again threw herself eastward into an obscure tracery of leads.

There on the margin of the shelf ice we had sighted from the air in 1929 the ship was completely blocked by impenetrable pressure ice. The glacierized coast of Marie Byrd Land was dimly visible in the light haze. The peaks of the Edsel Ford Range were only 100 miles away. But in between lay miles upon miles of fast ice, traversed by high pressure ridges, broken by craggy hummocky formations, the most dangerous ice against which you could throw a ship.

I glanced at Captain Johansen.

He shook his head. "Never," he said. "We get stuck for the winter."

So we backed off and retreated northwest and north, having two plans in mind.

First: the ship might be able to make a longer easting at a still lower latitude.

Second: to attempt to bring the ship's maximum northeasting into coincidence with the maximum southing attained by the *William Horlick* on its penetration along the 150th and 152nd meridians. In other words: to run clear to the continental margin the line of exploration and discovery between these meridians which first the *Ruppert*, and then the *William Horlick*, in their double attacks, had driven through the heart of the white lobe of unknown in the Pacific Quadrant.

The ship worked northwestward to the 154th meridian, where again she launched a northeasting.

It was no small task to complete the line.

The ice was severe, much heavier and denser than anything we had seen from the *Ruppert*. As evening came on and the misty sun declined, the low, gray shadows thrown by the upheaved pressure ridges and the gross hummocks gave this frozen sea the hard metallic aspect of moon craters. A host of bergs, many of great size, jostled among shallower formations. In the twilight of the mist the bergs had the dull shine of steel mountains.

The *Bear* made hard going of it. Her bow took a frightful pounding, but she gave as much as she took. The decks trembled to the shocks. You had to keep your senses alert. At the most unexpected moments she would hit hard; the decks would heave and tilt as the bow rode up; and unless you were in a position to grab something handy, you might be knocked off balance. Back again, then, for another try: another shock, the gentle sigh of rending ice. Then: "Steady as you go!" I had brought Ken Rawson with me on account of his knowledge of ice navigation. During our worse times he took his turn in the crow's nest conning the ship through bad pack. Second Officer Davis, though green at this work, did well also.

Roos reported the ocean bottom was dropping to 11,000 feet. Well, that was interesting. It went far towards settling the fate of the archipelago.

At Lat. 73° 22′ S., Long. 149° 34′ W., on the 11th, the carry of the northeasting was spent. The ship was stopped again by shelf ice. Progress eastward was impossible. The *Bear* swung northwest. Gaining the 73rd parallel and holding it she smashed westward to Long. 158° 12′ W.

When the ship cut the 152nd meridian the limit of vision from the *Bear's* crow's nest all but lapped the area we had in view from the bow of the *William Horlick* at the terminus of the flight along that meridian.

The south-seeking corridor of exploration driven by the *Ruppert* and *Condor* and the northeast-seeking corridor opened by the *Bear* had nearly met. For all practical purposes, a through line of discovery had been run along the 152nd meridian from Lat. 64° 40′ (Cook's record southing of 1773) to the Antarctic continent, a distance of 650 nautical miles (747 statute).

The hypothetical archipelago (at least insofar as it might exist west of 140° W.) seemed most unlikely. If an island exists in these seas it must be of negligible size. Roos's soundings showed ocean depths of 12,000 feet.

Now a word about these soundings. The *Bear* was equipped with a fathometer (or sonic sounding unit) for the taking of bathymetric profiles. The velocity of sound traveling in sea water is known: and by casting a sound downward from a ship, picking up the echo and noting the time lapse, it is possible to measure ocean depth. The fathometer is an instrument of four parts—power plant, oscillator, hydrophone and timing device—which combine these functions. Roos's apparatus was neatly arranged in what was called the sounding control room, just off the wardroom. The ship's generators supplied current, which was converted into alternating current by a special generator controlled directly in the room. The oscillator which produces the sound on a set of electro magnets on a tuned diaphragm and the supersensitive microphones of the hydrophones which pick up the sound as it returns from the bottom were both housed on the ship's bottom. Roos had only to press the key to evoke a deep, resonant musical note from the oscillator: out of a humming emptiness, moments later (depending, of course, upon the depths) would rise the very weary echo reflected from the bottom, but yet striking the hydrophones with the clear, clinking impact of a rain-drop on a tin roof. A timing device clocks the lapse within one-hundredth of a second and automatically converts time into meters of depth. It was a fascinating thing to hear and watch, but listening to these tell-tale whispers from the bottom you couldn't help feeling a trifle uncomfortable, the sort of feeling you get when you find yourself near a strange room and hear voices not meant to be heard.

These soundings were taken continuously along the *Bear's* track. As a rule they were taken at hourly intervals (or every 6 or 7 miles, according to the ship's speed). However, while the ship cruised along continental shelf or whenever any irregularity in bottom configuration was detected, they were increased to every five minutes.

As a consequence of the soundings taken on this northeasterly cruise, a substantial revision of the bathymetry of the seas off King Edward VII Land seems in order. On future maps the width of the continental shelf must be reduced. The ocean depths were considerably greater than had been theorized, on the continental shelf especially.

VI

From her westward thrust to Lat. 73° S., Long. 158° W., the *Bear* turned south, on February 12th, for Little America. Came now the most difficult phase of the voyage. The ice ahead became hummocky, much too heavy for the ship. We veered eastward, hoping to regain the out track and retreat as we had come. But that way was also closed. The ice had closed in around the ship, and, for a while, it looked as though we were trapped. The ship steamed and twisted in every direction, like a bird dog frantically trying to pick up a scent.

At 11 P.M. on the 13th the ship was critically beset. Pressure ice 60 feet thick, misshapen and upended, was working around her on the current—the wickedest ice I have ever seen in either the north or south polar regions. That night our spirits just about scraped bottom. It was too late in the season for comfort. Pack is an unpredictable thing. It has a queer mechanism of its own. Sometimes it will lie unchanged for days, heavy and stagnant. Or again it may suddenly begin to stir under mysterious and remote agitations, separating and expanding, creating broad waterways and leads through previously impregnable ice, with a general loosening and slackness as of decay.

But we were neither in the position nor the mood for waiting it out. Too much of a chance that a freeze-up would set the ice in a consolidated pack, perhaps imprison the ship. Moreover, *Discovery II* had advised by radio she would put out from Dunedin in the morning with the doctor on board, and would meet the *Bear* in the Ross Sea.

Captain Johansen, his hawk-like, weather-beaten face dark with worry, went into the crow's nest to direct the struggle to extricate the ship. You've got to keep your wits about you in pack. It can't be taken by assault; the *Bear's* pygmy engines couldn't prevail for a moment against such ice. What Johansen was looking for was the one weak place: an embrasure into which the ship could throw her bulk and where the floes had enough water behind them to give a little before her. He finally found it.

South of us, beyond a belt of thick ice, was a welcome horizon of water sky.

With just enough room to maneuver and get run on her, the ship charged in, jamming the shoulder of her forefoot against the leeward floe. A gap was opened: not very much, but enough to whet our hopes. The ship backed off, drove in again full speed, charging and fish-tailing, throwing the full weight of her charge against the lee floe. The moment way wore off her, she was withdrawn and launched again. I don't imagine that in her 60 years of service the white polar bear that is the ship's figurehead ever bit into more ice than it got on the morning of February 14th, 1934. She responded beautifully to every call made upon her.

Eventually she broke through. The wedge widened enough to let her slip into loose pack beyond, then finally she gained open water. I cannot say too much for the way Lieut. English and Captain Johansen handled the ship in the ice.

Pressing on full speed, we steamed for Little America, passing between the portals of the Bay of Whales at 6 A.M., February 15th.

VII

Throughout this voyage I was in daily communication with Commodore Gjertsen in the *Ruppert,* bound for New Zealand. I was gratified to learn that Captain Verleger was much improved (though ill health presently compelled him to resign his command and return to the States) and that the ship had emerged unscathed, except for the loss of her railings, through a storm of hurricane force. With waves breaking over her boat deck, she lay for a whole day in the trough of the sea, not having power to bring the head around (though in ballast, she was empty of cargo and therefore riding high) and was blown several hundred miles off her course before she could resume her northing. She reached Dunedin early in March.

Chapter VII

THE BOOM CITY

I

I RETURNED from the *Bear's* northeastern cruise to find Little America once more established as the capital city of Antarctica. It was a grand sight to travel down the Barrier rim and see the reborn city rising—the rectangles of the new buildings emerging in dark outline against the snow, the new tunnels reaching between the shacks, the mounds of gear steepening, and already in place the first of the diamond-shaped antennae, which would make it possible for us to talk, as easily as one could cast a cry over one's shoulder, to Buenos Aires, Honolulu, San Francisco, New York, London.

One saw taking form in the glittering white vaccum one of the most remarkable cities on the face of the earth—a city which would boast, among other possessions, of electric light and power, a complete broadcasting and field communications plant, a well-equipped aviation service enlisting four modern planes and skilled personnel, various machine shops, four tractors, nearly 150 dogs, a first-class meteorological station, a scientific staff and laboratory equipped to delve into twenty-two branches of science, a dairy plant with four head of cattle, adequate medical facilities, a well-stocked galley, library, a meteor observatory, even a motion picture theater wired for sound.

Eight new structures were in the process of building, a Mess Hall, Science Hall, Dr. Poulter's meteor observatory, cow barn, the radio shack which would house the radio unit and their rather extensive apparatus, the Kohler power plant, Dr. Bramhall's magnetic station, and the small domicile which Noville and Innes-Taylor had built for themselves. None of these buildings was quite finished. But Little America was taking root. It was rising. In the teeth of blizzards and cold it was growing like a boom town.

In overcoming the great obstacles confronting it, the expedition had demonstrated its inherent solidarity and self-reliance. With so many operations afoot, the leader couldn't possibly supervise every situation. Individual initiative and aggressiveness were essential. These the leader could encourage, but not create. In the struggle for survival it must have sometimes appeared to those in the ruck that the expedition's policy was to let the Devil take the hindmost. Yet out of the clutter and chaos, out of the confusion of personalities and talents, out of the small vexations and jealousies, out of the blinding white nightmare of unloading, out of the brutal physical labor and hardships, something hard and fine and spirited—that rhythmical purpose which is the *esprit de corps* of a polar expedition—had been crystallized.

It was proof that the expedition was on an even keel. And knowing this it was a lot easier for me, a month hence, to make the decision which would isolate me from the expedition for the duration of the winter night. Had I not had this confidence in the common sense and integrity of the expedition, such a decision could never have been made. No leader would dare leave exposed to the weakness-searching pathology of the long winter night an expedition which had not found itself.

Another thing: on the morning that I traveled up from the *Bear* I saw ahead of me three tractors crawl out of West Barrier Cache with the last cargoes of stores still on the far side of the Bay. Every ounce of it—food, clothing, coal, lumber, gasoline and general supplies—was either at East Barrier Cache or in Little America; West Barrier Cache and Pressure Camp were swept clean as a Dutch kitchen. No more the exhausting transit of the pressure. That purgatory had been requited. From East Barrier Cache to Little America was only a mile and a half, a down-hill haul, a blessed glide. How does it go? . . . and *Stout Cortez . . . upon a peak in Darien. . . .* Thus magically revealed from the summit of the last depot were the shining vistas of Little America.

Fatigue-lined faces, eyes reddened by sleeplessness, hoarse voices and frost-bitten cheeks, torn and oil-stained windproofs—all these things eloquently bespoke the galling ordeal. But even without these unbidden tell-tales a stranger might have guessed it from the trail alone. In the splintered, sagging bridges; in the broken crevasses and the flurries of footprints around them; in the snow blocks heaped around the hairpin turns, the story was clearly written. The tractors had ripped the trail to pieces. On the ridge crests the treads had ground down to solid blue ice; the troughs were morasses of soft, deep snow. For two whole days, Innes-Taylor told me, he had been obliged to suspend all dog transport until cold weather hardened the trail. Innumerable cracks and crevasses opened in the trail, which had to be filled with snow packed down from on top, to let the dog teams and tractors through. The game was not without its thrills. Healey's team of seven dogs disappeared entirely before his eyes; a simple sea-going man, he thought he was bewitched until he looked down and saw the dogs wrangling in their harnesses and a fifty-foot abyss where he had almost hourly traversed a surface as seemingly trustworthy as the asphalt of Fifth Avenue.

Such incidents became commonplace. The heavy tractors literally had to claw their way through the bottleneck. Roofed crevasses which were strong enough to accommodate dog teams broke through under the cars, and for a while, until they got hardened to it, the drivers drove with one hand on the wheel, the other on the safety lanyard on the door, and their hearts in their mouths. Fortunately, these crevasses (later on, they were to come upon crevasses through which the *Ruppert* could have steamed) were rather narrow, rarely more than four or five feet wide. It was just the nuisance of digging the cars out, of waiting for a passing shipmate to lend a hand.

How many times June and his men had to move the Bridge of Sighs he does not remember. "I lost count," he said simply, "but it seemed as though it had to be done every time I tried to get a bit of sleep." At least once, sometimes twice a day, the seaward drift of the ice, yielding to the enormous pressures building up from behind, would wrench the bridge from its westward abutment. The bridge was the key to Little America, the fatal thread through the labyrinth. And to defend and maintain the continuity of transport June and his crew would come out on the double quick with ice axes, crowbars, peaveys and shovels.

Nor is there any way of telling how many times the tractors and dog teams made the passage. No one kept records. There was no time for that. The dog drivers called it Misery Trail. Certainly several thousand trips were made. Considering the total tonnage moved and the average weight of the loads, there couldn't have been less.

Fri., Feb. 16, 11:20 P.M.

Today was declared a holiday for all hands. We can't easily spare it—so many things still undone!—but the men deserve it. More than that, they absolutely need it. The expedition has been driving at top speed for a month now, with no let-up. This brief respite is the least gratitude I can show.

In addition to the completion of the camp, the following projects must be launched at the earliest possible moment:

(1) Start of the Fall Southern Party under command of Captain Innes-Taylor: function—to advance food depots 200 miles south for the use of the spring exploring parties.

(2) Organization of the tractor division for a departure with the stores for Advance Base, the meteorological station which we shall establish on the Ross Shelf Ice and occupy throughout the winter night.

(3) A comprehensive seal-hunt. (Dr. Perkins and Lindsey have to date killed only 200 seals. We need at least 700 to provide the dogs with enough food to carry them through the winter.)

(4) Inauguration of the fixed scientific program. (Haines and Grimminger have already commenced their weather observations; Dr. Bramhall and Zuhn are constructing a new tunnel system for magnetic observations.)

During the day I had various conferences with June, Innes-Taylor and Demas over the most effective methods of prosecuting the two fall journeys. One insurmountable obstacle stands in the way of an early start—the need of maintaining all transport close at hand until Little America is secure for the winter. To send dogs, tractors and men into the field while ice conditions are critical and while the bulk of our stores are still out of reach would be folly. On this we are all agreed.

On the face of it, we must radically revamp our plans. I doubt very much if the Southern Party (which will be entirely a dog sledging affair) will be able to get off before the end of the month. The tractors (though June and Demas are more optimistic) aren't likely to get under way much before the middle of March. I had hoped for an earlier start.

Well, there's no use weeping over spilt milk. Considering the ghastly chore we had unloading ship, we're lucky to be as well off as we are. . . .

II

I was troubled; I admit it frankly. In any Antarctic operation you are never sure where you stand from hour to hour. Our situation was akin to that of a juggler with half a dozen balls in the air: one bad miscalculation, and the whole glittering edifice is apt to come tumbling down. All our resources were engaged; we had practically no reserves. And now a new threat insidiously intruded.

Shortly after I returned to the main base, a quick survey of local ice conditions persuaded me to the belief that Little America itself was in jeopardy.

During the ten days I had been at sea aboard the *Bear* the outrush of bay ice had persisted. The *Bear* herself was driven from her mooring a few hours after she tied up. A V-shaped lane of open water, the apex of which extended almost abreast of the abandoned Pressure Camp, had crept deep into the bay ice. One tip of the V rested on the north cape of Ver-Sur-Mer Inlet. From Little America one could see open water just beyond the pressure ridges bulging across the mouth of the Inlet. With the cementum of bay ice behind it gone, the pressure was loosely hung and sagging, and therefore at the mercy of the swell. It heaved and groaned as the swell sucked at its basement. Dr. Perkins remarked that the bloody pools marking the troughs in which he had killed seals just a week before had been flung up and tilted twenty feet or more. This will convey an idea of the forces at work.

With the interposed bay ice and pressure disintegrating, it looked as if the thin sheet of ice in Ver-Sur-Mer Inlet might go next. For the counterpoised forces were diminishing. The sea was creeping into Little America's front yard. And Little America was a house built on a raft. The sheet of ice on which it rested floated on 2,000 feet of water.

But what made the situation ominous was the discovery that wide looping cracks entirely encircled Little America. The cracks were not continuous lines, but a development of numerous progressive fractures. The first crack, an incipient crevasse, began in the vicinity of the north cape of the Inlet; it followed the lip of the Inlet eastward, passing Little America to the northward, and about a half a mile west of the camp joined a maze of cracks running in all directions. South of Little America ran a second cleft, almost parallel to the first, the western foot of which, like the other, touched open water. Drift had sealed these fissures, but when you scuffed your foot through the snow bridges you uncovered an opening from six to ten inches wide, which descended sheer to hard, blue-green ice. Ever so lightly, for you had to watch steadily to mark the movement, the lips of these fractures rose and fell, in an interval corresponding with that of the ocean swell. During the early morning of the 17th I was awakened in my bunk by a definite settling of the Barrier, as if the earth's crust had suddenly settled.

One fact was certain: the sheet of ice on which Little America was situated was definitely separated from the main barrier mass. The fanning cracks and the movement of the ice on the swell were tangible proof. Little America was a potential iceberg.

No inspired imagination is required to envisage the frightful consequences that might flow from this situation. The danger of a calving iceberg violently whisking the base to sea had always been recognized as the great, unpredictable risk of a Barrier base. Shackleton recognized it: the vast changes he had seen in this same Bay of Whales in 1908 had persuaded him to seek surer ground for his winter base.[1] Amundsen recognized the danger, but was able to establish his base farther inland than ours, due to the fact that the bay ice was nearly all out the year he arrived.[2] We also recognized it on the first expedition—more keenly, perhaps, than we ever admitted,—for the cruelest and the most effective practical joke of the whole winter night was the watchman's vivid cry that the Barrier had broken. Never were buildings more hastily evacuated; never had the Indoor Explorers reached fresh air more rapidly, dressing as they flew; and never were men angrier at being taken in. I can't say that I blamed them. No one who has seen the leviathan flat-topped bergs of the South Pacific Ocean, wrenched from Barrier coast like that upon which Little America rested, will ever be wholly convinced that it's the safest residence in the world.

So I had ample reason to be concerned. Still, I didn't wish to appear an alarmist, and I found that but few of the new men realized our predicament. Too many vital matters were hanging fire to intrude a disquieting factor which might mess up everything. Poulter, June,

[1] Shackleton, *Heart of the Antarctic,* i., 74-76.

[2] Amundsen, *The South Pole,* i., 49. A most interesting discussion of why he cast in his lot with a Barrier Base and, in light of Poulter's subsequent findings by seismic soundings, a keen prophecy.

Noville, Haines, Demas, Siple, Petersen and I had a quiet talk over the situation. The risk was admitted; but it was decided not to let it dominate the operations. We should wait and see. The next fortnight would hold the balance, one way or another. Either the increasing cold (the minimum temperatures, during the early mornings, were now dipping into the minus twenties) would weld the ice sheet together, or else the dispersion of ice would presently attain such dimensions as to recommend a definite set of tactics.

As a precautionary measure, it was decided to establish a tentative reserve cache on the high barrier about a mile southeast of Little America and about two miles east of East Barrier Cache. This site, the highest ground immediately within our reach, was selected because it seemed the most likely to survive a heavy movement of ice. Three tents were immediately dispatched to this cache, and under June's direction the tractor men on February 18th started hauling to it the food, clothing, gasoline and other stores in East Barrier Cache.

The emergency cache was called Retreat Camp. At one time, when the movement of ice was at its peak, we rather fancied that Retreat Camp would become the new headquarters of the expedition.

Thus, with this incalculable threat wavering like the sword of Damocles over our heads, we went about the daily tasks: on the one hand, strengthening and fortifying against the rigors of the winter night this alternative camp on the high ridge to the southeast; on the other hand, calmly proceeding with the reoccupation of Little America, nailing and hammering the new buildings together, and making ready for the departure of the two major field parties.

Captain Innes-Taylor, already in charge of dog teams, was promoted to chief of trail operations, in which capacity he was made responsible for the drafting of a campaign which would make it possible for these parties to achieve their ends in the most effective way. A difficult assignment. It called for careful planning and organization at a period in expedition affairs when conditions were scarcely congenial for either planning or organization.

Practically all transport units required for the southern operations were still wholly occupied with the movement of stores. Men and dogs were worn out, the tractors were decidedly in need of a thorough overhaul, sledges and trail gear had taken terrible punishment, and vital equipment was hopelessly scattered thither and yon. Altogether it was a mean job.

A semblance of order was gradually imparted to preparations. The two sailmakers, Kennedy of the *Ruppert* and Miller of the *Bear,* were put to work sewing the necessary tents, windproof clothing, medical kits, sledge tanks, etc. Demas and his tractor crew worked over their cars at night, behind a rude shelter constructed of the sides of crates in which the cars had been shipped. The carpenters, Cox and Tinglof, took over the broken sledges and renewed splintered runners and bridges. Having no other work shop, they dragged the sledges into the New Mess Hall and worked there between meals. Corey was burrowing into the scattered caches in search of missing trail equipment.

I still wonder how it was ever done. In February Little America was a mad house. Nothing was where you could lay hands on it. Men were no less elusive. Some were still tenting at East Barrier Cache. Even so, there wasn't enough shelter at Little America to house the rest, the new buildings being unfinished. Men were sleeping in tractor cabs, in the cabins of the airplanes, on the floors of uncompleted buildings, with fantastic burlap hangings to shield them from the wind.

On February 17th the wind shifted from east to south, and blew steadily for five days. In clouds of drift, penetrating, hateful and stinging, the outside work went on.

III

Shortly before midnight, February 18th, Lieut. English steamed out of the Bay of Whales in the *Bear* for the rendezvous with *Discovery II,* which on February 14th had put out from Dunedin with the doctor aboard. In the Ross Sea they entered extensive fields of pancake ice, indicative of winter's approach. Lieut. English reported by radio next day:

> "Sky overcast and wind increased to force six from southeast. Seas very high and rough and many icebergs buffeting about. Much water shipped aboard, immediately icing up decks. Snowing. At noon about 97 miles from Little America. Average speed 7.5 knots."

Solicited as we were by our own grave problems, still we followed with ever-rising interest the *Bear's* gallant race against time and darkness. In the three-score years she contended with polar seas the "White Angel of the Arctic" never ran a finer race.

Tuesday the 20th the *Bear* met the pack at Lat. 74° 30′, Long. 165° W.—heavy fields of it, with numerous bergs prowling the seas. In severe snow squalls the ship worked westward, with Watson, the radio operator, in constant communication with *Discovery II,* likewise feeling her way through dirty weather north of the pack.

The squalls deepened into a howling snowstorm. Visibility was reduced almost to a ship's length. The *Bear* heaved toward the rendezvous. In the evening of the 21st, at the northern edge of the pack—at Lat. 72° 05′ S., Long. 171° W., about 400 miles above Little America—the ships met. The dramatic circumstances of the meeting were told by Lieut. English in his report on the 22nd:

> "We had been exchanging positions and radio finder bearings every hour yesterday afternoon until the ships were within thirty

> miles of each other, then every ten minutes. Weather abominable, strong southerly winds, thick snowstorm, heavy pack ice, numerous bergs, very low visibility. Ships laid smoke screen, fired bombs and rockets, blew whistles at frequent intervals to insure contact under conditions. Kept altering course to approach on radio bearings at 1940 (7:40 P.M.) *Discovery* sighted *Bear* on port bow, radioed contact and blew whistle simultaneously.
>
> "Both ships swung in close aboard, then *Bear* swung head up into wind and stopped. *Discovery* then approached on parallel course and was skillfully placed alongside by Lieut. A. L. Nelson. A difficult maneuver on account of heavy sea running, strong winds, bad visibility and thick ice. Heavy fenders kept ships apart, though rolling heavily, and crews immediately jumped to task of transferring supplies."

About noon, February 22nd, dipping their colors in friendly acknowledgment, the ships cast off, *Discovery II* to pursue her Antarctic survey, the *Bear* to run the last and telling lap through the Ross Sea. Aboard the *Bear* was Dr. Potaka, the new medical officer, six tons of food and general supplies and 3,000 gallons of gasoline which Lieut. Nelson had generously offered to relay at the same time. (On account of the difficulties of unloading, the gasoline consumption of the tractors was far in excess of original estimates; and at the last moment we had made arrangements in New Zealand for this quantity to increase our reserves.)

The evening of the day the *Bear* plunged south for the Bay of Whales the sun set for the first time—a gorgeous burst of florid flame in a white chalice, long shadows reaching in the lee of every raised thing, and the opposite sky trembling with delicate rose-colored lights. Winter was coming on. With double-reefed stormsails and boilers under full steam, the *Bear* rammed into heavy seas.

Friday the 23rd the wind stopped blowing at Little America. During the early morning the temperature dropped to —24°. In the still air, with the seas quiet, a four-inch scum of ice sealed the Bay of Whales. With Dr. Poulter I traveled in a tractor along the east rim of the Bay, looking for a possible mooring place for the *Bear* in the event the freezing of the Bay should make it impossible for her to regain her old berth.

Once, while we were standing near the tractor, there welled up in the northeast the strangest sound I have ever heard—a vast, confused sound, like the roar of a great waterfall. It lasted a few seconds, then stopped. Though it seemed close by, Poulter and I searched the Barrier for six miles, but found no trace of the immense destruction that must have taken place. Somewhere a mighty slab of Barrier had calved. That alone could have produced such a sky-filling sound. Just a few days before Joe Hill from his tractor had seen a two-mile berg break off from the west wall of the Bay, near West Cape, and

The Bridge of Sighs

The First Days of the Occupation

Frontier Settlement

(Photograph by Joseph A. Pelter)

Main Street, Little America

float out to sea. Where before it had a straight bold line the east wall of the Barrier was terribly broken and jagged. A bight, three-quarters of a mile deep, in which the *Ruppert* had sought lee in January had entirely disappeared. The fifty-foot cliffs of ice which had walled in the bight had vanished as though erased. Poulter commented on how pale and light the sea smoke was. That meant that north of us the Ross Sea was freezing.

The *Bear* came on. That evening Lieut. English advised that at noon he was 240 miles off Little America, making 6.5 knots:

> "Bucking strong southeast gale and high seas. Seas breaking aboard freeze at once. Decks and rigging a mass of ice, but crew working hard chopping ice off ship. If *Bear* can fight her way south at present speed will reach L. A. early Sunday morning."

Saturday. Clear and cold at Little America. A party skied down to the Bay of Whales and found it fast with new ice. The quiet sea and air had done it. Now we prayed for wind and sea to break it up. Saturday afternoon a low bank of sea smoke crept over the Bay, shifting and restive, sullen and threatening against the white serenity of the Barrier cliffs.

That night Lieut. English reported:

> "Noon position 76° 33′ S., 167° 46′ W. Made average speed of 5.3 since noon yesterday, fighting way south in teeth of raging southerly gale, mountainous seas, snowstorm. Shipping much water which ices up ship at once. At noon 125 miles from L. A., but if can keep up battle will arrive Sunday afternoon. Large bergs blown before gale a constant menace to ship, particularly during night watches, which now quite dark. Firemen in stokehold doggedly keeping up steam in boiler while frequently thrown from feet by violent motion of the ship."

This same night I recorded in my diary that it would be touch and go whether the *Bear* made it or failed.

Sunday came in clear and cold, with a minimum temperature of —28°. In the morning we made radio contact with the *Bear*. Lieut. English reported:

> "From 0300 until 0600 (3:00 until 6:00 A.M.) fought way south foot at a time with ship giving utmost for a distance of three miles through very hard, newly-frozen close pack. We are twenty miles from Bay of Whales by DR (dead reckoning). Visibility poor, sky overcast, air temperature +2 degrees. At 0630 ice over six inches thick, no leads visible, nothing but one solid sheet as far as can be seen in all directions except thin dark pencil of wake which is also rapidly freezing."

A few minutes later he advised:

> "Ship stopped dead and unable to make another foot in this direction. I am endeavoring to get steerage way and on a northerly heading so as to fight way to open water in that direction. Johansen states this ice much worse than that experienced in 1929 and believes no ship could penetrate it. Pack is so heavy and widespread that I doubt if anything less than a northerly gale could break it up, and a gale from that direction would be hazardous to this ship. This command is unwilling to give up the attainment of any assigned mission, yet it is humanly impossible to get a ship beyond our farthest south."

At that juncture one of the electric generators we were using broke down, and for a few hours we were out of communication with the *Bear*. These Kohler lighting plants, donated by Governor Kohler of Wisconsin, however, held up superbly under the most rigorous possible conditions.

You can imagine our mood at Little America: the *Bear* not merely blocked off from us, but definitely in serious danger of not being able to fight her way out; perhaps beset thirty miles or so north of Little America, her crew ill-prepared to withstand the hardships incident to such a siege; Little America overcrowded with men slated to return on her; no doctor—all the makings of a disaster. The men who had been told they would return to New Zealand left off their packing. A fair chance now they would not have to leave at all. With the incredible velocity that bad news always gathers, word of the blocking of the ship flew through the camp, passed among the dog-drivers and tractor men plying between the caches, reached the men working in the outlying caches. Sobering news. For once there was little jesting.

Siple returned from a ski trip to the Bay of Whales. Heavy sea smoke, black as a Newfoundland Banks fog, lay over the Bay; but through the rifts he caught sight of lanes of open water. He saw a school of Killer Whales, too, a reliable sign of open water. The Bay of Whales, at least, was open again.

I asked McCormick to make the auto-gyro ready for flight. The tiny, spidery vehicle was dug out of the drift, and the engine heated. Shortly before noon McCormick and I took off for a survey of the Bay. Visibility was poor, much too poor for an extended flight; but by flying low through the sea smoke across the mouth of the Bay we saw enough to verify Siple's observations. Tide-rips had opened the ice along the Barrier.

If the Bear could extricate herself from her morning position, she could get through. When I landed I learned that Lieut. English (our radio unit was then in half-hourly communication with the *Bear*) had battered his way out ten miles to the northwest. His noon report said:

"Am hove to in open water among loose pack 30 miles NNW of Bay of Whales. Johansen and I agree that everything will be done to get doctor ashore. Hence will remain here until visibility improves, then will make repeated attempts on different meridians, including Discovery Inlet. . . . Of course this operation costly to us in fuel and time, and in view of pack stretched across Ross Sea to the northward we face a most difficult task in effecting our retreat at this late date. Submit that it would be dangerous to personnel this vessel and to relief of L. A. next spring if *Bear* were to be frozen in. This we will exercise all precaution to avoid."

The possibility of sending the *Bear* to Discovery Inlet, about 90 miles to the west, on the chance the Inlet might still be free of ice had been discussed. At least they might be able to land the doctor. We could pick him up either by plane (if weather were good) or by dog-team.

At 2:30 P.M. Lieut. English, encouraged by the news the Bay was open, started in again. Slick and dark as obsidian the new ice sealed the Ross Sea. It was harder to punch (English said later) than older and heavier pack. Even the densest pack is usually somewhat broken up and spaced by narrow leads. A ship can force it, or ease around it. But to new ice there is adhesive and rubbery bending rather than splitting at the impact of the ship's bow. The ship had to throw her full weight against it, punching a path, foot by foot. The cold air wafting across the roiled open water in her wake condensed as sea smoke; and instantly the wake commenced to freeze.

Afternoon flowed into twilight: still the outcome dawdled. The departing men lingered over half-filled dunnage bags, chatting, smoking, thinking much.

At quarter to midnight this message leapt through the pall of sea smoke covering the Bay:

"We are following West Barrier. Now two miles south inside Bay. What was open water this morning is now four inches of ice. We are doing our best to get as far south as old bay ice (in the vicinity of *Bear's* most recent berth) as you suggest. Visibility poor due to heavy frost smoke, hence cannot see old bay ice, but at present rate of progress ought to reach it about 0300 (3:00 A.M.)

An eleventh hour reprieve!

IV

Came now what was for many of the departing men (and no less for me) the bitterest hour of the expedition: the final weeding out of the Ice Party. Perhaps this phrase is objectionable, for the process wasn't so much a weeding out as of merely saying *no* to those we couldn't keep on the ice. It wasn't necessary to tell men they were assigned to the Ice Party and would therefore stay. They knew that already. The others had been told they would return with the *Bear*.

Now a great deal of nonsense has been written about the peculiar psychological dangers of the polar winter night, and the searching examination to which candidates for the wintering party are submitted prior to selection. Of course these psychological hazards exist, and care must be taken in the selection of men.

But the business isn't half so mysterious as superstition would have you believe. In my delvings in this particular branch of human psychology, as in all my other interests, I always strove for simplicity, common sense and faith. Above everything else—*faith.* I've had wide enough experience in the choosing of men for hazardous jobs to know that human behavior is unpredictable for the reason that the sets of circumstances in which it operates are also unpredictable: and that no wise man is so poor a judge of himself as to dare to call himself a good judge of men. Of a few men you can be absolutely sure. They are born with stability and loyalty. Some men are doubtful, either because of the absence of these qualities or because of other qualities which are bent to mischief. Occupying the far-flung middle ground is the remarkable amorphous aggregation of the average. Humans have baffled me no little. Of course, I have always had some men who from first to last try to tear things down; that I always expect. But I learned to credit the great majority of men who served under me at least with latent instincts toward honesty, honor and the other central Christian principles. These qualities, I have found, will generally triumph over the moral and emotional strain of a winter night or any other polar circumstance. Hence I make no pretentious claim to a unique power, such as the laying on of hands, by virtue of which obscure men are magically transformed into angels who will withstand, with unblemished record, the oppressions of the long winter night. I mostly hope for the best.

It's puzzling, but nearly all of them want to stay. I don't mean the scientists, the aviators, the specialists and the like. Why they are willing to accept the hardships and the risks is perfectly obvious: a sincere desire to explore little-known and exciting phenomena, to perfect themselves in the remote applications of their sciences; perhaps a touch of romanticism partly accounts for their appearance on a polar expedition's roster. For them at least there may be some tangible reward: a thesis, a monograph which may be the last word on the subject, perhaps a Ph.D. and a faculty appointment, or even a measure of fame.

But for the rest, the men whose only qualifications are willingness and a certain handiness in small tasks, there can be no lasting reward —only a long, unmitigated drudgery. Yet they wanted to stay, begged to be allowed to stay, as if a year in the caverns of Little America were the most desirable experience on earth. A variety of eloquent reasons were advanced, and I guessed a few that were secret. Two men wanted to get away from marriages which had turned sour. One, as I said earlier, was a fugitive from justice. Others were just drifters, men of certain general abilities, but who somehow failed to find a stable niche in civilization. One who had slipped from a high position sought the discipline and hardship as a means of accomplishing the rehabilitation of himself. Others, well-educated and gently born, with good families behind them and good jobs ahead of them, wanted the experience for its own sake. Still others didn't know exactly what they wanted: they just wanted to stay. Somewhere in their subconscious minds, I think, was the feeling that a polar expedition, the intimate experience of a polar camp, would lift them from mediocrity, would forever set them up as men who had done something *different*. In small towns that would go a long way.

What made it hard to say *no* was that so many of these fellows were worthy. They had worked hard and given a great deal to the expedition. As much as the others, they had created Little America. On my first Antarctic Expedition I could not find a place on the ice for one of my best men. His disappointment was so keen his mind became seriously affected.

Unhappily, there wasn't room for all of them. Food, stores, clothing and quarters were limited. The key jobs, such as radio, aviation, research, mechanical and executive assignments, required educated talents; these posts were assigned before we left the States. As for the dog-drivers and tractor mechanics, they had pretty well demonstrated their individual qualifications during the turmoil of unloading. Better than I, the killing daily grind had singled out the fittest. With these places filled, few jobs were left. These I tried to man carefully, taking into account a man's handiness (in a polar camp a handy man is the equivalent of three ordinary men), his service to the expedition, his spirit, and how well he fitted into the emotional tone of the expedition. You don't want a bad egg, and you certainly don't want a prima donna. In a polar camp both are equally offensive, one to the nose and the other to the intelligence. I must point out, in fairness, that many of the most capable men had important positions with the ships from which they couldn't be spared.

Yet sentiment as much as judgment bent the choice in more than one instance. The Ice Party, as it was finally constituted at 6:30 A.M. on February 27th, numbered 56 men, whereas when I left the States I had made up my mind it would not exceed 40. In addition to Dr. Potaka, who was arriving on the *Bear,* I kept two New Zealanders: Bob Young, retired torpedo man of the Royal Navy, quick with the practical knowledge of a first-class seaman, who had served on my first expedition and impressed me then, as he does now, as one of the squarest men I have ever known; and Bernard Fleming, whom

Dr. Poulter was anxious to have attached to the scientific staff. I kept the artist, David Paige, because I thought his paintings would be worth-while. Several others were retained because I had no other way of showing my gratitude for what they had done.

At the last moment another factor helped to throw the balance in favor of a number of deserving men. Captain English's reports strongly indicated that the *Bear* might have considerable difficulty extricating herself from the Ross Sea. She might be beset. Therefore I didn't wish to over-burden her with personnel. It was better that they should remain at Little America than perhaps become a tax upon the *Bear's* slender resources. This cold-blooded calculation had to be made.

Hence there were 56 men at Little America through the polar winter of 1934-35—the largest party ever to winter in the Antarctic. I credit myself with no generous motives for its size. It was the wisest mistake I ever made. Without the extra man-power we could never have done the things we did. For the expedition was never idle. It was in high gear all the time. So many activities were under way, so many parties were in the field that we had to make a wall map to keep track of their daily movements.

V

While the *Bear* crept unseen through the sea smoke toward the edge of the ice in the Bay of Whales, Little America left off everything for the ceremony of raising the last gangplank to civilization. Last letters were hastily postscripted, sealed and stamped. In the new Mess Hall June read off the names of the men (mostly crew of either the *Bear* or *Ruppert*) ordered to return. He finished crisply, "Take mattresses, blankets and personal gear. Leave your snow glasses for the Ice Party." We were short of snow glasses. Many had been broken or lost.

Outside, the tractor which would ferry them to the *Bear* was waiting, its engine missing in the cold. The twelve who were leaving hopped aboard, with friendly farewells and goodlucks. There was just one unseemly episode. One man, returned for chronic drunkenness, attempted to commit a minor sabotage as a kind of revenge because he did not want to go back. Somebody brought him up sharp, and that was the end of that. Hunched and silent, the man left without looking back. I really felt sorry for him. He was not a bad sort at bottom; only intensely anxious to stay in spite of there being no reward for him in doing so.

The sky was partly overcast, but where the sun lay submerged below the horizon pale, eruptive colors climbed the lower sky. Over the Bay the sea smoke was gathered like a truculent cloud. Ragged edges of it washed over the Barrier. Above the air was clear. But down in it Lieut. English had visibility of half a ship's length.

June counted heads again, then swung aboard the tractor. "All accounted for," he said to Skinner, the driver. "Let's go."

The tractor rolled off, with half a dozen dog teams flying in its wake. Down in the pressure all hands off to move the Bridge of Sighs. It had been twisted twenty-five feet out of position. On this side of the crevasse near Pressure Camp the tractor was stopped for good. The bridge which had formerly spanned it was gone—taken apart and removed to Little America where the telephone poles were raised for the directive antennae. But the lighter, flimsy bridge which the dog teams had used was still there. The dog sledges rocketed across. They would relay the stores aboard the *Bear* to the tractors: the tractors would haul into Little America. A game they knew by heart.

The *Bear* was already alongside the ice when the first teams got there. Her tall sticks and yards, her rigging and stays were solidly encased in ice. The bowsprit stays were swollen to treble their size.

"We got here," said Lieut. English, "but we don't know how we're going to get out."

Lieut. English and Captain Johansen had both been on the bridge twenty-six hours. Johansen said little. He was a man of few words. A shy greeting for a moment lighted up the cavernous shadows in his lined and weathered face, then he turned to direct the mooring.

The stores she had taken off *Discovery II* were stowed on the *Bear's* decks. The moment the ship was made fast Lieut. English began unloading, the men carrying the boxes of general stores down the gangplank to the waiting dog teams drawn up alongside. The heavy gasoline drums were rolled down. Wasted minutes meant thicker ice to overcome.

"This new ice at the edge of the Ross Sea is tough enough," Lieut. English said, "but the old ice 200 miles to the north is a damned sight worse. The same sort of heavy pack we got into on the northeastern cruise. Maybe it's the same ice. Maybe it has drifted over. No way of telling, of course. But we're going to need the breaks to get through."

Exactly eight hours after she touched the ice—at 8:30 A.M., February 26th—the *Bear* had discharged her cargo, over 21 tons of it, including the gasoline. There was a last toast in the low, smoke-filled wardroom to "A Speedy Northing."

"Let her go aft," Second Mate Davis shouted from the poop deck. The dog-drivers slipped the toggles. The *Bear* eased forward to take the strain off the bow line.

"Let her go forward," shouted Lieut. English from the bridge. The bow line was slipped. Clear, now, the *Bear* backed out and stood off for the northern run.

The men on the ice lingered only long enough to see her go. Little by little the sea smoke claimed her. Higher and higher it rose along the ship till only the topmasts were visible, vaguely and indefinitely floating long after the ship had been enveloped. For once Lieut. English had to forego tradition. There was no cheerful tootling on the whistle. The whistle had frozen solid. It couldn't even clear its throat.

The new medico—Dr. Potaka, dark, solidly built, with a good-humored face, an English accent and Maori blood in his veins—came to Little America on a tractor. He was liked from the start. No man could have justified himself in shorter order. Within a fortnight he successfully accomplished two operations, the second a major one.

By noon Lieut. English was pushing through the Ross Sea, with the engines wide open and all canvas spread to profit from the winds. The ice, he reported, was thicker, but not quite enough to stop them. But they had a hazardous time of it in the Bay of Whales. Lost in the sea smoke the *Bear* several times narrowly missed crashing into the Barrier. In the Ross Sea visibility was better.

Later the same day Lieut. English advised that after bucking new ice for nine hours, they had finally gained "open water filled with immense drifting bergs." But the wind had hauled into the northwest, forcing them to furl sail and pit the engines against high head winds and seas.

VI

Tuesday the 27th was overcast and drifting most of the day; but preparations for the departure of the Southern Sledging Party—the first field project of the expedition—were practically finished. Men and teams were picked, gear and equipment stowed in neat canvas tanks lashed to the sledges, everything ready except for the finishing licks. The party was supposed to start next day. But Rawson, who was to serve as navigator for the party, had meanwhile fallen ill with an obscure throat ailment. On Dr. Potaka's recommendation the assignment was withdrawn. Stuart Paine, who had been Rawson's roommate at Yale and, like himself, was a commissioned officer in the Naval Reserve, was made navigator.

Richard Black, a surveyor, who had had radio experience as an amateur and was a good man on skis (an indispensable qualification for a sledging party) was assigned the radio operator's billet.

These and other revisions delayed the start of the party until March 1st.

There was one aspect of our fall work, mentioned several times in passing, which might now be discussed in its fitting place. I have in mind the killing of seals.

The expedition required seals for three purposes: (1) food for the dogs (except on the trail, when they were fed pemmican enriched by seal blubber, the dogs were entirely fed on seal meat); (2) food for the men (there's no better preventive for scurvy than fresh seal meat); and (3) scientific data (the biologists were anxious to make as fine a collection of specimens as possible). Happily these three ends could be served at the same time.

Captain Innes-Taylor had earlier fixed 700 as the number of seal carcasses required to sustain his 150 huskies and their expected progeny during the winter. It was thought they would not be difficult to get. Seals had been common enough in the Bay of Whales. In 1929 I had flown over thousands of them basking in the pressure.

In the hurry and push of unloading ship, we had been able to spare only two men—Dr. Perkins and Lindsey, both biologists—for sealing excursions. They had a difficult time. Seals were very scarce. In fact, there was everywhere a marked poverty of animal life in the Bay of Whales, though it was celebrated as a haven for the flying and swimming creatures of high southern latitudes. Even penguins were rare. Dr. Perkins counted not more than fifty, where five years before we had seen them in hundreds. There were few whales cruising about the Bay, and only a few schools of the dreaded Killer Whales, which roam in packs, were seen. And though there were many heavy-flying, cannibalistic skua gulls, and dove-like snowy petrels (the fairest things that fly) and richly piebald Antarctic petrels, these by no means seemed so plentiful as they were in 1929-1930. I suppose that in some way not discernible to us food conditions in the Bay of Whales were subtly altered that season, and so these creatures which haunt the sun-washed zone of the Ice Age had sought more fertile fishing grounds (being wholly aquatic life, they are dependent upon the sea for food) either to the eastward or westward.

Anyhow, the few seals that the biologists found were for the most part secreted deep in the pressure. It was a hard day's work just to kill a dozen seals and drag the heavy carcasses, which weigh from 600 up to 1,000 pounds, to a flat place where the tractors could take them aboard. Nor was it the safest job in the world to be floundering in that morass of pressure, with its uncountable shallow-roofed crevasses and pitfalls.

Because the cold was deepening and animal life would soon be in full flight from the Bay, we had to act swiftly or go without. On February 17th McCormick and June were dispatched in the auto-gyro to reconnoiter for seals. Exploring the pressure southwest of the Bridge of Sighs, they sighted between 500 and 600 seals herded rather closely together. Dr. Perkins, Lindsey, Dane, Wade and Buckley immediately set out after them. They took with them two dog teams, camping equipment and a week's rations. In the course of a week they killed 191 seals, which they collected in five caches on the western edge of the pressure, where they could be picked up later by the tractors. No need then to worry about decomposition. The carcasses froze hard as a rock.

Dr. Poulter meanwhile killed nearly a hundred seals in the pressure ice between Ver-Sur-Mer Inlet and the Bridge. The others had seen and killed only Weddells; Dr. Poulter, on the other hand, had bagged mostly the small, and somewhat tastier Crab-Eaters. You ask: is it good sport? The answer is no. Not an atom of sportsmanship in it. Having no enemies on land except among their own kind, and then only when the bulls start brawling in the mating season, seals have no reason to suspect their glacial Eden is being upturned. A rifle shot through the brain at close range—hardly sport. The Norwegians favored the long knife.

VII

March gales kited the *Bear* along. A southerly gale, sheeted with blizzard, blew her out of the Ross Sea. March 1st Lieut. English reported he was at Lat. 71° 07′ S., Long. 179° 30′ E. By steering well to the westward he eluded the pack and escaped the risk of being beset. But it was a vicious passage none the less.

March 2nd the southeast gale behind him mounted to hurricane force, and for thirteen hours the *Bear* lay hove to. The barometer fell, in a few hours, from 29 inches to 27.82, at which point the pen ran off the chart.

In the afternoon the wind moderated to whole gale force and hauled into the southwest. Setting lower topsails and stopping the engines, they let the gale boost them along. Again on March 2nd, an hour before midnight, a second hurricane enveloped the ship. On March 3rd Lieut. English reported:

> ... Ship laboring heavily in mountainous seas, rolling fifty degrees each side. Green water breaking aboard. Have life lines stretched along weather deck in network pattern.... For three days no mess tables have been set ... well deck completely submerged, galley waist deep in water at times.... So violent has been lurching of ship that men unable to stay in bunks.... All hands have been remaining awake ... hanging on to any fitting available to support weight and prevent injury.... From 2300 (11 P.M.) made four knots with bare poles and engine stopped till 0300 (3 A.M.) this morning when ice seen ahead in pitch darkness, ship having been blown upon extensive field of massive bergs. Engines were started at once and ship pounded eastward in mountainous seas to avoid them. Ship then rolled almost on beam's end. Decks constantly awash. After two hours headed north working way between scores of ice mountains.... At 0700 weather again moderated to whole gale from east and seas now only very rough. Snowing and cold, visibility half a mile. Ship under steam and double reefed staysails.... Gusts of wind approached velocity of 100 miles per hour.... Noon position 67° 15′ S., 178° 55′ E.

On the 4th the winds diminished. But in the Fifties they passed through another gale. On March 12th the ship reached Dunedin—

completing what Lieut. English believed was the stormiest voyage in Antarctic annals. Seventy percent of the voyage, he said, was made in winds of 60 miles per hour. A year later when he sailed again into the Bay of Whales, he told me that at the height of the blow the ship was rolling 50° to either side, and tons of water poured below through broken skylights and sprung companionways. The real heroes of the trip, he said, were the youngsters, many of them making their first voyage, who were sent aloft, having to cling to icy handlines and work sails stiff with frozen spray, with the ship rolling through a hundred degrees of arc.

In all events, it was a magnificent first season's work for a ship supposedly tardy at the graveyard—six transits of the Ross Sea, two of them among the latest on record: 40,000 square miles of unknown seas explored, six lines of soundings and various hydrographic stations occupied. One couldn't have asked for more from the *Bear* and her gallant crew.

Chapter VIII

A LOUD AND STORMY MONTH

I

SOMEWHERE I read that the Anglo-Saxons called March the "loud and stormy month", and of course the Ides of March have always carried a fatal implication; so the succession of bewildering and sometimes appalling events that revolved around and within the expedition in March 1934 may partly be attributed to the melancholy character of the month itself. An airplane crash and a subsequent dangerous forced landing in fog, two operations on sick men, the *Bear's* violent efforts to make good her retreat, a fresh outbreak of the ice in the vicinity of Little America, a fire in one of the shacks, the foundering of the Cletrac 67 miles south of Little America, Dyer's fall from a 45-foot telephone pole—there may be a few mishaps that I've forgotten. March was indeed a "loud and stormy month." In its span of thirty-one days we launched and successfully completed two important field journeys. In March I also took leave of Little America and commenced my meteorological vigil at Bolling Advance Weather Base.

But let us take up these matters in order. Events were crowding hard and fast in March.

March 1st came in clear and cold, with a temperature of —15°. Innes-Taylor had his Southern Sledging Party toeing the line for the start: himself as leader; Paine, navigator and driver; Black, radio operator; Ronne, driver—four men and three nine-dog teams. Also on the mark was the Supporting Party—two men, Russell and Moody, and two teams.

The Southern Party had a double function: first, to advance rations depots at 25 [1]-mile intervals for the support of the major scientific parties which would take the field in the spring; and, secondly, to explore a safe passage south for the tractors which were to leave, presumably a week later, with stores and equipment for Advance Base. So late in the season, with winter night only seven weeks away, I could not honestly hope for a southing of more than 200 miles. Actually it was necessary to be content with less. The Antarctic March is one of the most punishing months for sledging: falling temperatures, lengthening nights, the rising fury of blizzards, and crystalline snow that grates like salt on the runners.

[1] The depot distances are given in geographical miles (1.15 statute miles).

The average load on the sledges was 950 pounds—not excessively burdensome as sledging weights go, but quite enough to impose upon weary men and dogs. These loads included the usual camping and trail equipment, radio and navigation gear, medical kits and rations. Beyond their own requirements the party also carried nine 30-day rations [2] (that is, units of rations sufficient to sustain 9 men for 30 days) which were to be distributed, in accordance with a predetermined plan, among the various depots.[3] The Supporting Party's function was what its designation implies: to accompany the main party, carrying part of its load, until a point was reached where the main party, its loads lightened by depot deposits, could take aboard the remaining weights and continue alone. At this point the Supporting Party, its purpose fulfilled, would turn back for Little America.

Actually the whole operation was a supporting movement preliminary to the major sledging parties which in the following spring would aim at the Queen Maud Range.

A physical obstacle stood squarely in the immediate path of the dog teams: how to get them through the pressure ice and onto high barrier south of Amundsen Arm. In 1929 Ver-Sur-Mer Inlet had offered a convenient exit for the first expedition's southern parties. There was then only a moderate amount of pressure across the mouth of the Inlet, which the sledges traversed with no great difficulty. Past the pressure the teams turned southwest, following the east wall of the Bay to Cape Manhue, whence they slanted across the mouth of Amundsen Arm, gaining high barrier on the south shore. The barrier

[2] The following were the constituents of a one-man, one-day ration as set for the fall operations:

9 oz. pemmican	.5 oz. tea
10 oz. eskimo biscuit	.59 oz. butter
4 oz. sugar	.29 oz. peanut butter
2 oz. oatmeal	.74 oz. malted milk
2 oz. chocolate	.5 oz. cocoa
2 oz. erbwurst	.236 oz. salt
1.33 oz. bacon	.029 oz. pepper

.355 oz. matches & toilet paper

Routine meals on the trail consisted of: Breakfast—2 mugs oatmeal with sugar & milk, 2 biscuits, 2 cups tea with sugar & milk; Luncheon—1 2-oz. bar chocolate, 2 biscuits with butter or peanut butter, 2 oz. pemmican eaten cold, 2 cups tea, cocoa, or malted milk; Supper—6 oz. pemmican in hot stew or *hoosh* with soup meal sausage, 4 biscuits with butter, peanut butter or bacon fat, 2 cups tea, 2 slices bacon.

[3] The distribution of the rations was as follows: 7 days' rations for 4 men at 25, 50, 75, 125 & 150-Miles Depots; and 30 days' rations for 4 men at 100-Mile Depot. The southern trail itself between the depots was marked with orange flags planted a third of a mile apart; and each depot was identified by flags running a mile to either side of it, pennants to the east, and burgees to the west, to guide a party which might be running toward it in heavy weather.

at this point rose in gentle terraces. Except for occasional crevassed areas, there was a clear run south to the Queen Maud Range.[4]

But this exit was completely closed in 1934-1935, barred off by the pressure ridges which had made the reoccupation of Little America so difficult. Likewise the mouth of Amundsen Arm was closed. So the connection to the Bay of Whales provided by the Bridge of Sighs was of no value to the southern operation. An alternative remained: to strike south from Little America over the rolling hills and down into Framheim where Amundsen had based, and look for a passage across the Arm.

Early in the morning of March 1st I dispatched Blackburn and Dane on this errand with a dog-team, and shortly afterwards McCormick and I took off in the auto-gyro to widen the search. We ranged south, east and west, scanning Amundsen Arm with close attention. The mouth of the Arm was impossible—a chaos of pressure ridges and crevasses; inside the Arm the sea-level ice was creased and broken by longitudinal furrows, like the corrugations of an iron washboard. Just east of Framheim was the region known as the Bad Lands, a broken, splintered confusion; only a skua gull would be safe in that.

But the search presently yielded what we were looking for. About seven miles south of Little America we marked a smoother channel across the Arm. There were a few crevasses and pressure ridges, but these could be negotiated. Indeed, proof that it was passable was immediately forthcoming, for there, on exactly the course I had in mind was a winding line of orange flags planted by Blackburn and Dane. A moment later we spotted their team toiling toward high Barrier to the south.

It was remarkable that these men on foot, with their limited vision, had unerringly selected the only accessible passage that we had seen in miles of flying.

McCormick slipped down almost vertically, landing beside the dog team. I congratulated Blackburn and Dane, and advised them there was no need to continue: clear sailing ahead.

McCormick and I took off to complete the survey. Crossing Amundsen Arm we studied the Barrier ascent. The ice in the Arm was depressed, so low that a dozen seals lay sleeping near a pot-hole. From the bay ice the snow terraces of the Barrier lifted in easy rises. At the bottom we marked a huge open crevasse trending east and west. I judged it was 75 feet wide in some places and quite as deep; from the air the open fissures were black and ugly. However, the crevasse narrowed sharply, and the snow bridge seemed staunch enough. Far in the south the white plain of the Barrier softly met the sky, rolling hills and gentle grades washing to the foot of the Queen Maud Range, 450 miles south. So far as we knew from our previous explorations across the Barrier there was only one serious obstacle intervening: the crevassed area

[4] Byrd, *Little America,* 282-283.

along the 81st parallel. The Southern Party's course was so directed, we thought, as to carry around it.

McCormick and I were back at Little America after an hour's flight. I was greatly impressed with the virtues of the auto-gyro. With its singular hovering instincts and its nearly vertical landings, it is a perfect instrument for short-range reconnaissance in the polar regions.

I had a short talk with Innes-Taylor and advised him to start at once.

"You have a hard journey," I said. "Bitter temperatures in a fortnight. You'll be suffering. That's when you'll want to be on the homeward run—not trying to push still farther south."

Getting a party off—whether it's sledging, tractor or aviation—is always a major expedition problem. The fault isn't hesitation or reluctance: nothing of that sort, of course. It's just the human quirk of tinkering, of altering and changing little things, sledges, rations, gear and the like. Something like trying to get the family organized for a picnic in the country.

At 6:41 o'clock that evening the party cleared Little America—six men, five dog-teams. They made a grand sight moving off. The air was clear and still; the horizon flamed with color. The pick of 135 dogs went south. Innes-Taylor's team was made up of heavy-shouldered, big-boned Manitoba huskies, descendants of the dogs used by Shackleton; Sam was his leader, a buff-colored giant, one of the most intelligent leaders in Dog Town. Moody's team consisted of white-eyed Siberian malamutes, small and wiry and vicious. The leader of this pack of assassins was Caesar, docile and ingratiating as a setter: his only fault was an insatiable appetite for harnesses. In a month he chewed fifteen of them to ribbons. The other teams were combinations of the unfathomable cross-breeds that made up the canine roster.

Fri., March 2, 10 P.M.

Snowing and drifting tonight. Min. temp. —20° : max. +11. An easterly wind brought snow and rising temperatures.

Hermann and Petersen, who accompanied the Southern Party to take motion pictures, returned this evening, reporting that the party camped at 3 A.M. this morning on high Barrier, 10.2 miles south, began breaking camp at 10 A.M. and started the second march at noon. They had no great difficulty crossing Amundsen Arm.

Now to get the tractor party organized. June and Demas will be co-leaders of this enterprise.

Demas tonight handed in a report on the condition of the tractors; they are decidedly in need of overhaul. The three Citroëns, he said, have traveled about 6,000 nautical miles since hitting the ice, and the Cletrac has added another thousand. Considering the difficulties, that's heavy mileage. The cars have been running steadily the past month, with one driver relieving another at the wheel. Partly on account of conditions, partly on account of the inexperience of the drivers, the cars have taken frightful punishment. The engines must be inspected, new clutches installed, gadgets invented for cold weather operation, and the body structures strengthened.

Little America has a night watchman now—Alton Wade. He makes an hourly tour of the camp, to watch out for fires; and also he keeps a sharp lookout for any change in local ice conditions. I'm still concerned over the safety of Little America. Petersen has likewise been detailed to make periodic inspection of the cracks around the camp....

Sat., March 3, 11 P.M.

Still drifting and snowing. This morning everything—dog kennels, caches, tractors—was half smothered. The men put in a hard day of digging. I told Dr. Poulter, on my return from the *Bear's* eastern cruise, that I had not favored the policy of constructing the new buildings on the surface. To be sure it's easier than digging a hole and raising a building in it, as we did before; but it does have the frightful disadvantage of piling up and collecting drift. The new buildings were half buried this morning, and the inevitable tailing ridges of drift were gathering to leeward. Before long Little America will be a series of small mountains.

Dr. Perkins and McCormick made another short flight today (I neglected to mention they flew yesterday for the same purpose) in search of new sealing grounds. June also left in one of the tractors on a test run across Amundsen Arm. The tractors, he said, are all right: they can get through.

Dyer, Bailey, Hutcheson and Waite put up the second of the directive antennae this afternoon. There will be three in all, I understand, separately bearing on Buenos Aires, New York and San Francisco; and a smaller one bearing on New Zealand, for contact with the ships. These are the focal points of the expedition's communications. All these telephone poles and wires crisscrossing the environs aren't calculated to ease the pilots' minds. Wasn't it Will Rogers who said you could always tell an American municipal airport by the high tension wires around it? Well, Little America has modern improvements.

Bailey happened to mention that Dyer tumbled from the top of one of these poles the other day—a clean drop of 45 feet. The pole was filmed with ice: Dyer's spikes slipped when his safety belt was unloosened, and down he came. A brace and bit hit a foot from his head. Dyer got up, Bailey said, and shook himself. All he said was, "Damn fool thing to do."

II

Sunday brought the first crisis of March. In the wisdom that always comes after the event it all seemed an unprofitable expenditure of

(Photograph by Joseph A. Pelter)

THE WRECK OF THE FOKKER, "BLUE BLADE"

AIRPORT

The Citroën Hits a Crevasse

"Pete" Demas

Captain Alan Innes-Taylor

thought and energy; yet I believe sincerely that were I again confronted by the same situation and the same set of circumstances, and having the same responsibilities as leader, I should do no differently.

The doubts with which I contemplated the ice conditions prevailing in the vicinity of Little America have already been described. Though the apprehensions which had arisen in February had passed from the general consciousness of the camp, mine were not calmed. The situation, if anything, had gradually become worse. After freezing lightly, the Bay of Whales had again broken open, and the bay ice was moving out with increasing velocity. Open water was only a few yards from the mouth of Ver-Sur-Mer Inlet, and only a little over three-quarters of a mile from Little America. A strong swell was pounding in from the Ross Sea, hastening the disintegration of the ice. The *Bear's* reports of hurricane winds and mountainous seas only a few hundred miles to the north were hardly calculated to be encouraging. The effects of that disturbance were bound to spread southward, building up and broadening the scope of the forces already hastening the destruction of the ice sheet.

Early that morning my cabin was jarred by a series of light shocks in the ice. A little later Dr. Poulter pushed open the door. The movement of the ice, he said, seemed to be increasing; he was a little worried. I got up and together we went out to look at the cracks. They were substantially larger. Where before they were only a few inches wide they now measured a foot or more. Ever so gently they expanded and closed; there was a barely perceptible horizontal movement as well—the effect, of course, of the swell surging under the basement of four or five hundred feet of ice. It was an uncanny thing to watch.

Wade, who had just finished his rounds, came up with the news that similar conditions prevailed in all directions around Little America. A huge chunk of pressure had just heaved out of the north cape of Ver-Sur-Mer. Returning to camp for a tractor, the three of us motored down to the mouth of the Inlet. The pressure ice across it, as Wade had said, was in considerable agitation, rising and sagging on the swell, with strange moanings and grindings, as if in agony. Now it was rotten and tumbling, with no backing of bay ice to hold it in place.

The day was overcast, and the wind, after boxing the compass, was making up its mind to steady in the northwest and blow up. Over the Ross Sea was a black billowing of water sky—the sea was again open, the ice smashed apart by the recent storms. One circumstance was encouraging. A solid white line of pack ran across the mouth of the Bay. The weight of it would dampen the swell.

It was plain to me—as it was to others—that the situation was critical. I decided therefore frankly to submit the facts to all hands, as their safety was involved, and work out with them a practicable plan which would best serve our needs, not only from the point of view of safety but also the preservation of our field program.

About 11 o'clock that morning we all met in the New Mess Hall. It was informal, as were all our common discussions. Occasionally I called such discussions in open forum, in which every man had the right to explore, criticize and recommend in respect to camp affairs. I doubt if a more interesting meeting was ever held. For we were met to consider the wisdom of evacuating Little America.

Dr. Poulter, Haines, Noville, Blackburn, Siple, June and myself all spoke briefly. The talks were general, turning upon an analysis of local ice conditions, the likelihood of Little America breaking out to sea, whether it was apt to break out suddenly or in a succession of break-ups, and what we would gain by evacuating the present site and retreating further inland.

The discussions lasted about two hours. Though we were all agreed the risk was real enough, it was decided that the evacuation of Little America, on the eve of the departure of the tractor party, would wreck the fall operations. It had to be one thing or the other. If the camp were evacuated, the tractors would have to shoulder the burden of the movement. The scientific work already under way, especially meteorological and magnetic research, would have to be dropped, the buildings uprooted and the camp transplanted bodily to a new site—a ghastly job. But to be on the safe side it was resolved to transfer to the emergency base—Retreat Camp—on the ridge to the south a certain minimum of essential stores, such as food, gasoline, coal, tents and the like, considerable quantities of which were already cached there. If evacuation became necessary—if it had to be done at a minute's notice—the expedition would have sufficient emergency stores to survive in tolerable fashion at Retreat Camp. Meanwhile the important work afoot would not be hindered nor the program impaired. We could count on a freeze-up before long.

June, assisted by Corey, Siple, Morgan, Haines and Blackburn, immediately took up the planning of the dump at Retreat Camp. The tractors, which had been laid up for repairs, were returned to service. By early afternoon dog-teams and tractors were plying between Little America and the cache. The remorseless drift was whirling across the Barrier by evening, but the transfer continued. That night headlights blazed on the ridge, and I suddenly realized how dark the nights were getting. Winter was coming on.

Mon., March 5, 10:30 P.M.

Still overcast, but the wind has dropped to a gentle N.E. breeze. The air is warm—a max. of $+25°$ today. We are praying for cold weather to cement the ice.

The movement of supplies to Retreat Camp continues. Out there the boxes have been arranged in a huge rectangle, with crossing connections. Bamboo poles have been laid across the top, and over them old tarpaulins have been stretched, making the cache serve as a potential shelter as well. At the rate we're moving stores we shall have sufficient supplies up there to release the tractors in a couple of days.

Incidentally, Dr. Poulter yesterday started to check ice movements with a device of his own invention called a tiltmeter. It is a modification of the McComb-Rhomberg seismograph, and before leaving the States Poulter himself built several for measuring the right angle components of tilting in the ice sheet, about which there has been much speculation and practically no definitive research.

Poulter has one of these gadgets rigged up in his shack, and today I had a chance to see it work. It consists of a pair of identical parts, set at right angles to each other. The principal parts of the apparatus seem to be a triangular cast iron base, a 27-inch column bolted to the base, a horizontal aluminum boom fitted to jeweled mountings, an aluminum vane swinging between the poles of permanent magnets which damp oscillation, and a movie-recorder. In effect, the instrument is a horizontal pendulum; any tilting is communicated to the sensitive vane which, passing over a strip of sensitized paper, automatically photographs its own oscillations.

Yesterday afternoon, Poulter said, the tilting at Little America was quite pronounced, so much so that he could see movement while setting the cross-hairs of a transit on a half mile horizon. The movement was irregular, but the tiltmeter showed a tilting of at least an inch. During the night the movement subsided, but a rising oscillation set in about noon today.

With this instrument we can at least keep our fingers on the glacial pulse....

III

On the evening of March 5th, having had no word from the Southern Party since its departure, we dispatched June and a tractor unit south to overtake it and find out what was wrong. The party was supposed to report twice a day—at fixed schedules in the morning and evening. At no time were we able to contact them. I had no cause to worry; it was inconceivable that they could have gotten into trouble so soon. More likely, the radio set was damaged. Still, silence was suspect. That's the psychological disadvantage of radio: you come to rely upon it completely. In other days sledging parties vanished into the unknown after leaving the main base and were unheard from until their return; this was in the nature of things. But when you send a party into the field equipped with radio and nothing is heard, not a call for days, you can't help being disturbed.

However, the trip was also made to serve several useful functions. It would give a line on tractor performance in the soft snow of the

Barrier: and the car was loaded up with 14 30-day rations for transfer to Innes-Taylor's party.

June's crew consisted of Skinner, driver, and Waite, radio operator. Skinner was an army parachute jumper, which should have fitted him temperamentally for the peculiar perils of operating a tractor over crevassed areas. Waite had been senior radio operator in the *Bear*.

Leaving Little America, the tractor ran south all night, following the small orange flags with which the Southern Party had marked the trail at third of a mile intervals. At 8 o'clock next morning June reported:

> "Arrived at 50-Mile Depot at 7:24. Innes-Taylor and party all well and ready to proceed. 24 miles from Little America found bad crevasse on trail. Marked with six flags. If any party passes must proceed with caution just east of flags. Surface from 25-Mile depot hard and rough. Bad for plane landing. Innes-Taylor taking 14 rations and kerosene with him.... Temp. plus four, calm, 90 percent overcast."

A subsequent message advised that the Southern Party had been held up by a severe blizzard, and that failure of communications was due to a minor fault in the radio transmitter which Waite had been able to rectify.

Taking aboard rations transferred by the tractor, a load of 1,280 pounds, Innes-Taylor promptly resumed the advance. 50-Mile Depot was situated on the crest of a rounded hill, the southern slopes of which descended into a shallow valley which was presently named the Valley of Crevasses. Across its flooring ran wave upon wave of crevasses, some gaping, others, lightly roofed. To pass around them the teams made an easting of five miles before again bearing south.

June and his unit pitched their tents at 50-Mile Depot and turned in.

> *Tues., March 6, 9:30 P.M.*
>
> I had intended to fly out to the Southern Party, but fog prevented it. A light impalpable fog, an indeterminate horizon, a low ceiling—so many days are like that! Drifting and snowing today. Temp.: min. —29°, max. +14°. Wind—South, 20 miles.
>
> Over the 8 P.M. radio schedule I asked June to set out after the dog teams and give them a hand to 100-Mile Depot. With tractor support, the Southern Party ought to be able to make better progress; at the same time the journey will give us a line on tractor performance in the field.
>
> ... Three men are on the sick list. Clark has a touch of malaria, apparently a chronic condition with him; Noville is laid up with a lame shoulder (he has a silver plate set in the bone close to the skin, the result of an injury received in a crash, and thinks that the cold works into it) and Rawson has been laid up for ten days with a puzzling condition which the doctor diagnoses as a septic

throat. Rawson has been in great pain: the glands are grossly swollen, and unless there is improvement the doctor may have to operate. An unhappy situation.

Ice conditions hereabout remain unchanged. The tractors today were hauling seals from the Bay to Retreat Camp, building up a meat reserve.

On Wednesday March 7th, the newcomers had their first taste of an Antarctic blizzard. During the early morning, with the temperature at —30°, a new low, the wind whispered from south into southwest, then abruptly swung into the east, and rose. The air became a flying confusion of drift and snow. Visibility dropped to a few yards. Life lines were hastily run between the buildings. Clark, who had left a sick bed to check the food stores at Retreat Camp, was marooned; Dane finally brought him in with a dog-team. A tractor stalled at East Barrier Cache; the driver had to make his way back on foot, groping between the flags. He stumbled into the camp just before the worst of the blizzard. The half built tunnels quickly filled, and a mounting tide of drift crept over the stores in the caches. I was then living in the shack which later moved out to Advance Base. A portable affair, Tinglof had practically taken it apart the day before to make a few alterations. Evidently he forgot to nail the roof on, because during the night I was all but blown down to Ver-Sur-Mer Inlet. Drift poured in and the roof heaved up and down like a bellows. The night watchman finally appeared out of the storm, and with his help and Tinglof's, for whom we had to send out an SOS, we finally got the thing battened down.

Meanwhile, 16 miles out of 50-Mile Depot, the tractor had again overtaken the dog party and taken aboard their loads. Their support no longer needed, Russell and Moody turned back for Little America. Innes-Taylor, Black, Paine and Ronne went ahead to complete the mission, with the tractor as convoy. At 82 miles south a 50-mile blizzard forced them to heave to.

There was, however, a fascinating sentence in June's evening report. A dark object sticking up in the snow attracted their attention; investigating it, they found the tip end of a sledge which had been abandoned by one of the southern parties of the first expedition, more than four years before.

Thurs., March 8, 10:45 P.M.

Blizzard moderating, after attaining a velocity of 40 miles this afternoon. Temp. rose (as it always does in the blizzard) to +29°. So near the melting point, the snow is soft and soggy. The shacks are all leaking through the roofs: there's a steady hissing drip of water down the stove pipes.

The blizzard means tough going for the sledging parties. June and Innes-Taylor still hove to at 71 miles. They said tonight it was doubtful if they could shove off before tomorrow. They reported heavy, soft snow, a max. temperature of +20°.

Wondering what effect this blast of northerly winds would have on the ice, I made a short trip with Poulter along the East Barrier wall. I remarked, as we left, that with all this wind the ice must be taking a terrific beating.

"I doubt it," he said. He explained that even at the height of the blow the tiltmeter showed very little activity. The reason for that, we soon discovered, was that the Bay of Whales and the Ross Sea as far as we could see were jammed with loose pack driven down by the wind. The pack had dampened the swell.

. . . Rawson had a very bad night: he was almost delirious.

Fri., March 9, Midnight.

Tonight Dr. Potaka operated on Rawson. It was not an easy operation, nor a very pleasant one: but Dr. Potaka went about his business quietly and efficiently. He was assisted by Jim Sterrett. I stood by to help where I could. It was the first time the knife was used at Little America.

The operation was performed at 9:20 P.M. in Noville's shack, where Rawson has shared a bunk for the past fortnight. Because the bunk was five feet from the deck, the operating table had to be a couple of tractor seat cushions which were spread on the deck. Rawson got down himself. He made no fuss whatever. Sterrett administered the anaesthetic and made the first incision. Dr. Potaka then operated on the cervical glands below the angle of the right jaw.

Boiling water stood on the stove, made from fresh snow collected to windward of the camp to avoid risk of contamination. A steady drip-drip-drip of drift ran down the stove pipes: and once a pack of dogs, which had gotten loose, tore around the shack, making a fearful racket.

Rawson was under the anaesthetic twenty minutes. He's pretty groggy now and quite sick, but the Doctor is confident there will be no complications.

I have made the difficult decision of not notifying Rawson's parents. His father, a close friend of mine, is himself not very well, and the sudden news of Ken's operation, no matter how encouragingly phrased, would worry him greatly. No parent is likely to bear with equanimity the news of a son's illness in the Antarctic.

. . . June advised this morning that they were digging out the tractor, and leaving immediately for 100-Mile Depot. . . .

Calm but overcast was the tenth day in March. The expedition shook off the drift and picked up the tasks it had dropped before the interruption. Now we made a shift in strategy. Uncertain how the tractors would fare in the impending march to Advance Base, we resolved to employ the Pilgrim and Fokker as cargo auxiliaries, dispatching them in advance of the tractors with the lighter stores. 100-Mile Depot (115 statute miles) was selected as a convenient cargo dump for the planes. This was the minimum distance I was prepared to accept for the Base. If the tractors could safely reach this point and were in condition to press still farther south, so much the better: they could take aboard the stores the planes had dropped and push on. So far as aviation could assist in the operation, weather was the controlling factor; if we had two days fit for flying we'd be lucky. What happened that day was an example of a heart-breaking routine endlessly repeated: planes dug out after freezing labor, heaters in place under the engines, then the decision of the meteorologists: sorry, gentlemen, not today.

At noon there was a joyful exclamation on a foreign sounding horn. June's tractor was back! Hard lumps of grease-stained ice were packed around the treads: drift was tightly wedged in the fenders. The men were jubilant over a remarkable run. In sixteen hours, with three stops, they had traveled 120 miles—a new day's record for surface travel in Antarctica, and the first successful demonstration of mechanized transport in field operations. They were also jubilant over a new kind of record. At 6 P.M. they had coaxed supper out of Paine and Black camped at 95 Miles; at 10 P.M. they had wheedled a bowl of soup from Innes-Taylor and Ronne at 90 Miles; at 50-Mile Depot they had cadged breakfast from Russell and Moody.

"Just get enough dog parties strung out in front of you," Skinner boasted, "and you can enjoy one free lunch after another."

The blizzard which had hit them at 82 miles, June said, had held up both him and the trail party for two days; but on the 9th the storm moderated and they broke camp. Sending Paine and Black ahead with one dog team in the guise of a bell wether for crevasses, June rumbled astern in the tractor, with Innes-Taylor and Ronne and their teams acting as convoy in case it came to mischief. Floundering in waist-deep snow, the dogs' speed dropped from four to two knots, and, becoming bored with traveling in low gear, the tractor crew finally pushed ahead on their own hook to 100-Mile Depot, where June cached the loads.[5] At 8 P.M. the tractor turned for Little America.

But what we were all impatient to hear was how the tractor stood up. June was greatly impressed by it. On smooth barrier surface, he said, it seemed infinitely superior to dogs on the basis of pay load and speed. Whether a tractor would prove as sure in the long run was another matter. Certainly the gain was not without new hazards.

"One idea we can discard immediately is that a dog team can scout ahead for crevasses for a two and a half ton tractor," June said. "Time after time we broke through roofed crevasses which had safely passed the much lighter teams. At 29, 58 and 70 miles we broke through bad holes. There's no warning whatever. The surface looks as solid as the Boston Post Road. For instance, on the way back we recrossed the

[5] In additions to the rations left at this depot by the Southern Party, the tractor left 14 30-day rations which were available for spring operations.

Valley of Crevasses, thinking we were carefully skirting the fissures we had noticed on the way out. Waite was driving. The car sagged violently aft. The rear treads had broken through. Waite gave her the gun and she crawled out, righting herself. Skinner took his turn at the wheel. Fifty feet later we cracked into another crevasse, and just beyond it a third.

"It's a funny experience—the same sickening sag you get when a plane hits an air pocket. You're driving along, thinking everything's all right; then all of a sudden there's a *b-rump,* then a loud *whroom* as tons of snow slide down a cliff: and you feel her tipping and sliding backwards as the treads grab for traction. If you have speed in reserve you're all right."

By altering course to the east and following a high ridge June thought that the tractors, even with full loads, could navigate around the Valley of Crevasses. He wasn't so sure as to the Cletrac, which was twice as heavy as the Citroëns. However, that was a chance we had to take.

The fate of Advance Base rested upon the Cletrac's ability to get through. Half the total weight of the stores had been assigned to it, an amount equal to the combined loads distributed among the three Citroëns. If the Cletrac were eliminated, so was Advance Base. The only cargo carrier that even approached the Cletrac's capacity was the *William Horlick.* And I was opposed to risking it in an alien project. Its loss (and that late in the season, with weather uncertain, the risk of damaging it was great) would rob the expedition of its main instrument of geographical exploration.

Sun., March 11, 10:45 P.M.

Russell and Moody got back this morning: and Innes-Taylor's party was making ready to leave 100-Mile Depot.

Bowlin made a short flight over the Barrier this morning, to find out if he could follow the trail from the air. The flags, he said, were little help, but the tractor tracks were quite easy to see.

He landed just in time to escape a blizzard. The drift was rising when he landed, and all hands were hurried out to secure the plane. A dozen men had to clamber on the tail to hold it down.

Mon., March 12, 11 P.M.

Blowing and drifting all day. . . . No report from the Southern Party. We are up to our necks in preparations for Advance Base and the tractor trip upon which it depends. Tractors are being overhauled, new sledges assembled, rations and gear collected—altogether we're extremely busy.

The tractor drivers are figuring ways to keep the cars running in the cold. Big Van Praag heaters are used for thawing out the engine block and rear end; the difficulty is in keeping the parts enclosed while the cars are being heated in the morning. Demas is having the sailmaker sew heavy canvas aprons which can be draped around the chassis. These aprons will serve the purpose of shielding the running parts from the wind while they're being heated, shielding the engines from drift while the cars are hove to in blizzards; and giving the driver some warmth and protection if he has to make repairs.

With Siple (for the past six months he had been working steadily on this problem) I've been checking and cross-checking the stores assigned to Advance Base. The variety of items required to stock an isolated base for the duration of the winter night can easily be imagined. Food, clothing, medical supplies, meteorological and navigational instruments, fuel, books, anti-scorbutics, radio equipment, fire-fighting devices—everything must be just right. And of course the old bugaboo of weight instantly intrudes from every side.

Siple, who started collecting stores for this project in Boston, has drafted a complete list of quantities and weights. For weeks we have been going over this list, checking each item, rejecting everything doubtful in an effort to reduce the gross total to the bare limit necessary for survival. Siple has done a splendid job.

Tuesday the wind mercifully stopped blowing, and the sun shone again. Thankful for these small blessings—even for the temperature of —20°—we again dug out the Fokker and Pilgrim, hopeful that the weather would hold good long enough for the pilots to squeeze in two freighting hauls to the 100-Mile Depot. The boxes were stacked up for them; they had been ready for days. The price of the respite was a crash.

The blizzards had left their marks on the planes. A solid block of snow was wedged within the engine cowlings: and a light layer of ice had gathered on the wings and fuselage. Light blows with the back of a gloved hand shook the latter loose; the snow around the engine was pried out: the hot breath of a blow torch quickly melted the ice on the propeller blades. Then heaters were put under the engines, and tins of oil were warmed over the galley stove.

The flying field lay in a shallow depression just north of the camp. The recent winds had raised long furrows of sastrugi, hard and bumpy. With a southwest wind, it meant a slightly up-hill take-off.

Schlossbach had the Fokker, *Blue Blade,* ready first. Before loading up, he decided to make a short test hop. Zuhn, Dustin and Young, who had helped him dig out the plane, asked if they might go along. None had ever flown before. "Ike" waved them in.

The plane got off very quickly—much too quickly, I thought. I was chatting with Bud Waite, and we happened to turn to watch the take-off. Exactly what did cause the crash is uncertain; several explanations were advanced, some of which may have been reasonable; but it seemed to me the decisive factor was that the plane was bounded into the air by a ridge of sastrugi before Schlossbach could get the right speed on the ground. The surface, as I said, was glossy-hard and roughened by sastrugi.

Anyhow, it was apparent the instant the plane got off that it was in difficulty. Drifting across the radio towers it seemed unable to gain altitude. The nose sagged, then the plane started to *hunt,* porpoise fashion. Schlossbach edged into a long swinging curve, evidently trying to make for smooth snow rather than risk crashing into the pressure in the Bay of Whales.

His fight to save the ship was in full view of the camp, which watched appalled and silent.

A tractor pulled up. "Get out with a load of fire bombs," I yelled at the driver. "Ike's going to crash."

About 500 yards east of the camp, still in the turn, the Fokker hit in an explosion of snow, ground-looping as the port ski tripped over sastrugi. The right ski smashed down with great force; the steel-tubed landing struts collapsed and the plane twisted awkwardly, stabbing the right wing into the snow.

The plane heaved as if about to flop over on its back, then fell back, skidded thirty yards or so, and stopped wearily. The right wing was practically torn off, the left wing pointed clumsily at the sky.

That instant all of Little America, by dog-team, tractor and on foot, broke for the wreck.

When we got there the four men were out of the wreckage. Nobody hurt, not even a scratch. Schlossbach had yelled to the others to brace themselves just before the crash; they had made fast to whatever fittings were handy. They were all suffering slightly from shock. Zuhn, still dazed, kept mumbling something about a pair of socks, no doubt the subconscious workings of his Iowan thrift. At Little America we measured a man's fortune by the number of clean socks in his sea chest.

The Fokker was a complete washout. The port ski and pedestal were torn off, the right wing (a monoplane cantilever wing of plywood construction) was splintered from tip to center. The longerons had buckled, and the stabilizer and flippers were destroyed. Engine, propeller and instruments were the only salvage.

A severe loss, but there was adequate consolation in the fact that no one was hurt, that no one was at fault. Aviation took up as if nothing had happened. An hour later Bowlin and Bailey made a brief test in the Pilgrim and before sundown completed two flights, supposedly to 100-Mile Depot, with a total pay load of 1,900 pounds of Advance Base stores. Next day they wedged in a third flight with a load of 1,100 pounds just before the ceiling dropped to zero, and June, having put the *William Horlick* through her test paces, was loading it up when Bowlin landed with word the weather south was too dirty for flying. The loss of the Fokker had persuaded me to risk using the big plane at least once as a freighter, in spite of my earlier objection.

Bowlin's three flights had an amusing aftermath. I became suspicious of the good time he made, and asked him if he were sure he landed at the right Depot.

"Well, I thought it was the shortest hundred miles I ever flew," he said, "but there was no more trail, so I landed."

It came out then that Bowlin had mistakenly landed at 50-Mile Depot. Past the depot the trail made a five mile détour due east, of which he hadn't been advised. He had been told to land at the fourth beacon. Pyramidal snow beacons eight feet high, heaped of snow blocks, identified each 25-Mile Depot. Rations, etc., were cached inside. Bill had faithfully counted four. Then June remarked, with a grin, that the dog party had also erected similar beacons to mark luncheon camps.

Bowlin cursed softly. "That accounts for it," he said. "Those beacons were strung out like picket fences. Luncheon beacons hell! These guys must have built a beacon every time they stopped to pump ship."

IV

But these were minor distractions; the night watches of March 14th saw a situation evolve that drove everything else into the background.

I had repaired to my shack after supper. Sterrett rapped on the door. When he came in, his face was grave. Pelter, he said, was ill, quite ill. He had been abed for several days in the Norwegian House (one of the original shacks which adjoined the Old Mess Hall), where he bunked with Blackburn. Sterrett said that Pelter hadn't wanted to stir up a fuss just over a "bellyache"; besides, he had no great faith in doctors. But Blackburn happened to mention it to Sterrett, who dropped in casually. After talking to Pelter, Sterrett came at once to me.

"What do you think it is?" I asked.

"I'm not sure," Sterrett said, "but I think it's appendicitis. Anyhow, Dr. Potaka should examine him."

We got hold of Dr. Potaka, who immediately went over and examined Pelter. Sterrett's diagnosis was right. A bad appendix, Dr. Potaka said, which would eventually require an operation, but perhaps not immediately. About 10:30 o'clock, however, Pelter had another relapse, and Dr. Potaka resolved to operate at once. Pelter, very pale and very weak, was boosted up the shaft of the Old Mess Hall; with Sterrett supporting him, he walked to the radio shack, which was cleaner and more comfortable than the other buildings. Walter Lewisohn cheerfully gave up his bunk.

Since his arrival at Little America a fortnight before, Dr. Potaka had had no time to unpack his instruments; he had been trying to convert the former library in the Administration Building into a medical office. Much of his medical gear was buried under five feet of drift. His surgical instruments, still unboxed, lay under a small mountain of things in the vestibule. Among these things the Doctor was pawing, when suddenly his pressure lamp went out. He started to fill it from a gasoline drum perched on a box nearby. The flame could not have died in the mantle; for there was a puff of smoke, the stream of gasoline ignited in Dr. Potaka's face and, startled, he dropped the lamp. In a moment the narrow vestibule was choked with smoke, and a pool of burning oil eddied around the boxes, setting them on fire, the crate of surgical instruments among them.

Tinglof and Von der Wall, who had heard Potaka's cry, hurried to the door. They acted with splendid promptness. Still in their underclothes (most of the men in the building had either turned in, or were undressing) they plunged into the vestibule, holding their breath as they scuttled up the hatch ladder. Tinglof dashed one way after fire extinguishers, Von der Wall made for the galley to get a gas mask. The others in the building, the doctor and a dozen or more, were cut off. Drift and ice had wedged down the skylights: the men couldn't open them from below. Smoke filled the long room. Demas slammed shut the door, to close off the draught down the hatch which was fanning the fire.

I had just stepped out of my shack when Tinglof went by on the dead run.

"Good Lord!" I thought, "what now?"

The smoke pouring out of the "Ad" Building hatch answered the question.

Fire and an appendectomy are just about the most unhealthy things that can happen in the Antarctic; but when they occur simultaneously, and when fire threatens to destroy the only tools you have to operate on a poor devil waiting to go on the table, you have a situation needing no description.

Thanks to the spontaneous action of the men in the "Ad" Building, there was no tragedy. The skylights were kicked in from above, and fire extinguishers passed to the men below. Von der Wall, a grotesque figure in flapping balbriggans and gas mask, dropped down the hatch to save the surgical instruments, the charred box of which was hoisted to the surface. The blaze was quickly extinguished. No great damage was done.

Even then Dr. Potaka was nearly at his wit's end. The sterile sutures were missing. He hurriedly broke open innumerable boxes which the men brought in from his smoking cache before he found them. *A table? What shall we do for an operating table?* Somebody remembered a table which Tinglof was building in the Science Building: it had no top, but stretchers could be laid across. *Where are the stretchers? Get Corey: he's the only guy who knows where anything is!* Corey knew: in the medical cache, under six feet of snow. Quickly they were excavated and thawed out over the galley stove. *Lights! What are you going to do for lights?* In his quiet way Dyer remembered the thousand watt lamp used to stabilize the camp load on the electrical circuit.

He got it, then ran a line across the ceiling over the operating table. *But suppose the generators conk in the middle of the operation! How about light then!* Bailey said he would stand by in the Kohler shack, with three generators running simultaneously, ready to switch the instant one spluttered. *How are you going to keep the room warm during the operation? You can't have an open coal fire with all this ether. It's twenty below. This room's going to cool off fast the moment you douse the fire!* Plug the cracks, then: seal the ventilators: get a good hot fire burning until the room temperature is up around 80°; then rake the ashes and carry them out. And to hold heat in the room, Cox and Tinglof fitted a door into the unfinished partition dividing the shack, while Pelter watched uneasily from the bunk.

At last matters were in hand, and at five minutes past midnight the anaesthetic was administered. I shall not quickly forget the scene—the narrow room with its rude bunks, the drifted skylights overhead, and the first pale aurora dimly seen through them, and Potaka, Sterrett and Perkins crisp in sterile white caps, gloves and gowns. The gleaming scalpels, forceps, retractors, hæmostats and scissors and the vials of sutures were racked on a small table which ordinarily served as a stand for the radio broadcasts. Wash basins, boiled and scoured till they shone, were spread out on the top of the small collapsible organ used in the broadcasts.

At Dr. Potaka's signal Sterrett started pouring the ether into the gauze-covered cone. Pelter answered to the count: "one . . . two . . . three." At first instantly, then draggingly: "twenty-four . . . twenty-five . . ." No answer at twenty-seven. Pelter stirred and in true navy fashion he murmured quite clearly:

"Quit kiddin', Doc. I can count, too. I'll let you know when I can't . . ."

Then he went inert, and the operation proceeded, with Sterrett gently dripping the ether with one hand while he held the other under the ramus of the jaw, one finger pressed lightly under the carotid artery to register the pulse action while he heeded the eye reflex, the breathing and the color of the blood; with Dr. Perkins handing the instruments which Dr. Potaka in his crisp British way called for, and with the Doctor himself, short, dark and dynamic, cutting deftly and with sureness. The small room was terribly crowded: Dr. Potaka was backed against the stove, and once, when he turned swiftly, he just escaped falling over it.

The operation dragged; it seemed to last forever, because, in the end, Potaka had to do most of the important details that trained assistants usually perform for surgeons. Before it was over we were all exhausted and shivering a little, too, because the temperature in the shack had steadily dropped. Then the fire was started and Pelter was gently transferred to the bunk, still unconscious.

Thurs., March 15, 11 P.M.

Overcast and drifting during the day, but clear tonight. Temperature is dropping fast.

Pelter is very weak, but Potaka is quite pleased by the way he pulled through it. The appendix, he said, was seven inches long and badly inflamed. I realize now that no enterprise I ever set afoot held a more fatal consequence than the race run by *Discovery II* and the *Bear* to deliver a doctor to Little America. Rawson, after several bad days, is slightly better tonight.

Innes-Taylor reports that he has reached Lat. 80° 56′ S., put down his last rations at 150-Mile Depot, and will start back tomorrow.

Demas and June are ready to leave with the tractors tomorrow. They're loading the tractors and sledges tonight. I've given up hope of using aviation in this project. The season's too late, weather's too dangerous. It must be the tractors or nothing. Tinglof and Siple are dismantling Advance Base shack, in which I've lived since February 15th.

Chapter IX

FALL JOURNEYS

I

ON Monday, March 16th, the tractor fleet, led by June and Demas, put out from Little America on its extraordinary mission. The advance was unique in the history of polar travel. Theretofore the Eskimo husky had dominated land travel. But this advance was entirely mechanical. The four tractors alone (the three Citroëns and the Cletrac) represented 13 tons of machinery. The crew numbered nine men—four drivers, Demas, Hill, Dustin and Skinner; two radio operators, Petersen and Waite, and Siple and Tinglof, whose particular job was to assemble Advance Base. The portable shack for Advance Base weighed close to two tons. The remaining loads were taken up with trail rations and equipment, lubricating oil, tools, clothing for the tractor crew, and the gear and stores assigned to the Base.

Just before the start I called the crew together and we talked briefly on the subject of trail practices: how to make the best use of sleeping bags and cold weather clothing, what to do about frost-bites and such matters. Six of the men were new to the polar regions; but June, Siple and Demas, veterans all of the first expedition, could be relied upon to enforce the rules and regulations of the trail. Two points we impressed upon them are subjects that I have always harped on: first, give heed to the feet, they are most vulnerable to frost-bite; secondly, hold fast to the trail, but if you do wander off keep your head; don't get frantic and, above all else, if you have the slightest doubt as to direction, stay where you are; it will make it easier for the others to find you.

All possible provisions were made for the crew's safety. The gear was so divided that each tractor unit had either in its car or on its sledges two 30-day rations per man; sleeping bags, tent, cookers and other essential camping equipment, man-hauling sledges and harnesses, alpine rope, kerosene for the primus stove, and gasoline for 300 miles of cruising. Thus each unit was independently self-sustaining. If it became separated in fog or blizzard, or if mechanical breakdown forced it out of the line, it was so contained that it could carry on alone. Crevasses presented the threat, as June's trial run to 100-Mile Depot had shown. Lanyards for springing the doors had replaced handles on all machines, to enable the crew to abandon ship more rapidly; and 200 feet of alpine rope was assigned to each unit for use in the crevasses. For the battleship like Cletrac, Demas had rigged up the most amazing safety device I've ever heard of. It was a remote control device for manipulating the driving levers and clutch. If that solid block of steel and iron ever started to plunge, the driver would have little chance of bailing out. Demas therefore hit upon the novel idea of attaching sixty-foot lines to the left and right steering levers and the clutch as well; these were led through small ports out in the rear of the driving compartment; and it was Demas's intention, whenever the vehicles approached a doubtful area, to disembark and "tool" the Iron Horse from a safe distance astern. Short of radio control, I could imagine nothing better. In fact, one wit asked Demas why not make the lines long enough to operate the machine from his bunk at Little America.

The four machines were drawn up in echelon in the center of the camp, each with three heavily-loaded sledges (the Cletrac had four) in tow. A man-hauling sledge was lashed to the roof of each car. A leaking gas line delayed Hill's car, and to save time the others went on ahead to gas up at Retreat Camp, where most of the tractor gas had been cached. The sky was overcast and a light snow fell. The temperature was —15°, and the exhausts hung in drooling white clouds in the wakes of the cars. June presently returned from Retreat Camp bringing the hand-pump which was frozen and out of order. A cry went up for Boyd, the machinist. He was sixty feet up in the air on one of the radio towers, rigging a platform for the wind-driven generator. The day before the doctor had called him down from the same perch to make a saline injector for Pelter. Always cheerful, Boyd descended and quickly repaired the pump. By that time Hill's car was ready, and the two left together. Gassed to capacity, four cars left Retreat Camp about 7 o'clock that evening. In the dark, with headlights blazing, the procession trundled across Amundsen Arm, having had to brake the sledges descending the steep slopes to the north. Just before midnight they gained high barrier, and squared away for the south. Next morning the fleet, including even the slower-gaited Cletrac, reported "all well" from 25-Mile Depot. In crossing the crevasses a mile north of the Depot, the Cletrac had crushed through three small crevasses without injury to itself or its huge load. Demas had employed the remote control device with good effect. An encouraging beginning. The telling test, however, would come in the Valley of Crevasses.

II

In order to understand the importance of this journey, an understanding of the purposes of Bolling Advance Weather Base is necessary: it seems to me that this is the right place to tell how the idea of this unusual base was born, what scientific purpose it was expected to serve, and in what manner it should be manned and equipped.

Polar meteorology is a subject in which I have always been keenly interested. It was one of the strongest scientific departments of both of my Antarctic expeditions. The department was twice headed by Bill Haines, of the U. S. Weather Bureau, who was also meteorologist for

(Photograph by Charles G. Morgan)

THE ADVANCE BASE TRACTOR PARTY

(Photograph by Charles G. Morgan)

THE ADVANCE BASE CARAVAN

(© Paramount Pictures, Inc.)

Laying the Foundations for Advance Base

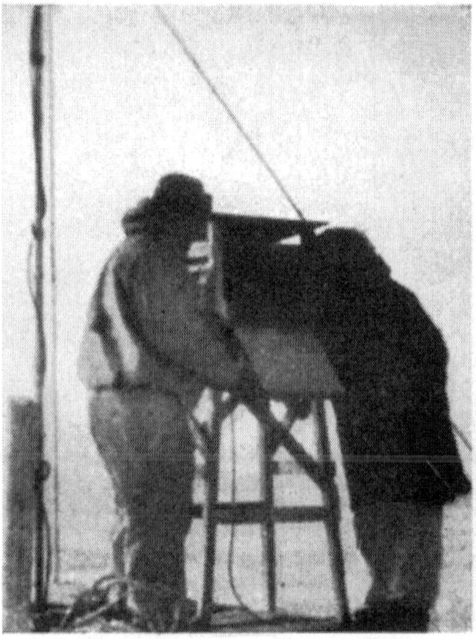

(© Paramount Pictures, Inc.)

Admiral Byrd and Siple (Left) Examine the Instruments

(© Paramount Pictures, Inc.)

Farewell—for the Winter Night

(© Paramount Pictures, Inc.)

The Tractors Depart for Little America

me at Spitzbergen, when Bennett and I flew to the North Pole. The meteorological data collected by Haines and his assistants (Harrison 1929-1930, Grimminger 1934-1935) are perhaps the most complete accumulated in the south polar regions, having benefited by the application of new technique; and it is quite possible, according to Haines, that when the combined data of the two expeditions are worked up, a task which will require several years, the subject of Antarctic meteorology, now obscure and exceedingly theoretical, will be to a degree illuminated in several directions.

It is also true that to the ordinary person, who can see little or no worth in polar expeditions, at least an investigation of weather seems to possess some practical merit. Recent years have witnessed a widening interest in polar meteorology especially that of the south polar regions; and as a consequence of the activities of various expeditions more people are beginning to realize that the great polar ice caps play a dominant—perhaps even a predominant—rôle in maintaining the broad circulation and movements of air on which depend the climates of the world, and with them all human activities. Most of us have a dim, schoolbookish understanding of the theory of simple circulation: an air current flowing over the earth from the Poles to the Equator, a return current moving Poleward above it, and that this endlessly renewed interchange is the breathing of the planet on which we live. It is interesting to note that in the nineteenth century (when the shining bulk of Antarctica had only just been raised above the horizon) the attention of meteorologists centered rather on the tropical regions as the mainspring of universal meteorology.[1] But little by little, as the scope of polar exploration widened and the accruing meteorological data became more meaningful, the emphasis slowly drifted Poleward to such a degree that a theory has been advanced that the key to southern hemisphere atmospheric circulation, which is the motivating power for weather, may be found on the lofty Antarctic plateau. There is, for example, Hobbs' theory of the glacial anticyclone, in which the downdrafts of cold air from the high plateaux of Greenland and central Antarctica are identified as dominating agencies in the manufacture of wind and control of planetary circulation.[2] Of very great importance is Bjerknes's theory of the Polar Front. This theory explains the mechanics of weather phenomena in terms of the reactions caused by the interaction of great masses of cold polar air, the so-called "polar fronts," with the masses of warm air of equatorial origin which they intrude.[3]

[1] H. R. Mill, Intro., *The Glacial Anticyclones,* by W. H. Hobbs, ix, xii.
[2] This theory is extensively discussed in Hobbs' own book, *The Glacial Anticyclones.*
[3] Charles Franklin Brooks, *Why the Weather?,* 50. U. S. Weather Bureau, *Monthly Weather Review and Annual Summary 1900,* "The Dynamic Principle of the Circulatory Movements in the Atmosphere," by Prof. V. Bjerknes.

The subject is highly complicated and controversial, and meteorologists are anything but unanimous in such matters. This much, however, is certain. Antarctica is one of the great "centers of action" of world meteorology: the changes that occur there affect the entire southern hemisphere.[4] In the world's atmosphere there can be no watertight compartments.[5] A refrigerator for the southern hemisphere, as like the Arctic in the northern hemisphere, Antarctica plays an important rôle in the heat economy of the atmosphere and oceans: and its meteorology is of especial interest in connection with the study of world periodicities and the development of long-range forecasting.[6] While the two polar regions are effective only in their respective hemispheres and Antarctica, therefore, has no influence on the weather of the northern hemisphere, nevertheless it is fairly certain that general observation involving the circulation of air or laws of weather obtaining in the south polar regions will probably hold good for the Arctic and the northern hemisphere. In this respect, at least, Antarctic meteorology is of world-wide interest.

Hence, Antarctic weather isn't something peculiarly annoying to explorers alone. A passion for martyrdom doesn't impel a meteorologist to expose himself to a 100° of frost, with one eye glued to an excruciatingly cold theodolite, while he tries to follow the capricious ascent of a pilot balloon, lit by a candle, which is bobbing up through the winter darkness. What he's looking for is data—data which will give us a clearer understanding of the mysterious processes that create the "cold waves" and the "polar fronts" which exert such a profound influence in the weather of lower latitudes. These data, in time, may make it possible for meteorologists to forecast broad seasonal changes.

So far as theory and such go, I claim no better than a layman's general knowledge of meteorology: but in discussing the subject with Haines during the first expedition it was plain to me that the most valuable source of Antarctic weather data was still unprobed. What data existed had largely been collected at fixed bases on the coast or on islands adjacent to the coast, on ships exploring coastal waters, and by parties, meagerly equipped for meteorological research, engaged in fast summer dashes into the interior.[7] Meteorologically, the vast interior was still a complete blank space. No fixed meteorological stations had ever been established in the interior; no winter observations had ever been made beyond the coast; the fragmentary data collected by field parties extended only over the comparatively mild summer months. Yet inland, past the moderating influence of the sea, was the greatest

[4] Griffith Taylor, "Climatic Relations between Antarctica and Australia," *Problems of Polar Research,* Am. Geo. Soc., 294.
[5] Hayes, *Antarctica,* 66.
[6] E. Kidson, "Problems of Antarctic Meteorology," Quart. Journal, Royal Met. Soc., Vol. lviii, No. 245, July, 1932.
[7] Hayes, *Antarctica,* 66.

cold on the face of the earth; it was there that one would expect to find typical continental conditions.

From this reasoning it was but a step to the idea of Advance Base; and I was determined that when—and if—I returned with a second expedition I should bend every effort to establish a well-equipped meteorological station in the interior and have it occupied during the winter night. Haines and I discussed the plan many times. In 1933, when the second expedition was being organized, the first practical step toward that end was taken. In a loft in Boston, from a blueprint worked out by Czegka with a few suggestions from me, Tinglof built the shack for the outpost. The necessary meteorological equipment was loaned by the U. S. Weather Bureau.

But between the original plan of 1929 and the accomplished fact of March 25th, 1934, there was considerable disparity. The Antarctic has a way of tripping up the best laid plans.

For one thing, we had hoped that by launching the project immediately after disembarkation at Little America we should be able to plant the base, if not on the polar plateau itself, at least near the foot of the Queen Maud Range, 400 miles or so south of Little America, in the heart of the weather-breeder.

But the disheartening conditions attending the unloading of the ships and the reoccupation of Little America, as you have seen, made this larger plan impossible. The tractors could not be spared a day earlier than they were. At that they took the field at a season when approaching cold weather and the impending winter night ordinarily called for the suspension of operations, when parties already in the field were homing for the security and comfort of the main base. How far the tractors would get, whether it would be fifty miles or two hundred, I had no way of knowing. The southing would depend entirely upon the capacities of these untested vehicles.

Another thing: according to the original plan, three men were intended to occupy the shack. Three bunks were installed in the shack, and supplies in proper proportions were collected for three. But the outcome of the tractor journey was to arrange it differently. Even before the tractors started I foresaw that it could not be otherwise. In the brief time remaining before the onset of the winter night, it would be physically impossible for the tractors to haul sufficient stores to maintain three men for seven months, and morally a mistake of leadership to ask them to attempt it. Therefore the shack had to be occupied either by two men or (as it finally happened) by one.

However, the circumstances upon which rested the fate of the base and its ultimate relationship to the expedition program were still evolving.

III

Saturday the 17th produced its triumphs and grief. Not pausing to rest, the tractor fleet pushed on to 50-Mile Depot, a hard, 24-hour march. Innes-Taylor's party, homeward bound from Lat. 80° 56′, made 125-Mile Depot in a temperature of —54°. And the *Pilgrim,* homing from a flight to 100-Mile Depot, was forced down by fog and for two days was marooned "somewhere" on the Barrier.

The *Pilgrim* had been dispatched on a multiple vision: to survey a better route for the tractor fleet around the Valley of Crevasses, and to carry certain supplies to 100-Mile Depot. Innes-Taylor had remarked that his party's sleeping bags were in pieces; the zippers had carried away and the bags were badly iced. One need never have sledged to appreciate the agony this imposed. The dogs were also doing poorly on the pemmican rations; so forty pounds of fresh seal meat was put aboard the *Pilgrim.* Also in its load were a few odds and ends for Advance Base.

In crystal-clear air, with unlimited visibility and ceiling, and a temperature of —32°, Bowlin, with Clay Bailey as radio operator, took off at 11:32 A.M. This time they found 100-Mile Depot, landing at 1 o'clock and taking off twenty minutes later, after dumping their load at the foot of the snow beacon. They were following the trail, flying at a low altitude. Bailey reported: "Very hazy, no horizon." An insidious mist gathered at Little America. It is extraordinary how swiftly it grows, seeming to rise out of the Barrier in vaporous exhalations. Before your eyes the horizon rolls up like a carpet, the ceiling vanishes and the spacing, depths and relationships of objects are bewilderingly distorted. Bowlin was advised of the change. Dyer, having established contact with New York and Buenos Aires for the regular Saturday broadcast, held a channel open for the plane; and the radio engineers at these remote stations had the novel experience of listening in on a plane groping in the fog of the south polar regions.

At 2:00 o'clock Bailey advised "All well;" they had circled the tractor party to drop a note to June telling of a better way round the Valley of Crevasses, then resumed their course. At 2:15: "OK QSK 225." Then, without warning, at 2:25: "Flying low. Landing on Barrier 2.25. What is WX (weather). We are land—"

Silence. Another crash? Or had Bailey just dropped the key to reel in the trailing antennae? Anxious minutes of waiting, while Dyer tried to regain contact. Then the welcome note of the plane's transmitter. A safe landing on Barrier surface near heavy pressure. I asked for their position. Bowlin was unable to say: simply that after losing the trail in heavy mist and with a solid wall of fog ahead, he had landed while he still had visibility for landing. He thought, however, they were west of the trail.

Bowlin, as usual, had used excellent judgment. The fog was drawn taut at Little America. At 100 yards the *Condor* in its pit at the head of Ver-Sur-Mer Inlet was just a darker shadow. Even the skua gulls, Haines observed, were walking. Had Bowlin flown another five minutes he must certainly have crashed. For his gas tanks, as it happened, were nearly empty.

The contact was purposely short, in order to conserve the plane's batteries; Bailey was afraid they would not last more than twenty-four hours. I advised them not to be impatient; if they lost contact, to wait at least five days before attempting to reach Little America on foot. Meanwhile we would make every possible effort to reach them by plane or dog team.

So long as they remained with the plane, the men were all right. They had a month's rations, tent, cooker and primus stove, sleeping bags, fur clothing—all the emergency gear made compulsory equipment on every flight for just such a contingency. I was more concerned over the safety of the plane. A sudden gale might wreck it. In 1929 we had lost a plane under similar conditions. Bowlin presently reassured me on this point. Taking advantage of a brief lifting in the fog he flew to high Barrier and "dug in."

In the afternoon the fog lifted a trifle. Hopeful that the air would clear rapidly enough to allow us to begin the search at once, McCormick excavated the auto-gyro. The heater was under the engine when the fog clamped down again; you could almost see it drop, a black weight pressing down. Frost crystals, the exquisite snow flowers of the Antarctic, were gathering on every exposed object, on the guys and the stays and the antennae cables.

Next day brought heavy easterly winds and drift; flying and sledging were impossible. But a heater stood under the auto-gyro engine all day. No word from Bowlin—batteries exhausted, of course.

Meanwhile we worked out methods for their relief. Dr. Poulter was put in charge of the operations. Two dog-team parties were detailed to comb the area east and south of Amundsen Arm on a ten mile front. The fewer men involved in a rescue effort, the better: that's one of the unwritten principles of the Antarctic. If anything goes wrong, it isn't half so difficult rescuing the rescuers.

The one doubtful element was the whereabouts of the plane. It might be anywhere in a gray emptiness of barrier. Fortunately, thanks to the meager information yielded by the radio, it was possible to calculate the position with approximate accuracy. Bowlin said he landed at 2:25 o'clock. He was over the tractors at 2:00 o'clock. Queried by radio, June said the tractors were 35 geographical miles south when Bowlin passed and dropped the note. Bailcy reported OK at 2:15. Presumably (though this was doubtful) they were still holding the trail. The plane's cruising speed was 90 knots, or 1.5 miles per minute. At 2:15, then, the plane was probably 13 miles south of Little America. Some time during the next ten minutes they drifted off the trail in the fog. Even if Bowlin flew steadily at right angles, the plane therefore could not be more than 15 miles off the trail. The chances were that he had circled—perhaps turned south again—trying to pick up the trail. Bowlin thought he was west of the trail. But the pressure he described might be the Bad Lands east of Amundsen Arm. However, no one could tell; I put no stock in my own guess.

Monday was sunny; but a stiff breeze was blowing at Little America. At 4 A.M. the members of the sledging party—Blackburn, who knew Amundsen Arm better than any man, having surveyed it in 1929-1930; Dr. Poulter, Dane, Russell, Moody and Guy Hutcheson, the latter as radio operator—were routed out by the night watchman: at 6 o'clock they left for Amundsen Arm, carrying 50 gallons of gas for the plane. McCormick and I embarked in the auto-gyro about two hours later. The temperature was —32°.

Rising above the protecting ridge encircling Little America, the gyro pitched and yawed in a wind of gale force. Beyond Amundsen Arm, we commenced the search. McCormick was watching to port and I to starboard. Out of the tail of his eye, McCormick saw something shine far to the east, called my attention to it. It was just a vague, meaningless speck, but we swung east because we were overlooking no bets. Ultimately the speck became the *Pilgrim.* I give McCormick entire credit for finding it; I would have missed it. For twenty-five minutes we bucked the wind, which at times seemed to be blowing us backwards, before we reached the plane. Drift had risen to the cabin, and fanned in long streamlined ridges, to leeward. Bowlin had indeed landed on the margins of the Bad Lands. Not far from the plane a crevasse gaped a hundred feet from lip to lip; just beyond were the uplifted blocks of pressure, as bad as any I have ever seen. Bowlin's stabbing descent in the fog was lucky not to have fetched up in that. The gyro dropped down the face of the gale, like a spider scuttling down a brick wall. I had the queer sensation of landing *backwards.* Bailey and Bowlin were asleep in a tent pitched in the lee of the plane; in the rush of wind they hadn't heard us arrive. Bowlin, rubbing the sleep from his eyes, greeted me warmly. Then a wry smile crossed his face; and with a twinkle, he asked:

"Did you fly?"

"Yes."

"But not, I hope—spare me that—in the gyro!"

I had to admit it. Bailey roared.

"Why didn't you just let us die out here, quietly and honorably?" said Bowlin.

Bowlin was a veteran Navy flyer, one of the very best; McCormick, a splendid pilot, was just a youngster, and the autogyro was the apple of his eye. But though Bowlin loved him like a brother and was quietly and wordlessly to sustain him when McCormick himself crashed and was hurt in the spring, still as a flying man he affected a profound and unmitigated scorn for the autogyro. He called it, among other things, "that tired windmill," and drove McCormick to despair by asking with acid innocence, how come its remarkable agitations in flight: was it just trying to scratch its back or choke itself to death? Indeed, the aviation unit was unable to explain how the autogyro flew at all, because they had proved by all the laws of aërodynamics that, with a full load of gas and emergency gear, the plane had a cruising range of *minus* 25 miles.

I paused only long enough to assure Bowlin that the dog teams were on their way with gas. The wind was knocking the auto-gyro around and McCormick was afraid it would blow over. We took off to find the dog teams. With the wind behind us it was a different story; twenty-five minutes going out, six minutes to get back. The dog teams had just crossed Amundsen Arm, about ten miles south of Little America. We landed alongside, and McCormick took Poulter and Blackburn to an altitude of several thousand feet to show them where the plane lay. The engine commenced to knock. McCormick, after an inspection, said that a rocker box stud was broken; the autogyro was grounded till spare parts could be brought from Little America. Ruefully I made a simple calculation: three planes left after the Fokker crash, two grounded away from base—total at Little America, one.

With one team three men departed with gas for the *Pilgrim,* and with the second team I hastened back to Little America to get the spare parts McCormick needed. Swan, the aeronautical engineer, left immediately with the parts. On the following afternoon, after a morning fog had dissipated, both planes flew to Little America, were berthed and made fast in their pits west of the camp.

Of his flight in the fog, Bowlin said:

"Immediately after we passed over the tractors we saw a low bank of fog far to the north. I thought it lay over the Ross Sea, but shortly after we passed 25-Mile Depot we stuck our nose in it. The fog was very low, not more than a few hundred feet deep, but dense as water. We went above it, hoping to find a hole, but there was none. About ten miles south of Little America we turned back. I was afraid that if I kept going I might get out over the Ross Sea. We retraced our course about five miles, then I came down through the fog, on the chance of getting a glimpse of the trail. Nothing doing. Visibility was just about zero. Gas was short, so I decided to land anyhow. It might be a lot harder if I put it off. I squashed in, fish-tailing to wear the speed off. No, I couldn't see very much. When it's gray like that you can't tell where fog ends and snow begins; it's just a milky broth. We sat down very nicely, and I was sitting there, congratulating myself, when there was a rift in the mist, and just off my port bow I saw a mass of pressure that looked like the Rocky Mountains. There was a big crevasse a few feet away. 'Let's go out of here,' said Bailey. Which suited me. Soon afterwards the mist lifted a bit, and we flew three or four miles and landed again on high barrier. That's how I got so far eastward."

IV

Meanwhile I followed with the greatest anxiety the progress of the tractors. March 18th, in a driving snowstorm, June and Skinner pushed ahead in a lone Citroën to test a new passage around the Valley of Crevasses. Bowlin, in the note he dropped from the air, had recommended détouring several miles to the east. On this tack, about 18 miles southeast of 50-Mile Depot, the tractor hit a crevasse. The right tread broke through, and the car heeled over at an angle of 45°. Though very deep, the crevasse fortunately was only four feet wide: the car lay cater-cornered in it, with the right side resting on the lip of the crevasse.

Not having radio, June couldn't advise the main body of the accident. Stormbound at 50-Mile Depot, Demas waited twenty-four hours, then at noon on the 19th pushed on with the other three cars, first taking aboard the 3,000 pounds of stores which Bowlin had mistakenly cached there. Visibility was abominable; the blizzard became a gale; the flags with which June had marked the new detour were blotted out, and the drivers instead relied upon the rapidly drifting tracks of his car. They couldn't see these tracks more than five feet ahead; unable to see through the windshields, the drivers steered with their heads stuck out the side windows. To add to their grief, frozen condensation in the fuel lines and the icing up of carburetors compelled frequent stops. The pin on the Cletrac's crank shaft had sheared off when they tried to crank it at 50-Mile Depot; they managed to start it by towing it in gear with one of the Citroëns. But the three cars held to their course, and shortly before midnight stumbled upon the fourth tractor. June had salvaged it after prodigious shoveling. First they had rammed down a tailboard where the walls of the crevasse pinched together, then packed snow on top until the sunken tread had surface to work on. The craft was restored to an even keel by excavating under the port tread, after which an incline was dug. Under its own power the car gained solid surface.

Unable to continue in the gale, the party camped there that night, Demas not daring to stop the Cletrac's engine. The strain of dislodging that mass of dead weight to start the engine would play hob with the Citroën's transmission. The Cletrac's fate was settled in the morning. The instant Demas gave it the gun the engine stopped. Though blow torches were played on the crankcase and rear end for two hours, though two Citroëns took the car in tow, the engine refused to start. A radio dispatch informed me of the breakdown. An extensive overhaul was in prospect.

Short of a disaster, a severer blow could not have been dealt the party. The foundering of the Cletrac had in a single stroke deprived the party of fifty percent of its load-carrying power.

I instructed June to redistribute the loads and proceed with the three

Citroëns to 100-Mile Depot, and return later for the rest of the Cletrac's load. Farther than 100-Mile Depot I saw no hope of conveying the Base. Even this distance was doubtful.

On the morning of the 20th, June and Demas reorganized their party on the wind-swept ridge. Hill would remain behind with Demas and work over the Cletrac, which Demas still hoped to salvage. Casting off his own sledges, Waite took in tow the sledge stowed with the sections of the portable shack. June and Skinner in the first Citroën hooked on the sledge holding the fuel for the base; and trailing astern of Dustin in the third Citroën were four small sledges of miscellaneous supplies. About half of the stores remained to be relayed.

Leaving Demas and Hill, June and his squadron bore southwest for 11 miles, fetching up with the Southern Party's trail on the southern heights of the Valley of Crevasses. The wind dropped, but the air chilled rapidly to —48°. In soft snow the tractors labored; many stops were made to rid the gas lines and carburetor jets of ice. But eventually, on the evening of the 21st, the three cars straggled into 100-Mile Depot. Innes-Taylor's party arrived almost simultaneously from the south, having been held up by heavy blizzards; only one day's rations of dog pemmican remained on the sledges for the dogs.

March 22nd was clear and cold, —52° where the tractors were. That morning Siple and Tinglof broke ground for Advance Base about 100 yards east of the snow beacon marking the depot. And that morning also I flew from Little America to direct the setting up of the Base.

V

As I have said earlier, we were not able to advance sufficient supplies to staff this meteorological outpost with three men. The alternative was either two men or one man. After gravely considering the choice for a long time, it seemed to me that to man the base with two men was impractical. My own experience in the polar regions, together with what I knew about men who had been isolated in the Arctic, convinced me that the chances were small that two men by themselves could achieve temperamental harmony. Remember, this outpost was to be sunk in the crust of the Ross Ice Barrier; and, as we gauged the risks then, whoever went out there had to be reconciled to isolation for at least seven months, no matter what came to pass. Four of these months would be in complete darkness, under the most unfavorable conditions that life contrives anywhere on earth. Life in that spot would resemble life on a dark, dead, and bitterly cold planet, and for some months would be almost as inaccessible as on that planet.

Two men, jammed together at arm's length in a tiny shack in this strange environment, living by the dim light of a lantern in a state of perpetual congestion and intrusion, staring at each other for seven months; hardly able to take a step without coming into collision; unable to express a thought without running athwart the other man's prejudices; small things taking on a monstrous significance! What man's nerves could stand the irritation? Could it possibly work out?

Under such a set of circumstances could a man predict the reactions of his best friend? Could he be sure of his own reactions?

Hating or being hated by a man you could not get out of your sight for long weary months would be a degrading experience, leaving the mark of Cain in your heart.

In all events, I was determined not to assume the responsibility for creating such a situation. Of course it is not impossible that two men could achieve harmony under these conditions. Few things are really impossible, least of all in human psychology. But I personally would prefer the risk of being alone at Advance Base to the hazard of having to endure the humiliation that a second man might involve.

In the woods it would be a different story. One would have diversions and familiar things. Even in the Arctic there is abundant life in places, as is so well described in Stefanssen's *Friendly Arctic*. It was necessary, as I said, that we should occupy the Base. Even if it had been possible to staff it with three men, I should still have had to be one of them; but since I felt it had to be one man, it seemed definitely up to me to go. I could not—and would not—ask another man to go. There was the advantage, too, of eliminating the need of having a second man beyond the services of a doctor.

But the decision wasn't really hard to make. The truth of the matter is, I really wanted to go and keenly looked forward to the experience. When I left Little America, I said I was going because I wanted to go. I could not bring myself to say I was going only in the interest of science because I sincerely believed I was as interested in the experience, for its own sake, as I was in the meteorological work for which the Base was designed. Therefore, I cannot say that I was making a sacrifice for science. That did not enter my head.

As for leaving the camp without a leader, well, I had confidence in the officers and men at Little America. No hazardous undertakings would be attempted during the winter night. Then there was a chance that I would have radio contact. Just before my departure, I wrote the following order:

> The following new appointments are made, to be effective during the absence of the leader:
>
> Second-in-Command................Dr. Thomas C. Poulter
> Third-in-Command........................William Haines
> Chief of Staff..............................Harold June
> Executive Officer.........................George Noville
>
> These officers will be obeyed and respected accordingly....
>
> During the absence of the leader the Second-in-Command will represent him. The Third-in-Command automatically becomes

the Commanding Officer during the absence from camp of the Second-in-Command. During the absence of both of the above mentioned officers, the Chief of Staff will take command. In the case of the absence of all three, the Executive Officer will assume command . . .

The principal instructions the leader leaves behind are few and simple:

1. Work industriously on obtaining scientific data and in making plans and preparations for the spring and summer operations.
2. Make and abide by strict rules for safety as to fire, getting lost in storms, or down crevasses during the night or thick weather of any kind.
3. As with all undertakings of this nature, conservation of food, fuel, clothing and shelter becomes of vital importance. Strict orders regarding the conservation of fuel will be issued and enforced.
4. Every man in this camp has an equal right to be treated fairly and squarely, and the officers are requested to hold this fact in mind.
5. More minute instructions will be given to the Second-in-Command.

Discipline must be strict, but unnecessary restrictions should be avoided. The acting commanding officer has the power to act upon cases of selfishness or infractions of camp regulations. He may, if he desires, turn over any one to the staff [8] for trial.

In addition to the above, the staff has two functions. First, to make plans as requested by the Commanding Officer. Secondly, the staff holds the power by two-thirds vote to overrule any order that any officer may give that may be considered unwise or unfair by the staff. As the staff now stands a vote of eleven members will be considered two-thirds. In such a case the good of the expedition from the broad standpoint should be the controlling factor.

The Chief of Staff may call his staff together at any time or place he may see fit, and the commanding officer may request a meeting when he so desires. . . .

In a sense, our status is primitive, where the humblest work takes on importance. That, I hope, you will always remember. We have no class distinction as in civilization. What a man is back home does not count at Little America. He who may have failed back there has his chance to make good here, and he will not be judged by the position he holds so much as by the way he plays the game and does his job, however humble it may be. . . .

The leader wishes for every man during his absence as pleasant a six months as he enjoyed during his last sojourn on the ice.

RICHARD E. BYRD.

[8] A staff, consisting largely of department heads and veterans of the first expedition, was appointed to assist and coöperate with the commanding officers.

VI

It took only a few hours to arrange my affairs. More detailed instructions had previously been given to Poulter, June, Haines, Noville and others.

Bowlin and Bailey waited impatiently in the *Pilgrim*. The engine was idling. Though hot oil had just been poured into the engine, it chilled rapidly. Blobs of black smoke were puffing out of the exhaust. The temperature was —43°.

We took off for Advance Base at 10:35 A.M. Gaining altitude across Ver-Sur-Mer Inlet, Bowlin made a banking turn around Little America, before squaring away for the south. I took in every detail, photographing the scene in my mind—the dark tracery of antennae, the dog crates and dogs tethered outside, the drifted caches, the unfinished, uncovered trenches of the tunnels, the lumpish mounds in which the buildings were pocketed and the plumes of smoke lingering over the ventilators and chimney pipes—a snug harbor in a vast rolling plain of white. Perhaps I felt homesick at the thought of leaving it; I'm not sure. I know that I should hesitate to describe what the place means to me.

A sweeping glance to the north showed the Ross Sea was frozen, a still, dark immensity. The whitish shimmer of ice blink laced the horizon.

The flight south was completed without incident. At 67 miles we flew low over the Cletrac. Demas and Hill, who were working on the engine, crawled out from under the canvas apron and waved a friendly greeting. Poor devils, theirs was an excruciatingly cold job.

Like welts in the unspoiled flesh of the Barrier, the tractor tracks ran south. Bowlin sped over them at an altitude of 50 feet. A dark speck on the horizon resolved itself into a cluster of tents and tractors—Advance Base.

Where Advance Base lay the Ross Shelf Ice was quite as flat as the Kansas plains. Snow rose to meet blue sky in an unbroken round of horizon. How spacious and empty it seemed, and how huddled and puny the aggregation of tractors, dog teams and men! A pin-pricking effort in infinity.

The plane landed at 11:55. It was quickly unloaded. Bowlin and Bailey wasted not a moment: too great a chance that cold would stop the engine. Fifteen minutes later they were off for Little America. In the super-cooled air the vapor from the exhaust trailed for miles behind the plane.

VII

When June led the three tractors north to recover the rest of the Cletrac's load, Captain Innes-Taylor, Paine, Ronne and Black of the

Southern Party and Petersen, Siple and Tinglof of the tractor party were hard at work on the Base. They had already excavated a pit deep enough to accommodate the shack, and Tinglof and Siple were laying the floor sections in the hole when I arrived. Brutal work, with the temperature sagging through the minus fifties. Nevertheless we stayed with it till 1 A.M., working by the bright glare of pressure lamps. Carefully we watched one another's faces for the dead-white patches of frost-bite, which one so rarely feels but which the other man can see. A solicitous molding of the flesh with the finger tips, fingers stinging the instant they leave the warmth of the gloves, the painful pulsing of blood in the affected zone: then back to work. Most of all I regretted having to delay the Southern Party's return to Little America. I gathered that they had had a rough time of it, especially on account of defective zippers on the sleeping bags. To sleep more than a few minutes at a time, Innes-Taylor said, was impossible; lying still meant slowly freezing to death. The bags were so stiff with ice that they had to be pounded before it was possible to roll them up.

During the night the temperature dropped to —60°; the kerosene froze in the primus lamps. Next morning, not far apart, the three Citroëns rolled into the Base, with the last of the Cletrac's load. Through that merciless cold they had traveled all night, dogged by the curse of freezing carburetors. Demas and Hill were aboard. After taking the Cletrac's engine down, Demas said, they had found that the magneto was dead. His hands and Hill's, I noticed, were painfully frost-bitten.

The Base was pretty well along by then; only the tunnels for food and fuel remained to be dug, and the food boxes and fuel drums stowed within them. That night we had a farewell "bon voyage" banquet for the Southern Party, which was free to resume its northing in the morning. Among the stores Petersen found several turkeys and chickens which Corey had handsomely contributed. Hard as armor plate, they were thawed out with blow torches. By unanimous vote Innes-Taylor was elected *chef;* and, presiding over five primus stoves, he concocted a princely feast. Fourteen men sat cross-legged on the deck, as intimate as sardines, genial and contented, and glowing with the filling content of something more delicately flavored than *hoosh.* Then we turned in, the hardy dog-drivers going topside to sleep in their tents, the rest of us unrolling our sleeping bags on the deck. Still do I recall that night with undiminished awe. In subsequent months of darkness I was to hear the disturbing phenomenon of snow quakes, a violent shivering of the crust and a deep, space-filling roar as great areas of snow sought a new equilibrium. But they were nothing more than the spent and declining echoes of the heroic snoring I heard that night. I might have said it was the mightiest demonstration of its kind ever played on human instruments, had not Dr. Poulter, Demas and

Waite arrived in concert in August, bringing their own unmuted horns and brasses upon which they played in the cool of the evening with rising exuberance and inventiveness, devising breathless runs, trills, pipings, blood-curdling strangulation effects, the virtuosity of which I never hope to hear excelled.

But to return to the theme: the banquet was somewhat premature, because on the 24th a stabbing westerly wind held the Southern Party at the Base. Heavy drift, visibility fifty yards, temperature —28° are too cruel a combination for sledging. But next day the teams departed, Black choosing to return with the tractors rather than let his game leg hold up their progress. The temperature was —48° and falling. In the evening, Demas, Skinner and Hill departed in a Citroën for the Cletrac, to make a last effort to salvage and drive it to Little America.

June, Siple, Waite, Petersen, Black and Dustin lingered long enough to make the Base shipshape. Waite installed the radio equipment, strung the antennae, and satisfactorily tested the hook-up with Dyer at Little America. With June's and Siple's help, I set up the meteorological equipment—instrument shelter topside, triple register in the shack. On the recording drums the whirring anemometer cups were already spinning out a tale of winds, the thermometers a tale of temperatures, at the coldest spot ever occupied. This day, March 26th, a numbing wind buffeted the Base. But the job was finished; at 5 P.M. the following day, after having dug out their cars and heated the engines for hours, the tractor crew finally departed, only to creep back a few hours later, having been stopped by mechanical breakdowns a few miles out. All that night, with the thermometers reading —59°, the drivers tinkered with frozen radiators and capricious carburetors.

At 12:10 P.M., March 28th, the cars again set forth for Little America. My isolation had begun.

Wed., March 28, Midnight.

The tractors are off at last. . . . For more than 200 days I shall see no living thing. But I'm in the midst of chaos with a very lame shoulder. I wrenched it when I fell while lifting a heavy box onto a tractor. It's very painful and an unfortunate handicap just now, because everything is in confusion, and days—even weeks—of hard work are needed to put things to rights.

Boxes, loose clothing, books, and odds and ends past counting are strewn about. I haven't the faintest idea where anything is. I've searched conscientiously for the alarm clock and the cook book, and the suspicion is growing that I left them at Little America. It would be an ironic joke if, in the pretentious planning for every contingency, we forgot these most commonplace and vital necessities.

Another thing: the fuel line from the tank to the stove is leaking and is therefore something of a fire hazard. Hope my shoulder mends soon. It's difficult to do anything with it. . . .

VIII

Bolling Advance Weather Base was situated at Lat. 80° 08′ S., Long. 163° 57′ W., within a hair's breadth of being due south of Little America. It lay near the heart of the Ross Shelf Ice, which itself is one of the grand natural wonders of the world, a vast sheet of ice rolling from the Ross Sea to the foot of the Queen Maud Range, 400 miles broad and upwards of 600 feet in thickness; its basement rests (we know now) on submarine ridges and depressed mountain tops in many places and much of it floats buoyantly upon the sea. Where the Base was no life had moved, nothing had stirred for centuries; the Ice Age was in complete ascendancy. In whatever direction I looked, north, east, south, or west, the vista was the same, a spread of ice fanning to meet the horizon. The shack itself faced west for no particular reason, now that I reflect on why this was so, since the Base lay locked within the Barrier crust. Anyhow, a hundred yards or so to the west was the eight-foot snow beacon and the orange-topped tent identifying 100-Mile Depot on the southern trail. But as the trail itself went, twisting and detouring to escape crevasses and profit by good surface, the Base was actually 123 statute miles from Little America. A thin line of orange flags, fitted to 24-inch bamboo sticks, fled northward to Little America. At first these flags were planted at intervals of a third of a mile, but June had later reduced the interval to one-sixth of a mile by doubling the number of flags.

The day my isolation commenced the shack itself was completely roofed by snow. It had been set up underground for three reasons: first, to benefit from the warmer and more constant temperatures prevailing within the crust; secondly, to shelter it from the penetrating winds which search out every crevice; and, thirdly, to protect it from the drift which mounts, with the velocity of a tidal wave, around every exposed object. Only the 12-foot anemometer pole with its silver wind cups and weather vane, the beehive-shaped instrument shelter holding the thermometers and barograph, and the radio antennae strung on 12-foot bamboo poles showed above ground. A double-action trap door set in the projecting roof of the shack, with a flat-runged ladder rising to it, communicated with the surface. This narrow projecting roof formed a small vestibule underground, from which emanated two narrow, parallel tunnels, 40 feet long, running east and west. In the southern tunnel was cached the food, the boxes themselves partly forming the side walls: in the other, the fuel drums. In the southern tunnel the small gasoline generator which powered my main radio set was disposed in a box set in a niche in the snow wall, with an exhaust pipe discharging on the surface. The toilet was at the end of the food tunnel. The beginning of a third tunnel, which I called the escape tunnel, had already been mined from the food tunnel; completed, it would give me an emergency exit if blizzards buried the trap-door.

As for the shack itself, it was a jewel of its kind. Tight, compact and of special fireproof construction, it measured 9x13x8 feet: the walls were only four inches thick, being built up of layers of special veneer and insulation which gave it the warmth of four feet of brick. So shrewdly had Tinglof matched the doweled sections that one could hear the air squashing out when they were fitted together. Unfortunately, however, several sections were damaged so that I could never completely shut the door. My bunk took up one corner of the room. At the foot of it stood a table upon which rested the triple register, which automatically recorded wind direction and velocity; the dry cell batteries, which powered it, were racked underneath. On the other walls were tiers of shelves, on one set of which my books were arranged; on the other, food. In one corner was a stand for the radio apparatus, with diminishing shelves, like a Chinese box, the lowest shelf holding the receiving set and key, with just enough space to serve as a writing table. The stove (a caboose type coal stove fitted with a single oil burner and a gravity tank for fuel) stood a foot or so out from one wall; the stack ran up and across the room, passing out through a small vent in one corner. A ventilator was cut in the roof: and to maintain a flow of fresh air an inlet had been let through the roof of the vestibule, through which a pipe conducted cold air under the floor of the shack, connecting with a second pipe inside the shack which discharged a few inches from the ceiling.

Altogether, it was a neat and not uncomfortable arrangement. Every likely source of risk that could be foreseen had been studied, and means made available for overcoming it. Against cold and blizzards the Base seemed staunch as a steel turret. But the small flaws which several months later were to make that place a living hell were present. For one thing, several stove-pipe sections were lost in the transportation of stores from Little America: and to fit the unequal sections together rough joints were made from empty fuel tins, which couldn't be rendered air-tight; so noxious fumes seeped into the room. And the stove itself was a make-shift affair. The oil-burning stove which had been brought from the United States was rejected as being defective after many tests at Little America; and at the last moment Siple had had the machinist replace it with an ordinary coal-burning caboose stove into which a burner had been inserted. Coal would have been the ideal fuel; but the weight and bulk of coal prohibited its consideration. The fumes leaking from these sources, together with the fumes thrown off by the gasoline engine which powered my radio set, were the cause of my subsequent misfortunes.

Still, in March 1934, the outcome was concealed. With confidence, even with keen anticipation, I turned to meet the oncoming winter night. There was much work to be done: the 40-foot escape tunnel to finish, and the stores to be sorted out. Meteorological and auroral observations occupied a substantial part of the day. The following

(Photograph by Charles G. Morgan)

Dog-Town

(Photograph by Charles G. Morgan)

Some of the New Buildings—"Dog Heim" and the Radio Shack

(© Paramount Pictures, Inc.)

BUILDING A SHELTER FOR THE PLANES

(Photograph by Joseph A. Pelter)

WINTER NIGHT—LOOKING UP THE GARAGE RAMP

meteorological records were made: a continuous mechanical registration of barometric pressure, temperature, wind direction and velocity; twice daily visual observations of cloudiness and the state of the weather; twice daily readings of maximum and minimum thermometers in the instrument shelter topside and twice daily visual observations of the barometer. The four instruments themselves exacted constant attention. In addition, I stood four or five auroral watches daily whenever the sky was clear enough for such displays. The intensity, structural form and direction of the aurora were noted, for subsequent comparison with the observations of observers who watched simultaneously at Little America. So I never had reason to complain of nothing to do.

Chapter X

UNDERGROUND

I

DIRECTLY after Admiral Byrd was established at Advance Base the expedition's fall operations drew to a close. The tractor fleet in fighting off at the end an epidemic of mechanical breakdowns, limped into Little America on March 29th, and two days later Innes-Taylor's Southern Party hove into sight. We were glad to see them all, and pleased that they had pulled off the operations as well as they had.

With the exception of Black, handicapped by a previous minor leg injury which was aggravated by cold and the strenuous demands of sledging, the men returned fit and well, though the dog drivers seemed to be trained down rather fine, and all of them, tractor drivers as well as sledgers, bore on their hands and faces the yellow, scabrous healing sores of frost-bite. Unremitting cold and the unremitting vindictiveness of blizzards had made March bitter for field operations. On this they were all agreed, however much they disagreed on other matters. During the last week especially, when the nights were rapidly lengthening, the cold was almost unbearable. "We just couldn't seem to keep warm," Innes-Taylor said. Commencing March 16th, when the Southern Party turned home, 178 miles south of Little America, the daily temperatures follow: —30°, —54°, —45°, —36°, —14°, —28°, —52°, —60°, —30°, —48°, —24°, —43°, —34°, —61°, —14°. During the 31 days the Southern Party was in the field, there were 18 days when blizzards or drift rendered traveling impossible: the average daily minimum temperature was —20°.

Nevertheless, the combined operations, tractor and sledging, were carried off with only one temporary loss—the abandonment of the Cletrac. Demas had finally hobbled the "Iron Horse" on the wind-swept ridge of the Valley of Crevasses. Mechanically, Demas said, the car was all right and could be recovered (as he proved) in the spring. All that kept him from bringing it back was the cold. In all events, the Cletrac had been an invaluable asset, and Admiral Byrd, thinking the men had suffered enough in the cold, advised them to leave the car till the spring.

Next to the accomplishment of their separate missions, the most striking contribution of the journeys was the contrast they presented between tractors and dog teams, between the new and the old, between steel and the finely strung, highly emotional content of heart and sinew that is the Eskimo husky. The issue between dogs and tractors as to which was superior on barrier surface had at last been joined; and in the first telling test, on the same sort of rolling surface on which he had reigned from the beginning of time, the dog came out second best. In the decisive matters of speed and pay load the tractor, pending the more rigorous eliminations of the spring journeys was well out in front. It was tireless, needing only a steady hand to guide it when the engine was running right: what "bugs" had cropped up, the drivers were sure, could be corrected with various adaptations; moreover, in gales that had beaten the dogs to the ground, the tractor had stoutly demonstrated its ability to hold a course so long as there was a trail to follow. Altogether mechanized transport had made off with the first season's honors, and the tractor pilots were jubilant over the spring prospects.

But the dog drivers, loyal to their craft, were very, very skeptical and the two groups were no sooner together than there commenced over the long pine mess tables a controversy between them and the cocky Citroën pilots that outlasted the winter night and lingered even after the tractors met their Waterloo, ten months later, in the crevasses past 81° S. There was talk enough over the matter of Dogs *vs.* Tractors to sustain a conference on naval pacts—and feeling, too, the same icy restraint and polite sarcasm that make for such agreeable intercourse between, say, aviation experts who would scrap all battleships and Admirals who would return the compliment to aircraft.

The tractor drivers, taking their cue from Al Carbone the cook, an unwilling neutral observer at these Mess Hall debates, referred to Innes-Taylor's young men as "dog catchers"; and the latter, drawing their inspiration from the same fertile source of invective, twitted the others as "limousine explorers." Passionately defending a heritage which they thought was being despoiled by machinery, the dog drivers exclaimed that the tractors, with their greasy droppings, were corrupting the traditions of polar sledging—which only excited from the tractor corps the retort that times were changing and that the "horseless carriage, boys, has come to stay in Antarctica."

Very fond was Captain Innes-Taylor of the story of the night the tractors passed him when he and his half-frozen dog drivers were trying to spoon the evening *hoosh* past their chattering teeth. The *beep-beep-beep* of a tractor born suddenly smote the Barrier silence. The sledgers got to the tent flap just in time to see the red-and-black cars flash by in a cloud of drift.

"You have my word for it, gentlemen," the Captain swore, "those bloated daredevils were lolling on cushioned seats, chewing gum and eating chocolate like so many millionaires on a tour. Stop? Hell, those fellows went by with their noses stuck up in the air as if they were passing a family of peasants having a humble dinner in their miserable hovel!"

Beneath this banter there was a vein of hard and solid truth. Perhaps that was why these shafts stung; both sides were right, and each knew it. Of course it was all good-natured. Then, as in the spring, the tractor and dog men pooled their resources and talents in a common effort for the success of the field operations. The two forms of transport, the new no less than the old, each had hardships and problems peculiar and unique to itself; for punishment there was little to choose between them, as the logs of their journeys showed.

On one hand, the sledging parties contended with the same unfriendly circumstances that have always gone hand-in-hand with sledging: bone-searching cold and physical hardships; the endless labor of pitching and breaking camp; fighting swaying sledges over razor-backed sastrugi; ice-filled sleeping bags and ski boots that must be kneaded and pounded and hammered before they can be put on; the agony of beating into super-cooled headwinds and trying to hold steady on a compass course while the dogs cringe belly-down and persistently pay off before the wind; and the scuffling of blizzards over quaking tents and the sudden torrent of snow bursting through a running rent in the cloth.

On the other hand, the tractor drivers had to meet conditions for which there were no prior experience or counsel: the misery of handling gasoline and metal in temperatures that shriveled the flesh; sucking and blowing the frozen condensation out of gas lines; playing blow torches over carburetors to melt the ice clogging the jets and float chambers, and to thaw the radiators after the last ounce of anti-freeze solution had vanished through enlarging leaks; the exasperating hours of waiting for blow torches to loosen the oil and grease in the crank-case, transmission and rear end, which congealed to the viscosity of rubber the moment the ignition switches were cut; and the chore of melting snow in the cookers to provide water for leaky radiators; the continual parting of tow-lines and the tipping of heavily-loaded sledges too narrow of beam; and the agony of making small, delicate adjustments with bare hands in remote parts of the engines, with cold robbing the hands of feeling and drift stinging the eyes. And the torture, finally, of sitting hour after hour in the freezing cars, unable to get circulation back into limbs numb with cold.

Cold and blizzards were leveling factors and both tractors and dogs had their heels of Achilles.

Let's glance at the Southern Party, breaking camp at 75-Mile Depot on the morning of March 27th. Homeward bound. Temperature —43°, and a 30-mile wind which was like a knife drawn across the face. All three men painfully frost-bitten before the teams were hitched up. And snow with no more run to it than sand. A short distance out, Harold, a black Labrador husky in Ronne's team, went down: dead in the harness. He was cut loose and the teams moved on. Then Skeelah, wheeldog in Innes-Taylor's team, collapsed: exhaustion and cold. The merciful judgment was to shoot him; he was slowly freezing to death. It took Innes-Taylor eleven minutes to thaw out the revolver in his glove. An hour later, Skookum, a wolf in Paine's team, keeled over. Same thing: cold and exhaustion. He, too, was shot. The teams struggled on. That day 13½ miles run. "The most awful day we've had," Innes-Taylor wrote in his diary. "Days like this will kill off our dogs in short order."

Now let's swing south to June's tractor, making ready to leave Advance Base a day later. After he, Dustin and Waite had pawed over the engines for hours to get it started, they found by taking down the carburetor that the high-speed metering jet had been sucked through the engine and was lost. No replacement nearer than Little America. Stopped? Not quite. To make it easier to blow out gas lines, Demas had inserted into the gas line close to the carburetor a small copper tubing with a pet cock attached. After tinkering with it, June found that by opening the pet cock and making a careful adjustment he could control the flow of air and with it the flow of gas drawn into the carburetor. But it meant a fresh adjustment for every change in speed, every change in grade. Thus crippled, they started the homeward dash. The temperature dropped to —64°. To add to their grief, the generator burned out; they were dependent upon batteries: then the radiator froze. In unscrewing the cap June first scalded one hand in the steaming spray that gushed up, then froze the other before he could regain the protection of the cab. If he got out once to make a carburetor adjustment, June swore he got out a hundred times. Waite, when he wasn't taking his turn at the wheel, dozed with a primus lamp burning in a bucket on his lap.

It was fascinating to compare the logs of the two parties. The tempo of the tractor driver was set, not by the sun as in March sledging, but by the moods and stamina of the drivers. Not for them the rhythmic routine of the dog drivers, the morning and evening camps, the luncheon stops, the fifteen-minute resting spells for men and dogs, regulated by the limits of physical endurance and the food reserves either on the sledges or in the depots. Hindered by the constant cropping up of small mechanical troubles and irked by the necessity of heating the engines every time they were stopped, the tractor drivers' philosophy of *keeping her* rolling was animated by the simple necessity of cramming in all possible mileage so long as things held together. However, since the cars traveled in convoy, these mechanical faults could be counted upon to occur at frequent enough intervals, as the dog-drivers helpfully observed, to keep the drivers from meanwhile starving to death for lack of time to eat.

Nevertheless the severity of the March journeys had had the invaluable effect of testing equipment to the breaking point; weaknesses and defects in tractors, sledges, trail gear and field strategy, even in the food value of the rations, had been exposed. During the winter night this hard-bought wisdom was turned to good account in fortifying the equipment of the spring parties.

II

Now that the pressure of field operations was lifted, the fifty-five men at Little America turned to the still formidable task of holing in for the winter. It was a pretty grim prospect. Here was April upon us, the sun to depart in a fortnight, and the three planes and all the tractors and dogs were still on the surface; a hundred tons of coal, gasoline, food and various general stores were still a mile distant at either Retreat Camp or East Barrier Cache; two hundred seals had to be hauled from the Bay caches beyond the Bridge of Sighs; one radio antennae and four telephone poles were still to be raised; a whole system of tunnels had to be mined for hooking up the scattered buildings in the camp; these and various other problems required immediate attention. Lord, we thought, will it never end! The burden was all the heavier by reason of the fact that half a dozen men were still on the sick list, and many others were so occupied with fixed daily routine that they couldn't be spared, except for brief intervals, for the common burdens upon which the well-being of the camp depended.

Yet profiting by a breathing spell conferred by a severe blizzard which for two days drummed with scarcely diminishing ardor out of the east, the expedition on April 5th lifted itself forward for the final effort. Long after the sun had set, well into the cold and darkness of May, the work continued. The tranquillity and peace which the winter night was expected to bring were somehow very elusive. The work never stopped. It just seemed to go on, and on, and on; before we quite realized it, day was marching into the northern horizon.

Unloading ship and ramming the stuff through the pressure had been unreal enough. Then the sun made its unhurrying round of the sky; even with the temperature below freezing one could still work outside as late as February with nothing more on than a light shirt, breeches, underwear, shoes and a single pair of socks. But in April the sun was dying; the cold came in and settled like a dead weight; the blizzards became more venomous; and a crazy, lurid, Hollywood orange moon, swollen by refraction, shoved its bulk out of the Ross Sea. And it was strange still to be working then; an unfathomable uneasiness permeated the camp, as if by leaving so much to the last we should be roundly chastised for our impudence, like the cricket who stridulated the summer away, while the wise squirrel stored his winter supply of nuts. But neither impudence nor improvidence had anything to do with it; the prostrating levies made upon limited manpower and transportation by more pressing needs had driven these jobs into the background. Now, as the sun rolled along the horizon, rising each day a little later and setting a little earlier, they exerted their own vehement demands.

Even the men who had just returned from the trail joined in without pausing to rest. The night watchman's ringing morning cry of "Rise and shine!" at six bells meant all hands. Then a painful, lingering exodus from the sleeping bags, fumbling and cursing over frozen boots, a hurried breakfast, then out in the cold gray dawn, as the poets say, for the orders of the day.

Once again dog teams and tractors were shuttling over drift-heaped trails between the outer caches, at long last returning to Little America for good the stores that had been accumulated there during the ice crisis of March. What got under the skin, what made much of it seem so useless and so utterly wearying, was the endless duplication and repetition. It was nobody's fault, nothing could be done about it; it's just in the nature of things Antarctic, like commuting to work back home, that the same job should be done over and over again. One day Skinner was seen to drop a case of tools he had just loaded on a tractor. Squarely in the center of it he planted a mighty kick. "Damn you," he said. "I know you. Twenty times I've moved you from one place to another. For God's sake, get back to Little America and settle down."

Drift is the curse of a polar camp. Like a fiendish, malignant enemy it fastens itself with the grip of the Old Man of the Sea, paralyzing every effort. Cold is tolerable, even the greatest cold. In clothing little heavier than we were accustomed to wear for barely freezing temperatures in cities back home, we worked outside for hours at a time, with no great discomfort at 60° below. But against drift there is no protection. Propelled by high winds, drift moves down with the solid rush and substance of a mountain river, a blinding and smothering confusion. The boxes of stores cached at Retreat Camp, the seal carcasses heaped in the five caches southwest of the Bridge of Sighs, the unemptied caches in the center of Little America, the planes anchored at the mouth of Ver-Sur-Mer Inlet, even Little America itself, had become monstrous heaps of hard-packed drift in which we prodded with the persistency, if not the passion, of archæologists. Even at the end of May, with the sun more than a month below the horizon, a company of men was still shoveling, still sounding the hard depths with twelve-foot brass rods, in search of machine shop equipment.

As Admiral Byrd had prophesied, Little America, on account of the super-imposing of the new buildings on the surface roofing the old, had become a minor Alps. Drift had risen to the nine-foot roofs, leveling off when there was no further obstruction to catch it, then building up in tremendously long streams to leeward, as a current will bubble up and fan around a bowlder. The prevailing winds are easterly; and the fanning ridges extended a hundred yards to the west, covering everything.

Through these cone-shaped mounds Commander Noville and Supply Officer Corey, early in April, launched the connecting tunnels which in time unified Little America's underground existence. Except for the prolonged labor involved, it was a simple business. The tunnels were just trenches, walled with boxed stores and roofed with waterproof paper laid across chicken wire and supported by wooden slats. Thus the camp had a safe means of communication during severe blizzards and the Supply Officer had convenient access to his stores. When the system was finally completed, it would have been possible for the expedition to work and live entirely underground during the winter night and never once come to the surface. A few men, who as the winter wore on became acutely sensitive to fresh air, were suspected of taking full advantage of it. Anyhow, toward the end of the winter night the cook was seen peering from one of the surface hatches with an interest and pleasure he took no pains to disguise. "Say," he remarked, "you fellows have a nice view from here, haven't you?"

In April, too, the dog-drivers not engaged in hauling fell eagerly to the job of completing the building of Dog Town, which had been spasmodically under way while the drivers were in the field. Not very much progress had been made, and with the nights lengthening and the cold increasing the dogs were beginning to suffer. They were still on the surface, being locked up at night in the wooden kennel crates in which they had made the voyage from Boston. Several had recently died of cold.

Fifty yards or so south of the new buildings, eight tunnels 100 feet long, in parallel and meeting at right angles a main tunnel running from the Seal Chopping House, were started. The side tunnels were about 6 feet deep and 3 feet wide. In these, at ten-foot intervals, the kennels were set in the walls, the kennels in one wall facing the center of the blank stretch between the kennels in the other. Thus each dog, within the orbit of his tethering chain, had a small ranging ground which he need not dispute with his neighbor. At any rate, that was the theory. In practice it worked out quite differently. One way or another there was always the devil to pay in Dog Town: dogs slipping their chains, or bursting loose to run the gamut of slashing teeth en route to liberty, or else foolishly switching their rear ends around in such a manner that a vigilant neighbor, by leaping the full length of his chain, could get in a slashing stroke. Dog Town was one long uproar: and yet for all the turmoil, and the blood-spilling, and the wild free-for-alls that broke out every time a couple of dogs got loose, it wasn't, as dog-lovers will instantly suspect, a terribly cruel place. Dark, yes; dark as the other side of the moon; wherever you looked, glittering eyes hung in an uncanny suspension. Cold, yes; but the air was always steaming with the heat from their bodies and breath. And smell! Oh, Lord, all the perfumes in France couldn't have rid Dog Town of its gamey aroma. It was appalling enough in its own primitive essences, but when Messrs. Paine and Russell stoked up the Blubber stove in the Seal Cutting cave at the head of Dog Town, the combination was richer than the lee side of a gas house. The air in the tunnels was thick enough not only to be cut with a knife; spiced with a dash of garlic from the bulbs that hung over Noville's door, it could have been served as pemmican.

Yet I dare say that if it were possible for the dogs to render their own account, they would say that as such places go, Dog Town wasn't too bad. Anyhow, they were always friendly, always eager to see you; the first glimmer of a light at the head of the tunnel was a signal for an ecstasy of sound; and you could hardly get through for the dogs leaping and twisting within the orbits of their chains for the passing caress. "Stu" Paine used to say that when he grew bored with the interminable controversies and the microscopic issues of humans he could always find something amusing, something lovable and fine in the simple society of Dog Town.

III

The wind blew on April 1st; it blew steadily on the 3rd and 4th; then it blew a blizzard on the 7th, lulling next day. It blew some more on the 10th and again on the 15th. Vigorous, blustery days, with lots of drift and men leaning to their tasks, cursing the particles that filled their eyes, sifted past their collars and melted clammily down their necks.

Steadily the work went on. By the time the sun went down Retreat Camp and East Barrier Cache were almost empty; the coal, food and some of the gasoline were stowed at Little America; the last of the seal carcasses had been hauled in from the pressure, the Bridge of Sighs torn up and the telephone poles promptly raised for the third directive antennae; and a good part of the tunneling was done.

Though the radio department was clamoring for its poles, needing the antennaę to improve communications, the Bridge was left in place until the tractors returned from the southern journey and finished hauling in the seals. About two hundred seals, mostly huge Weddells which had been killed by Dr. Perkins and his seal-chasing safari in February, were piled up in five caches along the western margin of the pressure. The farthest cache was about 8.5 miles from Little America, a long haul for the tractors and a shivering assignment for the body-snatchers. The aviators, Bowlin, Smith, Swan, McCormick and Schlossbach, who were invariably relied upon to hurry wavering tasks, cheerfully took over the assignment alone. Though it was a brutal job digging out the drifted carcasses which weighed from 500 to 1000 pounds each, they finished it in a week. The once sleek and sinuous bodies were stiff with frost; where the peavies took hold the flesh flaked off in bloody chips and splinters hard as wood. At Little America the tractors dumped the cadavers over the Seal Chopping House, where the drivers presently arranged them in flat, sardine-like tiers near the chute into the Chopping House, fifteen feet down. It took a seal a day to satisfy Dog Town.

After the seals were in, June departed in a tractor and uprooted the Bridge of Sighs. It had again been upheaved from its piers. How sustained was the shearing movement of ice along the face of the pressure was shown by the discovery that bits of lumber marking the original western abutment of the bridge had moved, since early in February, 400 feet nearer the sea. A certain melancholy attended the tearing up of the Bridge. Somehow it was the last surviving monument to the weeks of toil in the pressure. Of Misery Trail nothing remained but a few wind-shredded flags. Drift had effaced even the tractor tracks.

On April 19th the sun set for the last time. On that day Dyer, Hutcheson, Bailey and Waite, under Dr. Poulter's direction, raised the telephone poles for the last directive antennae—four 45-foot poles, and each of them a problem. The temperature stood at —53°. Laid in a shallow groove and teed against hatch covers sunk crosswise in the snow, the poles were each in turn hauled upright, with a block and tackle, by a tractor, then guyed to deadmen sunk deep. But in that temperature the tractor had a weakness for stalling, usually at the critical point of the pull: sharp cries, then, from all hands, and the pole teetering, swaying, deciding which way to plunge. Then the whole business of rolling the pole back into position, reeving the lines again, while Von der Wall, who was driving the tractor, struggled to work the ice out of the gas lines.

The sun departed without ceremony; in point of accuracy it must be said that it took French leave the day before, because the 19th was cast out of the same gray mold of fog as so many before it. The going of the sun isn't the sudden, spectacular event that so many people seem to imagine; there's no abrupt walling off between night and day. It's just a gradual, lingering passing of one, and a slow washing in of the other, like the ebb and flow of an infinite tide. Days after the sun set for the last time a gray twilight expanded at noon, diminishing a little bit each day until, by the middle of May, there was just a watery crimson smear at noon on the northern horizon. But even at midwinter day, when the sun was at its greatest northern declination, that stain, overlaid with a faint yellowish glow, still persisted on the frozen margin of the Ross Sea.

If the last day of the sun was drab and colorless, not so the several days preceding it. Day gave way to night not in the golden eruption of a New England fall, but in a lingering ecstasy of meeting. Lower and lower the bright wheel of the sun rolled along the northwestern horizon; more delicate and exquisite became the colors. The high cirrus clouds took on the extravagant opulence of tropical plants. Yellows, golds, greens, pinks, blues of a delicacy and novelty past describing: they are never the same and even as you watch they are in subtle distillation. The bold, solid Antarctic blue of the upper dome of sky; the rose-mist of the northern and southern horizons; the cliffs and the headlands of the Bay and the pinnacled pressure digging long furrows of shadows; and the soft swales of the Barrier luminous with a creeping sheen that seems alive. So the day dies, with colors waving and waning, then the night pours in, profound and vast, wheeling its lavish constellations and spreading the fluttering ballet of the aurora. It is an exciting thing to watch, this transition, if you don't mind the cold too much. On such clear days, especially when the sun is very low, no hour—no minute, for that matter—is ever the same. The colors of an infinite prism are in a state of flux, flowing, melting, merging, dividing in a lovely and intricate rhythm, as if the day were loathe to leave. You notice your shadow—a monstrous, inhuman thing, and the great shadows in the pressure, solid cones of blue seeming to have neither beginning nor ending. The spell of those hours never leaves you. I suppose that's why, in the writings of explorers, you come so often upon passionate descriptions of colors. How rare these days are you are inclined to forget until you look at your diary or riffle the daily meteorological reports: "overcast—light gray fog—poor visibility—horizon three miles. . . ."[1]

Of course by that time the animal life which in summer months flourishes in the Bay of Whales had long since taken leave. It seemed suddenly to melt before the cold of mid-March. In February the skies were raucous with skua gulls; they quarreled among the garbage heaps and over bloody seal carcasses. Lindsey, the biologist, counted as many as 160 disputing over a single dead seal. But they all vanished during the first week of March. With them went the snowy petrels. The first week in March a flight of one hundred of them fluttered moth-like in the haze above the camp. During the second week we saw one or two; after that, none at all. Early in March Lindsey saw a lone Emperor penguin and a couple of Adélies footing it northward along Barrier's edge, as if looking for an easy way down to the Bay. They were the last tourists of the season. After March 15th even the seals disappeared from their snoozing places in the pressure. But the day before the sun went down the biologists, Siple, Lindsey and Dr. Perkins, found three breathing holes in the new ice near the foot of the pressure, and a groove furrowed in drift which indicated that a seal had within twenty-four hours come to the surface. But otherwise Nature had packed up and abdicated. Only man was audacious (or vain) enough to remain.

IV

April 24th another blizzard drove working parties underground. Although some stores, notably aviation gasoline, still remained to be ferried from Retreat Camp, the tractors were summarily yanked out of service. A stock-taking of the gasoline cache revealed that only 3,000 gallons of tractor gas remained—scarcely enough, even with the

[1] Out of the 356 days represented in the meteorologists' summary only 97—or 27%—were clear. April was the cloudiest month, with only 4 clear and four partly cloudy days. July, in the winter darkness, was the clearest month, with 15 clear days.

strictest economy, to fuel the cars for the spring operations. On the 26th the dogs were brought to the surface, hitched up and sent after the last general stores. This done they were returned to Dog Town, freed from all further demands till spring. Though there were a few days of minus forties and fifties, the air was not punishing; the in-rush of gales from the east and north sent thermometers kiting to zero.

On the 25th the camp trooped out behind June to secure the Condor. With an upper wing span of 82 feet, a length of 48 feet plus, and standing 13 feet 3 inches from skis to upper wing, it required an enormous pit. "Like dry-docking a whale," Swan observed. Rather than unship the wings, June decided to drop her in the pit in which she was lined up with the Pilgrim and autogyro near the head of Ver-Sur-Mer Inlet, just north of the Old Mess Hall. Drift was wedged hard under the fuselage. She lay as she had been berthed, slightly cocked up, as a plane is on the ground. The way June brought her below the surface was to mine two deep trenches under the wings from the tips to the skis; then another trench aft to the tail, all wide enough to accept the plane in a glove-like fit. Then she was gently lowered by prizing away, little by little, the snow under the skis. As fast as the blocks of snow were sawed out underneath the wings, they were handed to men working on the surface, who fitted them into a bulwark which completely enclosed the wing. When the plane was down, there was just room enough for the mechanics to squeeze round it and make repairs during the winter.

Naturally it was a delicate, protracted operation; a bit of carelessness, or too much hurry on either side, might have brought that great weight crashing from its uncertain balance, perhaps smashing a wing or crushing the men underneath. Two tons of gas were still in the tanks making a total weight of eight tons. The job was done in the light of gasoline pressure lamps, which gave it an eerie aspect. Once the anchor lines were cast off and the plane started down the one great fear was that a blizzard might strike without warning. But it came off without mishap. While shovels plied noisily and June and Bowlin directed the work under the opposite wings, the plane twitched down, a groaning fraction of an inch at a time, like a fabulous winged creature of antiquity, captured and brought to earth, sinking resignedly into a vast prison. On May 1st, the temperature standing at —40°, the great orange wing disappeared at last behind the snow bulwark. With the wind rising, the hangar was sealed with a tarpaulin drawn across the upper wing and weighted down with snow blocks. Only the fluke-like rudder post showed above the surface. "And that," said Bill Bowlin, gently consoling the frost-bite on his cheek, "is that."

Compared with the Condor, the high-wing Pilgrim and the tiny autogyro were no trouble at all. Dropped the same way, by undercutting and walling around above, they were quickly secured in a day. Within a fortnight only a streamlined hump of drift remained to show where the three planes lay buried. East of the camp the Fokker lay where it had crashed, its unbroken wing probing above the drift in a dismal entreaty.

All that remained now were the jobs of building the machine shop and tractor garages, and bringing the cars below. Simple as this may sound, it took an agonizingly long time, partly because the cold was deepening, partly also because exhausted men were losing their stomach for prolonged sessions with dat old debbil snow shovel. Walter Lewisohn, observing the thinning ranks in the snow pits, said it reminded him of tropical armies—a brave display in the morning, the generals all out, flags flying and bands playing; and at siesta time a lone private moping on the battlefield. The twilight was thinning rapidly, just a grayness now at noon, sometimes with cold and remote eruptions of greens and reds and yellows low in the northern sky. Since we worked so much in the dark, the cold seemed to settle in the bones. Everybody got frost-bitten repeatedly; if it didn't yield readily, that is to say, if working the flesh and going into an abandoned gavotte didn't restore circulation, you repaired inside until the warmth of the fire did it, shooting red-hot pins into the nerves. It was a freezing business, all right: the aurora like a fine mist in a glittering sky, and a company of men digging furiously in enormous craters, by the light of gasoline lamps past which their breaths floated in streaming clouds of vapor.

Anyhow, that last bout was the toughest of all. It required an appalling amount of digging. What made it so difficult was that both the machine shop and the tractor garage had to be sunk in the mountain of drift in the lee of the new buildings. The machine shop wasn't so bad; it was only 14x11x9 feet, and was fitted smack against the Kohler shack without benefit of partition. But the tractor garage had to be built out of the walls of the packing cases in which the cars had been shipped from France, and whatever odds and ends "Pete" Demas could scrape up in a camp where no odds and ends existed. 24x24x14 were the dimensions of the pit dug to receive it. When you start on a hole that size you're just asking for trouble—daring a blizzard to come along and fill it. Every evening, when darkness and cold stopped work, in an effort to defend the ground so laboriously gained, the men roofed the hole as best they could with scraps of tarpaulin and long squares of galvanized iron stock which were spread in crazy-quilt fashion atop rickety bamboo poles. Sometimes it took half a day's hard work to undo the effects of a night's drift.

But on May 19th (the thermometers stood at −56°) the Citroëns were finally run down the ramp and into the garage. But not without considerable excitement. The cars had to be heated for hours before they would start; Skinner's engine burst into flames and was doused with snow; and the small snowmobiles were pushed down the ramp. There was room for only two Citroëns in the garage itself; the other, with the two snowmobiles, was parked on the ramp under a sagging tarpaulin shelter. A remarkable place, that ramshackle garage, as cold and big as the proverbial barn, with flimsy walls and ceilings which always seemed on the verge of tumbling down. Frigid draughts raced through it whenever there was wind on the surface, and drift sifted steadily through cracks ineffectually wadded with burlap bags, old shirts and socks. In that wretched shelter, shivering beside a stove made from an iron cracker drum, Demas, Von der Wall, Skinner and Hill labored all winter long over their cars, overhauling the engines, rebuilding the bodies, and experimenting with all sorts of gadgets to improve their efficiency.

With the tractors out of the way the men quartered in the Old Mess Hall and Administration Building at last had a chance to look out for their own comfort. Isolated from the tunnels connecting the new buildings, they had been in the habit of walking topside to the New Mess Hall and the other buildings. But lately the increasing darkness and rousing gales had made even that short walk a trifle too adventurous. Several men had become lost in the center of the camp, floundering around in the murk on the verge of panic till they stumbled upon a familiar landmark. So now the original 200-yard tunnel between these two buildings, which lay about fifteen feet below the level of the new tunnels, was partially reopened after four years. From their end the men in the Old Mess Hall pushed the tunnel under the machine shop, on the farther side of which they made a shaft. By passing through the machine shop, Kohler plant and radio shack they gained the main tunnel. From their side the men in the Administration Building reopened the original tunnel about 100 feet, then hewed a capacious staircase through the snow to join the main food tunnel running past the New Mess Hall. Naturally, all roads led to the refectory.

Thus by the end of May, more than a month after the sun went down, the expedition was finally secured. Rawson and Pelter, recovered from their illness, were on their feet again; and the health of the men was generally good. From Advance Base, whence he was in touch with us by radio—two or three times a week, Admiral Byrd reported "all's well." The decks were cleared for the task of preparing for the spring program.

V

What sort of place was this second Little America? And how did it differ from the first?

Well, these questions might be answered in various ways. For one thing, the second Little America was considerably bigger, owing to the increase in the size of the Ice Party. In all, there were ten new buildings, not counting the two small shacks which Bramhall used as magnetic observatories. Certainly it was more comfortable. There was much more elbow room for all hands, which made for more happiness and privacy (they go hand-in-hand in a winter camp), and a great many more conveniences: electric lights in all the main shacks; an electric coffee and meat grinder in the galley; electric saws and drills for the carpenters and machinists; a movie projector, sound equipment and over 150 films; rugs for the deck (end pieces donated by a generous manufacturer); etchings for the wall (the private wealth of a few who anticipated the pleasure they would bring); mattresses of an elegantly advertised make in which charming women are usually shown in attitudes of sweet repose (a masterly acquisition on Czegka's part, since it is difficult to see what satisfaction the manufacturer could derive from knowing that hardy explorers, in long baggy underwear not too frequently changed, were accommodated on the same luxurious pallets); electrically driven sewing machines; a wind-driven generator atop one of the radio towers, which, when the wind was brisk, was quite powerful enough to generate enough electricity to carry the camp load; a really voluminous library (Admiral Byrd's own polar library, *Encyclopedia Britannica, Modern Library,* a wide choice of classics and modern trash which friends of expedition members must have been only too glad to send to the Antarctic, *Dr. Eliot's Five-Foot Shelf, National Geographic Magazine, Atlantic Monthly* (1933), *Saturday Evening Post* (1932-1933 inclusive); a radio receiver in the galley to pacify the volatile Latin temperament of the cook (he was always threatening, by the great Jehovah, that he was through, knowing full well he had come to the one place where a man could neither resign nor be fired); telephones in all the main shacks (for the convenience, it was widely admitted, of the executive officer, who could thus from his own bunk rout out the shivering work details in the early morning—it also stimulated such bits of whimsy as ringing the general alarm signal, then asking, when a dozen excited voices answered as on a country party line, "Room Service? One Tom & Jerry, boy: no—make it two"); and three cows which yielded upwards of 40 quarts of milk a day (or did, until the yield diminished according to the workings of an inexorable natural law which the cowherd, Cox, tried in vain to explain to the simple souls of Little America—though Cox to the very end entertained high hopes for assistance from Iceberg, the young bull, and did everything within reason to initiate him in his expedition duties, Iceberg, either on account of his extreme youth or a congenital coolness, not surprising in one so named, was a complete disappointment; the yield diminished to a trickle which barely moistened the morning cereal).

These rambling recollections will perhaps serve to show that the second expedition was not lacking in luxuries unknown to exploring camps of the past. "A chicken in every pot," exclaimed "Cyclone" Haines, whenever the technically invidious comparison was drawn. Still, it was amusing how shocked the veterans were when the news got around that George Noville was using an electric razor. Cox threw the radio staff into a state of apoplexy by calmly asking for current to run an electric milking machine which the American Guernsey Cattle Club had pressed upon him as a parting gift, just why no one could fathom. In the matter of the movies, there was the same upending of the cornucopia. In the beginning there were movies only twice a week—a short and a feature. Then popular demand increased to thrice a week—Mondays, Wednesdays and Saturdays. It was but a step then to double features. The upshot of it was that by the middle of the winter night the films which were supposed to last another five months, with a bit of self-denial, were entirely exhausted—whereupon the camp cheerfully turned about and had the favorites run over and over again.

But even with these small luxuries and improvements life still remained hard and impoverished. Movies and electric lights helped to dissipate for a few hours the gloom and emptiness of the winter night, but they could never succeed in lifting it. Oppressive and taxing, the night remained, and you were steadily conscious of waiting—of waiting for the sun to come back—waiting for the replenishment it promised.

The Old Mess Hall and the Administration Building of the first Little America continued to serve as the main barracks. Not many changes were made in them, other than those Admiral Byrd has already described. In the Administration Building four new bunks were added, increasing its capacity to twenty-two men. It was just a long bare room, with twin rows of double bunks (upper and lower) projecting from the walls into the center, leaving barely room to pass about. The original stove, the kind you still occasionally see in country general stores, stood in the center of the room. Near it was a cleared space, to provide a bit of elbow room round the sink and allow a caucus of the Elder Statesmen who foregathered there in the cool of the evening to settle the affairs of the world. As before, the far end was partitioned off: but Dr. Potaka had converted what had been the library into a Doctor's Office. Anyhow, he called it that; when you dropped in for the monthly physical examination, it was difficult to see far enough in any direction to tell what it was. An intricate maze of clothes lines, festooned with thawing boots, old socks and whatever gear the Doctor had been unable to find room for, ran every whichway. It was evident, however, when you had stripped to the nude, stepped upon the scales and forced your head through a stratus roofing of moldy underwear, that June's bunk was near the ceiling. Abaft the Doctor's Office, in the gloomy cell which had served as Admiral Byrd's former quarters, Bill Haines had his bunk. His meteorological Bureau, a box-like cubicle in the double partition, was just a step away. There he and Grimminger watched over their complicated apparatus, worked up the daily reports, and talked dreamily of Washington, D. C.

In the first Little America the Old Mess Hall had served the quadruple function of a barracks, radio station, work shop, and common eating place. It must have been frightfully congested. We used it simply as a sleeping place. It slept sixteen. In the center of the room was the same scarred table at which 42 men, taking quick turns, used to eat. The sailmaker, Linwood Miller, had his sewing machines set up in the far corner. Even before the sun went down, his machine was whirring all day long, turning out the large quantities of windproof shirts, socks, parkas and pants; tents and canvas sledge tanks; first-aid kits and other articles for the spring field trips.

Adjoining the Old Mess Hall was the Norwegian House, also built by the first expedition. Pelter and Blackburn converted it into a private villa. Pelter had his photographic "dark room" in the rear. Two inches of hard ice plated the outer walls, and such was the strain of the ice on the roof that the tenants momentarily expected it to cave in on them. As a matter of fact, the rafters collapsed one night, with such ominous crackings that Pelter and Blackburn in full flight met simultaneously at the door. But they returned to brace up the roof and lived there till the ships came in.

Another old building in use was Blubberheim. Lying some distance south of the Old Mess Hall and having no connections with the tunnels, it was built by Walden and Braathen, who knew the joys of "a place of your own." Petersen and Ronne quietly inherited Blubberheim by the act of getting in first. It was a very tiny place, a mere pocket in the crust: to reach it, you dropped down a hatch and wound around a narrow, declivitous snow staircase, coming to a low door. The roof had sagged into a drooping curve; a trifle dubious that it would stay up, Petersen and Ronne never quite dared to bunk there. They used it only as a workship—Petersen to copy on his small receiver the daily radio press which he picked up from New York, London, San Francisco and other sources, and Ronne to repair skis and ski bindings. Because coal was scarce, they economically used the cinders from the galley stove. Blubberheim was a friendly, quiet place.

The new Little America lay in two parallel rows of buildings, roughly running east and west (the true bearing was 121°) south of the Administration Building and east of the Old Mess Hall. To attempt to give here their exact bearings and distances would involve a meaningless clutter of details; these are properly shown on the map of the town. In the north row in the given order, from west to east, were the New Mess Hall, the Science Hall and the small adjoining shacks of Dr. Poulter's meteor observatory and the Biological Department's Blubber House. In the south row, this time from east to west, came the cowbarn, Dog Heim (where Captain Innes-Taylor and Commander Noville had their celebrated *salon*), the radio shack, the

Kohler plant, machine shop and tractor garage. Past the doors of most of these buildings ran traverse tunnels, which ultimately connected with the central tunnel, variously called Fifth Avenue, Main Street and the Main Stem. This central tunnel, rising from the Administration Building vestibule, meandered, with various shoulder-rubbing turns and head-scraping grades, between the New Mess Hall and Science Hall, thence passed (about 20 yards farther on) between the cowbarn and Dog Heim, and finally dropped into the labyrinth of Dog Town.

Most of these tunnels were either lined with boxed stores, or else connected with various caches. For example, there were separate caches (just chambers hewn in the snow, sometimes braced, sometimes not) for coal, meat, fur clothing, trail gear, medical supplies, scientific equipment, hay, radio spare parts, machine shop and tractor equipment, and aviation stores. Naturally, there was no room in the crowded shacks for the plenitude of gear required for the expedition's sustenance. In fact, most of the men, having only the meager space of their bunks, stowed in the tunnels the personal gear not immediately in use. The main food dump lay between the New Mess Hall and the radio shack. This broad plaza was a honeycomb of marching lines of boxes from which each day "Steve" Corey pried out (with a jimmy and mallet) the food requisitioned by the galley.

Dark were these tunnels: if you were unlucky enough to have your flashlight go out, you had to stumble along, feeling your way with both hands out, trying to remember how many steps to this side cache, how many to the drop; if you miscounted a teeth-rattling collision was apt to refresh the memory. Because the shorter men had a great deal to do with digging them, the tunnels were rather hard on the six-footers. "Keep your head down" was the primary rule of tunnel navigation. As the snow got heavier, the tunnel roof sagged between the cross supports in ice-packed folds, hard as concrete. Thanks to them, most of the bald-headed men will carry scars to their graves. Still, one became accustomed to such cracks. The passing state of anaesthesia which they induced was, in fact, occasionally welcome. But oh, the misery of the dash of ice crystals down the back of the neck! Clear down, clear down to the boots, jingling all the way.

Until they were sullied by dirt rubbed off from passing parkas, these tunnels had a rare and exciting beauty. In a flashlight's glow the walls shone with the whiteness of alabaster, and each of the millions of ice crystals on the overhead was a radiant, dancing prism.

VI

The new buildings were all flat-topped, rectangular structures, primitive in their simplicity, with skylights (which were of course swiftly drifted over) and boxed-like ventilators cut in the roof. Most of them were portable structures, which had been knocked down for shipment, but several, notably the radio shack and the tractor garage, were built at Little America. Thinking that a peaked roof would bear up better under the weight of accumulating snow, the first expedition had favored ridge topped shacks: but this, they found, only defeated its own end. Though drift will mount with astonishing rapidity around any exposed object, once it has attained its level there is little accretion. A month or so after the new buildings were raised, nine feet of drift swelled over the camp. Thereafter, despite the heavy blizzards of the winter, not more than a foot of snow gathered over the roofs of the taller buildings. This, by the way, is the principal reason why meteorologists find it impossible to calculate Antarctic snowfall. An Antarctic blizzard is a gigantic torrent of falling snow and drift broomed up from the Barrier. The still flutter of snow that we are familiar with is rather rare. I remember remarking, one day, how odd it was to see snow gently falling and accumulating, and no drift.

NEW MESS HALL: 15x30x7½ feet. This was the common eating place, recreation center, movie theater and general workshop of Little America. The big galley stove, sink, dish racks and the cook's tables were all jammed together in the rear. Behind the stove lay a 150-gallon tank for melting snow, which was shoveled through a port cut in the back wall. Two long pine tables and benches sat 24 men shoulder to shoulder. Al Carbone's bunk was in one corner. On movie nights it became his box seat. Flat on his back, he was in an excellent position to take his drama or leave it alone. So close to the screen, he was, however, apt to be carried away by the illusion. One poignant night, in a scene where an officer (I seem uncertainly to remember that it was "The Eagle and the Hawk") had occasion to pass a magnum of champagne to a gorgeous thing in ermine under most agreeable circumstances; the bottle, for a heart-breaking second, seemed to pass directly into Carbone's hands. And as the lovely lady took it, we were all startled to hear the agonized cry from the wrathful cook, "Hey, gimme that bottle, scut. He gave it to *me*." The Mess Hall was transformed into a movie theater by pushing the tables against the walls, swinging the benches cross-wise, and dropping a small curtain down the front wall. I suppose this curtain was originally white. I remember it mostly on account of the variety of soup stains which carried a remorseless pattern through every film. Abaft the shack was a tiny cubicle which served as a projection room and quarters for Herrmann and Petersen. The movie projector peered through a loophole cut in the wall. Because the galley was the one place having a fair amount of open space, it was much favored by the sledge-riggers, the carpenters and the ration-makers. Even Skinner used it for packing parachutes. "The only thing you guys haven't brought in here," moaned the cook, "is an airplane, and I suppose you'll bring that in, just as soon as you can figure a way to get it through the tunnels."

Science Hall. Same dimensions as the New Mess Hall. Entering the door, which faced the latter across a capacious snow passageway, you first came to the library, which was set off from the rest of the building by a partition, in the center of which a gap had been cut to share the heat of the single stove. The library was about eight feet long, having a few chairs, a phonograph, and wall shelves, lined with books, running from the floor to the ceiling. Past the partition was the long room given over to the scientists. Each of them had his special small square of the rude counter tables running along the walls, a single electric light over his desk, and a place for his books. The biologists, Dr. Perkins, Siple, Lindsey and Sterrett occupied the south tables. Here Dr. Perkins, with his microscopes and Micro-Movies, pored uncounted hours over the singular tiny living things he hauled up from the black depths of the Bay of Whales. On Dr. Perkins' right, Sterrett had an impressive array of beakers, vials and test tubes, in which he was working up special bacteriological problems. On his left, Siple was usually engrossed in organizing his fine journey to Marie Byrd Land. Across the room were the geologists, Morgan, Wade and Blackburn, engaged, like Siple, in planning their spring journeys. Nearby Rawson had his table and charts stretching into the unknown, over which his eyes were wont to rove with a speculative and proprietary air. In the corner beyond him was what to us was always known as the Garret, where the artist, Paige, worked up, when the Muse had defrosted itself, the sketches he made outside. The physicists, Dr. Bramhall and Zuhn, had the corner opposite the Garret, from which, by means of a complicated control board, they kept their fingers on the pulse of their remote magnetic and thermal apparatus. On a table stood their cosmic ray gadget, provocatively interesting in a cloth shroud in which a light burned dimly, calling attention to itself by the peremptory ringing of the interval timer which summoned Bramhall from his chess games for new observations. (The nature of the scientific work will be discussed in a later chapter.)

Meteor Observatory: 9x12x7 feet. This shack lay just behind the Science Hall. How Dr. Poulter ever managed to dispose his own great bulk among the myriads of machinery and the complications of his meteor apparatus was one of the mysteries of Little America. In the roof of the shack Dr. Poulter had raised a turret-like transparent dome, facing the four quadrants of the heavens in which four observers, each with one eye glued to a tiny sighting operative, could be crammed. They sat on a revolving platform, an ingenious arrangement of folding chairs hooked into the outriggers of a shaft, which Dr. Poulter swung by hand at fifteen minute intervals during an observation period. In this way he rested the observers and by frequently exchanging them in the different quadrants had a check on the accuracy of their observations. Directly over his own bunk, Dr. Poulter had two binoculars set in the ceiling, with which he could simultaneously scan the zenith. On a bench underneath were the small lathes and drills with which he turned out so many remarkably fine things. Dr. Poulter was that rare combination, a true scientist with an extraordinary gift in practical handiness.

BLUBBER HOUSE: 9x12x9 feet. Constructed by Siple and Lindsey of spare lumber. Here they preserved and cured the skins and specimens collected during the fall, feeding the fire with oozing strips of blubber flensed from the seals. Apart from its biological significance, it was marked by a decidedly gamey smell, an oily detritus, and, in consequence, not highly favored except by biologists.

COW BARN: 15x31x8 feet. It lay nestled in a cache of hay. The three cows, the bull, the two carpenters, two Manx kittens (their shrift, however, was short on account of Dog Town's proximity) and Jimmy, a wolf-breed outcast of Dog Town, all dwelt here in simple rusticity. All in a row the cows and the bull stood in their stalls, nibbling at the frosted hay which Cox pitched in from the cache. To me one of the most melancholy sights of the winter was the spectacle of Cox, with the temperature —70°, trying to pry with a crow bar a bale of hay from a stalagmite of ice. Cox and Tinglof had their bunks in a partitioned space in the corner. The cowbarn, too, had its distinctive odor: but one which, when it permeated the tunnels, had a bouquet that evoked an unutterable nostalgia in the men from New England and the Middle West.

DOG HEIM: 12x12x8 feet. The "Castle in Spain" which Captain Innes-Taylor and Commander Noville had assembled in sections aboard the *Ruppert*. Originally built with the hope it would insure some privacy, it became (in tribute to Noville's skill as a cook) a sort of Antarctic Coffee Shoppe, always crowded, nearly always merry. On Innes-Taylor's bunk, George had painted in large letters: "This platform for trail practice," and, underneath his own, "Please don't talk to the motorman." Here George, in his capacity of executive officer, spun the web of intrigue that was called the Daily Work sheet; and here Innes-Taylor, in his capacity of Chief of Trail Operations, composed his Wilsonian notes on trail and operations. Dog Heim also had its aromas: the fragrance of the coffee always bubbling in the cream colored pot, and the still more penetrating fragrance of the sheaf of garlic above the stove, which George was inclined to favor as "an anti-scorbutic."

RADIO SHACK: 15x31x8 feet. Built on the ground by Waite, Bailey, Dyer, Hutcheson and Lewisohn who shared it. With Blubberheim it was the neatest, certainly the most comfortable building in Little America. The double walls were insulated with wool shearings, and a partition walling off the living quarters from the operations room, in which the complicated radio apparatus was neatly arranged, made it comparatively very comfortable. One corner was set apart for the weekly General Foods Broadcasts over the Columbia Broadcasting

System. It became a studio by the hurried acts of brushing the chessmen from the monitor board, advising Bailey please to pipe down on his snoring, plucking the reindeer hairs from the collapsible organ (the fur from the caribou sleeping bags got into everything; when you got up in the morning you looked like a moulting caribou), and carefully conveying from the vicinity of the microphone all coal bags, coal scuttles, pokers, stray pups, water buckets, etc., over which the agitated performers were likely to stumble.

KOHLER SHACK: 9x12x7½ feet. Connected to the radio shack by a tunnel. Three gasoline driver generators, with a power output of 2 KW, a bank of batteries. This was Waite's special province.

MACHINE SHOP: 14x11x9. It opened directly into the Kohler Shack. No polar expedition has ever had more complete equipment. A toolmaker's lathe (capable of turning a piece 14 inches by 6 feet), milling machine, power hack saw, a combination drill press, complete oxy-acetylene welding outfit, a blacksmith shop with a portable forge and hand-blower, anvils, hammers, combination table saw and joiner, jig saw and band saw—in short, a machine shop which could match any small shop in civilization. But without it, and without the ingenious modifications and adaptations which Boyd turned out, the tractor, aviation and scientific departments might have had a much harder time of it.

C.J.V.M.

Chapter XI

THE LUNATIC FRINGE

I

BY light of a kerosene lantern, Walter Lewisohn and one or two others (in all probability Dr. Potaka, as he was our foremost antiquarian) were rooting into one of the first expedition's caches. Half-hidden under a tiny glacial tongue they came upon a bundle, which they opened with lively interest. Some wonderful things had come out of the old ruins, fine old *Americana parva.* A whole set of chinaware (circa 1928) when the tableware was so depleted by the messmen's unhandiness that fifty-five men were reduced to 18 dinner plates, 16 soup plates, and 15 cups. A case or two of Dr. Baxter's Lung Preserver (alcoholic content about 28%, if memory serves) and, in the stratum, a neat little still. Little America was in a state of involuntary prohibition. Still it should be said in passing that no matter how often the elixir passed through the distillery and in spite of the combined technical abilities of the medical officer, biologist, geologist and senior aviation officer, all with their tongues hanging out, it still remained Dr. Baxter's Lung Preserver, a sweetish pulmonary petrifier with a delayed pickup.

Nor were the antiquarians disappointed this time. As the bundle fell open they brought the lamp closer to see better.

"Straitjackets—a dozen of them," exclaimed the doctor.

"Too bad," said Walter.

"They're in prime condition," said the doctor, testing the fabric.

"But they're not windproof," murmured Lewisohn.

Somehow that wistful appraisal summed up for men the new critical attitude on the "lunatic fringe" in high latitudes. The honest apprehensions which caused the inclusion of these canvas tranquilizers among the properties of the first expedition, together with a quarter of a ton of cough drops for a climate where colds are almost unknown, marked the passing of an era. Or perhaps I shouldn't be so sure. Among our own properties were a couple of bales of horsehair and a case of Lydia Pinkham's Vegetable Compound, for which even the supply officer couldn't render a satisfactory accounting. There would have been two handsome coffins as well, satin-lined and with a silver name plate, had not Admiral Byrd chased them back onto the *Ruppert.* It was a great disappointment to Carbone. He had hoped to use one as a bunk. "Look," he said, "it will keep out the draughts."

Perhaps it's heresy, yet now that I look back on it and see

things in their full perspective, the winter night, the four months of darkness, weren't half bad. Sometimes life was exceedingly trying; certainly it was cold and bleak and impoverished, and once in a while you were driven to say and do things you wouldn't have done if there were more scope to existence. "All of us are a little mad," John Dyer said. But surprisingly the memories that emerge now are how painfully long it was, how lovely were the hours when the moon bathed the Barrier with a light that must have ushered in the Dawn of Creation, how much you craved the sun and green vegetables, how stupid some of us were and how steadily fine were others, and what deucedly hard work it was. A confused and superficial inheritance. But that's how it went. There was little to draw on, either from the slow drift of camp life or the frigid rigidity of the world topside. A bit of froth and foam on the surface, Dr. Perkins observed, and no great still depths and strong currents underneath.

The oldest and hoariest of polar fictions is that of the consuming erosion of the artificial veneering of civilization. Nature seems rather to work in the opposite direction, contriving in explorers, as in seals and penguins, the accretion of protective and impervious layers of blubber beneath which the emotional and intellectual processes snooze in a state of profound hibernation. The Antarctic is a natural embalming medium. High up on a cliff where a Barrier berg had recently calved away, Lindsey saw exposed the body of a young Adélie penguin pinned in the ice. How many years it had lain hidden away, there was no means of telling—many, certainly, for so much ice to have accumulated around it. It was, of course, as perfectly preserved as the day the poor creature met its end.

Cold seems to perform the same sort of petrifaction for the spirit. When and if the incalculable stranger supposed to reside in all of us managed to struggle to the surface he was usually so spent as not to be very entertaining as a diversion. "It isn't worth the effort," said Jim Sterrett. The reason for it may lie in the good-natured tolerance, the easy-going, the what-the-hell-of-it attitude which is peculiarly American. Through the narratives of the British expeditions on this same continent runs a certain note of tragedy and spiritual enrichment. As a general thing Little America reached its emotional zenith promptly at 6:15 o'clock every morning when the sleepy and shivering messmen, reporting for duty in the galley, found the fire out, the snow melter frozen hard, the dish water all used up, and the sink stacked high with dirty dishes flipped there by the midnight diners. From the second-in-command down we took turn and turn about at mess duty; so every morning there was a fresh diapason of dismay and indignation from the galley. And nothing, of course, was ever done about it.

It really took a great deal to shake Little America out of its rutted unconcern. Though Petersen each day copied and distributed news flimsies from the world radio press, nobody seemed ever to get worked up over anything happening in the outer world. I remember only two instances wherein the news excited comment at the mess tables—Bruno Hauptmann's arrest and the assassination of Dollfuss. We were all shaken the day we had to tell Bill McCormick that his brother had been killed in a crash; and were shaken again when we learned what a close call Admiral Byrd had had at Advance Base. But, otherwise, nothing outside our own private concerns seemed to strike very deep, nor, what was even more fascinating, to be very important.

One way or another a small fire started in the galley. Ashes were smoldering under the stove, and the place was full of smoke. Rawson and Paine, who were on mess that day, went on washing dishes, showing no interest whatever in the cook's efforts to beat out the fire, though they were half suffocated. Foundering around in the murk and not getting anywhere with a fire extinguisher, Carbone whirled upon them in great agitation and inquired what-the-hell they were going to do about that fire.

"That isn't our job," said Rawson evenly.

"What ain't your job?" screamed the cook.

"Putting out fires," said Rawson.

The Marine in the cook for once was speechless.

"Certainly," said Paine, reaching through the murk for another bucket of fresh water. "Mess men are required only to wash dishes and set the tables. Anything else in the galley has to be done by the cook. Order No. 5, section one, Sergeant."

"Precisely," said Rawson. "Besides, you started the damn thing yourself."

By that time the fire was charring the floor boards, and Carbone dashed into the Science Hall across the way for volunteers.

No doubt the strain of the winter night was more intense in the past, when exploring parties were smaller, comforts were scarcer, and there wasn't the opportunity to take up the slack by overhauling tractors and airplanes and preparing for half a dozen major journeys. All winter long there was a buzz of power saws in the galley, a whine of drills in the machine shops, the click of Bailey's radio telegraph key, the smell of blubber from the Seal Cutting House where Russell, Paine and Stancliff were manufacturing dog pemmican, a litter of rations being sacked on the Mess Hall tables, the busy hum of Miller's sewing machine, the pulse-like beat of the Kohlers and calls for volunteers for this job or that—secure the tarpaulin over the big plane, haul gas in for the Kohlers, clean out the snow melter, shore up a caving tunnel or, as not infrequently happened, help Cox get the bull under control. The darn thing was growing like a weed, and it took three men to chivvy him into the stall whenever he got loose. After one exhausting bout, Noville said to Cox, "Listen, the next time that animal gets loose, don't call on me because I've got too many things to worry about, all of them having to do with getting home alive."

The sounds of the outer world were always there to hear. Dyer had only to throw a switch to bring into the shacks the note of Big Ben striking the hour in London and sending tiny shivers down your back with its world-filling authority of empire; or else, with a simple turn, evoke out of the same atmosphere the sounds of our crooning countrymen weeping expensively into the curdled milk of love.

II

Thus answered Eliphaz the Temanite:

Should a man utter vain knowledge and
fill his belly with the east wind?

Should he reason with unprofitable talk?
Or with speeches wherewith he can do no good?

I suppose each man will take the content of the winter night with a different measure; but for me, and I know for others, it was one of the most pleasurable periods of the whole polar experience. The dark months were the quiet months; there was not so much of the impatience, the hurry and push, that came with the sun. One had time again to breathe.

The night has a queer replenishment and dignity of its own. Nowhere on earth will you see anything lovelier, with more quiet strength and authority, than the Ross Ice Barrier by moonlight—foaming waves of pressure ice, the planed cliffs emerging from the darkness with classic purity of line, the sea-ice spreading into the shoreless night, and a pale strand of green-yellow light on the horizon, the longest lance the deep-sunken sun can throw.

Whether you stood on the flooring of the Bay of Whales or among the slender upperworks of Little America, you felt the beauty and the repose of the night, its immensity and movement, whole armies of stars and wheeling constellations, and the tidal movements of the aurora, now lying like a pale ocean river of light through the zenith, now bursting into insane displays, becoming searchlights, puckering and flying curtains, groping rays. And you could glance up from the wastes of the Barrier and see taking shape in misty showers of ice crystals, the magical refraction phenomena of the moon—haloes, paraselenae (moon dogs) and, rarest of all, the corona, with the moon a polished ancient silver coin framed between concentric rings of color, pale blues, greens and smoking reds.

When you look upon such things there comes surging through the confusion of the mind an awareness of the dignity of the earth, of the unaccountable importance of being alive, and the thought comes out of nowhere that unhappiness rises not so much from lacking as from having too much. Like Peter in *War and Peace,* something exclaims, though the words may not form: "All that is mine, all that is in me, is me." And you guess the end of the world will probably look like that, and the last men retreating from the cliffs will look out upon some such horizon, with all things at last in equilibrium, the winds quiet, the sea frozen, the sky composed, and the earth in glacial quietude.

Or so you fancy. Then along comes a walloping blizzard and knocks such night dreaming into a cocked hat. An Antarctic blizzard is like the sudden smashing of Conrad's Vial of Wrath. The peace is shattered as by a vast concussion; the world becomes a vindictive, brooding extravagance of plunging wind, foaming breakers of drift, furious shadows, as if the Barrier were disintegrating and flying to leeward. The blizzard has a queer taut sound, full and resonant, like the drumming of a mountain river in spring. And above and through it come rhythmic overtones, the creak and rattle of stove-pipes, the hiss of snow melting against hot metal, the clack of the wind-driven generator atop the radio towers, and the violin-like notes of the meteor reticles and the antennae wires.

The sound fills and dulls the ears until it ceases to hear them. But in the night, sometimes, a subtle altering in the texture of the atmosphere, something indefinable, like the lifting of a pressure, will awaken you out of a shallow sleep. Then you recognize it for what it is: the quiet, the creeping, rustling quiet of great cold—ah, the wind has stopped.

It was pleasant enough inside. Indeed, one of the peculiar pleasures of a blizzard was its vigorous reminder of the smugness and security of the shacks. All that ridiculous uproar and violence above, just a few feet above your head; and below the quiet currents of a deep pool. But God help you if such a storm catches you away from camp, or even walking topside.

You can become utterly, hopelessly, dangerously lost on a path you've traveled times past numbering. In a smother of wind and drift you flounder and seek, blinded by the impact of drift against the eyes, gasping for the air sucked out of the lungs. You bump against a pole, stumble over a box, a tin can, or a pile of rubbish; and for the life of you, however frantically you up-end your memory, they seem utterly strange and disconnected from the pattern in which you're trying to place them. And the panicky thought assails you that you may miss the upperworks of the buildings or the tunnel hatches, and pass blindly over the anchorage beneath the crust.

Coming from the Old Mess Hall in a 50-mile blizzard, "Ike" Schlossbach groped for half an hour over Little America before he finally tumbled, having no idea where he was, into the tunnel entrance above Dog Town. In the same blow Ronne, marooned in Blubberheim, headed overland for the galley. The wind soon twisted him round. Scared to death, shivering, trembling and talking to himself, he had given himself up for lost when he blundered, with a gratefulness he couldn't express, into the skis grouped around a tunnel hatch. In another blizzard Von der Wall, forsaking the roundabout passage through the tunnels which most of us favored in heavy blows, left the hatch over the tractor garage. It was only a few yards to the "Ad" Building. Being a deep-sea diver and accustomed to groping in the dark, he thought he could make it easily. Carefully taking a bearing as he left the hatch, he plunged into the drift. He couldn't see a thing—nothing at all. After what seemed a long time he glimpsed a light, which he judged to be Grimminger at the instrument shelter. He altered course accordingly. Then the light disappeared. Fifteen minutes later, completely befuddled, he tripped over the same hatch he had quit. In the worst blizzard of the year Grimminger had to go topside for the usual temperature reading. I doubt if any other man traveled on the surface that day. Haines stood by the hatch with a line on his assistant. Though the instrument shelter was less than a dozen steps away, Grimminger reached it by sense of direction alone. So fiercely was the wind driven into his face that he had to make his way backwards. In heavy blows you can't see a foot ahead; the particles of drift hit the eyes in level flight, hot and stabbing as sand.

Darkness gives a blizzard a terrifying power for panic. Drift envelopes you in overpowering rushes; it stings and batters the eyes until the eye-balls hurt: and the wind seems to suck the breath out of the body. Most terrifying of all is how quickly it can cause men to lose touch with each other. Five men went out to bring in gasoline for a broadcast. In a few seconds the wind rose from a whisper to small gale strength; though the men were walking together, the swirl of drift almost instantly isolated one from the other. Three men finally came together, and the other two reached the tunnel entrance just as a searching party was starting after them.

My only adventure during a year's residence at Little America was of a like sort. I started out alone for a ski trip down to the mouth of Ver-Sur-Mer Inlet. It was drifting a bit when I started, more perhaps than I realized, since the wind was at my back. When I turned at the edge of the pressure to go back, it was to meet a half-blinding flurry of drift. Luckily Perkins had planted a line of flags, 50 feet or so apart, all the way back to the camp. But, close as they were, even with a flashlight I couldn't make them out until I was within a few feet of them. The three-quarters of a mile back to camp is a confused memory. I was petrified with fear, I know that; and I started to run until the question flashed across my mind: where to? There's only one thing you can do, duck your head in the lee of a shoulder, and take it broad on the bow. But no matter how hard you try to keep going straight, knowing that the wind direction is the safest bearing, you pay off unconsciously, shrinking from taking the wind head-on. The upper part of the face becomes a solid mass of ice. Several flags were blown out in the line, which I hadn't remembered, and I made several stabs before picking up the next one. The green headlands of New Zealand were a no more welcome landmark than the black skeleton of the first radio tower miraculously evolving out of the storm.

However, there was no excuse for that sort of thing. Few blizzards struck that Haines and Grimminger didn't prophesy. The risk came from carelessness, or taking things for granted. On occasion, when the surface air was almost calm, the pilot balloon runs would show a high velocity wind just above the surface. I remember Bill's posting warning, one calm day, that a 35-mile an hour wind—a potential blizzard—was flowing over the camp at 700 feet. Sometimes these rivers of air suddenly licked down. The drift, raised by wind, much more than falling snow, gives vehemence to the blizzard. According to the meteorologists, a gale will fling drift between 100 and 200 feet high. In an attempt to measure precipitation, Grimminger mounted a bucket on one of the 60-foot radio towers, and quite often found it half full of drift. Sometimes when you couldn't see a man ten feet away, you could look up and see the stars shining dimly through the peel of flying snow.

But it would be a mistake to give the impression that Little America is an extraordinarily windy place. It is anything but that. Heavy drift —or blizzards—were rare. The meteorological records, which lack only a week of covering a year, cite 5 heavy, 15 moderate and 112 light blizzards.[1] The highest wind velocity during the stay on the ice was 60 miles per hour; the average was 11.7 miles. The prevailing wind direction was east. April, the windiest month, had an average velocity of 13.9 miles; August and December, the calmest months, an average velocity of 8 miles. The surprisingly low velocities may be partly attributed to the low protecting ridge encircling the town. The air was quieter in the valley. When the tiny sensitive wind cups on the 14-foot anemometer pole were barely stirring the ponderous blades of the wind-driven generator atop one of the 60-foot radio towers were often turning briskly. The hydrogen pilot balloons used for upper air soundings would lean hard the instant they towered above the ridge level.

A high wind, however, did not necessarily mean heavy drift or blizzard. Sometimes a strong wind raised very little drift; conversely, a

[1] The meteorologists did not use the term blizzard, indicating rather the days on which drift occurred; the terms light, moderate and heavy drift in their language meant mild, moderate, and severe blizzard respectively.

light wind might be accompanied by a great deal. The severity of the storm depended upon the barrier surface, whether it was packed hard or filmed with a loose, freshly fallen snow.

It is surprising how shallow the Antarctic snowfall is. In the previous chapter I mentioned how rare were the large snowflakes most of us were accustomed to, presumably on account of the small moisture content of the atmosphere. There was a relentless flutter, nevertheless, of tiny flakes and (in the colder weather) tiny crystals or ice needles. The records show that snow fell 135 days of the year. However, the amount was small. In August Grimminger planted two brass rods, of the diameter of a pencil, at points 8 miles apart, one to windward of the camp, the other on high barrier at West Cape, where no drift was likely to accumulate. When he took them up in January, five months later, they showed, within a tenth of an inch, an accretion of 6 inches of drift and snow—which amount extrapolated would indicate the Barrier was increasing at the rate of 14 inches a year. Grimminger was inclined to believe the actual increase was probably less.

III

As for cold, it was more tolerable than one might think. However brutal cold may be on the trail, it was no great hardship in the life of the camp. Some men were out every day of the winter, except when drift was too severe; we had some grand skiing parties down on the Bay of Whales even on the coldest and darkest days. On the three occasions the temperature crossed —71° (June 21st, August 30th and 31st) at least half a dozen men were out skiing several hours.

As a matter of fact, there was real joy in being out in such air, if only to rid the lungs of the stale, smoky fumes of the shacks. The air had an exciting taste to it; when you drew a breath it seemed to hit the back of the head, and the nose and throat tingled with the feel of it.

The tolerable quality of great cold, I mean in the low sixties, is that it almost invariably occurs in still air. The air is utterly quiet, and the anemometer cups over the "Ad" Building lie stopped for hours. Sometimes, when there is the barest breath of wind you can hear the breath freezing as it floats to leeward, a strange, rather uncanny sound, like the explosion of tiny Chinese fire-crackers.

Of course, in moving about or running on skis, you get nipped often enough. Most of the men who made a habit of skiing had scabrous, frost-bite sores on the cheek, hands and under the chin where the helmet strap chafed, which in the dim light of the shacks looked like leprosy in an incipient stage. But you accepted frost-bite in the natural order of things; it was as inevitable as sunburn at home in the summer, if considerably more annoying, since a good frost-bite leaves the skin sensitive, and for a long time afterwards a new bite is sore as blazes. So every little while you stop, slip a bare hand out of the warmth of the mitten and mold the flesh until the blood goes shooting through the veins.

Nor is it necessary to wear an excessive amount of clothing. Ski boots, two pairs of woolen socks, a woolen shirt, trousers, underwear (I found light silk and wool underwear quite satisfactory), helmet, mittens with double inner liners, and light windproof pants and parka (marvelous stuff for the cold) were all you needed for brisk ski running. This fact was most vexing to the cameramen, who were evidently under strict orders from Hollywood to photograph the explorers *in furs.* Furs were used only during flights when men had no opportunity to exercise, or in camp on the trail, or, finally, whenever the cameramen were able to muster a battalion for some special scene of hardship. In most cases the hardship came from wearing the furs. They're frightfully hot if you move around at all; worse than that, there lingers for days a singular musty odor suggestive of a civet cat making up its mind.

The veterans had a Paul Bunyan tale to the effect that Dr. Coman, stark naked except for boots and pith helmet, walked 200 yards at —53°. The antiquarians excavated the pith helmet from a pile of rubbish, but failed in every effort to persuade some hero to carry on the tradition. The feeling was that it called for risk above the line of duty. It should be mentioned, however, that the senior meteorologist survived the winter in B.V.D.'s. "I'd sooner freeze to death," he said, "than try to wash those long wool drawers."

The real agony of cold comes from wind. Though wind usually brought rising temperatures, nevertheless you seemed to feel the cold more intensely. Wind sucked the air out of the shacks and sent icy draughts through the tunnels. In a fair breeze at —30° we shivered more than in still air at —70°. When the wind blew it was hard to keep heat in the buildings, and the mechanics handling cold metal couldn't stand it for long.

Traveling up wind on a very cold day is undeniably bitter. The air cuts numbingly at the cheeks, throat, nose and the back of the neck, where the protection is lightest. When you stop to attend hurriedly to these areas, the freezing attacks the feet and hands, and a strange fiery metallic glow seems to spread over the whole body. No matter how you twist and turn, there's no getting away from it; the Barrier offers no more lee than the open sea. Cold clasps you as water enfolds a tiring swimmer.

So you beat and tack in the dark, shunning the full onslaught of the wind, watching out of the corner of the eye the tiny beacon light growing on the radio tower. What a friendly light it was!

In the beginning, of course, nearly every one was experimenting with face masks of one sort or another, ranging from simple vizors with eye slits to Rube Goldberg fantasies. Probably the most efficient was the mask, made by June, which Admiral Byrd took to Advance Base. Fabricated of windproof cloth stretched across a light padded metal frame, it entirely covered the face, leaving narrow slits for the eyes, nose and mouth. The commonest type was a mere patch of sheepskin covering the upper part of the face. However, these were more a bother than a blessing on account of the rime which collected from the breath; in short order they would freeze as stiff as cardboard.

The beauty of the cold of winter was the clarity of the night and the great joy of skiing. Never were the stars brighter than when the temperature was sagging through the fifties and sixties. We could see and hear for miles. The sky was chockfull of stars and if the moon was full we could barely make out the white bluff of West Cape.

Sounds carried with tinkling clarity. Way down on the Bay we could hear the Kohlers puffing at Little America. The clang of a hammer, even a loud shout carried for miles. The swish of skis on hard snow was startlingly loud. And often out of the darkness would float the round sounds of the pressure working—mysterious creakings and groanings, distant muffled sounds like those of a train running away off in the night, and sudden crashings and tumbling noises as unseen blocks let go. But the strangest noises of all were those of the seals under fifteen feet of ice—the thud of heads blundering against obstructions in the depths, the scrape of bodies, half-strangled gurglings, chipperings, pipings and a trill that was almost bird-like. On first hearing these sounds you could scarcely credit your ears.

The winter night is by no means a period of unmitigated cold. Inpourings of warmer air from the seas to the north and east kited the temperature to +20° or more. As a matter of fact, we were almost embarrassed in May and June by the onset of what the meteorologists referred to as a "heat wave." For 16 days in a row—from May 22nd to June 6th—the maximum temperature reached zero or higher; twice it soared to + 25°, and the minimum failed to drop lower than —20°. After a drop to —37° on June 7th, the "heat wave" resumed on the 8th, and during the next nine days the maximum only twice failed to cross zero. The snow got soft and was on the point of becoming slushy; the roofs were all leaking from the heat of the stoves, making the shacks rather miserable. In the "Ad" Building, the harassed tenants were resorting to intricate systems of drains and tin cans swung from the ceiling to keep the drip off the sleeping bags. Until the steady drumming of upper northerly and easterly winds stopped and the cold clamped down again, the meteorologists were in disgrace.

On July 27th, after more than a month of cold climaxing in a temperature of —71°, the miracle occurred—rain! Men who had scarcely seen the sky since the sun went down rushed to the hatches for a look. It was anything but a downpour—just a darker misting in the night, which wet the cheeks and the palm of an upraised hand.

"But I don't see no rain," protested the cook.

Grimminger put his flashlight down, to let it come to the temperature of the snow, which was colder than the air. When he switched on the light and held it upwards the miracle was confirmed—tiny droplets stuck mistily on the glass.

"Heat waves" notwithstanding, the climate was bracing enough for the most rigorous appetite. The mean minimum temperature of May was —28°; June —23°; of July —48°; of August, —49.7°; and of September, —47°. From March through September the temperature crossed —50° sixty times, —60° twenty-seven times, and —71° three times. January 1934 was the warmest month, with a mean temperature of +23.6°. The mean temperature of the year was —13.5°. In August, the coldest month, the minimum temperature on 23 days crossed —40°, and eight days in a row registered —60° or colder.

IV

In the slow river of darkness life flows pretty much by routine, confined and stayed as between a river's banks. After we finished securing camp for the winter night toward the end of May, with the darkness already a quarter spent, reveille was set by common consent at 8 o'clock, with breakfast from 8 to 9 o'clock. Too much work, however, was piling up in connection with spring preparations; so the rising hour was presently moved back to 7 o'clock.

At noon we had an institution called the "ob," a light lunch consisting as a rule of pea soup (or pea soup), salami, corned beef, the hash left over from breakfast, sardines every other day, coffee or cocoa, and occasionally a dessert, almost always canned fruit. The odd name was an inheritance from the first expedition. It evidently stemmed from the suspicion that every time Bill Haines excused himself from a snow-shoveling detail with the explanation he had to "take an ob," meaning a meteorological observation, he furtively ducked into the galley for a cup of coffee and a sandwich. This was a grave injustice to the senior meteorologist. Bill never ate sandwiches.

Supper was the heavy meal of the day—a soup, a meat course, two or three dehydrated vegetables, fresh bread, a dessert, and coffee. We had rather bad luck with the meat. A deal of fresh beef spoiled on the ship coming down, with the result that by the middle of the winter night, with six months still to go on the ice, we were practically out of beef. There were ample amounts of salt horse, ham, pig's knuckles, mutton (popularly called New Zealand chamois) and seal meat. Every once in a while we had chicken on Sunday, eking out the delicacy by each man limiting himself to a single portion. However, this self-denial was unavailing because the dogs got loose one night, broke into the meat cache (it was placed, fatally, just above Dog Town) and practically cleaned out the fowl. In the afternoon the doctor inspected the meat for the evening meal: there were few more melancholy moments than when he condemned a whole quarter of beef hauled into the galley for a state occasion. Even the medical survey didn't discourage those with a craving for a new taste, a different flavor. When the doctor's back was turned the least doubtful cuts would be stealthily cut away, and in the early morning an aroma of frying steak would pervade the tunnels adjacent to the Science Hall. It couldn't have been very bad because no one died; there wasn't even a good bellyache.

Three times a week, commencing at 7 o'clock, we'd have movies—as a rule a short and a feature. Like the books in the library, they were an extraordinary mixture of good and bad; but even the worst must have conveyed some pleasure, perhaps an hour or two of escape, because many men missed not one, not even the fifth or sixth showing of a picture. As the men arrived, stamping the snow off their boots and their clothing steaming as it met the warm air inside, Steve Corey would hand to each one the evening tidbit as he passed—a bar of chocolate, a bag of peanuts, popcorn or such. There weren't quite enough seats to accommodate all hands, so half a dozen men were usually clustered at the back of the room, peering past the dish racks. Hermann and Petersen, the Paramount cameramen, who put on these shows, and Dr. Poulter and Hutcheson, who re-wound the reels, were very good about the whole business, and these evenings were always pleasant. Afterwards half a dozen men stayed behind to put the galleys to rights, sweep up the deck and arrange the benches and tables for breakfast.

It is difficult to tell, and perhaps not very important, which movies were most popular. "42nd Street," a music show with lots of hotcha and Nebraska mountains, must have been shown at least six times; "Farewell to Arms" ran it a close second. Some men were most moved by a fine and deftly woven piece called "The Bitter Tea of General Yen." But the movies at Little America had certain aspects not found elsewhere, some of which quite took your breath away. If you happened to be returning from a ski trip down to the Bay of Whales, cold as the devil and your mind at peace, it was rather startling to hear, rising in waves of agitation through the Mess Hall ventilators, a woman's voice, ". . . don't, Zebulon, please . . . not now!" (My goodness, does that sort of thing still go on?)

The curfew was 10 o'clock. All electric lights out then, no more coal on the fire. The hour was fixed more by the need of saving coal and power than anything else. Most of the men had had small bunk lights —little lamps run from flashlight batteries or kerosene lamps made from fruit jars, or even lanterns—which made it possible to read for half an hour or so after the main lights went out. But when the fire died the air chilled quickly. The hands would get cold, the breath would begin to freeze, and one by one the bunk lights would wink out. From overhead, as the roof cooled, would come strange sharp cracklings and, carrying on the still air, the taut sharper reports of the ice contracting in the Bay of Whales.

A certain amount of work carried well into the night—Bailey's radio schedules usually lasted long after midnight, according to the luck he had getting through to New York or San Francisco; Bramhall and Zuhn were up all hours over cosmic ray and magnetic observations; and Perkins, a peace-loving soul, preferred the night watches for his microscopic work, since the Science Hall by day, on account of its spaciousness, was the common hangout for the dialecticians. "Perk" took to night work after "Ike" Schlossbach and Dustin had held forth at his elbow for five hours on the pros and cons of the anti-scorbutic properties of Lydia Pinkham's Vegetable Compound.

Exiled by occupation to the bituminous-breathing adventurers known as the Indoor Explorers, the writer is unqualified to speak for hardships in the field; but for his own kin he can say feelingly that the ghastliest ordeal of all was getting up in the morning. At night when we turned in, the doors were always opened into the tunnels; this made for circulation of the air and also had the good effect of secretly introducing fresh air to the slumbering *sourdoughs* in quantities not likely to be harmful. Still, certain care had to be observed. Sergeant Carbone came to one night exclaiming, "What's that funny smell in here!" Well, with the doors open the temperature steadily dropped: on colder nights, with a surface temperature of —60° or thereabouts, the shack temperature got as low as —25°. The washing water in the buckets froze, boots got hard as iron, clothing drying on the lines over the stove became stiff with ice, a coating of rime gathered on the sleeping bags where the breath fell, and beneath the ventilators and the cracks around the stove pipes there always gathered, when drift blew above, little heaps of snow which invariably lay between the bunk and where you dropped your pants and socks.

Into this dark scene of glaciation would come the night watchman at 7 o'clock. Different men took turns at the job; so the technique varied. Al Wade, big, blond and handsome, always cheerful, would stand in the middle of the room, shaking the stove and bellowing: "Hey, hey, hey, rise and shine, rise and shine," sometimes adding such timely information as, "Hot cakes and scrapple for breakfast. The cook's in a foul mood." Lindsey, the biologist, went in for doggerel: "To sleep, perhaps to dream, aye, there's the rub—for he who sleeps too long will miss his grub," delivered in full voice from the door. He was agile enough to escape without being marred. Lewisohn gently plucked at the sleeping bags, and you could always tell if Fleming were on watch by the uproar he contrived; either the stove pipe crashed down or else he fell over the coal scuttle. Dustin even went to the trouble of unhooking a siren from a tractor and dragging a storage battery after him from shack to shack. The novelty all but cost him his life.

Whatever the greeting, metrical or otherwise, the problem of getting up still remained. It's difficult to explain it, but what made it hard was not so much the cold as a sense of weariness, of physical depletion and attrition. Dr. Potaka, who remarked on it, said it was partly due to the abominable ventilation, partly to the enervation induced by great cold, the sluggishness of the physical system, the body's need of fresh food, and a drooping in vitality coinciding with the departure of the sun. It seemed to take a long time to come back from any sustained exertion, as if the mechanism of recuperation had slacked off. Even small cuts healed slowly. And I also believe now that the unmitigated toil of unloading the ships and securing Little America took more out of the men than they realized themselves. That the expedition was able to rise from that beating and carry on as brilliantly as it did, not merely through the winter's preparations but into the more sustained campaigns of the spring and summer, topping it all off with the slogging business of loading the ships in February, was the proof of its stamina and purposefulness.

Though the C.O.'s orders called for all hands out at reveille, no real attempt was ever made to enforce it. As a matter of fact, discipline in such matters was never rigid. Few orders were ever given and there was no harsh holding to the line. In this respect, I suppose, we differed most strikingly from the polar camp of tradition. Little America was mostly a group of individuals, each with a pretty fair idea of his job and the particular thing required of him, working informally and each more or less to his own taste toward the common end. Therein lies the particular genius of Admiral Byrd, that counting upon the pride most men have in their work he can afford to make allowance for the peculiar temperamental difficulties of existence without jeopardizing his organization. Men bred to rigid distinctions and regulations of military service distrust it instinctively, only to be puzzled by the fact that somehow, when the time comes, it all fits together. Perhaps no other system than this loose and genial fraternity could have survived the variety of temperaments and philosophies sealed in the caves of Little America.

At first, as the new department heads and officers felt the weight of responsibility, we were bombarded with memoranda, all signed in full, with title underneath. But this looked pretty silly: the fellow to whom you were addressing a formal communication was quite likely sitting in the bunk overhead, in the same sort of sleazy gray underwear, trying to compose one in the right severity of style to you. Besides, nobody had any place to file such things. John Dyer used to welcome such communications for the paper they provided toward starting the fire in the morning; we were awfully short of paper in the radio shack. So we naturally fell into the habit of casual dealings among ourselves.

If Bramhall needed a new gadget for his apparatus, or Bowlin a

Observing Meteors—Dr. Poulter and Smith, Lindsey Recording

(Photographs by Joseph A. Pelter)

Meeting of the Scientific Staff

William Haines, Senior Meteorologist

(Photographs by Joseph A. Pelter)

Dr. Bramhall and Cosmic Ray Machine

Grimminger Starting a Balloon Run

part machined for his plane, they would take it up with Boyd over the coffee at breakfast. If the supply officer needed help getting heavy boxes out of a cache, instead of going through the routine layers of authority he'd drum up his own volunteers. The same sort of informal exchange marked the fitting out of the field parties.

One of the grand sides of such an existence is the discovery of the indestructible generosity and courtesy in some men. No matter how much the rest of us tended to turn inward, shying without quite realizing it from the onerous burdens outside our province, a few were steadily carrying on, unasked and out of turn, the dirty work of the camp. Tramping out in a blizzard to dig out gas drums for the power plant, joining harassed messmen during the dinner rush to give them a chance to catch up, fixing broken things roundabout, digging out the tunnel entrances after a blizzard, stopping along the way to give a helping hand. At breakfast, perhaps, when harassed messmen were oppressed by the thought of chores still undone, there would come a rattle of coal in the galley box, the bang of snow against the metal wall of the snow melter, or perhaps two men on their way out would take the garbage—all chores on the messmen's agenda. One could be pretty sure that the anonymous benefactors were Dane, Dyer, Young, Von der Wall, Hutcheson, or Moody. But it is wrong to single out a few. When you were weariest and most despondent, lost in yourself and dullness, an unexpected act of courtesy or generosity would illuminate the day.

V

Above everything else the winter night was a period of preparation for spring enterprises. The big push was ordered for October, and for four months the order regulated routine. Little America talked, lived and, I dare say, dreamt field operations. They were the principal topic at meals; the subject of untiring conferences. Dr. Poulter, Innes-Taylor, Rawson and June worked closely with party leaders, and from time to time, over the thrice weekly radio schedules with Advance Base, various problems were taken up with Admiral Byrd.

Not counting the flights of geographical exploration, which will be discussed later by Admiral Byrd, three major sledging journeys, each requiring long-range support, were on the program. Although aimed into previously unexplored regions, the objectives of the several surface parties were scientific rather than geographical exploration. The purpose of the operation was to transport scientists to certain crucial areas for special and definite studies.

The program had been worked up by Admiral Byrd and Dr. Poulter, senior scientist; and before leaving for Advance Base Admiral Byrd had carefully gone into the operations end of it with Innes-Taylor, chief of trail operations.

In conjunction with the proposed flights of discovery, the field program was so designed as to throw a geographical network over the unknown areas to the east and southeast of Little America. In scope and range it promised to be the broadest attack ever launched in the south polar regions.

GEOLOGICAL PARTY

A three-man sledging party into the Queen Maud Range, having as its target a geological and paleontological reconnaissance of the unexplored easterly reaches of the Range.

In 1929-1930 the first expedition's Geological Party, under command of Dr. Laurence M. Gould, had run a reconnaissance survey eastward along the front of the Queen Mauds, from Liv Glacier, up which Admiral Byrd had flown to the South Pole, to Lat. 85° 25′ S., Long. 147° 55′ W. Here the party made the discovery of the easterly trend of the range, of two mighty valley glaciers—Leverett and Thorne—and of the fact that the range seemed to be declining in height. Arriving at the cited position after a long easting, and having neither time nor rations for a deeper penetration, the party was obliged to withdraw on the threshold of its discoveries.

The new Geological Party proposed to break past Gould's track by aiming at once for his farthest point, Supporting Party Mountain, a nunatak thought to form the northwestern portal of Leverett Glacier. Here they intended to put down a food base at the foot of the range, and from that point attempt to scale the glacier. The plan involved a 517-mile journey across the Ross Ice Barrier to the foot of the Queen Mauds, and a glacier ascent of at least 100 miles. If nothing miscarried, the party would have sufficient rations for 38 days' field work past this Mountain Base, and a total of 90 days out.

The associated objectives were (1) a geologic cross-section of the Queen Mauds, with an eye to crucial structural relationships; (2) an intensive search for fossiliferous strata, since a substantial find would help to illuminate the pale climatological history of Antarctica; (3) confirmation of the trend of the Queen Mauds; (4) the mapping of new mountains discovered during the ascent; and (5) a daily meteorological record in high southern latitudes.

Blackburn was leader and geologist; Paine was radio operator, navigator and driver; Russell was driver and would have charge of trail routine. The party's transport would consist of two teams, of nine dogs each.

PLATEAU PARTY

A four-man party having the double mission of running a seismic and magnetic survey across the Ross Ice Barrier to the Queen Mauds, and up the Queen Mauds to the polar plateau, in several respects the most ambitious research journey ever attempted in the polar regions.

The co-leaders were Morgan, geologist and geophysicist; and Dr. Bramhall, physicist. The men selected to accompany them were the two finest skiers in camp, Ronne and Eilefsen, since the glacier ascent with heavy loads called for the keenest sort of trail work. Four teams of nine dogs each would provide transportation.

The plan called for this party to travel in company with the Geological Party to the foot of the Queen Mauds. At the Mountain Base they would separate, the latter party proceeding up Leverett Glacier to the southeast, the former striking south up Thorne Glacier to the plateau.

Bramhall's magnetic survey was an extension of the study into terrestrial magnetism carried on at Little America. Its special purpose was to collect data bearing on the diurnal variation, the distribution of, and local anomalies in, the permanent field of the earth in a region where such data is exceedingly inadequate. His field equipment consisted of a dip circle (for the determination of the declination, total intensity and dip of the earth's magnetic field) an askania balance (for measuring variations in horizontal and vertical intensity), and a theodolite for astronomical determinations of the azimuth and position of observation stations. Such stations would be established every 25 or 50 miles along the route of march.

Morgan's seismic soundings project was a striking idea. Its primary objective was the determination of the thickness of the south polar ice cap by adapting a technique employed in petroleum geophysics. Estimates as to the thickness of the ice dammed back by the mountains encircling the Pole ran as high as 10,000 feet.[2] A successful series of soundings along the margin of the plateau would have the effect of suggesting the nature of the land smothered under ice and, what was of wider moment, might supply the first factual answer to the depth attained by ice over land during a period of glacial flood.

In principle, the seismic method is similar to that used by ships in determining ocean depths. It involved the measurement of the velocity and path of a sound wave beneath the surface. An explosion of TNT sets up the sound waves. Sensitive geophones (or vertical seismographs), planted at various distances from the charge, pick up the faint earth vibrations and convert them into electrical impulses. These impulses are amplified, filtered and sent through galvanometers with tiny mirrors attached, which vibrate with the electrical impulses, reflecting a light beam which photographs itself upon a rapidly moving strip of photographic paper. An electrically driven tuning fork, vibrating at the same time, impresses lines on the record at the rate of a hundred per second, making it possible to calculate the time factor within one one-thousandth of a second.

[2] Sir Douglas Mawson, *Unsolved Problems of Antarctic Exploration and Research, Problems of Polar Research,* Am. Geo. Soc., 262.

With this instrument [8] Morgan, who had had experience handling it in the Oklahoma oil fields, believed that the maximum error in the depth determination of 5,000 feet of ice would be less than 50 feet.

Morgan's apparatus with 220 pounds of powder and caps, alone weighed 832 pounds; and the fate of the party rested squarely upon the ability of the support to assist it to the foot of the Queen Maud Range, and upon the dogs to advance the load over The Hump to the 7,000-foot polar plateau.

The total load required for the operation, counting scientific instruments, man and dog-food, camping equipment and such, was in the neighborhood of 6,336 pounds, of which nearly half was destined for the plateau.

From every angle a difficult and hazardous journey.

MARIE BYRD LAND PARTY

A four-man sledging party having for its objective a mission of geological reconnaissance into the unpenetrated coastal mountains of Marie Byrd Land, east and northeast of Little America, which Admiral Byrd discovered by plane in 1929.

No exploring party had yet set foot upon this crucial area; and the party had a certain unique prospect in that it was destined to be the first scientific unit to penetrate a new land discovered by aircraft.

Save for the short journey of Lieut. Prestrud of Amundsen's expedition to the Alexandra Mts., 170 miles northeast of Little America; Admiral Byrd's flight of discovery to the Rockefeller Mts., 120 miles east of Little America; and his major flight northeast to the coastal margin of Marie Byrd Land, the vast region east of Little America was unknown.

It was this party's plan to strike past the Rockefellers for Mt. Grace McKinley, southwesternmost mountain observed by Admiral Byrd in the Edsel Ford Range, and from this point work northward along the front of the range to the coast. The distance to Grace McKinley was estimated to be 260 miles.

Since the responsibility of extended geographical explorations of the region would be taken over by aviation, this party was primarily concerned with definite research. The objectives included: (1) a study of the geology of the region with reference to its relationship with other continental land masses and, especially, to the much-discussed

[8] The set of instruments used on the journey was especially designed by the Seismograph Service Corporation for handiness and lightness. The oscillograph and three transformer-coupled amplifiers were built into one case; the tuning fork, control panel and batteries were in separate aluminum cases. Three seisometers and a five-element galvanometer were used. The recording instrument was hand-cranked. Apparatus was adaptable either to complete dry cell or partial storage battery operation. A second set of instruments was standard equipment loaned by the Geophysical Research Corporation.

problem of Andean connection; (2) an intensive search for biological and botanical specimens for which the presence of exposed rock so near the coast held out high promise; (3) a series of snow and rock dust samples for bacteriological analysis; (4) astronomical determinations of the positions of conspicuous landmarks along the route of march to provide ground control for aerial mapping on flights of discovery; and (5) the usual magnetic and meteorological observations.

The party comprised Siple, leader, biologist and navigator; Wade, geologist, radio operator, and driver; Corey, driver; Stancliff, driver, assistant radio operator and in general charge of trail routine.

The total load required for a 90-day journey was approximately 6,000 pounds, of which 3,600 was scheduled for transport by a supporting party. The party transport would consist of three teams, of nine dogs each.

So much for the main plans. To make them effective a strong, well-articulated system of support was necessary. Such a plan was worked out by Captain Innes-Taylor with the party leaders.

In advance of the Marie Byrd Land Party a tractor unit under June's command would put down a series of depots along the line of march from Little America to Mt. Grace McKinley, a support line 260 miles long.

On account of the great weights and superior distances involved, the joint operations of the Plateau and Geological Parties called for more complicated and hazardous supports, in effect a line of food depots across the Barrier from the Bay of Whales to the foot of the Queen Maud Range, a distance of 517 miles.

As the plan was worked out during the winter, the support would proceed in a series of waves, employing both dogs and tractors. The first wave would be the advance by tractor of 3,000 pounds of dog food to 100-Mile Depot. The second wave would be a sledging operation, having for its purpose the establishment of dog and man food depots at 25-mile intervals from 150-Mile Depot, termination of the fall depot-laying journey, to 300-Mile Depot. The third wave would be tractor, having for its purpose the delivery of 300 pounds of dog food to 300-Mile Depot, and the advance of 2,200 pounds of dog food and 850 pounds of scientific apparatus (principally the seismic instruments) to the Mountain Base at the mouth of Thorne Glacier.

Between 300-Mile Depot and the Mountain Base the two main parties were expected to put down the food depots covering their own retreat.

The main tractor party consisted of three men and two cars—Demas in command and driver of one car; Hill, driver of the second car; and Waite, radio operator.

The Supporting Party involved three men and three dog teams—Captain Innes-Taylor, leader; Moody and Dane, drivers.

Altogether the entire southern operations, counting support, involved 13 men, two tractors, 81 dogs and the movement of approximately 29,000 pounds of load.

VI

Little America scraped the war-chest bare to outfit the trail parties. In spite of all the planning many shortages developed. The most serious was gasoline for tractors. Thanks to an ingenious swap contrived by Commander Noville, the strain was relieved. Aviation had a surplus of high octane gas which was unsuitable for tractor operation; the radio department, on the other hand, had a supply of gasoline which approximated the tractor requirements, but was itself on short rations. Noville therefore borrowed 1,500 gallons of gas from the radio department which he turned over to the tractors; replacing it with a thousand gallons of gas taken from aviation which, compounded with 500 gallons of kerosene, gave a mixture suitable for the Kohlers. This wangling made available to the tractors barely enough fuel for their requirements.

It was interesting how far-reaching these economies were. Anxious to turn over every possible ounce of gas to the tractors, Waite reduced the use of the Kohlers to a minimum. He and Noville made a tour of the camp eliminating all electric lights not absolutely necessary: we were put on a diet of 10-watt bulbs, awful things for close work, mere misty glows in darkness. Into the movie projector they popped a 400-watt lamp in place of the magnificent 1,000-watt affair which had hitherto powered it. These economies were hardly popular—no more so, at any rate, than prohibition. The cook wanted to know what the devil they expected him to do—cook in the dark? "It might be an improvement," said the Exec unfeelingly. The carpenter demanded power for his saws. "The first carpenters on this continent," said the Exec, "got along quite nicely with elbow grease." In the end, after a flurry of bootlegged lights, the economies prevailed.

But there were other shortages. The spark plugs for the Kohlers having been hopelessly lost in a mountain of drift, Waite was running the engines on second-hand plugs borrowed from aviation. Demas likewise was turning the camp upside down for spare plugs for his cars. If you mentioned fan belts to him his cheeks turned pale and a feverish light leaped into his eyes. The rubber-impregnated fabric with which the cars were originally equipped disintegrated in severe cold, and the tractor department was manufacturing spares out of everything they could lay hands on. Cox accused Demas of thus making off with his only pair of suspenders. Anyhow, by the greatest stroke of luck they found a roll of webbed belting in the tractor cache which, it seemed, was earmarked for the *Bear of Oakland's* air compressors. Nobody knew how it ever got to Little America, but Demas welcomed it as a gift from Providence. To be on the safe side, the drivers manufactured any number of experimental belts out of rubber cables and strips of leather, cemented and riveted together.

Dyer was squeezing dry the resources of the radio cache for parts with which to finish the trail sets—four sets for the sledging parties,[4] two sets for the tractors.[5] At the fag-end there developed a shortage of plywood (a strong, but light, laminated wood) needed for trail boxes and housing radio equipment. In our profligate way we had used the stuff for all sorts of private conveniences. Now the carpenters were raiding the shacks for any good piece fit for their purposes. For the Citroën, burned during the unloading, Dyer constructed a new instrument panel, cleverly converting a volt meter into a gas gauge. Because the windproof material was needed for trail parties, the Indoor Explorers were notified their spring wardrobe would be limited to new patches. Grimminger, as a matter of fact, was holding his pants together with bunion plasters. Snow glasses had been lost or broken; levy was made on the camp supply for the field parties, leaving the rest to shift for themselves. Dr. Poulter and Fleming stewed for days over this problem, experimenting with all sorts of inks and dyes, before they hit upon a mixture of pigments made from ordinary writing inks and indelible pencil, dissolved in acetone and alcohol, which could be applied to pyrolene, a composition glass. When the sailmaker said he was running short of material for trail flags, Dr. Poulter came forward again with the suggestion that heavy black photographic paper be used, a huge roll of which had been found in one of the old caches.

Still I scarcely realized how acute the needs were until the day I saw Von der Wall and Demas sneak through the radio shack with a piece of wood which I was horrified to identify as the door—the only door—to our only toilet. An hour later, crescent moon and all, it was being nailed into the sides of Tractor No. 3.

During the winter night all the sledges, nearly 50 of them, counting trailers, were overhauled. Ronne and Eilefsen were busy at it every day. Immediately after the breakfast dishes were cleared, one or the other of them would poke his head into the galley and politely ask the cook if it would be all right to bring in a sledge. Regardless

[4] The sets built by Dyer for the sledging parties consisted of a push-pull self-excited oscillator and a simple two-tube receiver built into one unit. The transmitter was adjusted to operate on three frequencies —4797, 6425 and 8655 KC, with an output power of five watts. The receiver was operated from batteries and the transmitter from a hand-cranked generator. Total weight about 110 pounds.

[5] The tractor set consisted of a self-excited oscillator with dynamotor plate supply. The receiver was similar to that used by the sledging parties. The dynamotor was supplied from a heavy-duty 12-volt battery charged from the car's generator.

of what the cook said, they promptly returned with a huge sledge which they swung onto one of the big tables. Almost always one sledge was thawing on the ceiling, where the air was warmer, giving off a deadly drip of seal gore which accounted for the twitchings and acrobatics at the meals.

Designed by Czegka and built by Tinglof, the sledges used by the second expedition were a new wrinkle in sledge structure. Most Antarctic types utilized straight upright pieces from the runner, and the bridge was a separate member lashed to the uprights. Czegka's design had a single arch-shaped bridge, countersunk in the runner grooves; it had the merit of eliminating an extra member and two extra lashings, making for greater strength without sacrifice of flexibility, important factors in view of the strain put upon a sledge pounding with heavy loads over furrowed sastrugi. The sledges were built of hickory. For the sake of flexibility, no metal other than the gee-pole socket was used in them. The lashings were of rawhide, tightly reeved. Weighing 78½ pounds (that is, the lead sledges; the trailers weighed 65 pounds), they were capable of carrying over 2,000 pounds between the fore and after bridges.

In the punishing transit of the pressure during unloading (we fell into the habit of thus dividing the seasons—Unloading, Fall Journeys, Winter, Spring Journeys, Loading), Czegka's sledges stood up beautifully. No structural weaknesses appeared, in spite of the wicked surface and heavy loads. The tractors had crushed one or two; but most of them came through with no heavier damage than broken slats, sprung lashings, or perhaps a broken bridge. Tinglof had raw stock on hand for replacements.

Indeed, the strength being substantially in excess of requirements, Innes-Taylor decided to reduce the weight about 16 percent, sparing the dogs that much dead weight to carry. This was done by paring a bit of wood from the bridges, shaving down the tops of the runners, and slicing away part of the runners between the fore and after bridges. In this way the weight of the lead sledges was reduced to 66½ pounds, and the trailers to 53 pounds. Another thing: some of the parties shod the runners with a light sheathing of metal to make for better running on the granular surface characteristic of low spring temperatures and to withstand the wear and tear of glacial ascents.[6]

A shrewd saving was also made in the tractor sledges. The original tractor sledges had proved to be too big and heavy, being nearly 14 feet long and 5 feet wide, and weighing 750 pounds. Such weights ate into pay load. In the haul to Advance Base the drivers also used dog sledges, but they were too narrow of beam to be much good;

[6] The full dimensions of lead sledges follow: length, 11 ft., 6 in.; width, 25 in.; runner width, 4 in.; length between fore and after bridges, 7 ft. Dimensions of trailers: length, 9 ft., 6 in.; width, 25 in.; other dimensions, same as lead sledges.

The Fireside Philosophers

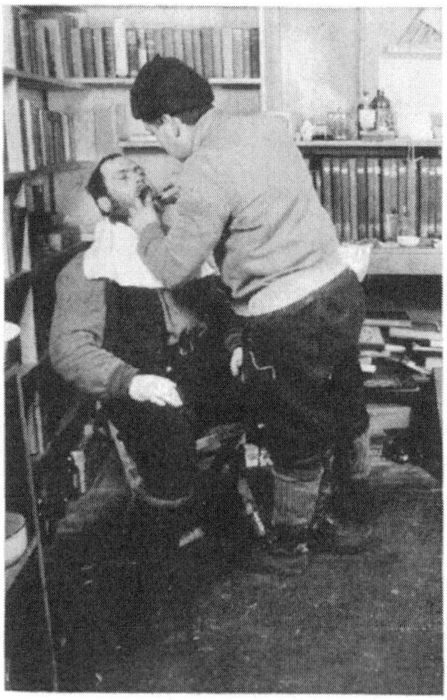

Dr. Potaka Uses "Painless Dentistry" on Corey

(Photographs by Joseph A. Pelter)

George Noville, Executive Officer

INNES-TAYLOR AND MOODY TAKE TO SURGERY

(Photographs by Joseph A. Pelter)

THE PRESSURE BY TORCHLIGHT

tipping over constantly in the ruts left by the treads. Having insufficient lumber to build new sledges, June hit upon the scheme of constructing a new triple-runner carrier by joining two leader sledges in parallel. It worked out very nicely. A solid centerpiece section was passed through the bridges across the width of the sledge, which was locked into place by a small key; this made for lateral rigidity yet preserved the flexibility of the whole. The new invention, which was successfully used on all subsequent tractor trips, had a beam of 50 inches, a length of 11 feet, 6 inches, a loading weight in excess of 4,000 pounds, and weighed approximately 160 pounds, a saving of 600 pounds each over the original sledge.

Rations were another problem. In the original estimates prior to leaving Boston, 3,000 man-food days had been fixed as the amount required to take care of all operations, and food reserves set up accordingly. However, a larger number of rations had been consumed during the fall operations than had been anticipated—8 complete rations (30 days' rations for 8 men) and 1,200 man-food days of Eskimo biscuits vanished during the unloading operations alone. Fall operations used up another 12 rations. According to Innes-Taylor's calculations, a total of 93 additional rations were required for all spring and summer operations, counting main parties, support, tractors, planes, reserves and local journeys. Practically all of these had to be made up during the winter.

What added to the difficulty was the necessity, as a result of the fall journeys, to modify the rations. A new formula was devised by Dr. Dana Coman, medical officer with the first expedition, and Dr. McCollum, both of the staff of Johns Hopkins.[7] Dr. Malcolm of Dunedin, New Zealand, who rendered a similar service to the first expedition, also helped. To provide the new rations the expedition's resources were strained to the limit. The greatest lack was fat; and for months Carbone scrupulously saved the fat left over from the meats. The camp limited itself to bacon once a week to build up the field parties' reserves. Even then it was impossible to fulfill the formula for all purposes, consequently separate rations were worked up for the tractor and plane crews, differing from sledging rations

[7] The Coman-McCollum formula consisted of the following ingredients:

Pemmican	1.5 oz.	Bacon	1.5 oz.
Fat cereal	5.5 "	Butter	2. "
Eskimo Bis.	10. "	Tea	.5 "
Sugar	3.5 "	Cocoa	.5 "
Klim	4.5 "	Dried Apricots	.5 "
Oatmeal	2. "	Dates	.5 "
Chocolate	2.5 "	Spinach	.25 "
Erbswurst	1.5 "	Salt	.5 "
Lemon Powder	.35 "		
		Total	37.5 oz.

only in the replacement of fat cereal with pemmican. Naturally the sledging parties, theirs being the heaviest physical strain, had preference.

The shortage of Eskimo biscuits also made it necessary to invent a new biscuit having all essential ingredients, yet which could be supplied from limited commissary stores. Here, again, by radio Drs. Coman and McCollum worked up a most satisfactory formula.[8] In all, 370 pounds of the new biscuits, amounting to 20 monthly rations, were made up by Carbone, who baked at night because the galley stove was steadily in use for the day's meals. The biscuits were made in fairly thin one- and two-ounce cakes, and sacked in rations bags.

In the depths of Dog Town, in the Seal Chopping House, a third division of trail supply was hotly engaged. In that cavernous chamber, lit up by the ghastly glare of a gasoline pressure lantern and the flames hissing and leaping from the blubber stove, Russell and Paine were manufacturing dog pemmican—six tons of it for trail and reserve needs. Seal blubber was melted for fat, and the stuff was set to harden in molds providing pound-and-a-half briquettes, a day's ration for a dog. It was a devil's chore. The stinging, acrid, pungent, penetrating smell of the boiling blubber (I can still taste it), the bloodless fragments of frozen seal kicking around the snow floor, and the thick haze which hung about the place caused nearly every one to give it a wide berth.

"Still, it's really quite nice," said Paine. "At least no one ever interrupts you."

But marvelous things were meanwhile happening in the garage. In that ice-box of a place, Demas and his drivers—Von der Wall. Skinner and Hill—buckled down early in June to the task of putting the cars in shape for the spring journeys. It was undeniably bitter labor. In an effort to make the shack halfway tolerable by the time the crew arrived after breakfast, the watchman used to light the fire at 6 o'clock. So much work lay ahead of them that the tractor unit waived the usual Sunday holiday. By the close of fall operations in May the three Citroëns had logged 6,796 miles, including 1,115 miles for the burnt car. During the winter all three were given a thorough going over, engines, running parts and skis. In fact, new bearings were poured and refitted on one engine.

Profiting by the hard lessons ground in by the March journey to Advance Base, the drivers tinkered and experimented with all sorts

[8] The Coman-McCollum biscuit consisted of:

8 parts entire wheat flour	8 parts oatmeal
2½ parts white sugar	2½ parts powdered milk
2 parts minced dried beef	1 part lard
½ part bovril	½ part bio-vegetin
1/10 part soda	1/10 part milk of magnesia

of gadgets for beating cold. The deadliest source of grief was the formation of frozen condensation in gas lines. In March, when that happened, they had no choice but to take the lines apart, with bare hands, and blow the ice out. Handling cold metal and gas at —60° was sheer agony. The flesh covering the drivers' finger tips had sloughed off. Now they inserted a small line with a petcock into the gas line just ahead of the fuel pump. With this attachment they counted on being able to blow out the lines in a few seconds.

A special oil tank was installed under the hood on the dashboard, with a line running to the crankcase; thus the heat of the engine would keep the reserve oil warm and it would be available at the turn of a petcock. Drain cocks were installed in accessible positions on the engine block and radiator to facilitate draining oil and anti-freeze solutions during halts. A metal shield was fitted across the bottom of the crankcase to keep the heat within the hood and prevent super-cooled air from striking the crankcase directly. The exhausts were so deflected that the hot exhaust gases were expelled directly against the differential housing, to make for steadier circulation of oil. Racks for oil cans and grease guns were built under the hood so that the crew would have warm lubricants handy while under way. Special switches were installed in the battery leads to the generators to reduce the risk of burning up the cutouts. During the March journey the generator cutouts had a tendency to stick and were burned up by the current flowing from the battery. Another thing: a toggle switch was inserted into the ignition so that the driver could instantly cut the ignition if a gas-line broke or the car plunged into a crevasse. Fire was a grave hazard on account of the large quantity of gas aboard.

But the cars themselves were meanwhile so altered as to be scarcely recognizable. The original canvas-topped bodies abaft the driving cab were torn down. Mindful of the nuisance of unloading tents and setting up camp, the drivers determined to convert the cars into rolling camps. In June they fell to work building a new superstructure, 5 feet high, 8 wide, and 6½ long, consisting of a framework of angle iron with wood three feet up the side. There wasn't enough spare lumber in camp to enclose the cars entirely with wood, therefore the roof and upper walls were covered with canvas laid across wood and metal slats. Narrow folding bunks, constructed by the carpenters out of odds and ends of lumber, were fitted to the side walls, each car sleeping two. When they were finished each car had a galvanized iron oven for the cooker; and an incongruous domestic touch was added by the capped smokestack jutting above the roof. In a false deck an aluminum airplane gas tank, capacity 145 gallons, was installed, giving each car, with the small tank aft, a capacity of 172 gallons. The new superstructures were painted a lurid orange not only for visibility but also because it was the only paint available.

When Demas's iron cavalry finally wheeled out into the full view of the camp, they were anything but lovely. "Gaudy," some one remarked, "but not very neat." More than once the ugly, seemingly top-heavy superstructures were to save a driver's life in the spring.

VII

Some men are committed to orderliness, and a change in latitude isn't likely to alter them. One might have set his watch by the regularity of certain tasks. At 8 o'clock in the morning, fair weather or foul, a flash-light beam playing eerily over the instrument shelter atop the "Ad" Building—Grimminger taking the 8 A.M. observation. At 9 o'clock the thud of an axe from the direction of Dog Town—the dog watch chopping up seal meat for the dogs. At a minute to noon, a peremptory winking of the lights in the shacks—Bailey's warning to shut off all electric drills, the meat grinder, power saws and the like while he handled the New York radio traffic. And at the stroke of midnight the clashing of a hammer in the Administration Building—Dr. Potaka making boxes. Why? Nobody knows. The "doc" just had a passion for making boxes. He made hundreds of them.

We had certain institutional habits too. School, for example. Under Dean Perkins, the University of Antarctica got off to a spectacular start. In spite of such formidable topics as the Purpose of Antarctic Meteor Research, the Origin of the Theory of the Polar Front, and the Cosmic Ray Program, the galley was crowded on the first day. It was Noville who accounted for the phenomenal enrollment, who noted the correlation between the passion for education and the chill of a work detail. "Every time I try to muster a couple of snow-shovelers," he complained, "they tell me they've got a class in shorthand."

However, in short order the University was reduced to the strictly utilitarian purpose of training men for the spring sledging missions—Rawson's daily course in navigation, Waite's classes in radio, and Innes-Taylor's course in sledging methods.

In this manner Little America worked toward the sun. Grief? There was no end of it. Unhappiness? Yes, I dare say we all had our moments of deep unhappiness; in June, when the sun was farthest away, one's spirits seemed to be rattling around in one's mukluks. Disagreements? Oh, Lord, it was Babel underground. Did it seem long? Quite. But most of the time it was great fun, and a vast amount of solid work was accomplished which bore fruit in the spring.

C. J. V. M.

Chapter XII

NIGHT JOURNEY

I

THE pertinacity with which most of the scientists carried on throughout the winter night was amazing. Technical difficulties weren't the most overpowering. A peaceful and quiet place for work was a real problem. Little America lived, ate, slept and talked in noisy congestion. Privacy in the ordinary meaning of the term did not exist. This want was presently driven home by the accessory apparatus installed on the outer wall of the flimsy sanctuary which, at least in all civilized communities, is respected as a place for peace and meditation. This accessory was, in truth, a punching bag! The quaking walls and the machine-gunning impact of the bag were enough to frighten one out of a year's growth. Perceptions so insensitive to the decibel quantities as to contrive such widespread horror were hardly apt to humor the smaller yearnings of a handful of scientists. It was a case of being sardines in a goldfish bowl. Rudeness was rarely intended. All things considered, life at Little America was surprisingly courteous. Just as nature abhors a vacuum, so we abhorred the sight of a man sitting alone at his desk.

I recall one day checking off the extraordinary confusion of enterprises under way at one time in the Science Hall: Cox, the carpenter, operating a power saw; the phonograph going full blast; Bramhall and Dr. Potaka playing chess in one corner with three kibitzers giving counsel; a noisy rift in the lute in another corner where a tractor driver and dog driver were contending over trail matters; Morgan calling hopelessly into a five-meter radio telephone for Black, who was half a mile away with the seismic sounding equipment; Blackburn washing his underwear in an iron bucket, and falling over it; Perkins and Boyd tinkering with a movie device for photographing microscopic specimens the biologist had just brought up out of the frozen depths of the Bay of Whales; Sterrett snoozing peacefully with his feet on the desk; Innes-Taylor, with half a dozen consultants, sewing up a dog slashed in a Dog Town squabble; Siple and Lindsey examining a couple of plant bulbs they were trying to grow; and Walter Lewisohn arriving crashingly with a hundred pound sack of coal for the stove.

In spite of the uproar a great deal of work was accomplished.

Meteors

Dr. Poulter first introduced meteor observations into Antarctic research. Always keenly interested in the subject, he determined to make it one of the main points of the winter program. The extraordinary clearness of the amosphere, due to the relatively small amounts of water and dust particles, promised excellent results. In order to widen the importance of the work, he invited various observatories and stations throughout the world to coöperate with the observatory in Little America. Some 70 stations accepted. They were divided into chains extending along certain meridians. The 80th meridian group included those falling between longitudes 70° and 90° W.; the 20th meridian group was made up of those between longitudes 10° and 30° E.; and the 140th meridian group comprised those between 130° and 150° E. The system was so constituted, geographically, that as one chain in the lower latitudes moved with the earth's rotation from darkness into daylight another chain would be moving into darkness, thus making possible synchronous and continuous observations with the observatory at Little America during its four months of total darkness. Arrangement was made for subsequent exchange of data.

The general purposes of the observations were to determine more exactly the quantity of meteoric matter striking the earth's atmosphere, observe meteor showers not already known, locate radients more accurately, seek to correlate the directions of meteoric movement with the earth's motion, and measure the altitude at which they appear and disappear in the earth's atmosphere.

In the previous chapter mention was made of Poulter's observatory. Like everything else he made at Little America it was a masterly improvisation. Even his own bunk was cannily used. The bunk was raised almost to the ceiling; a set of binoculars, fixed in the roof, was aimed at the zenith. Stretched out full length on the bunk, he could make his observations without putting a foot on the floor. The arrangement excited the praise of even the most grudging Bunk Director.

But the really marvelous thing was the revolving platform for observers. It was a small structure made of angle iron, revolved by hand around an iron column which was fitted with outriggers for folding chairs. Four observers sat back to back, with their legs dangling in mid-air. There was just room for their heads in the tiny transparent dome. With one eye glued to a round hole serving as an eye-piece, the observers faced the four quadrants of the heavens. Outside on the roof and over each eye-piece was a reticle, invented by Dr. Poulter to provide a convenient arbitrary system of coördinates for measuring meteor tracks. It took the place of the more common star chart. Poulter's reticle was a simple structure of steel wire arranged in five concentric circles, with six cross wires radiating from the center, dividing the circles pie-shape into twelve parts. For convenience these were numbered from one to twelve, as on the face of a clock. An alert observer, catching a meteor in flight across the sky covered by the reticle (a solid angle of 50°), can almost instantly flip off the coördinates at which it appears and disappears.

Dr. Poulter commenced observations on April 22nd, just a couple of days after the sun went down. At one time or another nearly every one got a try-out as an observer. Some were quicker and more reliable than others. The watch required a keen eye. Most meteors were visible only for a tenth of a second or so. Bits of blue, red, green, yellow, orange, red and white streaks diving through a spangled sky, they exploded across a reticle before an unwary observer had time to mark them.

As the winter wore on Poulter reduced his staff to a crack unit consisting of aviation pilot Smith, assistant biologist Sterrett, and Fleming, assistant to the scientific staff. So long as the darkness held they lived like firemen. The instant the sky cleared, no matter what hour of the night, they were hustled into the observatory. Lindsey and Clark alternated as recorders, setting down the data called off by the observers.

It was quite an impressive business to watch: the shack utterly dark except for a sliver of light falling upon the recorder's watch and notebook, no sound except the creak of chairs as the observers eased slightly from a cramped position, and an octopus-like confusion of legs descending from the ceiling. Then the crisp call of "time!" as first one, then another, observer marked the fleet waxing and waning of a meteor, followed hard by the coördinates, "one-point-five, forty-five degrees—seven-point-three, twenty degrees. Magnitude—three." But it was even stranger to pass it on the surface. The sloping dome, the town's only turret, was barely awash; and there was an eerie solemnity to the ritualistic language of coördinates floating out, broken by some such human note as, "Oh, boy, that was a sonofabitch!"

The results far exceeded Poulter's most sanguine expectations. In spite of the cloudiness of Little America, the station obtained data on approximately 7,000. The coöperating stations have already reported data on 11,000. On clear days the sky could be very clear; and under such conditions the meteor count rose spectacularly. On July 11th-12th the meteors were appearing so rapidly that it was impossible for one recorder to remain abreast of a single observer. The sky was virtually alive with swarms of ruddy travelers exploding earthward. By midnight on the 11th they were appearing at the rate of 300 per observer. Though observations were not continuous, data on approximately 1300 meteors were collected during a 15-hour period, probably the greatest number ever recorded by a single station in so short a time.

"We have noticed an interesting correlation between the visibility of meteors and temperature," Dr. Poulter said. "When the temperature fell between —50° and —60° we saw from two to more times more meteors than when the temperature was between zero and —40°. Moreover, at the lower temperatures the magnitude, or brightness, rose sharply. The increase is due, of course, to better visibility."

On the basis of the observations Poulter estimated that the earth's atmosphere is catching meteors at the enormous rate of a billion or more a day.

Cosmic Ray

The study of cosmic ray intensity at Little America was an extension of similar studies made during the *Ruppert's* southerly voyage. This likewise was an innovation in Antarctic research. Dr. Bramhall and Zuhn made a prolonged series of visual observations, amounting to 800 hours distributed over fortnightly intervals, between April 1934 and February 1935. The expedition acted as a coöperating unit in Dr. A. H. Compton's world-wide survey of the geographical distribution of the cosmic ray. The instrument was one used by him in 1932.

The principal purposes of the expedition's cosmic ray research were to measure, if possible, the absolute intensity of cosmic ray radiation at the southernmost latitude at which such measurements had been made; to determine in a region where prolonged winter darkness was especially favorable for such observations a possible diurnal variation in the intensity; and, finally, by means of observations at high altitude, either on the polar plateau or by an airplane flight, to collect data tending to prove or disprove the universality of the Lemaitre-Vallorta theory of electrons approaching the earth at high speed from remote space, the paths of which are bent by the magnetic poles.

The travels of the instrument—from the Equator to New Zealand, through the ice and gales of the Devil's Graveyard to the underground caverns of Little America—were among the most adventuresome in the pursuit of this subtle phenomenon since its discovery by Rutherford and Cook in 1903.

The peculiar value of the observations derived from their being undertaken in a region several thousand miles nearer the magnetic pole than such measurements had previously been made. Little America was about 828 statute miles from the magnetic pole.

The experiment was nearly ruined at the outset by an odd accident. After the apparatus was transported by dog team from the *Ruppert* to the camp, Bramhall was chagrined to discover that due to low temperatures the ionization chamber, holding argon gas at 450 pounds pressure per square inch, had sprung a leak and allowed the gas to dissipate. The blow seemed fatal when he found that the reserve cylinder of argon had also leaked and was empty. Luckily the expedition stores contained sufficient quantities of carbon-dioxide gas which could be substituted for the argon. One of the miracles of our daily existence was the manner in which the tunnels always yielded up something which ingenuity could convert into an adequate substitute.

The displacement of argon with carbon-dioxide gas is not expected to affect the values obtained, since the use of a standard radium capsule for comparison renders the data independent of the nature of the gas in the ionization chamber. However, there was no assurance against radioactive contamination of the chamber during the refilling. A crucial test for such contamination will be made before results are published.

Magnetism

In addition to the studies of the field parties, the magnetic program called for the establishment of a complete magnetic station at Little America for continuous registration of magnetic elements. As on the first expedition, this research was sponsored by the Department of Terrestrial Magnetism of the Carnegie Institution of Washington. Dr. Bramhall was in charge; he was again assisted by Zuhn.

On February 1st, 1934, well in advance of the reconstruction of the town, the two physicists started building their magnetic tunnels and shacks. It was a masterly piece of tunnel construction. Virtually unaided they dug and roofed a tunnel an eighth of a mile long, in which they constructed two buildings, the "variation building" and the "absolute building," both of non-magnetic materials. This tunnel was later connected with the central tunnels via a shaft dropping from the Science Hall.

The "variation building," completed on February 12th, housed the instruments which would record continuously on sensitized paper all the variations in the earth's field, both in direction and intensity. The instruments were disposed on a large, specially designed pier, the base of which was sunk deep in the snow and frozen into place by pouring water around it. The shack had an outer vestibule, on the door of which was printed the command: "Divest yourself of magnetic materials." Peering in, one could see the faint glow reflected from the instrument mirrors which were converting the movement of magnets into beams of light photographically registered.

One hundred yards north of this came the "absolute building," a small box-like structure with double walls and floor. The magnetometer, which was used to determine periodically the absolute values of the magnetic elements, was mounted on a daïs-like pier in the center of the room. For heating the place the physicists had a primus stove, with radiators made from copper gasoline containers. Bramhall used to say that it was "reasonably warm."

From this building they ran a narrow tunnel, 300 feet long, past the crushed remains of one of the buildings used by Davies, physicist with the first expedition. At the very end of the tunnel they set up a timber on which they mounted a small mark light, visible from a window in the "absolute building." The true bearing of the line through the lamp and the center of the magnetometer pier was determined astronomically; having such a reference line, they were enabled, regardless of weather, to ascertain the magnetic declination simply by noting the difference of the direction of the line and that of the magnetic meridian as shown by the magnetometer.

Over the "absolute building" the physicists built a flat-topped wooden shack known as the "star observatory." In this chill shelter Bramhall and Rawson throughout the winter night took an involved series of observations, fixing with all possible precision the astronomical position of the station (Lat. 78° 34′ 05.5″ S., Long. 163° 55′ 55″ W.) and the azimuth of the mark light in the magnetic tunnel. The light that used to burn in the shack was a welcome beacon for night travelers. Perkins used to say that every time he saw it the shack put him hungrily in mind of a hot-dog stand.

The records of the magnetic station, when it was finally closed, lacked only a fortnight of covering a whole year.[1]

Meteorology

The meteorological observations were the extensions of similar observations launched by the first expedition. As various aspects of this study are discussed elsewhere by Admiral Byrd, it is unnecessary to do more than outline them here. Counting both expeditions, a total of 2,700 surface observations, 1,200 pilot balloon observations and 50 airplane and kite soundings were made. A continuous record of relative humidity, pressure, wind direction and velocity were made. These data are now being worked up by Haines and Grimminger for the U. S. Weather Bureau.

Altogether the meteorologists had a fairly busy time of it throughout the winter night. The first of every month, when the reports had to be prepared, Bill Haines would be around all the shacks, trying to drum up clerical assistance in exchange for a haircut. Bill was widely regarded as the finest barber at Little America. The abundance of amateur barbers eager to try their hand and such depraved tastes as were indulged by men like Dyer, who cut their own hair ("It's quite evident, John," said the meteorologist), virtually extinguished trading opportunities.

Cold and lonely chores were the pilot balloon runs, especially during

[1] The records indicate a mean value of inclination, or dip, of about 82°. The horizontal intensity of the earth's field is not far from 0.09 c.g.s. units, and the magnetic declination (the direction assumed by the compass needle) remains about 107°.5 east of north. All these values exhibit regular fluctuations of various periodicities as well as transient disturbances, or magnetic storms, of considerable magnitude (E. H. Bramhall).

winter darkness. If the clouds weren't too low, three runs were made daily, using a small rubber balloon inflated with hydrogen and carrying a lighted candle within a paper lantern. Grimminger was the outside man. He stood on the surface following the balloon with a theodolite, reading off the angles and calling them into a telephone head set. Haines was below in the Weather Bureau, with another head set, recording the data and plotting the results. Pilot balloon runs gave the wind direction and velocities aloft. To give Grimminger some protection from the wind, the theodolite was placed on a ledge in a shaft rising near the vestibule of the "Ad" Building. Only Grimminger's head showed above the surface.

Cold was annoying to more than flesh. As the temperature dropped, Grimminger found that frost from his breath formed on the theodolite lens as soon as he commenced to observe, making it impossible to follow the balloon unless he was continually scraping the ice away with a small stick. This was awkward because he needed both hands to operate the theodolite. He remedied the difficulty by taping a small electric light bulb along the theodolite barrel just below the object lens and by winding a resistance coil around the eye-piece, the first hooked into the camp lighting circuit and the second fed by a storage battery. They threw off enough heat so that the moisture from the breath no longer condensed on the lens.

This was considered one of the most successful boondoggles, ranking favorably with Bailey's automatic radio calling device. In order to dispense with the physical effort of calling New York and San Francisco stations, Bailey persuaded Dr. Poulter to make him an automatic key, turning on a wheel driven by electricity, which uttered the required address while Clay snoozed in the bunk, with the loud speaker on full blast, waiting for a man 10,000 miles away to come in.

Seismic Soundings

During the winter night Morgan, assisted by Black, made a number of tests with the seismic sounding instruments which in the spring were employed to such excellent purpose. The first soundings were made early in May. At first they set up the apparatus in the cabin of the crashed Fokker east of the camp. Finding the cold too punishing, they finally rigged up a sort of remote control device whereby they could operate from the laboratory. The seismometers were buried outside the camp and connected by cables to the amplifiers and oscillograph on Morgan's desk in the corner of the Science Hall. He had a five-meter radio telephone with which he talked to Black.

The principal purpose of the test was to measure the effect of cold upon the instrument, and on TNT, caps and blasting equipment. Good profiles, according to Morgan, were obtained at temperatures as low as —65°.

Biology

Before the sun went down, Dr. Perkins, Lindsey, Sterrett and Siple pitched a tent at the edge of the pressure on the new ice of the Bay of Whales, just beyond Ver-Sur-Mer Inlet. Perkins was eager, if he could, to continue his plankton hauls throughout the winter night, in order to study plankton distribution through the period of darkness. Near the tent they started a hole through the ice which they thought they might be able to keep open. Every so often throughout the darkness Perkins, sometimes alone, sometimes with his colleagues, would head down the dark shallow depression of Ver-Sur-Mer, carrying in a rucksack strapped across his shoulders a plankton net, 2,000 feet of line, bottles for sea water samples, a gallon thermos jug for the plankton sample. I used to ski down to the Bay of Whales to watch him. On May 15th, nearly a month after the sun went down, he made a successful haul from a depth of 800 feet—copepods, several types of diatoms, radiolarians, many small gastropods and a few algal fragments. As the net broke out of the water Perkins' flashlight happened to go out; in the sudden darkness the silken net and the brass-ribbed bucket at the bottom gleamed with hosts of luminescent microscopic copepods. Even the biologist's hand glowed when he withdrew it from the net.

For two and a half months Perkins labored to defend the hole to the open water below the ice. On April 17th, two days before the sun set for the last time, the new ice was two and a half feet thick. A month later it was four feet thick. By the light of a lantern he hacked and chipped at the ice, often working hours before the water came up through the hole. After the hole was cleared they had to bail out the mush of ice crystals welling up from under the ice. It was no fun getting wet in mid-winter temperatures. On several occasions Perkins had to race severe frostbite all the way back to Little America. The instant the net came clear of the water the samples had to be transferred to the thermos jar; the net froze almost instantly.

On May 28th Perkins made another successful haul from 700 feet —no diatoms but many copepods. He had to cut through five feet of ice. On June 26th, with the temperature —26°, he started to reopen the hole. The ice was much thicker. After four days' hard chopping, the last in temperature of —51° and a razor-edged wind, he finally got through; but the rush of water drove him out of the hole before he could make an opening wide enough to admit the net. He returned to camp and fashioned a long-handled chisel with which he pried the hole open, but the masses of ice crystals under the ice resisted the net. Even a 15-foot pole failed to reach clear water. This dense layer of ice crystals under solid ice effectively halted plankton studies during the winter darkness.

In the middle of the winter night Siple led an expedition across the Bay of Whales to look for seals and collect snow samples for bacteriological analysis. He also thought such a trip would be good training routine for the party which he would lead to Marie Byrd Land in the spring. The four of them—Siple, Wade, Corey and Stancliff—on June 26th set out with the intention of camping a week at the foot of the hill of haycocks south of Floyd Bennett Bay. The air being too rigorous for dogs, they manhauled their own equipment. However, they made camp instead near the entrance of Chamberlin Harbor, about four and a half miles northwest of Little America. On a ski trip to West Cape the second night out, Wade froze his face and hands severely and the party was obliged to return with him to camp on the 29th. Because he was in considerable pain and the temperature had dropped to —51°, the others, much against his will, insisted on hauling him back on a sledge.

Wade was certainly a shocking sight when he arrived—his face grossly swollen, the right eye tightly puffed under puffy lids. He looked exactly as if he had stuck his head in a hornet's nest. No one, including the veterans of the first expedition, had seen a worse case of frosting.

Dr. Potaka applied soothing medications and in time Wade's face healed without leaving a scar. He lost 18 pounds—probably from shock and toxæmia, the doctor said.

The foregoing were the principal subjects in which data were collected by the scientific staff during the winter. In addition, routine auroral observations were made, Paige, the artist, sketching the more interesting structures. Bramhall and Zuhn also rigged up an apparatus for observing temperature gradients at different depths of snow, which was later taken over by Fleming.

II

Nature has a curious way of working seemingly aimlessly and to no apparent purpose; then at the right moment something happens and all the disconnected and remote things fly together, forming a significant design.

Toward the end of June, in the middle of winter darkness, such an obscure motivation was to turn our minds with heightening misgivings and anxiety toward Advance Base.

Poulter's unexpectedly good results with the meteor observations—the remarkable things Demas was doing with the tractors—the general progress made in spring preparations, all had their rôle in the hidden purpose.

From the day Admiral Byrd commenced his isolation on March 28th we were in frequent radio communication with him. Three times a week, Tuesdays, Thursdays and Sundays, Dyer contacted him at

KFY, Advance Base, speaking to him on the telephone and the Admiral responding in code.

Everything seemed to be going very nicely. Admiral Byrd was unfailingly cheerful. As a rule, the contacts were quite short, and would have been even shorter if he were a better operator. His sending speed was about ten words a minute. For the most part the time was given to an exchange of personal messages. Occasionally, however, the officers of the camp took up with him various aspects of the field operations. Captain Innes-Taylor several times discussed with him knotty problems on which only he could render the final decision, such matters as trail personnel, the feasibility of abandoning one of the supporting tractors at 300-Mile Depot to increase the gas reserves of the through car, the best approach the through car should take past the crevasses at the foot of Thorne Glacier.

Occasionally, too, Admiral Byrd made passing reference to the sort of life he was living—the steady demands of his meteorological records, the little things he was doing to avert monotony, the pleasure and peace of the place, the weather. On the whole his temperatures seemed to be running from 8° to 10° colder than Little America. For example, on May 20th, when our own thermometers stood at —62°, he reported a temperature of —72°.

Throughout the winter night, while an observer made simultaneous observations at Little America, he studied the aurora, standing as many as five watches a day when the air was clear.

Toward the end of June Demas was getting along with the tractors. No. 1 was nearly ready for a trial run on the surface. He also had to make room in the garage for No. 2, which since May had lain buried on the ramp leading down into the garage.

Dr. Poulter followed these preparations with keen interest. Encouraged by the success of the meteor program, he considered using No. 1 as a rolling meteor observatory, taking it on a journey 30 or 40 miles south for synchronous observations with the main observatory at Little America. While exploring the value of such a trip he was awakened to the possibility of pushing through to Advance Base. Advance Base would give him a longer base-line for calculating the paths and altitude of meteors and, at the same time, a more congenial shelter than the tractor. So far as cold's being a hazard, Demas was confident the journey was within the capacity of the cars. After all, even without the improvements now being installed for cold weather, the cars had survived the minus sixty temperatures of March.

The senior scientist and the tractor crew were eager to try the journey while darkness still made meteor observations possible. The only question was whether or not Admiral Byrd would approve it. Mindful of the not inconsiderable suffering and perhaps disaster that might attend failure of a night journey, he had given the most explicit orders that under no conditions should an attempt be made to reach him so long as the darkness held.

Here, then, is where the hidden motivation first made felt its purpose.

On June 21st Poulter took up the meteor project over the usual Thursday morning radio contact. As vigorously as he could, he outlined the benefits to the scientific program. He explained what was being done with the tractors, the increased safety factors, the probability that in a day or so No. 1 would be ready for a trial trip.

Dyer copied down Admiral Byrd's brief comments. If Poulter thought the project feasible and essential to his program, he was perfectly willing to approve the trip—in fact, might himself take advantage of the tractor's arrival to return earlier to Little America to assist spring preparations. However, he recommended withholding final decision until the test run gave a line not only on the tractor's performance, but also on how readily the trail flags planted in March could be followed.

At that time, we know now, he was at the end of the tether—dying from the effects of the poisonous fumes cast off by the stove and gasoline generator, scarcely able to walk, existing on half-frozen foods he was too ill and too weak to prepare properly.

Admiral Byrd was then approaching the fifth month of isolation, and in the third month of darkness.

But in June we had no such insight. The design was still concealed. Code is impersonal and, unlike a voice, does not give one away.

In a day or so No. 1 was ready, but cloudiness and high drift held it underground until the 26th. In the morning the wind dropped, and Noville promptly mustered all available hands for digging out the ramp. A mean job in darkness, working by the blinding light of pressure lamps. As the picks, shovels and saws dug deeper, scores of boxes cached there in the hurry of securing the shack in May came to light. The moon was obscured by a dry, cold fog, and there was a vague smear of a moon dog to either side. The temperature was —15°.

Presently No. 1, with Skinner at the wheel, backed up the steep grade, complaining and balking as the treads spun for traction it couldn't find. With twenty men pushing wherever they could thrust a shoulder the car finally gained the surface. As soon as No. 1 was out, No. 2 was dug out of the snow and shoved into the garage.

That evening, about supper time, Poulter, Demas, Skinner and Waite left in No. 1 for the trial run, taking the flag-marked southern trail past Retreat Camp toward Amundsen Arm. The darkness and mist quickly swallowed up the car, but long after it vanished we could see the flow of its lights above the ridge.

They were back about midnight, enthusiastic over the car's performance. Between Retreat Camp and the northern shore of Amundsen Arm, Poulter said, a good many flags were either drifted over or blown away. They had to reconnoiter on foot to locate the big depot flag marking the transit through the crevasses across the Arm. The few miles across Amundsen Arm were very good; the flags stood out prominently, and such upheaval as had occurred did not hinder the passage. In the pressure at the foot of high barrier sloping down to the southern shore of the Arm they stopped to fill a small crevasse. Gaining the crest of the Barrier about 11 miles south, they found the flags still visible, though many were drifted up to the cloth.

On the schedule of June 28th Poulter reported to Admiral Byrd the results of the test run. He said the trail appeared to be good and that he foresaw no great difficulty in following it to Advance Base.

On the strength of this report Admiral Byrd tentatively approved the journey. He insisted, however, that the departure from Little America be regulated by weather, that no undue risks be taken with personnel, that above everything else the tractor should hold to the flags put down in March, rather than risk stumbling upon new crevasses in the dark.

These safety precautions virtually doomed the success of the first attempt, and with it his own relief.

Departure was set for the full moon period of July 18th-23rd, at which time the party, if the air was clear, would have the benefit of moonlight and the enlarging twilight of the south-swinging sun as it boosted itself a little bit nearer the northern horizon at noon each day.

July must have been an unspeakable ordeal for Admiral Byrd. Fighting off an infinite weakness, though despairing of ever recovering, he was ever so meagerly gaining strength;—enough, anyhow, to keep up his observations, to be able to get food into his stomach, to defend his line of communications lest the slowly evolving, unenlightened meteor venture be converted into a reckless relief effort. The mild weather of June crumpled under a fresh onslaught of cold. At Advance Base July rounded the corner frostily. Twenty-five times that month the thermometer level crossed —50°; four times it passed —70°; once it stood at —80°. And this man at Advance Base, too helpless to do anything about it, watched the drift wash up over the roof of the shack, assailing his only exit.

III

In the wisdom that comes after the event, a blinding light falls upon things that once were meaningless and removed from purposeful design. Weeks later we at Little America were to feel cold shivers running up and down our spines when we saw how everything added up, and how unthinking, how undiscerning we were.

There was haste enough in the preparations, but only the haste of meeting the July 18th deadline. The tractor men, assisted by Boyd, were hurrying to overhaul and finish No. 3, to have it available as a stand-by unit in case anything happened to No. 1. If time permitted, they hoped to have No. 2 also ready, which would provide two mobile units for whatever emergency needs might arise out of the trip. In such temperatures and darkness it would have been slaughter to use dogs.

Innes-Taylor and his dog drivers were making up and sacking rations, assembling the pick of the camping equipment. Ronne, Eilefsen and Tinglof were coming along with the new tractor sledges. Corey was collecting the necessary field equipment, fur sleeping bags, fur clothing, special kits. Lights burned in the tractor garage past midnight.

It was decided that the party should number five—Dr. Poulter, leader; Skinner, driver; Waite, radio operator; and Fleming and Petersen, the last two being assigned to Advance Base as observers. They would occupy the base until spring, carrying on the meteorological observations and making meteor observations as long as the darkness lasted. Both men were meanwhile being given the necessary instruction.

On July 5th (the schedule having meanwhile been moved up to 2 o'clock in the afternoon) Admiral Byrd for the first time failed to come in. The following afternoon Dyer reëstablished contact over the emergency schedule. As he spelled out the code on the typewriter, Dyer remarked the Admiral was using his hand-cranked generator.

"How do you know?"

"I can tell by the sound. It's unmistakable.

Admiral Byrd said that his main set was "shot." A coupling on the gasoline-driven generator powering his main transmitter sheared off, disabling it. He was obliged to fall back upon the emergency set, a trail set, the transmitter of which was dependent for power upon hand-cranking.

It must have been a frightful blow. In his weakened condition cranking the set called for strength it was almost impossible to muster. He collapsed after signing off that day, his diary shows.

Again, though we called twice a day over the emergency morning and afternoon schedules, we failed to contact him until July 15th. On this day, after having patiently given his always courteous and soft-spoken call—"KFZ calling KFY Advance Base. Good afternoon. We shall stand by for you, Admiral Byrd. Please come in"—Dyer switched hopefully to the receiver. He turned to the typewriter just in time to catch Advance Base in the middle of a message:

> ". . . above all tractors must be absolutely certain not to lose trail or give out of fuel . . . and (take) no chances with lives of men . . ."

Poulter, who was standing at Dyer's elbow, didn't bother to ask the cause of the week's silence. (We learned later that something was wrong with the transmitter, that Admiral Byrd struggled desperately to fix it, that at the cost of strength he should have saved for his own needs he broadcast reassuring messages.) Various small details in respect to the journey were cleared up. Poulter said he expected to start in four days, if weather allowed. Admiral Byrd said that from the 20th on he would keep a beacon light burning on the anemometer pole. In the dark the tractor might pass fifty yards to either side of the tiny upperworks of the buried shack and never see them. He also advised them to take along plenty of flags to cover their retreat. Poulter said the tractor's tracks would be excellent things to steer by if they had to turn back.

Foreboding as was the week's silence, it failed to impress most of us very deeply. We talked about it and speculated; some thought it meant one thing, some another. But restoration of communication brushed away some of the uncertainty. The night has a lethargy that dulls perception. Besides, Admiral Byrd was unfailingly cheerful. There was utterly no hint of his distress. Invariably he signed off with an "OK cheerio."

The next month was a long nightmare, intensifying as shadowing meanings came out of the darkness.

The hurry of the last phase of preparations turned the town upside down. A great jagged hole breached in the tunnels to get the sledges out. Sleeping bags being overhauled. Face masks. Rations being sacked, weighed, counted and weighed again. Heaping mounds of things on the galley tables.

For picking up flags in mist Poulter was constructing a searchlight. The bulb was a 400-watt projection light from the movie booth, the reflector a piece of aluminum stripped from a primus stove, the housing made of sheet aluminum found in one of the first expedition's caches. It would be run from a special generator carried in the tractor cabin. This also would power Waite's radio, with which he expected to maintain continuous contact.

On the 19th Innes-Taylor, Dane and Wade loaded the sledge and tractor, carefully dividing the loads. If one plunged into a crevasse, they could survive from the other. In the tractor went five weeks' rations for five men, meta tablets, complete medical kit, large primus and cooker and spare parts, 400 trail flags, 40 extra gallons of gasoline, complete radio equipment, 2 shovels, 1 snow saw, 50 pounds of fresh seal meat (an anti-scorbutic), and a trail box containing bowls, spoons, candles, cups, etc. On the sledge were stowed ten 30-day rations, sleeping bags, primus stove and spare parts, meta tablets, three tents, alpine rope, 100 feet af alpine rope, shovels, 60 gallons of gas, emergency radio set.

Gusty and snowing, temperature —41°. Haines didn't like the look of the weather. Too much wind aloft. Poulter decided to wait a day. Soon that upper air licked down, and by midnight a blizzard was blowing. But two blow-torches burned under the car all night.

The 20th came on fair and cold. On the verge of noon the slow-swinging sun washed up a pale rosy smear on the northern horizon.

At 2:20 o'clock in the afternoon, No. 1 started south, a grotesque, misshapen monstrosity drooling great plumes of vapor from the exhaust. By then the pale hint of oncoming day had drained from the north, and the darkness had closed in. The headlights dug deep furrows into the night. Skinner was at the wheel, and Poulter, looking like a Mongol in a yellow face mask with a contorted mouth, sat astride the hood, playing a searchlight over the trail. The others were sprawled out in the heaping mounds of gear in the cabin. None of us envied them. One couldn't imagine anything much more oppressing than to sit for hours in that freezing cabin, not able to see, not able to tell what lay ahead, bouncing over flinty sastrugi like peas in a pod.

Atop the car were lashed two man-hauling sledges.

Through radio's sorcery Little America followed the car southward into polar night. Waite was reporting every hour to Dyer. Haines, who had moved up to command, left the engineer's elbow only to scan weather. On the blackboard in the galley Innes-Taylor had rubbed out the rations formula and drawn in a rough map of the southern trail. Every hour he checked off the car's progress. A crawling line, a painfully inching line. Only men who had slogged over that trail by daylight knew the punishment that went with every yard won by night.

At 6:45 P.M. the car reached the end of the tracks of the trial run. On high barrier they squared away for Advance Base. The first setback came almost instantly. They circled an hour before they found the tall snow beacon just beyond. At 7 P.M. Haines took a balloon run—12 miles of northeasterly wind on the surface, switching into a 36-mile westerly at 4,000 feet. "A mite suspicious," said Haines. The moon was barely visible, obscured by a shower of ice crystals. At 9 P.M., unable to pick up the flags beyond, Poulter retreated to the beacon. Fleming and Waite got off with a lantern; taking a bearing from the light, Skinner and Poulter groped south till they came upon a flag barely awash nearly half a mile beyond. A few inches of cloth on a dark ocean. To make good 11.8 miles they had cruised nearly 24 by the speedometer, searching for flags.

Midnight, and the bottom dropping out of the thermometer: —58° below at Little America and still dropping. The tractor was 17 miles out,—"snowing, viz. zero, flags sticking out two inches, but finding them all right." Poulter was sitting astride the hood, fanning the trail with a searchlight. A brief contact with Admiral Byrd at Advance Base. All well.

The second day came on, the seconds ticking by on the radio clock. At 3 A.M. the tractor was at the edges of the crevassed area north of 25-Mile Depot. A mile détour to the east, then south, then west. Dyer held close contact with Waite. At 6 o'clock—"at 25-Mile Depot. Clear." Petersen and Poulter were relieving each other outside on the hood, then ducking into the cabin to thaw out. The heat from the primus stove filled the place with steam. The instant one left the cabin his furs froze to the hardness of armor. Poulter's sheepskin mask *cracked* when he banged the ice from it.

A cup of oatmeal and crackers. At 8 o'clock Waite advised: "30 miles out. Cold—clear. Cannot hear you." (Unknown to him the antennae cable dragging behind had turned brittle in the cold and disintegrated.) The line moved forward on the galley blackboard. But on the trail the interminable groping for flags continued, right to left, back and forth, with the men skiing ahead of the car to widen the search. How much brisker it would have been to cut loose and make a straight run of it for Advance Base! However much he was torn, Poulter faithfully held to his instructions: "above everything else be absolutely certain not to lose the trail."

The second day wore on. At Little America the temperature sagged to —71.6°; out where the tractor was, to —75°, the coldest day of the year. That afternoon a gain in hope—"arrived 50-Mile Depot. Cold." (Unable to find any more flags, they had still pressed on; the searchlight picked up a burgee about 400 yards west of the depot, just at the edge of an enormous crevasse. Wheeling east they ran smack into the depot, eroded by wind from a square block to a drooping cone from which stuck out a gas drum and several bags of rations.)

No pause for rest. The critical stage of the journey lay dead ahead, the détour around the Valley of Crevasses. Little America had a sober discussion at mess. As the last sitting got up from the table, Innes-Taylor printed on the blackboard:

"6:30 P.M. Tractor returning from 54 Miles to 50-Mile Depot to make fresh attempt pick up trail."

"What's the dope, Alan?"

"Evidently the flags are drifted over or blown away," he said. "Looks tough now."

Dyer's radio log follows:

"6:30 P.M. QSK 9:30. Looking for flags. Soon back at 50. We are going to start again from Depot."

7:30. Tractor unheard. (No juice from the batteries—frozen: the receiver, too, was short-circuited by the moisture from the primus stove.)

8:00. Unable to contact Admiral Byrd at Advance Base.

8:30. Tractor unheard.

9:30. Tractor OK. (With the headlights blazing at their backs, Poulter, Waite, Fleming and Petersen traveled four miles east of the Depot, skiing abreast and 200 yards apart trying to locate the flags. Not a flag survived, though once or twice they found the drifted tracks from the March journey.)

The outcome was inevitable. The tractor had already traveled 173 miles to make good 62 (statute miles).

Admiral Byrd at the Radio (Advance Base)

(Photograph by Joseph A. Pelter)

Demas, Poulter and Waite Start for Advance Base

(Photograph by John Dyer)

Spring Comes to the Antarctic

At 12:30 A.M. on the third day, Dyer intercepted a message that Waite was broadcasting "blind" to Admiral Byrd:

"We are at 50-Mile Depot unable to locate trail around crevassed area in six hours. Apparently snowed under. . . . Many flags completely covered. Think it inadvisable to proceed through crevassed area without more light since present trail can't be followed. POULTER."

Admiral Byrd didn't hear it. Too weak to crank his generator, he was harboring his strength to keep the beacon light blazing on the roof of his shack.

No word then for hours. A pitiless cold. The wind was steepening. Perkins froze his face badly just walking overland from the "Ad" Building to the galley. Haines mistrusted the weather.

"Take my word for it," he said, "it's going to blow like hell."

About two hours later, when the tractor was running at full speed for home, the blizzard struck—a gentle rustling in the ventilators, then a rattling of the stove pipe. Half a dozen skiers tumbled into the tunnel entrances, exclaiming that they barely made it. The first warning was a wavering white cloud, moving with incredible speed across the Barrier.

For a while Skinner tried to push into the storm, but the engine was stalling as drift penetrated to the carburetor. The temperature was still in the minus fifties, and the air was molten metal. When Dyer reëstablished contact with the car, it was hove to 28 miles south in a wind close to hurricane force. Even in the sheltered valley of Little America the wind hit 60 miles an hour, the severest of the year. In the shacks the draughts backed down the stove pipes, filling the rooms with smoke, and the pipes themselves were rattled from the stoves.

Thus ended the first attempt to reach Admiral Byrd at Advance Base—an attempt the failure of which was in a large measure made inevitable by the precautions that Admiral Byrd imposed for the safety of the crew. Had these men known or guessed the suffering and illness that lay south of them that night east of 50-Mile Depot, when they sat in the freezing cabin over bowls of *hoosh* and debated whether to hold to the letter of instructions or make a run for it, taking a chance on the darkness and crevasses, the car would never have been pointed north.

The blizzard blew out on the 23rd. Digging out the car, and the sledges, the latter from under four feet of snow, the tractor crew resumed the retreat that afternoon, arriving home about 8:15, having been guided all the way by the big beacon light Dyer and Hutcheson had installed on one of the radio towers.

Dr. Poulter's first question was, "Has Admiral Byrd been informed we had to turn back?"

He was told Dyer had been unable to contact him since midnight on the 20th.

"That's a pity," Poulter said. "I can imagine nothing unhappier than to be in that isolated place expecting some one to arrive, and then waiting hours and hours, wondering what happened."

It was, we know now, something more than disappointment. Admiral Byrd's receiver was disabled, and the messages we were broadcasting "blind" were all but unintelligible. His last certain news was that the car was outward bound. As the hours dragged into days and the northern horizon yielded up no sign of its coming, the fear possessed him that either the crew had met with disaster or else was still trying to get through. Steadily he broadcast reassuring messages most of which Dyer was unable to decipher; they were too dimly heard.

Admiral Byrd's diary said:

> "Can't keep up these blind broadcasts much longer. . . . I've tried cranking the radio set with my feet, when my arms give out, but it wasn't made for the feet and I can't keep it from jumping around. Worst of all, I can't seem to repair the receiver . . . I'm afraid that if I don't keep the beacons alight at the stated hours, he may never find the shack. . . ."

IV

The truth of the matter is that the fear was creeping through Little America that the leader was in distress. There was utterly nothing to base it on. It had root in nothing tangible. Nobody had a name for it, —intuition or logic; but there it was, a crawling uncertainty. Things were beginning to add up. The silence itself was suspect, and the simple explanation that Admiral Byrd was having trouble with his radio set didn't entirely account for it. After he became dependent upon the hand-cranked generator, Dyer remarked how slow and ragged his sending was. The messages filtered through in groups of three and four words. In between he would spell out "wait." Minutes would elapse before he resumed. The same hesitation occurred in the dim, reassuring messages he broadcast "blind" after the tractor turned back.

Were these pauses meaningful? One couldn't tell. When asked about it Admiral Byrd explained he had a "bad arm" which made it difficult to crank, but insisted it did not otherwise inconvenience him.

But it was a ghastly feeling to look southward into the depths of the night and think that a man, a close and beloved friend, was isolated out there, perhaps too proud to call for help or unwilling to place another man in jeopardy.

In all events, Poulter now determined to make a run of it to Advance Base, ignoring instructions to hold to the trail. He reduced his crew to three—Demas, Waite and himself. It was Demas' turn to drive. He and Skinner had tossed for the right to make the first trip.

The weather, however, was uncertain, squally at times, cloudy. On

Haines' recommendation Poulter deferred the start until conditions stabilized.

On August 2nd Dyer heard Advance Base—"Where is tractor? I have heard nothing for days."—repeated over and over again.

Dyer broke in and miraculously restored contact.

Hutcheson hurried out and got Poulter. In the calmest sort of way the scientist reviewed the journey. He planned, he said, to leave on the first break in weather, being hopeful of getting through in time for satisfactory meteor observations. He said nothing that might give Admiral Byrd an inkling of the rising concern at Little America.

"Can hear only few words," Admiral Byrd replied. "I have lights outside from three to eight P.M. Everything okay. Sorry to be so much trouble. Good luck."

On August 4th there was a liquid apple-green hint of dawn in the northern sky. The temperature was down to —13°. Conditions weren't exactly of the best, but Poulter thought he could risk the cloudiness. With two sledges in tow, No. 1 shoved off again at 10:30 A.M. so that the driver would have the benefit of the dim twilight of noon in steering through the pressure across Amundsen Arm. They ran into difficulties right in the back yard. The great blizzard of the 22nd had overwhelmed the flags marking the transit across the Arm. Unable to find the passage, they probed to the eastward, looking for a way. Darkness trapped them in a nest of huge crevasses. A blind crevasse let go under the car; as it sagged Demas zoomed out under full throttle. The second sledge, holding rations and other gear, plunged in. Several hours were lost recovering the sledge and restowing cargo. A spare storage battery on the sledge spilled acid over the canvas tanks holding the rations. Luckily it did not penetrate to the food. Visibility dropped to zero, and a rising wind harassed them with drift. So they camped for the night. Not until next day were they able to find the way through the pressure.

At noon on the 6th Waite informed Dyer that they were 21 miles out and that the clutch was slipping. Four hours later Poulter advised Haines that he was turning back on account of a slipping clutch—that he had dropped the sledges at 23 miles. He asked Haines to have No. 3 tractor on the ramp and ready to go.

His orders, however, had already been anticipated. A dozen men under Dr. Perkins had excavated the ramp; Von der Wall and Hill had run the car to the surface; it was standing there with the engine running.

With the temperature plunging to —58°, Demas coaxed the crippled car back to Little America. The slipping clutch forced them into second speed. All the fan belts were used up, the rubber-impregnated fabric having turned brittle and parted in the cold. Poulter and Waite were fashioning makeshift affairs out of alpine rope, but in a mile these would turn so slack as to be almost useless. The engine overheated, the anti-freeze solution boiled away and they were obliged continually to stuff snow down the steaming radiator. Thus vexed and beset they made their way back to Little America, arriving there at 3 A.M. on the 7th.

Chilled to the bone, grimy from grease and oil, too weary and disgusted to talk about their troubles, the three men got out of the car.

"We'll wait for noon when the light is better," Poulter said.

After talking it over they decided not to use No. 3. This was the car which had caught fire during the unloading. It lacked headlights and the instrument board was a makeshift affair. The overhaul of No. 2 wasn't finished and the car was therefore unfit for the trail. Luckily there was a spare engine in the garage. The clutch, Demas said, could be shifted to No. 1. While Boyd fell to work on this, Hill and Von der Wall got to work on No. 1.

A cruel blow fell. The clutch wouldn't fit. The engines were of a different size.

Hill went into the "Ad" Building and awakened Demas.

"All right," said he, "get No. 3 ready."

While Wade, Innes-Taylor, Moody and Dane shifted the gear from the cabins of the first car to the second, June, Dyer and Hutcheson transferred the headlights from No. 2 to No. 3, fixed up a new dashboard light, checked the ignition, installed a new battery. These and other matters carried through the day. Siple, who was assisting Poulter, got a nasty cut on a finger, just missing a tendon. Potaka took six stitches in it. It was hurry now, a grim, driving business.

For the first time there was something to go on besides meteors.

Over one of the schedules, Admiral Byrd made a suggestion as to navigation. The message being garbled, he was asked to repeat. He had always been most courteous about that. He commenced again. Then abruptly the code call thinned out and faded.

Dyer waited for him to come in. The seconds passed. Dyer fidgeted nervously at the dials, but nothing came through.

"Are you ill? Are you hurt?"

The tired answer drifted out of the south, spelled out with infinite slowness: "Please don't ask me crank any more. I'm okay."

At that instant the fears and intuitions, the speculations and apprehensions of July were confirmed.

No. 3 squared away with the same crew at 1:20 o'clock on the morning of the 8th. Dyer, looking terribly thin and haggard with great dark circles under his eyes, stayed up again for the radio watch. Hutcheson would relieve him in the morning. An hour later the car was back—a balky oil pump. Von der Wall, Skinner and Hill, who were still working over No. 1, rushing it for standby duty, gave them a hand. Maybe they stayed half an hour. Nobody kept a stop-watch at such things.

Anyhow the car, with the engine wide open, struck again into the mist. The temperature was —44°, and the sky utterly dark.

At 7:45 o'clock Waite advised they had picked up the sledges at 23 miles.

For three days Little America didn't draw a happy breath.

In spite of poor visibility Poulter made 30 miles the first morning, camping at that point. In the early evening of the 9th, having fetched up with 50-Mile Depot, they headed around the Valley of Crevasses. Poulter was lining the car up on the course with flashlight bulbs and lighted candles stuck in perforated tin cans planted on snow beacons.

At 7:45 on the morning of the 10th a bewildering impact of good and bad news. They had picked up the flags of the old trail, had come upon the drifted hulk of the Cletrac, but . . . "generators going haywire, ignition failing every few minutes. Been going since 8 A.M. yesterday. Save daylight."

The last meant they intended to remain under way rather than lose the gray twilight hours of the forenoon. Though they were headed into the darkness of the south, there were a few hours now before noon when the lower northern horizon was suffused by a rosy light.

At 3:45 that afternoon they were at 81 miles. The generator burned out, the brushes on the spare were badly worn; they were whittling tiny blocks of wood to hold them in place. Waite told Dyer they were freezing hands and face every few minutes. Fagged out, too. "Eating and going right through," Poulter reported.

Then we lost contact with them. Advance Base was also silent.

Shortly after they pushed on from 81 miles south, Poulter, sitting atop the cab, had seen the blue light of a magnesium flare well up in the south, linger, then die away.

Two hours of what seemed to be creeping progress, though they were making five knots, then a winking light on the port bow. Just before midnight, a livid burst of flame split the darkness as they topped the last rise.

The searchlight picked up a man in furs walking slowly toward the tractor. "Come on down, fellows. I have a bowl of hot soup for you."

Slumped over the key, Dyer was calling, calling, calling. Flashes of liquid light welled up in the tubes, and on the racks various needles sprang to attention like startled grenadiers.

"Nothing yet?"

Dyer's tired eyes framed a negative. From time to time he would swing around in his chair, cut off his own transmitter and listen gravely. As he turned the dial the whole world piped up—London, New York, Frisco, ships at sea, aircraft reporting to ground stations—you could hear them all bustling with cheerful confidences.

But from the south—nothing.

Midnight came, went by; the flame went out under the primus stove and the coffee froze in the pot.

"Try Advance Base, John," somebody suggested. "They may have gotten there."

Not hopefully Dyer went to the new frequency. Out of the background murmuring of the atmosphere there boiled up, like a trout smashing at a fly, a vibrant note, deep, surging, welcome: "KFZ de W1OXCD . . . KFZ de W1OXCD. . . ."

"Here's the tractor," Dyer said, wheeling to the typewriter. Words hurried across the message blank. "Heard you calling me on REB's receiver. Will go back to shack to finish schedule. Confidential. Found him weak from fumes. WAITE."

First-class news was never broken in a more oblique way. Exasperated, confused, wondering what tale the next few minutes would bring, we waited and counted the minutes it took Waite, more than a hundred miles away, to descend the shaft at Advance Base, speak to Poulter, and fall to with the hand-cranked generator.

Ten minutes by the clock. Up came the familiar mounting whine of the hand-cranked set and the code calls ripping cleanly across it. ". . . The fumes from the stove got REB down about June first. . . . Please don't publish as it would be hard on his wife. POULTER."

"For God's sake," somebody snapped at Dyer, "tell Poulter we want to know how Byrd is."

The answer floated back: "Pretty weak now, but think he will pull through."

And with that we shut down for the night.

Later on we learned what had happened—the gradual poisoning from the fumes of the stove; the almost fatal blow on May 31st when the gas from the gasoline-driven generator running in the tunnel felled him; the ghastly struggle to live through the cold and darkness of June and July and finally into August; the obvious reason he declined to call for help and yet steadily tried to hold communication; and, finally, the things the tractor crew found, the litter of cans under the bunk, the instructions hanging from a nail.

The pattern at last had come together. The coalescing clue was a man's sense of dignity, honor and responsibility. Through the chilling realization of what might have happened during the two and a half months Admiral Byrd lay ill at Advance Base welled up happiness that it had finally worked out all right.

"The meteorological records are complete," Poulter advised. From him, a scientist, it was the highest compliment he could frame. They would remain, he said, until Admiral Byrd was well enough to travel.

How long would that be? He didn't know. At least a month, anyhow.

V

Slowly the oncoming day was rising phantom-like out of the night, unreal and soundlessly; and in the eastern sky a carpet of cold, lustrous sheen was being spread for the sun. On August 21st we glanced up from the wash basins to the enthralling discovery that a perfect light was growing in the ventilators and the skylights, a light you couldn't call mauve, or pink, or rose, or any other color—just the loveliest, most significant color you can imagine. Standing about in their baggy underwear, the amateur navigators were disputing as to whether this day or the next was the official date for the sun's return, some holding that this day the sun would rise above the Ross Sea, and the hair-splitters holding that the high ridge to the north would keep Little America from seeing it until the following day. Officially or not, Pelter, Petersen and Bramhall skied out along the Barrier and saw it—saw the shining bulk of the sun hoist itself clear of the white smoothness of the frozen sea. It was the real thing, they said. The whole sky was suffused by a rose-pink glow, and the clouds on the horizon were opaline ships. And from the caverns of Dog Town, where the blue refracted light of day was shining through the chinks in the roof, broke a frenzied yapping among the 121 survivors.

The temperature was —71°. A bracing spring day.

It was unbelievable how rapidly the darkness seemed to dissolve, and how in daylight anything was endurable. During the last ten days of August the minimum temperature only once failed to cross —50°; three times it hit —71°. But every day saw an increased activity on the surface. On the 29th the autogyro emerged from its winter hangar and Noville mustered all hands to drag it to the surface. They swarmed out of the hatches with a will, the first time the whole population was seen on the surface, Dick Russell said, since the sun went down. I believe that we all stared at one another with spontaneous curiosity and a measure of amazement. In the fair clean light of day no one seemed the same as in the smoky gloom of the shacks. Odd how pasty and yellow the skin looked. No matter how cleanly it was scrubbed the soot from the stoves seemed to impregnate the skin. Ragged, untidy, with torn windproofs flapping about our legs, we were anything but impressive, probably the most desperate looking company of ragamuffins in the southern hemisphere. The last issue of pants had gone to the trail parties. "The rest of you," said the supply officer, "will have to hold out till the ships come in." There was no question of the men holding out; the real problem was whether the pants would hold together that long.

September, for all its cold, saw affairs get under way with a rush.

On the first day of the month, with the temperature —50°, a working party under Schlossbach traveled to the high ridge to the east and commenced excavating the old Ford plane. The first few cuts of a pick confirmed what had always been suspected—that bringing the plane to the surface would be a lingering campaign. Only the rudder post was awash. Beneath the top layer of compact drift a stratum of blue-green ice, two to three feet thick, enfolded the metal wing and engine.

"See that haycock over there?" said Ike. "Well, on it I'm going to erect a snow monument to the guy who punches the most holes in this wing. And the guy," he finished gravely, "will be under it."

In the afternoon an exciting sound flooded every corner of the underground town—the autogyro was flying. A grand piece of work to have a plane in the air just nine days after the return of the sun.

Since August 11th, in the most punishing cold of the year, Bowlin, Swan, McCormick and Smith had been overhauling the "windmill." It took a whole day of heating with blow torches just to rid the fuselage and engine of snow. A shell of ice a quarter-inch thick lay over the blades. In digging them out of the drift a shovel punctured the fabric in several places, necessitating a rather difficult repair. Moreover, McCormick decided to install new rubber mount washers, which involved moving the engine forward. Nevertheless they were ready on the scheduled date, and on September 1st McCormick took off on the first of the high altitude atmospheric sounding flights, an innovation in Antarctic research.

On such flights the plane carried outboard a small instrument resembling a bird-cage, called the aero-meteorograph, which automatically records the temperature, pressure and humidity of the various strata of air through which it passes. This data, together with wind directions and velocities obtained from pilot balloon runs, would give the meteorologists a complete picture of atmospheric circulation. Haines was anxious to have as many such flights made at maximum altitudes as were possible before the summer season set in.

Towering into a cloudy sky and fighting a bitter breeze from southwest which was pushing him out toward the Sea, McCormick climbed to 7,200 feet, the best he could get out of the craft. He landed near the head of Ver-Sur-Mer Inlet after a flight of 45 minutes. The propeller was immediately unshipped and taken into the Science Hall, where June reset the pitch. With this alteration and by reducing the amount of gas, the plane's ceiling, and with it the effectiveness of the soundings, was increased.

Throughout September, seizing every day fit for flying, squeezing his hops in between blizzards and through rifts in the cloudiness, McCormick managed to complete nine such flights to an average altitude of 8,646 feet, not counting several which, for one reason or another, did not attain the required height. The sound of the engine and the spidery thing crawling up the sky sometimes across a wafer of moon became familiar aspects of the spring. Bill took off in temperatures as low as —55°, mean temperatures for flying. Cold also imposed hardships on the aviation unit. The engine had to be heated an hour and a half before it would turn over—in all, four hours or so just to get the gyro ready, gassed, checked and hot oil poured in. As the surface temperature at the time of the take-offs was never lower than —45° one need never have been to the polar regions to appreciate that this is torture in a minor key. Working in the propeller slip-stream a man could freeze his whole face in a second. June advised McCormick not to fly in temperatures lower than —55° on account of the chance of structural failure. The gyro had certain rubber parts and oil dampers; oil hardens at —55° and rubber turns brittle.

However, thanks to a peculiar phenomenon he was recording, the air aloft was not quite so rigorous. Above the surface there occurs at times a region of inversion wherein up to a certain altitude the air grows much warmer and thereafter steadily grows colder again up to the stratosphere. According to our observations, this inversion was reached about 3,000 feet above the surface.[2] On the way up McCormick rejoiced fleetingly in a not particularly bland hint of summer, entering air as much as 44.8° warmer than on the surface. In this region the air temperature was generally close to zero. Past it as he climbed the air again steadily grew colder.

On September 28th this series of observations ended abruptly so far as the autogyro was concerned. It crashed and McCormick was lucky not to have been more seriously hurt.

I did not see the crash. With Dr. Potaka and several others I was a mile away on the ridge to the east, helping to excavate the Fairchild. We all heard the autogyro take off, and Blackburn remarked, not hearing the engine again, that Bill must have decided he didn't like the weather. However, no one bothered to look. We were eight feet deep in the trenches.

A little while later we heard Moody yelling: "Is the doctor there?"

"Here I am," said the doctor, coming out of the hole. "What's the matter?"

"The gyro's crashed," Moody gasped, "and McCormick's hurt."

"Badly?"

Moody nodded, having no breath for speech. He had run all the way.

Dane's team arrived on the run, and Dr. Potaka went back with him. Just west of the camp we could make out the crumpled wreckage of the gyro.

They were just taking McCormick below when the doctor got there. There was no way of getting him down through the narrow tunnel entrance without half killing him; so they breached the tunnel roof

[2] The average altitude of inversion, based on 9 flights, was 2,895 feet; the maximum was 5,020 feet, the minimum 948 feet. The average increase of temperature was 34.3°; the maximum was 44.8°, the minimum 22.9°. The average surface temperature at take-off was —45°.

near the cow barn and gently lowered him into the tunnel, whence they carried him to the Science Hall, because the tunnel ran straight towards it and there wouldn't be so much hurt in moving him.

McCormick was still in furs with the parachute strapped around him when they put him on the table. His forehead was bruised, a nasty cut on his right wrist was bleeding, and his left arm was manifestly broken. As the doctor cut away the parachute and parka, Bill kept asking:

"Won't somebody tell me what happened?"

Bowlin, who was deeply affected, said: "Everything's all right. Now just keep quiet."

No one was better liked than Bill McCormick. Men stood around in the galley waiting to hear the doctor's report, discussing the crash. Dustin and Smith, who were working on the Pilgrim, saw it happen. They said that after taking off into a westerly wind, McCormick had started across the pressure intending to gain altitude up wind. Then they heard him directly overhead. He was swinging around as if to land. The engine sounded quite all right. "It seemed to flutter and fall away on its tail from an altitude of 75 feet," Smith said. "The plane seemed to roll up like a ball when it hit. McCormick," he said, "must have known he was going to crash because he cut the switch and attempted a deadstick landing."

Smith and Dustin came out of the Pilgrim's pit with fire extinguishers. Moody and Wade, who were nearby with dog teams, legged it too; and the sound of the crash choked the tunnel exits.

The gyro lay ten feet from where it hit, a tangle of fabric, twisted parts; the rotor blades were broken off where they had thrashed. A complete washout.

Half thrown out of the cockpit, McCormick was unconscious when they reached him. His left arm was pinned under the plane. They managed to get him out and carried him to a sledge.

In the midst of this telling Dr. Potaka came into the galley; he was smiling.

"It might have been a lot worse," he said.

"Not bad then?"

"A simple fracture. And, of course, some shock. But he'll be all right."

Later on they moved Bill into the library where Cox had just finished constructing a bunk for Admiral Byrd. The doctor fitted a splint, and Boyd rigged a pulley with a five-pound weight for pulling the bone into place. It was hardly necessary to point out how wretched a broken arm can be under these circumstances: the cold working into it; the frustration of being helpless in a camp made up of active men; and the appalling boredom of waiting to get well. But during the six weeks of convalescence, Bill's spirit was never snowed under. After all, Bowlin, Smith and Swan were thoughtful men: and the watchman was always around at night.

Later on, the pilots figured out what must have happened. The tail was found to be full of snow which must have collected during a heavy drift. Drift penetrates everything. With the ship out of trim the crash was inevitable.

McCormick never knew the plane was washed out until the November day he walked out and saw the wreckage. Nobody had the heart to tell him.

VI

September was really cold, with minimum temperatures almost steady in the minus fifties or sixties during the first three weeks. There was a fair amount of drifting, too, a bad combination. Dr. Potaka recommended no prolonged physical labor be undertaken in temperatures lower than —45° on account of the danger of frosting the lungs. Several of the men who had been up digging on the Ford and Fairchild for hours at a time came back coughing their heads off. Still, one way or another, the work never really stopped. A polar expedition is 99 percent physical labor and one percent perspiration, at least until the air warms up, at which time the proportion tends to become less extreme.

The clocks were moved back an hour to profit by the better light of morning, and once more Noville's work lists for the next day's jobs were appearing on the galley blackboard at night.

There was a matter of pride, I think, in having affairs in readiness for Admiral's Byrd's return.

On September 12th, in the salubrious temperature of —52°, the Pilgrim was dragged to the surface by a tractor. Except for the crushing of a fork connecting the shock absorber to the tail ski pedestal, it had come through the winter undamaged. When the snow was shoveled away from the tail the spring bounced it four inches.

Next day all hands were standing by to fall to on the big plane; but with the temperature —66° that day and —67° on the next, Bill Haines suggested, "Let's wait till it warms up a trifle." It blew a blizzard on the 15th; the following day the air cleared in the forenoon and June led forth the army, the greatest turnout of man-power since the grim days of reëstablishing Little America. Even the trail parties left off with their weighing and packing to man the ice saws and shovels.

Just a glance at the amount of snow to be moved from the buried giant was enough to send your heart right down to your boots. It was one thing dropping it for the winter, digging under wings and letting it drop into a neat-fitting oversize outline of its own shape. But now a ramp 83 feet wide, 40 feet long and with a 30-percent grade had to be dug to bring it to the surface. The rudder section was the only part that showed above the surface; drift had piled over the wing, leveled off, and formed an enormous swollen ridge running several hundred yards to leeward.

The temperature stood at —33° when Smith formally and factually broke the ice by taking the first spadeful, and —53° when he knocked off about 4:30, just after the sun had set in a golden sky. Or, I should say, after the third setting, for it was twice popped up breathlessly by refraction. We were hard at it next day, a wonderful clear day—so clear that Haines and Grimminger got the highest balloon run recorded in more than a thousand such ascensions, approximately 8.8 miles. At that altitude the tiny balloon was hovering well into the stratosphere. Grimminger had it in sight through the theodolite lens for 77 minutes. He had no desire to repeat it. All this time he scarcely took his eye from the eye-piece. The temperature was —65°. Haines said he had to chop Grimminger away from the theodolite. "If this is going to keep up," Grimminger said, "let's put a time fuse on these darned things."

On the morning of the 18th, the ramp was dug; only a thin veneering of snow enclosed the plane. On the evidence of a balloon run, which promised "dirty weather," June decided not to break through lest a blizzard strike in the middle of it and drift crush the wings before the plane could be gotten onto the surface. It was a prudent decision. The blizzard struck and lasted two days, nullifying, as blizzards usually did, a good deal of the work.

Not until the 22nd were we able to resume the job; but by midnight the great plane stood on the surface, securely anchored. Just before darkness shut down Hill and Von der Wall, in tractors Nos. 1 and 2, finally dragged it out of the pit, after the steel towing cable had parted at least a dozen times. The whole expedition could have been housed in the hole.

Unhappily, the prodigious shoveling around the plane had scarred it; more than forty rents were discovered in the fabric, all of which must be patched before the plane was fit for flight.

VII

With this chief manual task out of the way, preparations for trail operations again took precedence. Thanks to the planning of Innes-Taylor, the industry of his dog department and the coöperation of the camp, these affairs were prospering.

On September 27th, June opened the field campaign. In tractor No. 1 he started eastward for Mt. Grace McKinley on the double mission of marking a trail and putting down a series of depots clear to the Edsel Ford Range for Siple's Marie Byrd Land Party, and at the same time picking out, in the vicinity of the mountain, a likely landing field and refueling base for aircraft. Such a base would extend the plane's operating range on an exploring flight just that much more.

Ken Rawson was navigator; Von der Wall, driver; and Petersen, radio operator and cameraman.

The tractor carried 3,600 pounds of dog and man food and other trail stores for the sledging party.

Rawson and June, after carefully considering the problem of navigating a tractor, had hit upon a sound idea. The principal difficulty proceeded from the circumstance that the large amount of steel engine parts, framework, radio generators, etc., made it impractical to mount a magnetic compass in the car. Heretofore the drivers had relied upon getting out of the car every little while with the compass and checking the course. But this was costly in time and fuel, especially where a devious course was followed. What June and Rawson wanted was a device which would enable a tractor to make prolonged and fast runs over a country without a trail.

They solved it by mounting an aperiodic compass (which is less susceptible than an ordinary boat compass to the oscillation conveyed by the swinging of a sledge) on the last of two trailing sledges from which all iron had been excluded. Two switches were installed close by, and cables were carried through the tractor to two electric lights on the dashboard on either side of the driver. Lying on this sledge, partially protected from the wind by a screen made from windproof cloth, Rawson could direct and hold the driver on the course, flashing him either to left or right.

On clear sunny days he counted on navigating by sun compass.

Although the minimum temperatures were still quite severe, the sun, each day climbing higher in the sky, brought more warmth. On the 28th all the dogs, except for a few cripples, were brought to the surface for good. It was a delirium. Out they came, one by one, with a driver's hand firmly holding the collars—Russell's white-eyed, slinky Siberians, black and wiry; Coal, the furtive pint-size assassin who slew four dogs half again as big as he in the dark ambushes of Dog Town; Paine's great leader, Jack, with a windproof bandage around a stump of a tail; Navy, alas, hopelessly crippled; Nero, the bouncing MacKenzie River husky, who rocked back and forth on his feet when he pleaded for chow; Rattle, who traveled the pitch-black length of Dog Town, running a gauntlet of slashing teeth all the way, to kill slow-witted Olav; Tobey, the monstrous Shamboul who roamed the Barrier for ten days in the middle of winter and lived to find his way back to Little America; Taku's seven pups, now grown to great size, with rich golden coats and fine strong paws. One after another, 121 of them. Many were missing —Marve, Cæsar, Don, Weedy. The "wolves" had come off badly. Of Corey's team of nine wolves, only five survived. Good-humored Pony, driven to distraction by their slashing attacks, went berserk and knocked off two in succession.

The instant a dog topped the hatch he blinked at the unaccustomed brightness of the day, looked frantically about as if searching for something dimly remembered, while the drivers roared: "Yes, sir, old boy, it's still there!" Of course, the telephone pole hard by the hatch.

There was the inevitable hullabaloo. Dogs broke loose from the tethering lines, tangling immediately with other dogs. Soon bright scarlet stains appeared on the snow, and drivers were storming in with the butt end of the whip. But the wild strain soon played itself out. Unused to such violent ranging, the dogs tired rapidly and their tongues hung out like red flags.

"It will take a while to harden them up," Innes-Taylor said.

Every day, now, the drivers had their teams in harness, bringing them back into condition and inculcating afresh the discipline of the trail. An exasperating business for the drivers, but a constant joy to the rest of us. All day long the air resounded with the entreaties and supplications, the wheedlings and blandishments, the oaths and threats of men from Harvard, Yale, Groton, New Hampshire State, Cambridge (England), Columbia, and the Northwest Mounted Police. Now that spring was on the wing the dogs' spirits rose. No matter where you looked you could always see far off on the horizon a dog team in full flight, and a disgraced driver in pursuit.

Around the first of October we were pleased to learn that Admiral Byrd was sufficiently recovered in health to make the return trip to Little America. He asked to have the Pilgrim dispatched at the first decent weather. Bowlin took it aloft on a test flight on the 2nd, but the weather shut down, bringing low, overcast skies and steady northerly and easterly winds.

Meanwhile "Ike" Schlossbach and his gang finally chivvied the Fairchild to the surface from five years' entombment. No. 2 tractor hauled it down to the camp, where it excited as much curiosity as one of Caligula's galleys. There was gas in the tanks, food rations stowed in the cabin. The plane looked ready to fly until you examined it closely. Two wing struts had been crushed by the weight of ice on the wing, and the wing fabric was flabby, loose and torn in many places.

"Going to fly it, Ike?"

"Not today. But I'll bet you I have it in the air before Christmas."

On October 6th Commander Noville, Skinner and Hill started for Advance Base in tractor No. 2 on the second supporting operation, carrying 3,000 pounds of dog food to be depoted there for the southern parties which would later take them aboard. The main sledging parties were stowing their trailer sledges, intending to advance and depot them a day's run out, for the sake of a better showing when they took formal departure—in front of the movie cameras.

"Well, I saw the first bird today," said Young at the evening meal. The uproar of talk stopped.

"Oh, yeah?"

"Where? What sort of a bird?"

"Over the camp," said the British sailorman. "A sort of a brownish bird, very fast of flight."

Lindsey remarked that would be an Antarctic petrel.

Two days later Ronne saw two Antarctic petrels wheeling through a blizzard. And on the 9th, the same day that Noville reported sighting a lone snowy petrel 38 miles inland, Lindsey and I saw two snowy petrels precipitated out of mist above the pressure ice in the Bay of Whales—two lovely white moth-like creatures which hovered an instant on timid wings, then melted into the fog. A moment later two Antarctic petrels came out of nowhere. And along the foot of the pressure ice Lindsey counted five seals, slick, lazy things, all of them, so Lindsey announced, pregnant.

VIII

On October 12th, after nine days of overcast skies and drift, the sky cleared. Bowlin took off in the Pilgrim for Advance Base, with Schlossbach as navigator and Bailey as radioman.

Shortly after one o'clock Waite flashed word from the base that the plane had taken off for Little America, that Admiral Byrd and Poulter were aboard, that Schlossbach would return with him and Demas in the tractor, and that they would shut down Advance Base.

An hour later the plane grew in the sky and we went forward to meet it. Seven months is a long time anywhere.

C. J. V. M.

Chapter XIII

THE SPRING CAMPAIGN

I

It is hardly necessary to add to what has already been written in the foregoing chapter about my experiences at Advance Base. What happened out there was substantially reported. From June on, till the tractor arrived in August, it was very tough sledding. The chances of my survival seemed very slim. But March, April and May were more than all right. I had a great time. The trying months that followed have never succeeded in taking away the joyful memory of the earlier period. However, that's neither here nor there. When I went out to Advance Base, I expected it to be hard—not quite so hard. I'll admit, as it turned out to be—but in all events, I had no reason to be surprised or rueful, whatever the turn in affairs. The meteorological records are now in the possession of government meteorologists. If they add only a little to present knowledge of Antarctic meteorology, I shall consider myself rewarded. With the exception of a few blank pages and a few observations missed, the data were complete and continuous from the day the Station was occupied (March 25th) until it was abandoned (October 12th).

As for Dr. Poulter, Demas and Waite, I cannot say too much for them. Theirs was a hard, dangerous journey. It was one of those indescribable moments when, looking north over the black ocean of the Ross Ice Barrier, I suddenly saw far off (I tried to tell myself, as I had so often done before, that it was just a star) the wavering pinpoint of a tractor searchlight.

In the two months that followed, while I tried to recover strength enough to withstand the return trip, these three men were always thoughtful, always generous. It was deucedly uncomfortable in that ice-box of a shack, sleeping on the deck at night, politely getting out of one another's way during the day. With four of us in the tiny place, it was impossible to take a step without colliding. Waite generously did all the cooking, took infinite pains with it, a real help to me in my wretched condition. Dr. Poulter and Demas occupied themselves with meteorological observations and (as long as darkness lasted) with auroral and meteor observations. Very much of a man, this Dr. Poulter: physically a giant, as fast in action as he is slow in words. He was hardly at Advance Base before he unshipped the meteor reticle and set it up on a stand atop the shack. No cold was great enough to cool his ardent interest in his meteor research. Bundled up in furs, he used

(Photograph by Joseph A. Pelter)

THE SLEDGERS START OUT

(© Paramount Pictures, Inc.)

PLANTING A FLAG ON THE EASTERN TRACTOR TRIP
(Note signal cable—for blinker lights—between tractor and sledge)

(Photograph by Joseph A. Pelter)

PRESSURE ICE AT THE MOUTH OF VER-SUR-MER INLET

THE SEALS PROVIDE ENTERTAINMENT FOR TWO SKIERS

to stand for hours under the iron reticle, once with the temperature as low as —75°, watching the skies for the swift-burning tracks of meteors, and calling the magnitude and coördinates down to Demas, who stood at the bottom of the shaft with a notebook and watch in his hand. Back at Little America observers in the main observatory were simultaneously scanning the same strip of skies. Demas is always a good fellow to have around. He spent most of his leisure time, as he always does, in study and reading. In a way I'm responsible for that. Pete has been trying to complete his education for the past ten years, but what with interrupting it to serve on four of my expeditions, including two wintering expeditions in the Antarctic, he has had to take his studies on the fly. If either he or I do not give up exploring, I'm afraid he'll be attending college with a long gray beard.

Impatient as I was to return to Little America and direct preparations for the field trips, it was physically impossible for me to leave much sooner than I did. I was a bit too flimsy to attempt the trip in the tractor; so I had to wait for the plane to be dug out and, after that, for decent flying weather. The long wait helped me to get back some of my strength; and modesty compels me to say that it did the expedition no harm. Thanks to the daily radio communication that Waite held with Little America, I was continuously in touch with the state of preparations at the main base and was able to advise and direct where it seemed necessary, though I cheerfully concede they really had no great need of it. The main parties were on the mark and set to go; local scientific work was under way, aviation was tuning up, and June and his party in Tractor No. 1, already with one fine discovery behind them, on the evening of my return to Little America flashed warm greetings by radio and word they had that day ascended Mt. McKinley.

No leader could have asked for a better state of things. To return abruptly after a separation of nearly seven months and find the field parties poised and ready was proof enough that everywhere along the line the expedition had looked to the task. That is why I shall not single men out for praise. To do so would be an injustice to many. Behind the small parties lined up for the start were, I knew, men who in countless and inconspicuous ways had helped them—the machinist, the radio engineers, sledge riggers, ski instructors, the navigator, senior scientist, meteorologists, the cook who helped prepare their rations, the mechanics, the sailmaker and men, like Bob Young, who had no titles.

I hope none of us forgets these debts. Civilization has a way of making us forget the homely coöperation, the unspoken give-and-take, the quiet sharing and the other like things which make a polar expedition so different from the jungle warfare of most collective enterprises. All this running down of one another, so common with polar explorers when they get back to civilization, is usually without justification. The

Antarctic code with decent men is pretty much above meanness and pettiness.

Returning to Little America was like returning to life. To mingle again with the men, to hear familiar voices and almost forgotten sounds, the ring of telephone and the steady, rhythmic beat of the gasoline generators, the barking of the dogs intruded a new existence. The tunnels had all been driven after I left for Advance Base; so it took me a day or so to get my bearings. I felt like a stranger, having to stop somebody in one of those pitch-dark corridors and inquire: please, sir, would you mind directing me to my own residence? Captain Innes-Taylor was kind enough to offer me his share of Dog Heim; so I moved in with my old friend and associate of three expeditions, George Noville.

It was good to join afresh the life of the expedition, and to feel under my hand the lively stir of a variety of enterprises. With the main parties whipping their gear together, the camp was pretty much in an uproar. Fortunately I had time enough to have a look at the gear and to have a general conference with each of the parties. Their gear was in excellent shape (for which Captain Innes-Taylor and his dog department and Demas deserve the highest praise); the men knew exactly what was expected of them, and a sound system of rations, depots, weights and support schedules had been worked out. All they needed was the word to go.

On October 14th, one day ahead of schedule, the Marie Byrd Land Party (Siple, leader, biologist and navigator; Wade, radio operator, geologist and driver; Corey, supplies and driver, and Stancliff, driver) started eastward with four teams. Departure time: 11:15 A.M. An abominable day—heavily overcast and snowing, a muggy north wind, a mile horizon and an air temperature of +2°. Dane, who accompanied them a short way, returned to camp before supper with the news that seven miles out they had taken in tow the loaded trailers depoted earlier, then pushed on. The fog, he said, was very heavy. "They just walked into it," he said, "and vanished as if they had dropped into a crevasse."

The fog was apparently distributed over a wide belt. Both tractor parties—June in No. 1, 208 miles to the east; Demas, Waite and Schlossbach in No. 2, 575 miles south—reported they were hove to in zero visibility. Next morning, however, Demas arrived with the gear from Advance Base. The Base, he said, was empty, except for a small supply of food and the meteorological instruments. His last act was to wind up the thermograph and insert a fresh recording sheet.

On October 16th, one day behind schedule, the Geological Party (Blackburn, leader and geologist; Russell, in charge of base laying, and driver; Paine, navigator, radio operator and driver) with two nine-dog teams, and the Plateau Party (Morgan and Dr. Bramhall, co-leaders—the former geologist and the latter physicist and navigator;

Ronne and Eilefsen, drivers and ski experts) with four teams, departed simultaneously for the south polar plateau. Departure time—11:15 A.M. The same somber conditions: milky fog and light sifting snow, a gusty northerly wind, and a temperature of +2°.

Notwithstanding the dullness of the air, the six teams made a grand spectacle as they moved off, one behind the other, well-spaced, with a nice spread to the dogs and a clean run to the sledges. I noticed with quick understanding how soon, after the emotional impetus of the start was spent, the teams slowed down to a walk on the slight rise to Retreat Camp. So long as the temperatures remained warm, they would have hard going, especially in the soft, loose barrier snow farther south. Siple that morning reported he had made only 16.5 miles in two days. "Soft surface, hard going, taking it easy until the dogs harden to it," his radio message said. "Bar. 28.35, temp. plus 3, overcasts, vis. 2 miles." A subsequent message said they were manhauling, too; that is, the men themselves had gotten into harness and pulled with the dogs. Well, they all had to do that.

Wed., Oct. 17, 10 P.M.

With the main parties safely launched, the next step is to get the supporting parties off. Siple is extremely well off; he's fortunate in having had the tractor lay his depots in advance. He's much better off in that respect than the southern parties. I believe there's a 50-50 chance the tractor support planned for the Plateau Party will come a cropper in the crevasses at Lat. 81°, in which case we shall have to make a radical change in plans. However, circumstances will decide.

No word from June's tractor tonight. Last night he reported they were camped 11 miles east of 120-Mile Depot: "Bar. 27.50. Have gone down 2800 feet from 150-Mile Depot. Temp. minus 7, Wind ENE, force 1, some fog, 80 percent overcast." Expect them in tomorrow. They must have a story to tell.

Herrmann and Moody, who went with the Southern Parties to take movies, returned with the news they camped last night on high Barrier 10.7 miles south. Dogs fagged out, he said, and the men, especially Morgan and Bramhall, who have had the least experience with dogs, took a beating the first day. Surface very soft, Herrmann said, and the men were planning to pack 50 pounds each in a knapsack to ease the loads on the sledges.

October 18th, at 2:13 P.M. o'clock, Tractor No. 1 rolled into camp, ending a voyage of 525.5 miles, which carried the crew of four (June, leader; Rawson, navigator; Von der Wall, driver; and Petersen, radio operator and cameraman) to the previously unpenetrated western margin of the great Edsel Ford Range in Marie Byrd Land. The major results of the journey were: (1) discovery of a broad elevated plateau rolling unbrokenly from the Rockefeller Mountains to the Edsel Ford Range, and south and east of Mt. Grace McKinley to the limit of vision; (2) the first penetration into a new land which enjoyed the unique distinction of being the first new land discovered by aviation; and (3) the establishment by Rawson of new ground control points by astronomical observation, which had the valuable effect of shifting the peaks of the Edsel Ford Range approximately 37 miles west of their estimated position[1]: and (4) the stocking of a series of depots for the Marie Byrd Land Party clear to Mt. Grace McKinley. No less impressive was the fact that the tractor had succeeded brilliantly in a season too cold for sustained travel with dog teams.

When the tractor halted on the outskirts of Dog Town, there remained but a pint of oil in the engine and 25 gallons of gas in the tanks. The men looked quite tired; their faces were yellowed from frost-bite, but they were all in high spirits. I shall recount the story as they gave it to me that evening, and as they later confirmed it in their formal report.

After leaving Little America September 27th, they ran one mile south to near Retreat Camp, where they bore east on a great circle course laid to fetch them up a trifle south of the Rockefellers. The first day out they made 40.7 miles. Twelve miles east the surface was a series of rolling hills and valleys; June thought that an indentation, structurally like the Bay of Whales but now filled in, lay south of Kainan Bay on the coast. Next day, with visibility sometimes at zero, they cruised 23.6 miles. The temperature was —42°. A heavy crust, into which the sledges and tractor sank four inches, broke repeatedly under the car; they traveled almost constantly in second speed. At 69 miles a depot was put down for Siple's party. Every 34.5 miles also, an aviation panel beacon, of the type described in an earlier chapter, was hoisted on a 12-foot pole; and drums of gasoline were cached for the return.

In the early afternoon of the 29th, when about 80.5 miles east of Little America, they raised for the first time the dark peaks of the Rockefellers on the port bow. That day they ran 44 miles, establishing another depot at 103.5 miles, where they camped. Visibility was bad, the temperature —15°. After breakfasting next morning on cocoa and oatmeal, they were underway again at 8:30 o'clock. At 2:30 P.M. they passed 14 miles south of Mt. Helen Washington, a peak of the Rockefellers. That evening, 138 miles east of Little America, according to the sledge meter. they camped about two miles west of frowning pressure ridges, deciding to wait for morning before attempting to navigate them. From their camp the low peaks of the Rockefellers were plainly visible, black rock thrust above the snow piled around them.

Worried by the obstacles the pressure ridges might contrive, all four of them were up at 4 P.M. October 1st, for a survey of the area on foot. The fog, however, was too dense for them to dare to leave before

[1] See Rawson's *Notes on Maps and Surveys.*

noon. On skis, and roped together with long stretches of alpine rope, they pushed into the pressure, penetrating it for four miles before they discovered a likely transit farther south. What puzzled them was that northeast, east and southeast of the pressure the *barrier* seemed to rise gently, and that the disturbances thereabouts seemed to be caused by the ice riding over low, buried peaks. Though they didn't realize it then, nor for several days, they had discovered the western front of the new plateau. That night the sky was clear enough for Rawson to get his first sights; because the sun was still too low during the day for observations, he took star sights, which fixed their position at Lat. 78° 21′ S., Long. 154° 15′ W. The temperature was —42°.

October 2nd was clear. June and Von der Wall were up at 3 A.M. to fire the blow torches under the engine. They were under way at 6:30. Steering along the face of the pressure, they ran 7 miles due south, then southeast for two miles through the milder transit they had marked before. In the pressure they marked many deep crevasses on their left, but fortunately met none. Changing course to 81° true, they started to climb what they later found to be a broad and elevated plateau. Crouched behind the canvas shield on the trailing sledge, with the compass before him, Rawson held Von der Wall on his course with his clever blinker light system. Petersen lay beside him, reaching out every third of a mile by the sledge meter to jab in a trail flag. At first the ascent was gradual, merely rolling folds of snow, each one a little bit higher than the other. But at 1900 feet by the aneroid barometer the ascent stiffened. The car was running steadily in low gear. The temperature was —20°. Above the shining dome shimmered the mirage of the mountains, which they were later to recognize as identical reproductions of Mt. Grace McKinley and Haines Mt., 69 and 92 miles away respectively. At 3 P.M. a bad oil leak stopped them, after a run of 39 miles. Here, while June and Von der Wall worked in a tent to fashion a new gasket, which they cut out with a knife, Rawson and Petersen unloaded the stores for Siple's 150-Mile Depot (173 statute miles). With the rations they had depoted and the gas they had consumed up to this point, they were now able to stow everything on a single sledge. The other was left at the depot, to be picked up on the return. By aneroid the altitude of their present position was shown to be 2,624 [2] feet. Well below and behind them (nearly a thousand feet, according to Rawson's observations by theodolite) they could see the craggy peaks of the Rockefellers. To the northwest the peaks of the Alexandras and the LaGorce group were barely visible.

Having worked most of the night over the gasket, they shoved off again at 11:40 A.M. on the 3rd, still climbing, with a rising wind on the port bow. At 5:20 that evening, no longer able to see through the drift, they hove to, having logged 29.8 miles and attained an elevation of 3,120 feet. The flags disappeared in the storm almost as soon as Petersen's

[2] This and subsequent readings are corrected readings.

hand left them. A rapidly falling glass worried June. First unloading dog and manfood for 180-Mile Depot (207 statute miles), they hurriedly pitched their tents and secured ship for the blizzard they knew was in the making. The barometer, which had run off the scale, read 25 inches, the temperature was —5°, the wind northeast 20 miles, and rising fast.

None too soon did they finish. That evening the wind reached a velocity of 40 to 50 miles per hour, according to June's reckoning. It oscillated between northeast and east. In the afternoon of the next day came a short lull; the sun broke through, and they considered breaking camp and running a few miles before dark. At 6 P.M., with the suddenness of a thunderclap, a wall of wind cracked down. In a very few minutes it built up to hurricane force. At its height, the velocity, they estimated, was over 100 miles per hour. "Anyhow it blew bloody murder," Von der Wall said. The barometer dropped to 23 inches.

When the storm struck, Von der Wall was asleep in the tractor; June, Petersen and Rawson were in the cook tent, which had been pitched in the tractor's lee. The radio tent was only a few feet ahead.

"I tell you, she blew and blew and blew," June said. "I never heard a more solid rushing sound, not even that time in 1929 when Gould, Balchen and I lost the Fokker in the Rockefellers. It made my ears sore just listening to it. First thing we knew, the tent poles were driven clear through the roof, and Rawson, Petersen and I were scrambling around in the dark trying to keep the tent from being blown down on top of us. Finally we stood with our backs braced against the sloping ridge of the tent—I guess we did that most of the night. Petersen didn't dare leave for his radio schedule: the wind would have swept him off his feet in a second. As for drift, the air was so thick you could have walked on it. We tried to plug the holes in the roof with socks, windproof parkas, shirts—anything we could get our hands on in the dark. The tent was full of snow. Above the wind we could hear the radio tent whipping and tearing itself to pieces—an ugly sound, sharp as the cracking of a whip. We were worried, too, about Von der Wall. But though he was only ten feet away, he might just as well have been a hundred miles. I tried twice to leave the tent, but the wind was too much. That ten-foot trip wouldn't have been safe in a submarine."

Von der Wall took up the story, chuckling:

"I was asleep when the hurricane hit. What awakened me, the sound of the wind or the shaking of the tractor, I don't know; but both were awful. The tractor had a 10 degree list, and she was shaking and rising, like a small ship in a heavy sea. I got worried; it seemed about to take off any minute, so I decided I'd try to reach the other fellows. There must have been a dead spot just behind the cab, because I thought I could make it. I took just one step out of the lee, when something hit me and down I went. Drift filled my mouth: I seemed to be smothered and choking, but I didn't dare to get to my feet, knowing I'd be blown clear off the plateau. I had no idea then where the tractor was; I couldn't see it, and I had lost all sense of direction the moment the wind spun me around. The air was full of black shadows and noise. But I had to go somewhere, so I started crawling, flat on my belly. After two or three feet my hands hit the treads; I felt my way around aft and finally got to the door. 'Any port in a storm,' I said to myself. The wind pounded the car all night. I could feel it lift and give, as though the wooden body was on the verge of being torn off. Anyhow I put everything on and got in my sleeping bag, to keep warm if it blew away."

It was eleven hours before the others could reach Von der Wall, ten feet away. About 5 A.M. on October 6th the wind subsided enough to let them out of the tent. They found Von der Wall all right, but the radio tent was in shreds; Petersen's radio gear and sleeping bag were buried in drift. The front end of the tractor, which was listing heavily, was a solid block of ice. Petersen dug out the radio set; the antennae had been blown away, but fortunately he had a spare length of wire.

However, they had to wait six days before they could resume the journey. The wind blew steadily till the morning of the tenth, with a velocity of up to 50 miles per hour. These easterly and northerly winds having brought rising temperatures, the heat from the stoves now melted the snow on the tent: clothing, sleeping bags, everything was soaking wet. To make up for the loss of Petersen's tent, he and Rawson took turns sleeping in the spare bunk in the tractor, Petersen by day, Rawson by night. They had one good laugh, however, when they needed it most. Petersen rigged up the radio so they could listen in on one of the regular broadcasts to Little America. Joe Rucker, a member of the first expedition, was speaking from New York; and not knowing that June was 180 miles to the east, he sent him cordial greetings, saying that he had only to close his eyes to see Harold stretched out in his bunk, pipe in hand, a picture of solid comfort.

About 9 o'clock on the morning of the 10th, the sun broke through the clouds of drift. Anxious to be off, because waiting was costing 1 gallon of gas a day in the stoves, they fell to digging out the tractor, which was buried to the roof on the lee side. The sledge likewise was buried. At 4:45 P.M. they resumed the easting. Nine miles out a sticking gear shift lever stopped them. By 11 P.M. they had the transmission down, but it was too cold and drifting to finish repairs.

Up at 4 A.M. on the 11th, assembled transmission before breakfast, leaving at 9:45 A.M. Still climbing (the aneroid registered 3,477 feet at this last camp), they pressed eastward. About 11 o'clock, on their port bow, June and Von der Wall sighted one of the mountains they had seen in mirage on the 2nd. In fact, they paused to debate whether it was a mirage, and though it seemed authentic enough they held their course. They had risen another 400 feet since 180-Mile Depot. The plateau at this point was decidedly rolling, with high ridges and valleys. Wary of crevasses, they sidestepped the valleys where they could, following the curve of the ridges. Shortly after 1 o'clock, behind the saddle-back mountain which they had in sight all morning, they sighted another, a long, irregular ridge, snow-covered except for a few outcroppings of bare rock. The first, they decided, must be Grace McKinley, the second Haines; so at 1:25 P.M. they altered course toward the first. The elevation, at the turn, was 3,577 feet.

Now as they turned north, steering about 346° true by compass, the surface became exceedingly rough, corrugated by irregular waves of polished, glazed sastrugi, very hard at the crest and soft in the hollows. The car took a frightful pounding, June said. Slamming across these ridges, it sometimes listed 20° by the inclinometer. Von der Wall braced himself at the wheel, to keep from being thrown out of the seat. The sastrugi trended NW and SE—an indication of the prevailing wind direction. Steadily the plateau dropped, descending to the nearest mountain (Grace McKinley) in a succession of terraces, with steep slopes from one to the next. At 7 P.M. that evening they reached the foot of the mountain, having dropped 1,400 feet since turning north. Now they steered the tractor up the southeast slope of the mountain, making camp an hour later about a quarter of a mile from bare rock, the first any of them had seen in ten months. The elevation by aneroid was 2,496 feet, and the peak towered another 600 feet above them.

October 12th was, they said, wonderfully clear and fair. All four of them, that morning, ascended the peak, first to set foot on the northern reaches of the newest of American possessions.[8] At 11:30 o'clock they raised a flag on the lowest patch of bare rock. They were quite appalled by what they saw. South of the mountain the snow rose gently within a few hundred feet of the top; the tractor, in fact, had itself climbed halfway to the summit. But the north face was a sheer precipice of 1200 feet, with a treacherous overhang, which they didn't quite dare to approach. Remembering the fog, they remarked how easy it might have been to blunder right over the precipice.

That afternoon they climbed the peak. The entire northeast horizon was filled with the black tops of the Edsel Ford Range. Rawson counted 42 mountain masses, dark outcroppings of rock with long, glacierized ridges: behind these, he thought, lay others. The descending terraces south of Mt. Grace McKinley seemed to have been produced by downfaulting. North of the mountain and spreading across the crescent of the western front range was a wide belt of shelf ice, terribly broken up and crevassed, which, through a transit telescope, they made out to be the broad channel of Sulzberger Bay. A line of snow-submerged peaks seemed to run from Mt. Grace McKinley to the Alexandras, 80.5 miles to the west.

To fix its position and establish a control point for a subsequent realignment of the Edsel Ford Range and also the mapping of the

[8] The Geological Party of the first expedition entered the central region of Marie Byrd at Lat. 85° 25′ S. Gould, *Cold,* 208.

mountains which impending flights would likely discover farther to the east, Rawson took a series of star, sun and moon sights on the peak of Mt. Grace McKinley. Its position was found to be Lat. 77° 55′ S., Long. 148° 10′ W. Two time ticks picked up by radio from the Naval Observatory at Washington, D. C., gave him an exact time setting. So bright was it then even at midnight that Rawson could take observations only on the brightest stars; he read the arc on the theodolite with the aid of a flashlight, the batteries of which had to be re-heated every five minutes to keep it burning.

October 13th they commenced the homeward journey. About a mile back on their old trail they laid out an emergency landing field, identified by three large orange flags planted in a triangle. The height of the plateau at once extinguished hope of using the area as a refueling base; it meant too hot a landing, in the pilots' words. Here they put down the last of Siple's depots, 2,400 pounds of dog and man food, 10 gallons of kerosene. Shortly after they got underway an amusing, but potentially dangerous, incident happened. Once when the tractor slowed down, Rawson jumped off, intending to overtake the cab and tell June the signal lights were out of order. Before he could make it, the car lunged forward again. Rawson tried to throw himself on the sledge, but missed. The car went merrily on, June and Von der Wall having no inkling of what had happened. Petersen, who had been riding with Rawson on the sledge, yelled himself hoarse, but couldn't make himself heard above the roar of the engine. Rawson, footing it for all he was worth, ragged wind-proofs flapping scarecrow fashion about his legs, was rapidly disappearing from Petersen's sight when June stopped, as he made it a practice to do, whenever there was no blink on the lights at least once every 15 minutes; this was one of their safety precautions. Petersen stumbled to the cab, weak from yelling, and told him what had happened. They turned round and picked up the derelict, who was puffing too much to berate them. "I suppose you guys thought I could hitch-hike my way in," Rawson said, jerking his thumb in the familiar roadside gesture.

In order to save gas, they took a short cut south-southwest (204° true) up the terraces of the plateau, fetching up with their original trail 23 miles on. For 18 miles they climbed steadily, rising another 1,850 feet, then dropping for two miles to reach the trail. That afternoon the wind made drift, and frequent stallings of the engine, caused by snow and ice in the intake manifold and carburetor, forced them to halt two miles east of 180-Mile Depot.

Drift and zero visibility held them in camp most of the 14th. The wind was East, force 3, the temperature −9°. About 4.30 a lightening in the mist persuaded them to start, but after 4.5 miles they heaved to. Though drift and fog were still heavy, they resumed the homing next day, running 42.5 miles. Visibility was never better than one-sixth of a mile, just half the distance between the flags; and they lost much time trying to pick up the trail. The hurricane of the 4th had either torn most of the flags to bits, or bent the bamboo so that the fabric was smothered in drift. The torn flags were removed, and the others straightened up. The temperature was zero. On the dome of the plateau, between 180-Mile and 150-Mile Depot, where the hurricane apparently blew with greatest force, the surface was a continuous rumpling of sastrugi, five feet from crest to trough. "It was slam-bang all the way," Von der Wall said. Rawson and Petersen on the sledge were hard pressed to keep from being thrown overboard. But they had to keep running as they had no gas to spare for reheating the engine before 120-Mile Depot, where fuel had been cached on the outward journey. The real hardship, the torture of tractor travel, Rawson said, was having to sit still so long without being able to restore circulation to the hands and feet. These would freeze again and again.

Off at 5:45 P.M. October 16th, they rode steadily for 28 hours in light ground fog and drift, descending the plateau, passing the Rockefellers and camping finally, in heavy fog, about 9 miles east of Little America. Till they were within 34.5 miles of Little America, they saw behind them a perfect mirage of the peaks of the Rockefellers. That single run they logged 159.4 miles, a new record for a single march in the polar regions. On the 18th, as I have said, they made Little America. The day before, 29 miles east of Little America, they met Siple's party, pretty much down at the mouth. In the light crust the dogs and sledges were sinking four or five inches every step. All the men were in man-hauling harness, pulling with the dogs. They made an extraordinary picture, the giants Siple and Wade and the shorter Corey and Stancliff, all pulling like draught horses.

In the matter of tractor operation, the most vexing fault, June said, was the continual formation of ice in the gas lines and carburetor. No matter how careful they were, even straining the gas through chamois, water collected in the lines. Most of it, of course, was produced inside the metal lines by condensation. June said that he and Von der Wall blew ice out of the lines till they were dizzy.

Dr. Potaka immediately weighed in the men to see how well they had fared on the new rations. The weights follow:

	Before	*After*
June	192 lbs.	185 lbs.
Rawson	162 "	153 "
Petersen	175 "	164 "
Von der Wall	138 "	130 "

II

With Siple's party forging eastward along the line of depots which June had put down for him, the next important step was to provide the same support for the Geological and Plateau Parties. In some respects, this second was treble the job of the first. Whereas the depot system for the Marie Byrd Land Party was only 253 miles, the two southern parties would require a line at least 517 miles long, from the sea to the foot of the Queen Maud Range. In addition to the supplies carried on their own sledges, and the stocking of the depots along the line of their retreat, the parties, in order to achieve their missions, required the delivery of 3,000 pounds of dog food and scientific apparatus at the mouth of Thorne Glacier in the Queen Maud Range. An enormous weight as sledging weights go, since it must be all pay load, above and beyond the requirements of a supporting party which must itself be self-sustained over a 1,037 mile journey.

How that support was originally planned, what purpose it would serve, and how necessary it was to the defense and maintenance of the main parties, have been described in an earlier chapter. However, in order to clarify the changes that altering conditions soon made necessary, I shall review them briefly. The attack in the southern sector was to be made in three waves, first the main parties, then two waves of support. Captain Innes-Taylor's Supporting Party of three dog teams was expected, in the original plan, to stock the depots between Little America and 300 miles south. It will be recalled that preliminary depots had been run as far as 150 miles by the Fall Southern Party. Two tractors would continue the second wave of support, one as far as 300 miles, the other to the foot of the mountains.

In the last analysis, the success of the movement hinged squarely upon the tractors. If they failed, the Plateau Party, at least insofar as the attainment of the Polar Plateau was concerned, was defeated. Morgan's seismic apparatus alone weighed 850 pounds.

The least load with which each tractor was expected to leave Little America was about 8,000 pounds.[4] These loads, of course, would vary as gasoline was consumed; on the othr hand they would be increased at Advance Base by taking aboard 2,200 pounds of dog food. The gasoline required to fuel the cars weighed, with containers, approximately 11,640 pounds.

Mechanically, the journey was within the capacities of the tractors.

[4] The gross load for the tractors leaving Little America follows:

3 men @ 185 lbs. ea.	545 lbs.	1160 gals. gas in tin containers	9260 lbs.
Equipment for 3 men	300	4 sledges at 170 lbs. ea.	680
Trail gear, etc.	250	Radio equipment plus emergency set & spares	360
Cylinder oil	128	2,000 trail flags	440
Prestone non-freezing radiator solution	102	Total	15,965 lbs.
340 gals. gas in tanks	2380		
Tools & spare parts	150		
2 spare batteries	220		
Dog food	300		
Seismic sounding apparatus	850		

The drivers had repeatedly demonstrated their ability to keep them going under the worst sort of handicaps. The loads weren't excessively heavy. On the Eastern trip No. 1 had left Little America with a load of 7,600 pounds. Gasoline was something of a problem, but not critically so. Barely 1,500 gallons of tractor gas remained for the operation (counting the gas previously depoted on the trail)[5] which was barely enough to fuel the cars. The consumption rate, however, was fixed on the arbitrary figure of a gallon per mile, which allowed for prolonged travel with heavy loads in low gear, idling, distance lost in circling for the trail, and the gasoline used in the cookers and the blow torches. For example, June's party used 45 gallons in their cookers and blow torches alone.

The only *x* in the equation was the incalculable topographical hazard —crevasses! If the test were to come at all, we were convinced, it would come in the crevassed area just south of the 81st parallel. I knew how severe this area was, having flown over it several times in 1929. The crevasses lay in a serpentine belt, from eight to fifteen miles wide, running east and west. Immense black pits, very long and twenty fathoms deep, they were far worse than any crevasses the tractors encountered between Little America and Advance Base. Dog teams could thread them; Amundsen got through them, as did the southern parties of the first expedition.[6] But the heavy tractors—well, we didn't know: we couldn't tell without trying. How far east and west the belt ran we had no way of foretelling. Our flights in 1929 had revealed they lay at least between the 173rd and the 155th meridians W.[6a] To the west the crevasses were more severe, plunging into upheaved blocks of pressure; but to the eastward, at least from the plane, they had seemed to be diminishing. In all events, the course of the southern parties had been laid toward this seemingly more favorable terrain.

It has always been a first principle in my ABC's of field operations never to leave, where it could be avoided, the success of a pioneering party dependent upon a single doubtful circumstance. Where a purely scientific party has an alternative—say, between a spectacular objective with a large risk, and a less spectacular but equally valid objective with a smaller risk—it seems to me that the latter is the right choice. This reasoning I tried to impress upon the party leaders in the planning of their journeys. The temptation is to try to do too much, to overreach one's self, to risk everything on a single cast. On the loftiest branch the grapes are always most inviting, but the fable points the moral. Greediness is a fatal quality in the polar regions. The ice has

[5] The gas available on the trail follows:

50-Mile Depot	......	80 gals.
75 " "	......	250 "
Advance Base	......	240 "

[6] Byrd, *Little America,* 298-301.

[6a] Ibid., 377.

buried many men—and, in even great numbers, the plans of men—that reckoned too much on hope and too little on percentages. In the present state of Antarctic knowledge, where so little is known and so much is challenging, it seems to me that a leader should select, from the myriads of opportunities available, those objectives which are at once valuable and *reasonably accessible.* Piece by piece, Antarctic research is too costly to chance failure. It should be modeled on the business-like principles of concentrating in those territories which promise the most effective results. After all, scientists will still be grubbing in the Antarctic long after all of us are dead.

These conditions were beautifully met in the Geological Party. Well-knit, well-manned, not too heavily burdened, it was capable, no matter what happened to the tractors, of detaching itself and pushing ahead on its geological reconnoissance of the Queen Maud Range with just a moderate amount of support. It was as fine a sledging party as ever hit a trail. Had it cared to sacrifice its scientific mission, the Geological Party might have made the Pole with a machine-like precision that would have astonished the world.

But in the case of the plateau party, as I have said, the weight of Morgan's seismic apparatus, easily the most cumbersome and weightiest instrument ever used in polar field operations, was a deciding factor. Without tractor support the project was impossible. Even if the operation had been feasible with dog teams alone, we lacked dogs for it. The pick of Dog Town went into the teams of the three main parties. Innes-Taylor's Supporting Party was left with second-class material, the lighter and poorer dogs, and the sickly and wounded dogs which the main parties, at the last moment, had demoted from their teams. Aviation was out of the question. With the flying season at hand, the *William Horlick* would have to use every fair day for long-range exploration; and the Pilgrim, the only plane reserve (the Fairchild was too flimsy, lacking a factory overhaul, to be risked on a long flight) had to stand by in reserve. So the fate of the Plateau Party in consequence had to rest on the tractors; and the fate of the tractors, in turn, would be settled, as it was, at Lat. 81°, 345 miles from the mountains.

Luckily we had an ace in the hole—an objective *at once valuable and reasonably accessible* toward which the Plateau Party could be instantly swung if the crevasses were impassable. This objective was the new plateau which June's party had just discovered. On this great dome of ice Morgan's seismic, and Bramhall's magnetic, research could be prosecuted with undiminished value. Morgan and Bramhall had discussed it with me as a possibility the morning their party took the field. Their minds were set on reaching the polar plateau, but they had a weather eye cocked for the alternative.

One important change was made in the support plans before the tractors left on October 26th.

After a resurvey of the operation, Captain Innes-Taylor recommended that his own Supporting Party be cancelled and its function taken over by the tractors. Above its own gear and rations, this party was to carry for the main parties only 162 pounds out of Little America, and 1,169 pounds (mostly man and dog food) from Advance Base. Taking aboard these loads wouldn't tax the tractors. They would leave Little America with about 8,000 pounds, and Advance Base with approximately the same loads. But from Advance Base on, as a consequence of depoting and gas consumption, these peak loads would rapidly diminish. At a consumption rate of a gallon a mile, the tractors would each blow away 100 pounds through their exhausts every 15 miles or so.

The recommendation was excellent, since it would consolidate the support, cut down the number of men in the field and broaden our reserves. The truth of the matter is, I had some misgivings that we were a trifle lean on the safety side. Had Innes-Taylor's three teams taken the field, the main base would have been left with only one tractor (and practically no fuel for it), no skilled dog-drivers, and only five grown dogs, several of them crippled, which the biologists needed for their work in the Bay of Whales. With the Supporting Party withdrawn from the operations, we now had available in reserve a reliable mobile unit which could be called upon to assist either the main sledging parties or aviation, if an emergency arose.

But more than the common sense of the suggestion, the spirit in which it was made pleased me. There were no more ardent sledgers than Innes-Taylor, Moody and Dane. They had all worked hard; they had shouldered much of the drudgery of preparations in order to equip their companions on the main parties; and they had looked forward to this journey, with an eagerness that only sledgers will understand, as a reward. As chief of trail operations, Captain Innes-Taylor, in the planning of the whole operation, had modestly assigned himself an inconspicuous rôle. Now these men came forward, volunteering, for the good of the whole operation, to eliminate themselves. I should rather find such bigness in my associates than discover a mountain range.

While the southern parties struggled across the Barrier, slowed down by soft snow and the need of again breaking the dogs to hauling, Demas, Von der Wall and Hill worked night and day to have the tractors ready to leave in time for the rendezvous at Lat. 81°, where the dog teams would escort them through the critical area. Citroëns Nos. 2 and 3 were Demas' choice. Both having had hard usage in the journeys to Advance Base, they were overhauled from top to bottom, fore and aft. Treads were tightened; the engines were taken down, valves ground and reset, generators overhauled, batteries recharged, body bolts and shackles tightened—in short, a complete overhaul.

At 10:30 A.M., October 25th, the two tractors, their square orange cargo cabins and trailing sledges piled high with gear, started south in the wake of the southern parties. Demas was alone in No. 3; Hill and Waite, the latter again serving as radio operator, were in No. 2. The day was cloudy, the temperature —6°, and a light snow was falling.

A few hours later Demas was back, ruefully bearing a broken sledge. Going down a long hill this side of Amundsen Arm, the bridle on the leading sledge had parted, allowing the heavily burdened sledge to slew and smash against the tractor treads, breaking a runner and a cross-bar. A hole was broken through the tunnel roof, and the sledge carried into the galley, interrupting the noon meal. Cheerfully the camp gave up one of the tables; the broken sledge was thrown on it and Innes-Taylor, Dane and Moody quickly installed a new cross-bar and runner. Even Demas fell to washing dishes, to enable Dr. Poulter, who was on mess duty, to leave and make an awl with which to work the rawhide lashings.

On that day the two Southern parties were at Advance Base; Siple's party was 115 miles east, almost at the Rockefeller Mountains. Both were a trifle behind schedule, heavy drift and soft snow having taxed them greatly. Siple reported "surface terrible on dogs," and to lighten the loads he had dropped 300 pounds—200 pounds of dog food and 100 pounds of gear.

Otherwise all was well. The surface would improve, the dogs would harden up to their jobs, depoting would lighten loads, and the time would be made up. In the last march to Advance Base, the two Southern parties had made 29 miles.

III

Now aviation, which would carry the burden of long-range geographical discovery, made ready for its opportunities. The plans for the aerial attack had long since crystallized.

First off, a thrust into the 517-mile gap of unknown between the Edsel Ford Range to the north and the Queen Maud Range to the south.

This white gap, running north and south along the 147th meridian, between the mountains of the coast and the mountains rimming the south polar plateau, held one of the most crucial secrets in Antarctic geography—the secret of the great Ice Strait. Of the unsolved geographical riddles of the modern world, this was one of the most challenging, perhaps the most important. For this theoretical Strait, if proof of its existence could be found in the undiscovered interior, held out the promise of a great potential waterway connecting the Atlantic and Pacific oceans across the bottom of the globe.[7]

In the first chapter I called attention to this problem as one which animated the organization of the second expedition. Until the existence or non-existence of this Strait was confirmed, the structural integrity

[7] Sir Douglas Mawson, *Geogr. Journal* (London), Vol. 37, 1911, 609-620.

of the Antarctic continent must remain a mystery. From the point of view of geographical discovery, of defining the geographical identity of Antarctica, I regarded it as perhaps the most valuable single problem falling within our program. It's a curious but readily accredited fact that long after most astronomers had settled to their satisfaction that there were no canals on Mars, no geographer nor geologist could have told you whether Antarctica, only 10,000 miles away, was one continent or two.

Let me cite a famous Antarctic geologist, Mr. R. E. Priestley, who served under Shackleton (1907-1909) and Scott (1910-1913): "... First of all, the geologist is faced with the question: am I dealing with one continent or two? Do the Antarctandes of Graham Land stretch across the continent to Victoria Land? Alternatively, is the Ross Ice Barrier continued across Antarctica as a great ice strait? ..." [8]

And also the distinguished Sir Douglas Mawson, scientist with Shackleton's first expedition (1907-1909), leader of the Australasian Antarctic Expedition and subsequent expeditions: "Is (Antarctica) one continuous rocky land above sea-level, merely veneered by ice? Is it a number of epicontinental islands which have been overwhelmed and united by a flood of glacier ice between which the sea would flow were the ice to melt? In the latter case, are the inter-island channels choked to the very bottom with glacier ice so that the ice rides on a rock bottom below sea-level. Or does the sea water, in some at least of these, maintain a through-flow deep under the capping ice so that the inter-island ice caps, though very thick and of land origin, are yet afloat on sea water? ..." [9]

Associated with this problem of the Ice Strait, as the foregoing citations indicate, was the equally important problem of the Andean fold chain. A glance at a map of the south polar regions will show why this is so. South of Cape Horn the diminishing backbone of the South American Andes, after vanishing under the South Atlantic Ocean, seemingly rise afresh in the mountainous islands of the Antarctic Archipelago (sometimes called Graham Land and Graham Land Peninsula) which impinges on the Antarctic continent at Hearst Land, recently discovered by my friend, Sir Hubert Wilkins. That this ridge, referred to by some authorities as the Antarctandes, is a continuation of the Andean fold chain, tectonically and petrographically, many geologists believe.[10] The crucial question was: Is this chain continued across Antarctica; and, if so, in what direction? Does it march into the heart of the continent, as some authorities believe? Or does it after recurring on the coast of the Antarctic continent make a broad sweep to the west, skirting the South Pacific Ocean, finally to join the mountains of Marie

[8] R. E. Priestley & C. E. Tilley, *Problems of Polar Research,* Am. Geo. Soc., 324-5.

[9] Mawson, *Problems of Polar Research,* 258.

[10] Priestley & Tilley, op. cit., 324.

PLANNING A FLIGHT—ADMIRAL BYRD, RAWSON, PETERSEN, JUNE, PELTER, BOWLIN, AND SMITH

(Photograph by Joseph A. Pelter)

THE "WILLIAM HORLICK" COMES OUT OF ITS WINTER COCOON

(Photograph by Joseph A. Pelter)

The Condor Plane "William Horlick"

(© Paramount Pictures, Inc.)

The Condor in the Air

Byrd and King Edward VII Land? And finally, in either case did "an arm of the sea," [11] the so-called Strait, separate these mountain chains?

There was the double problem, as fascinating to me as a modern search for a short-cut to Cathay, a new northwest passage.

I shall attempt here only to suggest the general nature of the evidence out of which the problem rose. Being no geologist, I shall outline some of the arguments of scientists who have given special attention to this subject. In order to show the evolution of the problem, and the rôle we played toward its solution, I shall summarize the evidence as it existed in 1928, when our first expedition took the field.

For the Strait:

(1) The discovery by geologists, notably Nordenskjöld, that the geology of the Graham Land Peninsula is significantly different from that of South Victoria Land, the massive mountains of which form the western margin of the Ross Ice Barrier.[12] The latter is "a great elevated land mass which, so far as yet explored, is a region of block uplifts on a grand scale and has nothing in its tectonics corresponding to the folding in late geological times evidenced in . . . the Andean cordillera.[13] The geological and structural dissimilarity between these opposite regions of the continent was favorable to a dividing strait.[14]

(2) The occurrence in the nearly opposite sides of the continent, of the broad corridors of the Ross and Weddell Seas, facing each other across 1,300 miles of utterly unknown interior, and each advancing in the general direction of the other great sheets of some sort of water-borne shelf ice.

(3) The behavior of tides in the Ross Sea persuaded some authorities, notably Sir George Darwin, that a through passage was possible.[15]

(4) The apparent existence, between the high ice-covered land just southeast of the Bay of Whales and the "appearance of land" reported by Amundsen at about 82°, of a stretch of low-level ice, over a hundred miles across.[16] The existence of such low-level ice gave rise to the notion that a sea-level channel, if it did not extend across the continent, might therefore isolate the mountains of King Edward VII Land from the continental mainland.[17]

[11] Mawson, op. cit., 260.

[12] Otto Nordenskjöld, "Antarctic Nature," *Geographic Journal* (London), v. 38 (1911), 278.

[13] Mawson, op. cit., 260.

[14] Ibid., 260.

[15] Darwin, *Tidal Observations of the British Antarctic Expedition,* 1907: cited by Mawson.

[16] Hayes, *Antarctica,* 312-13.

[17] Ibid., 313.

(5) The comparatively calm air at the edge of the Ross Ice Barrier discounted the likelihood of much elevated land to the southeast. Highlands in that direction would spill a strong outward wind flow.[18]

Against the Strait:

(1) The sheer distance between the Ross and Weddell Seas—roughly 1300 miles—was too great for any channel.[19]

(2) Amundsen's report of "appearance of land" at Lat. 82° and discovery of Carmen Land between Lat. 84° and 86° east of his route across the Ross Ice Barrier to the Pole[20] seemingly interposed a solid bulwark of land athwart the route such a Strait would have to take.

(3) The likelihood, on the basis of the scanty geological and geographical evidence available, that the great bulk of the continent "is one tectonic unit forming a great shield against which the Antarctandes of Graham Land are folded as a continuation of the Long South American and South Antarctic ridge."[21]

(4) The possibility (a lucid deduction, so far as our subsequent investigation was to show) that the Andean line of crustal weakness on the far side of the continent would be found to skirt the coast toward King Edward VII: that the boundary of the plateau block of East Antarctica would be found to stretch across the continent to the east side of the Weddell Sea: and that sandwiched between these two belts and extending between the Ross and Weddell Seas there might be, crumpled against the massif of East Antarctica, undulating and moderately elevated land. . . ."[22]

All this, however, the pros and the cons, was, in Sir Douglas Mawson's own phrase, "pure speculation."[23] Though he, Priestley, and other authorities on the Antarctic, definitely inclined to the view that the strait was the less likely hypothesis, the solution awaited definitive discovery, and especially the delineation of the wholly uncharted eastern shore of the Ross Ice Barrier. If a Strait existed, it must somewhere enter that unknown shore.

Curiously, the discoveries of the first expedition, rather than settling the issue, served rather to pile new questions atop the already towering edifice of questions. Carmen Land and the "appearance of land" reported by Amundsen were non-existent. Where we looked for them,

18 Mawson, op. cit., 261.
19 Hayes, *Antarctica*, 313.
20 Amundsen, *The South Pole*, ii, 170, 171.
21 Priestley & Tilley, op. cit., 325.
22 Mawson, op. cit., 261.
23 Ibid., 261.

from the air and from the ground, we found only extensions of the undulating and supposedly largely water-borne barrier or shelf ice.[24] Thus the bulwark of land seemingly interposed between the Ross and Weddell Seas was removed; and once more, with the widening eastward of the Ross Ice Barrier, the way was open for the theoretical Strait.[25]

But was it really? The surveys of my first expedition had radically changed the charted direction of the Queen Maud Range: had shown that instead of bearing south-southeast, they bore almost due east, gradually diminishing in size.

But south of the coast of King Edward VII Land, in 1929, we had discovered a new range, the Rockefeller Mountains[26] apparently structurally related to the Alexandra Mountains of King Edward VII Land nearer the coast; and, east of this range, a far more extensive and significant range, the Edsel Ford Range of Marie Byrd Land.

It was the discovery of this second range, after the elimination of Carmen Land, which threw the problem of the Great Ice Strait into fresh confusion. So far as we could tell from the air and from photographic angles, the new range seemed to bear north and south. Did it trend south and join up with the new mountains of the Queen Maud Range, the mountains of which it appeared to resemble,[27] thereby blocking off the Strait? Or did it follow the coast eastward to provide the long-sought link to the Andean chain?

This, then, was the state of the double problem when we returned with the second expedition in an attempt to close with it. It remained, as it was at the beginning, a fascinating opposing array of arguments utterly lacking the polarizing impetus of discovery at the source. Short of actual *seeing* and *finding,* the problem could no more be settled by the analysis of remote data than the character of a man could be determined by a study of his cousins twice removed.

In the earlier chapters you have seen how we tried to gain, in the double attack by ship and plane, the unknown coast to the eastward, in an effort to fill in the coast, and determine its trend and structure. I shall emphasize here, what I did not emphasize then, that a coequal objective in this *frontal* attack was to determine, if we could, the trend of the Edsel Ford Range, with particular reference to these problems of continental structure.

But, of course, one must not lose sight of the fact that our main purpose as an exploring expedition was the extension of the geographical network of discovery over the whole vast region between the South Pacific Ocean and the Queen Maud Range. Irrespective of theoretical speculation arising out of such problems as the Strait, our mission was

[24] Byrd, *Little America,* 315, 344; Gould, *Cold,* 205.
[25] Griffith Taylor, New York *Times,* Jan. 3, 1930.
[26] Byrd, op. cit., 124-25.
[27] Gould, op. cit., 211-212.

to bring back the raw material of detached, objective observations from which theories are made.

The discoveries of June, Rawson, Petersen and Von der Wall in the tractor trip across the previously untraveled ice of Scott Land to Marie Byrd Land forged two new links in the chain of evidence. First, the Edsel Ford Range, instead of bearing south, appeared rather to stream off to the northeast. Mt. Grace McKinley, they reported, was the southwestern anchor of the western front range. Secondly, the new elevated plateau appeared to roll to the south and southeast. From the peak the tractor party's range of vision was possibly 50 miles. Hence, new questions were excited. How far south then, does this plateau extend? Does it roll to the foot of the Queen Maud Range? Does it destroy the concept of the Ice Strait?

So, the issue, now, was sharply drawn. If the Great Ice Strait existed, it must of necessity debouch somewhere through that 517-mile gap of unknown along the 147th meridian between Mt. Grace McKinley, anchor peak of the Edsel Ford Range, and the loftier masses of the Queen Maud Range.

So, after careful consideration we laid a flight course which would strike in the heart of this gap, and enable us, for all practical purposes, by running north to the Edsel Ford Range, to close the gap from the coast halfway to the Queen Maud Range.

The flight track, as it was planned, roughly described a scalene triangle, with a base line running from Little America to Mt. Grace McKinley, and the apex resting at Lat. 81° S., Long. 147° W., the latter serving as the halfway point.

The discoveries of this first flight would shape the course of the following flights. If low-level barrier ice were found south and east of the new plateau, then subsequent flights within the practical limits of the plane's range, would search out the depression until either its eastern limit was defined, or the direction of the trough affirmed. If the plateau were found to lie between the sea and this halfway point, then the subsequent flights would be launched in an effort to close the gap entirely between this point and the Queen Maud Range.

But you will protest: but here you have a land smothered in ice. Suppose a passage does exist. It would be frozen to the bottom under a heaping mass of ice riveted to the ice cap doming the whole continent. How, then, from an airplane could you expect to isolate and define an Ice Strait from an immense and anonymous sheet of ice?

The answer is: we purposed to *sound* all doubtful areas with the plane's altimeter, and delicate barograph brushing low over the ice to get the elevation as registered by barometric pressure.

Which must instantly excite the second protest: but even so! Granted you find a significant area of low elevation. But what more will it be than *ice* elevation? The thickness of the continental ice cap is absolutely unknown; estimates run from a few hundred to several thousand feet.

How then could you possibly tell whether or not you merely have, at low elevations, just a thin veneering of ice over land above sea-level, or a deep heaping of ice over land well below sea-level?

The answer to the second question is: from the seismic soundings which Morgan would take on his journey, together with those Poulter would take roundabout Little America, we hoped to be able to determine something about the thickness of the Antarctic ice cap and of the shelf ice (that is, ice over water). This data would be a pretty good check against altimeter determinations. Let's put it this way: if, for example, the altimeter showed the ice elevation of a region to be 1,200 feet above sea level, and Morgan's soundings showed an ice thickness of 400 feet generally prevailing at such an elevation, we could be pretty sure that the land underneath was about 800 feet above sea level. The altimeter soundings would also indicate where the step gradients were, thus indicating the junction points of shelf ice and upthrusting shoals. In fact, thanks to the tractor party's change of course, we were to have as well a series of seismic soundings and a continuous set of elevations by aneroid across part of the crucial area.

Anyhow, there was the problem, and we were eager to try our hand at solving it. My deepest interest has always lain in exploring from the air. A successful flight would polarize the problem of the strait, but I was counting on the data of the other field parties. Remember, at this period as aviation made ready, we had three parties running toward strategic areas—the Marie Byrd Land Party headed eastward for a geological reconnoissance of the Edsel Ford Range, the Geological Party headed on a similar mission toward the Queen Mauds, and the tractor and plateau party, for reasons which shall be explained shortly, on the verge of making a shift to the new plateau, thus giving us three main units engaged in a flanking attack on the same broad sector. On the evidence accumulated by these three units, together with the discoveries by flight, we would rest our case for or against the Great Ice Strait.

IV

All through the cold and drift of October, Bowlin, Swan, Smith, Skinner and Dustin (the latter having been assigned to aviation as apprentice mechanic) strove steadily to put the *William Horlick* in shape for flight. Much of the mechanical overhaul had been done during the winter night, but a long, lingering, painful process was the job of patching the rents in the fabric. After the plane was dug out of its winter hangar, an inspection revealed some forty tears in the fabric sheathing the wings and fuselage, almost entirely caused by picks and shovels. Each of these rents had to be patched and sewn together, then doped to draw the surfaces together, taut and smooth.

"Doping" was a mean business. Airplane dope, in order to dry properly, should be applied and dried in quiet air with a constant temperature of 80°. Usually it's done in a closed hangar or factory. Well, the aviators had neither; and as for temperature, they started their patching at —60°. They had the sailmaker sew together a small windproof tent, which fitted quite snugly over that part of the wing on which they worked. For heat they used two big blow torches. Dope has a high, sweet, sickening stench; it used to give the men headaches and make them sick. I remember once seeing Smith on his hands and knees, with his head stuck out from under the flap, gulping in deep breaths of fresh air. The part of him that stuck out of the tent at that moment, I reflected, was in air —50° cold: his stern sheets in air +80° warm—a swing of 130°. While the torches were on, one man always stood in the tent, lest the plane catch on fire.

In patching the holes on the under side of the upper wing they had a peculiar problem which they solved quite cleverly. There seemed to be no way of using the tent; but, after much head-scratching, Bowlin and Swan finally hit upon the idea of making a long, draping skirt which could be tied around the waist of the man doing the patching and drying. With this thing around him, one of them would mount a platform, take a position under a rent: then the hem of the skirt would be passed over his head and lashed with long cords around the leading and trailing edge of the wing. He had a 500-watt electric lamp on a long cord running to the Kohler plant with which he dried the dope after it was applied. It couldn't have been very pleasant standing on that precarious platform, with your head as in a sack, not able to move, the hot, sickly smell of the dope rising in the nostrils, and the feet freezing from standing long in the same spot. That's the sort of quiet, self-effacing effort I had in mind when, earlier in this chapter, I mentioned the myriads of small, inconspicuous labors that go beforehand into the making of a spectacular journey, or a flight of discovery.

These repairs took a long time, the more so because, as Bowlin said, the slightest wind seemed to suck the hot air out of the heating tent and render proper drying impossible. Another thing: Swan, after examining the rigging and control wires, found that the aileron wire passing through the wing between the ailerons, was badly frayed, probably on account of the beating the ailerons took during the storms aboard the *Ruppert.* This wire had to be renewed, which involved opening up the wing fabric.

On October 26th—the day after the tractors departed—the *William Horlick* was finally ready and conditions were agreeable for flying. In the morning, immediately after breakfast, Noville led a squad out to dig out the plane, which the recent blizzards had again buried almost to the lower wings. The day was sunny and clear, with a temperature of —30°, and a light southwesterly breeze. After the plane came out of the pit, a two-foot rent in the fabric which had escaped notice was found under the lower wing. It took an hour or so to repair it; so it was mid-afternoon before the plane could be flown.

The flight was a routine test flight—a test for alignment, stability, control, engine performance and instruments. For two hours and twenty minutes, June and Bowlin put it through its paces, maneuvering it into heavy turns, flying "hands off" to see how quickly it returned to trim, and dropping for hard landings to test the staunchness of the ski pedestals and landing gear. Swan, as airplane constructor, was aboard to observe rigging and wires for tautness and vibration. So were Rawson and Bailey, the former to calibrate the compasses and the latter to test the radio installation. The flight was made with two-thirds of a full load. June, on landing, said that the ship, except for a final inspection of all wires, a top-overhaul of the engines and a general tuning up, was ready to go.

Well, that would depend upon weather.

That after both the *William Horlick* and the Pilgrim, which Smith also had aloft on a brief test flight, were secured on the Raymond Fosdick Flying Field—a flat stretch of barrier surface on the south shore of Ver-Sur-Mer Inlet, about 200 yards southwest of the camp. The surface thereabouts was flatter, with a long run in any direction for a take-off with heavy loads.

The flight had its amusing side. For the compass calibration tests, Rawson and Black had earlier laid out on the ground various courses, marked by beacons, over which the ship was to be flown when there was no wind to cause drift. Rawson, puzzled by the eccentric behavior of the compasses, suddenly asked Bailey if, by any chance, he had any iron tools in his pocket. Bailey had been moving about, checking the radio installation. Rawson was appalled to see the radio man produce, in quick succession, a monkey wrench, two pliers, and a screw driver, all highly magnetized from being used on electro-magnetic devices.

V

In October the hints of summer were multiplying on the frosty air. On the 22nd the sun became the Midnight Sun by the simple process of ceasing to dip below the horizon, the beginning of four months of continuous daylight. On clear days, when the air would fill with ice crystals, there would sometimes occur exquisite haloes of the sun.

More and more seals were appearing near the edge of the pressure as the pregnant Weddells, dreading the pursuit of Killer Whales, worked in under the basement of the ice in the Bay of Whales and came into the rookery to bear their young. The biologists—Lindsey, Dr. Perkins and Sterrett—spent most of their time on the Bay, taking notes on the returning life. On the 15th Lindsey was delighted to find the first two Weddell pups on the ice, apparently just born. They were drawn up on the lee side of their mothers' bulging bodies. From that day on the pups arrived fast; in a month there were three hundred seals, with their young, just beyond Ver-Sur-Mer Inlet. Perkins used to welcome visitors with a grand gesture of the hand; "The maternity ward, gentlemen, extends for the next two miles to the left."

Lindsey and Sterrett, assisted by Bob Young, were kept pretty busy weighing in the new arrivals and keeping track of their growth and habits. Weighing the pups was a very serious business with the biologists, and very annoying to the seals. The pups weighed from 57 to 85 pounds at birth, so the biologists had certain practical difficulties in getting a wiggly, squirming, shapeless, furry thing that size onto a set of scales slung from a rickety tripod, especially with a belligerent mother crashing around in the neighborhood. After a while, the biologists reduced it to a system. While Young engaged the mother from behind, shouting and yelling and brandishing a ski pole, Sterrett, the instant her attention was distracted, would shove the pup into a sack, and try to get it on and off the scales (with Lindsey meanwhile taking rapid notes on the weight, moult and dental development) before the mother noticed the disappearance of her offspring. But it wasn't always carried off quite so smartly. Sometimes a shrewder Weddell would suspect what was going on behind her back, and wheel suddenly, trumpeting like a bull elephant. With half a ton of enraged motherhood bearing down upon them, the biologists were quick to drop the torch of science (and the pup, to boot) and take to their heels. However, Weddell seals, according to the biologists, are pretty dumb. So long as they actually see their pup in jeopardy, they'll put up a vicious defense; but the chances are the moment their attention is distracted they promptly forget all about it and, with the first quiet, slump into a profound sleep. In order to keep track of the seals and to collect data on their rate of growth, dental development and the moulting of the young, the biologists marked some 250 and periodically took a census of the Bay.

With this brood to watch the biologists had their hands full. In fact, after October they practically lived down on the Bay. The pups were constantly interesting. They grow extraordinarily fast. Some that Lindsey marked weighed 260 pounds a month after birth. They commence to moult within a fortnight; the soft buffy wool falls out in great patches and they soon look like something the moths got at. They seem to take to the water quite handily, though sometimes you'll see a mother gently hustle a timid pup in, or else, if she is in an especially whimsical mood, seize him by the scruff of the neck and pull him in. Just a matter of breaking the ice, as it were. As a rule, Junior got his (or her) first ducking in a pool of slush ice near the pressure ice, where the mother could either break through the thin crust or else saw a place open with her teeth, using vigorous sidewise strokes of the head. Ordinarily, Lindsey said, they didn't enter the water before they were two or three weeks old, but some were swimming eight days after birth. Not until the ice started to break up in January did they start retreating into the pressure; in a certain staid and unimaginative way, they seemed to fall into routine like the rest of us, using the same old exits through the ice.

On October 22nd Lindsey and Moody traveled with a dog team to the mouth of the Bay, in the hope of finding an early penguin. Stopped by a belt of pressure ice near West Cape, they tethered the sledge and went ahead on foot. Though the day was otherwise dead clear, thick clouds of sea smoke lay over the mouth of the Bay. Walking through this pall they came suddenly upon a colony of 47 seals, huddled together in the lee of the barrier, sheltered from the wind. Of these 25 were males and 18 were females, none of the latter, curiously, either pregnant or with pups. Just beyond where they lay, so far as Lindsey could tell in the fog, was a broad open lead; and it was thought that the pregnant seals had come in under the bay ice, so far as they could, to gain the surface through a vent and there calve their young, knowing that the Killer Whale, which shuns fast ice, would not pursue them. All the bulls he saw were battered and bleeding from numerous wounds, with shallow, raking gashes in their sides and mangled flippers.

All along the east Barrier wall the ice was in the process of change; the sloping angles of ice foot, built up by the accumulation of drift during the winter, were breaking away at the Barrier crest, leaving steadily widening crevasses as the ice foot crumpled, buckled, or slumped under the bay ice. The pressure, too, was molding, intruding steadily into the mouth of Ver-Sur-Mer Inlet; and the skiers were hard-pressed for a decent place for down-hill running. The first Fulmar was seen in arrow-like flight through sea smoke on October 22nd.

Still, it was hardly summer weather. Though the maximum temperatures were getting higher, the minima were rather chilly. Beginning October 19th, the latter registered, on consecutive days: —47°, —46°, —45°, —30°, —38°, —31°, —12°, —30°, —38°, —42, —17°, —32°, —33°. On the 28th we had a heavy blizzard, with a wind velocity approaching 50 miles. But when the Condor was dug out on the 26th, with the temperature —30°, I saw Bob Young and several others stripped bare to the waist, all complaining of the heat, though the breath freezing on their whiskers had formed miniature ice falls. Still, summer was on the way.

Chapter XIV

PAST THE RIM OF DISCOVERY

I

ON October 31st the Geological and Plateau Parties, running south well ahead of the tractors, drew near the fateful crevasses lying between the 81st and 82nd parallels. Over their fixed radio schedule,[1] just before they shoved off for the day's march, they advised:

> Now 192 miles . . . dogs doing fine but getting thin from cold . . . turned south at 159.5 [2]. . . pressure showing in mirage to west. Nothing showing ahead . . . all well but thoroughly blistered.

Since leaving Advance Base on the 25th they had sledged in temperatures averaging about —30°, and often dropping to —45°. At Advance Base they had increased their loads 1,600 pounds between them; the heavier loads and the soft, deep snow of the central Barrier taxed the dogs.

No word came that day from the tractors, which the day before, having taken aboard the fuel and rations cached there, had put out from Advance Base. Reaching the Base on the 28th, Demas, Hill and Waite had spent two days overhauling the cars, taking up the bearings.

November 1st would tell the tale. With some misgivings I awaited the next report from the southern parties. Dyer was up at 7 o'clock for the radio schedules.

At 7:30 A.M. Wade of Siple's party reported in from the high dome of the new plateau:

> Camped 195.5 (miles) good surface, altitude 4,000 feet . . . excellent visibility. . . .

Paine checked in for both Southern parties on the dot at 8 o'clock, reporting they were encamped at Lat. 81° 22′ S., Long. 161° 24′ W., about 209 miles south of Little America (see map). Between 199 and 202 miles, Blackburn advised, they passed a three-mile belt of crevasses, most of them small cracks, but with several open fractures 30

[1] Every party had a fixed radio schedule. The Marie Byrd Land Party reported in at 7:30 A.M. on Tuesday, Thursday and Saturday; the Geological Party at 7:30 A.M. on Monday, Wednesday and Friday; the Tractor Party twice daily at 8:30 A.M. and 6:30 P.M. All parties, of course, were familiar with these schedules and were therefore sure of being able to contact the main base at least twice a day in case of emergency.

[2] This was the site of the Beacon which will hereafter be identified as 159 (geographical) Mile Depot (173 statute miles).

feet or more across. If the drivers exercised great care and prudence, he thought the tractors could pass through. He had marked a trail with flags, detouring around the worst holes.

Encouraging, but mention of 30-foot crevasses wasn't exactly tranquillizing. I asked both parties to remain in their present position till noon, pending word from the tractors, which again failed to make contact.

Another schedule at noon. Paine advised:

> No tractors in sight. Have built high beacon. Shall we go back to crevasses?

A good suggestion. Russell and Paine, presently followed by Blackburn, left with their teams to await the tractors' arrival on the other side of the crevassed area. The Plateau Party remained in camp at 209.

At 6 P.M. that evening the first blow. Waite of the tractor party came in on schedule:

> Sorry missed sked last night—watch broke—now at 193 . . . one machine in process of being pulled out of crevasse—dog teams now approaching. More later.

An hour later a second message:

> Paine, Russell and Blackburn report impossibility of going ahead with the tractors. Dog teams no use on these blind crevasses . . . tractor is safe but we think we better go to 180 (miles) then east. . . .
>
> Demas

Even from this meager report we had a pretty fair idea of what had happened. The dog teams in advance reported good surface up to 199, then a three mile belt. Yet here was Demas bogged down at 193, five miles away from the main belt, manifestly so thoroughly stymied that he saw no alternative but to retreat 13 miles and try a new attack farther to the east.

Blind crevasses—that is to say, crevasses roofed over with thin snow bridges, often so smoothly knit that the keenest eye can't mark the tell-tale shadowy hollowing—had safely passed the dog teams, which crossed all unsuspecting, then had dropped under the heavier tractors. This was the meaning behind Demas's reference to dog teams being useless for reconnoitering a tractor trail. It only confirmed what we had so painfully learned in the fall journeys.

Later on, we learned exactly what had happened. In low gear the two tractors, one about 200 yards behind the other, crunched south in pursuit of the dog teams. Hill and Waite were ahead in No. 3. The surface seemed perfectly safe. With no warning whatever the car sagged sharply, and from underneath welled up the awesome sound of tons of snow breaking and streaming into great depths. Without knowing why he did it, Hill jammed on the brakes, violating the one law of tractor driving—*speed, full gun* over a crevasse. The act saved the car, and perhaps themselves from serious injury. The car sprawled cater-cornered over a ragged fracture, supported only by the port rear tread and the starboard front ski. The car was well down by the starboard tread, with the body jammed hard against the crevasse wall. Neither Hill nor Waite had had time to get the doors open.

Fortunately, about ten feet down the walls of the crevasse pinched together; by making a foundation of snow blocks they were able to shovel in snow to make a surface for the treads. In the middle of this task the Geological Party, which had started back to look for them, arrived. The instant the sledgers saw what had befallen the tractors on surface they had appraised as solid, they realized Demas had absolutely no hope of penetrating the main belt of crevasses five miles on. The wisdom of that judgment was presently shown. Rethreading the belt next day, Bramhall had the experience of seeing a blind crevasse collapse a second after it had passed him, the dogs and the lead sledge. The trailer, with about 500 pounds of dog food on it, crashed through and hung vertically. The combined efforts of four men were required to salvage it. The hole was 100 feet deep and six feet across.

Next morning—November 2nd—from the tractor:

> We consider it best plan for all concerned to have all dog teams and tractors return to 159-Mile Depot and proceed 10 miles east then head for point 10 miles north of Leverett Glacier. We feel that all men and dog power should be with tractors till we are clear of crevasses. Dog teams are not much use for finding blind crevasses. The bridges have a hard crust which the machines break through. We feel, however, that we can find a way through them and all parties should be together. . . . This will enable the dog teams, if tractors cannot get thru, to devise plan and distribute weights so as to continue themselves, save time and prevent unnecessary chances. Please ask Morgan return to this point, bringing everything Geological Party left behind and all flags on trail. . . .
>
> Blackburn-Demas

Since the future career of both parties, the Plateau Party's irretrievably and the Geological Party's in a minor degree, depended upon the ability of the tractors to make a break-through, this suggestion of keeping all three units together through the critical period impending seemed prudent. The Plateau Party was still camped on the far side of the crevasses, 14 miles farther south. Ronne, radio operator for the party, was listening in on all the schedules. A message was immediately dispatched to Morgan and Bramhall, acquainting them with the situation and recommending their return to the tractor. They started back immediately, Waite announcing their arrival at 6 o'clock that evening. If I seem to be tediously detailed, it is partly because I wish to illuminate the peculiar perils and difficulties that attended this enterprise, to show how desperately the tractors tried to break past that terrible obstacle, and also to show how with radio a leader could follow and take part in the remote problems of scattered units.

That evening, when the parties were again united, I sent the following message:

> Blackburn, Demas, Bramhall, Morgan:
> If tractors try to go through any crevassed area, do not take unreasonable risks with personnel. Take time calmly to think things out. You have come to one of those situations which arise in Antarctic where the medicine called for is patience.... Good luck.

On the morning of the 3rd—the same day Siple reported his successful arrival at Mt. Grace McKinley and the commencement of his field work—the Southern parties, 10 men, 2 tractors and 9 teams, retreated 8 miles to 159-Mile beacon, where now they headed southeast, hoping to find a passage about 10 miles east of where the cars first came to grief:

> *Nov. 3, 7:30 P.M.*
> On trail at 171 Miles.[8] Course 135°. Camping at 201 Miles tonight and proceeding with dog teams again tomorrow.... Three teams lead tractors and three follow. No sign crevasses so far. Regards.
>
> Demas

But the signs, though unseen, were present. The objective of 201 miles was never reached. Fourteen miles out of 159-Mile beacon, at Lat. 81° 09′ S., Long. 161° 07′ W.—(the 173-Mile beacon).

> *Nov. 4, 6 P.M.*
> Stopped after cracking numerous small crevasses and seeing evidences of many large ones last night. Two parties reconnoitering today. Geo. Party just returned, reports southeastern area impassable by tractor. More news 9 P.M. Regards.
>
> Demas
>
> *Nov. 4, 9:10 P.M.*
> Report Demas western party indicates no chance of tractors getting thru between old and present trail. Sked at 11 P.M. Regards
>
> Trail Parties
>
> *Nov. 4, 11 P.M.*
> Passage impossible here and crevasse looming indicates they continue eastward....
>
> Morgan-Bramhall-Demas

[8] These are not airline distances from Little America but the reading of the sledgemeter. The various backtrackings, etc., must be borne in mind to keep track of their movements on the map.

The tractors were again completely blocked, on the threshold of the area we had feared from the beginning. I shall reconstruct the situation as it was revealed in subsequent messages and the final reports of the parties.

On the night of the 3rd, an hour or so after Demas had advised all clear ahead, fresh misfortunes beset them. Every few yards the tractors broke through crevasses that had safely passed the dog teams. Most of the breaks were narrow, just two or three feet across. The cars would sag, thump down aft as the treads broke through, then slowly crawl out, caterpillar-like, while the dog teams hovered round. Luckily the fractures lay at right angles to their course, so that the drivers could carry them head-on, always the safest approach.

Nevertheless they resolved to push ahead, though the *looming* of pressure, a queer refraction phenomenon which usually means trouble ahead, was visible in all directions, a glassy horizon of broken, upheaved ice hemming them in. Demas's car was in the lead, and Ronne and Eilefsen, with two teams, were in escort ahead and astern. A blind crevasse let go under Demas's treads. As the car tilted back, Demas opened the throttle wide. Just enough of the treads clung to the front wall to give him traction. For a second or two the treads spun uselessly; then the car inched forward and righted itself. Ronne and Eilefsen said they just stood and held their breath. "That made three of us," Demas added quietly. Ronne went back to look down the hole. It was, so far as he could see, bottomless and wide enough to take the tractor bodily. Another foot and the car would have been lost.

The dog teams returned with the news that dead ahead the crevasses were broader and much more dangerous.

So they made camp and, after conferring over the evening hoosh, decided to divide into two parties in the morning and explore for a passage east and west of their position. The results of that all-day search were summarized in the messages of the 4th. Teams and men roped together in single file with 60-foot lengths of alpine rope, Blackburn, Eilefsen and Paine searched out the crevasses eight miles to southeast and east. Similarly roped together, Demas, Russell and Ronne traveled eight miles to the west, feeling out the area between them and the first position on the 161st meridian. There was no loophole. Ten miles wide, an inchoate pattern of slithering furrows ten stories deep, with the domed tops of haycocks rising everywhere like monstrous pimples, the belt stood them off. Some of the open holes, Eilefsen said with awe, were big enough to swallow all the dogs, the men, and the tractors in Little America. There was a constant hollow drumming under the runners, a soft swishing of ice crystals swirling into great depths, as they worked into the area. Once while he waited for Ronne, Russell idly picked at the surface of the snow with the point of a ski pole. The pole broke through, and Russell jumped back.

Ronne came along and jabbed open the hole with his pole. The whole bridge collapsed; where Russell and his team had been standing was a 5-foot hole, sheer blue walls slanting into incalculable depths.

Now the question was—for the discouraged men grouped around Waite's radio set as well as for the men gathered around Dyer's receiver at Little America—what next?

There was utterly no hope to the westward. And the only chance of making a break-through to the eastward lay in withdrawing, as they had done before, to 159-Mile beacon, then making another long easting into the unknown.

It would have taken time—several days—and there was no assurance even then of getting through. The belt, so far as they could tell, seemed to trend east-northeast by west-southwest. Time was pressing. Field schedules called for the arrival of both parties at the foot of the Queen Maud Range 29 days out of Little America. 19 days were gone: only 10 days remained to travel 293 miles. Eastward the Barrier was entirely unknown. They were already 30 miles east of Amundsen's route and the route of the southern party of the first expedition.

All day November 5th the frosty air was agitated with messages flying between these units and Little America. On one point—the imprudence of wasting more time searching for a passage—agreement instantly crystallized. The Geological Party had to be detached at once, or else its mission would be jeopardized. There was only the problem in its case of borrowing support to lay down food depots to 300 (345 statute) miles. The Plateau Party, on the other hand, was in exactly the box we had feared.

The first thought of Morgan and Bramhall, whose hopes and ambitions were still set on seismic and magnetic reconnoissance on the polar plateau, was to cut loose from the tractors with their four teams and push on to the mountains. Morgan wanted to leave his seismic apparatus with the tractors, which on their own hook would endeavor to worry through farther to the east. If the tractors failed, Morgan thought the geological work he was capable of carrying out on the mountains west of Blackburn's survey would make up for the wiping out of the seismic program. It was proposed that the dog teams take aboard all supplies required to provision them beyond 300-Mile Depot, leaving the rest to be relayed beyond their present position to the Depot either by airplane or by reviving Captain Innes-Taylor's Supporting Party.

One of my firm principles of field operations is never to attempt to run a remote field party by radio. Nowhere in the world can a mere desk director, telling distant parties how to operate in the form of rigid orders, contrive more mischief and perplexity than in the polar regions. The conditions encountered in the unknown are so novel, and so subtly involved with incalculable factors of human safety, that the judgment of the man on the spot must always be weighed with the greatest respect and consideration. In this particular instance, holding as it did the fate of three of our most valuable scientific missions, I tried to heed that rule. Besides, I had full confidence in my party leaders. For the most effective gain to the scientific program which could be had from the reorganization of the parties, I left it with the party leaders to work out with their chief, Dr. Poulter, senior scientist. For a recalculation of food and support requirements, I left it with them and Captain Innes-Taylor, who, as chief of trail operations, knew these requirements better than any one else.

In Dr. Poulter's judgment, the flaw in the Plateau Party's proposal to cast off from the tractors was the obvious penalty of sacrificing the seismic field program if the tractors failed to get through behind the dog teams. I seriously doubted that they would. Dr. Poulter was counting heavily on the seismic data. His own experimental soundings in the vicinity of Little America had been very successful. A line of soundings in the interior, he thought, might turn out to be one of the finest contributions of the expedition. His idea was that the Plateau Party would profit most in the end by consolidating its forces with the tractors and prosecuting its seismic and magnetic research on the new plateau to the eastward.

With this idea I was in complete accord. You will recall the earlier discussion of the Ice Strait and the alternative objective therein presented to the Plateau Party. Well, that alternative was again available. Moreover, the crevasses which had stopped them, the breadth and length of the disturbances, together with its seeming folding back to north-northeast, were themselves of significant geographical value. Why this broad belt of disturbance across the heart of the Barrier? Creeping ice riding over land, most probably. But how deep was the ice? Was the land above or below sea level? Folding to the northeast, could it possibly mark the western frontier of the new plateau and, correspondingly, the still undiscovered shore line of the Ross Ice Barrier and the Ross Sea which flowed under it? Not far to the southeast was the "appearance of land" that Amundsen had reported, which we had failed to find in 1929. All these matters had a bearing on the Secret of the Strait. Morgan's seismic apparatus, tapping the ice cap, could explore this area as could no other instrument. With any sort of luck at all, he and Bramhall were in a strategic position to convert a defeat into an attack of first-class importance.

In accordance with my determination not to be a desk director, I embodied these ideas, as suggestions, which were transmitted to the field parties, which, after some discussion, accepted them. Reorganization of the parties and a redistribution of loads and dogs proceeded on the spot. The Geological Party remained intact, but Ronne and Eilefsen, with their teams, were attached as support, to

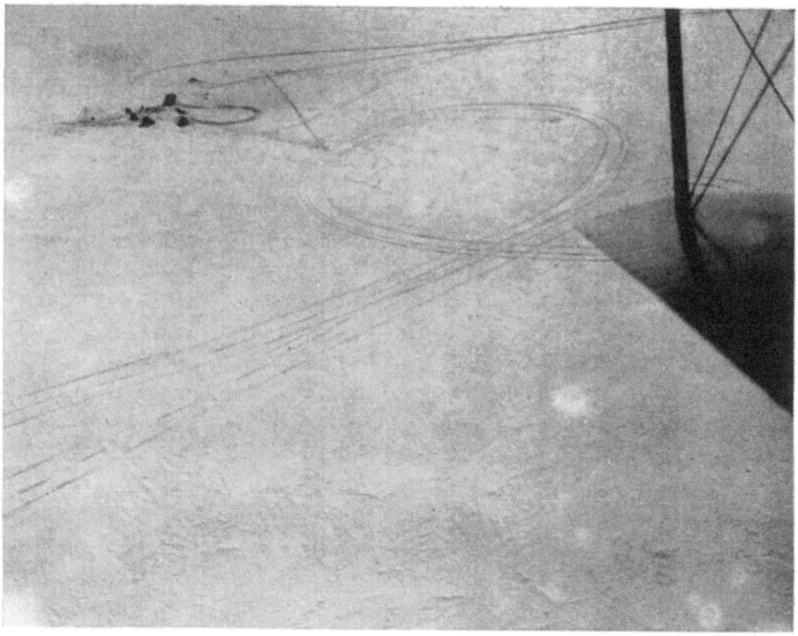

(Photograph by Carl A. Petersen)

THE PLANE VISITS THE TRACTORS

HAROLD I. JUNE, CHIEF PILOT

SNARED

HEATING THE MOTORS

(Photographs by Joseph A. Pelter)

THE RADIO STAFF—BAILEY, WAITE, DYER, HUTCHESON

lay down ration depots between that position and 300-Mile Depot.[4] Morgan's and Bramhall's dogs were absorbed by the Geological Party, Blackburn taking one team and the other being divided all around among the drivers, giving four 11-dog teams and one 10-dog team. The loads per team averaged about a thousand pounds. Though the Geological Party had generously offered to ferry him and his magnetic apparatus south, Bramhall ultimately decided to cast in his lot with the tractors. Besides his magnetic research, he would act as navigator for the new party. Accurate fixes of position were important to Morgan's soundings.

On November 6th the reorganized parties separated. The Geological Party, with its support, struggled through the crevasses, bearing 2.3 miles on a southeasterly course, then 4.7 miles due south. "Dogs all in," they reported. "Got through crevassed area extending about 6 miles OK, but worse here than where we crossed before. Loads very heavy." As soon as the Geological Party was safely through the two tractors commenced the retreat to 159-Mile Depot whence, on an easterly heading, a third attempt would be made to break through the crevasses. By taking aboard the gas he had previously cached at the Depot, Demas still had enough gas to fuel both cars 200 miles. If he started to run short, he could still abandon one.[5]

II

Meanwhile aviation waited for weather to fly.

Smith tuned up the Pilgrim for a cosmic ray hop to a high altitude. the final step in this particular research. It will be remembered, from the earlier discussion of cosmic ray observations at Little America, that Bramhall had turned to such a flight as an alternative when the practical difficulties of transporting equipment necessitated the cancellation of his project to take cosmic ray observations on the Polar Plateau. For observational purposes approximately the same results, he hoped, could be had at a 12,000 foot altitude over Little America.

With Bramhall on the trail, Zuhn took over preparations for the flight. He, Dr. Poulter and Boyd worked a long time to overcome

[4] Borrowing from the Plateau Party's stores the following depots were put down by the Supporting Party: 173-Mile Depot: 81 lbs. dog food, 2 gals. fuel, 1 30-day rations. 200-Mile Depot: 27 lbs. dog food. 250-Mile Depot: 1 gal. fuel, otherwise same as 173-Mile Depot. At 300 the Supporting Party turned over the balance of its loads, giving the main party a total of 1,440 lbs. of man food and 450 lbs. of dog food for the rest of its operation from this Depot.

[5] On account of the small scale of the map, it was impossible to show in complete detail the tracks of the parties. For instance, the return of the tractors, to the 159-Mile Depot, is not indicated, and their easting is not shown until they are east of the longitude of the 173-Mile Depot.

certain practical difficulties. To damp the vibration of the plane a bedding of soft felt was laid on the deck of the cabin for the apparatus, which was bolted in place. An electric heater was constructed to keep the instrument warm, and chemical heating pads were to be packed around the batteries operating it to keep them from freezing. The problem of bringing the instrument first within and then without the influence of the radium standard they solved by imprisoning the radium capsule in a small brass cylinder which could be lowered 125 feet below the plane by means of a fisherman's reel borrowed from the biologists.

November 2nd was clear. Clear long enough to allow June to get the Condor off on two brief test and photographic hops over the Bay of Whales. It was being gassed for the first main flight and Smith was getting ready to take off on the cosmic ray flight when the sky clouded over.

And clouded it remained till November 15th.

Weather is simultaneously the greatest hazard and the greatest obstacle to flying in the polar regions. Most of all it is an obstacle. Day after day of waiting, day after day of intransigent cloudiness, low stratus clouds packed solidly 500 feet or so overhead, no horizon, just a meaningless fuzzy blur in all directions. Flying in that stuff, I once observed, was like flying in a bowl of milk. Occasionally one gets caught in it on a long flight; but no one in his right senses would deliberately take off in it. The soft gray rolls of the Barrier melt meaninglessly into the gray roof of the sky; there is nothing to mark the joining; even with a mile visibility, in that suffocated perspective a pilot, flying low, could crash into a hill and never know what hit him. Men running on skis are bewildered and confused by the shapeless aspect of things before them.

And so you wait, hopelessly consulting a sky that seems to be pressing down upon your temples. The twenty-four hours of daylight make the waiting seem all the longer. You can't imagine how discouraging it is to poke your head out the hatch, no matter what the hour, and find the world exactly as it has been for days, with no outward evidence of growth or change, no sign of waxing or waning—nothing but an accretion of unprofitable hours. Sometimes a hole will appear, patches of deep blue sky bursting through the gray; and just when your hopes rise the holes will close as rapidly as they appeared. It is amazing how swiftly conditions will change, under certain conditions of wind. I have seen an utterly solid clouded sky dissolve and become crystal clear in less than half an hour, and clear skies become impenetrable masses of black billowy clouds in the same time. That's why, in waiting for a flight, you must be on your toes to seize the break the instant it appears and ram through the flight with all possible dispatch, lest the opportunity vanish entirely or the return be jeopardized by a change for the worse. When Bill Haines, after plotting his weather data, gave the word to go, the pilots could be fairly certain of 12 hours of stable weather; after that, it was in the laps of the gods. I have never known Bill to be very far wrong. Wise in the ways of Antarctic weather and knowing the hazards of flying, having for years plotted weather conditions for air mail pilots over the Alleghany Hell Stretch, Bill was always prudent, deliberate and patient. Being a meteorologist, he accepted weather as a dictator whose whims and caprices he questioned but respected. Bill took nothing for granted, and in a camp where everything was hurry and push, he alone, blandly indifferent to his nickname *Cyclone,* lived in a state of profound mental calm. If the aviators were irked or made despondent, he would say: "Well, you can't push Nature around." With Haines the right weather was a mathematical equation. When it proved, he would come in, as he always does, with a report written in a neat and bookish hand, stocking cap cocked on one side of his head and a quiet smile in his eyes that was always infectious. If conditions were just about ideal, he might yield enough to his inner enthusiasm to say rashly, "It looks pretty good now. Don't know how long it will last, but if you get off fast I think you can squeeze one in." Bill never rushed the weather: he never let it rush him.

Throughout this period, pilot balloon runs, which were entirely for meteorological research, took on an immense practical significance. They were the only reliable method of forecasting weather for flights. The barometer, ordinarily the best tell-tale in lower latitudes, was not so useful in the south polar regions. Drops in pressure as violent as half an inch or more in twelve hours on one occasion would bring clouds and wind, on the next clear skies and calm air. The pilot balloon runs, on the other hand, were generally more accurate forecasters. Northerly or easterly currents aloft were warning of low clouds and most likely a blow; southeasterly or south winds aloft ordinarily brought clear skies and stable weather. At the same time the surface weather observations of the field parties, which were routine elements in their radio reports, were carefully studied. Whenever a long flight impended, the parties nearest the plane's track flashed in daily weather reports, and stood by while the plane was in flight. Siple's party and the tractor unit were especially valuable in this connection, as most of the exploratory flights passed through the area in which they were exploring. We were fortunate in having so planned an interlocking series of operations that on nearly every flight the pilots had the benefit of weather information and potential agencies of rescue somewhere near their flight tracks.

Thurs. Nov. 8, 10:20 P.M.

Still overcast, visibility about one mile. Siple this morning reported a blizzard at Mt. Grace McKinley. No word from the tractor party....

But the talk of the camp is John Herrmann's adventures in the purlieus of Little America. Having within the past month gotten lost, and on another occasion ripped open his hand with a can-opener, he again demonstrated the hazards of local exploration by falling into a crevasse at the mouth of Ver-Sur-Mer Inlet which was marked with more warning flags than Main Street on Memorial Day.

Grimminger was telling the story in the galley this afternoon. John and he were skiing along, he said, when suddenly he heard a gasp. He turned around just in time to see a flurry of snow and the cameraman sinking by the stern. A moment later, John was at the bottom of a sheer-walled 12-foot crevasse, trying to get upright, and not succeeding very well, according to Grimminger, on account of his skis being wrapped around his neck.

"By the way," said Grimminger, putting down his coffee cup, "has anybody got a rope handy?"

"Why do you want a rope?" asked Noville. "To hang him with before he kills himself?"

"Well, it's like this," Grimminger drawled. "He's still down there."

Fri., Nov. 9, 10 P.M.

Still overcast. Temp. —18° this morning, but rose to +4° during the day.

McCormick got up last night—the first time he's left the bunk since he crashed. Looked quite well. It's splendid the way the boy stood up under the ordeal. Never lost his cheerfulness, never complained. And I'm grateful to Bowlin for helping him along.

Lindsey has sighted the first skua gulls of the season—three of them in flight over the pressure at the foot of Ver-Sur-Mer Inlet.

Sat., Nov. 10, 11:10 P.M.

And still overcast. Siple, who this morning advised he was starting eastward toward the unpenetrated front range of the Edsel Fords, reported temp. zero, wind E 15, barometer 26.10, slightly cloudy. Tractor party said tempt. —8°, wind SE 8, barometer 28.08, visibility fair, partly overcast.

For a few hours today it looked as if it might clear up. The sky actually drained very rapidly, but soon black clouds crept over the western horizon. Within an hour the air was gray with the same deceptive, engulfing, tantalizing fog.

The camp is inclined to be despondent, but Haines reminded the aviators they "ain't seen nothing yet." In 1929 we had one stretch of 30 cloudy days.

Bill hasn't been able to get any decent balloon runs lately, on account of low banks of stratus clouds. Judging by the short runs, the upper winds for the past week seem generally to have been easterly and northerly winds of low velocity, between 15 and 20 miles per hour.

Bill remarked today that a principal reason for the uncertainty of the weather is that November is a period of transition. In this month the barometric pressure, after falling to a low in October, commences to rise rapidly. This was evident in the meteorological records of Amundsen's expedition, the British expeditions at McMurdo Sound, and the records of our first expedition. One of the reasons for the constant cloudiness is that the temperature on the ice cap in the interior, benefiting by the southward swing of the sun, is going up and up, gradually overcoming the tremendous temperature differential that exists between high and low latitudes during the winter months. Temperature gradients give rise to wind: and as the temperatures in these regions tend to equalize over large areas there is less wind, less of the robust inpourings and outpourings that clear the skies. The prevailing summer winds are light northerly and easterly winds, warm winds which bring fog and cloudiness....

Sun., Nov. 11, 9:45 P.M.

Clear today, and many alarums and excursions, but nothing accomplished. Too much wind at first, and not enough later on. Haines took a balloon run right after breakfast—at the surface the wind was SW, velocity 14 miles. Above the surface the direction was uniformly SSW, rising in velocity to 27 m.p.h. at 700 feet, 38 m.p.h. at 2500 feet, then diminishing steadily to 8 m.p.h. at 15,000 feet. Still, conditions were encouraging enough to prompt us to ask the field parties to stand by for weather bulletins at 10 A.M. When 10 o'clock came the winds aloft had dropped to nothing, and Haines was apprehensive a change for the worse was making. Anyhow, the aviators were greatly disappointed. They had started to warm up the engines when Haines said nothing doing. The memory of the bitter hardships and cold they endured to get the planes ready for early flying must gall them now, when there's nothing to do but twiddle their thumbs or tinker with gadgets that have already met every requirement.

However, with nearly everything else standing still, the scientists are busy. Dr. Poulter and Black are out on seismic soundings every day. They have their apparatus rigged up on a sledge, hauled by dogs, and are running a series of soundings along the Barrier to determine the thickness of the local ice and the depth of the ocean bottom. Poulter is delighted with the way this instrument is working. Too early now for anything but the most general conclusions, but he's confident we're on the right track. In a little while we may have a clew to the mystery of the Ross Ice Barrier.

Dr. Perkins, Sterrett, Dane and Bob Young took leave with two teams for a three day trip into the Bay of Whales. Perkins hopes that somewhere in the pressure he'll be able to find an open crack through which he can let down his plankton net. The substrata of ice buckled under the top layers of new ice, together with the ice crystals welling up, have made it almost impossible for him to sink his net into clear water. Sterrett went along to collect samples of aseptic snow for bacteriological analysis.

It remained for Lindsey to capture the day's honors. He and Young saw and captured the first Emperor penguin of the season, eight days ahead of the earliest arrival recorded for the Bay of Whales. They were on their way to the seal rookery near the pressure when they were brought up short by the trumpet call of an Emperor. They caught sight of her waddling into the pressure toward the seals. Young brought her down with a flying tackle, and Lindsey clamped on a headlock just after she had dealt the British tar a shrewd buffet with the port flipper. It was no way to treat the first lady of the summer, but a biologist inflamed with quest of specimen P-24A is scarcely in a mood for chivalry. Anyhow, the old girl is on exhibit in the Science Hall tonight—63 pounds in all her plumage, a silvery-blue coat, creamy white breast, jet black head and throat, and a splash of orange on the sides of the neck. . . .

Mon., Nov. 12, 10:30 P.M.

. . . Another day of disappointment. Skies miraculously clear here this morning. Marie Byrd Land Party reported fair visibility and .6 cloudiness over the Edsel Fords, and the tractor party, 223 miles south-southeast of Little America, reported good visibility, with but a few clouds. It looked just right. But the morning balloon run showed an unsatisfactory reversal of currents aloft. Haines was uncertain: he recommended getting the planes ready and deferring final decision till the noon weather reports. Both field parties were instructed to stand by and radio weather reports at two hour intervals.

Instantly the camp sprang to the demands that a flight always exacts. Dog teams off to Retreat Camp for gas; a gang to dig out the plane; Swan and Smith rigging heating tents over the engines; Bowlin checking the engines; Rawson working on the charts; Abele, supply officer in Corey's absence, making a check of all emergency gear in the plane.

At 10 o'clock Siple reported good visibility, but drift on the southern horizon. The tractor party reported unlimited ceiling, a slight haze on the horizon. At noon clouds were gathering over the Edsel Fords, and the wind was making. The tractor party, which was lying east of the apex of our triangular course, continued to report unlimited ceiling, good visibility.

Conditions at Little America persisting unchanged, we resolved to fly the southeasten leg of the triangle to Lat. 81° 05′ S., eliminating, if necessary, the northern run to the Edsel Ford Range. There was a chance, Haines said, of being pocketed and perhaps cut off by the disturbance over the mountains. However, since our first objective is about 247 miles south of McKinley, I thought we could chance it.

After a quick luncheon the engines were started and the Condor was taxied out of the pit. The flight crew was just getting aboard when Haines ran up. A mass of clouds was moving in from the west. "Not today," he said. In less than an hour the sky was solidly overcast, the ceiling dropped to a few hundred feet, and visibility shrunk to nothing.

And from the field parties at 4 P.M.—

Marie Byrd Land Party—clouding over, McKinley already in fog. Wind E-15.

Tractor Party—wind E-12 increasing. Viz. 1 mile, thick haze overhead.

It is that easy to get your neck out.

Tues., Nov. 13, 8:25 P.M.

No change. A bit of sun this morning and again this afternoon, but otherwise the same dead grayness.... The local temperature rose to +12°, the highest since October 6th. It is almost uncomfortably muggy.... The tractors are again blocked by crevasses; and Siple advises that having been unable to relay his loads along the front of the range, he is using Corey and Stancliff to relay from the main depot at McKinley....

Wed., Nov. 14, 7 P.M.

And still we wait. For a few hours this morning the sun staved off the cloud wrack. Though conditions were anything but auspicious, Smith warmed up the Pilgrim, thinking that he and Zuhn might be able to sneak in a hop over Little America for cosmic ray observations. Before he could get the plane out of the pit, the skies clouded over again.

Haines' balloon run showed a wind direction of ESE up to 3,000 feet, a shift to NE up to 5,000, then a switch into ESE above 5,000. The clouds, he said, occurred at the layer of shift, as they have in the past. It is curious to watch clouds form under such conditions—first a scattered blossoming, then patches here and there, then a gradual coalescing, then a swift consolidation covering the sky.

Geological Party reports: "18 miles Monday. Tuesday nerve-racking day with wind from SE up to 50 m.p.h. Taking on Supporting Party loads here and Supporting Party turning back. Will continue with 39 dogs, leave 6 at 300 Mile Depot and continue with 3 11-dog teams for 5 days. Figure 10 days to mountains from here. Get time ticks direct now so OK. DR position 300-Mile depot 7 miles from here (Lat.) 83-09, (Long.) 157-06. Finn and Albert (Ronne and Eilefsen, who acted in support) did great work. All well."

III

Shortly after midnight, November 15th, the break came. The clouds vanished as if erased. Fleming, night watchman, who every half hour was supposed to look at the sky, roused Haines and Grimminger. At 4 A.M. they took a balloon run, the most encouraging in a fortnight, a light southwesterly wind at the surface which gradually shifted through south into southeast at 3,000 feet with a velocity of 5 to 10 miles per hour, then above that at 7,000 feet a layer of southeasterly wind increasing in velocity to 35 m.p.h.—headwinds on the outward track, but drying winds, the winds we had been waiting for.

The aviation gang was awakened at once. Bowlin, Swan and Dustin fell to on the *William Horlick*. The heater tents were rigged over the engines, and the blow torches started.

The cosmic ray venture opened the day's flight operations. At 5:54 o'clock in the morning, before breakfast, Smith and Zuhn took off—the first flight of its kind in the south polar regions. Climbing slowly to an altitude of 12,000 feet, Smith held that level for three hours while Zuhn made his observations. They landed at 10:01 o'clock. Zuhn said that everything functioned satisfactorily.[6]

At 6:30 o'clock all hands came piling out of the bunks to stand by for work details in connection with the main flight. Though the temperature was —9°, the air had such a bland warmth to it that the men working were presently stripped to their underwear.

An hour later, the Marie Byrd Land Party, camped 30 miles northeast of Mt. Grace McKinley, reported: "Clouds—none, wind—none, viz.—excellent."

As Wade went off the air, Waite broke in from the south: "Tractor Party WX—temp.—12°, wind S 15, increasing rapidly. Clear, viz unlimited, no clouds, looks good for flight if that wind doesn't bother you."

It wouldn't. Orders were given for a departure as soon as June finished gassing the plane.

This brings up the matter of a decision which I have deferred mentioning here, as I staved it off in my own mind at Little America, until the hour of choice arrived—the decision of whether or not I should fly.

The truth of the matter is, I was still pretty flimsy. Though I had come up a long way from my physical low at Advance Base, I was still far from being well. My whole system was torn to pieces from having been subjected to the poisonous fumes thrown off by the stove for more than half a year; and even in November my muscles seemed to

[6] The final report on cosmic ray observations has not yet been completed; but Zuhn informs me that at this altitude the intensity was 15 times greater than on the surface at Little America, and 8 times that of any observations made in the United States.

have little tone and no recuperation. The muscles of the heart, which had become unspeakably tired, still had little reserve. Dr. Potaka urged me strongly not to attempt a long flight.

On these counts the hazard was entirely mine. The objections to my taking the risk were of a nature too personal to discuss here. But what made the decision doubly difficult was the knowledge that in the event of a forced landing, especially under conditions that might make it necessary for the flight crew to foot it back to Little America, my weakness would render me a burden upon my companions.

Nevertheless I decided to go. I shall not try to justify the decision. My reasons for going would take more space than I am warranted in giving to a problem which, however painful it may have been at Little America, ceased to be a problem the instant the flight was completed without mishap. One can measure such a choice in many ways.

I couldn't honestly claim that I was needed on the flight. On the long exploring flights of my previous expeditions I had done all the navigation; it must be done rather carefully while flying near either Pole. But for the first time I now had with me, in Rawson, a man who could navigate and navigate well. Perhaps it was a reasonable caution to make the flight to test him out, as he had never navigated a plane; but I had found him brilliant at surface navigation and of a cool temperament, so there was no reason to doubt his ability in the air. Which was how it turned out.

But it was human to want to go. Of all the various missions of the expedition, geographical discovery was that which, more than any other, had drawn me back to Antarctica. I was keen to look into the problem of the Strait and I was no less eager to study afresh, and from a more advantageous and perhaps more revealing position, the mountains of Marie Byrd Land which we had discovered in 1929.

As for the likelihood of a forced landing, the big plane, thanks to the aviation unit, was in corking shape; and with the Pilgrim in reserve and two field units near our track, we weren't apt to walk back.

The flight crew consisted of June, chief pilot; Bowlin, co-pilot; Bailey, radio operator; Pelter, aerial cameraman; Rawson, navigator; and myself.

At 11:53 A.M. June raced the big plane across the Barrier surface into a light southerly wind. The skis slammed and jolted over hard, glazed ridges of sastrugi, but the engines had a rich, full sound. Easily, at the end of a short run, they cleanly lifted a gross load of 17,000 pounds. The foaming pressure ridges of the Bay of Whales swirled under the great wing as June banked.

Over Little America for a navigation departure, at 11:56 we squared away on the course, a long beat to windward in the currents aloft to our first objective—the halfway point in the gap.

A beautiful day, a perfect day for flying. A fleckless sky, visibility that seemed to run on forever, and the plane's shadow running ahead of it across the wind-riffled Barrier. Over the smashed and contorted pressure of the Bad Lands in the upper canyon of Amundsen Arm, holding a southeasterly course. All that broad white plain running to the horizon, whiter than any white on earth, and all untrodden, unexplored.

Just beyond the Arm there lifted the broad bulk of the huge island which, Poulter's seismic soundings were later to show, is the nearest upraised land to Little America. Though 1,200 feet above sea-level and more than 100 miles long, it is wholly ice-covered, just a smooth lofty swelling in the Barrier. We crossed its southern reaches.

Making 80 knots we ran down the southeastern leg of the triangle. Like a ship lifting and sending on a long, easy swell, the plane swayed in the surge of the high, cold currents pouring off the polar plateau. The side benches over the long, flat tanks on either side of the cabin were stowed high with emergency gear—rations neatly sacked, trail gear, cookers. Overhead two very light, very shrewdly made manhauling sledges, skis, and tents were lashed in place.[7] Bailey had his radio apparatus aft, behind the main bulkhead. He was working with Dyer at Little America; but Siple's party in the Edsel Ford Range and the tractor party 165 statute miles south-southeast of Little America, a fair distance west of our course, were both stopped and listening, watching the weather. Rawson had the charts spread on a folding table dropped from the port side. No simple job is navigating a plane in the Antarctic. Just as at sea there are frequently no conspicuous landmarks with which to check course and direction. But the polar regions give rise to their own peculiar problems. Owing to the proximity of the Magnetic Pole the magnetic compass is unreliable; it is sluggish, reluctant to settle down, subject to wide swings. There is the problem of direction caused by the rapid convergence of meridians toward the Pole. In any direction but due north or south in high southern latitudes a plane flying a straight course cuts rapidly across meridians at quickly changing angles. Thus direction changes constantly: time, too, with the same rapidity, an hour every 180 miles on an easterly or westerly course in Little America's latitude. So between making compensations for changing time and direction, resetting

[7] The following emergency gear was carried on all flights (varying, of course, according to size of crew) for use on a forced landing:

2 trail tents, 1 6-man cooker and primus stove with spare parts, 5 soup bowls, 5 wooden spoons, 5 enamel cups, 10 gals. kerosene (for cooker), 2 snow knives, 2 snow saws, 1 ice ax, 5 sets skis and poles, 5 sleeping bags and 40 pounds clothing, each; 8 ice anchors and securing lines, 1 oil funnel and drain hose, 1 tool kit, 2 light manhauling sledges, 1 sledge meter, spare rawhide ski repair outfit, 100 feet alpine rope, 24 smoke bombs, 5 manhauling harnesses, Sennaegrass (for boots), 5 pr. crampons, sewing kits, 5 rucksacks, 50 trail flags, gear for securing plane controls, 2 Van Praag torches (full), for heating engines, 1 hand-cranked radio trail set and spare batteries, 1 tent for heating engines, first-aid kit.

the sun compass, checking drift with the drift-indicator, calculating ground speed, plotting positions and laying new courses, a navigator, in Bill Bowlin's phrase, "is busier than a barber's cat."

At 1:26 o'clock, 93 miles out of Little America, I caught sight of an interesting formation of crevasses, an irregular pattern of them, lying directly across our course. We dropped low to study them. At 400 feet by the altimeter the surface was still well under us, 100 feet at least. All low Barrier. Far, far away in that crystal clear air the ice lifted and met the horizon in a shining golden encirclement.

A few minutes later a second wave of crevasses, still at right angles to the course, still very low.

At 2:06 o'clock a third wave of them, more confused and broken than the others. Ah, we were getting close to something. I asked June to drop low and sounded the elevation with the altimeter—400 feet, and the surface still considerably below us. This sounding by plane was something new in polar exploration. It would give us an idea of the altitude of the ice cap above sea level.

Practically at the end of the first leg of the triangle, we had just risen again when, over June's shoulder, I sighted dead ahead another grossly disturbed area, a great swirling whirlpool of pits and fractures, coming in from the west and folding back through north to west in the shape of an enormous horseshoe. As a matter of fact, that was the name we gave it—the Horseshoe. We made for it. Near this area we again dropped low for an altimetric sounding—again little over 400 feet. The crevasses lay in a band from half a mile to several miles wide. Many had caved in; and the regular furrows and the dark colors in the depths put you in mind of earth turned over by spring plowing. Curiously, within the horseshoe the snow seemed to be of a subtly different texture, quite discolored, almost dark, as if just under a film of translucent ice lay a spreading of soot.

Here, I decided, must be the eastern extension of the broad belt of crevasses running through the heart of the Ross Ice Barrier which had blocked the tractors.

East, west and south, to the limit of vision, the Barrier seemed to roll at the same low level, so low the ice must surely be resting, if not on water itself, at least on land below sea-level. And here, it seemed to me, beneath this glittering carapace of ice must be if it existed at all, the trough of the Great Ice Strait. Did these crevasses mark the southern reaches of the new plateau? We were nearly 4,000 feet below the highest altitude calculated by June and Rawson when they crossed the plateau on the way to Mt. Grace McKinley.

At 2:16 o'clock we turned north, to run down the second leg of the triangle to the Edsel Fords. The turn was made at Lat. 81° 05′ S., Long. 146° 30′ W., 275 miles southeast of Little America.

The second leg would carry us abeam and east of Mt. Grace McKinley, just within the western margin of Marie Byrd Land.

North of the Horseshoe the surface was broken up in many places by crevasses. And here, it seemed, was the southerly flank of the new plateau: the pressure and crevasses must mark the ice riding down from the high summit to the north to the low-level gap we had just found.

Odd how difficult it is, under certain conditions of light, to judge relationships, depths and distances. The snow becomes an intricate and deceptive arrangement of flashing planes. Though the surface seemed to be rising underneath I should have hesitated to swear to it. So, between the 78th and 79th parallels, we dropped down again for a sounding by altimeter. The elevation had risen to 1,975 feet—the dome of the new plateau.

At 2:56 o'clock another east-west belt of crevasses, about half a mile broad. Ten minutes later still another. At 3:27 o'clock, Bowlin, who had taken over the wheel, swooped down and brushed the surface once more—3,200 feet by the altimeter, a rise of nearly 3,000 feet in 110 miles.

Drawing within range of the Edsel Fords we commenced to climb, steeply, with the engines lustily digging in. At 10,000 feet Bowlin leveled off. At 3:31 o'clock the pyramidal peak of Mt. Grace McKinley, a glistening cone on an ivory plain, swept up on the port bow; the sugar loaf of Haines came up on the starboard bow. Five years before we had first seen these mountains from 100 miles to the northwest. Now we were striking at them from the south. I trained my glasses on the horizon, waiting with a keenness I should hesitate to describe the momentary rising of the other mountains.

Now they appeared—one, two, three, four... faster than I could tick them off mentally, a swift and violent eruption of black peaks, popping up like heads behind a fence in a ballpark. Dozens of them, streaming off behind the western front range.

A fascinating discovery. Most significant of all was the massing of the peaks in the northeast and east. Why, we had been all wrong! In 1929, when we had approached this land from the northwest, I was sure this range ran north and south. The mapping camera, which supposedly never lies, had so attested. But the lens, no less than our eyes, had been deceived. The front we discovered and photographed in 1929 was only a cross-section of a much greater range. Instead of running north and south the range bore east, peak upon peak.

Making 100 knots with a quartering wind, and again climbing a little, we approached the heart of the second problem.

At 11,000 feet we passed by Mt. Grace McKinley. A bow and beam bearing put us 23 miles east of it and exactly on our course.

From this lofty perch we had a full view of this refrigerated world, a view which, once seen, can never vanish from the mind, but lingers with the unrelaxing clarity of something at once so terrible and still so beautiful that it impoverishes all other spectacles. Gray masses of rock that a giant hand might have strewn about like so many pebbles filled the northeastern horizon. Battered, eroded, carved and splintered by an ice sheet which still drowned all but their highest shoulders and ridges, they looked what they were, the shattered derelicts of an Ice Age, the remnants of the land which had stood off the warring assault of the ice. Somewhere down there (though we failed to see him, and he failed to see or even hear the plane) Siple was grubbing above the ice line for traces of life—mosses and lichens, bird rookeries, and microscopic things. It was hard to believe that any life could find nourishment on that bleak landscape.

What we had seen as we approached from the south was confirmed. At 11,000 feet we had vision of 130 miles. The trend of the new mountains was definitely east and northeast. Moreover, the plateau, passing Mt. Grace McKinley, seemed to roll endlessly to the east along the axis of the range. Forty miles on our beam I raised an enormous mountain, a block of steel-gray rock, apparently granite.

My original conception of the Edsel Ford Range and Marie Byrd Land I had to revise. This newest of Antarctic Lands is a mighty elevated land, domed by a 4,000 foot plateau and traversed by a great coastal mountain range, as stately and beautiful in its architecture as any of the known lands to the westward. Sulzberger Bay, which in 1929 I thought to be a small indentation in the Barrier, now emerged in its true identity of an enormous arm of the sea biting clear to the foot of Mt. Grace McKinley and finding its eastern shore line along the front range of the Edsel Fords and its western shore at the foot of the Alexandra Mountains of King Edward VII Land.

At 4:30 o'clock we turned west, on the homing leg to Little America, a run of 255 statute miles. The turn was at Lat. 77° 30′ S., Long. 146° 30′ W.

A straight run, now, for home. The sky continued flawless.

As we drew near the Rockefellers something tumbled out of the recesses of memory. On the southern slope of Mt. Helen Washington, in the Rockefellers, the Fokker, which Dr. Gould, June and Balchen had flown there in 1929 on a geological survey, had been destroyed in a hurricane. There was the barest chance the wreckage might still be visible. I mentioned it to June.

So we altered course a few degrees to pass the mountain, and presently banked sharply around a bare shoulder of rock.

June was gesticulating and shouting, "There she is, right where she hit!"

Twisted and crumpled into a ball of metal, the wreckage lay imprisoned in a lake of green ice at the foot of the mountain. It was remarkable to find it awash after four and a half years of blizzards. There was practically no drift around it, no doubt because of the steady down-drafts of wind.

Whereupon another idea emerged. The Fokker had an excellent motor. No reason why, as soon as a small party was available, it couldn't be salvaged. That morning my New York representative and friend, Leo McDonald, had advised me in melancholy prose that "rocks are showing in the bottom of the expedition treasury." We could sell the motor back home. "Well," I shouted to Rawson, "maybe it's rather odd to end a flight of exploration with a junk survey, but in these times an explorer can't be fastidious."

At 6:43 P.M. we landed at Little America. Altogether we had been in the air 6 hours and 43 minutes. We had flown 777 statute miles and surveyed, within our range of vision, approximately 50,000 square miles of unknown Antarctica—a very satisfactory beginning of the flight program.

But because the sky still remained miraculously clear and because Haines thought it might last, there was no resting on the oars. Before the flight crew sat down to supper, Smith and Swan were working over the engine. An oil leak in the starboard engine made it necessary to pull the propeller and remove the thrust plate. There were the routine inspections as well—landing gear and all control wires had to be checked, the covers removed from the rocker arm boxes and the oil pads taken out, dried and washed with gasoline and resaturated with oil (to rid them of the ice and water produced by condensation) and the plane had to be regassed. All night long, while the rest of the camp slept, aviation labored over the plane.

I was anxious, while the weather still held good, to send the plane to the relief of the tractor party which was again bogged down in the crevasses.

IV

That evening, when we sat down for dinner, there confronted us on the bulletin board in the Mess Hall, a spectacular chalk drawing of a plane in flight over a range of mountains, ostensibly the Edsel Fords, and issuing from the cabin, in the balloons of the comic strip, were the words: "Don't leave me now." The flight crew looked blankly at one another, but a sheepish grin on Clay Bailey's face gave him away.

While we were at 11,000 feet near Mt. Grace McKinley the engines suddenly sputtered. One set of tanks had run dry, and for a few seconds the engines coughed and missed before Bowlin could switch to another set of tanks. Bailey, who was way aft and just finishing transmitting a message to Dyer at Little America, heard the engines stop, and on the chance it might be engine failure flashed Dyer: "Don't leave me now."

V

And, meanwhile, the biologists had plucked a brand from the burning. Quietly behind the uproar around the flying operations, Dr. Perkins, Sterrett, Young and Dane, had disappeared into the inner recesses of the Bay of Whales. Discouraged at not being able to force his plankton net through the submerged levels of the new ice between Ver-Sur-Mer Inlet and the Sea, Perkins had organized an expedition of his own to search for a better place on the west side of the Barrier. He had the notion that in the older bay ice he might find a pressure crack, or a tide-rip or a seal's breathing hole through which he could drop his net into deep water. With a dog team the four of them crossed the Bay and on the western shore started up an inlet between two extensions of Barrier which in 1929 we had identified as McKinley Plateau and Braathen Peninsula. At the head of the Inlet, about 15 miles southwest of Little America, they entered a gorge, which had been created since 1929 by the calving of a huge berg which, after drifting about 100 yards, had been beset and frozen in, forming a narrow cañon several miles long. Perkins named it Echo Cañon because of the four or five echoes it gave to a shout. Here they pitched camp.

On the way in they had seen numerous seals, and in the cañon itself they found a herd of 40 or more, some with pups, including half a dozen that had been branded by Lindsey near Ver-Sur-Mer Inlet, showing that they had traveled under at least 5 miles of hard fast ice to reach their present breathing holes. In the morning Perkins heard a seal scraping at a hole in a water-filled crevasse, slapping his head to and fro as he ground the ice down with his teeth. Perkins hurried into the tent to get a camera, but the seal was gone before he got back. Sterrett, however, was peering into the crevasse.

"Look, Perk," he called, "there's a dime."

Perkins saw something shiny move, like a coin side-slipping through water. He looked more closely, and together they were excited to see at least half a dozen small fish, with long, delicate dorsal and ventral fins and streamy tails—some the color of coral, others having seemingly transparent bodies which absorbed the colors in the ice—hovering in the crannies of the ice, or darting in and out of tiny clouds of ice crystals. The biggest was not more than 5 inches long, and they were all exceedingly timid and furtive, venturing out, apparently, only to feed, then twisting back with the swiftness of light to their hide-outs in the ice. The slightest disturbance in the water sent them in frantic flight into the clusters of ice crystals.

The crevasse itself, they said, was an interesting structure. It ran down the center of the cañon, being about a fair jump in width at the top, and narrowing, 30 feet or so down, to a thread-like gap through which these fish swam in and out. The walls were rich blues deepening into an emerald green, and with their richly painted caverns, sensitively frond-like clusterings of ice crystals and delicate ice formations they were remindful of a tropical lagoon. But the water temperature was barely above freezing.

Having no luck catching the fish with the plankton net, they returned to Little America where they built a fish trap; then Sterrett and Moody sledged back to the cañon. It was all they could do to restrain Dr. Potaka from going. "Will they rise to a fly?" he wanted to know. He was a passionate angler, and was counting the days before he would again be wading his favorite trout stream in New Zealand. Several days later Sterrett and Moody came back.

"Any luck?" asked the Doctor, bursting into the Science Hall.

"Fair," said Sterrett. "They weren't rising very vigorously."

"How big do they run?"

"Oh, this one will go, I should say, about one hundred and fifty-five . . . millimeters!"

Well, there was the lone specimen on a plate—a curious, blunt-headed thing, just a few inches long. Transparent and colorless except for a few brownish spots near the gills.

"At least," said Jim, "you fellows can say you have seen fresh fish."

Noville grinned.

"Do you mean to tell me," he demanded, "that all you scientists and dog-drivers—you, Perkins, Moody, Dane and Young—with all the implements of modern science, dog teams, shotguns, fish nets—do you mean to tell me that that poor fish, so starved you can see right through it, is all you have to show for ten days' work!"

Still, the fish created great excitement for a while. Perkins stayed up all night examining it: in appearance, he said at the time, it seemed to resemble a species called *Notothenia scotti,* described in a monograph by Dr. Wilson of Scott's expeditions, which had been caught in 300 fathoms of water.[8] However, Perkins was no less interested by what he found in its stomach, coming upon half a dozen kinds of copepods and plankton quite different from anything he had ever seen before.

[8] The fish has since been identified as a new genus, *Pagothenia antarctica.*

Chapter XV

AGAIN THE DOUGHTY TRACTORS

I

AND again the doughty tractors, fighting for a passage through the crevasses along the 81st parallel, came a cropper—their third setback in ten days.

After the reorganization of the southern parties at the 193-Mile Depot (199 statute miles) on November 6th, the two cars, with the scientists Morgan and Bramhall aboard, retraced the trail to 159-Mile Depot on the southern trail. Here they bore east, running through the night, putting down flags every third of a mile. Fog stopped them early next morning. For three days they were fog-bound. The morning of the 10th, however, brought improved visibility, and, breaking camp, the party got under way at 11:30 A.M., steering 105° true by compass for a third thrust toward the belt of crevasses.

On this course the drivers traveled slowly and warily. During the day they broke through a few small crevasses, most of them from 6 inches to 3 feet wide, not quite wide enough to bother the cars. That evening they attained Lat. 81° 06′ S., Long. 157° 28′ without mishap. Their hopes were rising, though ahead of them they now could see numerous haycocks with tiny plumes of vapor floating over their summits, and the looming of pressure.

Halting for a quick supper of *hoosh,* they got underway again. Morgan went ahead on skis to scout the area. The course was still 105° so as to strike at right angles whatever blind crevasses the tractors should hit. Demas's car was in the lead. Bramhall was braced on the navigation platform on the port side, guiding him on a compass course. Morgan was ahead on skis, and Hill and Waite, in the second car, brought up the rear. The cars were making about 2 knots. For the past 20 miles they had been jolting over a washboarding of sastrugi.

Shortly after midnight, when their apprehensions were all but lulled, Demas's car broke through a 6-foot crevasse. Again there was no warning: just a convulsive shudder to the car, then the *whroom* of tons of snow collapsing and spilling into a narrow abyss, and the appalling sag aft, with the floor boards rising under the driver's feet and the wrenching rush of loose gear in the cabin sliding against the bulkhead.

Bramhall hauled himself off the navigation platform, landing sprawling on the far lip of the crevasse. That was the "abandon ship" rule of the tractors—every man for himself. Crevasses let go too fast under a tractor for a man to help anybody else. The more men on the surface, the more hands for hauling somebody else out.

Demas, jammed in behind the wheel, couldn't move, though he had his hand on the safety lanyard. He said he just sat there, for what seemed to be forever, watching the radiator rise up and up till he couldn't see over it. Instinctively he cut the switch, to prevent fire in the crash. There were 147 gallons of gas in the flimsy airplane tank bolted to the false deck in the cabin. Just when he thought the car was going straight down by the stern, it stopped. The back of the wooden superstructure had caught and was wedged against an overhang of the bridge which hadn't carried away. There the car held at a 60° angle, with its front skis in the air, and the after part sunk in the crevasse. Hill and Waite, approaching from behind, could see the headlights over the cab roof.

Very gingerly, lest a heavy movement disturb the fragile balance of the car, Demas crawled out and took stock of the damage. A smell of gas rose out of the crevasse. All the gas in the rear tank—40 gallons of it—had spilled out, itself a severe loss. The frame of the wooden superstructure was wrenched around, and the canvas fabric was ripped in several places, but otherwise everything held fast. Demas quietly congratulated himself for having built the superstructure so staunchly, and for having made them so high.

Though salvage seemed hopeless, they had no recourse but to try it. A bridge couldn't be built with snow blocks under the treads, as they had done before. The walls of the crevasse, instead of pinching together, bellied out a little way down. Later on, Morgan descended the crevasse on a rope and found it to be 100 feet deep, a V-shaped chamber of hard blue ice at the bottom.

Sounding the crevasse to right and left, they found a narrower place where Hill could cross with No. 2. He came around cautiously, cracking several small crevasses on the way. Then he backed up in front of No. 3 and tried to haul it out with a line. It scarcely budged. To lighten the load they cut a hole in the canvas roof of No. 3 and dragged out all the heavy gear and instruments they could reach. Still No. 2 couldn't stir it. Now they hacked away the lip of the crevasse under the car, to bring it level. And still no use.

"Well," said Demas, "here goes nothing."

Ignoring the warnings of his companions, he climbed into the car and started the engine. The treads barely had traction. With No. 2 straining on the line, and Waite, Bramhall and Morgan throwing their weight across the hood to bring it down, Demas rocked the car out, inch by inch. All this took them four hours, and at 4 o'clock on morning of the 11th, when the "Black Maria" once again stood on firm ground, they could scarcely believe their luck.

They made camp on the spot. During the next two days Bramhall occupied himself with magnetic observations, and Morgan, assisted by Waite, made several seismic soundings. Demas and Hill meanwhile overhauled their cars. It was necessary to drop the pan on No. 3 and take up four bearings. The strain of heavy loads and steady traveling in low speed were knocking the engines to pieces. Hill said the work was brutal. The temperature was —26°, and a wind which rose to blizzard strength finally drove them to their tents.

Still hopeful of breaking through, having already passed through six miles of crevasses, they reconnoitered ahead on skis November 14th, only to find the area utterly impassable. Blind crevasses, which they estimated to be 20 to 30 feet wide, lay across their course, many caved in, leaving ragged, crater-like holes. There were a great many high polished sastrugi and crumpled masses of pressure.

On the 16th, after Demas had finally succeeded in restoring his engine to rights, the party commenced to retreat, intending now to strike a little north, then due east, in an attempt to gain the new plateau. The crevasses still seemed to trend east-northeast across the Barrier. At the point where they commenced the third retreat they were approximately 37 miles east of the position where they had met their first set-back. Incidentally, they were also about 70 miles south and a trifle west of the southeasternmost point reached by the Japanese expedition of 1911, which had reported a 1,100 foot elevation.[1]

The tractors had retreated two miles when we halted them by radio, on the 16th, with word that the big plane was leaving immediately to survey the crevasses for them.

II

With the utmost sympathy I had followed the day-by-day career of the tractors, and though it meant sacrificing weather which might have been exploited for geographical exploration, I resolved to help them with aviation if I could.

Besides, the flight could be made to serve two other useful purposes: (1) to survey the triangular wedge of unknown area between the southeastern leg of our flight track of the 15th and the main southern trail: and (2) to locate Eilefsen and Ronne who had acted as support for the Geological Party to 300 miles.

The Supporting Party carried no radio, Ronne having depoted his to cut down weight. Though they had a well-marked trail back to Little America, still, as they had no navigational instruments other than a compass, it seemed prudent just to see how they were faring. The Geological Party had advised us on the 14th that the two men were turning back.

Fortunately the weather held good and aviation had the *William Horlick* ready for flight by evening. It was in the air at 7:30 o'clock.

June was chief pilot and in command; Bowlin, co-pilot; Rawson, navigator; Bailey, radio operator; and Pelter, cameraman.

[1] Hayes, *The Conquest of the South Pole,* 307-308. Sir T. Edgeworth David, *Geographical Journal,* June, 1914, 220.

For the time being, I felt, I had better stay behind. Though it was disappointing to give up the satisfaction of discovery, there was compensating satisfaction in being able to pass on the honor to able and conscientious men who had shared my burdens. June was a reliable flight commander, cool and practical. As for Rawson, he had, on the earlier flight, demonstrated his mastery of air navigation. For a man of 24 years, he was competent in many directions. Not only in the field, but in the organization and demobilization of the expedition, he, as much as any man, contributed to its success.

Wheeling over Little America, the crew bore south along the 169th meridian, which course would strike the bulge in the southern trail around the Valley of Crevasses. From over the drifted hulk of the Cletrac, they struck straight for the 159-Mile beacon, whence they followed the trail to a point just south of the belt of crevasses. Here they rose to 5,000 feet, and though they had vision southward of 90 miles or more, there was no sign of Ronne and Eilefsen. However, the trail was clearly marked. The tall snow beacons with their orange flags, the aviation markers and the trail flags stood out boldly and clearly. Ronne and Eilefsen, June decided, would have no difficulty following it.

As the plane turned they scanned the crevasses to the west. From where they were on the 161st meridian, the crevasses, a belt eight miles or so wide, ran steadily west, seeming to bend a trifle to south-southwest. Rawson said they could see to the 167th meridian. What seemed to be great blocks of pressure threw back splinters of sunlight.

They now retraced the trail to 173-Mile Depot, then swung east to pick up the tractors. At 9:55 o'clock they were over the tractor party. Demas and Waite were signaling them with smoke pots and flares. The cars were drawn up together, about two miles away from the crevasse in which Demas had had such a close call.

Sweeping over them, June headed over the crevasses. It was a mumbo-jumbo of broad scars and fissures, according to the flight crew. They could see the hole that Demas's car had made—"a hell of a big hole," June said. What impressed the flight crew most was that the cars had gone as far as they had. Under right conditions of sun you can mark crevasses quite plainly from the air. There's a subtle darkening, a curious riffling effect of shadows, that is lost on the ground. And Rawson estimated that the tractors had unknowingly traversed several hundred such blind crevasses before reaching their present position.

So far as they could tell, the belt seemed to bend north-northeast, in the general direction of the Horseshoe crevasse we had sighted to the east.

Convinced it would be fatal for the tractors to attempt to break through the main belt, and seriously concerned as to their ability to extricate themselves from their present position, the flight crew now wheeled to look, first, for a retreat for the tractors and, second, a reasonable approach to the new plateau.

For 25 miles they retraced the tractors' inward course. The welted trail was easy to follow. Here, at Lat. 81° 01′ S., Long. 159° 45′ W., they picked up a snow beacon which the tractor party had raised. The surface was good at this point, and if their luck held the tractors should be able to make good a retreat without too great danger. Some of the blind crevasses on their course, however, seemed to be 15 feet wide, and June said Demas would have to proceed with the greatest caution.

From the beacon, they now flew northeast 55 miles to Lat. 80° 27′ S., Long. 156° 30′ W., seeking an approach to the plateau. The surface all the way was low barrier, smooth and unmarred. June brushed over it, sounding with the altimeter—600 feet by the instrument, though 100 feet, June thought, ought to be allowed for lag in the instrument.

Bearing due east, they headed for the plateau, crossing the flight track of the 15th. Slowly the rounded dome of the plateau lifted before them. All along the western plateau shore, where the ice riding down from the plateau met the Barrier ice anchored to its foot, were irregular and isolated patches of crevasses barring approach.

But between these patches were corridors of good surface, through which, the flight crew thought, the tractors could zig-zag their way up to the roof of the plateau.

A message announcing the discovery of a safe transit was immediately flashed by radio to Little America and to Waite of the Tractor Party, who was listening in.

With that job done the crew now struck south along the 151st meridian, to rub out the slice of unknown in that sector. But clouds massing in front of them and a wind rising to gale force finally compelled them to turn after 58 miles on this course.

At midnight, at Lat. 81° 20′ S., Long. 151° W., approximately 230 miles south-southeast of Little America—about 72.3 miles east of the tractors and 43 miles west and 15 miles south of the apex of the flight course of the 15th—they came about. They rode a gale for 207 miles to within 20 miles of Little America, where they landed, much surprised, in a dead calm.

The plane was in the air 6 hours 46 minutes, flying approximately 770 miles.

Besides charting a safe route for the tractors, that roving flight had had the fine effect of further defining the eastern shore of the Ross Ice Barrier.

Another important result of the flight: it continued the charting of the belt of crevasses running through the heart of the Ross Ice Barrier along the 81st parallel. Like a monstrous wound, it runs continuously from an unknown distance west of the 173rd meridian to beyond the 140th meridian to the eastward, surely one of the major topographical obstacles in the Polar regions.[2]

[2] Due to the small scale of the map and the congestion of flight tracks in this area this flight is not shown on it.

So far as the problem of the Ice Strait was involved, it remained in status quo after the flight of the 15th—a potential waterway until a blocking land mass should be found east of the depression we had sounded at the apex.

Talking over this problem with June and Rawson after they landed, I could find nothing to strengthen our case, one way or the other. As nearly as they could tell, the same low-level Barrier seemed to roll south at their turning point.

III

Friday, November 17th, was cloudy, with a minimum temperature of —23°. The tractor party reported a blizzard which "nearly blew us out of the tent." In the afternoon the wind hit Little America, bringing clouds and ground drift. With flying out of the question at least for twenty-four hours, aviation made capital out of the break by rushing a twenty-hour check on the *William Horlick's* engines.

That evening, the blizzard abating, the tractors got under way again, retreating along the course June had recommended—28.7 miles northwest to the beacon at Lat. 81° 01′ S., Long. 159° 45′ W., then a 52-mile sweep to the northeast within a curving scimitar-reach of crevasses and finally good surface upon which to launch an easting toward the plateau.

Shortly after midnight they reached the beacon, where they halted only long enough to refill the tractor's tanks from the drums on the sledges. Seventeen miles out on the new course they had to stop to install new brushes on the generator of Hill's car; 40 miles out a bearing let go on the same car.

By that time Little America was in the throes of launching another flight.

After conferring with Dr. Poulter and Rawson (Rawson was always most helpful in the discussion of geographical problems) we decided to aim the next flight due east of Little America into Marie Byrd Land. Within the limits of the plane's range, we wanted to confirm the easterly trend of the new mountains of the Edsel Fords and observe the easterly reaches of the new plateau.

Apart from the value of such a reconnoissance to the allied problem of the Strait, a peremptory reason recommended a temporary shift of attention to this quarter. This sector was the weather breeder, the home of the dirtiest fogs and storms. Being near the coast, it was earlier affected than the interior by the inpouring of clouds and fog that marked the advent of summer. If we ever expected to get into the east at all, we had better seize the first break to ram a flight in that direction, leaving the southeasterly sector to the last.

The opportunity broke almost before we were ready for it. During the early watch of the 18th the wind veered into the south and dropped to a gentle breeze; the clouds drained, leaving a sky as clear as my lady's looking glass. At 6 o'clock the watchman was banging heartily at the doors, jabbing into formless sleeping bags—"Rise and shine, gentlemen. Clear as a bell! A flight to the mountains!" We always referred to the eastward as "the mountains," an exciting implication of land.

Aviation had been up most of the night, slaving to finish the overhaul before weather improved. Nowadays the entire unit—June, Bowlin, Smith, Swan, Dustin, Skinner, even Boyd, the machinist—were bivouacked in a tent colony near the planes. Smith and Swan, in fact, were sleeping in the *William Horlick* itself. Up at the watchman's shout, they hurried to the Mess Hall for a quick breakfast before they finished the assembly of the engines.

At 7:30 A.M. Siple, in the Edsel Ford Range, advised a gusty southeast wind, clear skies and excellent visibility. The tractors reported a mere breath of northwesterly wind and *cavu*—ceiling and visibility unlimited. At noon Siple said no wind, no clouds, excellent visibility: and the tractors said again *cavu*.

Aviation, sweating from hurry, at last fitted on the cowlings. Dog teams arriving with gas from Retreat Camp—900 gallons pumped in by hand, strained by chamois, two hours' work; oil bubbling and seething in a cauldron in the aviation shack—heated over blow torches to a temperature of 120°, to be called for just before the pilots were ready to start the engines; the square heater tents drawn over the engines and the blow torches started—an hour's heating at a temperature of 110°. A quick inspection of control wires and landing gear. Drift brushed and pounded from the fabric, wings, fuselage and tail structure (as much as 200 pounds of snow were taken off the plane after a severe blizzard).

All ready, now. Tents whipped away from the engines. Men hurrying from the shack with steaming buckets of hot oil. From June in the cockpit, "Clear?" From Swan on the ground, "All clear. Let her go." The lugubrious whine of the engine starter, then, gratefully, the explosive retort of the engines, first one, then the other.

Leaning against the blast from the propeller, the flight crew scrambled into the cabin—Bowlin, Rawson, Petersen, Pelter. A raffish looking crew. June bulking at the bow port, stripped down to his shirt-sleeves, with a beard that made him look more like General Grant than Grant ever looked himself. Petersen tall and lean, uncombed reddish hair falling past his helmet, looking like one of those strange, undernourished ascetics of the fifteenth century. And Rawson, with a thin silken beard, like a Manchu gone to seed. Scare-crows with oil-stained windproofs flapping about their legs.

Off at 2:37 o'clock in the afternoon, with a load of 18,000 pounds. Over the camp a few minutes later for a navigation departure. You can't imagine how beautiful it is to see a plane in flight against an Antarctic sky. In fact, you never realize how deep and spacious, how infinitely blue that sky can be till you look up and see a plane moving across it. The grimy wings become the color of wheat and the plane seems not to move but to be drawn by a power not of its own making through a buoyant blue fluid, with a tautness of space-filling sound dislodging resonant echoing overtones in the ground under your feet.

In a little while there was just a faint diminishing speck in the eastern sky.

IV

For the first time in the unaccustomed rôle of a listener *seeing* remote discoveries through another man's eyes, I followed by radio this flight through a region which I looked upon as peculiarly my own. Dyer had hooked up a loud speaker in my shack. For an hour or more, till the plane moved too far away for the words to remain intelligible, I could hear Petersen reporting on progress on the telephone set. Afterwards, he and Dyer turned to code; bulletins came to me every 15 minutes. It was the first flight of exploration launched by any of my expeditions in which I had not participated. It was not easy to turn away from it. I was acutely conscious of my own invalidism. Years ago, I used to play football, and I learned how hard it was to sit on the bench after you have gotten used to carrying the ball.

Petersen's voice, blurting through the static, and the hum of the generator, filled the room: "We're five miles north of Amundsen Arm, flying at 90 knots and climbing to 10,000 feet. . . . Okay. . . . Yes, werry clear. Some clouds, that's all. . . . Ross Sea is still frozen. . . . There's a lot of sea smoke, though, on the noddern horizon. . . . Boy, wouldn't it be great to see the ole *Yacob Ruppert* steaming into the Bay. . . ." Petersen, though an American citizen, was Norwegian born; his j's and the w's were the delight of the radio engineers.

Across Scott Land into Marie Byrd Land to Mt. Grace McKinley they kept to a great circle course. By the time they had the Rockefellers abeam they had attained their altitude objective of 10,000 feet. Here, over the position where Rawson on the eastern tractor journey had gotten an astronomical fix, they flew a complete circle, so that Pelter, with his mapping camera, could compass the horizon. At that great height all the prominent features of that region—the Rockefellers, the Alexandras and Scott's Nunataks on the coast of King Edward VII Land, Okuma Bay, even the summit of Mt. Grace McKinley—were in view. Later on, by the application of an ingenious system of mathematics to these photographs, the distances and geographical relations, and the height of the new mountains to the eastward could be established.

At 4:06 o'clock they again headed east. Skeletal imprints on the plateau underneath drew their attention—several new ridges not quite awash, their tops barely buried in snow.

Over Mt. McKinley at 4:56, still at 10,000 feet, they circled for another round of photographs. At 5:01 they struck east, breaking past the limits of the flight track of the 15th. All ahead of them, now, was new, undiscovered and uncharted.

On their port hand the new peaks of the Edsel Fords were marching past, massed in a wedge streaming to the northeast. The exposed peaks, weathered to a yellowish-gray, bitten and raked by ice, were only the starved and eroded remnants of the mightier blocks that stood on that land before the ice came. Even now, though the ice is in retreat, only the tallest peaks have struggled through the frosted capping. Their ridges and shoulders lie mantled by glacial ice, and the bulging in the snow that marks them is like the swelling of muscles under flesh.

The big mountain mass I had raised through binoculars on the 15th was rising to the north and east. At 6:40 o'clock they drew abeam of it and circled again for another round of photographs, to tie this peak [3] in with the mountains astern.

Very definitely now, in the altering perspective, the bulk of the mountain masses were seen to be gathered in a tight jumble of peaks to the northeast, which dissolved presently into a single, thinning chain of smaller peaks, bending little by little through east to southeast.

Somewhere behind that rim of rock lay the undiscovered coast—the coast we had struggled so often to attain. Perhaps it was quite near. The whole northern horizon, the flight crew said, was laced with a dark ribbon of water sky.

Now they slanted south a little, to resume their easting on the 78th parallel. The scattered panels of cirrus clouds on the southern horizon were giving way to gross storm clouds. The air was getting rougher, and a fuzziness on the horizon was indicative of cloud.

The plateau, curving in behind the western front range of the Edsel Fords, seemed to be rising under them. June started to write a note on scratch pad, "flat as . . ." Bowlin leaned over, ". . . as the plains of Kansas," he submitted.

North of their line of flight, about 100 miles away, a magnificent peak appeared,[4] dwarfing the thinning line of peaks flowing about it. They were then about 150 miles east of the previous limits of discovery. The straggling chain of peaks far down on the northern horizon appeared now to be trending southeast. Mere dots on the horizon of the great white plain, they were too far away—too indistinct—to be photographed, but they were visible through 7-power glasses.

Ahead of them, about 30° on the port bow, a monstrous mountain mass was shouldering through the white roofing of the plateau. They thought it must be close to 10,000 feet, to bulk so prominently over the plateau. June was impressed, too, by the curious structure of the mass.

[3] This peak was named (see map) after Mr. Clarence Mackay, friend and benefactor of the expedition.

[4] This peak was named Mt. Hal Flood (see map).

It seemed to him to be an extinct volcano, the southern side of which had been blown out. A not improbable surmise, since Siple was presently to come upon the ice-eroded remnants of a volcano in the eastern reaches of the Raymond Fosdick Mountains (see map).

They were holding a course to pass close by this mountain,[5] and were about 69 miles off, when June, observing that the clouds had closed in to the northeast and were thickening ahead, decided to turn.

At 7 o'clock, at Lat. 78° 00′ S., Long. 135° W., approximately 448 miles east of Little America, they wheeled for home.

Shortly after turning they dropped to sound the plateau elevation, skimming the crust for a mile to let the altimeter settle—4,486 feet by the corrected pressure. Then they rose sharply, running for Little America at 9,000 feet, with the clouds threatening to cut them off.

At 9:30 o'clock, when they were just abeam of the Rockefellers, Waite, with the tractor party, advised "WX looks bad now . . . wind NE 5 and increasing . . . black clouds in NE . . . slightly overcast . . . viz still good."

Bowlin at that moment was climbing through a thick bank of clouds so that Rawson could continue to hold the sun with the sun compass. Half an hour later, just after Waite had rapped in a warning that the sky was 50 percent overcast, Petersen, his voice once more booming in the loudspeaker, gayly announced: "The Bay of Whales is now in sight. We'll land in about 25 minutes."

In a little while the sound of the engines was heard in the ventilators. At 10:32 o'clock the Condor landed on the south side of Ver-Sur-Mer Inlet, having been gone 7 hours and 36 minutes.

V

June and Rawson came below to make a report. George Noville had a fresh pot of coffee for them steaming on the stove. Still deafened by the engines, they were shouting at us at the top of their voices. We got the charts out from behind the stove and started roughly to fill in the new discoveries.

"Any sign of the coast?"

"Couldn't see it," June said. "The mountains blocked it off, for one thing. But for 100 miles across the plateau on the way out there was a decided water sky on the northern horizon."

Rawson confirmed this. "It may have been a cloud formation," he said, "but in color and character it was the same sort of horizon we saw over the Ross Sea, all the way from the Bay of Whales."

"How did it bear?"

"Well, it seemed to curve in behind the mountains," June said.

Of course, this was the purest speculation, but it was the first tangible hint of the trend of the unknown coast.

[5] This peak was named (see map) Mt. Mabelle Sidley.

When we had summarized the results of this flight, together with the discoveries of the flight of the 15th, these striking facts emerged:

(A) Definite discovery and confirmation of the easterly axis of the Edsel Ford Range and the forging through 15° of longitude of a 230-mile link in the hypothetical chain of mountains rimming the coast.

(B) The extension of the new plateau from the Rockefellers through 24° of longitude to the 130th meridian, establishing it as a major topographical feature. We had already driven a 332-mile line of exploration through it.

(C) Conclusive proof of the continental character of Marie Byrd Land and its clear-cut emergence from the fog of the archipelago theory as an enormous land mass capped by a 4,500 foot plateau spreading and apparently rising (though naturally, this was only a guess) to the south and east.

(D) The apparent—but admittedly speculative—outlining of the trend of the unseen coast. For all immediate practical purposes of geographical reconnoissance, the coast could be considered as very probably paralleling these new mountains, somewhere between the 75th and 76th parallels.

There rose now the question how these facts, and especially the implications of the plateau, would affect the problem of the Strait.

"Did the plateau appear to continue indefinitely when you turned?"

"So far as we could tell, yes," June said. "It was definitely rising. The altimeter sounding, which was nearly 900 feet higher than any we got on the tractor trip between the Rockefellers and the Edsel Fords, proves that."

"How about to the south?"

"Same thing," said Rawson. "The clouds were getting heavier, but as far as we could see the plateau rolled unbrokenly in that direction."

Odd that we should have found that apparently sea-level trough 215 miles south of Mt. Grace McKinley. Could it be that on the 15th we had stumbled upon a mere indentation—an embayment—in the western shore of the plateau? On the basis of the fresh evidence, it seemed unlikely that between this massive plateau flowing south from the coast and the great mountain structures of the Queen Maud Mountains damming back the 10,000 foot Polar plateau there could exist a sea-level strait.

June and Rawson thought it unlikely. I wasn't sure. But my belief in the significance of the low elevations we had found in the Horseshoe crevasses at Lat. 81° 05′ S., was shaken.

The next step toward the solution had already suggested itself—a deep thrust southeast to attempt to define the great sweep of unknown south of Lat. 81°, and to verify the trend of the Queen Maud Range.[6]

[6] The point had been raised by Dr. Gould of the first expedition as to whether or not the unknown extensions of this range, which he had explored to Lat. 85° 25′ S., Long. 147° 55′ W., might be found to

If we could raise these factors into the realm of discovery, we should know more clearly where we stood. The flight would also have the effect of closing the southern half of the corridor.

For three days unsteady easterly winds and clouds at Little America, together with the unfavorable reports of the field parties, grounded the plane. But on the 19th, in the routine progress report of the Geological Party which was bearing toward the Queen Maud Range far east of any previously traveled track, there occurred an illuminating sentence:

> Held in camp Saturday by high SE Wind. Yesterday made 12 miles to 350 (Mile) Depot, then 7 miles about SW. Built high beacon topped by two flags. Ran south 9.7 miles. Obs (observed) Lat. this A.M. 83° 57′. DR (dead reckoning) Long. 154° 20′. Continuing south to 375 Depot, 8 miles yet to go. *Appears to be high land east of 350. Very large crevasses running NW to SE commence there and continue for 7 miles.* Had some difficulty. Dick's trailer went down nose first. . . .

It was the mention of high land 100 miles north of the Queen Mauds that riveted my interest. This was of commanding importance to the problem of the Strait. The crevasses were a definite suggestion of land. I got into the radio shack as soon as I could, but Dyer informed me that Paine had just signed off. I had to wait for their next schedule on the 21st.

On the 21st, in reply to my query, Blackburn advised:

> Apropos crevasses area between 350 and 375 Miles. Crevasses with NW to SE trend. Fragile bridges, rows of haycocks. Pressure must be active here because of insubstantial bridging. *Along trend of this pressure area to east of 350 appeared definite rise in shelf ice commencing within a mile of that point.* From 350 southerly our course has crossed roll after roll with crests from 2 to 10 miles apart and up to 100 feet in elevation above troughs. . . .

It was as exciting as building up the causational chain in a problem of induction—sleuthing for a continental mystery concealed in an ocean of ice.

VI

In the late afternoon of the 21st the air commenced to clear and aviation took the drift covers off the engine. About 6 o'clock the tractors reported excellent weather 161 miles out, a little east of the plane's course. Bill Haines deferred judgment till the 10 P.M. balloon run. The air aloft yielded its signs and portents. "Good enough, now," said Bill, with his characteristic caution, "but I don't know how long it will last.

swing north and connect somewhere with the Edsel Ford Range. *Cold,* 211-212.

It's a mite skittish. If you don't waste any time," he said to June, "you ought to be able to get this one in quite nicely."

Bill has rarely called a closer one.

June was again in command, Rawson was navigator, and Pelter again manned the cameras. But Smith sat in Bowlin's seat as co-pilot and Bailey replaced Petersen as radio operator. There was, of course, no question of competence in the shift: merely a sharing of the honor of making important flights.

At 12:10 o'clock on the morning of November 22nd they took off with a load of 19,400 pounds—the heaviest load, to my knowledge, ever flown on skis. A full capacity of 900 gallons of gasoline largely accounted for the increase.

A couple of spare connecting rods, lashed together and made fast to a parachute, were included in the load. Demas, a few hours before, had advised that the tractors had used up all spare connecting rods, and that if Hill's car burned out another bearing he would have to abandon it. June offered to parachute them down on the homing leg. We certainly were taking such matters in our stride, those days.

Now for the flight log as it grew on Dyer's typewriter. Dyer maintained almost continuous watch on the plane, breaking off at scheduled periods to snatch weather reports from the Marie Byrd Land and tractor parties which were hove to.

12:15 A.M. OK. Taking navigation departure.
12:30 OK.
12:45 OK.
1:00 56 miles out on course 141° (true).

(June had the engines throttled way down, and with the leanest possible mixture, to extract the last possible ounce of southeasting out of the gas. The engines were turning up 1500 rpm's, 90 knots air speed, about 75 over the ground. They were steering a few degrees off the eye of a fresh upper wind. Tractor reports "WX unchanged," and the information is transmitted to the plane.)

1:15 "Everything OK. WX looks fair. There is a bank of cumulous clouds about 50 miles SW. Nothing but high cirrus (elsewhere). PX (position) 75 miles course 141° at 1:15 A.M. JUNE

(They were across the Island, then, and over the Barrier surface, steering between the flight tracks of the 15th and 16th.)

1:30 OK. Changed course to 133° true. 94 miles from LA (Little America). (Tractor weather same.)
1:45 OK. Course and speed same.
2:00 OK. 131 miles out.

(The Geological Party, practically at the foot of the Queen Maud

Range, breaks in on schedule with a weather report: "Bar. 1420 feet.[7] Temp. plus four. Viz good. Few alto stratus clouds to E. Wind SE 5." Bailey, in the plane, is contacting Waite with the tractor. Dyer interrupts to pass on the Geological Party's weather. A striking instance of how our field communications functioned under Dyer's superb direction.)

2:15 OK. At 2:05 passed tractor trail at intersection of NE and E legs.

(At the "intersection" meant, presumably, the beacon to which the tractors retreated on the 17th, after the flight to locate a passage for them. June passed the tractors unseeing and unseen, about 40 miles to the west, though Bailey was in contact with Waite.)

2:40 OK. Motor spitting (a pause, then a reassuring) OK. QSK10 (meaning will see you in 10 minutes).

3:00 PX at 2:55—(Lat.) 81° 10′ S., Long. 152° 30′. Changed course to 126°. Tested altitude—1600 feet.[8] Tractor weather same.

(They were on the threshold of the critical area, and this abrupt rise in elevation meant high land—land well above sea-level—land that held the fate of the Strait. A quick calculation placed them about 267 miles southeast of Little America and about 28 miles southwest of the trough in the Horseshoe crevasse we had marked on the 15th.)

3:20 OK. No mountains in sight yet.

3:40 PX (Lat.) 81° 42′ S, (Long.) 146° 15′ W. Came down at 3.29. Elevation 2000 feet.[9] Surface steadily going up. No topographical features.

(So this blank white surface rising ahead of them, unmarred and unbroken by exposed rock, must be plateau—high land entirely capped by ice. Part of the same high land, certainly, that Blackburn, Russell and Paine had raised near Lat. 84°, between 350 and 375 Mile Depots. The southwestern margin of the Ross Ice Barrier.)

4:00 OK. QSK 4:20.
Tractor WX: "Bar. 28:40. Wind S—5, viz good. Ceiling unlimited, a few clouds. . . ."
Geological Party WX: "Bar. 14:60. Temp. minus 1. Clouds and viz same.

[7] The Geological Party had a hypsometric barometer which was graduated in feet instead of inches. Due to weather changes their altitude would seem to vary, though when corrections were applied it was found to be practically the same all the way across the Barrier.

[8] Subsequently corrected by calibration of the barograph to 1370 feet elevation.

[9] Subsequently corrected to 1840 feet.

4:20 PX at 4:15 (Lat.) 82° 02′ S., (Long.) 142° 30′ W. "Nothing in sight but great smooth level plain as far as can see. About 2,000 feet high and exactly like area to east and south of Haines. Gas consumption low—72 gals. per hour. Weather perfect. All well." JUNE

(At 4:15 they were 356.5 statute miles out—more than 184 miles beyond the crevassed area—and with vision of more than 50 miles over the snow surface in all directions beyond that point. The identical nature of this "great smooth level plain" they were exploring to the broad plateau swirling around Haines, a sugar-loaf mountain group in the Edsel Ford Mountains, was already inclining the flight crew to the belief that these plateaux were one. Well, we'd withhold decision till the next elevations. They can probably still go several hundred miles. And there was still that trough, now narrowed to a slit, near the Horseshoe at Lat. 81°.)

4:45 DR PX at 4:45 (Lat.) 82° 19′ S., (Long.) 138° 20′ W, "Averaging 75 knots. Tested elevation at 4:35. 2,000 feet." [10] RAWSON
CORRECTION PX. (Lat.) 82° 21′ S., (Long.) 137° 40′ W.

5:05 Geological Party WX: "temp. zero, wind and viz same. Bar, 17:70 QSK 6.
TRACTOR WX: "unchanged."

5:10 Plane says: OK.

5:35 OK.—reeling in again. BAILEY

("Reeling in" meant that Bailey was cranking in the plane's antennae. June must be dropping for another sounding—brushing low over the ice to test elevation by altimeter. Really a new technique in exploration, a shrewd tactical method in the search for the strait.)

5:50 DR PX at 5:45 (Lat.) 82° 52′ S., (Long.) 125° 15′ W. Tested elevation at 5:40 (o'clock)—2,850 feet.[11] At 5:30 (changed) course to 104° true. On basis of right angle wind test find ground speed last hour and half around 82 knots. Increase 4:45 and 5:15 (o'clock) mileages proportionately. RAWSON

("Right angle wind test" meant that they had flown at right angles to their course, to obtain the true direction and force of the wind. By correcting for drift as shown by the drift indicator the plane can be kept on the course, but it is necessary to know the force and direction of the wind to determine the ground speed and, hence, how far the plane has gone. Still, they would be turning back in a few minutes—

[10] Corrected to true elevation of 1,760 feet.
[11] Corrected to true elevation of 2,480 feet.

they were approaching the outward limits of their gas, allowing a 20 per cent safety margin.)

6:00 Geological Party WX: "Bar. 1600. Temp. zero. Viz excellent. Stratus clouds in east." Tractor Party WX: "perfect."

6:25 Turned around at 6:05 in (Lat.) 83° 05′ and (Long.) 119° W. Sighted high mountains in S. Judge to be Queen Mauds. Tested elevation at 6:15—3,350 feet.[12]...
...Yes, turned at 6:05. Then had 500 gals. gas. WX perfect. Many thanks for message. All well. JUNE

(I had flashed them a message congratulating them on discovery. Discovery of the plateau and with it the further definition of the eastern shore of the Ross Ice Barrier was by itself a superb achievement: but discovery of a new mountain group approximately 170 miles east of the last known extension of the Queen Mauds was a capping triumph. Yet, as it turned out, this last hung by the proverbial eyelash. They had decided to turn a few minutes before 6:00 o'clock. But with weather so excellent and headwinds diminishing, they were tempted to prolong the flight a few minutes more. Smith had spelled June at the controls. About 6 o'clock, just when they were about to wheel, Smith made the landfall—a cluster of snow-clad peaks 45° off their port bow, barely awash on the horizon line. Smith excitedly called June's attention to them: Rawson hurried up forward with the field glasses. The peaks must have been well over 100 miles away, Rawson said, when Smith first saw them—too far away for Pelter's mapping camera. But the flight crew held their course long enough to be absolutely sure of what they saw. Then, at Lat. 83° 05′ S., Long. 119° W., 552 statute miles southeast of Little America, they turned for Little America.)

6:45 OK. QSK 7 (o'clock).

7:00 OK. PX not ready. QSK 7:15
Geological Party WX: WX same except for wind which south 5 miles.

(I wonder what thoughts are going through the minds of the Geological Party—poor devils, as they listen in on the plane's progress bulletins. For 36 days they've been footing it toward the mountains, with a day's full journey still to go; yet in less than six hours a flight crew overtakes and passes them 200 miles to the east, wheels and heads back for luncheon at Little America. Without once lifting a foot. Without a twinge of the agony of sledging. Well, flying is faster, and, for that matter, its risks are greater.

[12] Corrected to true elevation of 2,810 feet.

7:15 Plane PX: (Lat.) 82° 23′ S., (Long.) 136° W. WX perfect. Viz and ceiling unlimited.
7:30 OK. QSK 7:45.
7:45 OK. QSK 8.
8:00 OK. QSK 8:15.
8:15 OK. QSK 8:30.
Marie Byrd Land Party WX: "7:30 A.M. Bar. 27.20. Falling clouds—50 percent overcast. Wind E—35 m.p.h., viz fair. We are camped on blue ice and antennae won't stay up. . . .

(Siple's party thus breaks in with a warning—clouds and a blizzard over the Edsel Fords. Haines, who throughout the night has sat at Dyer's elbow, appraises the report anxiously, then hurries topside for a glance at the sky over Little America. It remains fair, but low down on the southeastern horizon, between the plane and the Base, a smudge of cloud is broadening. Haines decides to take an immediate balloon run.)

8:40 Bailey asks for tractor weather report. Tractor unheard.
9:00 OK. Plane PX: "(Lat.) 81° (Long.) 148° 30′. QSK 9:20."
Tractor Party WX: "perfect."
9:20 We have not passed tractors yet. Still have 300 gals. gas at 9:10. Have recognized crevasses at 81°. All well, weather fine. JUNE. QSK 9:40.
9:40 KHNGHT (the plane) calls Waite and sez cannot find tractors because of low ceiling.

(Curious. The plane must be over ground fog too heavy for June to risk breaking through it. Yet only 20 minutes before the tractor party reported perfect weather. That's how quickly weather can close in on you on a flight. Well, Demas would have to do without his connecting rods.)

9:40 (cont.) We sighted tractor trail thru hole in clouds but surface instantly obscured again so have headed for LA. MSG (for) Haines: "Please give WX and upper air, also surface barometer at LA." JUNE

(They wanted the barometric pressure in order to set the altimeter at proper pressure in case they had to make a blind landing at Little America with ceiling zero. Haines instantly sent the reading—advised them that Little America was still clear, but low clouds were gathering on the southeastern horizon, on their line of flight. With 140 miles still to go, June was apprehensive the plane might be cut off.)

10:00 Engines wide open. Still over clouds.
10:10 Plane PX: (Lat.) 79° 37′ S., (Long.) 158°. QSK 10:30.
10:30 Clearing up. Can see surface now. Very thin clouds. Guess we can beat it in. BAILEY. OK. QSK 10:45.

10:45 Amundsen Arm ahead. QSK 11.
11:00 Am securing to land. See U few mins.
11:05 LA in sight. Now.
11:09 Landing . . . landing . . .

VII

Thus, racing the fog, they brought to conclusion an 1100-mile flight of discovery which carried to Lat. 83° 05′ S., Long. 119° 00′ S., 552 miles southeast of Little America. Just before they were due to cross the tractor trail, they came upon a solid layer of black, puffy clouds, half a mile thick and pressing down on the Barrier. After sighting the trail through a hole in the vapor, June pushed into it, flying blind for a few minutes, hoping to find the tractors. He soon gave it up; too risky. There was the chance, too, that if he lingered the overcast would meanwhile close in around Little America; cut off, he would have no recourse but to race southward to find a place to land. So, giving up the project of dropping the connecting rods, he headed for the base. For 125 miles they flew over a sea of clouds, never once seeing the surface. But near Little America the fog thinned out: about 20 miles out they found a groove dividing thick masses of fog. Down this groove Smith, who had taken his trick at the wheel, dived with the throttle wide open; the plane burst into view almost over the camp. A half-hour after they landed the sky over Little America was solidly overcast.

The achievements of that flight—the discovery of the plateau south of 81° and the mountain landfall at the turning point—have already been outlined. According to Rawson's calculations, these new peaks lay approximately in the vicinity of Lat. 85° 30′ S., between Long. 110° and 115° W. He, June and Smith were agreed the peaks, of which they counted perhaps half a dozen, were grossly iced: at their great distance no bare rock seemed to show. Though they saw no mountains to the westward, probably because of a bank of haze which they saw along the mountains, there was every reason to believe that this group must be a prolongation of the Queen Mauds which Dr. Gould of the first expedition had traced eastward to Long. 140°.[13] In position and character, and especially in their heavily glacierized aspect, they fitted into the pattern of peaks Dr. Gould and his companions, Goodale, Crockett, Vaughan and O'Brien, had seen to the eastward of Supporting Party Mt.[14]

This same afternoon, Dr. Poulter, June, Rawson and I had a

[13] Gould, *Cold*, 208: *Little America*, p. 406.

[14] "Throughout the whole of our eastward journey . . . we had found the Queen Maud Mountains getting ever progressively lower and the covering of ice so much thicker that we could not help speculating upon the possibility of the range disappearing beneath the ice farther to the east. . . ." Gould, op. cit., 210.

thorough discussion on how much this flight affected the status of the Strait. This much was certain: discovery of the plateau and with it the sounding of a 1,370 foot elevation just across the belt of crevasses along the 81st parallel seemed virtually to abolish the Strait.

In the whole eastern coastline of the Ross Shelf Ice there remained, now, for all practical purposes, only a 40 or 50 mile slit, between the 81st and 82nd parallels and a similar gap between the limit of surface vision of the plane crew on the southeastern flight and the new mountains. In the first gap we had found low-level ice; north and south of it were steadily rising plateau elevations. The problem was reduced to one of elimination—to wipe out these slits as rapidly as possible. They held the rapidly expiring destiny of the theoretical Antarctic Strait.

Therefore we resolved, as soon as weather lifted, to ram home another flight.

Next morning—November 23rd—the fog commenced to lift, and aviation hurried preparations for departure in the afternoon.

VIII

On the flight to close the gap I was again in the plane. My strength was slowly coming back and I felt up to another effort. I was also anxious to have a talk with the tractor party, and see how well they were bearing up under the strain of their appalling journey. Also we had the connecting rods aboard. The decision to go, I must confess, wasn't exactly what the doctor ordered. As a matter of fact, I came very near being left behind, chiefly because I neglected to tell the flight crew I was going. After the noon "ob," I lay down for a while, thinking it would be several hours before the plane was gassed and ready. The next thing I heard was the plane in flight over Little America. "Yes," said George Noville, chuckling, "it's the plane and it looks as if you've missed connections." However, a radio message brought the plane back. At 5:16 P.M. we were off for the southeast.

The flight crew consisted of June, Bowlin, Rawson, Petersen and myself.

The afternoon was clear, the wind a light southerly, the temperature $+6°$.

Rawson laid a course for the tractors, which the night before were at Lat. 80° 29′ S., Long. 151° 33′ W., about 207 miles southeast of Little America.

The beauty of the evening was past describing. The Barrier was an enchantment of pure gold. On the way we crossed Roosevelt Island. I conned it now with field glasses. It is a very large island—nearly 100 miles long and close to 50 miles wide; it rises just south of Amundsen Arm and extends past Advance Base. The Valley of Crevasses beyond 50-Mile Depot on the main Southern trail is a narrow bight in its western face: and though they hadn't realized it at the time, the high ridge the parties followed around the Valley was actually one of the lower slopes of the island. We brushed the crest of the island as we flew over it, and got an altimetric sounding of 1,070 feet.[15] A little later we took another sounding and got 1,237 feet.

About 80 miles southeast of Little America, well beyond the island, we dropped for a third sounding—275 feet. Low barrier ice here and numerous crevasses.

At 6:45 o'clock Petersen came forward with a message from Morgan and Bramhall, relayed by Dyer at Little America, saying that the tractors had moved 23 miles east during the day. So we altered course for the new position. Ten minutes later another sounding—200 feet elevation. We were then about 17 miles southeast of the area where the Japanese expedition of 1912 had reported high Barrier, but we could see no sign of a rise anywhere in the vicinity.

At 7:36 June picked up the tractor trail, a thin track bearing east. We soon had the orange cars underneath. Petersen was in radio contact with Waite, and instructed them to stand by for the connecting rods. The bundle was parachuted down and, as we squared away on the course again, I saw two men hurry after it. I decided not to risk a landing until we had finished our exploration.

Making close to 90 knots, we struck directly for the Horseshoe crevasses which had yielded the only sea-level elevation we had found in the whole broad stretch between the Edsel Fords and the Queen Mauds.

Shortly after leaving the tractors we were over that rumpled, crumpled crescent. We coasted down for an elevation sounding, skimming the ice for a mile or so to allow the altimeter to settle—771 feet above sea-level.

The ice was rising—rising toward the 2,000 foot plateau elevation the others had discovered, the day before, just a few miles south.

The slit was narrowing.

We swung east, flying low. Even as we came around, I realized that the Strait was in all likelihood doomed.

Above our flight level, above the swinging nose of the ship, rolled the rising silver folds of the plateau.

Nevertheless we steadily bore east for 60 miles on the parallel of 81° 10′ S. Three times we stooped for soundings—1,105 feet, 1,204 feet, 1,338 feet. It was an exhilarating piece of detective work: the quarry all but cornered, the judgment crowding in. East of the Horseshoe the crevasses were petering out: there were fewer black holes. And past the point where we turned, approximately on the 140th meridian, the land was still rising, a silver bulwark in all directions.

Nevertheless, to satisfy the last lingering doubt, we ran north about 16 miles. A sounding here of 1,591. Then west again, paralleling the outward course and completely squaring the line of inquiry about the

[15] These and subsequent elevations, are corrected readings.

crucial gap. Three more soundings—1,138 feet, 1,085 feet, 669 feet, this last just a little north and east of the Horseshoe.

I think that when we took our eyes off the flickering needle of the altimeter we all drew a sigh of relief.

"That's it," somebody shouted above the sound of the engines.

The trough—the sea-level depression we had blundered into on the 15th—was nothing more than a bight in the eastern shore of the Barrier.

As we soared once more above the shining carapace I took stock of the findings.

The eastern coast of the Ross Shelf Ice was now filled in. Rimming it was a massive and unbroken plateau, 4,500 feet high behind the Edsel Fords, drooping to a moderate elevation near the center, then rising again to 3,000 feet near the foot of the Queen Maud Range. A solid barrier to the Strait. It was land, all land: land overridden by ice, to be sure: but land which, were the ice to melt, would stand as solidly interposed to the questing keel of a ship as the Atlantic coast stood before the 16th century navigators seeking a Strait to Cathay.

Antarctica, almost beyond a shadow of doubt, is one continent. There is almost certainly no Strait between the Ross and Weddell Seas. A glance at the map with its network of flight tracks, together with the more significant soundings by altimeter, will show that this is no idle prophecy.

The one region not observed in the whole long stretch between the South Pacific Ocean and the Queen Mauds is the southern half of the stretch of plateau between Lat. 83° 05′ S., where the flight crew of the 22nd turned back, and the Horlick Mountains discovered on that flight. Though the crew had uninterrupted vision over the northern part of this region and saw the surface steadily rising toward the mountains, recognition of the axiom that nothing is certain in geography till it is proved persuades me to set this area apart as possibly (though in all probability not) doubtful in relation to the non-existence of the Strait.

But you may ask, as the question was posed in the preliminary discussion of the problem of the Strait: aren't these just *ice* elevations? How can you tell the character of the land under ice, or how deep it may lie?

There are the seismic sounding records compiled by Dr. Poulter and Gill Morgan—a whole dossier of them, including soundings on a north-and-south line across part of the new plateau. These will be discussed more fully later on; it is sufficient for our purposes here to say that the general results show that with an *ice* elevation of 1,200 feet above sea-level (as on Roosevelt Island) the ice capping is about 400 feet, which gives a land elevation underneath of 800 feet. With ice elevations of between 2,000 and 3,000 feet (as in back of the Alexandra Mountains, where the upraised land appears to dam up the ice) the ice layer may be as thick as between 1,000 and 2,000 feet, but elsewhere appears to be thinner.[16]

On this data we rested our case.

A little while later, Blackburn, Paine and Russell of the Geological Party, from their lofty perch in the Queen Mauds, were to see that the so-called Leverett Glacier was actually a structure which, for want of a generic name, they called a *sub-plateau.* This new plateau was rising over the diminishing nunataks of the mountains and seemingly preparing, farther eastward, to merge with the great polar plateau probably forming from the coast to the South Pole a continuous reach of land.

I named this land Rockefeller Plateau, after John D. Rockefeller Jr., who has generously supported my expeditions.

IX

At 9:55 o'clock we landed alongside the tractors. It was good to see the men again; in spite of all the hardships, they were all in good spirits. However, there was time for little more than an exchange of greetings; we were too anxious to settle on the best course they should pursue to gain the plateau. Demas and Hill remarked that they had had no end of mechanical difficulties, owing to cold and the strain put upon the engines by heavy loads in soft snow, but were confident they could keep the cars running. I noticed that Demas's face had been burned raw by an explosion: the eyebrows and eyelashes were singed and the skin under his beard was peeling. He made no mention of it, but Waite told me that it had been caused by a small gasoline explosion.

Since leaving the beacon to which they had been directed by the flight of the 16th, the two cars had traveled 172.5 miles on the new course, 56 miles on a sweeping curve to the northeast, then 80 miles due east toward the plateau. When we overtook them they were at Lat. 80° 28′ S., Long. 149° 04′ W., about 23 miles from the edge of the plateau, and about 33 miles northwest of the Horseshoe crevasse. Directly between them and the plateau was a severely crevassed ridge through which, I was convinced, after surveying it from the air, they could not pass. It would be necessary, I felt, for them to retreat to the north again, before they could find a safe ascent to the plateau.

Anyhow, I invited them to go aloft for a survey of the region with the pilots. Morgan, Bramhall and Hill flew about 20 miles along the edge of the plateau. The lower reaches of the plateau were everywhere fringed with crevasses, but Bramhall and Morgan thought that by bearing north a way and carefully picking their spots they could squeeze the tractors through. In all events, they were encouraged by

[16] The greatest thickness of ice reported by Morgan was 2,100 feet at a 3200-foot elevation just back of the Alexandras.

the reconnoissance: it greatly simplified the problem by saving time that might have been lost in fruitless searching. They hoped to be able to run their line of seismic and magnetic observations across the plateau to Mt. Grace McKinley, which was almost due north of them. However, they were doubtful as to their gas supply: and the crevasses on the roof of the plateau were also incalculable obstacles. I give them—Bramhall, Morgan, Demas, Waite and Hill—full credit for resourcefulness and determination. Few exploring parties in modern times have had to put up with greater difficulties and perils.

We wished them luck on the new course: and at 10:49 took off for Little America.

Past the radiantly white line of the Barrier, as we drew near Little America, we joyfully marked blue water in the Ross Sea. Pack still littered it, but the sea was breaking open under the mild persuasion of summer. It gave you a lift to see it.

A few minutes before 1 A.M. we landed at Little America.

Chapter XVI

NEW LANDS

I

AFTER the flight to close the gap, aviation moved for a while into the background of expedition affairs. There remained unliquidated only one important flight of geographical exploration on the program—a long thrust to the northeast to attempt to fill in the coast behind the Edsel Ford Range. Whether we should ever be able to execute it, I could not say. Weather in that sector was too treacherous, too uncertain. Haines was anything but sanguine. The stagnant conditions of summer, the fogs, the overcast and the light summer snows, were already upon us. The day after the flight the fogs again clamped down: for 13 days the skies were overcast, snow fell on every day but two. On November 24th the wind rose and for seven days blew steadily, warm but robust winds out of north and east, gusty and loud, with velocities up to 34 miles per hour. On the 25th the temperature climbed to + 22—the warmest temperature, by a substantial margin, since a freak day in July: and the fifth day since June 4th that the minimum temperature had not hit zero or lower. Actually the "dog days" of the Antarctic summer were at hand; thereafter, until Haines dismantled the weather station on January 31st, 1935, the temperature would only twice drop below zero, and four times would rise above freezing.

Profiting by wind and fog, aviation gave the big plane another scrupulous overhaul. There could be no cutting of corners on this last flight. As the season progresses, the risks against aviation mount proportionately—partly on account of the instability of weather, partly on account of the diminishing potential usefulness of field parties for relief work as their rations and dogs are used up, and, finally, because a crash landing away from base may require dangerous rescue operations and perhaps a second winter in the Antarctic for those involved. These factors were carefully considered in the calculations for the coastal (or northeastern) flight.

About midnight on the 22nd, Finn Ronne and Albert Eilefsen, who had acted as support for the Geological Party to 300-Mile Depot, returned to Little America, having made the return journey in nine days—very fast sledging time. So quietly did they enter the camp that no one, except the night watchman, knew they were back till next morning. But they were given a glad welcome at breakfast. Both were windburned to the color of copper: they were worn down rather fine, and the bones showed in Eilefsen's usually chubby face. "They look like a couple of turkey buzzards," Noville said. Actually Eilefsen had lost 15 pounds, and Ronne only three. A curious fact, but sledging seems to take most out of a bigger man. They turned over their loads to Blackburn, Russell and Paine at 300 Miles, they said, and started back at 9 A.M., November 12. The return dash was uneventful except for the speed. Their best day's march was 47 miles—on the 19th, when they ran all the way from 150-Mile Depot to Advance Base in 13½ hours' traveling. At Advance Base they rested 18 hours, resuming the journey on the night of the 20th. In spite of being held up half a day by blizzard, they made the run from Advance Base to Little America in about 75 hours, really excellent time all the way. The journey was made with a single team of 11 dogs, Eilefsen having turned over all but two of his dogs to the Geological Party at 300-Mile Depot. I think that Ronne's real pleasure came not so much from showing the camp what a couple of Norwegian ski experts could do on the trail, as from the vindication of his claim that between him and his argumentative Manitoba leader, Power, there existed a perfect understanding. All the other dog drivers used to say that Power wore the pants in that team: that whenever Power had reason to suspect the team wasn't being run properly, he'd sit down on his haunches and bark furiously at Finn, declining to budge till the matter was adjusted then and there. Such fast time, said Finn, wouldn't have been possible if Power had stopped to argue. In the team also, lined up side by side as files, were the seven fine pups born at Little America the previous February: and, backing them at wheel was Ski, the only veteran of both expeditions. But of Paine's great leader, Jack, Ronne spoke as another man might speak of genius. "There," he said softly, "is a dog—a dog that's half man. All the way south that dog broke trail for the whole party. I've never seen a dog do that before."

"How was the Geological Party getting along?"

"Very smoothly," said Ronne. "That's one party you won't have to worry about."

"Pretty hard going, wasn't it, after you cut loose from the tractors?"

"For the first few days, yes. The loads were quite heavy, and the sledges were breaking through a light crust. We had to ice the runners twice a day to get a run on the sledges. It was cold, too. I remember Paine saying one day, when it was 20 below, that it seemed like mid-summer."

"How about wind? They say they've had winds all the way to the mountains?"

"We got a bellyful of it between 200 and 300 miles. The worse blow hit us on the 13th, the day before we reached 300-Mile Depot. It was a fifty mile wind, cold as the devil. It cut right through you."

Ronne brought back a message from Blackburn, saying that he was leaving 300-Mile Depot with three 11-dog teams, and expected to reach the Queen Maud Range in 10 days. He had aboard his sledges

1,440 pounds of dog food and 450 pounds of man food which, with the surplus dogs, was enough to provision them for 33 days' field work beyond the mountain base.

Blackburn actually reached the mountain base a day ahead of schedule, advising us on the 23rd that he was that morning camped near the foot of Supporting Party Mountain. In spite of the loss of 5½ days escorting the tractors, they were all but on schedule.

As for the crevasses, especially those they traversed while reconnoitering for the tractors, Ronne and Eilefsen were almost speechless trying to find words to describe them. Altogether, they crossed the belt six times in three weeks. I shall only quote Eilefsen, since his remark struck me as being the last word on the subject. "No gude," said Albert, "no gude," shaking his big head. After being exposed to the English language for a year, he could find no better description.

II

December of the second season is always a critical period in the life of an Antarctic expedition. For it usually finds all the field units either approaching or at their greatest distances from the main base, and aviation standing by, night and day, to seize the rare break in the eternal fog and cloudiness. In the career of the second expedition, December 1934 was no exception. It found us with our resources fully engaged. On the evening of December 1st the tractor party reported they were at last through the crevasses and on the lower western reaches of the plateau, after a journey of 445 nautical miles out of Little America. Siple's Marie Byrd Land Party was deep in the Edsel Ford Mountains, having divided in order to accomplish the greatest possible work in the time remaining to them, Wade and Stancliff going north along the western front range on a geological reconnoissance, and Siple and Corey striking northeast on a biological mission. There was no direct word at that time from the Geological Party. A freak magnetic storm during the last three days of November—the most violent of the year—interrupted communications. For nearly 48 hours the air was dead. On the 30th, Waite with the tractors very dimly overheard Paine with the Geological Party trying to get through to Dyer at Little America. He copied the message, which was garbled, but was himself unable to relay it until atmospheric conditions improved on December 1st. The message said:

> Sorry were unable to reach you last sked, probably due to x x x x . . . Have traveled part . . . ice with rippled and crevassed surface for last three days . . . yesterday stopped at . . . we are about 23 miles up Thorne Glacier. Unsatisfied with mantled nature of mountains tributary to Leverett. . . .

I cite this message principally in evidence why the leaders of polar expeditions gray prematurely. Here at the critical stage of his journey

Blackburn is suddenly isolated from Little America by remote atmospheric events. A survey of the region he has traveled 517 miles to reach (not counting the mileage lost reconnoitering for the tractors), persuaded him that the route up Leverett Glacier which he originally selected is unsuitable. The sentence saying "unsatisfied with mantled nature of mountains" must mean he decided at the time that the mountains are too heavily iced for geological inspection. Therefore he suddenly decided to swing up Thorne Glacier, a route he had previously rejected. Unhappily for my larger purposes, the interruption of communications came just at the time when I was about to recommend to Blackburn that instead of ascending the Queen Maud Range he swing along the foot of it and explore the Range eastward. At Supporting Party Mountain he was already at the easternmost limits of discovery: he had only to sledge a few miles to be in wholly unknown area. The geographical importance of further locating the trend of the Queen Mauds and of definitely establishing the relationship of the new mountain group (the Horlick Mountains) seemed to me to hold out a more valuable prospect to the party. It was also of great importance to obtain detailed observations on the junction of the Rockefeller plateau and the mountains. It was, however, too late to do anything about it. When we next regained contact with the party on December 3rd, after a silence of six days, they were already 70 miles up Thorne Glacier. I must make plain, however, that this is no criticism of Blackburn's choice. It was just the difference between two points of view—Blackburn's interest as a geologist naturally gravitating him toward the route most effective for geological research, my interest in geography turning toward the expanding opportunities for discovery. If the weather held out any prospect of a successful flight in that direction, I should not have been forced to consider modifying Blackburn's program. However, his geological data was so excellent that I was reconciled to the geographical loss. No matter what direction he steered, he could not have executed a more brilliant journey.

Thurs., Dec. 6, 11 P.M.

Still overcast. Aviation is very pessimistic. June remarked today that he expected the next—and last—flight would be to deliver the planes to the ship.

We are definitely at a crucial point of our operations, with all parties at close to their peak distance away from the base. If anything should go wrong now—if one of the parties should happen to stub its toe—we might be hard put to it to find a way to extricate the men. Aviation is an unreliable reserve factor, on account of its dependence on the weather. Of the four dog teams in camp, three are constantly in use for seismic and biological errands. Our reserve tractor is mechanically prostrate. Dane started south with it the other day, intending to salvage

Advance Base, but a short distance out he was first stopped by a crevasse, then by the disintegration of the shaft. No spares could be found here. Innes-Taylor then radioed Demas for the whereabouts of spares. From the remote dome of the plateau, where he certainly must have enough vexations of his own, Demas said they were in case No. 5, in a cache near the tractor garage. For the past two days a squad of men under Innes-Taylor's direction have been making prodigious excavations in the drift about the garage, trying to find the case. Innes-Taylor was taken to bed with a bad ankle. The doctor put a cast on it, and Innes-Taylor will therefore be out of action for a couple of weeks. Over his bunk somebody scrawled the words: "CASE NO. 5—practically hopeless."

The Geological Party advised yesterday that it was 85 miles up Thorne Glacier. ". . . there are several hundred new peaks and many glaciers to map. Our dogs in no condition to go on an extended trip east." Which extinguishes the opportunity of filling in the area between the 140th and the 115th meridians. If we should get a break in weather, and succeed in mapping the coast, I should like to make a flight in that direction.

Siple reported this morning that his party is again reunited and homeward bound with a heavy cargo of geological specimens. However, he's short of dog food and is asking to be met by a supporting party at 150-Mile Depot, between the Rockefellers and the Edsel Fords. Well, the tractors may be able to give him a hand. They are now about 65 miles from the 150-Mile Depot, which is their next objective. Siple and Wade can turn over to them their rocks, which will enable them to make better time and perhaps eliminate the need for support.

But I don't know. The tractors themselves are again in a jam. Bramhall and Morgan yesterday reported being stopped by poor visibility in a badly crevassed area at an elevation of 1,400 feet, at (dead reckoning) Lat. 79° 07′ S., Long. 149° 24′ W. The crevasses run in a northeast-southwest direction. In reporting to Dyer, Waite added that both cars had gone into crevasses but were now OK. It's been a rocky voyage for the Iron Horses. On top of that, it now appears they have scarcely gas to carry them within a hundred miles of Little America. We've got to get gas out to them some way. Demas is reluctant to abandon one car. Two cars, he maintains, are absolutely essential, one to pull the other out of crevasses. He's perfectly right. Evidently, as summer progresses the bridges are weakening and the crevasses are opening up. This partly accounts for their increasing difficulties. Ronne said that when he and Eilefsen recrossed the belt at 81° the holes seemed considerably wider.

Thus with three parties we have three potentially dangerous situation spots on a 600-mile front, from the Edsel Fords to the rim of the south polar plateau. Anything may happen. The next fortnight will either bring serious trouble or a quick winding up of field activities. Another thing: Dyer says that he can't tell how long the Geological or Marie Byrd Land Party will be able to hold two-way communication. The latter party's receiver batteries are nearly used up, principally on account of transmitting daily weather bulletins for aviation. Paine says that his spare set of batteries was damaged—just how, he didn't explain.

Fri., Dec. 7, 10:20 P.M.

At last the sun—a warm, fine day, with a temperature of 15°. Aviation was all set to go, but conditions weren't stable enough to launch a flight. In the afternoon, the tractor party advised heavy fog and visibility of only a hundred yards on the plateau. Apart from its bearing as a safety factor, this flight requires good visibility for effective mapping of the coast—its main objective. Without good visibility the mapping camera is useless. As a matter of fact, this is the principal reason we are so dependent upon weather. Haines and June today brought up for discussion the alternative of a flight southeast to the Queen Maud Range. The weather in that sector is usually better, and they were inclined to think that the chances of making it were superior to those of the coastal flight. However, the experience of the southeastern flight shows that there is no great assurance that we can defeat the clouds this way. The prospect is tempting, but I'm disinclined to involve the Condor in another operation until we've cleared up the coastal problem. Definition of the coast of Marie Byrd Land is of major geographical importance.

We are all following, with utmost sympathy and interest, Ellsworth's efforts to complete his transcontinental flight.[1] We are now furnishing him with daily and sometimes twice daily weather reports. Ellsworth and Balchen face a long and difficult flight. Their probable track and what they're likely to find on the way are a lively topic of conversation here. Bill Haines was talking about it today. This late in the season, Bill says, the chances against the right conditions for the flight are about 100 to 1. Weather, of course: the same sort of thing we're up against, but on a much larger scale. Where we need a clear stretch of only 400 miles or so, they need clear weather between two hemispheres. The weather experts and pilots here seem to think that Ellsworth's only hope this season is to ignore weather at his end and seize the first stable weather at Little America, gambling on the chance of breaking through and finding good weather for landing here. Well, there are two objections to that. If he and Balchen take off in poor weather, they cut themselves off from an avenue of retreat. Secondly, Ellsworth's mission is

[1] The Ellsworth-Balchen Trans-Antarctic Expedition in October 1934 returned to the Antarctic for a second effort, this time basing across the continent, first at Deception Island then later at Snow Hill Island. Continuously bad weather made it impossible for Ellsworth and Balchen to fulfill their purpose of a transcontinental flight to the Bay of Whales. Early in January 1935, Ellsworth notified us at Little America that he was postponing the flight another year.

exploration—you can't explore if you haven't visibility to see. God knows what will happen to them if they come down in the interior. In that whole 2000-mile stretch of unknown coastline, there's only one place to which they can walk with the faintest hope of being picked up by a ship—Little America on the Bay of Whales. We have quietly laid plans how we might best assist them in such a contingency. That's one reason why I am anxious to have our own field enterprises wound up as expeditiously as possible. Anyhow, they can count upon a warm welcome at Little America.

The sick-list is up. Innes-Taylor will be laid up for a fortnight with his foot in a cast. Dr. Potaka thinks an operation will be necessary—not here, fortunately, but in the States. Noville is temporarily out of action with a stomach disorder, Von der Wall with a wrenched back (too much heavy lifting), Perkins with a painful carbuncle which the doctor had to lance. Dr. Poulter came in tonight, after fourteen hours' sledging with his seismic outfit, in great pain from snow blindness. Black and Fleming, who were with him, were similarly affected. They'll be laid up for a day or so.

I had no sooner finished this entry when Haines knocked on the door. "It looks pretty good," he warned. An upper air sounding had yielded the fair-weather currents he and Grimminger were waiting for. The night watchman was sent after the flight crew—June, Bowlin, Rawson, Pelter and Petersen, all of whom were sleeping. The hour was nearly midnight. The air was clear, but there was still falling the diminishing rain of one of the most copious and beautiful ice showers I have ever seen. For several hours the upper air swam with myriads of sifting, drifting, glinting atoms of buoyant color, like those colloidal things one used to see in the windows of old-fashioned apothecaries. But ever so much lovelier; every one of these minute particles was a prism and all together they turned the air into an ocean of rainbows. From the sun fell a pillar of cascading platinum, and there was a like splashing of radiance at the foot of the parhelic "dogs" on either side.

A fair omen. The plane was off at 2:37, with a load of 19,800 pounds and fuel for 14 hours' flying at economical throttle. Though the snow was soft and there was no help from the wind, the air being almost dead, nevertheless the big ship strove clear after a run of 23 seconds. June swung low over the camp before he squared away, on a course which would carry him along the coast of King Edward VII Land and the coastal peaks of Marie Byrd Land. The Marie Byrd Land Party and the tractor party were again standing by for weather bulletins. I should point out here that it was desirable this flight to the northeast be started as near midnight as possible, in order to have the sun in a favorable beam position for navigation by sun compass. Otherwise at mid-morning Rawson would have the sun over the bow, and by early afternoon over the stern on account of the rapidity with which time and longitude change in high latitudes.

But the auspicious omens, the clear take-off with full load, the fortuitous hour, were all unavailing. Scarcely 15 minutes after the plane took off, a low bank of stratus clouds dirtied the southwestern horizon. Bill Haines and Grimminger, who were standing by in the radio shack as they always were in every flight, went topside every few minutes to see if it was increasing. It was—steadily and remorselessly, like a malignant growth. Still, the plane reported clear air except for "clouds to the south." It was hard to order them back while the way ahead was clear. But by a quarter past three—less than an hour after the plane took off—Little America was almost entirely roofed over. The ceiling, Haines calculated, dropped to 500 feet.

Nothing to do then but order them back, before retreat was cut off. They were within 15 miles of Okuma Bay, and the air ahead was bright with sunlight. They were excited, too, by finding the Ross Sea, from the Bay of Whales to Cape Colbeck, open to the horizon, with just a few patches of ice—"no more ice," Rawson said, "than you could put in a cup." Just before they landed, June dumped 200 gallons of gas to lighten the landing weight. With a perversity it does no good to rail against, the air was already clearing when the plane landed at 4:20 A.M., though heavy rolls of clouds still lay on the northern and western horizon. Five minutes before the skis touched the tractor party reported zero visibility on the plateau. Tired and disappointed, the flight crew repaired to the galley for a warming cup of cocoa, where they talked of the pleasure of finding the Ross Sea open, while the Great Carbone, stretched out on the hard wooden table behind them, snoozed and snored no doubt in gentle dreamy speculation of the hour the arrival of the ships would bring him reprieve.

The afternoon was clear and, the hour being unfavorable for the major flight, the crew took off again to put down a gasoline cache for the tractors at 120-Mile Depot on the eastern trail, just a little south and east of the Rockefellers, and at the foot of the western margin of the plateau. McCormick, happily recovered from the broken arm, was again in the air as co-pilot. The tractors were then striving to reach 150-Mile Depot on the eastern trail. Demas estimated he had enough gas to carry him west along the trail at least to 120-Mile Depot. By scraping into the reserve he had set aside for such a contingency and draining the last drops from gas drums which had long since been aside as empty, Noville managed to collect 150 gallons of tractor gas nobody knew he had. The flight was uneventful. After carefully picking a spot, June landed near the edge of the crevasses, then taxied up to the Depot, where they stacked the containers of gas. Sasturgi made it a bumpy landing. What appalled June, Rawson and Petersen was the startling disclosure from the air of the crevasses they had unwittingly traversed on their eastern tractor trip. A 20-mile stretch on either side of the trail from the Rockefellers to 120-Mile Depot, which they had appraised as entirely trustworthy surface, fairly crawled with blind crevasses. The tractor's tracks had almost miraculously threaded through the one gap in this broad region of trenches. Another thing that impressed them was the prominence with which the mountains—the Rockefellers, the Alexandras, and LaGorce—now stood out. When they had gone here on the 1st of October, the sun had been so low that distant objects were almost obscured in the near twilight. There was a great deal more bare rock showing now. The melting around exposed rock, hastened by radiation, had raised more of the land into view. They were back at Little America at 5:15 o'clock.

III

And now, with waiting, days commenced to drag. Gloomy gray days of fog and snow; and days suddenly and briefly illuminated by warm, rich surgings of tropical colors across the sky. Days of balancing as on a tight wire, scanning the meanings of the balloon runs (on most of which the balloon was lost to sight after a thousand feet or so in the overcast), and the weather reports from the field parties, hopefully clearing one hour at Little America and bad elsewhere, then clear with the field parties and hopeless there. Days of almost hourly false alarms, hurried heating of the engines, last-minute conferences, and ending almost always with the aviation unit trooping off to the Mess Hall to resume the poker game that was still, so far as I could tell, flourishing on the original capital of $43.20.

The air was getting warmer, though the temperature had yet to rise above freezing; the swings between the daily minima and maxima were diminishing—a few degrees, fifteen or twenty at the most. When the sun broke through you could feel the warmth penetrating to your bones. Summer brought its nuisances. The radiated heat caused melting around every wooden or metal object. Things which for months had been hidden by drift appeared like rocks exposed by an ebbing tide. The ghastly garbage dumps to the leeward of camp slowly emerged, offending the eye and the nose. The snow melted on the roofs, and the shacks leaked like a ship taking water at every rivet. There was a lively trickle of water through the roofs, defeating the precarious and complicated systems of drains and buckets which the tenants had constructed. In the Mess Hall we ate to the accompaniment of drops of water tinkling in soup already too thin for further dilution. Dyer, Bailey and Hutcheson in the radio shack had awnings stretched over the radio apparatus. Bailey went to answer a telephone and a gallon of water which had quietly collected within the roof chose that moment to seek a lower level. Noville exclaimed grumpily that he didn't mind the water coming through the roof: but when it started gushing through the walls it was time to man the pumps. As the crystalline cementing of snow over the older shacks collapsed and the full soggy weight came upon the roofs, the tenants feared the whole business might any moment come crashing down. Ever and anon would come strange and intimidating creakings and snappings from overhead. Shorings of boxes, timbers and steel frames—anything that was handy—were hastily thrown up to brace the sagging roofs. More than half the inhabitants of Little America took flight to the surface: a whole colony of tents sprang up around the camp. Dyer and Sterrett had a tent more than a mile away, on the Barrier heights overlooking the Bay of Whales. "Shore front," they called it and, trying to promote it into a substantial suburb, they advertised among its advantages "the first view of the ships when they come in." And the night watchman, wearied by his lengthening rounds, finally complained to the executive officer that he couldn't be expected to rout out work details in the early morning unless the tents stayed put. Just when he'd get the new residences memorized, the fellows would fool him by moving somewhere else.

All this melting, this softening of the snow, was more than a nuisance: harder pulling for the sledging parties on the home stretch, and a distinct peril for aviation. About noon on the 11th June tried to get the *William Horlick* off on a photographic hop over the Rockefellers. Though he had only 500 gallons of gas in the tanks, and half the weight of rations ordinarily carried, he couldn't rock the plane into the air. The air was dead calm, the anemometer cups were motionless, the temperature +25. Blobs of snow as big as a man's head clung to the skis, and the skis, instead of rising up and riding high, dug in and plowed. The best speed June could make on the ground was 45 knots, whereas 63-70 knots were needed to lift the plane with a full load. After two tries, June gave up. Thus another condition was imposed upon the projected coastal flight—a helping breeze and cold air to firm the snow.

Meanwhile, however, aviation scored a certain minor triumph. Ever since the old Fairchild had come to the surface in September, "Ike" Schlossbach and his faithful collaborators, Johnny Von der Wall and Bob Young, had been mysteriously puttering around it, their goings-on concealed by a wind-torn tent thrown around the plane. The rest of the camp had long ago dismissed the plane as useless, and regarded Ike's vow that it would fly as just another whimsical manifestation of the milder forms of Antarctic pathology. Well, one day in December the camp rubbed its eyes at the spectacle of the Fairchild emerging chrysalis-like from the grimy concealment of the tent, with a heater going full blast under the engine and Ike, Von der Wall and Young contemplating their handiwork with a solemnly delighted air of proprietorship. The broken struts had been welded together, the shattered ribs in the starboard wing section renewed, the flabby and torn fabric patched and drawn taut. There it stood ready to fly after five years under the snow. I ducked up through the hatch to come upon all hands, including the cook, assembled in grave convention. "What's this?" I asked. "Somebody hurt?" Not exactly; just a sitting of the Crash Board to consider the *status in quo ante* of the sad fate of Commander Schlossbach and his flying machine. I really believe that nearly every man there fully expected that Ike, like Darius Green, would be hoist on his own petard, and the morbid prospect of seeing him crash drew them more than the wonder of seeing the plane in the air. With its impressionistic patterns of fabric patches and lurid daubs of paint, the plane was hardly calculated to inspire confidence. And Ike himself hardly looked the part of a former squadron leader of a crack Navy fighting group. His beard was bushy and red and uncombed; his clothes were bafflingly held around him by a complicated system of horse-blanket pins and antennae wire which somehow simultaneously stood off gravity and disintegration. I had complete confidence in Ike. A man who could keep up his pants with such inventions would have no difficulty keeping the Fairchild up.

Ike took off with gusto, slamming over a haycock near the end of the run, and climbed, with the old engine screaming triumph in the full breadth of its power. Over Little America he put it through its test paces—steep climbs and dives, sharp turns, then down to brush the Barrier surface several times, and finally, as pretty a three-point landing as any one could ask for. The Crash Board meekly dissolved into congratulations instead of condolences, and Ike, Von der Wall and Young were the cocks of the walk. Thereafter Ike had the Fairchild in the air nearly every good day.

Wed., Dec. 12, 4:10 A.M.

Up all night, all of us, slaves to the weather. It was promising in the evening, then steadily grew worse. The Marie Byrd Land Party and the tractor party were reporting every two hours—the aviators and meteorologists huddled around the table in the radio shack, with the fire out and a pot of stale coffee humming on a primus stove. Because it looked fair here, Haines was reluctant to wash out the flight till the 4 A.M. reports from the trail. At that hour the tractors reported thick clouds to north and west; Siple reported 90 percent overcast. We called it off then.

Bad news from the tractors—Hill's car is out of commission. Demas advised, between weather reports, that a connecting rod pierced the crankcase and block casting. So they're abandoning it and will proceed in No. 3—Demas's car, after stripping the other of all salvageable parts and of course, all gasoline. No. 3 itself is so badly used up that it can probably use these parts to advantage. They even intend to salvage the drive shaft and universal joint. Lord, we're certainly being frugal.

The car foundered just after Bramhall and Morgan had cheerfully announced both cars were safely out of the crevasses in which they've been struggling since gaining the plateau. All clear ahead—then this. Their px is Lat. 79° S., Long. 150° 31′ W., which put them about 57 miles south-southeast of 150-Mile Depot on the eastern trail. They're just about 173 miles from here on a straight line.

Same day—10 P.M.

All parties are now in the home stretch. Blackburn advised that they started down the glacier, after completing their geological work at the rim of the south polar plateau. "Made ascent of Mt. Weaver and obtained cross-section, valuable fossils and rocks. Heading for Home Sweet Home this morning. Wind has never let up," was the message they flashed this morning, from within 207 miles of the Pole.

And Siple this morning checked in from 214 miles, homeward bound across the eastern plateau.

And the tractor party says it will be under way tomorrow for 150-Mile Depot. A suggestion that Siple's party be deflected to their assistance was politely declined as they were confident they could finish the journey as they began it—under their own power.

However, I dispatched Dane, Moody and Swan with two dog teams to the Rockefellers tonight, principally to salvage the engine and instruments of the Fokker. At the same time my mind will rest easier if we have two fresh teams available for emergency use on the eastern line of retreat. Siple is running short of dog food.

We have every reason to rejoice. All the scheduled field work has been successfully put through, the local scientific work has meanwhile prospered, the results have quite equaled our most sanguine speculations—*and no casualties!* Yet I can't help feeling as if we were walking on eggshells—probably because one mishap now might wreck everything.

Fri., Dec. 14, 9 P.M.

Partly cloudy today—and the northeastern flight still hanging in the balance. The tractor party this evening reported heavy fog—"viz 20 yards" on the plateau, and Siple, not far away, reported overcast skies. As a matter of fact, the two parties should meet tomorrow. Siple tonight was camped 6 miles east of 150-Mile beacon and the tractor party was only 10 miles south of it. I shall be greatly relieved to have these two units together after their distant and dangerous journeys. . . .

Saturday December 15th was exactly like so many other days—an ocean of milky fog. But about noon the sun burned through, revealing a flawless sky. The balloon runs were encouraging—good air aloft. If weather held good, it was decided the plane should take off in the early evening. Luckily there was no change. At Little America conditions were just about ideal. The day was the coldest in three weeks—with a maximum temperature of 12°, a minimum of zero. The surface was hard and fairly fast for a take-off.

A quick supper, and they were off at 7:27 o'clock—June in command, Bowlin, Rawson, Petersen and Pelter. In spite of its great load, the plane easily drew its bulk into the air. Rawson laid a course east by north through King Edward VII Land, following just within the coastal cliffs of the Barrier, and aiming for Scott's Nunataks. The flight track would more or less parallel the track of December 5th, 1929, when the coastal reaches of Marie Byrd Land were first discovered, but would attempt to surpass it several hundred miles to the east. Again I followed their progress by radio—with a map in front of me on which I checked off their positions from the frequent reports which Dyer brought in from the next room. And in between I settled down to a chess game with Hutcheson in the radio shack.

At 7:50 they were over the southern tip of Kainan Bay; at 8:24 they crossed Okuma Bay at an altitude of 3,000 feet. Climbing gently as they angled across King Edward VII Land, they had the wine-dark expanse of the Ross Sea on their left hand—"all open except for scattered patches of pack." At 8:48 the Rockefellers were abeam. Half an hour later the twin peaks of the Nunataks were 6,000 feet below them. A round of mapping photographs here, then, at 9:20 they changed course to 52° true, which would fetch them about 30 miles north of Bernt Balchen Glacier, a broad channel of ice in the western flank of the Edsel Fords.

Now they struck the mouth of Sulzberger Bay. Though the ice in the Bay was still fast, the northern edge was beginning to break out. Imprisoned in the bay ice were numerous ice islands, probably grounded icebergs, the domed summits of which were split and riven. Massive ice tongues licked toward the sea from the coast, thrusting their weight through the lighter ice. The shelf ice of Sulzberger Bay was grossly pressure-ridden and disturbed.

I followed their progress with real anxiety. So close now to the goal, I wondered if again the storm witches which have defended that coast from the dawn of time would turn them back. Over two expeditions, this was the eighteenth thrust we launched into this crucial area.

At 9:40 o'clock (just when Hutcheson had my king all but pinned between a rook and two pawns) Petersen flashed word:

> "Heavy clouds ahead. They seem to extend from water along front of Ford Range to Haines (Mt.). Will continue until we are closer. Present Px. at 9:41 (o'clock) 76° 45′ S., 150° 45′ W."

A solid block of clouds pressed down almost upon the peaks of the Edsel Fords. Ten minutes later, Siple, on the plateau and well west of

THE RAYMOND FOSDICK MOUNTAINS BREAK OUT OF THE CLOUDS

(Photographs by Joseph A. Pelter)

THE PILGRIM PLANE "MISS AMERICAN AIRWAYS"—THE ROCKEFELLER MOUNTAINS IN THE BACKGROUND

(Photograph by John Dyer)

CREVASSE

the mountains, reported a steady barometer, no clouds, a light easterly wind and good visibility.

At ten o'clock they resumed the climb, and never stopped, except to level off for brief intervals, till they reached 14,500 feet. The first stratum of grossly swollen cumulous clouds they mounted at 8,000 feet. Above that was a layer of wispy stratus clouds, which they hurdled at 10,000 feet. A little later they brushed through another stratum of heavier cloud vapor at 13,000 feet.

At 10:41 Rawson advised:

> "We are flying above clouds now. Clouds everywhere to eastward to south but can see surface occasionally through holes. Can't see any mts. yet. Px at 10:40 (Lat.) 76° 08′ S., (Long) 148° 45′ W.

They were still over the Ross Sea. In a little while Rawson's reckoning put them over the western front range. Yes, there were the mountains. Through occasional holes in the clouds they glimpsed snow-swathed summits of rock, then Balchen Valley sliding along a shoulder of the Fosdick Mountains.

But the clouds covered everything. It was just a matter of time, now, before they conceded defeat.

> 11:05 (at) 11:00 Balchen Mt. abeam.
>
> 11:15 Msg. REB. We are flying at 14,000 feet over heavy clouds to SE and S. Saw Balchen Glacier through hole in clouds (at) 10:15. June Mt. abeam. Can see water through cracks in ice and to north of us. Course unchanged. RAWSON
>
> Guess should be 11:15. Yep, make it read 11:15 (this from Petersen).
>
> 11:25 PX at 11:30—(Lat.) 75° 28′ S., (Long.) 145° 00′ W.
>
> 11:35 We are changing course to 22° true for Mt. Washington. Can't see anything. That can't be right. Will check. He meant 222°. Wait—Rawson writing out some dope. Had to put on parka as got cold up here above clouds (this from Peterson to Dyer). Here Msg. Turned back at 11:35 on account heavy clouds closing in ahead of us. Course 222° for Mt. Helen Washington (in Rockefeller group). Px. at 11:35 (Lat.) 75° 22′ S., (Long.) 144° 30′ W. RAWSON. Msg. REB. Ran into heavy fog bank at 14,500 feet. Visibility very poor. All well on board.... If clouds let up will follow west face of Edsel Fords south. JUNE
>
> 11:57 All OK. Fine sight of mnts. with white clouds hanging over them.

Just before they turned they topped a cloud bank at 14,500 feet; light scud was streaming across the wing tips. Still another bank of clouds, black and formidable, loomed on the course. June thought it must be 25,000 feet high. He and Bowlin debated for a second whether to knife through it, then decided nothing was to be gained.

As they wheeled, June and Rawson scanned the clouds for a glimpse of the coast. They were then 360 miles northeast of Little America—just about 45 miles beyond our maximum northeasting of 1929. Where we had seen streaks of open water in 1929, north of the Edsel Fords, they again had glimpses of them, about halfway between the 75th and 76th parallels.

There was a lively moment as they turned. Just after they had knifed into a bank of cloud, the starboard tank ran dry. Before Bowlin could switch to another tank the engines got cold and missed fire. They lost altitude fast. A forced landing on that mountainous coast would have been fatal. There was no flat landing surface nearer than a hundred miles. They nursed the engines carefully and presently the port motor took up its rhythm, but it was some minutes before the starboard one resumed. The feeling one gets at such a time must be felt to be understood.

At Little America, just about that time, Cox poked his head in the door of the radio shack. "Don't get alarmed," he said, "if you hear a shot." It was Klondike's finish. The frost-bite she had gotten in the winter had spread into a ghastly sore; Dr. Potaka finally recommended that she be destroyed. I do believe there were tears in Cox's eyes. "I've put away a lot of 'em, Admiral," he said, "but it never got me before. I guess I got pretty fond of that cow."

Meanwhile the flight crew, boring down through the clouds, flew in a southerly direction along the face of the Edsel Ford Range—the first flight directly along the western front range. Though the clouds lay flat almost on top of the peaks, there was a slit of midnight sunlight in between, cast up by the sun, which was low on the southern horizon. Pelter mapped the Range from a new angle. Over Haines, they altered course for Mt. Grace McKinley, where they circled for a last round of mapping photographs.

At 1:15 they headed for Little America, landing safely at 3:21 o'clock on the morning of December 16th. The barograph, when calibrated by Haines, showed that it was the coldest of the main flights—with a temperature of −19°.

IV

This flight actually terminated the geographical explorations of the second expedition. Though we continued to stand by in the hope of favorable weather, and actually made another attempt New Year's Eve to break through, little further was gained. The cloudy season had set in in earnest. From then on aviation made capital out of rare and short-lived spells of weather by furthering Dr. Poulter's seismic work and engaging in photographic reconnoissance locally.

With the hustle and bustle of flight preparations over and the main parties withdrawing from the field, life at Little America relaxed into quiet and familiar grooves.

Mon., Dec. 17, 11 P.M.

The hottest day of the year: the thermometer soared to +38°. Really uncomfortably warm. The paths between the buildings are shin-deep in slush. Shacks are all leaking like second hand umbrellas. A heavy snow storm came up in the afternoon, the wettest snow with the largest flakes I've ever seen in the south polar regions. They stick to everything they touch; the dogs curled up near the hatch were transformed into huge snowballs.

Siple met the tractor party yesterday at 150-Mile Depot, and this morning resumed the march to Little America. He should arrive in ten days. Morgan and Bramhall held the tractor for seismic and magnetic observations. They will head for home tonight. Blackburn was 50 miles down Thorne Glacier this morning—expects to reach here January 15th. All's well.

Tues., Dec. 18, 12 P.M.

Cloudy and cooler today, with a max. of +28°. I think we'd all welcome a cold snap to end the infernal leaking in the shacks....

A fresh complication in the affairs of the tractor party. No. 3 —their last car—is broken down 157 miles east of Little America, on the eastern trail. The cam shaft follower let go; and Demas says he also requires new piston rings and tools for grinding valves. These, and other parts he asked for, were collected, and Von der Wall, just to make sure nothing was overlooked, threw in what was left of a spare Citroën engine. We'll try to fly them out tomorrow, but if weather is unfavorable, we'll send out dog teams. This last setback, hard upon the loss of the other car, must be irksome to the tractor crew, but there's no hint of defeat in their messages. In fact, their one fear seems to be that I may be tempted to turn Dane, who is almost at the Rockefellers, to their relief. They're determined to come in under their own power, if they have to carry the car in. They are well provisioned—they still have 8 full 30-day rations.

Wed., Dec. 19, Midnight.

A fairly stiff easterly blow this morning, a light snowfall in the afternoon. Unfit for flying. If we don't have right weather tomorrow, I shall dispatch Ronne and Black with dog teams to carry spare parts out to the tractor.... We're making plans for the evacuation of Little America. Noville has been put in charge of the operation.... Lieut. English advises that both ships have been overhauled and are ready for the southern voyage. English has shown himself an efficient and able officer. I am no less pleased with the work of Captain Rose, commanding the

Ruppert. The tentative plan is for the *Bear* to sail about January 1st; the *Ruppert* will follow about a fortnight later, the time and course depending upon the state of the pack ice met by the *Bear.* If circumstances are favorable, the *Bear* will coast the western side of the Ross Sea on the way in, to extend the oceanographic survey Roos so successfully prosecuted last season. Another thing: Lieut. English is anxious to make a new survey of the front of the Ross Ice Barrier between McMurdo Sound and Cape Colbeck. This has not been done since 1911, and the survey will have the very real value of shedding light on the periodic recessions and advances of the Barrier Ice. However, these matters are beyond calculation. A bad ice year may ruin everything. I pray there be no repetition of the first expedition's ordeal.[2]

Thurs., Dec. 20, 11:10 P.M.

Overcast and cloudy—snowing, too, a wet, straight-falling snow. The peculiar darkness of the sky and the gently sifting character of the snow had something of the quiet air of a November snowfall in Boston. Of course the shacks are leaking all the more. Wherever you go, you find the decks strewn with pots and pans and old tins to catch the drip. Sterrett remarked he hasn't had to empty one in a month. Somebody always falls over a can before it's full.

Black and Ronne started out today with spare parts for the tractors. Exactly 16 dogs are left in Little America. Of these, Poulter has 9 steadily employed on his seismic travels, and the biological department borrows the others whenever they're available. Once a full-strength team was available for general camp duties. Fights decimated it, and levies for other purposes finally reduced it to one lone, miserable creature named, as I remember, Friday. Innes-Taylor posted a melancholy obituary. "The camp team died today. *He* will be buried with full military honors."

Fri., Dec. 21, 10:30 P.M.

Overcast—light snow and drift, a 25-mile east wind. The light snow of recent days, which made a soft layer on the Barrier, is being rapidly blown away....

Thus December wore through its clammy cycle. A towering cloud of water sky was climbing over the Ross Sea, like smoke from a great forest fire. Toward the end of the month the aviators discovered that the ice was slowly breaking out between East and West Capes. The bay ice was cracked and broken and the biologists found it more diffi-

[2] Blocked off for a month by heavy pack ice and, after breaking through, harried and pounded by a hurricane, the *City of New York* was unable to reach the Bay of Whales until February 18, 1930. *Eleanor Bolling,* the small iron supply ship, found ice conditions too severe to attempt the transit. *Little America,* chapter xvi.

cult to sledge across the Bay. The mild manifestation of a polar summer! In December snow fell 16 days; 8 days were foggy; 20 days were cloudy or partly overcast. The lowest temperature was —1°, and the highest +38°; the mean was +16°. To be comfortable outside one needed only the lightest of clothing—light shirts, underwear, trousers, a single pair of woolen socks, ski boots. Indeed, when the sun was out, one would usually see the skiers traveling with backs bare and the tops of their underwear tied around the waist.

Christmas arrived in the lull after a blizzard, a bright lift out of the rut of routine. A holiday, of course: the galley decorated with tinsel and balls and streamers which Abele produced from one of the caches. Pots and kettles were polished until they glittered and the long tables scrubbed to a shining brightness. That old Scrooge, Carbone, resplendent in a new apron and chef's cap of white windproof, presided over the festivities, cheerfully bellowing Christmas carols in one breath, then cursing in the next as a dash of ice spray from the roof found his neck. There really was a Santa Claus at Little America in 1934. Way back in the long disused meat cache, where it had been hidden under a small glacier, Noville happened upon a quarter of beef—"the last of the Mohicans," Carbone named it. Stiff with cold and white with frost, it was borne with the ceremony of a Yule log into the galley, where for two days it thawed out over the stove, with Carbone standing guard over it, lest the prize cuts vanish while his back was turned. And in an innocent pile of drift a haphazardly adventuring sounding rod struck pay dirt—a case of sherry lost for ten months, a grand discovery. Vegetable soup à la Bay of Whales (fair warning to be prepared for anything, from seal to plankton), fried steak Carbone style (if the first mess ate too well, the second mess would dine on memories), creamed corn, dehydrated potatoes, cranberry sauce, apple pie and ice cream (mixed directly with fresh snow, another one of Dr. Poulter's inventions), and a bouquet of sherry. Out on the trail, the main parties paused to feast on the hamburger steaks which, in anticipation of this day, they had slipped into their rations before departing in October.

Affairs were prospering as December ended. The Geological Party was off the Glacier and swinging home across the Barrier. Dane, Moody and Swan had salvaged the Fokker engine in the Rockefellers and were on their way back with it. Ronne and Black had reached the tractor with the spare parts on the 30th, and twenty-four hours later the tractor was again under way. On New Year's Eve a flight crew commanded by Bowlin, with McCormick as co-pilot, made a last bold attempt to break through to the Edsel Ford Mountains, only to be halted just west of them by an impenetrable wall of clouds.

And at 3 P.M., December 29th, the Marie Byrd Land Party came down the ridge to Little America, ending a journey of 862 miles (not counting side-trips) and 77 days, unique among polar journeys in being the first scientific reconnoissance of land discovered by aircraft. The four men—Siple, Wade, Corey and Stancliff—were burnt the color of mahogany. The big fellows, Siple and Wade, looked very thin. The dogs, too, were down very fine, and went wild at the sight of a seal carcass. Siple said they had scarcely a day's ration of dog food left on the sleds. Dr. Potaka weighed the men in:

	Before	*After*
Siple	181	173
Wade	195	173
Corey	152	149
Stancliff	141	138

The main accomplishments of the Marie Byrd Land Party in its travels through the western front range of the Edsel Fords, approximately between the 76th and 78th parallels, can be divided into three sections—geological, botanical and biological. Wade specialized in the first, Siple in the latter two. In these fields there was a rich harvest of information, which was to be expected in a new land. In addition, the party fulfilled its other purposes of meteorological and magnetic observation, and collected numerous samples of aseptic snow and rock dust for bacteriological analysis.

Of course, a great deal of definitive research—especially in the matter of collation, correlation, classification and identification of rock and biological sample—must be done before any sort of final judgment can be rendered upon the "finds" of the party; but certain general results can be outlined here. Wade's research was particularly important for such light as it may throw upon the problem of the Andean connection. He was the first geologist to set foot on this region of potential linking. His geological survey carried him north along the front range, between Mt. Grace McKinley and Saunders Mt.[3] His observations were generally substantiated by Siple's reconnoissance in the peaks behind the front range.

The northern mountains of Marie Byrd Land consist of highly metamorphosed and severely folded dark sedimentary rock, composed for the most part of pink and gray granites of great age, and very old, intensely folded schists, all of which have been intruded by dolerite dikes. The land could not have been very resistant to the ice, for the oceans of glacial ice pulsing across it have worn away the mountains, as a stream wears river rocks, carving and sculpturing them with a violent hand, eroding the softer enfolding strata, and exposing a core of coarse-grained pink and gray granites. Throughout the region the resistant granites stand boldly above the ice level, dwarfing the smaller, grossly eroded peaks of softer material. They found no sedimentary beds topping the folded layers of schists and granites, and Wade did not

[3] Named after Commander Harold E. Saunders, U.S.N., chief cartographer of the first and second expeditions.

believe they could have been entirely denuded by glacial action. The only trace of a recent orogenic (or mountain-building) period was the finding, by Siple and Corey, of the ice-shattered remnant of an extinct volcano, in the Raymond Fosdick group. The rock structure, like that of Graham Land, is highly folded, and seems quite definitely to lie in the hypothetical axis of folding extending from the Andes to New Zealand. But whether this connection is more geographically apparent than geologically real only further investigation and correlation can prove. Preliminary study indicates that these rocks are chemically dissimilar to the Andean and Graham Land rocks. The rocks of Graham Land are very acid in character and distinctly an Atlantic type, while those of Marie Byrd Land are true Pacific rocks and have a more basic character. On the other hand, the latter did not appear, on first examination, to be related to the towering Antarctic horst traversing South Victoria Land and continuing to the eastward. In the matter of minerals, traces of galena, pyrites and molybdenum were found.

Siple's biological finds were perhaps more spectacular. Traveling among these half-drowned peaks, upon which human foot had never trod, he discovered no less than two dozen or more different species of mosses and lichens. Pieces of algae-flecked ice, chopped from frozen pools in the Edsel Fords and transported through 400 miles of hard sledging to Little America, were found under a microscope to be inhabited by myriads of microscopic organisms—rotifers, water bears, varieties of infusoria and numerous types of unicellular and filamentous algae. Rookeries of both the snowy petrel and the skua gull were found on three of the peaks they explored. In places the exposed cliffs were bright with the color of lichens, bright as paint; and occasionally, while tracing small veins, they had to scrape away the lichens to get at the structure of the rock.

How rich a discovery this was can be emphasized only in terms of the poverty of Antarctic flora and fauna. Antarctica, compared with the Arctic, is lifeless. More than 400 species of flowering plants flourish in the Arctic regions, and "myriads of ephemeral insects, the land birds, the reindeer, musk oxen, polar carnivora and rodents, which penetrate to the northernmost land projections of the globe." [4] So far as such life is concerned, the Antarctic continent is practically a vacuum.

Away from the few known penguin rookeries on the Antarctic coast, in the vicinity of which occur "mites, such lowly organized insects as Collembola, and a wingless Chironomid fly, together with a few rotifers, a tardigrade, and two or three protozoans in the moss," [5] life is almost unknown. In 1903, Dr. Wilson of Scott's expedition had found only one insect: [6] Dr. Taylor of Scott's second expedition had come upon a

[4] Robert Cushman Murphy, *Problems of Polar Research, Antarctic Zoögeography,* 359.

[5] Ibid., 364.

[6] Hayes, *Antarctica,* 89.

second species:[7] tiny red insects were uncovered under the bowlders at Cape Adare:[8] and on the bleak, windswept coast of King George VII Land one of Mawson's parties found myriads of mites clenched to uprooted stones.[9] The only species of insects with any sort of a wide distribution in the Antarctic appear to be parasites of seals.[10] No land mammals exist: no marsupials have been found in the fossiliferous beds of the continent. "Only a handful of true land birds reach the sub-Antarctic islands, and beyond the 55th parallel or thereabouts there is not a single species. The only Antarctic birds, indeed, which take even a portion of their food from anywhere except the ocean, are the skua, the sheathbill, and the giant petrel. . . . Only about 32 species of birds penetrate beyond latitude 60° S., and most of these are sub-Antarctic wanderers rather than polar species."[11] Of the varieties of pelagic birds which visit the continental margin during the summer months, only three—MacCormick's skua gull, the Adélie and Emperor penguin—are exclusively Antarctic. Inland, except for birds occasionally sighted by field parties in the summer months, no life meets the eye, no sound is heard.

The same impoverishment characterizes continental plant life. It is almost non-existent except for patches of mosses, lichens and fungi clinging to emergent rock, which awaken briefly for a few weeks in summer to fulfill their life processes, then for months lie rigid in a frozen state, in temperatures as low as —70°. These mosses and lichens and fungi, with a few fresh-water algae and certain microphytes which exist only in ice and snow, are, so far as we know, the entire terrestrial plant life of Antarctica.[12] Meager and starved as it is, it is nevertheless audacious. Priestley, for example, on the mountainous slopes of Ferrar Glacier, on the western side of the Ross Sea, found a yellow lichen at 3,100 feet, a black lichen at 3,800 feet, and a green lichen or moss at 4,200 feet.[13] And on the rocks of Mt. Nansen in the Queen Maud Range, the geological party of my first expedition stooped to scrape off bits of lichens—the nearest life had then been found to the South Pole.[14] Only two flowering plants—a species of grass and a small caryophyllaceous plant, both dwarfed and primitive and rare—have been detected in Antarctica, and then only in the less rigorous climate of the sub-Antarctic islands.[15] Ferns do not exist: of the Antarctic lichens some

[7] *Scott's Last Expedition,* ii., 243.
[8] Priestley, *Antarctic Adventure,* 192.
[9] Mawson, *The Home of the Blizzard,* i., 341.
[10] Murphy, op. cit., 365.
[11] Ibid., 371.
[12] Ibid., 363.
[13] Shackleton, *Heart of the Antarctic,* ii., 54.
[14] Gould, *Cold,* 185.
[15] Rudmore Brown, *Problems of Polar Research, Antarctic and Sub-Antarctic Plant Life and Some of Its Problems,* 343.

(Photograph by Olin Stancliff)

THE MARIE BYRD LAND PARTY IN THE EDSEL FORDS

(Photograph by Richard S. Russell, Jr.)

THE GEOLOGICAL PARTY 230 MILES FROM THE SOUTH POLE

(Photograph by Richard S. Russell, Jr.)

THE "ORGAN PIPES" OF THORNE GLACIER—PAINE ON SKIS

100 species,[16] and of the mosses 63 species [17] have been recorded, by far the greatest number of them occurring on sub-Antarctic Islands. Whether Siple's finds will include new species it is too early to say. That will be a long-drawn-out process of comparison and elimination. He thinks they will. In all events, the discovery of life existing in comparative luxuriance at such a high latitude (77° to 78° S.) was quite unexpected. I can say for myself that one of the exalting moments of the second expedition was when Dr. Perkins called me over to the Science Hall, a day or so after the party returned, to look at some of the things Siple had brought back—small vials of ice, now melting in the warmth of the building, which had been chipped from the slime of a mud flat exposed by a receding glacier, from a pool of slick blue ice around a heap of lava ashes at the foot of an extinct volcano, and from the frozen muck atop a windswept ride where skua gulls had made a rookery. In the silver plain of the microscope field these daubs of water on the slides suddenly became the busiest of worlds—with myriads of competent, amazingly agile things, faring and fending for themselves among tiny masses of rusty-colored vegetable matter strewn about like autumn leaves, alive with the swarming energy of things doomed to ill-favored places. And this from a land which five years before was just a haze of peaks on the horizon of discovery.

Certainly life nowhere has had to contend with and overcome harsher environment—a land buried under hundreds of feet of ice, which offers no sanctuary except on rocky emergences: terrific winds super-cooled by the refrigerator of the central plateau; a prevalent cloudiness which diminishes the sunlight of the summer months; and a temperature which even at the height of summer rarely rises above freezing. This fact, more than the great cold of winter, accounts for the meagerness of Antarctic plant life, just as the comparatively hot Arctic summer accounts for the comparative luxuriance of life. What life has clutched a foothold on continental Antarctica must be capable of existing upwards of 10 months of the year (perhaps years at a time) in a frozen encystment, rushing its cycle in the few weeks of summer when the warmth of the sun's radiation brings thawing around the rocks at the ice line.

No less mystifying is how these tiny life forms, the mosses and lichens especially, found their way to these bleak grounds, from 50 to 100 miles from the coast. Everywhere on its circumference Antarctica is separated from the main land masses of the southern hemisphere by at least 500 miles of the stormiest oceans in the world. The nearest land that might have served as a bridge for the propagation of these life forms from more temperate regions is more than a thousand miles distant from the Edsel Ford Range. Science has not satisfactorily explained the distribution of Antarctic flora, which appears to be com-

[16] Ibid., 344.
[17] Murphy, op. cit., 363.

posed of three elements—endemic, Arctic and Fuegian.[18] It is generally believed that the present flora is post-glacial; the last great onrush of ice must have overwhelmed every vestige of vegetation, and with it the means to sustain life.[19] Elaborate theories of former land bridges connecting Antarctica with Australia, New Zealand and South America have been constructed to account for its revival. Fossiliferous fragments have indicated that before the ice came, Antarctica possessed a luxuriant flora which is reflected in many respects in the present-day plant life of these countries.[20] Another theory is that these life forms may have been transported by the rivers of upper air, or ferried by such carriers as the petrel and tern, which wander up and down the earth. All this, however, is speculation.

V

As for the physical nature of the Marie Byrd Land Party's journey, it presented no great difficulties, according to the reports of the men. They had their share of fog, crevasses and trail drudgeries, but owing to the fact their trail more or less lay toward the coast the temperatures were less rigorous than those endured by the other parties. Of the 27 dogs with which they left, only three failed to come back: Will Rogers, a magnificent Manitoba, perished of wounds received in a fight with Leatherneck; Corey's leader, Marve, died one night on the tethering lines; and Dewcla, a file dog, foundered near the end of the outward journey.

On the 200-mile run to the Edsel Ford Range, the party followed the trail and depot system which the Eastern Tractor Party under June had blazed through Scott and Marie Byrd Lands, past the Rockefeller Mountains and across the plateau to Mt. Grace McKinley. Soft snow, and heavy loads slowed them up on the outward run. Even manhauling with the dogs, they could make no better than 4 or 5 miles a day. They had to jettison several hundred pounds of dog food to lighten their loads 30 miles out: the dropping of the food, together with subsequent losses, compelled them to curtail the trip and accounted for the shortage on the retreat. A blizzard improved the surface and with the lighter loads they made better time, arriving at McKinley a day ahead of schedule, and 20 days out of Little America.

They camped six days at McKinley, investigating the rocks and lichens, and transmitting frequent weather bulletins for the first flight, then impending. On the second day Corey had a narrow escape from death. He and Stancliff had climbed the eastern ridge to take photographs. The ridge sloped quite steeply to the northwest. Corey went a little bit ahead. Stancliff, finished with his photography, said some-

[18] Brown, op. cit., 348.
[19] Ibid., 349.
[20] Murphy, op. cit., 363.

thing to Corey. No answer. He was nowhere in sight. First puzzled, then frightened, Stancliff looked wildly down the slope. About 700 feet below, he was appalled to see one of Corey's ski poles on the snow. Thinking he must be dead, Stancliff was casting about for a quick way down, when Corey popped out from behind a bowlder and yelled he was all right. How severe a drop it was may be judged from the fact it took Stancliff nearly an hour to get down to him. Corey said his feet just flew out from under him on slick ice; the next thing he knew he was rolling down the cliff, head over heels, grabbing at rocks to arrest the descent. Except for getting badly bruised and injuring a small bone in the left wrist (the doctor thought, after examining it on his return, that it might have been cracked) he was unhurt, and his companions said his escape was miraculous.

On November 9th, after being delayed a day by a blizzard, they stocked up with supplies from the depot and steered east, aiming for the Haines Mountains and intending to work northward along the front of the range toward the coast. A northerly course would have been the direct approach, but they could see no safe descent to the shelf ice of Sulzberger Bay. The ice at the foot of the mountains was badly crumpled and upheaved by the ice creeping down from the plateau through glacier channels. A short distance on this course, after leaving McKinley, they were obliged to drop part of their loads; and a few days later, while Siple and Wade concentrated on collecting specimens on the Haines Mountains, Stancliff and Corey relayed the loads. From this point they progressed, by easy stages, over various small mountain groups, to Mt. Rea in the western front range, about 69 miles north-northeast of McKinley, arriving on the 21st. Between the Haines and Mt. Woodward they crossed a broad valley glacier.[21] They traveled cautiously, often in fog, and the terrain was difficult. Snow and ice were heaped deep over the southern sides of nearly all the mountains, but the northern exposures were bare and sheer, with straight drops of several thousand feet from the taller peaks. Wade and Siple stopped frequently to collect rock specimens and lichens.

One quality was marked in the conversations of these men, after months of the blank desert of the Barrier: the land had cast a spell on them, which they were a long time losing. On the few sunny days, they said, the sheer beauty of the region alone repaid them for any hardships. Pink and gray granites, black upthrusts, flashing snow and blue glacial channelings; patches of white lichens standing out breathlessly against black rock; scarlet lichens—a cochineal scarlet—pulsing with thawing rivulets, causing the rock to appear dripping with red paint.

In almost every crevice where life could lodge and benefit by the moisture released by thawing, they found it, Siple said. Superficially, the older rocks showed more evidence of having been weathered by plant life than by other forces. When they broke open loose crust

[21] This valley has been named John Hays Hammond Inlet.

of crystals covering rocks, they uncovered these tiny plants underneath, the tiny rootlets of which were breaking the rocks by pressure and absorbing the minerals necessary to their life processes. They found moss beds two inches thick.

There was ample evidence of deglacierization—that is to say, recession of ice. They found a number of moraines. In the vicinity of Rea Mt., Siple thought, the ice has receded about 2,000 feet. Three glaciers working around this mountain have carved away and polished its sides: the side facing Haines was so sheer and flat-topped that they named it The Billboard.

On account of the shortage of dog food, and in order to make the most out of the time left, Siple thought it necessary to split his party at Mt. Rea, he and Corey striking behind the front peaks toward the Raymond Fosdick group to the northeast, and Wade and Stancliff pushing along the front range toward the coast. After dividing the rations, they separated on November 23rd, agreeing upon a rendezvous December 5th at the Haines Mountains, a 1,300 foot group just south of them where they had made a depot.

Wade's side-trip was cut short by an accident that might have ended tragically. Three days after leaving Siple, he and Stancliff rounded Mt. Saunders in a heavy fog. The load being light, both men were riding the sledge. The sledge gave a lurch, and in the second between the *sensing* and the actual collapsing of the crevasse they flung themselves off, landing in opposite directions. When they regained their feet, only the gee pole was visible; the dogs were belly-down, groveling to keep from being dragged after the sledge.

The two men carefully crawled to the edge. About 50 feet down was a snow ledge over which the sledge dangled: below that the crevasse bellied out to form a bottomless pit wide enough, Stancliff swore, to turn a dog team around. Aboard the sledge were all their gear, food, instruments and the only radio set. With a right angle pull the sledge was too heavy for them to haul out. They must first lighten the load, a tricky and perilous salvage.

They brought the dogs round at right angles to the crevasse, to keep a strain on the line. It was their good luck that Wade had several lengths of alpine rope coiled over his shoulder when he jumped. Stancliff, being much the lighter man, offered to go down on the line and try to pass the gear to the surface. Wade braced himself as anchor man, and Stancliff lowered himself into the crevasse.

With the utmost care he cast off the lashings around the canvas tank. He worked patiently and delicately, pressing his weight against the canvas to prevent the gear from spilling out when the flaps were opened. He managed to pry out the tent, then Wade's sleeping bag, and finally the sacks of man food. He had just salvaged his own bag and most of the radio set when he slacked up a second on the line. The sledge lurched, the tank flew open, and the contents—dog food, cloth-

(Photograph by John Dyer)

ADMIRAL BYRD WELCOMES THE MARIE BYRD LAND PARTY ON ITS RETURN

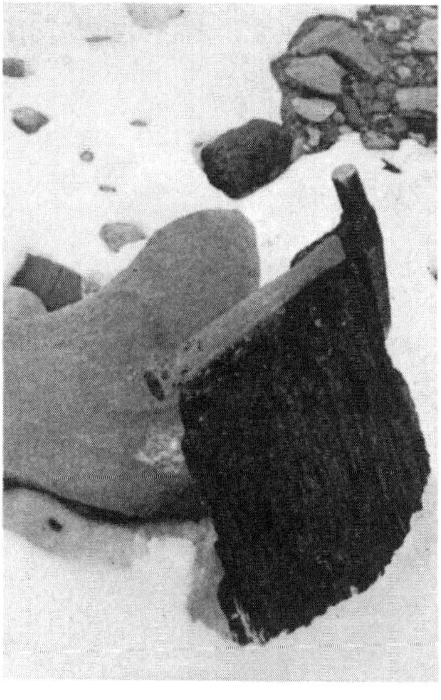

FOSSIL TREE FOUND AT MT. WEAVER —207 MILES FROM THE SOUTH POLE

(Photographs by Richard S. Russell, Jr.)

JACK THE GIANT KILLER, WHO BROKE TRAIL FOR 1400 MILES

THE BAY OF WHALES FROZEN—THE WHITE LINE OF THE EAST BARRIER IN THE BACKGROUND

(Photographs by Joseph A. Pelter)

LITTLE AMERICA FROM THE AIR

ing, radio spare parts, and the head of the hand-generator—fell past him. He looked down and saw the stuff bounce on the ledge 50 feet below him.

They had no choice but to go down after it. After pulling the sledge to the surface, Stancliff went down again. The line was just long enough to reach the ledge. Clinging there he recovered and passed up on a handline the generator head, which lay just an inch or so from the edge, what was left of the clothing, and about 25 blocks of dog pemmican. Some of the clothing, the spare parts and 65 blocks of pemmican (five days' dog rations) had missed the ledge and disappeared into the lower pit. Stancliff said he could see no bottom.

The loss of the pemmican left them no choice but to retreat to the depot at the Haines Mountains. As it was, the dogs had to travel on half-rations. Nevertheless, while waiting at the rendezvous, Wade found in a three-inch quartz vein slanting down one of the mountains in this group a deposit of galena in which he thought might be associated silver, zinc, lead and copper.

Meanwhile Siple and Corey had sledged past the sheer face of Mt. Rea, skirting Saunders Mt. (4,450 feet) a striking alpine structure of culminating peaks. A broad outlet valley, pitted with crevasses and violently upheaved, stretched between them and the peaks of the Fosdick group. They crossed it with difficulty, logging ten miles in doing so. After passing various small peaks, meanwhile climbing to an altitude of 2,000 feet, they finally gained the central mountains of the Fosdick group.

At this point, while scanning the mountains for the most promising area to work, their attention was attracted by several puzzlingly dark peaks near the easterly termination of the group. Toward the nearest they sledged next day. They were astonished to find it was an extinct volcano, the remnant, evidently, of a huge cone. The cliffs on one side were nearly vertical; and the black lava beds striating them were spangled with patches of bright green olivine crystals. Scooped up in the lee were mounds of lava ashes, which tailed out more than a mile behind the peak. The dust still rose, Siple said, when they scuffed their feet.

These ash beds must be most interesting formations. They were strung out, so Siple said, eight of them all in a line about a mile to the leeward of the volcano, so regularly "that they looked like coal dumps on a wharf,—as if a string of tiny railway cars had run along and dumped their loads." The beds themselves were roughly conical and stood about 15 feet above the ice, with bridges of loose ashes connecting them.

Here they camped November 28th. For the three days the wind never stopped blowing. Siple estimated that the velocity never fell, except in brief lulls, below 40 miles, and at times was much greater. Because of the slick, hard ice, they were unable to sink the tent stakes.

So they anchored one end of the tent to a sledge, which was laid head-on to the wind, and loaded down with rocks. Even then the sledge was tossed about, and several times the tent blew down on them. At the height of the blow they could hear rocks, lifted and blown by the wind, slithering past their tent. Their greatest fear was of being caught themselves, when returning from forays for specimens, by a strong gust and sent spinning down the glacier. On that ice, slippery as a ballroom floor, and against wind of that strength, crampons were useless. Once started, they said, neither would have had much chance of regaining the tent. Yet even in this inhospitable place—in a pool of blue ice in a bed of lava ashes, not yet commenced to thaw—Siple found bits of algae which he chipped out with an ax. Noticing a faint pinkish discoloration to the ice, he collected samples of this also: the color, he found under the microscope at Little America, came from myriads of rotifers.

December 2nd, with only 5 days' dog food left, they started back for the rendezvous with Wade. In an attempt to shorten the journey, they struck across the main glacier south and east of the original crossing. At this point it was swollen to a breadth of 34 miles. The going, Corey said, was frightful—all blue ice, heavily crevassed; the dogs were hard put to it just to keep their footing. They were crossing crevasses at the rate of two a minute. The day was calm, with a brilliant sun, and though the temperature was about +25°, the sun was blistering. Both men had stripped to trunks, socks and ski boots and were bare from the waist up.

At this juncture about 10 miles out on the glacier, the lead sledge, holding all the man food, clothing and most of their specimens, smashed into a crevasse. The surge of the dogs and the braking effect of the trailer saved it from going to the bottom. But it hung out of reach, and they couldn't bring it to the surface. Conscious of their nakedness and the fact no food or clothing was nearer than 80 miles, they worked desperately to save it. As Wade and Stancliff had done, Corey went down on a line snubbed by Siple. Five hours' hard work finally salvaged the gear. They lost five days' man food, a stop watch and most of the mess gear. After that they took turns eating from a single cup and spoon.

Doubtful as to the wisdom of continuing on this course, they retreated as they had come, recrossing the glacier near the original route. The diversion yielded its own record. About 25 miles east of Saunders, on the northeast slope of a glacial valley, at an elevation of about 2,000 feet, they came upon a mud flat (so Siple called it) which yielded some of the most interesting biological specimens. What it was—whether it was a moraine, or perhaps a mountain top just being exposed by the recession of ice—Siple wasn't sure. It was several hundred feet below the nearest exposed rock. The blue ice over it was very thin, a mere veneering, and where it was just commencing thawing strips of mud, like a soft clay, were appearing, the first thing of its kind they had seen. Siple carefully filled several bottles with samples of the mud.

Approaching Mt. Saunders Corey sighted the first birds—two skua gulls in full flight. Siple watched them with curiosity; instead of hovering, as was their habit, they were making a bee-line for the interior.

Presently they climbed a low ridge, surrounded by a moat of ice. Corey came first upon the skeleton of a bird—a gull. A moment later Siple found another. They topped the ridge, and enclosed in the hollow of it, on the margin of a small glacier, was a small lake of ice, thawing at the edges from the radiated warmth of rock. In this pool they found a thick deposit of guano muck and all sorts of bird refuse. Fresh claw tracks were visible in the snow. The disgorged skeletal remains of a snowy petrel, upon which the robber skuas prey, were found in the lee of a rock. Before they left half a dozen skua gulls suddenly arrived from nowhere and hovered overhead. Just about that time the same species were first appearing in numbers in the Bay of Whales. From what he saw Siple believed that the lake had served as a skua gull rookery for many years.

On the night of December 5th Corey and Siple made their rendezvous with Wade and Stancliff at the Haines Mountains. The consolidated party started for Little America next day. Except that the increasing softness of the snow made travel atrocious, and the shortage of dog food worried them a little, the return was accomplished without mishap. On December 18th, after having met the tractor party, they left the trail to make a brief excursion into the Rockefellers, to look for geological and biological specimens for comparison with those collected in the Edsel Fords. It was a happy thought. On one of the conical peaks of Mt. Helen Washington they discovered not only a profusion of botanical specimens, including several species not found in the Edsel Fords, but also populous Antarctic and snowy petrel rookeries. Thousands of birds—flights of piebald Antarctic petrels swirling through clouds of the beautifully white snowy petrels—wheeled over the peaks. The loose rocks on the summits, wedged together in such a manner as to offer innumerable sheltering caves, made it a perfect sanctuary, Siple said. They found one hen nesting, sitting tranquilly on an egg half as big as herself.

Before they left, Dane, Moody and Swan arrived to salvage the Fokker engine. Not long afterwards they met and passed Ronne and Black on their way to the tractor. The eastern trail, Stancliff remarked, was becoming almost as populous as the Lincoln Highway.

VI

Down on the Bay of Whales, just two days before the Marie Byrd Land Party came back with its tales of life clinging to the land, Dr. Perkins finally broke through to his own distant objectives. After trying in vain to blast a hole through the bay ice with heavy blasts of dynamite—after trying to suck water up through the cracks with a long hose connected to a pump mounted on a gasoline drum—after even trying to attract plankton to the surface with bits of seal meat, he finally got his plankton net past the ice layers into the deep waters of the Bay.

It was his first haul since June 15th.[22]

[22] Thereafter, until the *Bear* arrived, Perkins made vertical hauls from 300 feet. Several Euphausia, amphipods and a few medusae were obtained with a dip net. On the whole, a disappointingly small amount of plankton was obtained because of the difficulties of getting the net into clear water.

Chapter XVII

THE LONG SLEDGE JOURNEY

I

ON January 1st, 1935 (our date), the *Bear of Oakland,* with a new jib-boom, main lower mast and topmast, new rigging and steering gear, with seams freshly caulked, sailed from Dunedin on the afternoon tide. Her bunkers, Lieut. English reported, were crammed with coal, and a generous deckload of sacked coal set the vessel deep in the water, with barely 20 inches of freeboard. Aboard her were several new faces, including Charles F. Anderson, well-known postal inspector, sent by the U. S. Post Office to handle the cancellation of Little America's mail, and Glenn H. Bryant, geophysicist with the Seismograph Service Corporation, making a voyage of 20,000 miles for a fortnight's study of our seismic sounding methods. The deck officers were: Captain Johansen, first officer and ice pilot; Alfred Robinson, second officer; and Rudolph Van Reen, third. The engineering watch: Seth Pinkham, chief; Thomas Litchfield, first assistant; and Victor Niewoehner, second assistant. Directly out of Otago Harbor, the *Bear* dipped her forefoot in a strong southerly swell, and for a week plunged into robust southerly winds, rain squalls and fog.

At Little America the year turned quietly, with both the Condor and the Fairchild in the air, the former under Bowlin's command making a last gallant attempt to cleave through the fog over the Edsel Fords, and the latter, with Smith at the controls, pursuing it to the Rockefellers on a photographic mission. After six clear days—the next to the longest clear stretch we had at Little America—the weather turned foul in the evening. By midnight it was snowing and drifting, with a gusty north wind. Near the head of Ver-Sur-Mer Inlet, where the pressure was flattening out, Dr. Perkins found and marked a trail, about half a mile long, which he thought might be used as a road to the ships. Winding over folds of pressure, past white mountains with bright blue caves and glittering needles and obelisks of ice, with the emerald folds of Barrier visible from the rises and the expanding thunderhead of sea smoke over the Ross Sea, it was the most beautiful road in the world. Whether we should be able to use it or not would depend upon the state of the ice in the Bay of Whales and the pressure itself on the arrival of the ships. In summer these things were in flux. The old road to the bay ice was completely smashed.

II

At 4:30 o'clock on the morning of January 2nd, struggling through drift and pea soup fog, Tractor No. 3, almost at its last mechanical gasp, arrived at Little America—under its own power, as the crew had vowed it would. The last 28 miles of an 815 mile journey took nearly eleven hours. A valve had broken, one cylinder had cut out, a connecting rod bearing was burned out, the pistons, Hill swore, were swapping cylinders every other stroke, all the anti-freeze radiator solution was gone, and they had to stop every hour or so to stuff snow down the radiator and pack more around the housing of the rear end, which was overheating. Only Lewisohn, then night watchman, was up, and he stared incredulously at the ghostly thing evolving out of the fog, with its ill-proportioned and hideous home-made cabin, sledges racked on the roof, and the sledges towing behind top-heavy with a weird cargo. As for No. 2, abandoned on the western margin of the plateau, if all their ingenuity and ardent supplications failed to bring it back under its own steam, at least they brought back everything that was movable—treads, pistons, rods, drive shaft, universal, clutch, even the carburetor and distributors.

The night watchman grinned softly. "Dr. Livingstone, I presume?"

Waite stepped gingerly off the navigating platform, flexed his muscles tentatively, then gave a long sigh.

"Walter, the Amazons were terrible, but we finally got through."

The end of a journey the like of which has never been seen in the polar regions.

Unlike the sledgers who came back looking quite as clean as when they left, the tractor crew were stained with grease and oil. Working over the engines, of course, made the difference. Bramhall, Hill and Waite seemed in tip-top condition, but Demas looked pale and unwell. Demas had been sick at his stomach, Waite said, for a month: couldn't keep food down. Morgan wasn't with them. After Ronne and Black had arrived with the spare parts, he had taken them to the Rockefellers on a brief geological errand.

Dr. Potaka immediately weighed them in, as he had weighed in others. Interestingly, with the exception of Demas and Morgan (the latter weighing in after 130 miles or more of sledging) the others either held their weight or gained during the 69 days they were with the tractors.

	Before	*After*
Bramhall	166 lbs.	167 lbs.
Morgan	161 "	158 "
Demas	167 "	163 "
Waite	176 "	181 "
Hill	144 "	144 "

So far as the major results of the journey are to be estimated, they, with those of the other wider scientific investigations, must await further study. The whole function of the party, after the consolidation of the tractors with the Plateau Party, was scientific—seismic and magnetic reconnaissance over the untraveled eastern reaches of the Ross Ice Barrier and northward across the new plateau. Through this unexplored region Bramhall made magnetic surveys at intervals of from 25 to 50 geographical miles along their track, occupying 19 stations in all, and Morgan made frequent seismic soundings, establishing the ice thickness at about ten points on the plateau. More, they ran a barometric survey along the edge of the plateau, determining elevations as often as every hour, and checking elevations of submerged land against ice thickness determinations. Morgan made a substantial haul of geological specimens in the Rockefellers, and Bramhall accurately located the mountains by triangulation from four control points fixed astronomically with precision. Sound work, all of it.

The general terms of Morgan's seismic data (not yet completely worked up) have already been stated—the evidence showing that while the ice thickness on the eastern plateau varies considerably, all of it is consistently above sea level, that at elevations of from 2,000 to 3,000 feet, preliminary calculations indicate ice thicknesses ranging from 1,000 to 2,000 feet respectively.

Dr. Bramhall, at this writing, was working up his report for the Carnegie Institution at Washington. Here, also, final judgment must be held temporarily in abeyance, but a partial analysis of the data presages certain conclusions. The journey lay through a region magnetically unknown. Bramhall's instruments and methods were probably the most precise ever used in south polar field operations. Absolute values as well as relative variations of horizontal and vertical intensity and direction in the earth's magnetic field were measured. It appears that existing isogonic charts of the south polar regions, constructed from very meager data and necessarily theoretical, generally conform to the present state of the earth's magnetic field; but a uniform shifting of the lines of equal variation through two or three degrees of longitude is indicated by the new data. In the vicinity of the Edsel Ford Range Bramhall found some evidence of a local anomaly, probably due to the presence of metal.

I admired the way this party carried on in spite of the most crushing sort of physical oppressions; and I liked especially the way the scientists adapted themselves to the abrupt displacement of objectives. Defeated on one course, they rebounded to push through in another. They brought back the data, which, when you come right down to it, is the Antarctic bacon.

Throughout their wandering, circling odyssey, preyed upon hourly by all sorts of topographical and mechanical incertitudes, and traveling at odd hours in all sorts of weather, they nevertheless kept a certain orderliness in their affairs. Every 25-50 geographical miles they would stop for scientific observations. Bramhall would pitch his special magnetic tent, in which he set up his instruments—askania balance and dip circle. Waite usually assisted him as recorder. The geographical position and azimuth at each station were determined by theodolite. As a rule it took four hours or more to occupy a single station; and on foggy days or during blizzards, when travel was impossible, Bramhall would lie for hours in his sleeping bag, absorbed in endless calculations.

While Bramhall was occupying a magnetic station, Morgan got ready for seismic soundings. Demas and Hill always gave him a hand. It was a rather elaborate business. A line was measured off and flagged, reels of firing and recording cables were dragged out and placed in position; the cookers and blow torches started to melt snow for water; holes for the four seismometers dug or sawed out at intervals of 150-200 feet and the seismometers frozen into position by pouring water on them; and the TNT charge placed either in open holes or tamped four to six feet deep. Morgan had his apparatus set up on a bunk in the tractor, where he could barely squeeze in around it. On the cry of "Ready, everybody," Demas would ram home the plunger of the hand-blaster—then a geyser of snow as the charge exploded.

Morgan required anywhere from 8 to 15 hours to occupy a single station. As many as a dozen charges were exploded before he got clear reflections. He made a practice of developing the records on the spot, usually after every third or fourth shot, so that, if a new series was necessary, the charges could be varied on repeat shots without having to set up the instruments again. He developed the traces in the cook tent, using blow torches to melt snow for water. In the severer temperatures the hypo and wash water often froze in the middle of the operation, a nuisance in that the freezing and reheating of the solution altered its characteristics and the clarity of the prints.

Cold was more than physical hardship. In the coldest weather the rubber sheathing on the firing and recording cables lost all pliability; below —20° the dry batteries which supplied the plate and filament current for the amplifiers froze and gave no juice: they had to be warmed over a primus stove. Yet the effect of this trifling amount of heat on the air caused the formation of frost crystals on instruments having metal parts, such as the galvanometers, with a consequent dispersion of light. Until the warmer temperatures of December made it possible to eliminate the pre-heating of the batteries, it was all but impossible, Morgan said, to secure good results in a limited amount of time.

Even in December his operating temperatures ranged from —10° to +30°

III

The story of the trip itself is a saga of marches and counter-marches, advances and retreats, fog and blizzards, harried excursions among the vertical ambushes of crevasses, and cruel, unremitting labor over the "Iron Horses." Their adventures among the crevasses at Lat. 81° have already been outlined. At first, Waite said, the rumbling collapse of a crevasse and the sickening lurch of the car would almost transfix him with horror. The fear that the next blind crevasse might be as big as one of the 40 and 50 foot open cracks they were evading deprived them of any feeling of security. Later on, when the cracking of crevasses became commonplace (one day they broke through sixty small ones) they accepted them casually; the cry "there she goes" stimulated only a brisk and practiced jump over the side. A hint of the besetting mechanical difficulties came in Demas's casual mention of having eight times dropped the pans on the cars to take up bearings and such; once they did the job with the temperature —44°, eight hours stretched under the engine, with a strip of tarpulin under them and a blow-torch for warmth. Demas and Hill finished the trip with a deep respect for the cars. They were impressed that the cars had held together so long. Brutal handling by inexperienced drivers during the unloading of the ships, and thereafter the burdens of huge loads in soft, deep snow, unbroken travel in low gear and the wrenching strain of crevasses took the guts out of the cars. When they left Advance Base late in October, Demas said, both cars carried loads of 8,000 pounds—huge burdens for 22 horsepower engines, especially with the treads sinking four inches in the crust.

As the journey has already been sketched in up to the time we landed beside them after the flight to close the gap, November 23rd, I shall resume it at that point. At that time they were only about 20 miles west of the edge of the plateau, but held off from direct approach by impassable crevasses. The survey of the region from the air had recommended a slight northing toward better ground. A blizzard and poor visibility held them in camp three days; at 6 A.M. on the 26th the cars were underway, steering 15° north of west. Bramhall, of course, did the navigating; on clear days he stood on a navigating platform built out from the running board, holding Demas on a course with a sun compass; when they were running in fog, he used the magnetic compass, directing the driver from the trailing sledge by blinker lights, as Rawson had done on the Eastern Tractor trip.

Forty miles on this course—at Lat. 79° 38′ S., Long. 149° 22′ W.—they stumbled into a shallow valley of crevasses, really immense crevasses, full of huge "pot holes." They were only two miles from the edge of the plateau; the surface just beyond the disturbance seemed good. Fog and mists held them up three days. They celebrated Thanksgiving in the interim—a forlorn chicken thawed out over a blow torch and shared by five ravenous men. Bramhall and Morgan meanwhile explored the area on skis. Progress to eastward was impossible: but to the north the crevassed area seemed quite narrow.

December 1st, on a northerly heading, they carefully worked through the last crevasses, gaining what they thought were the lower reaches of the plateau. For 11 miles they climbed over a succession of hills and terraces to 1,900 feet elevation, a rise of 1,300 feet from the Barrier. Clear sailing ahead, they thought. Bramhall set course for 150-Mile Depot on the eastern trail. But instead of gaining altitude the aneroid showed they had lost several hundred feet. They camped after a run of 28 miles, and went on station. Demas and Hill meanwhile tightened up the treads of No. 3, which had gotten very loose. The last stock fan belt had been used up, and they were dependent upon the home-made affairs Boyd and Poulter had fabricated at Little America.

On the 4th they moved on in heavy mist, Bramhall directing Demas by blinker lights from the sledge. The course was 25° east of north. Hill and Waite were about 50 yards astern in No. 2. A few cracks, one or two feet wide, broke open—nothing serious enough to warrant stopping. Then Bramhall was appalled to see a yawning chasm open under the treads. Demas jammed the accelerator to the floor and barely managed to clear it, stopping short on the other side to save the sledge. Bramhall had rolled off.

The crevasses was lenticular in shape, 15 feet wide at the crossing, just three feet narrower than the car, the widest the car had yet opened under it. It was 120 feet deep. Morgan went down on a line and verified it.

Again the two scientists reconnoitered for a transit. The region was impassable to north and east; to the west it seemed risky but passable. The place was full of open "pot holes" and lightly roofed crevasses in which their skis awakened frightening echoes. "When the weather cleared," Bramhall said, "one felt unsafe even on skis."

Two days later, after retreating about three miles, they struck along a ridge to the west. A few miles in this direction brought them into more crevasses. Painstakingly Morgan, Bramhall and Waite took turns probing the ground ahead for blind holes with long iron rods, while the cars came creeping behind. Even this precarious détour soon petered out into a maze of crevasses running every which way, around which no satisfactory passage was to be found. The surface was rough as the crust of a gigantic French loaf.

After Bramhall and Morgan had set up their stations, Demas and Hill skied to the top of a long hill about 11 miles west, to which attention was attracted by what seemed to be waves of pressure ridges. The pressure turned out to be high sastrugi. From this eminence, however, they marked a likely route to west-northwest, parallel to a line of crevasses following a slight rise. Such a course was hazardous; practical experience had shown over and over again that safety lay in hitting crevassed areas at right angles to the general trend. But there was no choice: the attempt had to be made.

Again with men probing ahead, the tractors inched away. About 5 miles on this course, Lat. 79° S., Long. 150° 31′ W., they were fetched up by a crevasse which Bramhall, never given to over-statement, indeed rarely given to any unnecessary comment at all, described as "large enough to be the grandfather of all crevasses." Where the roofing had caved in, it gaped forty feet wide in places: the bottom was so deep as to be out of sight: the walls were sheer. Elsewhere it narrowed to fifteen feet, with a snow bridging three or four feet thick.

There was no dodging it. Either take it, or turn around and retreat for good. Diminishing gas left them no opportunity for extended reconnoitering. They resolved, therefore, to attempt to "jump it" at high speed.

That night the drivers went over the cars, tightening them up. The governors were removed. Down to the crevasse licked a gentle slope. In the evening of the 11th the cars moved up to it.

Demas started down first, with Morgan on the navigation platform and Waite riding the swaying sledge. At top speed, which was about 10 knots, they made for the crevasse. Demas had his foot jammed down on the throttle, one hand on the safety lanyard on the door.

"For about ten seconds I didn't breathe," Demas said. "But nothing happened. We couldn't believe it. The bridge held."

Then they signalled to Hill, who had waited to see how they fared. At full throttle, he slammed across the crevasse. But just as he cleared the bridge a frightful din of loose and clashing parts rose from the engine: the car jerked to a stop a few yards beyond the crevasse. The bearings had let go, and a connecting rod slashed clear through the crankcase. The piston was hopelessly bent.

If that had happened over the crevasse, No. 2 might have dug its own grave.

As it was, the car was past rehabilitation. Though it had gallantly died with its boots on, Demas thriftily removed them before *rigor mortis* set in. Mindful of his own needs, he stripped the car of everything salvageable, treads included. All that he left were the naked chassis and a pylon of dry gasoline cans, a monument to tractor navigation in the Antarctic.

On the 13th, No. 3, loaded to the gunwales, took up the march alone. Waite and Hill rode the sledges. It was good going now; after slamming and banging through a broad field of sastrugi, some of it more than six feet high, they gained elevation rapidly—3,000 feet above sea level at Lat. 78° 34′ S., Long. 150° 34′ W. They were at last on the plateau. Morgan stopped for more frequent soundings, and Bramhall extended his series of magnetic stations.

The rest of the story—their arrival December 16th at 150-Mile Beacon, the meeting with Siple's party, the break-down of No. 3 about 15 miles west of the beacon, and the arrival on the 29th of Ronne and Black with spare parts—have been told. Bramhall's navigation hit the beacon right on the nose. I have only the highest praise for the men of the party, and for the tractors as well.

IV

With the Geological Party the only main unit still in the field—on January 2nd, the day before the tractor arrived, they were 225 miles out, having made 28 miles in the last 8 hours—we were rapidly cleaning up the last lingering jobs.

Thurs., Jan. 3, Midnight.

... Quite a bit of excitement roused today by a request from Ellsworth's radio operator please to stand by, the plane was in the air. The operator said he had no idea where Ellsworth and Balchen were bound. In the afternoon a message from the New York *Times,* saying the plane had taken off and would we please give them any news of the flight. We couldn't understand it. Our meteorological report to Ellsworth couldn't have encouraged him—partly overcast, a 26-mile SE wind on the surface, an unfavorable north wind aloft, and the barometer diving. Then we got word from the *Wyatt Earp* that the plane had returned after a brief trip of exploration.

We have resumed the aerological flights interrupted by the auto-gyro's crash. On recent flights the big plane has carried a barograph to high altitudes. About midnight last night the Pilgrim went up to 15,800 feet. A temperature of −24° was registered at the peak altitude (+29° on the surface). In order to increase the plane's ceiling, all emergency gear—rations, sleeping bag, tent, etc.—was removed.

Fri., Jan. 4, 11 P.M.

Wind moderating today in SE. Cloudy. Max. +29, Min. +17, exactly yesterday's range. Men are already packing up personal gear in anticipation of a speedy passage by the ships. Corey and Noville are ransacking Little America for expedition supplies worth salvaging. I must save everything to pay off my debts. Demas, Boyd, Hill and Skinner are trying to put tractor No. 1 in shape for a trip to Advance Base, to recover the shack and instruments, and at the same time bring back the Cletrac which foundered last March. Demas said the car is mechanically all right. We're all tired out, and looking forward to the voyage to New Zealand—land and friends.

Noville has just handed me an amazing summary of the distance traveled by some of the units up to January 1st, 1935. Thinking the figures would be much larger than we realized, he got estimates from June and Demas. Since the first flight over the pack ice in Dec., 1934, aviation has flown over 16,700 nautical miles—counting test flights of all kinds, photographic hops, navigation checks, freighting, and the autogyro's aerological hops. The Condor has flown 4,673 miles in exploration missions alone.

Demas estimates that the tractors have logged a gross distance of about 11,500 miles since they hit the ice.

> Innes-Taylor hasn't yet made an estimate of dog mileage. I doubt if he'll be able to. There was no way of keeping track of the countless journeys made during unloading of the ships, nor of the multitude of small errands run in the vicinity of the camp. Probably the sledging parties will prove to have traveled 3,000 miles in the fall operations alone.

The next few days were strenuous. On the 5th Demas, Boyd, Skinner, Tinglof and Wade, the latter as radio operator, departed in No. 1 for Advance Base; and not long afterwards Dane, Swan and Moody returned from the Rockefellers with the Fokker engine, propeller and instruments. A day later Morgan, Ronne and Black also arrived from the Rockefellers, Morgan pleased at having found that the mountains were capped by black mica schist through which granite had intruded. Dr. Gould of the first expedition, limited to Mt. Helen Washington in the group, found only granite. Morgan scaled Mt. Nilsen, a peak to the northwest, and a small peak in between, finding the latter topped with a five-foot layer of mica schist and the former of the same structure from the ice line to the summit.

I was gratified with the salvage crew's success. They found the Fokker turned over on its back, the engine sealed in hard blue ice, which took them several days to chop away. Traces of camp where June, Gould and Balchen had waited 12 days for rescue were still visible—the poles of the tent, but the fabric gone, ski poles, fur clothing—moldy, rotten and spoiled by sun, a carton of cigarettes too stale to be enjoyed, a cooker and bricks of slightly gamey pemmican. The engine, though rusty in spots, was in good shape.

Meanwhile, in the background of the more spectacular field activities, Poulter's seismic soundings in the vicinity of Little America were prospering. I have from time to time made passing reference to them. The first soundings were taken during November in the vicinity of Little America, and confirmed what had long been suspected and Morgan's test soundings had proved—that Little America and the local Barrier ice were afloat, with bottom depths ranging from 1,800 to 2,000 feet. But Poulter also got the first thickness determinations—an ice thickness of 500 feet on the low ridge to the east. Curiously, in Ver-Sur-Mer Inlet the ice was so shallow that he couldn't fix its thickness with any degree of accuracy.

From this beginning Poulter proceeded with a close-profiling of the Bay of Whales region, one of the most illuminating enterprises of the whole expedition. He ran a series of seismic stations along the Barrier first up to East Cape, then up the other side to West Cape, then more soundings at strategic points in the vicinity. By December 10th he was in possession of the first clues toward the solution of the mystery of the Barrier. At four points—on high barrier behind East and West Capes, near Cape Manhue and on the rise south of Amundsen Arm—the soundings showed that the Barrier was grounded, resting apparently on ridges, reefs and skerries 200 feet below sea-level. The records disclosed ice thicknesses up to 500 feet. These ridges, reefs, or a shoaling of the bottom accounted, then, for the persistence of the Bay of Whales as a fixed structure in the inconstant front of the great Ross Ice Barrier. Poulter was especially encouraged by the discovery of double reflections in the water layer beneath the ice. In other words, the reflected wave bouncing from the bottom was again reflected by the under side of the ice sheet. Several instances of triple and quadruple reflections were recorded. This data gave an absolute thickness determination for floating ice.

Late in December, after journeying by dog team across Amundsen Arm to sound the ice on the lower slopes of Roosevelt Island, 23 miles southeast of Little America, he was astonished to find in the records as he developed them in his shack, the first indisputable evidence of land above sea level in the vicinity of Little America—land 500 feet above sea level, sheeted with 300 feet of ice.

In November and December, Dr. Poulter relied upon dogs for transporting his instruments. He had ingeniously rebuilt a sledge to house the camera, amplifiers, tuning forks and batteries. The seismometers were disposed on a neat rack; for the firing and recording cables, he had a special reel mounted outboard. With its red flags flying and shining apparatus, the thing looked like a circus calliope; but "Doc" ran it like a fire engine. He and his assistants, Black and Fleming and later Moody, were sledging 20 miles a day in good weather and foul. Always efficient in his work, Poulter reduced the operation itself to a science. Behind the main sledge were towed two light sledges fixed at various distances on a measured cable equivalent to determined shot-point intervals. On these sledges the powder and caps for the next shots were ready. As they moved from one station to the next, Black and Fleming skied, each along a sledge; the instant the sledges stopped, which meant that Dr. Poulter, with the instrument sledge ahead had reached a new profile location, they rapidly planted the charges and fired in turn on the signal. Black said they hardly spoke a word all day. But it saved a lot of time. Poulter finally got it down to a point where he was able to occupy a station in 20 minutes. He developed the records when he returned at night.

The big plane having been withdrawn from long-range flights on account of the lateness of the season, Poulter now asked permission to borrow it to transport him and his instruments on quick dashes to certain strategic points for soundings. With a plane, he could occupy in a few hours stations that would take days to reach with dogs. The plane and crew were placed at his disposal. He quickly installed his apparatus, and on the evening of the 5th the Condor departed on its first seismic errand. June and McCormick were in the pilots' seats, Petersen was radio operator, Poulter and Fleming were aboard for the soundings, and Rawson to fix by astronomical observation the exact position of each station. Haines installed a barograph in the plane for an aerological sounding to 13,000 feet just before they landed—another example of the varied use to which we put aircraft, exploring the land under the ice by seismic soundings and the pressures and temperatures aloft by other means. On subsequent flights Pelter was aboard for mapping purposes.

The seismic sounding flight roughly described a semi-circle of 25-mile radius east, south and west of Little America; the plane was out 6½ hours, 7 landings were made and 7 stations were occupied. I shall briefly summarize the results in order to show how Poulter went about this business:

First station—5 miles south of Kainan Bay. Elevation by altimeter 180 feet.[1] Ice thickness about 250 feet, grounded below sea-level.

Second station—25 miles east of Little America on eastern trail. Elevation 220 feet. Ice thickness 250-300 feet, grounded below sea-level.

Third station—½ mile south of Amundsen Arm, on slope of Roosevelt Island. Elevation 720 feet. Ice thickness 400 feet, *land above sea-level.*

Fourth station—On the dome of Roosevelt Island, about 30 miles southeast of Little America. Elevation 1,400 feet. Ice thickness 400 feet, *land 1,000 feet above sea-level.*

Fifth station—25-Mile Depot on Southern Trail. Elevation 180 feet. Ice thickness 300 feet, grounded below sea-level.

Sixth station—25 miles due west of Little America. Elevation 140 feet. Ice thickness 500 feet. Barrier afloat and ocean bottom 1,200 feet.

Seventh station—25 miles west of Floyd Bennett Bay. Elevation 140 feet. Ice thickness 500 feet. Barrier afloat and ocean bottom 1,200 feet.

This series of soundings Poulter quickly followed up by soundings, on two subsequent flights, at Discovery Inlet, 100 miles west of Little America, at Advance Base and at 75-Mile Depot on the Southern trail. On January 13, the Condor having been dry-docked for a complete overhaul in anticipation of the possibility it might be required to ferry stores to the ships during the evacuation of Little America, Poulter, with Moody and Black, departed for Discovery Inlet with a dog team, to run a line of soundings along the northern edge of the Barrier, where they were eventually picked up by the *Bear*. During the last fortnight on the ice, he and Dr. Bryant, the seismic expert who arrived on the *Bear*, filled in the profile around the Bay, and carefully checked earlier data.

In all, 510 seismic soundings were made by the expedition—425 by

[1] Instrument set at zero for Little America, which was about 30 feet above sea level.

Poulter and 80 [1a] by Morgan on the tractor trip. Summarizing the results, Poulter said four facts emerged: (1) Little America and immediate vicinity are afloat on a 250-300 foot sheet of ice in 1600-1800 feet of water; (2) much of the Barrier east of a line running straight south from Little America is grounded; (3) in this region the land reaches an elevation at Roosevelt Island of 1,000 feet above sea-level with a capping of 400 feet of ice; and (4) the great Ross Ice Barrier, supposedly water-borne, is in all probability largely grounded or held in by ice that is grounded in many places.[2] Later on when the data have been fully worked up, we may be able to draw a profile of the land under the ice.

V

About 7 o'clock on the morning of January 11th the news flew over Little America: the Geological Party's back! A rush for the exit hatches, and there they were—Blackburn, Russell and Paine—quietly tethering the dogs, looking extraordinarily fit after a journey of 1,410 statute miles, the longest thrust of the expedition, farther even than the longest flight. They lacked just 5 days of being three months in the field. Paine came back from the south polar plateau with the finest set of mutton chop whiskers ever cultivated by man or beast; all he needed was a pair of moleskins, maybe the background of the famous Yale fence, or maybe just a tandem bicycle, to be the incarnation of the spirit of the 90's. Blackburn's honest countenance was transformed by a tweedish efflorescence which reminded us all at the same instant of Ben Turpin; the roars of laughter brought a blush of dismay through the frost-scarred tissue of his cheeks. As for Dick Russell, he was utterly unchanged, the same quietly half-smiling eyes, the same Puckish deviltry. They all insisted the night watchman had failed at first to recognize them, that he had looked at them blankly, and said: "Now, don't tell me—I'll think of it in a minute—you're the Geological Party!" The camp heard with wonder that Coal, most murderous of the white-eyed Siberians, had come up for judgment at the foot of the Queen Maud Range, had come up for judgment at a drumhead courtmartial and been

[1a] Morgan's soundings were begun at the point the tractors turned east and were continued to 150-Mile Depot on the eastern trail.

[2] One interesting phase of the soundings was the velocity determination tests, which showed a wide variation in the velocity of sound in snow and ice, ranging from 1080 ft/sec in freshly fallen, light snow to 12,200 ft/sec at greater depths. The difference, of course, is due to compression, which increases the rigidity and density of the snow and its change in character at the basement layers to hard blue ice. At the 12,200 ft/sec horizon the time-distance curve for the sound impulse remained constant, indicating that at this depth the ice becomes nearly constant as regards density, rigidity and incompressibility. Morgan, who descended a crevasse to 120 feet, said this point was not reached at that depth, which conforms with the depth estimates of the 12,200 ft/sec horizon.

THE GEOLOGICAL PARTY—RUSSELL, BLACKBURN, AND PAINE

(Photographs by Joseph A. Pelter)

THE SOUTHERN TRACTOR PARTY—HILL, DEMAS, AND WAITE

A Seismic Sounding

Lindsey and Young Weigh a Baby Seal

Black, Ronne, and Morgan at the Top of Mt. Nilsen (Rockefellers)

sentenced to death. "Which squared a lot of old accounts," Blackburn said. The hero of the trip was Paine's long-legged, pepper-and-salt leader, Jack the Giant Killer, who broke trail and set the pace for all but a hundred miles of the journey—as fine a performance by a sledging dog as you'll find in the history of sledging. "Jack was equal to another man," Paine said.

The outstanding findings of the journey fall into three divisions—geographical discovery, geology and paleontology.

Ascending the untraveled pass of Thorne Glacier and carving out at the same time a new route through the Queen Mauds to the polar plateau, they discovered and mapped several hundred new mountain peaks. But eclipsing this in importance was the discovery east of their ascent that the great stream of ice which Dr. Gould had identified as Leverett Glacier, was no glacier but instead a sub-plateau—a mighty terrace of ice intermediate between the polar plateau and the new plateau of Marie Byrd Land.

At Lat. 87°, Long. 152° 30′ W., on the summit of an 8,200 foot mountain, the party stood within 207 statute miles of the Pole. From the top of this mountain, which they named Mt. Weaver, they had vision over the gleaming expanse of the plateau to within 100 miles of the Pole itself.

So near the Pole, in moraines and gulleys around the mountain and on the summit itself, they came upon numerous fossils of plant leaves, fossiliferous traces and imprints, perfectly formed plant stems, and even fossilized tree trunks up to 18 inches in diameter. In the sides of the mountain Blackburn counted 15 seams of coal, interbedded with shales and limestones.

All magnificent material for the paleontological record of Antarctica. By a substantial margin this was the nearest such finds had been made to the Pole.

In all, 460 pounds of geological specimens—representing a cross-section of Mt. Weaver as well as other important formations in the Queen Maud Range from Barrier level to the rim of the polar plateau—were collected and brought back to Little America. During the descent 14 triangulation stations were established for locating the new peaks, and mapping photographs were taken on various bearings. A meteorological record was kept throughout the trip.

At Lat. 86°, at an altitude of 5,000 feet, where the unslackening, bitter-cold gales funneling down the glacier made human effort an agony, they found patches of green, white and blackish lichens defending existence in the crevices of rocks—the farthest south life has ever been found.

Here, again, I must point out, as I did in summarizing the results of the other parties, that final judgment must be suspended until data and specimens can be studied with more precision than was possible at Little America. There is another point it would be well to emphasize here: and that is that this party, like the others, was essentially scientific. Pioneering exploration was a by-product, rather than a main objective, of their journeys. Blackburn's party, for example, was primarily shaped toward a certain geological mission. That he made important geographical discoveries was the happy outcome of his having to break past previous horizons to reach special regions. His real objectives were the sedimentary beds of rock holding the fossiliferous and geological keys of a doomed continent.

The paleontology of unknown Antarctica is a fascinating problem. Compared with the fossil-history of the rest of the world, it is almost as blank as the ice that enfolds it. Involved in it is the dawn history of this remote continent.

The only parallels to the pulsing tides of ice which in Pleistocene times overwhelmed Europe and the United States are the ice sheets now clamped upon Greenland and Antarctica.[3] In these two areas modern man, so sure of himself on the land and sea and in the air, can study humbly and discerningly, according to his philosophical mood and technical gifts, the majestic mechanism of obliteration that operates an Ice Age.

At any rate, there for me is one of the grand excitements of polar exploration, the sensing of things that once were.

The difficulties facing the geologist and paleontologist must be perfectly obvious. The ice hides the land and, creeping everywhere toward the sea, drops unseen in the ocean the accumulated débris of the Ice Age.[4] But little by little from the rock strata exposed by the receding ice and from fossiliferous fragments picked up here and there, science is piecing together a fascinating picture of the continent that used to be.

Antarctic fossils have been dredged from a depth of 1,775 fathoms in the Weddell Sea.[5] The stomachs of penguins and seals captured off coasts where no rock is exposed have yielded valuable information.[6] In Granite Harbor the scientists of Scott's last expedition found in Devonian shales and sandstones fragments of fossilized fish scales.[7] At Lat. 85° S., in the Beardmore Glacier, Shackleton on his first dash toward the Pole, came upon seven seams of coal.[8] Scott, on his fatal journey, confirmed it; and Wilson picked up plant impressions "with beautifully traced leaves" and "impressions of thick stems." [9] Dr.

[3] R. E. Priestley and C. S. Wright, *Some Ice Problems of Antarctica, Problems of Polar Research,* 332.
[4] Ibid, 335.
[5] Hayes, *Antarctica,* 23.
[6] Priestley and Wright, op. cit., 336.
[7] *Scott's Last Expedition,* ii., 262; Taylor, *With Scott,* 386.
[8] Shackleton, *Heart of the Antarctic,* i., 327, ii., 299.
[9] *Scott's Last Expedition,* i., 389.
Cherry-Gerrard, *Worst Journey in the World,* 523.

Gould found coal in Mt. Nansen.[10] And in the vicinity of Terra Nova Bay, on the western shore of the Ross Sea, Priestley happened upon fossil stems 12 to 18 inches in diameter and impressions of even larger trees.[11]

All this, of course, is very sketchy and somewhat heterogeneous to boot; it is cited merely as general evidence in proof of what so few people seem to realize—that at one time Antarctica possessed what must have been a comparatively mild and humid climate,[12] a climate, at any rate, genial enough to support "a flourishing land flora, with strongly developed trees and with swamp or forest vegetation capable of forming beds of coal" which probably extended across the Pole.[13]

But no less enigmatic is that in Antarctica, now the most formidable example of refrigeration surviving on the face of the earth, such glacial conditions are the exception rather than the rule.[14] Sir Douglas Mawson has called attention to the anomaly of the polar continent which in its geology exhibits no trace of glaciation earlier than Cretaceous times, whereas a present temperate land, such as Australia, shows marked manifestations of repeated glaciation.[15]

It is in this special and highly speculative field that Blackburn's fossil finds are of eminent importance, amplifying as they do the extent of the known area of these fossil-bearing formations.

VI

Russell remarked at breakfast, that morning, if they ever wrote a book about the journey, it would be called *Wind*. The wind had bitten into their memories as acid bites into an engraving plate. From the time they cast off from the tractors at Lat. 81° 09′ S. they sledged into steady down-drafts from the polar plateau, blowing across the Barrier with the persistence of the trade-winds—all southeasterly winds, with a velocity of from 20 to 60 miles per hour, perhaps more. Blackburn's face was whipped to the color of raw beefsteak. "It was just one big blow," he said. He pulled out his log and showed me an entry: "December 31. Today the wind let up for the first time. It is blowing only 10 miles per hour and seems like a dead calm." Up the glacier, the mountain walls of which made a funnel, the wind was even worse. It buffeted them like a solid force. It never blew less than 20-40 miles per hour, and at times approached hurricane force. Men and dogs suffered exceedingly.

[10] Gould, *Cold,* 189.
[11] Wright and Priestley, *Glaciology,* **427.**
[12] Ibid, 425.
[13] Priestley and Wright, op. cit., 331.
[14] Wright and Priestley, *Glaciology,* 442.
[15] Sir Douglas Mawson, *Unsolved Problems of Antarctic Exploration and Research: Problems of Polar Research,* 264.

On November 14th, after leaving Ronne and Eilefsen at 293 miles south, Blackburn, Paine and Russell pushed on for Supporting Party Mountain, with three 13-dog teams. That afternoon, before they camped at 309 miles, they glanced up from the dogs to see the frosted peaks of the Queen Mauds—which they later identified as the white hood of Mt. Nansen, the pyramidal cone of Don Pedro Christophersen—rising handsomely on the southern horizon. Curiously, just before they turned their faces to Little America, Ronne and Eilefsen saw in the south what they thought was a perfect mirage of the Queen Mauds.

The run from this point to the Supporting Party Mt., was a brutal ordeal of headwinds, heavy loads, drift and blizzards, crevasses. The southeasterly winds never stopped; the air was turbulent with drift. It was difficult to hold a course. The dogs in their misery kept paying off before the wind, and the men traveled with faces averted, tucked in behind the cowls of parka hoods. Several dogs foundered, poor things, and were shot. The surface was gritty and they continued to halt twice a day and ice the runners. But the mountains were rising and rising in the south, fold upon fold, and flashing peaks.

November 15th and 16th they were pounded by a 60-mile blizzard. On the 17th they ran to 350-Mile Depot, where they raised on their left hand the high land already described. Just after they shoved off from the beacon, where they depoted food for the retreat, they sighted pressure and crevasses ahead. They stopped to rope themselves together, man to man, and team to team. They changed course to southwest to strike the crevasses at right angles.

A mile out of the beacon, they hit the first crevasses, mostly blind, but with a few deep, open pits. The bridges seemed insecure, trembling and giving as the dogs went over them. Russell cracked the first; the trailer dropped in after the lead sledge had safely run across. Half an hour's work to get it out. A mile on, Paine was appalled to see his dogs swallowed up in one convulsive gulp; the leader and six dogs hung straight down in their harnesses, and the wheel dogs were backtracking furiously to keep from being dragged in. Paine went down on a line, and, with a second line, passed the dogs to the surface, one by one.

Paine said:

"My team then went into the lead. Blackburn and Russell followed in that order, about 50 feet apart. We were going along quite nicely when I felt a sharp shock on the gee pole. Before I quite took in the meaning, I noticed, with mild wonder, that my dogs were digging in furiously: but instead of going forward, actually were going backwards. Instinctively I grabbed the tethering pole from the sledge and rammed it home behind the runners. Out of the corner of my eye I saw Russell braking his lead sledge.

"Blackburn's sledges were nowhere in sight. His dogs were belly-down, scraping for all they were worth: and Quin himself was crawling from the edge of a hole which had opened right under his feet.

"Well, there were the two sledges—with all of our navigational and geological gear, and a good part of our food and clothing,—hanging straight down over a 60-footer. It took us 7 hours to get them back on the surface. Blackburn and Russell took turns going down on a line and passing the gear back to the surface. The wind never let up; it was a freezing business."

This was at Lat. 83° 58′ S., Long. 154° 30′ W.

On the 21st the teams moved into another dangerous area. The Barrier became upheaved with huge white billowings, forced up by the compression of ice pouring off the glacier. Paine likened the troughs to sunken highways. The rolls occurred from one to three miles apart, and measured 100 feet from crest to trough. Slam-bang descents, followed by abrupt and tiring climbs. Down in the hollows the mountains disappeared from view. Warily they navigated the blind crevasses at the bottom.

Next day their best run—33 miles, which carried them to within 12 miles of Supporting Party Mt., a peak flanking the eastern foothills which border on the northern side of the sheet of ice named Leverett Glacier. Here, on a mile-square stretch of smooth surface, they marked out with flags an emergency landing field for aircraft and depoted supplies for the return. This was the Mountain Base (see map). High winds and drift held them in camp several days; on the 26th they ran to the foot of Supporting Party, gaining the land after 42 days of Barrier sledging. Next day, ascending the 1,300 foot peak, they happened upon the rock cairn which Gould, Crockett, Goodale and Vaughan had raised in December, 1929; and within it, sealed in a cereal can, they found the note which briefly set forth the details of their journey, the fact they were the first to set foot on this land, and claiming "in the name of Admiral Richard E. Byrd this land as Marie Byrd Land, a dependency or possession of the United States." [16] This point likewise was the farthest south and east reached by the first party.

From the peak of this mountain hopefully Blackburn scanned the mountains east of Thorne Glacier for the most attractive opportunities for geological investigation. He was instantly disappointed. West of the glacier the main scarp front of the Queen Mauds is made up of superb and lofty tabular and domed mountains rising to altitudes of 10,000 to 14,000 feet. The longest valley glaciers in the world pour through them. But looking eastward Blackburn saw that the mountains were almost drowned under the ice pouring down from the Plateau. Few bold mountains appeared even in the higher escarpment

[16] Gould, *Cold*, 209.

behind Leverett.[17] There were no great valley glaciers: merely narrow and precipitous ice falls of the alpine type.

Convinced these mountains were too heavily mantled for successful geological examination, Blackburn and his companions, after a long discussion, finally resolved to strike up the broad white stream of Thorne Glacier.

November 28th they ran in a southwesterly direction across a glacial outlet from Leverett [18] to a peak which formed the northeastern portal of Thorne Glacier. Next day, Thanksgiving, they commenced the ascent, hugging the easterly margin of the glacier. At the mouth the stream was about 15 miles broad, with slick glare ice, blue as sapphire when the sun was on it, and everywhere cracked and riffled. The men donned crampons; the dogs were hard put to it to find footing, slithering and slipping all over the place at times. The wind funneling down the pass, of course, made it difficult; it struck them full in the face: the higher they rose the colder it got. Paine said that the wind spun the dogs off their feet.

It took them 10 days to climb the glacier, which they calculated to be 120 miles long. The first three days of climbing they rose 3,000 feet. The wind bit to the bone. Even with furs and windproofs on top of these, they couldn't seem to keep warm when they stopped to camp. The wind flapped and pumped the tents all night. The one comfort was the absence of drift; the winds had broomed the surface clean. But curling sheets of drift from the plateau were flying over the topmost peaks.

December 2nd, 40 miles up the glacier, they established a midway rations depot. A belt of crevasses on their course shunted them toward the western margin of the glacier. Here they encroached upon the most dangerous ice they had seen—masses of folded, jumbled pressure and crevasses a hundred feet across, where the ice had been torn away from the mountains. Finding no passage here, they retreated several miles, then steered again for the east wall. That day they made 7 miles, rising only a few hundred feet. On the 3rd they equaled the distance in a gale, the aneroid showing a climb of 800 feet. The 4th was likewise squally, but they made 13 miles. Halfway up the surface commenced to flatten out; the blue ice gave way to firm, gritty snow. On the 5th they were blocked by heavy ice walls, past which they found passage to the west after Blackburn and Paine had reconnoitered 12 miles on skis. After making 7 miles they regained the eastern shore of the glacier, where the surface was better. The center

[17] The four peaks running east of Supporting Party Mountain were named Harold Byrd Mts.; the upper group were named Thomas Watson Escarpment (see map).

[18] As a consequence of Blackburn's observations here and from another vantage point on the west side of Thorne Glacier, Leverett Glacier has been renamed Leverett Plateau.

of the glacier was badly crevassed. On the 6th they made the best run of the ascent—19 miles, climbing 1,000 feet.

When they camped on the night of the 6th they were all but at the head of the glacier. Their tent was pitched near the mouth of a small tributary glacier passing out from the half-submerged peaks on the east wall of Thorne. Just about 5 miles to the southwest was a first-class peak which had beckoned them on during the last half of the ascent. Its northwestern face was all exposed rock; and the banded structure held the promise of the horizontal sedimentary beds Blackburn was looking for.

Next morning Russell hiked over to the mountain to have a look. Shortly after noon Blackburn and Paine saw him coming back, leaning against the wind which sometimes spilled him flat on his back, often hidden in whirlies of drift.

"What's the news, Dick?" Blackburn yelled the instant he was within calling distance.

Russell waited till he reached them, then he brought a dark lump of rock out of his windproof pocket.

"It's coal," said Blackburn. "Real coal. It's a sedimentary mountain."

"The coal is all over the place," Russell said. "One part of the moraine is nothing but coal."

Quickly they loaded the sledges, hitched up the dogs and headed for the mountain which they named Mt. Weaver. The surface was slick ice with occasional patches of snow. Wind of gale force puffed around the mountain. "We fell flat on our faces trying to make headway," Paine said.

That evening, in the lee of the northeasterly shoulder of Mt. Weaver, they made camp, 727 miles from Little America, and 53 days out. Here, at the junction of two moraines, black with the glacial débris and detritus carried off the mountain, they pitched their tent. They had only to walk a few yards to what Russell insisted on calling "the office."

In these and other moraines, among the litter of stuff washed down by the glacial streams, they found finely grained argillaceous and carbonaceous sandstones, weathered to delicate pinkish-white shades: perfectly cast fossiliferous impressions of leaves and stems, and numerous fossilized fragments of tree trunks, from a foot to 18 inches in diameter. They could hardly credit their luck. In the sides of the mountain itself they counted 15 seams of coal, of which 12 were cleanly defined. This find, taken in conjunction with previous discoveries of coal, gives fresh meaning to Griffith Taylor's prophecy that the Antarctica may be found to possess the greatest coal reserves, next to the United States, in the world.[19]

The coal appeared to range from lignitic to sub-bituminous.

[19] Griffith Taylor, *Antarctic Adventure and Research,* 100-101.

After waiting in vain for the wind to diminish, and having food for only two more days, according to their time schedules, they started up Mt. Weaver on December 10th to run a cross-section of the sedimentary layers. The temperature was zero. The maximum temperature recorded during their stay at the mountain was 5°. Making ready for the ascent, Russell said they put on everything but the primus stoves—3 pairs of socks, gamoshes, heavy woollen underwear, heavy woollen shirt, fur parkas and pants and windproof over these, fleece-lined helmets, two pairs of woollen inner liners and windproof gloves. Thoughtful of blizzards, they carried a light tent, Sterno cans for melting water and cooking food, and a day's rations of chocolate and pemmican. They also had a medical kit, compass, barometer, thermometer, ice axes, alpine rope and several hundred specimen bags.

They climbed a northwest spur, which seemed to offer a ridge of exposed rock a good way to the summit. The wind increased as they climbed. They scrambled up, squatting or throwing themselves on their bellies until the heavier gusts lessened. A sheer drop fell on the lee side. The wind frosted their cheeks every few minutes and seemed to suck the breath out of their lungs. Halfway up they had to mount a steep snow slope, sometimes cutting foot ledges with ice axes. Gratefully, when they had climbed a fair distance above the plateau elevation, the wind moderated. But Blackburn called attention to the fact that the drift was whirling with undiminished strength around their tent. A curious phenomenon, that: a film of cold air pouring like a fluid off the polar plateau, given velocity by gravity down the steep passes.

Gaining the summit, the first sledging party to advance the American flag to the plateau, they took stock of the known and unknown. In the west they marked, with glasses, what they took to be the peaks which were prominent landmarks in Amundsen's ascent toward the Pole—Mt. Helland Hansen, Oscar Wisting, Olaf Bjaaland, Sverre Hassel—even, they thought, the glittering reflection of blue ice in the Devil's Glacier.

In the south and southeast were a few ridge outcroppings—nunataks, smothered in the snow, fanning out from the head of the glacier. Otherwise the unsullied spread of the plateau, golden in the sun.

Looking north and east from this eminence, Blackburn had a profound view of the new mountains in that direction. Again he marked the easterly trend of the Queen Maud Escarpment. To the east the plateau was gradually dipping. At the head of Thorne it probably did not exceed 7,000 feet, several thousand feet lower than at the head of the western passes.

"The mountains which fringe the valley of Thorne Glacier," Paine wrote on his return, "stood in serried ranks, like matched soldiers, the shorter in front with the bigger and huskier well back of the front rank. The main escarpment of the plateau stood higher than the rest. It seemed to form a background to the soaring granitic peaks nearer the main glacier, making them look lean and tall against its own massiveness. Each of us felt a sense of elation as he took in that panorama of mountains, glistening snow domes, glaciers and skies. There was a serenity and peace on the land.... Soft blues and greens merged into the dazzling whiteness of snow above, and purple lines told of fissures and grottoes.... Sweeping around the northern base of our mountain from the east was a tributary glacier. From our lofty perch the broken waves of ice and crevasses appeared like ripples on the smooth waters of a slowly moving river. Many of the crevasses must have been over a hundred feet across, and we shuddered to think of crossing them. We had come over so many that we were exceedingly crevasse-conscious."

Before starting down to commence the cross-section, they lunched on chocolate and pemmican. The temperature was —14°, but the air at that altitude was almost calm, though drift was still blowing around the foot of the mountain. They built a cairn; and a laconic note, giving their names and an account of their journey was put into a cocoa tin and wedged in the rocks.

A few feet below the summit Blackburn found a stratum holding hundreds of imprints of fossil leaves. While he bagged the specimens, Paine took down with pencil and paper the notes he dictated. The transition from one species of rock to another was rapid; they had to move only a few feet to reach the next layer. The rocks had to be handled and bagged with bare hands, and Blackburn froze his fingers severely. On the way down they again entered the wind level of the southeast Antarctic "trades."

So loaded with specimens they could hardly walk, they reached camp at 8:30 o'clock that evening. The sequence could not be continued to the base, the talus and broken rock fragments concealing the outcroppings.

The mountain, Blackburn said, was synclinal in character, with buff-colored sedimentary beds of sandstone and bluish shale resting upon a weather-reddened base of igneous rocks and, in turn, capped by them.

At 9 o'clock on the morning of December 12th they started the descent of the glacier, glad now to have the wind at their backs. They paused on the way down to occupy triangulation stations and collect more specimens. At Latitude 86°, about 5,000 feet up the glacier, Russell found the patches of lichens already described. For the most part they clung to the northern faces of the rock, where they had sun and were out of the wind. And in this vicinity, also, they had their first glimpse of alien life since leaving Little America—two honeymooning couples of skua gulls, who flapped out of nowhere, scarcely 240 miles from the Pole and 450 miles from the sea on a great circle course.

Evidently the gulls were hungry (there is no known food source nearer than the sea) for they fretted awhile overhead, then landed nervously near the dogs, who, being tethered, went frantic at the sight of fresh meat. But the dogs couldn't get them, and neither could the drivers, though Russell and Paine, likewise anxious to convert this natural phenomenon into a change of diet, shied rocks at them until their arms were sore. After a while the gulls wheeled and vanished to the north, probably for the coast, perhaps for the rookery Siple had discovered in the Edsel Ford Range.

There's a curious question behind the migrations of the skua. Whither are they bound? Possibly there is a well-traveled air route for such birds between the Ross and Weddell Seas; possibly they migrate into the continent to die.[20] Other exploring parties have seen them—Amundsen at Lat. 84° 20′ S.,[21] Scott as far as Lat. 87° 20′—184 miles from the Pole.[22]

Safely off the glacier, with 450 pounds of geological specimens on their sledges, they quit the Mountain Base two days before Christmas. A haul, then, of 527 miles to Little America and the sea. With the wind at their backs, Russell and Paine made sails out of a torn tent and bent them to ski poles, using bamboo for booms. They called it Barrier sailing, and said it was equivalent to having two more dogs on the gangline. They traveled mostly at night, to have the sun at their backs and the glare off their eyes. In all events, they made marvelous time northward across the Barrier—527 miles in 16 sledging days, the fastest time ever made on a long-distance trip in the Antarctic.

There was only one untoward incident: one of Russell's dogs strangled to death in harness when the team broke through a crevasse.

A clean-cut, beautifully tooled job; and a wonderful thing about it is that neither Paine nor Russell had ever handled a team of dogs until they landed at Little America. Blackburn had driven dogs with the first expedition, but on this trip he rarely put his hand to a gee-pole. "We insisted," Russell said, "that he keep his mind unclouded for geological reflections and contemplations."

The weights of the men follow:

	Before	*After*
Blackburn	159 lbs.	159 lbs.
Russell	163 "	157 "
Paine	168 "	163 "

VII

On the afternoon of January 15th a remarkable procession, crawling like a caterpillar, appeared over the southeastern ridge—Demas and his salvage crew from Advance Base. Not only did they have the sections of the shack aboard: but in the van was the revived Cletrac, chugging along under her own power; and cocked up on a sledge trailing

[20] Hayes, *Antarctica,* 101.
[21] Amundsen, *South Pole,* ii., 164.
[22] *Scott's Last Expedition,* i., 528.

astern of the Citroën was the ice-encrusted snowmobile, resurrected from the glacierization of five years.

Except for Dr. Poulter, Moody and Black, who were westward bound to Discovery Inlet on the seismic sounding mission, the expedition was once again completely assembled at Little America.

Meanwhile the *Bear of Oakland* was steadily cleaving south, after lying hove to for a day in a gale. On the 13th, at Lat. 72° S., Long. 180° E., she entered the Ross Sea. Up to then she had met only a few bergs and scattered pack. Even now there was no sign of closed pack. A southeasterly swell was almost unimpeachable evidence to Lieut. English and Johansen that the sea was clear, and the way open to Little America. He immediately flashed a message which set afoot more excitement and joy at Little America than any tidings in a year:

"No ice of any kind during day and night."

With the *Bear* swinging westward to extend her sonic survey of the Ross Sea along the continental shelf of South Victoria Land, I immediately got in touch with the *Ruppert's* officers at Dunedin and ordered them to start with all possible dispatch. On the 15th she raised steam and put out of Otago Harbor. Commander Gjertsen had returned from Norway to resume his post as Commodore; Lieut. Commander Rose, U.S.N.R., was acting Captain; Muir was promoted to first mate, Van Reen was second and Healey was third.

Little America came up by the roots. Noville and Corey, with their gangs, were tearing the tunnels apart to bring the unused stores to the surface. A clattering and hammering of boxes rose in every shack, and a wild confusion, made buoyant with the almost incredible intelligence that a ship would presently steam into the Bay of Whales, rose in the town. On the Bulletin Board in the Mess Hall the noon and midnight positions of the *Bear* were enthusiastically printed in huge letters; and Carbone each day crossed off one day, one day less to go on the longest sentence, he said, he ever had to serve.

Chapter XVIII

THE SHIPS ARRIVE

I

UNDER Lieut. English's command, the gallant *Bear of Oakland* launched what may be recorded as her last polar mission. Standing in along the western shore of the Ross Sea, where the great British expeditions have stamped the land with a heritage as lasting as the rock itself, the *Bear's* crew, on January 14th, raised the majestic mountains of South Victoria Land. Course was laid to carry the ship north of Coulman Island, so that Roos could sound the bottom between the Island and Lady Newnes Shelf Ice with his sonic sounding apparatus. But heavy pack jammed between Cape Wadsworth, northern cape of Coulman Island, and the mainland held the ship off; Lieut. English therefore steered south, passing the island to eastward.

Wide fields of pack ice, probably recently broken out of the inlets and bays, were jammed along the western shore. Some of the fields, Lieut. English estimated, stretched 100 miles long to seaward. The day was brilliant, and the temperature rose to +55°. However, on the night of the 15th, the thermometer tumbled; and the ship had to fumble through a blizzard. Early next morning, the air cleared and Franklin Island was sighted. Before noon Beaufort Island and Cape Bird, northwestern extremity of Ross Island in the Ross Archipelago, appeared on the horizon. And as afternoon wore on the great volcanoes of Ross Island appeared—Erebus, Terror, Bird and Terra Nova, one of the most superb scenic views in the world. Most of all they were struck by the massive beauty of Mt. Erebus (13,200 ft.), an active volcano standing at the gateway of the Barrier, its flanks veined with glaciers and a plume of vapor floating above its cone. Three famous British expeditions wintered near its foot.

Steaming as close to the north shore of Ross Island as the pack would permit, Lieut. English turned the *Bear* eastward, skirting Cape Campbell. Under the knoll of Cape Crozier the vessel went on hydrographic station, Roos getting specimens from the bottom and samples of water and temperature readings at various depths. Shortly before midnight, January 16th, the *Bear* headed east, beginning at that instant a 460-mile survey of the Ross Ice Barrier, between Cape Crozier, the western seaward hinge of the ice sheet, and West Cape, in the Bay of Whales.

The survey of the Barrier front was itself a major piece of research. Simultaneously Roos ran a line of sonic soundings of ocean depths along the ship's track, and en route 12 hydrographic stations were occupied and bottom cores collected for mechanical and chemical analysis.

The movement of the Ross Ice Barrier, no less than the structural mystery now clarified by Dr. Poulter's seismic soundings, has for a long time puzzled scientists. There was the question whether it were retreating or receding, whether the amounts of ice surging and pushing out through glaciers from the interior plateaux overbalanced the loss at the edge brought about by calving—that is to say, the breaking off and dispersion in the form of icebergs.

Since its discovery and charting by Ross in 1841 and his subsequent extension of it in 1842, the Barrier had only twice been surveyed, both times by Scott's expeditions, first by himself in the *Discovery* in 1902, then by Pennell in the *Terra Nova* in 1911.

After his first survey, in which he found that Ross had exaggerated the height and uniformity of the Barrier,[1] and having sailed well south of the position of the edge as fixed by Ross, Scott was of the opinion that during the ensuing 60 years the Barrier front had receded between 15 and 20 miles.[2] This seemed to argue for the deglacierization of the continent. But later investigation indicated that it was perhaps less a proof of recession than of straightening out Ross's understandably faulty estimates.[3] Shackleton had found the Barrier's edge moving seaward at the rate of 500 yards a year in certain areas. More to the point was the evidence of Pennell's survey in 1911, which demonstrated that while there had been slight recession at certain points since 1902, the Barrier along the greater part of its length was advancing northward—the only direction the sheet could move—at the rate of approximately a mile a year.[4] In other words, accumulation and growth at the edge were progressing faster than the loss through the seasonal breaking up and calving.

Lieut. English conducted the 1935 survey with characteristic efficiency. He was equipped with a gyro compass, pelorus, range finder, sextants, of course, plotting sheets, recorders, etc. Just before he commenced the survey he carefully swung ship to determine the error of the gyro compass on various headings.

Almost immediately he found evidence of gross changes since the *Terra Nova* survey. Throughout the first 150 miles of the western reaches of the Barrier Lieut. English found the edge 13.8 miles *north* of the position fixed in 1911. The whole aspect and contour of front had gradually altered since Pennell's coasting.

This gain—or extension—was confirmed all the way from Cape Crozier to West Cape—a distance of 460 miles. The average annual rate

[1] Scott, *Voyage of the* Discovery, i.
[2] *Scott's Last Expedition*, ii., 408.
[3] Hayes, *Antarctica*, 55.
[4] Debenham, *Report on Maps and Surveys, British* (*Terra Nova*) *Antarctic Expedition*, 1910-1913.

of movement, therefore, was half a mile. An accumulation of 6,348 square miles of ice in 24 years.

On the afternoon of January 18th, Lieut. English entered Discovery Inlet, where he took aboard Dr. Poulter, Moody and Black. He notified Little America that he expected to enter the Bay of Whales next morning.

II

For weeks, the arrival of the ships and the consequent problem of evacuation and loading had been an inexhaustible topic of conversation at the base; but with the *Bear* almost in, and the *Ruppert* pressing hard upon her heels, we found we'd have to do something about it. Various tentative routes had been flagged through the pressure; a careful survey had been made of the eastern wall of the Barrier; and Captain Innes-Taylor was in the habit of sledging once a day to the Bay of Whales to report on the state of the ice.

It was, in many respects, the original problem in reverse.

Very little ice had moved out by the middle of January 1935. Whereas the year before, to the day, the *Ruppert* had been able to steam within 3 miles of Little America, the edge of the ice on January 17th ran in a line almost due east across the Bay from a point just south of West Cape.

All new ice, of course, one-year ice, about 12 feet thick, quite rotten and soft for a good distance south of the edge. Even a moderate swell, we saw, would rip it to pieces. On the 18th, for example, half a mile of it went out in a few hours. Wedge-shaped cracks were penetrating deep along the western and eastern Barrier margins: here disintegration was setting in.

We had, as I have said, tentative trails outlined through the pressure from Ver-Sur-Mer Inlet. But they were steep, almost alpine passages, impassable to the tractors. And even the dog teams, once they gained the bay ice beyond, faced five miles of sledging to the water's edge, over miserable surface, badly cracked and fissured. The biologists, Perkins, Lindsey and Sterrett, who had done more sledging on the Bay than any one else, said their dogs took ducking after ducking between the cracks.

Not a very encouraging prospect. And again, in leaving Little America as in reoccupying it, there was just one feasible exit along 10 miles of Bay front.

At Eleanor Bolling Bight, 4½ miles north of Little America, Innes-Taylor found a gentle descent down the ice foot to the Bay. There was a narrow roofed crevasse at the top: and at the foot a shallow pool of slush ice. From Ver-Sur-Mer Inlet to the Bight it was the only descent to the Bay. Elsewhere the ice foot had collapsed or disintegrated, leaving sheer drops.

So it meant, again, the punishing and tedious business of relaying—

the tractors hauling between Little America and the Barrier, the dogs between the Barrier and the ships. Or so it appeared at the time. Later the bay ice broke out and we had to load direct from the Barrier.

Yet, curiously, the appreciation of the difficulties scarcely dampened the camp's joy. The ships were on their way, and that was quite enough. The mere physical problem of getting aboard, every man must have measured in his heart, with a sigh of anticipation, would evolve its own solutions at the proper time.

"Listen, you guys," announced Carbone to the morning mess, "just you show me a packet out there and I'll show you how to get aboard."

III

About 10:30 o'clock on the morning of the 19th a distant explosion shook the air—the *Bear* was in! Dane and Herrmann had fired the dynamite signal which meant she was rounding West Cape.

I shall pass briefly over the ensuing events. Though, for safety's sake, a small party under Captain Innes-Taylor's leadership had been assigned to meet the ship and bring in the mail, that portent striking on the ecstatic air almost emptied Little America.

Out of the hatches, out of caved tunnels, out of the ventilators, out of recesses I hadn't known existed issued a spontaneous eruption of humanity as might have risen to greet the Millennium. The ridge to the north was fairly crawling with explorers, hot-footing it for the ship, on skiis, afoot, by dog team and tractor. If they had moved in such lively fashion toward the unknown, there wouldn't be an unsolved problem in Antarctica today. The cook was in the van, a Moses leading the Israelites across the Red Sea. In fact, in the cool of the evening we had to dispatch a dog team and a master-at-arms to bring him back, lest we meanwhile starve to death at Little America. He returned to the galley singing, once again contemplating the world through rose-colored glasses, and from time to time permitting himself the luxury of a hiccough which was the envy of all who heard it.

Lieut. English warped the *Bear* in for a mooring halfway between the Barrier cliffs, about 7 miles from Little America by way of Eleanor Bolling Bight. When she came alongside the ice, the cargo gear was already rigged to the foreyards, the winches were warmed up and ready, the hatch covers were off, the supplies needed for Little America were on deck, and the mail pouches, a great pile of them, were stacked at the head of the after companionway.

She was fast to deadmen at 11:30 o'clock, and the first dog teams, bearing the mail in charge of Mr. Anderson, were soon on their way in.

Practically everything stopped the instant the sacks were carried into the galley. Noville took over the distribution of the mail. "Abele . . . Blackburn . . . Bramhall . . . Corey . . ." In 20 minutes the throng in the low building had melted away: and for the next few hours there was scarcely a sound except for the tearing of envelopes, the riffling of pages, and occasional sudden bursts of confidences.

"Look at this picture of my kid. He's certainly grown a lot."

"Say, I don't like these new automobile designs—they're too . . ."

"Yeah, a Bible. Just what I wanted, goddammit."

"Beer, boys. Just rest your eyes on that picture of contented suds."

"Here's a swell new joke. A traveling salesman . . ."

"That's a tough break about Eddie So-and-so. Yes, crashed. Wings came off. Well, I guess his number was up."

"That's what my father says. The depression's over."

"Well, I'll be damned. All my girls have gotten married—Susan, Margaret, Mary Anne . . ."

And so it ran, life bursting into a long-stagnant pool, small joys and disasters, the hopes and fears of a year and a half of ignorance and uncertainty all crammed into a few minutes of reading. Radio communication is marvelous; but mail is a miracle.

From the *Bear* the dog-drivers returned singing the praises of Tony the cook, and of the rare viands in his galley, pork chops that tasted finer than terrapin, lettuce of an incredible green, and potatoes that met the palate in lingering ecstasy. I found Dr. Perkins in the galley exclaiming over the green, earthly delicacy of raw onions, and oranges and apples were being passed around as the rarest of gifts.

Meanwhile Innes-Taylor's dog drivers were relaying from the ship to the Barrier summit, and Demas's tractor drivers were steadily plying on the trail between there and Little America. Just about midnight the *Bear* finished discharging, and the movement promptly reversed itself, with the equipment to be embarked now moving from Little America.

The tractors had started a cache on the Barrier summit at Eleanor Bolling Bight, a hundred yards or so from the edge. The dogs were hauling from the cache to the ship, 2½ miles away. Lieut. English sent in six of his crew to assist in the evacuation.

Hurry—hurry—hurry was again the order of the day. Get out and shove off as rapidly as possible, while the Ross Sea was still open, before the incalculable movements of the pack interposed fresh obstacles.

It was the repetition of the white nightmare of unloading, except that now our steps were turned in the opposite direction. There were the same flogging imperatives, the same exhausting tasks, the same conspiracies of pack and wind and swell, the inconstancy of the ice, and the icebergs loping down from Marie Byrd Land to harry the ships in the Bay.

The wind blew most of the time; days when it would be almost calm at Little America the *Bear* would be plunging in a gale tearing across the Bay of Whales, fighting for her skin among the pack bursting out of the Bay or heaving down from the northeast. Our old friends, the east and northeast winds, hummed steadily. The temperature was almost stagnant in the plus twenties. The surface grew fearfully soft, and the dogs were sinking to their bellies. On the 26th, with the temperature at +32, a snowstorm for a little while became the finest of rains—a wet, steamy sort of misting which almost instantly froze and covered the antennæ wires and stays, even boxes and upended skis, with a thin veneering of clear ice. From January 9th to February 2nd we never saw the sun except for a few minutes at a time.

Between the 19th and the 23rd the *Bear* was five times driven from her berth by outrushes of ice or the threat of pinching pressure of ice wafted down from the northeast. Once Ike Schlossbach, taking a last flight in the Fairchild, flew over the ship and found her moored to a floe which had broken away a quarter of a mile south of her. We warned the ships' officers by radio. About 3 o'clock on the morning of the 23rd she was again driven out by a wind of whole gale force from east-southeast, and it was seven days before she could find a berth. Lieut. English was marooned at Little America, while Johansen worked the ship, already short-handed by the absence of six of her crew on detail at Little America. The ice was crumbling like very ripe, very old cheese.

The only ones who profited were Roos, the oceanographer, and Perkins, the biologist. Pooling their efforts, they got a number of rich bottom hauls with the dredge.[5] If the storm gave "Perk" the opportunities he so richly deserved, it was one of those rare ill winds that somewhere do a kind service. No man on the scientific staff worked harder, or under more discouraging circumstances, than he.

With the winds showing no signs of abating and the *Bear* drifting aimlessly in and out of the Bay, we gloomily awaited the *Ruppert's* coming.

Choosing to run down the 177th meridian W., well east of the *Bear's* track, Commodore Gjertsen stubbed his toe on heavy pack

[5] Dr. Perkins has since advised that the first haul was made on January 22nd, in 540 meters of water between East and West Capes. The dredge brought up one complete crinoid, and several stalks, four holothurians, and several species of polychaetes—some with complete mud cases. Another dredging shot at 480 meters off West Cape, where the bottom is rocky, brought up tunicates, lamellibranchs, many small sponges, polychaete and sipunculid worms, colonial bryozoans, asteroids and ophiuroids. Off East Cape the bottom animals at a depth of 490 meters included polychaetes, tunicates, holothurians, pycnogonids, a large sponge, bivalve molluscs and brachiopods. Other hauls in the Bay brought up much the same variety.

In addition, the dredge brought up a good quantity of rocks, pebbles and blue and yellow clay. The rocks, Roos said, were fresh and angular, glacial débris. Most of them were acid igneous rocks with occasional fragments of more basic varieties. Sedimentary rocks were represented by small quantities of green shale, friable sandstone. There was one piece of conglomerate cemented with iron.

just north of the Ross Sea on the night of the 22nd, and was obliged to steer west before he broke into the clear on the 24th.

The *Ruppert* entered the Bay of Whales late in the afternoon of January 26th, groping through a driving snow storm on radio direction finder bearings from the *Bear*. Cheerily the ships exchanged greetings, whereupon the steel ship, having no choice, joined the barkentine in her prowl up and down the Bay, steaming up to the Barrier for lee, then lying and drifting, then up to the Barrier again, two elusive phantoms weaving in and out of the confusion of fog and sea smoke. You can perhaps imagine what a gay parade this was for the men watching from the Barrier cliffs.

In the whole stay at Little America this was probably the most wretched week. It was like having a reprieve handed on an elastic band. Again we were in the familiar situation of being confronted by one of those sullen, glacial moods of Nature against which human ingenuity and engines are powerless. All you can do is sit and wait and let the winds and the pack fight it out. The men who came back from the Barrier said the ice was going out fast—had broken past Eleanor Bolling Bight. We were in almost hourly communication with the ships. The masters reported high seas, pea soup fog and heavy outrushes of ice. The wind-driven generator above the camp clacked night and day.

At Little America we hadn't been idle. The tractors and dog teams, under the direction of Demas and Innes-Taylor were steadily ferrying stores to a cache near Eleanor Bolling Bight. June and Bowlin had finally excavated the Ford and brought it to the surface. All the dog crates were ripped out of the caved-in tunnels of Dog Town and piled on the surface for transfer to the *Ruppert*. Noville and Rawson were brooding over the great piles of equipment and the scientists over their expensive apparatus and specimens, all strongly crated and boxed, speculating on the chances of losing them on the bottom of the Bay of Whales.

Merely waiting didn't worry me. I try to take such situations philosophically. Patience is one of the best tools I've ever been able to level against the polar regions. But this was eating up the ships' fuel; it was wearing on the nerves of the men; worse than these was the mounting danger that the steady northeasterly winds, if they continued to hold in strength, would fill the Bay of Whales with pack blown down from King Edward VII Land and hopelessly block off the ships for days, perhaps weeks more.

From this stalemate there was only one escape—to rely once more on the *Bear's* ancient hull, to send her into Bolling Bight and use her as a ferry between our shore transport and the flagship.

When the ice broke out past the Bight, it swept away the only descent to the bay ice available to the dog team. Even if we were in the mood to try to force a new route through the pressure south of

Ver-Sur-Mer Inlet and accept the killing burden of a long haul, the rotten new ice north of the Inlet offered neither safe surface for the dogs nor safe moorings for the ships.

The only alternative was to bring the ships into the Bight and load from the Barrier, a proceeding quite as risky in prospect now as it was during the unloading in 1934. However, there was this in our favor now, which wasn't present then—that our exploring was over, and a mishap, whatever other inconveniences it might entail, wouldn't ruin our program.

Nevertheless, we resolved to keep the *Ruppert* out of the Bight until the *Bear* had moved to the *Ruppert* all but the heavier stuff she couldn't take aboard with her light tackle—the airplanes, tractors, etc. I had no desire to hold the flagship in the Bight a second more than was necessary. A triangular cove perhaps two hundred yards long and about 50 yards wide, it was a dangerous pocket for a metal ship.

IV

On January 26th, just a few hours before the *Ruppert* arrived, Captain Johansen tried to force the *Bear* into the Bight, only to be driven off by heavy ice. Two days later the seas moderated enough to let him go alongside the flagship to coal ship. On the third day, in a snowstorm, he gained the Inlet, holding the berth a few hours, just long enough for Lieut. English to rejoin his ship and for the dog drivers to get a few loads aboard. The ice stirred and started to close in around the Bight. The *Bear* backed out hastily to avoid being crushed, and the dog drivers, hurrying up with new loads, stopped their sledges and cursed profoundly.

The 30th brought a lull—quieting air, quieting pack, but a heavy snowfall. English flashed word by radio he was heading in for the Bight. Tractor and dog drivers put out in a rush.

The *Bear* crept into the Bight and socked her forefoot against the ice at the head, where she was made fast to ice anchors and deadmen. The Barrier at this point—one of the lowest elevations along the whole eastern wall—sloped gently to 15 feet above the water line, just about flush with the *Bear's* gunwales, a lucky thing, as it turned out.

Innes-Taylor's dog teams were relaying from the cache, about 100 yards back, to the ship's side. The ship's crew, assisted by members of the Ice Party, were unloading the sledges and shouldering the stores across two narrow gangplanks. It was all done with great haste and dispatch. Engrossed in their jobs, the men forgot about the ice.

With the always appalling silence, just a whisper of something rending and giving, 50 feet of the Barrier broke out alongside the ship. Royster of the *Bear's* crew, trapped on the seaward side of the crack, flung himself across the widening fracture. Dr. Poulter, half way across the gangway with a heavy box on his shoulder, made the ship's deck in a flying leap as the walk twisted under him. The ship heeled with a groan, lay over a second until the weight of the ice let up, then slowly righted herself. Somebody aft, using his head, rapidly paid off the stern line fast enough to lessen the shock. Men below decks said her timbers shook as if she'd been rammed.

But it was accepted in the natural order of things. Lieut. English backed out to let the current carry away the ice: then he steamed in smartly to take a new position a ship and a half's length away. Had the flimsy plating of the *Ruppert* received that blow, the outcome would not have been so casual.

The embarkation was one of the most remarkable, I believe, in the history of the Antarctic.

For six days the tractors out of Little America discharged on to the dog sledges at the cache, the dog sledges discharged into the *Bear* lying in the Bight, and the *Bear* discharged into the *Ruppert* hove to beyond the pack near the middle of the Bay. Along that eight mile endless chain of transport—tractors, dogs, auxiliary ship and steamer—Little America, bit by bit, was vanishing into the *Ruppert's* capacious holds.

Lord, it was work. Lieut. English's men worked 60 hours without stopping, one stretch. I believe that some of the men ashore equaled it. Innes-Taylor, Rawson, Demas and Poulter, when I saw them, seemed on the verge of dropping from exhaustion. At Little America men were sleeping on the tables in the galley and Science Hall. There were no fires in the shacks because no one had time—or strength—to care for them. All the time a monstrous threat lay poised over the line of communication. A huge river of pack, blown down from the northeast, was creeping along the east wall till it got within a mile of the Bight. Commodore Gjertsen in the *Ruppert* followed it to East Cape and, even through glasses, couldn't see the end of it. It was not slushy, new ice, but masses of bergy bits and bay ice two years old. "If it should completely block the Bay," the Commodore advised by radio, "no ship ever built could force it." Fortunately the wind died, edging into the west and south. But even so, on every relay to and from the *Ruppert,* the barkentine had to smash and hammer her way through belts of pack.

February 1st was overcast, with a lightly sifting snow; but I noticed that for the first time in weeks the blades of the wind-driven generator were still. On the 2nd all the planes were started toward the ship—the Ford and the Pilgrim towed by the Cletrac; shortly after midnight the Condor and the Fairchild taxied out of the camp and up the ridge to the Bight under their own power. The uproar of the engines practically sounded the death knell of Little America. On the 2nd Haines and Grimminger dismantled the weather station, and two days later Bramhall and Zuhn formally closed their magnetic station. Dyer, Hutche-

THE "BEAR" TIES UP AT BOLLING BIGHT

THE CLETRAC HAULS THE "FLOYD BENNETT'S" WINGS TO THE SHIP

Admiral Byrd and Lieut.-Commander Noville (Left) Lower the Flag for the Last Time at Little America

son, Waite and Bailey uprooted the cumbersome radio equipment and power plant on the 3rd, leaving Little America dependent upon a trail set for communication.

On the night of February 3rd all that remained on the beach were the four airplanes, two Citroëns, the Cletrac, three aircraft engines, two machine lathes, the sections of two houses, the cows and the penguins, and about 15 tons of miscellaneous gear, most of it too heavy or too big to be handled by the Bear's hoists.

Shortly before midnight the *Ruppert* moved into the *Bear's* berth, the first time she had touched shore, the first time we had seen her crew, since she put into the Bay eight days before. The sea for once was quiet as a millpond, but a light snow was falling.

With telephone poles thrust out from her sides to hold her off from the ice, and the *Bear* moored on the opposite side of the Bight to act as a buffer and tug if she were thrown out by a calving of the Barrier against the opposite side of the Bight, the *Ruppert* started to clean up the job. One by one the planes were hoisted aboard—the Condor and Ford aft, the Pilgrim and Fairchild forward. A deuce of a job. Even with the Cletrac snubbing her, the Condor got away for a second and all but dashed into the side of the ship just before the boom took a strain. At that her ski broke through the edge. Then the wings were hoisted aboard and lowered into No. 2 hold. A touch of bad luck, here. A strong back being swung across the hatch crashed into the hold, damaging the wings of the Pilgrim and Condor, and smashing through the Fairchild's fuselage. And after these the cows, jerked up one by one in a crate into which they were peremptorily jimmied by the impatient shore crew, were deposited on the forward well deck. They trooped into their stalls on the shelter deck, with not even a lightening of the melancholy with which they had contemplated the whole expedition. "Cheer up, old girl," said Cox, thwacking Deerfoot heartily on the stern sheets, "you'll soon be in clover." I don't know what hopes were held out for the penguins. The 19 of them came over the side in dog crates.

The *Ruppert* could hold the berth just 17 hours. A fresh surging of the pack—curiously like the action of a flood tide—swept an eddying mess of growlers and floes across the mouth of the Bight. Lieut. English interposed the *Bear* astern of the *Ruppert,* and tried to fend them off. Commodore Gjertsen became apprehensive. He recommended casting off. Stuck in that narrow cul-de-sac, with no room for maneuvering, able only to back out with her vulnerable stern presented to the ice, she stood a fair chance of being cornered. So the *Ruppert* cast off about 6 o'clock in the evening of the 4th, after Captain Innes-Taylor's dog-drivers had rushed their dogs up the gangway.

Still ashore were the tractors, the aircraft engines, a large mound of empty gasoline drums, hay for the cows, and the sections of several houses. Forty-five minutes later Lieut. English drove the *Bear* into the Bight, and his men, entering their third day without sleep, strove to salvage what they could.

Little America had meanwhile closed its second phase. In the afternoon I returned with Demas in a tractor to collect the last of my things. The shacks, for once, were utterly silent. I can't say that the place looked beautiful or even attractive. The tunnels were broken up and smeared with dirt, broken boxes, cartons of bunion plasters, tooth paste, bottles of mouth wash, frozen cans of food. The shacks, with one or two exceptions, were little better—littered with the débris that only a polar expedition seems able to accumulate. Already the ice was collecting on walls and ceilings. But there is something about the place—something for which I can find no trustworthy words—that made me hesitate. In the radio shack, with the fire out and the place almost in darkness, I came upon Hutcheson, the most serene, and most undisturbed, and certainly one of the most decent minds I've ever met; he was sitting in a corner, puffing at a pipe.

"Glad to leave, Hutch?"

"Well, I'm not very sure," he said, in his soft Texan way. "I've really liked it here."

Noville and Rawson, who had remained at Little America to direct the loading of the last tractors, said everything was all set. Sisson notified Bailey on the flagship that he was shutting down KFZ. Boyd came out of the machine shop with a handful of tools. With Demas we traveled for the last time the road to the ship, and Little America receded except for the shining radio towers.

V

All the night of the 5th and into the morning of the next day the *Bear's* splendid crew, assisted by Innes-Taylor, Poulter and a few hands from the *Ruppert,* labored to clean out the cache. The weather turned surly: the wind freshened to small gale force, and from the *Ruppert,* cruising in the Bay, we could see the men moving to and fro in sheets of drift. About 8 o'clock the *Bear* cast off and steamed out of the Bight out to trans-ship cargo, in the lee of the Barrier. Happily the wind lulled. Every inch of the *Bear's* decks clear to the lower foreyards was taken up with the oddest miscellany of cargo imaginable—sections of Advance Base shack, boxes of geological specimens, aviation engines, gasoline drums, tents, personal sea chests which were cheerfully known among the Ice Party as "loot boxes," dog crates, small gasoline engines and—miraculously—one of the Citroëns, No. 1.

"Just name it," Lieut. English called up from the bridge, "and we've got it."

Unable to take the tractor aboard on his hoists, English boldly resolved to try to run it aboard. The guard rail was dismantled, a cribbing was assembled on the deck over the steam winch, planks were run out to the shore; over this precarious runway Skinner drove the tractor from the Barrier onto the deck. A matter of pride with them, for this was the car the *Bear* herself had carried to the Antarctic, which Skinner had piloted on the first winter trip and Von der Wall, both of the *Bear,* had driven to the Edsel Fords.

I can't say too much for that grand ship, her officers and men. Almost single-handedly, they accomplished the embarkation of the expedition.

By 3:30 o'clock that afternoon the *Bear* finished discharging. The wind had meanwhile blown the ships, as they lay together, well out of the Bay.

"Do you want us to go back and try to get the rest of the things?" asked English.

"No, I think not. No use pushing our luck. Let's shove off."

On the Barrier remained only the Cletrac, Citroën No. 2, the two snowmobiles, a number of gasoline drums, a bit of hay and a small mound of nondescript things.

Five minutes later the *Ruppert* headed westward along the Barrier, bound for Discovery Inlet to make a catch of live penguins. The *Bear* was on our quarter, under sail and steam. Though the sky was partly overcast, still it was a lovely afternoon, with a creamy green and gold paneling at the horizon and so bright and cleanly shining were the Barrier cliffs above the wine-colored sea that they seemed to have the buoyancy of a mirage. We passed growlers almost black with birds, which soared wildly at the unwonted intrusion. I heard some one cry out from the bridge, and turned in time to see a huge piece of the Barrier calve miles ahead, dissolving soundlessly, in a cloud of rosy mist. But these matters, in a sense, seemed of no large consequence. I happened to see a fly in my cabin, and its busy enterprises so fascinated and bemused me that I forgot everything else.

Elsewhere on board men too exhausted to sleep were absorbing the new smells and new sounds of the *Ruppert,* the conversations of men from the outer world, a sensing of expanding existence which was already causing Little America to recede into the miasma of memory—and some, not quite so expansively and certainly without the same enrichment of the senses—were absorbing the motion of the ship and foundering with dreadful laments.

VI

On February 7th, having picked up twenty more penguins at Discovery Inlet, both ships put out for Dunedin, New Zealand. The formal departure was made in fog so dense that visibility was hardly a ship's length. Gloomy as the day was, I drew a measure of happiness from it: it was *so long!* again to Antarctica, and no one left behind.

The *Bear,* because of her slower speed and also needing time for sonic soundings and plankton hauls,[6] quickly fell astern. Except for continuous squalls, storms and a wind of near hurricane force which assailed the barkentine, the voyage to New Zealand and its jovial heartiness and warmth was ended without incident.

[6] This research was continued on the subsequent voyage across the South Pacific Ocean to Panama, via Easter Island and the Galapagos.

NOTES ON THE MAPS AND SURVEYS

By KENNETT L. RAWSON

THE two small scale maps appearing in the book were prepared during the summer of 1935 in the cartographic department of the National Geographic Society to show in a general way the geographic work of the Second Byrd Antarctic Expedition.

Before going into a detailed description of the maps, I want to take this opportunity to express the great debt which this expedition and the preceding one owe to Commander (C. C.) Harold E. Saunders, U. S. N., expedition chief cartographer. It is hard to conceive of any one's handling the survey material with greater skill or more devoted perseverance. His work, especially on the aerial photographs, represents a distinct advance in the technique of constructing maps from oblique photographs.

The South Pacific map (reproduced elsewhere in this book) constructed by Lieutenant (J. G.) R. A. J. English, U. S. N., shows the tracks of the two ships, the *Jacob Ruppert* and the *Bear of Oakland* and the flights from the *Jacob Ruppert* of the airplane *William Horlick*. Both the cruises of the ships and the flights have been described in detail elsewhere.

The map shows primarily that the geographic results of our work at sea were purely negative. No new land was discovered anywhere in the previously unknown area which was penetrated. But the results, while negative, were none the less significant. The southern known limits of the Pacific Ocean were moved considerably farther south in the vicinity of the flight tracks and along parts of the route of the *Jacob Ruppert*. The *Bear of Oakland* also drove a wedge into a section of the Ross Sea and Pacific Ocean which had previously been considered likely to contain an archipelago. No trace of such was detected and none probably will be, because of the great depth of water found there. Of even greater significance was the restriction of the possible area in which the continental coast line can lie. Coupled with the flights to the eastward of Little America, the work at sea has narrowed this down to a fairly small compass.

Lieutenant English in the *Bear of Oakland* made a careful survey of the Ross Ice Barrier during January 1935. It is interesting to note that the Barrier has advanced on an average of 12 nautical miles (13.8 statute) along the whole front between Ross Island and the Bay of Whales. The 1911 position is taken from Pennell's charts and Debenham's *Report on the Maps and Surveys*, British (*Terra Nova*) Antarctic Expedition (1910-1913). The Victoria Land topography is taken from the British surveys of the region. The King Edward VII

Land and Marie Byrd Land features, including Roosevelt Island, south of the Bay of Whales, are derived from the surveys of the present expedition, with the exception of the section from Okuma Bay to Cape Colbeck, which comes from Scott.

The map on the lining pages at the front and back of this book was constructed by Commander Saunders and the writer with the invaluable help of Mr. Albert Bumstead and Mr. James Darley of the cartographic staff of the National Geographic Society. It is based primarily on the surveys of the present expedition and the hitherto unpublished final chart constructed by Commander Saunders from the aerial surveys of Admiral Byrd and Captain Ashley McKinley in the Queen Maud Range on the previous expedition. Supplementing these, the surveys of the expeditions under Captain Scott, Sir Ernest Shackleton and Roald Amundsen have been drawn on, also the surveys of Dr. Laurence M. Gould of the previous expedition.

It is necessary to point out here that this map, both on account of its small scale and its preliminary nature, includes only the more prominent topographic features. Commander Saunders hopes in due time to bring out large scale maps which will do full justice to the various surveys.

The surveys fall into three categories, aerial, surface, and subsurface or seismic. The surface triangulations were carried out in the Edsel Ford Mts. by Paul Siple, leader and navigator of the Marie Byrd Land Party, in the Thorne Glacier area by Quin Blackburn, leader, and Stuart Paine, navigator, of the Queen Maud Geological Party, and in the Alexandra and Rockefeller Mts. by Dr. Ervin H. Bramhall, co-leader and navigator of the Plateau Party (Tractor Party).

The aerial surveys were made by Joseph Pelter, aerial mapping cameraman and the writer, who navigated the plane on these flights.

The seismic surveys were carried out along the route of the Plateau Party by Charles Morgan, co-leader and geophysicist of the party. Dr. Thomas C. Poulter also carried on an extensive series in the vicinity of Little America.

The seismic data had not been sufficiently worked up at the time of completion of this map to render desirable the inclusion of the detailed figures. But, as has been pointed out in earlier chapters, even preliminary study was sufficient to give us the necessary correlations between ice thickness and the elevation of the surface to confirm the other evidence pointing toward land above sea level along the eastern side of the Ross Sea.

The surveys were plotted from the notes on large scale polyconic charts of the appropriate areas. The data were then consolidated on a general sheet of the entire region and such portions as were suitable were transferred to the aerial survey work sheets for establishing gound control points.

The vertical control was obtained from comparisons of the aneroid barometers in the field with the standard mercurial barometer at Little America. In the eastern section the elevations were based largely on the barometric readings obtained on the Grace McKinley tractor journey in September and October 1934. For one week this party was held in camp at the 180-Mile Depot by unfavorable weather. The night and morning readings of the tractor barometer were plotted against the corresponding readings at the base camp. George Grimminger, meteorologist, was able to establish a very close correlation between the changes in the barometer at both stations and to work out a practically constant pressure difference for the entire week. The other barometric elevations were adjusted to conform with this station as far as Mt. Grace McKinley. Siple's elevations were also adjusted to these values. The elevations of the peaks in the Edsel Ford Mts. were obtained by trigonometric leveling, using the barometric elevations of Siple's triangulation stations as a base. Some check on the accuracy of these assumed base values and of the leveling in general is afforded by the fact that we were able to level certain of the peaks on Mts. Rea and Saunders from four of these stations with widely differing base elevations and the results agreed within one hundred feet.

On Blackburn's route across the Ross Shelf Ice we could find no significant changes in elevation between Little America and Supporting Party Mt. in the Queen Maud Mts. The elevations seemed to run consistently in the neighborhood of 300 feet. The values obtained at Supporting Party Mt. and vicinity agreed well with those determined by Dr. Gould in 1929. The elevations of Blackburn's stations on the glacier were obtained in the same manner by barometric comparisons between the Little America standard barometer and his instrument. The elevation of Mt. Weaver at the head of the Glacier was obtained by barometric readings on the summit.

It is unnecessary to point out the uncertainty of barometric leveling in general, but it should be borne in mind that the great distances involved between Little America and the Queen Maud Mts. render the barometric differences liable to serious and ineradicable errors due to vagaries in the weather. The Geological Party never stayed in one place long enough to allow any attempt at plotting systematically the pressure differences as was done in the eastern theater. There may also be a permanent condition of low or more probably high barometer in the interior caused by meteorological factors and not by any corresponding change in elevation. This would introduce material errors in any assumption of elevations based on atmospheric pressures.

A word may not be amiss as to the degree of accuracy that should be expected in these surveys. In the first place, the time in the field was so limited and the extent and multiplicity of the topographical features so great that one or even a dozen sledging parties could work the areas in question and even then barely scratch the surface. To try to survey adequately an area of many thousand square miles in a month when the means of transport can cover at best an average of twenty miles a day is manifestly impossible. In addition, surveying was not the sole purpose of any of these parties. Each had an extensive program of other investigations to be carried on which necessarily curtailed the time and energy which could be expended on this work.

But above all one must not lose sight of the conditions under which they labored. To work with bare fingers or the lightest of silk gloves, which the delicacy of adjustment of the tangent screws requires, on frost stiffened instruments at far below zero temperatures, is a real ordeal. It is even worse when the time must usually be subtracted from much needed rest at the end of an exhausting day's march, when every muscle and nerve craves the warmth of the sleeping bag. The struggle to keep a transit level on an unstable snow surface when the slightest shift of weight from one foot to the other, or even no apparent movement, will throw it off level is enough to try the patience of a saint.

In view of all this, it is not surprising that some discrepancies and errors were found in working up the survey notes. Due to bad weather, Siple was unable to make complete astronomic determinations of position and azimuth in the northern part of his journey from Saunders Mt. to the Raymond Fosdick Mts. His stations therefore had to be located largely by resection from the previously located peaks and the triangulation angles laid off from these peaks to the new ones in this section. There were also other minor discrepancies. But after careful adjustment the final results seem satisfactory.

In the Queen Mauds the greatest problem was one of identification. This is always one of the most trying problems in any totally unknown area, as mountains, etc., usually look entirely different when viewed from different angles. To keep positive track of a large number of topographic features under these conditions, and in addition to pick out the very same points on each feature to triangulate, is well nigh impossible. The Queen Maud Mts., being of the block type, rendered this even more difficult, as clear cut peaks, or features which can be identified from many stations are rare. This led to some confusion in the triangulation. The fact that the track of the party was very nearly in a straight line also gave less favorable conditions for surveying. But even taking fully into account these factors the results were very good in the major part of the survey.

Dr. Bramhall's survey of the Alexandra and Rockefeller Mts. was the most satisfactory of all. Here he had a relatively small number of clearly defined targets and ample time to carry out a very full set of observations at each of his four triangulation stations. Above all, he was favored with mild weather.

It is worth recording that the astronomical observations of the writer on the Grace McKinley tractor trip agreed closely with those of Siple at Mt. Grace McKinley and with those of Bramhall at the 120-Mile Depot on the Eastern Trail, thus providing an independent check on the work.

All in all, it is felt that these surveys reflect real credit on the devotion and skill of the men who carried them out, and that they compare favorably with any previous surveys in the Antarctic.

The aerial surveys, as has been already noted, were carried out on the eastern, northeastern and southeastern flights principally, by Pelter and the writer. In addition, Pelter and Bowlin made an attempt to amplify the survey of the Edsel Fords on January 1st, 1935, but were blocked by clouds.

The first major surveying flight was the one eastward of Mt. Grace McKinley. This resulted in carrying the photographic survey onward to the 130th meridian West and recording the eastward extension of the Edsel Ford Mts. In this connection it should be stated that Mounts Hal Flood and Mabelle Sidley appeared in only a small number of pictures taken quite close together. This did not provide a base line long enough to fix their position with the precision obtained with most of the other features.

The second major flight, the southeastern, resulted in the discovery of the Horlick Mts. At the time of discovery the wings of the plane were in the way, hence it was impossible to obtain pictures. By the time we turned and the mountains were within view of the camera, a bank of mist had obscured them; so unfortunately no photographs of this important group were obtained. They were located on the basis of pelorus bearings taken by the writer, which were admittedly too close together to afford a very accurate fix of the position of the mountains. It must therefore be considered as only approximate.

On the northeastern flight, the other major photographic reconnaissance, the work was greatly hampered by clouds and the scope of the flight much curtailed. We were able, however, to observe approximately the trend of the Jacob Ruppert Coast and to obtain some excellent photographs of the western part of the Edsel Ford Mts. after emerging from the clouds and turning southward.

The construction of a map from oblique aerial photographs is somewhat too complicated to be described in detail here. Suffice it to say that on any picture if the apparent horizon show, and the altitude of the plane and the focal length of the camera be known, by the application of certain principles of optics and solid geometry the angles subtended from a calculated center point in the plane of the negative by the objects in the field may be worked out. These angles are then drawn on celluloid sheets, one for each picture, and laid down on a polyconic chart along the flight track at appropriate points as indicated from the navigational data. The time that each picture is taken is marked on it for this purpose. The intersection of the bearing lines of the same object on the different plots serves to fix the position of the object. If one or more features located by ground surveys appear in a picture the appropriate bearing line is anchored on the chart and if three such features appear the plot is positively anchored in both orientation and position. Hence the importance of ground control.

The ground control was scanty at best. The Rockefellers were well located by surface surveys but were somewhat too far west to be of tremendous help in the present surveys. The same applied to the Alexandras. In the Edsel Fords we had some peaks located by Siple, but all of these were in the western part. There was also great difficulty establishing the identity of some of the peaks on the aerial pictures from Siple's ground photographs and descriptions. A mountain looks so entirely different from the ground and from the air that it is a matter of great difficulty many times to make a positive identification.

We feel that the present map, while far from complete or final, does give a reasonably accurate depiction of the major topographic features of the regions surveyed.

The most striking addition to this map as compared with previous ones is the Rockefeller Plateau. The methods by which it was discovered and traced have been described by Admiral Byrd. The western margin of it, or in other words the actual coast line, from Okuma Bay to the 120-Mile Depot on the Eastern Trail can be considered as very nearly accurate. From there to beyond the crevassed region near Latitude 81° S., the geographic network laid down was dense enough to confine its possible position to a very small area. But from the vicinity of the elevation marked 1370 feet to the Queen Maud Mts. there is only one control point, the high slopes reported by Blackburn near the 350-Mile Depot on the Southern Trail. The position of the coast line therefore is highly uncertain especially in the section from the 350-Mile Depot to the Queen Maud Mts. Here Blackburn did not make direct contact with the Plateau. Either the slope was too gradual to be detected from the trail or the coast bends too far to the eastward. Its position therefore is speculative and is based on inference from his descriptions, the altitudes observed on the southeastern flight, etc. The actual junction of the Rockefeller Plateau and the Leverett Plateau has not as yet been actually observed. There is strong reason to believe that such junction does take place, however.

This inevitably brings us to the question of the Ross Sea-Weddell Sea Strait. This question has been thoroughly discussed in chapters XIII, XIV and XV. The map shows clearly that the possible position of such a strait, if it does exist, although the probabilities against its existence seem overwhelming, must be between the termination of the southeastern flight at 83° 05′ S., and the Horlick Mts. The limit of visibility from the plane was in the vicinity of 75 nautical miles. Within this range the Plateau seemed to maintain its elevation without visible diminution or without any appearance of crevassing or irregularity that would lead one to suspect any interruption. But the remaining territory between the surface horizon as visible from the plane and the base of the Horlick Mts. is still *terra incognita.*

In the northern region the surveys showed that the Rockefeller Mts. as plotted on the Reconnaissance Map of King Edward VII Land, and part of Marie Byrd Land (American Geographical Society, 1933), were about twelve miles too far to the east. This is not surprising, as the whole position of the group was dependent on the very brief survey made by Dr. Gould in March, 1929, during which the weather was very bad. Several peaks in the Alexandras were also shown to be too far east by Dr. Bramhall's survey.

Scott's Nunataks, which were the only point in King Edward VII Land which had been located astronomically prior to the first Byrd expedition, were also found to be nearly a degree too far to the east. These peaks had been located by Prestrud in 1911, but there were discrepancies between the several publications put out by Amundsen's expedition in which the position of this mountain is given, and Prestrud remarks that his time pieces had been unchecked so long that his longitudes were probably in error. It is not surprising, therefore, that the position assumed by Commander Saunders for the Reconnaissance Map was in error. The present position was assigned on the basis of the aerial surveys. The Nunataks showed on a large number of pictures taken from many different angles and with ample ground control.

The displacement of the Edsel Fords has already been discussed in chapter XIII. The whole western face of the range seemed to be about 30 to 35 nautical miles too far east. As Scott's Nunataks were the only available ground control point between Little America and the Edsel Fords, this is not surprising. Almost half of the error was caused by the erroneous position of the Nunataks. The astonishing thing is that Commander Saunders was able to come so close to the true positions.

Roosevelt Island was delineated on the basis of the seismic work conducted on it by Dr. Poulter and the altimetric readings taken within its confines on the frequent aerial traverses of it. In addition to the tracks shown on the chart, the first flight to the tractors on November 16th crossed the southern half of the island both on the outward and homeward legs. (This flight and the one of January 1st to the Edsel Fords were omitted from the map on account of the congestion of flight tracks in these areas and the small scale of the map.)

The presence of a high ridge southeast of the Bay of Whales had been known since Amundsen's day and he correctly surmised the existence of an island. There had been no attempt, however, before this expedition, to trace its outlines systematically, and the seismic soundings were necessary to supply the first scientific proof that the land was actually above sea level. We were much astonished to find how large the island is. The fact that the magnitude of such a feature could go unsuspected for so many years shows how scant is our knowledge of Antarctica in even the most frequented areas.

I wish to express to Mr. W. L. G. Joerg of the American Geographical Society our profound thanks for his assistance in interpreting the geographic data.

The total area brought within the range of vision of the aerial or surface parties operating from Little America as a base was approximately 450,000 square miles. Of this 290,000 were previously unknown. At sea, in the neighborhood of 160,000 square miles of unknown waters were explored. Thus a grand total of new land and sea of roughly 450,000 square miles was added to the map. This area is equal in size to the northeastern United States from the Canadian border to the Ohio River including Pennsylvania and New Jersey and west to include Illinois.

For those who are interested, a comparison of any standard map of the Antarctic such as the American Geographical Society or British Admiralty charts up to 1928 with the present map will demonstrate far more clearly than any amount of description the geographical significance of the first and second Byrd Antarctic Expeditions.

APPENDIX

Ice Party

C. A. Abele, Jr.
Clay Bailey
R. B. Black
Quin A. Blackburn
E. H. Bramhall
V. Boyd
W. H. Bowlin
Richard E. Byrd
A. Carbone
Leroy Clark
Stevenson Corey
E. F. Cox
F. S. Dane
E. J. Demas
Frederick G. Dustin
J. N. Dyer
Albert Eilefsen
Bernard Fleming
George Grimminger
W. C. Haines
John Herrmann
Joe Hill, Jr.
Guy Hutcheson
Alan Innes-Taylor
H. I. June
W. P. Lewisohn
Alton A. Lindsey
W. S. McCormick
L. T. Miller
E. L. Moody
C. G. Morgan
C. J. V. Murphy
G. O. Noville
David Paige
J. A. Pelter
E. B. Perkins
Carl O. Petersen
Stuart D. L. Paine
L. H. Potaka
Thomas C. Poulter
Finn Ronne
Kennett L. Rawson
Richard S. Russell, Jr.
Paul A. Siple
Bernard W. Skinner
Olin D. Stancliff
J. M. Sterrett
Isaac Schlossbach
Ralph W. Smith
Paul Swan
Ivor Tinglof
J. H. Von der Wall
F. Alton Wade
Amory H. Waite, Jr.
H. R. Young
Arthur A. Zuhn

Additional Expedition Personnel

Victor Czegka, Supply Manager, on duty U. S. A.
Thomas C. T. Buckley (Resigned, February, 1934)
Byron Gay "
S. D. Pierce "
G. O. Shirey, M.D. "

Officers and Crew, *Jacob Ruppert*, First Trip to Bay of Whales, 1933

Commodore Hj. Fr. Gjertsen
W. F. Verleger, Master
H. Bayne, First Officer
P. Dempster, Second Officer
J. J. Muir, Third Officer
W. K. Queen, Chief Engineer
B. W. Paul, First Assistant Engineer
J. A. Ellis, Second Assistant Engineer
Peter MacCurrach, Jr., Third Assistant Engineer
J. G. Sisson, Radio Operator

Peter Barbedes
B. O. J. Bradley
H. R. Burt
L. P. Colombo
L. W. Cox
A. B. Creagh
E. W. Christian
J. B. Desmond
P. O. Dornan
P. Dymond
H. L. Fleming
Philip Gargan
W. P. Gaynor
F. W. Giroux
E. H. Griffiths
J. Hawley
J. D. Healey
T. Johnson
L. H. Kennedy
G. Kerr
G. P. Lindley
W. H. Lowd
T. McLennon
John McNamara
M. P. MacKintosh
G. M. Mitchell
B. P. O'Brien
M. Pilcher
J. Robinson
T. Sanderson
W. C. Stewart
S. J. Sullivan
E. L. Tigert
F. C. Voight
G. B. Wray

Officers and Crew, *Bear of Oakland*, First Trip to Bay of Whales, 1933

Lieut. (J. G.) R. A. J. English, U.S.N., Master
B. Johansen, Sailing Master and Ice Pilot
Stephen D. Rose, First Officer
N. B. Davis, Second Officer
Leland L. Barter, Chief Engineer
S. A. Pinkham, First Assistant Engineer
T. E. Litchfield, Second Assistant Engineer
R. D. Watson, Radio Operator

J. D. Albert
J. A. Callahan
A. Christensen
T. J. D'Amico
H. Dickey
W. H. Dornin
George J. Frizzell, Jr.
Robert Fowler
Paul Kallenberg
Howard Lawson
Walfred Miller
John Murphy
Victor Niewoehner
J. Edward Roos
W. A. Robertson
R. S. Robinson
C. P. Royster
Rudolph Van Reen

Officers and Crew, *Bear of Oakland*, Second Trip to Bay of Whales, 1935

Lieut (J. G.) R. A. J. English, U.S.N., Master
B. Johansen, Sailing Master and Acting First Officer
A. G. B. Robinson, Second Officer
Rudolph Van Reen, Third Officer
S. A. Pinkham, Chief Engineer
T. E. Litchfield, First Assistant Engineer
Victor Niewoehner, Second Assistant Engineer
R. D. Watson, Radio Operator

J. A. Callahan
A. Christensen
T. J. D'Amico
W. H. Dornin
Gordon Fountain
Robert Fowler

George J. Frizzell, Jr.
C. J. Garner
Edw. A. Griswold
H. A. Hambleton
W. B. Highet, M.D.
T. W. Joss
Paul Kallenberg
J. V. Mathias
Wm. McCristel
Walfred Miller
John Murphy
Neville Newbold
W. A. Robertson
H. B. Robinson
S. Edward Roos
C. P. Royster
J. W. Sorenson

OFFICERS AND CREW, *Jacob Ruppert,* SECOND TRIP TO BAY OF WHALES, 1935

Commodore Hj. Fr. Gjertsen
S. D. Rose, Master
J. J. Muir, First Officer
Thomas Van Reen, Second Officer
Joseph D. Healey, Third Officer
James M. Gillies, Chief Engineer
B. W. Paul, Chief Engineer (Expedition)
Leland L. Barter, First Assistant Engineer
Peter MacCurrach, Jr., Second Assistant Engineer
W. C. Stewart, Third Assistant Engineer
J. G. Sisson, Radio Operator

W. H. Clement
L. P. Colombo
O. E. Davis
Gordon B. Desmond
Percy Dymond
Philip Gargan
W. P. Gaynor
F. W. Giroux
Wm. McL. Loudon
W. H. Lowd
D. R. Mackintosh
John McNamara
Cecil Melrose
G. M. Mitchell
John H. Morrison
Irving Spencer Ortiz
P. E. Round
F. H. P. Schonyan
F. W. Smoothy
E. L. Tigert
F. C. Voight
Max Winkle

Leo McDonald, General Manager
John McNeil, Business Representative
Hazel McKercher, Secretary

INDEX

INDEX